MW01712588

March, 2010

To the Children's Council,

Thank you for your participation in the Kids in the Atrium Project.

We couldn't have done it without you!

The KITA Team.

Studies in Childhood and Family in Canada

Studies in Childhood and Family in Canada is a multidisciplinary series devoted to new perspectives on these subjects as they evolve. The series features studies that focus on the intersections of age, class, race, gender, and region as they contribute to a Canadian understanding of childhood and family, both historically and currently.

Series Editor
Cynthia Comacchio
Department of History
Wilfrid Laurier University

Manuscripts to be sent to
Brian Henderson, Director
Wilfrid Laurier University Press
75 University Avenue West
Waterloo, Ontario N2L 3C5, Canada

DEPICTING CANADA'S CHILDREN

LOREN LERNER, editor

Wilfrid Laurier University Press

This book has been published with the help of a grant from the Canadian Federation for the Humanities and Social Sciences, through the Aid to Scholarly Publications Programme, using funds provided by the Social Sciences and Humanities Research Council of Canada. We acknowledge the support of the Canada Council for the Arts for our publishing program. We acknowledge the financial support of the Government of Canada through the Book Publishing Industry Development Program for our publishing activities.

Canada Council for the Arts | Conseil des Arts du Canada

ONTARIO ARTS COUNCIL
CONSEIL DES ARTS DE L'ONTARIO

Library and Archives Canada Cataloguing in Publication

Depicting Canada's children / edited by Loren Lerner.

(Studies in childhood and family in Canada)
Includes bibliographical references and index.
ISBN 978-1-55458-050-7

1. Children—Canada—Pictorial works—History. 2. Children in art—History. 3. Childhood in art—History. 4. Photography of children—Canada—History. 5. Children—Canada—Social conditions. 6. Children—Canada—History. 7. Art, Canadian. I. Lerner, Loren R. (Loren Ruth), 1948– II. Series.

N7640.D46 2009 704.9'4250971 C2008-906593-X

Waterloo, Ontario, Canada
www.wlupress.wlu.ca

Front cover image: *Diego Asleep #2*, 1972 (oil on wood, 48 × 48 inches), by Jack Chambers; Toronto Dominion Bank Collection. Back cover image: *Andrea and Dewi, 1973* (1973); photo by Robert Minden. Cover design by David Drummond. Text design by Catharine Bonas-Taylor.

∞
This book is printed on Ancient Forest Friendly paper (100% post-consumer recycled).

Printed in Canada

CONTENTS

vii LIST OF ILLUSTRATIONS

xiii ACKNOWLEDGEMENTS

xv INTRODUCTION
Loren Lerner

SYMBOL AND REALITY

3 Iconography of the Child in Early Quebec Art
François-Marc Gagnon

27 Shaping Modern Boyhood: Indian Lore, Child Psychology, and the Cultural Landscape of Camp Ahmek
Abigail A. Van Slyck

49 Haunted: First Nations Children in Residential School Photography
Sherry Farrell Racette

85 A Land of Youth: Nationhood and the Image of the Child in the National Film Board of Canada's Still Photography Division
Carol Payne

109 Mapping a Canadian Girlhood Historically through Dolls and Doll-Play
Jaqueline Reid-Walsh and Claudia Mitchell

OTHERS AND OUTSIDERS

133 The Raw Materials of Empire Building: Depicting Canada's Home Children
Alena M. Buis

153 Immigrants, Labourers, "Others": Canada's Home Children
Margaret McNay

173 Re-Visioning the Girl's Narrative for the 1980s: The Case of the Short Story "Jack of Hearts" and Its Film Adaptation
Elspeth Tulloch

201 Locating Children in the Discourse of Squeegee Kids
Derek Foster

219 A Child's Place in Ottawa's Commemorative Landscape
Susan Hart

SUBJECTS OF CARE

233 Frocks and Bangles: The Photographic Conversion of Two Indian Girls
Sharon Murray

259 Pictures of Health: Sick Kids Exposed
Annmarie Adams, David Theodore, and Patricia McKeever

279 Healthy Bodies, Strong Citizens: Okanagan Children's Drawings and the Canadian Junior Red Cross
Andrea N. Walsh

305 Children and School Interiors: The User-Material Culture-Environment Nexus in Late Nineteenth-Century Toronto
Kai Wood Mah

INNER VISIONS

325 George Reid's Paintings as Narratives of a Child Nation
Loren Lerner

347 James Wilson Morrice's *Return from School*: A Modernist Image of Quebec Children
Sandra Paikowsky

365 Something Resembling Childhood: Artworks by Jack Chambers, Daniel Barrow, and Rodney Graham
Johanne Sloan

387 The Child in Me: A Figure of Photographic Creation
Martha Langford

415 Paterson Ewen's *Portrait of Vincent*
Monique Westra

425 CONTRIBUTORS

429 INDEX

LIST OF ILLUSTRATIONS

Fig. 1.1 Montagnais woman in the *Carte geographique de la Novvelle France*, 1612, and Huron woman in the *Voyages* of 1619 4

Fig. 1.2 *Historiae canadensis seu Novae Franciae Libri Decem*, 1666, by François Du Creux 6

Fig. 1.3 *Codex canadiensis*, c. 1700, by Louis Nicolas 7

Fig. 1.4 *Historiae canadensis seu Novae Franciae Libri Decem*, plate V, 1666, by François Du Creux 8

Fig. 1.5 *Sainte Famille à la huronne*, c. 1671, by Claude François (Frère Luc) 11

Fig. 1.6 *L'Ange gardien*, 1671, by Claude François (Frère Luc) 13

Fig. 1.7 *Ex-voto de Madame Riverin*, 1703, Anonymous 14

Fig. 1.8 *Cyprien Tanguay*, 1832, by Antoine Plamondon 17

Fig. 1.9 *Cyrice Têtu et sa fille Caroline*, 1852, by Théophile Hamel 18

Fig. 1.10 *Madame Têtu et son fils Amable*, 1852, by Théophile Hamel 19

Fig. 1.11 *Evelyn Pleasant, Clark Street, Montreal*, 1936, by Louis Muhlstock 21

Fig. 2.1 Map of Camps Ahmek and Wapomeo, Algonquin Provincial Park, Ontario, c. 1928, by Harold V. Shaw 28–29

Fig. 2.2 Camp Ahmek council ring, 1922 34

Fig. 2.3 Jack Ridpath with totem pole, Camp Ahmek, 1922 34

Fig. 2.4 Ernest Thompson Seton and Woodcraft Indians conducting a council and war dance at Wyndygoul, in Connecticut, 1908 36

Fig. 2.5 Jousting tournament at the council ring at Camp Ahmek, c. 1923 37

Fig. 2.6 The medical cabin at Camp Ahmek, from the brochure for the 1931 season 43

Fig. 3.1 Thomas Moore, before and after tuition at the Regina Industrial School, 1896 53

Fig. 3.2a "Parents and Children Attending Qu'Appelle Industrial School," 1900 55

Fig. 3.2b "Father and Children Attending Qu'Appelle Industrial School," 1900 55

Fig. 3.3 Girls arriving at Spanish Indian Residential School from Manitoulin Island, c. 1950 58
Fig. 3.4 Pupils of the St. Joseph's Industrial School, High River, Alberta, 1900 60
Fig. 3.5 Students of the Anglican residential school at Pelican Falls watching a fisherman 62
Fig. 3.6 "The Indian Boys of the Duck Lake Boarding School Working at the New Addition to Their School," 1900 66
Fig. 3.7 "Sewing Room," Qu'Appelle Industrial School, 1895 66
Fig. 3.8 "Old Pupils of All Hallows' School, Yale, B.C., Now in Domestic Service," 1902 67
Fig. 3.9a Boys working on building construction, Spanish Indian Residential School 70
Fig. 3.9b Adam Roy and Peter Cooper hoist their shovels, 1945, Spanish Indian Residential School, 1945 70
Fig. 3.10 Children praying to a statue of the Virgin Mary, Holy Angels Residential School, Fort Chipewyan, Alberta, 1931 71
Fig. 3.11 Girls' Calisthenics Club, St. Paul's Indian Industrial School (near Winnipeg), 1900 73
Fig. 3.12 Boy and girl holding hands, Duck Lake Residential School, c. 1905 75
Fig. 3.13 Empty beds, Spanish Indian Residential School dormitory 76
Fig. 3.14 Cree children playing in the snow at residential school, Sturgeon Lake, Alberta, c. 1946 79
Fig. 4.1 "Canada's Future Belongs to Them," National Film Board, Still Photography Division, 1964 86
Fig. 4.2 Mrs. E. Marr, physiotherapist, with Dorothy Gifford, 2½, at the walking bars in the polio clinic, Sudbury General Hospital, 1953 93
Fig. 4.3 "Canada Will Start Trials of Polio Vaccine April 18," National Film Board, Still Photography Division, 1955 95
Fig. 4.4 Child behind crowd at Grey Cup Parade, May 1965 100
Fig. 5.1 Joan with her Eaton's Beauty doll, Christmas, 1939 117
Fig. 5.2 Claudia with her rubber "wet-ums" doll in carriage 121
Fig. 5.3 Bride doll 122
Fig. 6.1 "The Raw Material as We Find It" 137
Fig. 6.2 "The Situation," *Canadian Illustrated News*, 1870 139
Fig. 6.3 "E.E.J.M. Home for Working & Destitute Lads" 143
Fig. 6.4 "A Boy Ploughing at Dr. Barnardo's Industrial Farm," Russell, Manitoba, c. 1900 144
Fig. 6.5 "T.B with a Young Steer," 1915 146
Fig. 6.6 Frontispiece to R.M. Ballantyne, *Dusty Diamonds, Cut and Polished*, 1884 148

Fig. 7.1 Mr. Quarrier and a band of young emigrants, 1878 157
Fig. 7.2 Group of immigrant girls en route to Stratford, Ontario, 1908 158
Fig. 7.3 "Party of 84 girls from Bridge-of-Weir, Scotland," 1905 159
Fig. 7.4 Group of immigrant boys and girls from Scotland arriving in Canada, 1921 161
Fig. 7.5 "A Boy Ploughing at Dr. Barnardo's Industrial Farm," Russell, Manitoba, c. 1900 163
Fig. 7.6 "Four Barnardo Children," in front of their Canadian classmates at Cavan School, Durham County, Ontario, 1912 165
Fig. 7.7 Boys' Canadian party at Fairknowe, 1920. Inset: James McNay, April 1925 168
Fig. 8.1 Elizabeth Kessler peers out at the audience prior to going onstage as the male lead of her ballet recital, *Jack of Hearts*, 1986 178
Fig. 8.2 Elizabeth looks downcast as her fine-boned peers titter, *Jack of Hearts*, 1986 183
Fig. 8.3 Aunt Eadie gives Elizabeth life lessons, *Jack of Hearts*, 1986 185
Fig. 8.4 Elizabeth hides in her closet, tearfully leafing through images of ballerinas, *Jack of Hearts*, 1986 187
Fig. 8.5 Trudy, perched on Elizabeth's knee, kisses Elizabeth as they take their bows, *Jack of Hearts*, 1986 189
Fig. 8.6 Elizabeth springs with her ballerina peers during the ballet recital, the arms of the girls in front reinforcing her exclusion, *Jack of Hearts*, 1986 192
Fig. 9.1 Squeegee kids in *Weltschmerz*, June 26, 1997, by Gareth Lind 205
Fig. 9.2 Sloppy dressing in *Weltschmerz*, February 11, 1999, by Gareth Lind 207
Fig. 9.3 Wild meat in *Weltschmerz*, May 27, 1999, by Gareth Lind 211
Fig. 9.4 Starvee kids in *Weltschmerz*, August 6, 1998, by Gareth Lind 212
Fig. 10.1 *Monument to Canadian Fallen* (Korean War Memorial), Ottawa, 2002, by Yoo Young Mun 221
Fig. 10.2 *The Response* (National War Memorial), Ottawa, 1939, by Vernon March 224
Fig. 10.3 *Refuge—Mother and Child* (Vietnamese Commemorative Monument), Ottawa, 1955, by Pham Thế Trung 227
Fig. 11.1 "Muktie [and] Savitni, 1898. Little Hindoo Girls adopted by Miss Minor & Miss Jefferson" 236
Fig. 11.2 "Group of Missionaries in the Kolhapur Mission, India, Jan. 1892" 239
Fig. 11.3 "One of our Christian Families. Kolhapur," 1892 240
Fig. 11.4 "Sewing Man," 1892 241
Fig. 11.5 "Indian Mode of Sawing Wood," 1892 242
Fig. 11.6 "Famine people; workers on Miss Jefferson & Miss Minor's Compound, 1897" 247
Fig. 11.7 "Mary Hannum & Robert Henry Hannum, 1896" 250
Fig. 12.1 Tea party in a ward at Montreal's Royal Victoria Hospital, 1894 260

Fig. 12.2 Hospital interiors were typically shown as orderly and bloodless 262
Fig. 12.3 The exteriors of early twentieth-century hospitals were photographed as welcoming and urbane 262
Fig. 12.4 A pneumothorax is performed at the Children's Memorial Hospital, Montreal 263
Fig. 12.5 Young patient on a stretcher at Toronto's Victoria Hospital for Sick Children 264
Fig. 12.6 The open-air school in February: Royal Edward Institute for the Study, Prevention, and Care of Tuberculosis, 1913 265
Fig. 12.7 Exterior scene on Mount Royal, 1912 267
Fig. 12.8 Sewing hour, 1912 268
Fig. 12.9 Boy drawing in bed, 1912 269
Fig. 12.10 Toronto cityscape from inside SickKids, photographed by a seventeen-year-old boy 273
Fig. 12.11 Tunnel-like image of SickKids by a sixteen-year-old girl 274
Fig. 12.12 View outside the hospital by the same sixteen-year-old girl 275
Fig. 13.1 The Rules of Health, card distributed by the Canadian Red Cross, 1944 283
Fig. 13.2 Stick figures illustrate the story of how one family entered the Kingdom of Health 293
Fig. 13.3 Inkameep health rule drawings from *Canadian Red Cross Junior*, 1938 294
Fig. 13.4 Inkameep health rule drawings from *Canadian Red Cross Junior*, 1939 295
Fig. 13.5 Scene or rehearsal of an Inkameep drama recorded by an Inkameep student drawing 296
Fig. 13.6 Inkameep students, in costume, rehearsing one of their dramas, c. 1941 297
Fig. 14.1 Georgetown School, 1953 306
Fig. 14.2 Student teachers practise teaching kindergarten at the Toronto Normal School, c. 1898 308
Fig. 14.3 Wellesley Street School, 1873 310
Fig. 14.4 Wellesley Street School, 1873, ground floor plan, by William G. Storm 311
Fig. 14.5 Wellesley Street School, 1873, showing site plan, play sheds, and privies, by William G. Storm 312
Fig. 14.6 St. Lawrence Ward School, 1873, by William G. Storm 313
Fig. 14.7 Wellesley School, St. John's Ward, plan of ground floor 314
Fig. 14.8 Basement plan of Wellesley School 317
Fig. 14.9 Wellesley School, alterations and additions, ground floor plan, 1908 319
Fig. 15.1 *The Story*, 1890, by George Reid 329
Fig. 15.2 *The Other Side of the Question*, 1890, by George Reid 331
Fig. 15.3 *Mortgaging the Homestead*, 1890, by George Reid 333

Fig. 15.4 *The Foreclosure of the Mortgage*, 1934 replica, by George Reid 337
Fig. 15.5 *Patriotism*, 1929, by George Reid 342
Fig. 16.1 Detail from *Return from School,* c. 1901, by James Wilson Morrice 348
Fig. 16.2 *Sketch for "Return from School,"* c. 1897–1901, by James Wilson Morrice 349
Fig. 16.3 A country school in 1915 353
Fig. 16.4 *Girl Wearing Clogs*, c. 1896–1898, by James Wilson Morrice 357
Fig. 16.5 *Sugar Bush*, c. 1897–1898, by James Wilson Morrice 359
Fig. 16.6 *La Communiante*, 1899, by James Wilson Morrice 360
Fig. 17.1 *Diego Asleep #2*, 1972, by Jack Chambers 367
Fig. 17.2 *Margaret Keane Trading Card*, 2004, by Daniel Barrow 377
Fig. 17.3 *Awakening*, 2006, by Rodney Graham 381
Fig. 18.1 Untitled snapshot, 1936, by Denyse Snow Rynard and Michael Snow 389
Fig. 18.2 *Lark and Her Children, Vancouver*, 1974, by Robert Minden 392
Fig. 18.3 *Andrea and Dewi, 1973*, by Robert Minden 393
Fig. 18.4 Untitled, from *Staying Home*, 1981–1983/1900 by Michael Mitchell 397
Fig. 18.5 *Co-operative Self-portrait: Rowenna and I*, 1979, by Sandra Semchuk with Rowenna Holden 399
Fig. 18.6 *Pinery Net Fishing, Pinery, Ontario*, 1984/2005, by Sandra Semchuk with Rowenna Holden 401
Fig. 18.7 *Gribouillage sur la photographie – Autoportrait à la table lumineuse*, 1988, by Michel Campeau 403
Fig. 18.8 Detail from *Maybe Wendy's Right*, 1979, by Carol Condé and Karl Beveridge . . . 404
Fig. 18.9 Detail from *Mnemonicon (the screen)*, 1988, by Marian Penner Bancroft 407
Fig. 18.10 *Quintet*, 1984, by Michael Snow 409
Fig. 19.1 *Portrait of Vincent*, 1974, by Paterson Ewen 416
Fig. 19.2 *The Bandaged Man*, 1973, by Paterson Ewen 421

ACKNOWLEDGEMENTS

I was fortunate throughout this project to receive support from a large number of individuals and organizations. A special thanks is owed to Cynthia Comacchio, series editor of Studies in Childhood and Family in Canada, for encouraging me to be editor of this book. My sincere gratitude goes to the authors who have contributed to the publication. I also want to thank Annmarie Adams, Kristina Huneault, and Martha Langford, who as members of the editorial board helped to develop the content of this anthology. I am especially indebted to Martha Langford, whose support and advice guided this publication at each stage to completion.

Graduate students in the master's program in the Department of Art History, Concordia University, merit special recognition. Suzanne Rackover assisted in the research, Alena Buis in the preparation of the manuscript. I would like to express my appreciation to Victoria Dickenson, executive director of the McCord Museum, who invited me to curate the exhibition *Picturing Her: Images of Girlhood / Salut les filles ! La jeune fille en images* at the McCord Museum of Canadian History. This exhibition and the accompanying symposium precipitated the call for papers for this book.

I also wish to stress the valuable assistance provided by Lisa Quinn, acquisitions editor of Wilfrid Laurier University Press, who has played a crucial role in supporting this publication, and more recently, Rob Kohlmeier, managing editor, whose excellent supervision facilitated the editorial process.

This book would not have been possible without the contribution of the various agencies and institutions that have provided funding: the Aid to Scholarly Publications Programme of the Canadian Federation for the Humanities and Social Sciences, the Canada Council for the Arts for publishing programs, and Concordia University.

LOREN LERNER

INTRODUCTION

DEPICTING CANADA'S CHILDREN IS AN ANTHOLOGY of essays on the visual representation of children drawing on imagery from the seventeenth century to the present. The purpose of this volume is to bring together a rich array of subjects to encourage a critical perspective in the analysis of pictures of Canadian children. Recognizing the importance of methodological diversity, these essays discuss understandings of children and childhood that encompass a wide range of media and contexts. In the process, they provide a close study of the evolution of the figure of the child and shed light on the defining role children have played in Canadian history and our assumptions about them. The topics address many issues, including child imagery, the ideologies of childhood, race, class, gender, architectural spaces, children's bodies, sexuality, and the commercialization of childhood.

The subject of childhood has been studied from differing viewpoints, covering such disciplines as art history, history, anthropology, developmental psychology, sociology, and literary criticism. Indebted to the findings of these studies, this volume has as its objective to demonstrate the significance of visual culture within this field of inquiry.[1] More than an examination of images in formal settings such as art galleries and museums, visual culture takes into account the components of an image and the role of the making of pictorial works in everyday life. It also looks at how the making of images relates to intellectual, cultural, and political history, as well as to theoretical constructs such as semiotics, psychology, and feminism. All types of pictures—oil paintings, children's drawings, architectural renderings, photographs, snapshots, commercial reproductions, cartoons, advertisements, and films—are given equal weight in this treatment. Whether canonical or not, the images discussed here advance our understanding of Canada's children and Canadian childhood.

The visual representation of children has been the subject of a number of important studies, but this attention is still relatively new. Further, these studies have been devoted mainly to works of art. Robert Rosenblum's *The Romantic Child from Runge to Sendak* is one of the first monographs on this theme.[2] In this short text, which covers the late eighteenth century to recent times, Rosenblum looks at the romanticized vision of children in paintings and book illustrations as observed reality and allegorical symbol. In *Pictures of Innocence: The History and Crisis of Ideal Childhood*, Anne Higonnet takes another point of view.[3] She notes that the emphasis on the child's body in the mass production of illustrations and photographs beginning in the late nineteenth century led to the transformation of the Romantic child into the "knowing child" possessed of a more complex, ambiguous, and problematic constellation of attributes. Focusing on national identity, David Lubin, in *Picturing a Nation: Art and Social Change in Nineteenth-Century America*, explains that the portrayal of middle-class children in genre paintings during that century relates to America's image of itself as a national entity in how it thought it was or should be.[4] Claire Perry, in *Young America: Childhood in Nineteenth-Century Art and Culture*, broadens the scope by showing that nineteenth-century America saw within itself a wide range of children: male and female, white and Indian, truant and studious.[5] European artists from the nineteenth century to the beginning of World War I—Gustave Courbet, Jacques Henri Lartigue, Oskar Kokoschka, Edouard Manet, Auguste Renoir, and Egon Schiele—are the subject of a series of essays in *Picturing Children: Constructions of Childhood between Rousseau and Freud*, edited by Marilyn R. Brown.[6] These essays discuss how images of childhood that were central to the production of modern art coalesce with the emergence of the modern concept of childhood, which began with the publication of Jean-Jacques Rousseau's *Emile* in 1762. In a more wide-ranging survey of images of children in the history of Western art, Erika Langmuir's *Imagining Childhood: Themes in the Imagery of Childhood* addresses themes such as the family, aging, loss of innocence, illness, and death to explore how childhood is visualized.[7]

Although *Depicting Canada's Children* favours a more inclusive corpus of images than do the publications cited above, it shares with these texts two premises: the idea that the child is a historically changeable social construction that can inform our learning about actual children, and the warning not to interpret these representations simply as illustrations of a verifiable external reality. Making images presupposes the agency of a creator and the individualized activity of visual inventiveness, leading us to assume that complex meanings are embodied in pictures of children. In a departure from previous explorations, however, this anthology aspires to demonstrate the possibilities of interpretations that take into account the shifting social, cultural, and political contexts defining the history of the Canadian child. As such, *Depicting Canada's Children* owes a debt of gratitude to the historians of Canada's children and youth. Landmark studies of childhood and family history have delved into the living environments of families; the upbringing of children; and the laws, policies, and practices governing child care and protection.[8] These texts, in considering public records, parliamentary debates, child-rearing manuals, autobiographies, anecdotal writings, oral histories, and theoretical concepts of youth and familial relations, are foundational in the academic study of the Canadian child. Curators of museums and historic sites from across Canada have also contributed to this work. Studying archaeological evidence and the material culture of clothing, household objects, manufactured goods, built forms, physical spaces, and landscapes, these scholars have uncovered illuminating evidence of past and present cultures.[9]

The McCord Museum of Canadian History in Montreal has a long record of achievement in researching Canada's material culture: two exhibitions, *Growing Up in Montréal* (2004) and *Picturing Her: Images of Girlhood* (2005), helped shape this collection of essays.[10] Starting with the close of the nineteenth century and spanning the twentieth, *Growing Up in Montréal*, produced under the direction of Victoria Dickenson and Moira McCaffrey, examined the activities and behaviours of young Montrealers at home and school and in hospital, and in the outdoor spaces of parks, playgrounds, and back lanes. Through toys, games, books, furniture, children's clothes, and historic photographs and documents, the exhibition highlighted the role children played in shaping Montreal's rapidly expanding urban environment and the medical and technological innovations that changed their lives.

The exhibition *Picturing Her*, which I curated primarily with selections from McCord's holdings of paintings, prints, drawings, and photographs, considered the expressions of Canadian girlhood from the 1860s to the present. Sketchbooks, diaries, and albums were included to provide access to the private rituals of girls, while works by contemporary artists explored vulnerable girls and girls who radiate potential and promise for the future. The symposium held in conjunction with the *Picturing Her* exhibition precipitated the call for papers for *Depicting Canada's Children*.[11] The members of the book's editorial board—Annmarie Adams, Kristina Huneault, and Martha Langford, all participants at the symposium—were most instrumental in shaping the content of this anthology and encouraging the interdisciplinary vitality that characterizes the essays.

Depicting Canada's Children is organized into sections to emphasize the continuities as well as the changes in images of children over time, and also to promote comparative discussion. Within this thematic structure, each article has its own merits and raises a specific set of questions about pictures of children.

Symbol and Reality

From the time the concept of childhood as a distinct developmental stage was introduced by Enlightenment philosophers such as John Locke and Jean-Jacques Rousseau, children have been both projections of society's fondest desires and evidence of its worst failures. The first chapter of *Depicting Canada's Children* considers this split image of children, reflecting on how adult ambivalence toward children has taken on different forms.[12] In "Iconography of the Child in Early Quebec Art," François-Marc Gagnon introduces the image of the child as it was drawn in Quebec even before the writings of Locke and Rousseau. These early seventeenth-century depictions of nonconverted Aboriginal children contrast with the religious paintings of white children produced during the same period. This structure of comparison persists into the modern era. Whereas nineteenth-century Quebec artists treated bourgeois children more as complacent types than as individuals, modern paintings of rural children in Quebec began to reflect the harsh realities of poverty and climate and the strict ideology of the Catholic Church.

"Shaping Modern Boyhood: Indian Lore, Child Psychology, and the Cultural Landscape of Camp Ahmek" by Abigail A. Van Slyck explores the first Canadian-owned private summer camp in Ontario's Algonquin Park, opened in 1921, and its close association with two innovations introduced to summer camping in the 1920s. The first was the integration of First Nations motifs into camp routine, particularly the practice of encouraging white campers to impersonate Native Americans in elaborate council ring ceremonies. The second was the application of scientific methodologies to the camp program, especially the use of behavioural psychology to shape the character of individual campers. Drawing on a number of archival sources, including extant buildings and brochures from Ahmek's archives, Van Slyck shows how camps in general and Ahmek in particular constructed a model landscape of childhood that was inevitably complicated by interrelated ideas about gender, class, and race.

Ironically, as Ahmek's boys were being taught to idealize Native Americans in camp settings, federally sponsored residential schools for First Nations children begun in the late nineteenth century were being driven by the national goals of cultural and racial assimilation. In "Haunted: First Nations Children in Residential School Photography," Sherry Farrell Racette merges photographs with oral testimony to expose this disastrous social experiment. Racette's essay unpacks the aesthetic and communicative power of these images, including government photographs and photos taken by the children at the schools, to show how they have acquired new significance in recent years. Giving voice to the generations of children who were forced to attend residential schools and whose experiences have rocked the Canadian conscience, she explains that photographs of this kind have been used by historians and lawyers as documentary evidence, by survivors as tools for healing, and by contemporary artists in evocative and inspiring works.

Racette's essay uncovers the process of marginalization and exclusion by which the majority culture was able to control minority peoples and assign symbolic value to their exploitation. Photographs taken by government-appointed photographers were used to support federal policies and illustrate official publications. Pictures of children have often been manipulated as an ideological superstructure to both reflect and determine the circumstances under which children live their childhoods. In "A Land of Youth: Nationhood and the Image of the Child in the National Film Board of Canada's Still Photography Division," Carol Payne looks at how government photographs served the project of Canadian nationhood. She explains that the changing approaches to documentary photography by the National Film Board of Canada's Still Photography Division show shifting attitudes toward the national citizenry. From the didactic and formalized models that captured a malleable citizenry in the 1940s and 1950s came the seemingly unobtrusive and spontaneous photographs of the 1960s that expressed the carefree spirit of liberal individualism.

With children as distinct targets of consumerism, a burgeoning industry in children's toys, books, magazines, songs, and clothing has helped market the child as a symbol of progress and the future.[13] Jacqueline Reid-Walsh and Claudia Mitchell's "Mapping a Canadian Girlhood Historically through Dolls and Doll-Play" demonstrates how the visual codes of industrially manufactured dolls might have been countered by the memories of the girls who played with the dolls. Situating doll-play within the study of Canadian girls and popular culture more generally, the authors use recollections and photographs of themselves, relatives, and friends playing with dolls to graph this type of play onto the historical material reality of Canadian girlhood.

Others and Outsiders

In this section the essays explore how the oppression of children was at odds with a paradigm that promoted society's obligation to train and educate the child.[14] Between Confederation and the interwar years, eighty thousand British child apprentices came to Canada from poorhouses, orphanages, children's homes, and other institutions to work on farms and as domestic labourers. Immigration to a new and less crowded country would, it was believed, give these poor children the opportunity for a better life. In "The Raw Materials of Empire Building: Depicting Canada's Home Children," Alena M. Buis explains that the term "artistic fiction" is often used to discuss the creative licence child welfare agencies in Great Britain used to dramatize the promotional imagery they circulated. The term also applied to the theatrical enactments these agencies employed to create emotionally charged, highly symbolic photographs. Bearing in mind not only the goals of the child welfare movement but also the larger imperialistic aspirations, Buis presents the visual and literary imagery and metaphors used to "paint" a picture of the destitute child and the transformation of Great Britain's "orphans, waifs, and strays" into Canada's home children. Considering the same topic from a different point of view, Margaret McNay's "Immigrants, Labourers, 'Others': Canada's Home Children" offers a personal reading of this history. As the daughter of a father who was a home child but never spoke of his youth, McNay analyzes several photographs of these "little immigrants" to explore how they reveal major themes in the children's lives, including their status as immigrants, labourers, and "others," and how they helped McNay create a "narrative inheritance" and "absent memory."

By the 1970s, the evolving concept of the family, the advent of a new feminism, the growing acceptance of sexual difference, and the development of urban modernity helped introduce a more active, self-determining notion of the child.[15] Concurrently, one of the principal goals of parents was to raise their children to be acceptable to society at large. As such, the "other" child came to mean the child who failed to fit into society's controls and expectations. Elspeth Tulloch's "Re-Visioning the Girl's Narrative for the 1980s: The Case of the Short Story 'Jack of Hearts' and Its Film Adaptation" relates how, from 1984 to 1986, Atlantis Films and the National Film Board of Canada, in reaction to North American feminist concerns about the creation and propagation of positive role models for young women, co-produced a series of twenty-five adaptations based on Canadian short stories that focused positively on the otherness of the new Canadian girl. Wishing to document the ways in which Isabel Huggan's film *Jack of Hearts* reflected attempts to diversify representations of adolescent forms of femininity, Tulloch's essay examines the female adolescent protagonist in the film adaptation by director Cynthia Scott and scriptwriters Jack Blum and Sharon Corder. Tulloch's analysis shows how *Jack of Hearts* sought to correct the precursor text by having the protagonist embrace so-called masculine traits or responsibilities, or at least adhere to less passive feminine behaviours.

Derek Foster, in "Locating Children in the Discourse of Squeegee Kids," also takes on the task of studying adolescents as an "other" category. In the late 1990s, the Ontario government became concerned with the social issue of squeegeeing, where motorists were approached while stopped at intersections and asked if they wanted their windshield cleaned, with the expectation of a donation in return for this brief labour. Foster argues that the public's understanding of childhood at that time was a crucial determinant in the way this issue took shape. As more "kids" took up squeegeeing, they were portrayed as hardened by the streets and thus more adult. Foster's essay shows how the activities of squeegee kids shaped their public identity and influenced the media's subsequent characterization of them as dissident, alienated, dirty, rebellious, delinquent, and deviant. This depiction in a political cartoon strip, *Weltschmerz*, by Gareth Lind, suggests a reversal in that it was not youth who required the protection of society but society that required protection from youth.

In "A Child's Place in Ottawa's Commemorative Landscape" by Susan Hart, the child as "other" is a political metaphor for the child as nation. Hart explores two public monuments commemorating the Canadian Forces that depict children, the *Monument to Canadian Fallen* (2002, Confederation Park, Ottawa), a statue group representing Canada's military contribution to the Korean War and subsequent peacekeeping mission; and *Refuge—Mother and Child* (1995, Preston Street, Ottawa), referencing the Vietnam War. Although superficially these monuments acknowledge the importance of the child in the national narrative, indeed, as the future of the nation, on deeper consideration a more complicated picture emerges. The children represented, Hart explains, are not Canadian children but abstract symbols of underdeveloped countries or infantilized nations that have not yet reached the maturity that Canada imagines it has attained.

Subjects of Care

Since the nineteenth century, children's bodies and emotions have been seen as vulnerable, needing both protection and discipline by parents, schools, and other organizations.[16] This section addresses the supervision and control of children in spheres thought to be essential to improving their lives: an effective educational system, a good family life, child and family welfare, and quality healthcare. The first essay, "Frocks and Bangles: The Photographic Conversion of Two Indian Girls" by Sharon Murray, situates the beginnings of this discourse in the religious morality typical of the nineteenth century and in Canada's presumed role in international affairs. Murray's essay is a close study of an 1898 photograph of two girls in India, Muktie and Savitni, who are dressed in Western frocks. The photograph is attached to the last page of an album assembled and captioned by Amanda Jefferson of Berwick, Nova Scotia, who, along with her lifelong companion Emily Minor, worked in western India as a missionary. This essay addresses how the photograph generates an image of Muktie and Savitni's conversion. It pictures a cultural conversion as much as a religious one since it adopts the two girls as naturalized Christian citizens of Jefferson's home culture, regardless of the actuality of their circumstances at the moment the image was created.

Droughts and famines, with their attendant sickness and death, probably led to this Canadian missionary's adoption of Muktie and Savitni. Meanwhile, in Canada, with paediatrics advancing as a distinct field of medicine, the proper care of sick children in hospitals built especially for them was becoming a serious priority. "Pictures of Health: Sick Kids Exposed" by Annmarie Adams, David Theodore, and Patricia McKeever juxtaposes photographs taken in Montreal and Toronto hospitals prior to World War II with recent photographs taken by patients of Toronto's SickKids hospital.

The earlier photographs present the hospital either as a therapeutic centre where physicians use new technology to cure children or as a welcoming place where the sick play and study, imitating everyday life despite their illnesses. The latter part of the essay positions the children as the image-makers: they take their own photographs of the hospital's Atrium and are willing to expose themselves in Canada's largest paediatric facility.

The childrens' photographs of Toronto's SickKids transgress the passive representations of children in hospital interiors. Here, the children are active interpreters of their own visual landscape. "Healthy Bodies, Strong Citizens: Okanagan Children's Drawings and the Canadian Junior Red Cross" by Andrea N. Walsh introduces an earlier example of agency and transgression, this time by First Nations children aged ten to seventeen who attended the Inkameep Day School in British Columbia. The children's drawings, made between 1936 and 1942, present their interpretations of the Red Cross Rules for Good Health. The drawings were sent to the national office of the Canadian Junior Red Cross in Ottawa, and a certain number were published in 1938 and 1939. In this essay, Walsh explores the evidence of agency in Aboriginal children and youth as witnessed in these drawings, and shows how the drawings interrupted the dominant paradigms of health and models of citizenship during the interwar and World War II eras.

The public health movement in Canada was a nation-building process that attempted to erase differences in the upbringing of children. At classroom desks from coast to coast, compliance and preservation of the social order were part of the pattern for children learning to be citizens.[17] Prior to the 1870s, education was voluntary and erratic, especially for the poorer ranks. But as children ceased being workers on farms and in factories and became instead schoolboys and schoolgirls, institutionalized education emerged as a carefully regulated instrument of conformity. In "Children and School Interiors: The User-Material Culture-Environment Nexus in Late Nineteenth-Century Toronto," Kai Wood Mah explores the modern school plan by tracing Toronto's Wellesley Street School through three decades of physical transformation in the late 1800s. The essay demonstrates the shift in emphasis from school exteriors to school interiors, creating the intimate link between children and healthy, safe learning environments that is so well established today.

Inner Visions

The idea of the child is closely identified with adult selfhood, which itself was the product of a new subjectivity peculiar to the late nineteenth century.[18] This section shows the ways that relatively recent inventive notions of childhood have been linked to understandings of the adult self. In "George Reid's Paintings as Narratives of a Child Nation," I argue that Reid invested memories of his own agrarian childhood in his art to create a vision of Canadian nationhood. Reid's paintings from the 1890s into the twentieth century, which his fellow citizens understood because they were participants in the same narrative, were devoted to inculcating young Canadians with the civic and moral responsibilities thought to be essential to maintaining a recently established nation.

Reid's Canadian boys are situated in rural Ontario, in contrast to the Quebec country girls depicted in *The Return from School* (1901) by James Wilson Morrice. Sandra Paikowsky, in "James Wilson Morrice's *Return from School*: A Modernist Image of Quebec Children," explains that this is an unusual subject for Morrice, although it displays his modernist pictorial language with the same sensitivity and acuity seen in his European images. The condition of Quebec rural life and the education of its children form the subtext for his visual thematization of the everyday act of walking.

If the Enlightenment gave its inheritors the concept of childhood as a separate stage of development, the latter part of the twentieth century may have succeeded in complicating perceptions of adulthood by introducing the idea of the child who is forever present in the adult. In "Something Resembling Childhood: Artworks by Jack Chambers, Daniel Barrow, and Rodney Graham," Johanne Sloan examines the ways artists from the 1970s to the present have penetrated children's inner psyches. Sloan explains how these artists, fascinated by their own childhood or the childhood of their children, generate a set of associations linked to memory, perception, play, technology, and culture with the purpose of remembering and representing childhood from the viewpoint of the adult subject.

Countering the burgeoning industry of commercial photography and the growing documentation of family life in home photographs, photographic art offers another outlook on the visual construction of childhood by contemporary artists. "The Child in Me: A Figure of Photographic Creation" by Martha Langford looks at the ways the depiction of a child can create a photographic illusion that takes us from the real into the imaginary, there to meet "the child in me," a composite of the artist and the spectator. Langford considers the work of Michael Snow, Robert Minden, Michael Mitchell, Sandra Semchuk, Michel Campeau, Carol Condé and Karl Beveridge, and Marian Penner Bancroft to discover the observational, intuitive, and accidental sources of their images and to reveal how the children in their works are not innocent but active, knowing agents of artistic creation.

Monique Westra's "Paterson Ewen's *Portrait of Vincent*" is the last essay in the collection. Westra reminds us that since all accounts of childhood are in some measure depictions of ourselves, the topic can never be as objective as we would hope it to be. In this essay, Westra compares Ewen's portrait of his son Vincent, made in 1974, to *The Bandaged Man*, a symbolic self-portrait completed one year earlier, discussing their resemblance in mode of execution, media, and scale. Linking Ewen's depression with his son's difficulties, she explores how the artist–sitter relationship is extended and interpersonal dynamics complicated when the parent of the represented child is the artist who creates the work.

Depicting Canada's Children is innovative and far reaching in its cross-disciplinary approach and range of analyses and interpretations. With a focus on images, imagery, and representations and on the centrality of vision and the visual world in creating meanings, the essays encourage the reader to recognize the critical scope of this new area of research. The contributors understand the complexities inherent in depictions of children and point the way to advancing the subject within the rich field of visual culture.

Notes

1 See Nicholas Mirzoeff, "What Is Visual Culture?" in *Visual Culture Reader*, 3–13 (London: Routledge, 1998).

2 Robert Rosenblum, *The Romantic Child from Runge to Sendak* (London: Thames & Hudson, 1988).

3 Anne Higonnet, *Pictures of Innocence: The History and Crisis of Ideal Childhood* (London: Thames & Hudson, 1998).

4 David M. Lubin, *Picturing a Nation: Art and Social Change in Nineteenth-Century America* (New Haven, CT: Yale University Press, 1994).

5 Claire Perry, *Young America: Childhood in 19th-Century Art and Culture* (New Haven, CT: Yale University Press, 2006).

6 Marilyn R. Brown, ed., *Picturing Children: Constructions of Childhood between Rousseau and Freud* (Aldershot, UK: Ashgate, 2002).

7 Erika Langmuir, *Imagining Childhood: Themes in the Imagery of Childhood* (New Haven, CT: Yale University Press, 2006).

8 A sampling of recent publications includes Xiaobei Chen, *Tending the Gardens of Citizenship: Child Saving in Toronto 1880s–1920s* (Toronto: University of Toronto Press, 2005); Nancy Janovicek and Joy Parr, *Histories of Canadian Children and Youth* (Don Mills, ON: Oxford University Press, 2003); Françoise Noël, *Family Life and Sociability in Upper and Lower Canada, 1780–1870* (Montreal: McGill-Queen's University Press, 2003); Mona Gleason, *Normalizing the Ideal: Psychology, Schooling, and the Family in Postwar Canada* (Toronto: University of Toronto Press, 1999); Cynthia R. Comacchio, *The Infinite Bonds of a Family: Domesticity in Canada, 1850–1940* (Toronto: University of Toronto Press, 1999); and Neil Sutherland, *Growing Up: Childhood in English Canada from the Great War to the Age of Television* (Toronto: University of Toronto Press, 1997). The Studies in Childhood and Family in Canada series from Wilfrid Laurier University Press has published pivotal works, such as R. Brian Howe and Katherine Covell, eds., A *Question of Commitment: Children's Rights in Canada* (2007); Cynthia Comacchio, *The Dominion of Youth: Adolescence and the Making of Modern Canada 1920 to 1950* (2006); Brian J. Low, *NFB Kids: Portrayals of Children by the National Film Board of Canada, 1939–1989* (2002); Norah L. Lewis, ed., *Freedom to Play: We Made Our Own Fun* (2002); Katherine Covell and R. Brian Howe, *The Challenge of Children's Rights for Canada* (2001); Neil Sutherland, with a new foreword by Cynthia Comacchio, *Children in English-*

Canadian Society: Framing the Twentieth-Century Consensus (2000); and Denyse Baillargeon, *Making Do: Women, Family, and Home in Montreal during the Great Depression*, trans. Yvonne Klein (1999).

9 For example, Christina Bates, "Beauty Unadorned: Dressing Children in Late Nineteenth-Century Ontario," *Material History Bulletin* 21 (1985): 25–34; May Tivy, "Nineteenth-Century Canadian Children's Games," *Material History Bulletin* 21 (1985): 57–64.

10 Coincidentally, two other exhibitions on children took place in 2005: *Childhood Revisited*, depictions of children by Canadian artists over the past one hundred and fifty years, at the Varley Art Gallery, Markham, Ontario; and *Nobody's Child: Canada's Home Children*, consisting of objects and visual documents borrowed from the descendants of these children, at the London Museum, London, Ontario.

11 The symposium took place on December 1, 2005. The keynote speaker was Anne Higonnet, whose address was "The Image of Childhood Today." The participants and titles of the talks were Annmarie Adams, "Constructing Girlhood," Kristina Huneault, "How Close to Me? Mothers and Babies in Canadian Art," Martha Langford, "The Assembled Self: A Photographic Memoir of Girlhood," Loren Lerner, "Picturing Canada: Allegorical Images of the Canadian Girl and Family," Charmaine Nelson, "Racing Childhood: Representations of Black Girls in Canadian Art," and Leah Sherman, "Anne Douglas Savage: The Artist as Teacher and the Teacher as Artist: Modernism in Canadian Art and Art Education." Most of the papers from the symposium are already in publication; those who chose to participate have preferred to offer new essays for *Depicting Canada's Children*.

12 John R. Gillis, "The Birth of the Virtual Child: A Victorian Progeny," in *Beyond the Century of the Child: Cultural History and Developmental Psychology*, ed. Willem Koops and Michael Zuckerman, 83–95 (Philadelphia: University of Pennsylvania Press, 2003).

13 Gary Cross, *The Cute and the Cool: Wondrous Innocence and Modern American Children's Culture* (New York: Oxford University Press, 2004), and Lisa Jacobson, *Raising Consumers: Children and the American Mass Market in the Early Twentieth Century* (New York: Columbia University Press, 2004).

14 George Dimock, "Children's Studies and the Romantic Child," *Picturing Children*, 189–198.

15 Linda A. Pollock, "Foreword," *Picturing Children*, xv–xix.

16 Philippe Aries, *Centuries of Childhood: A Social History of Family Life* (New York: Knopf, 1962).

17 Neil Sutherland, *Children in English-Canadian Society*.

18 Carolyn Steedman, *Strange Dislocations: Childhood and the Idea of Human Interiority, 1780–1930* (Cambridge, MA: Harvard University Press, 1995).

SYMBOL AND REALITY

FRANÇOIS-MARC GAGNON

ICONOGRAPHY OF THE CHILD IN EARLY QUEBEC ART

To better understand the representation of children in early Quebec paintings, it is necessary to look at how the theme of the child was secularized over time. The acceptance of children as legitimate pictorial subject matter happened only gradually, and the earliest representations were entirely within the context of religious imagery. There was, however, one exception, and as is often the case, this exception proved the rule: the depiction of Aboriginal children, or more precisely the way that Aboriginal mothers carried their children. These fascinating images were not always understood. In the monolithic culture of New France, the Aboriginal child, or at least the nonconverted child, was positioned in the sphere of the profane while the white child was placed exclusively within the domain of religion from the moment of baptism.

The Aboriginal Child

Much can be learned from studying two engravings of women made from a presumed drawing by the explorer Samuel de Champlain (fig. 1.1). The first, which seemingly served as an inspiration for the second, is found on one of Champlain's maps engraved by David Pelletier and published in 1612. The second was published in 1619 along with accounts of Champlain's voyages. The fact that the slightly earlier engraving claims to show a Montagnais woman while the second female figure is called a Huron does not seem to have troubled Champlain or his readers. A comparison of the two engravings suggests that the second image could be an interpretation or reworking of the other. In the first image, it is difficult to understand how the mother could breastfeed the nude child on the verge of slipping to the ground. However, the other mother carries the child in a kind of bag slung across her shoulder, and this child looks much more secure. This mother wears a skirt, not a dress, and the belt that encircles her waist has only a decorative purpose.

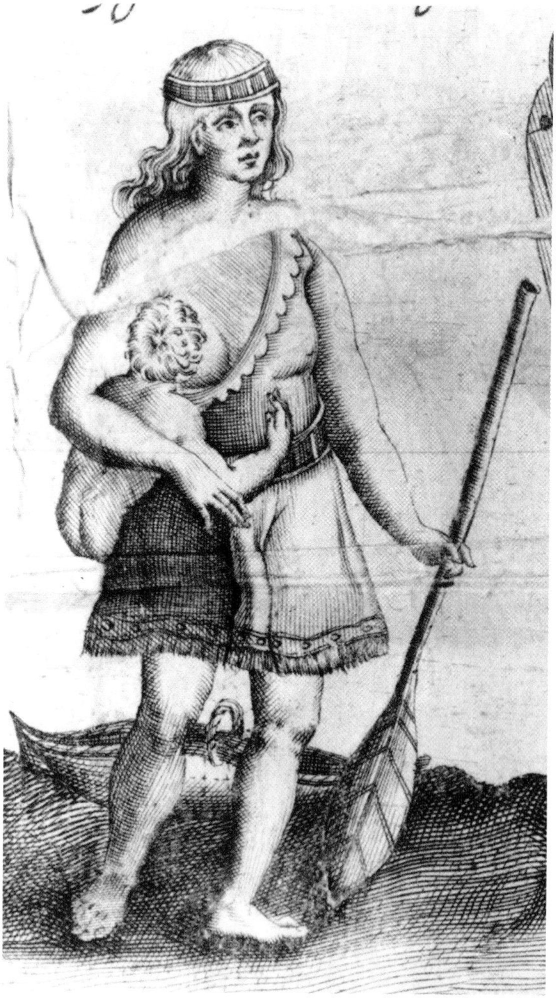

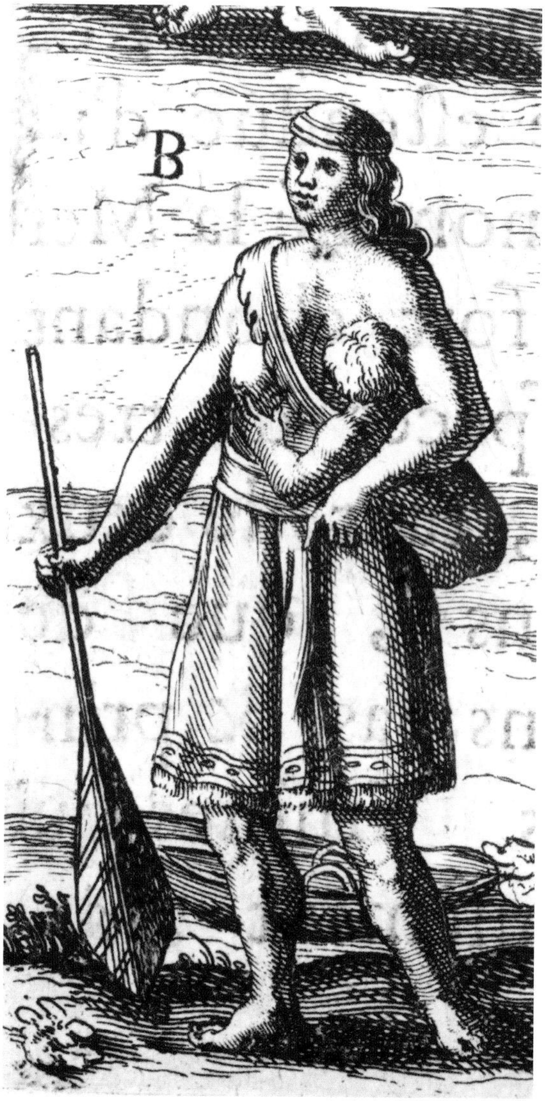

FIGURE 1.1
Depictions of a Montagnais woman in the *Carte geographique de la Nouvelle France*, 1612, and a Huron woman in the *Voyages* of 1619, folio 88.

Such disparities suggest that the engravings were done by different engravers and raise two questions: which image is the closest to Champlain's original drawing, and which one is closest to the reality observed by Champlain? Using the testimony of a seventeenth-century Jesuit missionary, the ethnologist Marc Laberge has proposed a plausible reconstruction of the costumes Aboriginal women and children wore.[1] Indeed, the *Jesuit Relations of 1657–1658* contains a remarkable comparison of French and Aboriginal use of clothing that betrays a European aesthetic:

> In France, men and women have their clothes made rather tight-fitting to impart a lighter appearance, the girls especially priding themselves on their slenderness. In Canada, the people dress to look large, both men and women wearing robes that they gird in two places, below the navel and above the stomach, tucking up these ample robes so that the folds hang down. Thus, they have a great sack, as it were, around the body in which they stow away a thousand things. Mothers put their children there, to fondle them and keep them warm.[2]

Also of interest is the way Aboriginal mothers carried their children on their backs in *naganes*, or cradleboards. The *Historiae canadensis seu Novae Franciae Libri Decem*, written by François Du Creux, a Jesuit, and published in 1666, was illustrated with a few engravings that caught the imagination of his audience.

Facing page 22 is a plate showing Aboriginal women at work (fig. 1.2). The engraving, however, does not reflect Du Creux's text, which discusses how Champlain fought off famine during the siege of Quebec City by the Kirke brothers. Nonetheless, the image is important because it shows more clearly than anything else found in Champlain's work how Aboriginal women prepared corn flour by using two stones that archaeologists have named *mano* and *metate*. However, the woman on the right who grinds corn in a mortar is not completely convincing since her pestle seems too thin for the task. Of greater importance is the *nagane* leaning against a nearby tree; how the baby is secured to the small cedar board remains a mystery. The engraver depicts the crisscrossing leather strips that tightly hold the infant, but he does not show how these thin cords are attached to the board.[3]

Figures 35 and 36 on page 21 of the *Codex canadiensis*[4] show a "portrait d'un Enfant au bersseau" (portrait of a child in a cradle) and are reminiscent of Du Creux's engraving. The "Branle pour Endormir les Enfans" (a swing to rock children to sleep) (fig. 1.3) is a type of hammock suspended between two trees and may be an invention, but it also is taken from a Du Creux image, plate V, facing page 70 (fig. 1.4).

Nevertheless, this image of a baby in a horizontal hammock is strange. As Lafitau explains, the *nagane*'s head strap was normally used to suspend the board vertically from the branch of a tree.

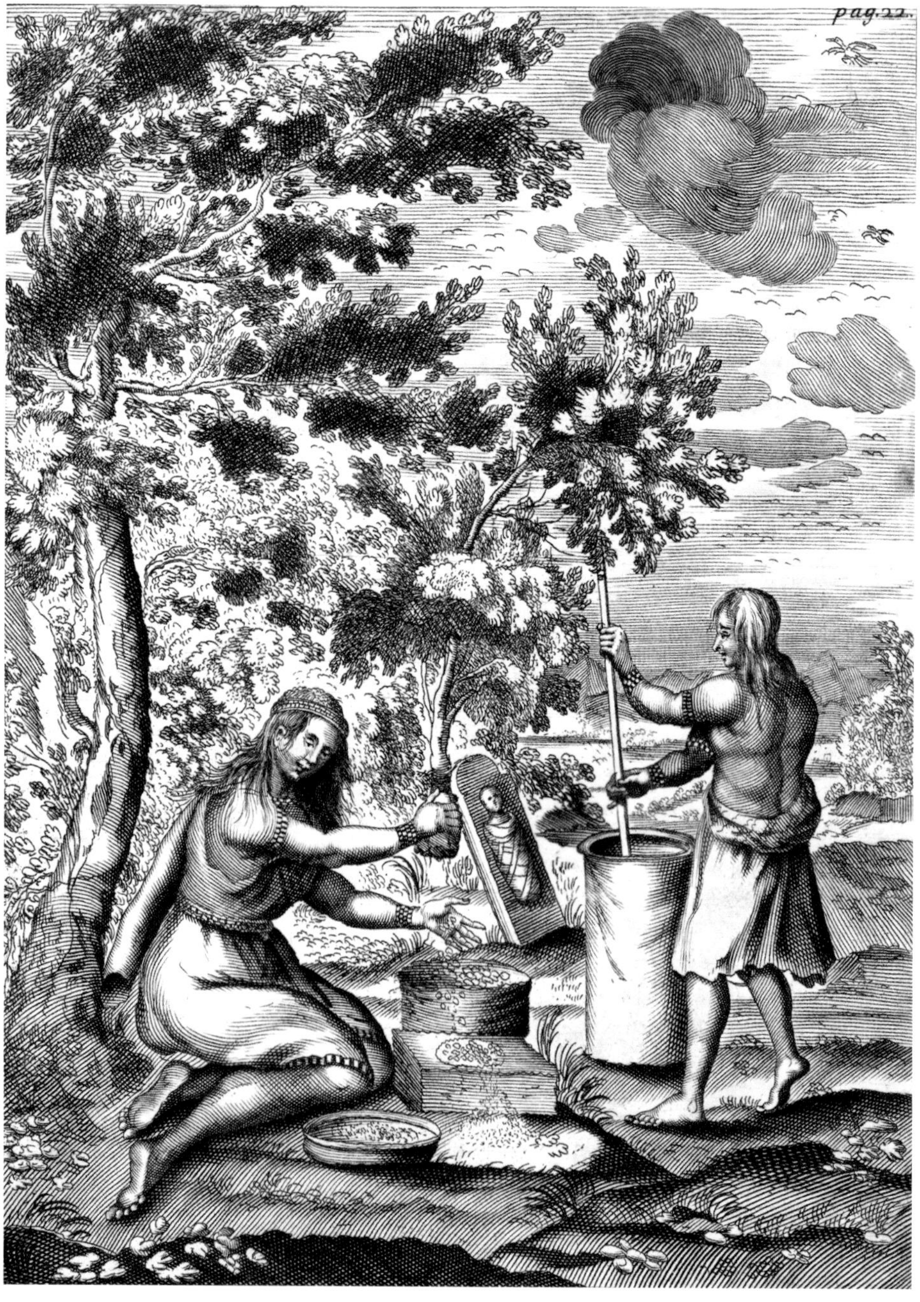

FIGURE 1.2
François Du Creux, *Historiae canadensis seu Novae Franciae Libri Decem*, 1666, engraving facing page 22.

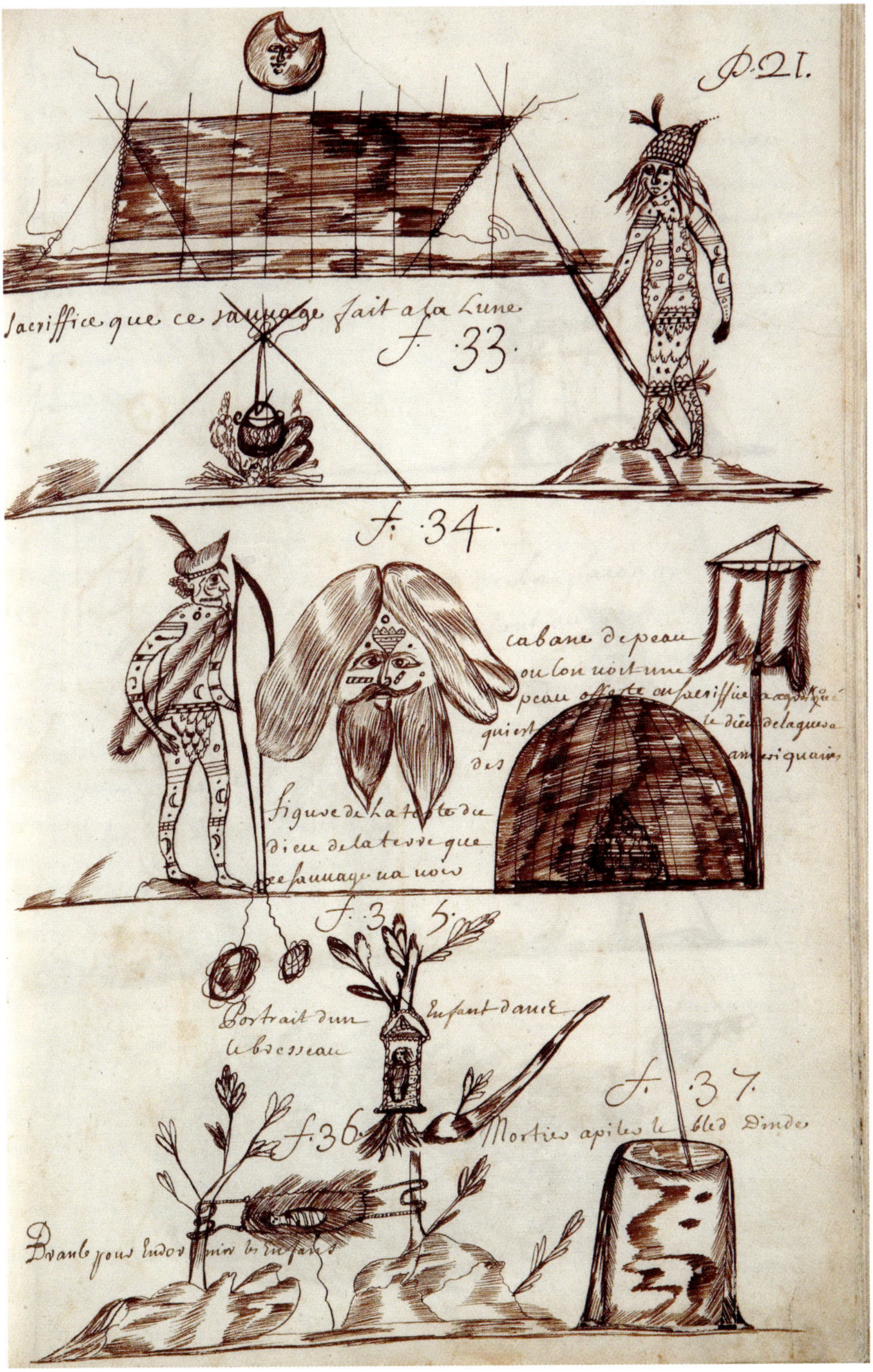

FIGURE 1.3
Louis Nicolas, *Codex canadiensis*, c. 1700, 21. Gilcrease Museum. (Photo courtesy of the Gilcrease Museum of Tulsa, NLC-12158)

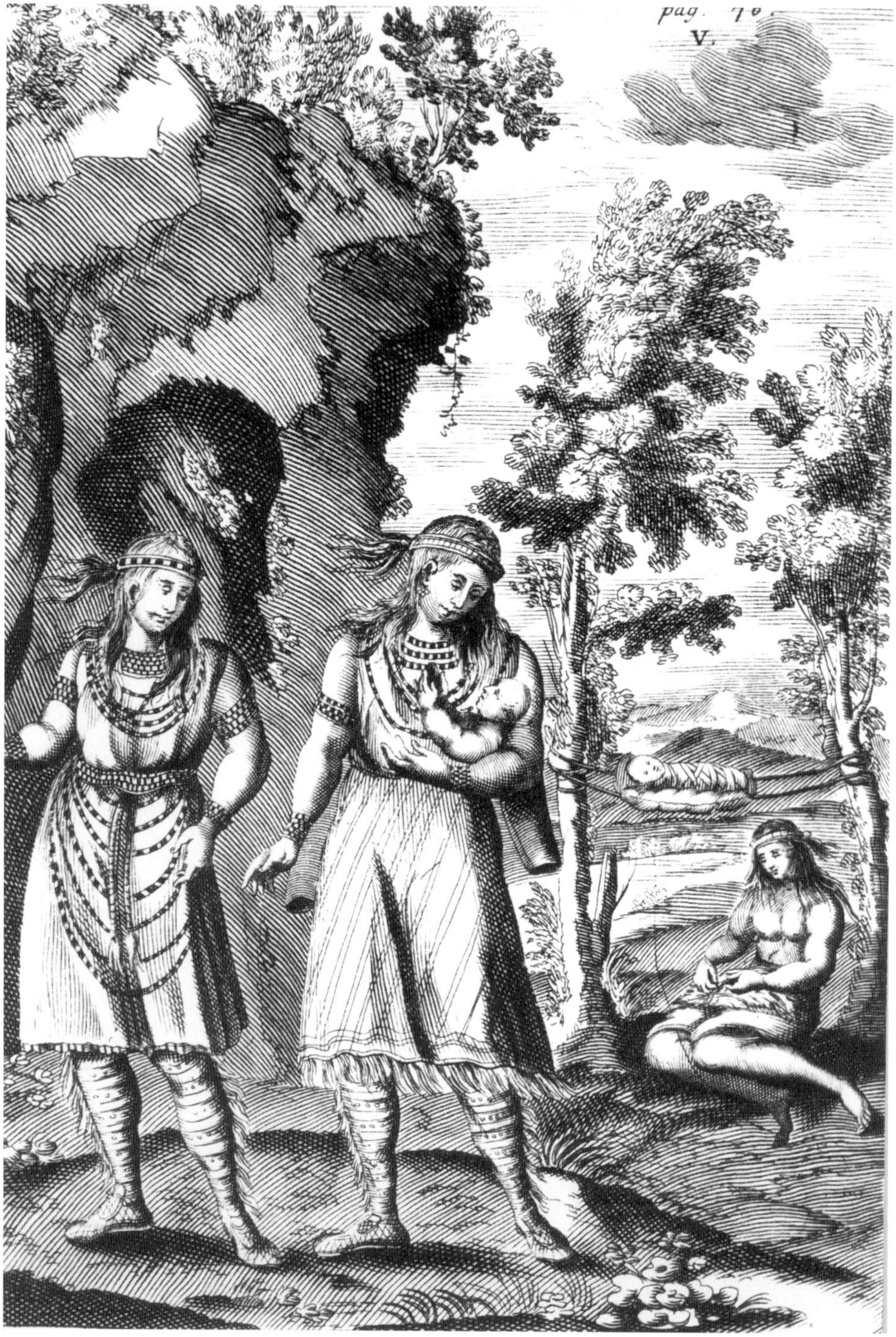

FIGURE 1.4
François Du Creux, *Historiae canadensis seu Novae Franciae Libri Decem,* 1666, plate V, facing page 70.

> Two great straps of strong leather that come out of the top of the cradle make it possible for the mothers to carry it everywhere with them ... or to hang it on a tree branch so the child can be rocked to sleep by the wind while the mothers work.[5]

Du Creux's engraving also poses the question of how the mother, who is swinging the hammock by a string attached to her toe, could keep her child from falling to the ground. The way that Aboriginal women carried their children would continue to be a fascinating motif for artists. Depictions of this practice are found, for example, in the work of Paul Kane, in which he tried to explain the Caw-wacham custom of flattening the skulls of children.[6]

The *Novae Franciae Accurata Delineatio*, a map attributed to the Italian Jesuit missionary Father Joseph Bressani, features an Aboriginal family kneeling before a shining cross. The family is not identified, but as the image is placed immediately to the left of the *Huronum Explicata Tabula*, one can assume they are Huron.[7] The positioning of the group in their own separate space, as well as their larger size when compared to the figures on the map (with the exception of the martyrs in the bottom right inset), indicates that they no longer belong to the Aboriginal world. Rather, they are positioned in opposition to other Natives who represent the unconverted. Classifications of this type were highly important to missionaries in the New World.

Conversion has made this family familiar to modern Christians by virtue of the fact that they are kneeling and have clasped hands. Our souls are kindred, but the discourse of difference is not completely absent. While these Hurons are converts, they are "converted savages," and their detailed Aboriginal costumes are a distinct reminder of their status. On the mother's back, and attached to her hair, is a plate "d'un pied en carré, couvertes de ... pourceline qui pend par derriere" (a foot square covered with ... wampum that hung behind) as described by Champlain.[8] Gabriel Sagard, a Récollet brother, also noted their use, although he described these "plates" a little differently: "And I have seen other women who also wore bracelets on their arms and great plates in front of their stomach, with other plates on their back, circular in shape, like a teasel for carding wool hanging from their hair plates."[9] Considering the converted Huron family on Bressani's map, the comparison to a teasel is an apt one. The father carries a tobacco bag on his back, a Huron practice that was mentioned in the *Relations*.

> Their only covering is a beaver skin, which they wear on their shoulders like a cloak; shoes and leggings in winter, a tobacco pouch on their back, a pipe in hand; around their neck and arms bead necklaces and bracelets of porcelain; they also suspend these from their ears, and wind them around their locks of hair.[10]

The sleeves of the woman's costume are not a part of her dress but separate entities, as Champlain explains: "they have a robe of the same fur, shaped like a cloak, which they wear in the Irish or Egyptian fashion, and sleeves that are tied behind by a cord."[11] The mother no longer carries her children on her back, which is not surprising since they have become more mature. The children are now integrated into the religious sphere of the whites and they also act like white people, clasping their hands together and looking toward heaven.

The White Child

The earliest portrayals of children in New France were purely religious images. This is true not only in the context of representations of the Holy Family or the Christ Child but also when it came to depicting individual children. The importance of the cult of the Holy Family, introduced in Canada by the Jesuits and encouraged by Mgr. Laval, is remarkable. As Honorious Provost has shown, Laval established the rules of the confraternity of the Holy Family between 1664 and 1666 and clearly enunciated its objectives:

> The design and goal of this devotion is to honour the Holy Family of Jesus, Mary and Joseph, and the Holy Angels, and to show Christian households the example of this Holy Family, which must be the model above all others; to sanctify marriages and families; to abolish sin, especially the sin of impurity, which is the scourge of marriage and the source of so many ills and fills the Earth and Hell with the children of Satan, who will curse their Creator for all eternity; to instil in them Christian virtues, especially chastity, humility, tenderness, charity, the union of hearts, patience during tribulations and true devotion.[12]

Evidently, Mgr. Laval was obsessed with the sexual life of his colonists. The Holy Family, consisting of the Virgin Mary, who conceived the Christ Child through the Holy Ghost, and St. Joseph, who played the earthly role of the family provider, was an extreme model of chastity and did not reflect the realities of family life in New France or for some time to come. In order to enforce the intentions of this highly impractical model, the Church inundated the colony with depictions of the Holy Family in a variety of forms, including paintings, sculptures, and engravings in prayer books, as well as liturgical celebrations.

One of the most touching representations of the Holy Family is a painting attributed to Frère Luc (fig. 1.5), a Récollet painter who travelled to New France in 1670 and stayed for a year and a half. The painting depicts a converted Huron girl (indicated by the Christian medal she wears on her belt) confiding in the Holy Family. It is easy to imagine that for Aboriginal children, who were taken from their families and brought to Quebec City to be educated in seminaries or convents, the Holy Family offered a kind of substitute for the families they had left behind. However, it is less certain to what extent these images of the Holy Family responded to the children's psychological needs.

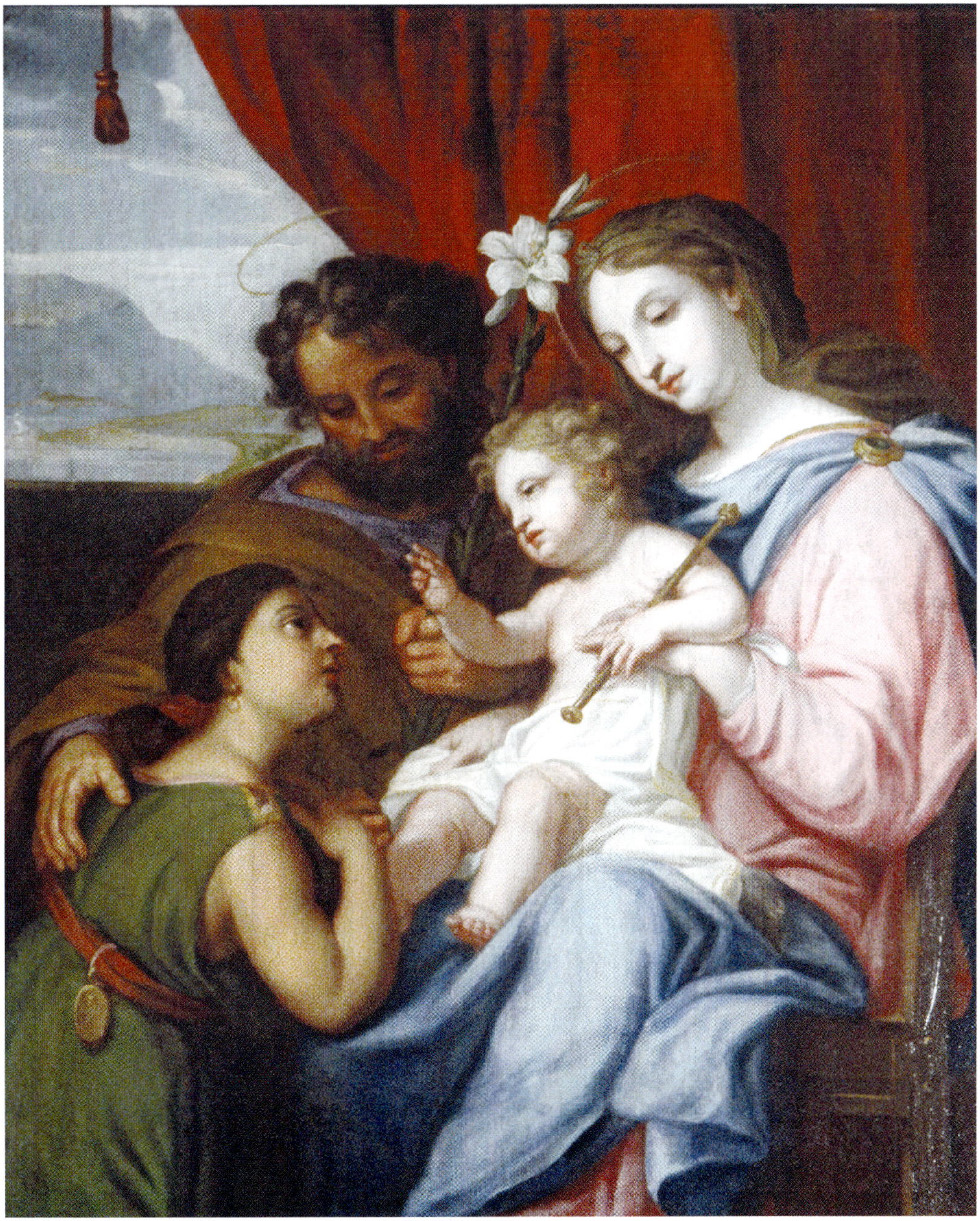

FIGURE 1.5 Claude François (Frère Luc), *Sainte Famille à la huronne*, c. 1671, oil on canvas, 121.9 × 106.7 cm. Ursulines Convent, Quebec City.

There is evidence that some Aboriginal children experienced such images almost as a physical presence. For example, Sagard writes of the reaction of "petit Naneogauachit, appelé à son basptesme Louys" (little Naneogauachit, named Louys at his baptism), who ran to the Récollets in Quebec City because he was distraught over the eternal fate of Oustachecoucou, who had been killed and eaten by two Montagnais women.

> Quick, quick, my brother, he said to one of our Religious brothers, open the door to your room so that I can see if Oustachecoucou is in Hell, for he died without being baptized. He sought a large engraving of the Judgment, of the Hell in which he thought he would find him depicted with the other damned, since our Religious brothers had made a habit of showing them this image to make them better understand the future of man, the glory of the blessed, and the punishment of the wicked.[13]

For little Louis, it was as though the print were actually alive. Is it possible that representations of the Holy Family evoked this same belief? At least their images had the merit of reassuring rather than provoking terror.

A second religious theme depicting adolescents was that of the guardian angel. In fact, according to the rules of the Brotherhood of the Holy Family, Mgr. Laval associated "holy angels" with the Holy Family and saw their worship as being of equal importance. In another painting by Frère Luc, commissioned for the high altar of the parish church of L'Ange-Gardien near Quebec City and now in the Musée National des Beaux-Arts du Québec (fig. 1.6), a guardian angel saves an adolescent from the snake bite of impurity. A similar theme is found in the *Ex-voto à l'ange gardien*, attributed to Michel Dessailliant de Richeterre and conserved at the Hôtel-Dieu in Quebec City. Here, the child Marie-Andrée, the frail youngest daughter of Madame Regnard-Duplessis, is protected by a strong-legged angel. Marie-Andrée's untroubled face greatly affected Gérard Morisset, the important French-Canadian art historian of early Quebec painting.[14]

The Church constantly worried about the purity of the young men and women under its care. As the French cultural historian Philippe Ariès aptly demonstrated, this preoccupation first appeared in educational institutions where great importance was placed on "discipline." According to Ariès, educators interpreted discipline to mean a constant monitoring of the pupils, both day and night—at least in theory.[15] Because the instructors could not be everywhere at all times, guardian angels would take over when the need occurred. As early as the sixteenth century, during the time of Erasmus, the simple mention of possibly being seen by angels was enough to cool the passion of young Sophronius, who was tempted by the prostitute Lucretia.

> SOPH.: Can we escape here from the eyes of God?
> LUC.: Of course not, for He sees everything.
> SOPH.: And from the angels?[16]

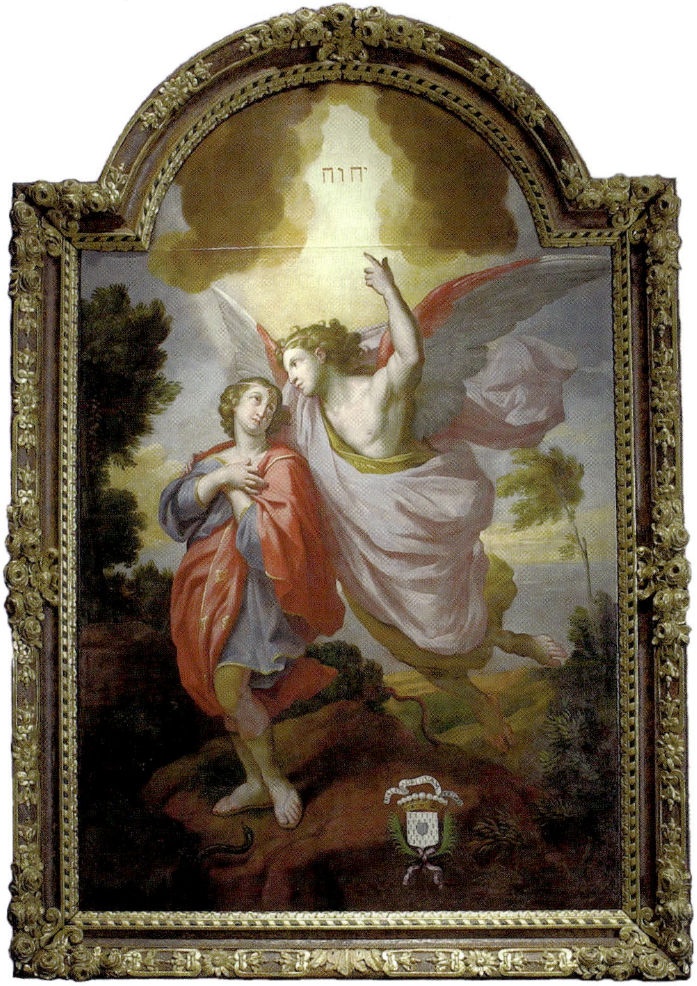

FIGURE 1.6
Claude François (Frère Luc), *L'Ange gardien*, 1671, oil on canvas, 248 × 159.5 cm. Musée National des Beaux-Arts du Québec, Quebec City.

In general, the children and young adults represented in these paintings were treated more as types than as individuals. This is not the case, however, with *ex votos*, particularly the famous portrayal of Madame Riverin and her four children (fig. 1.7). The work was commissioned as an offering to Sainte-Anne-de-Beaupré by Angélique Gaultier, the wife of Denis Riverin, a Quebec City merchant who came from the region of Tours. At the same time, it is also a family portrait of Madame Riverin and her four children, including (from left to right) Marie-Clémence, born in 1700, Marie-Madeleine, born in 1699, Angélique-Jeanne, born in 1697, and Denis François, born in 1698. Everyone is

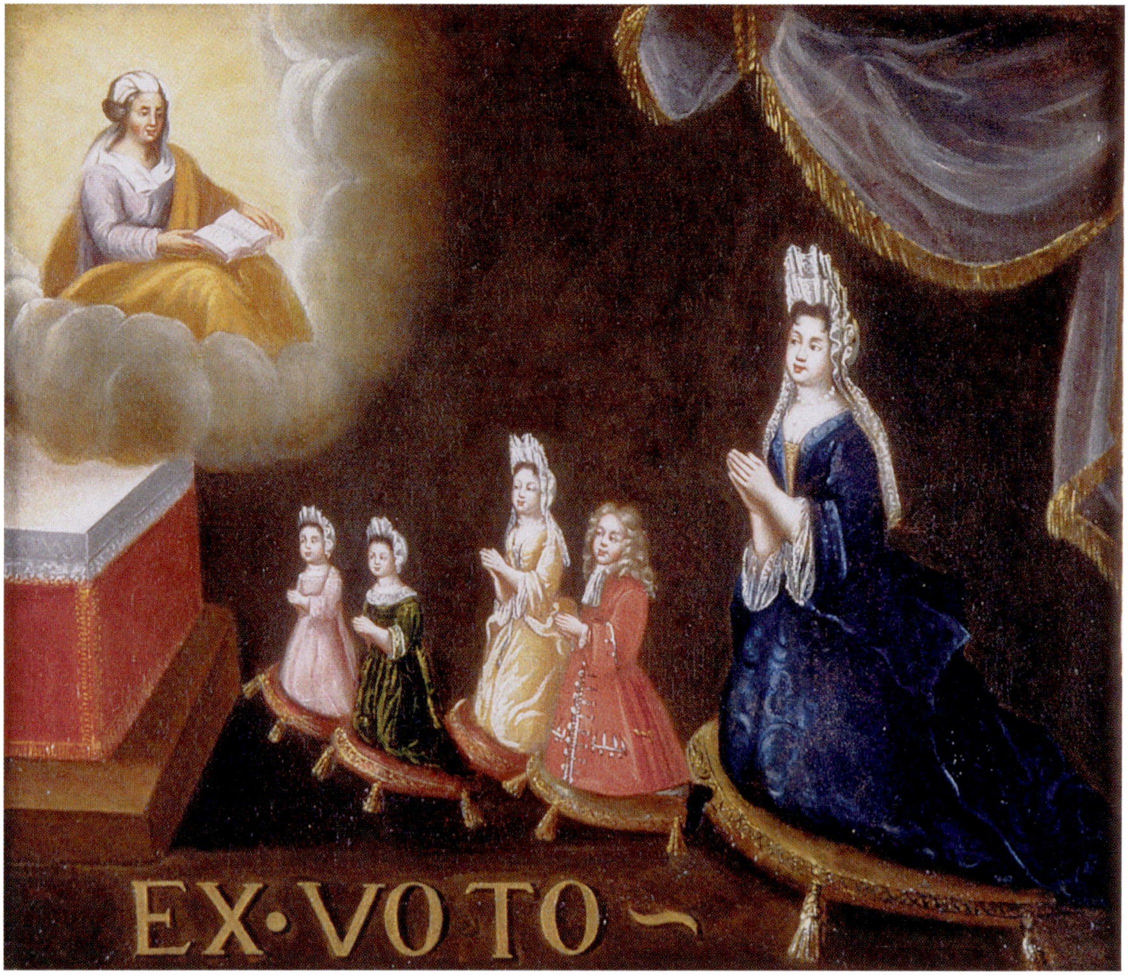

FIGURE 1.7 Anonymous, *Ex-voto de Madame Riverin*, 1703, oil on canvas, 45.6 × 52.7 cm. Musée Sainte Anne, Sainte-Anne-de-Beaupré.

dressed in their Sunday-best clothing. Exactly what prompted Madame Riverin to offer this *ex voto* in 1703 remains a mystery; however, between 1700 and 1702, her husband, who was the director of the Compagnie Mont-Louis in the Gaspésie region, stood a series of trials that undoubtedly affected his social status.[17] Furthermore, Denis Riverin left the colony in 1702 for France and never returned. Because of strong support in his native country, he was later named a representative of the Compagnie de la Colonie in France. In 1706 his mandate was renewed and he held that position until his death in 1717.[18] With her husband's departure, Madame Riverin must have felt abandoned and left with little choice but to entrust her fate and that of her children to Saint Anne, the mother of the Virgin Mary and one of Quebec's holy patrons.

Another *ex voto* is devoted to a single child, little Marie-Anne Robinau de Bécancour.[19] Until recently the work was attributed to a certain Monsieur de Cardenat,[20] who was associated with the mythical École des arts et métiers in Saint-Joachim.[21] However, recent restoration work has revealed a signature on the side of the piece of furniture at the right of the *ex voto*. The artist has been identified as Jacques Galliot, a student of Frère Luc who is said to have frequented Frère Luc's Paris workshop in 1675.[22] Like Madame Riverin's *ex voto*, this painting is in the Musée de Sainte-Anne in Sainte-Anne-de-Beaupré. Marie-Anne was the youngest child of René Robinau de Bécancour (1625–1699), the first baron of Portneuf and the first road surveyor in New France, and Marie-Anne Leneuf de la Poterie, who bore him twelve children. Marie-Anne would have been three years old if this *ex voto* actually dates from 1675. As with the Riverin *ex voto*, the reason for René Robinau's commission is unknown. It is true that he frequently travelled to France, but unlike Riverin, he always returned to the colony. He died in Quebec City and was buried on December 12, 1699, at the Récollet church.[23]

The theme of both of these works is protection, which designates a specific type of *ex voto*. Unlike working-class families and ship captains, members of the bourgeoisie refrained from directly acknowledging any misfortune they had been spared or feared would happen. It is also possible, especially in the case of the *Ex-voto de Mademoiselle de Bécancour*, that the piece was simply a request for protection by her patron saint. What is striking in all these depictions is the great familiarity of its subjects with the religious world. For example, Saint Anne appears in a cloud or stands with her daughter the Virgin Mary and is positioned close to the patron; in the case of Frère Luc's young Huron woman, she leans against the Virgin's knees. Even small children do not seem frightened by the winged apparitions that are their guardian angels. In general, there is a deep interplay between the religious and the profane, the imaginary and the real, the supernatural and the ordinary. Deconstruction of the earthly and heavenly realms of *ex votos* can reveal a wealth of symbolic and visual content. To cite only one example, after the English Conquest, Abbé Antoine Aide-Créquy painted the large altarpiece for the church of Saint-Joachim in 1779 and appropriated the figure of Mary from the *Ex-voto de Mademoiselle de Bécancour*, placing her in the arms of Saint Joachim, who presented the young Virgin to the temple.[24]

The Child in Nineteenth-Century Paintings

It was only in the middle of the nineteenth century that major steps were taken in Quebec toward secularizing the visual image of children, and these changes coincided with a new enthusiasm for portraits by the bourgeoisie. When wealthy merchants from Quebec City and Montreal began sitting for portraits, alone or with their wives, they frequently included their children in the paintings.

In other instances, the subject might be a child on his own, as occurs in the charming image of twelve-year-old Cyprien Tanguay by Antoine Plamondon (1832) (fig. 1.8). The boy wears the school uniform of the Séminaire de Québec, and he is probably in his second or third year of the high school program known as the "Cours classique." His expression is rather serious as he sits with one hand on the writings of Cicero, while with his other hand he writes the Roman orator's name on a sheet of paper with a goose quill. We do know that Cyprien Tanguay would later have a brilliant career. Ordained in 1843, he became renowned as a historian and genealogist, and his monumental *Dictionnaire généalogique des familles canadiennes françaises* (1871–1890) is still consulted today.

In the case of family portraits, children are almost always associated with their mother. This could be interpreted as a reference to the popular religious theme of the Madonna and Child. Antoine Plamondon provides an example of this motif in his double portrait of the Louis-Joseph Papineaus. In one image, Louis-Joseph Papineau (1786–1871), the popular orator and leader of the Patriote Party, is shown seated in the Legislative Assembly.[25] He wears the long, black orator's robe with the double band associated with lawyers. He has slipped the index finger of his left hand between the pages of a book resting on his left thigh; his right hand is placed on a document. On the table are richly bound books by Aristotle, Demosthenes, Montesquieu, Jefferson, and others, as well as a tray of inkwells. In the background on the left is a well-stocked library.

Its companion portrait of Papineau's wife, born Julie Bruneau (1795–1862), includes his eldest daughter, eight-year-old Ezilda (1828–1894), who is more interesting in this context.[26] Dressed in their finest clothing, mother and daughter have interrupted their music lesson to acknowledge the presence of the painter. The mother holds a small musical score on which Ezilda's name is written, and the child looks toward the spectator with a gently mischievous smile. Between the two figures is a bouquet of flowers, and on the wall hangs a lyre, which was often used to symbolize harmony in family portraits.

Théophile Hamel slightly bent the rules when he depicted the Cyrice Têtu family. In a kind of light-hearted allusion to the Oedipus complex, the first portrait shows the father with daughter Caroline (fig. 1.9), while the companion piece presents the mother, née Caroline Dionne, with their son, named after his grandfather, Amable Dionne (fig. 1.10). The little girl plays with her father's watch as he holds her by the waist, and the boy is holding an open book. While the motif may be a tribute to Amable's scholastic abilities, it could also be an allusion to traditional images of the *Education of the Virgin*, in which Saint Anne teaches her daughter to read. Religion is never far off when children appear in Quebec paintings.

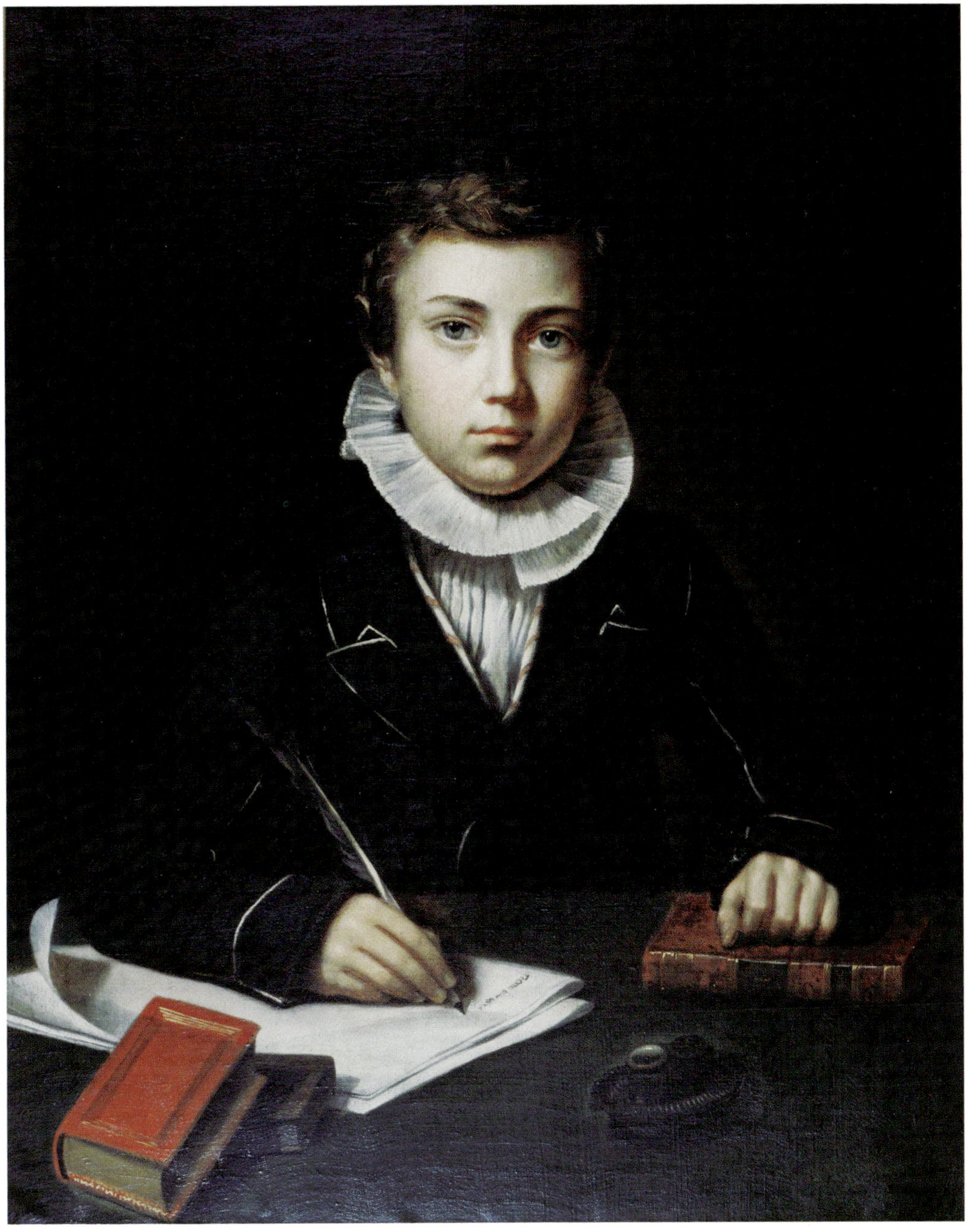

FIGURE 1.8 Antoine Plamondon, *Cyprien Tanguay*, 1832, oil on canvas, 73 × 59.9 cm. Musée de la Civilisation, Collection Séminaire de Québec, no. 1991.74. (Photo: Ida Labrie Perspective)

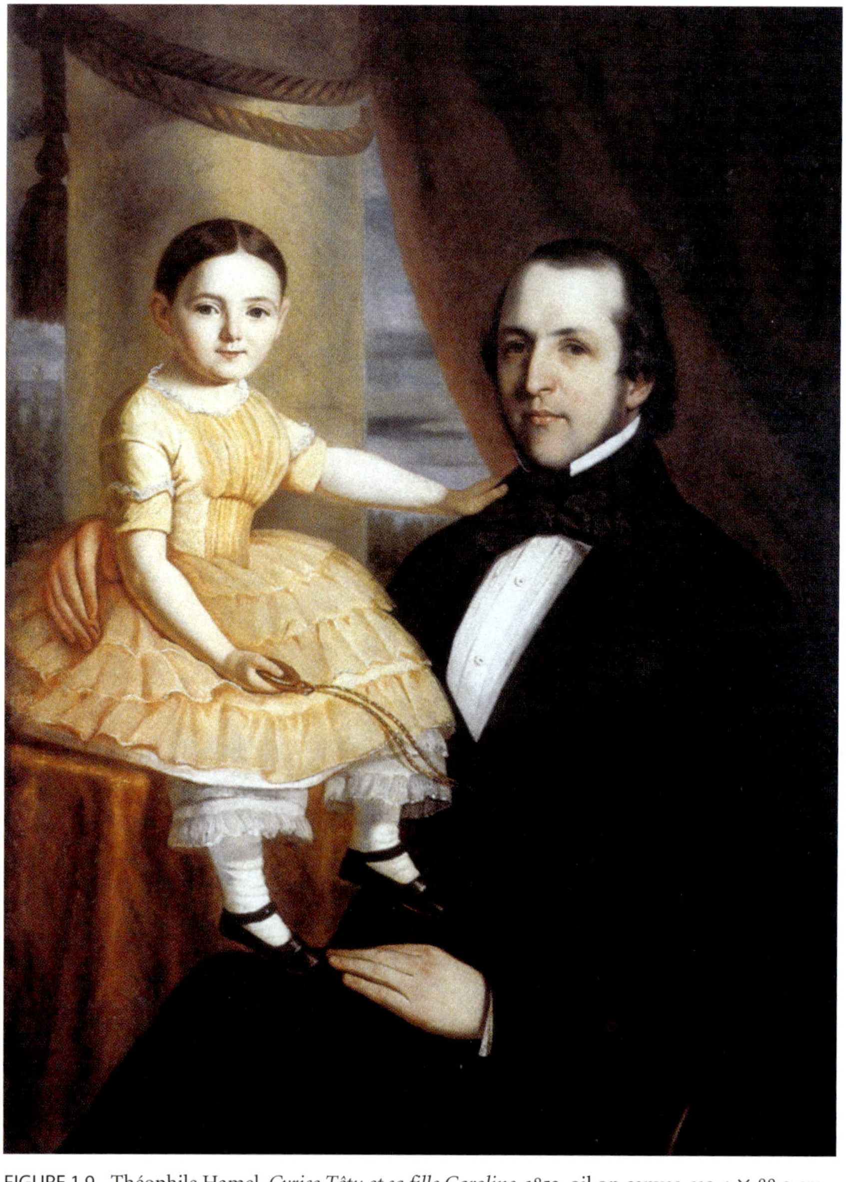

FIGURE 1.9 Théophile Hamel, *Cyrice Têtu et sa fille Caroline*, 1852, oil on canvas, 119.4 × 88.9 cm. Musée National des Beaux-Arts du Québec, Quebec City.

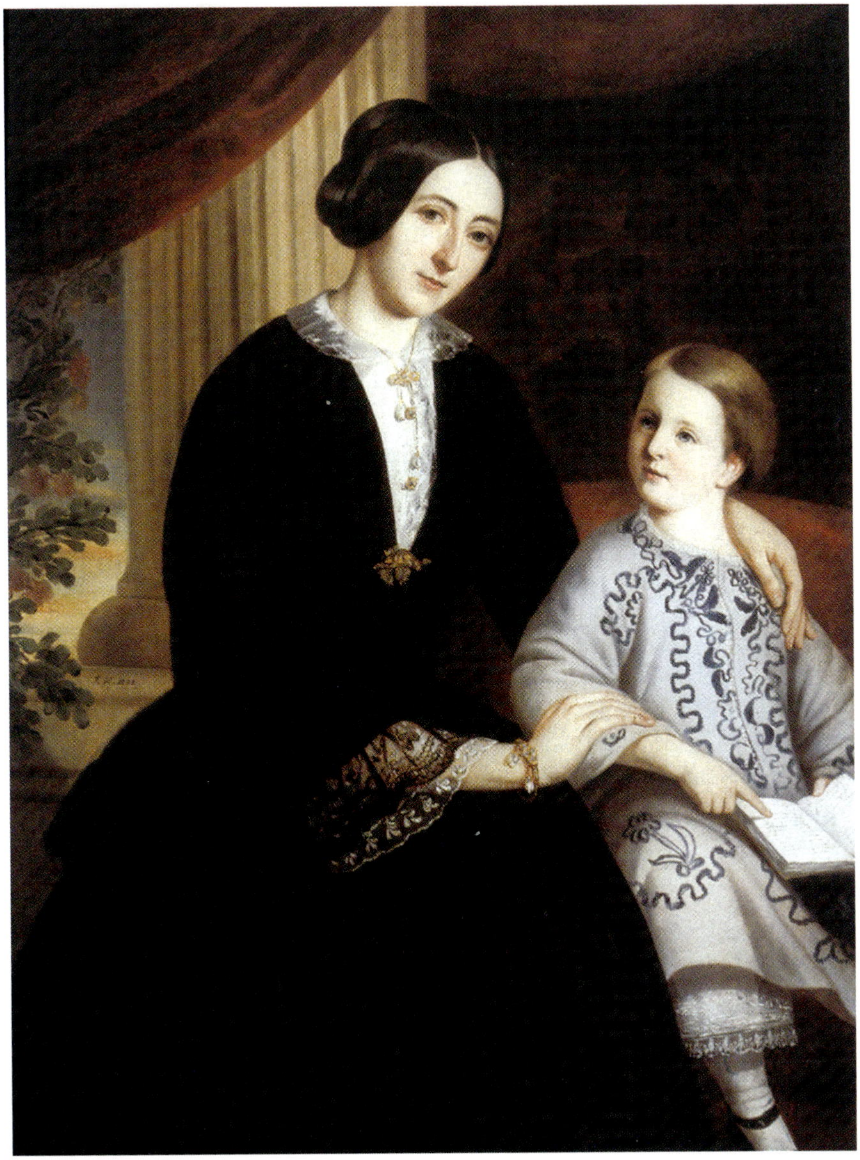

FIGURE 1.10 Théophile Hamel, *Madame Têtu et son fils Amable*, 1852, oil on canvas, 119.4 × 88.9 cm. Musée National des Beaux-Arts du Québec, Quebec City.

Antoine Plamondon's so-called fantasy compositions are less satisfying, particularly *Perdus dans la forêt*, 1836; *Les Petits Savoyards*, 1844; and *Les Petits Jardiniers*, 1857.[27] These sweet scenes, painted in the sentimental manner typical of the nineteenth century, convey an idea of childhood that Freud would later turn upside down by his theory of the "polymorphous perverse" that resides in every child. The vulnerability of the sleeping children in the first painting, the glasses of wine in the hands of the Petits Savoyards, and the slightly equivocal gesture of the big sister lifting up the baby's shirt in the third all suggest that Freud was quite correct.

In considering the theme of Quebec children, it is important to look at William Berczy's admirable and widely discussed *Woolsey Family*, painted in 1809.[28] A famous "conversation piece," the painting shows the Woolsey children with their parents: John William Woolsey; his wife, Julie Lemoine; his brother-in-law, Benjamin Lemoine (with a flute); and the children's grandmother Josephette Rottot. The four children are shown from left to right, William Darley with a book, William Henry with the dog, the baby John Bryan, and Eleonora with a hoop. The "conversation piece," invented in eighteenth-century England, was an informal family image painted in reply to highly formal portraiture. Everyone wanted to know the identity of the people in the painting and what had happened to them since the portrait's completion. In this case, the questions were answered thanks to a long inscription glued to the back of the piece that William Woolsey himself wrote in 1848. He stated that everyone in the painting, with the exception of himself and his brother-in-law, Benjamin Lemoine (the man holding the flute), had since died. Such news would have been read with great sadness had not Woolsey had the somewhat absurd idea to include "the eight portraits cost ten pounds each," although "the dog Brador was added at no additional cost."

Conclusion

It was only in the period of modernity that the subject matter of childhood in Quebec painting became truly secular. When Prudence Heward painted *Farmhouse Window* (1938)[29] and *Sisters in Rural Quebec* (1930),[30] when Louis Muhlstock did the portrait *Evelyn Pleasant, Clark Street, Montreal* (fig. 1.11),[31] and when Alfred Pellan painted *La Fillette en rouge* (1941),[32] they may not have realized they were part of a long tradition in Quebec of portraying children. Working in a straightforward manner, without taking into account how religion had shaped their subjects, they often produced distant, some would say even hostile, images of children, as is the case with Heward's *Sisters in Rural Quebec*. The artists may not have understood that their subjects' mistrust arose not only from the fact that they were sitting for an artist for the first time, but from their religious education, which if not outright xenophobic, taught them at the very least to be

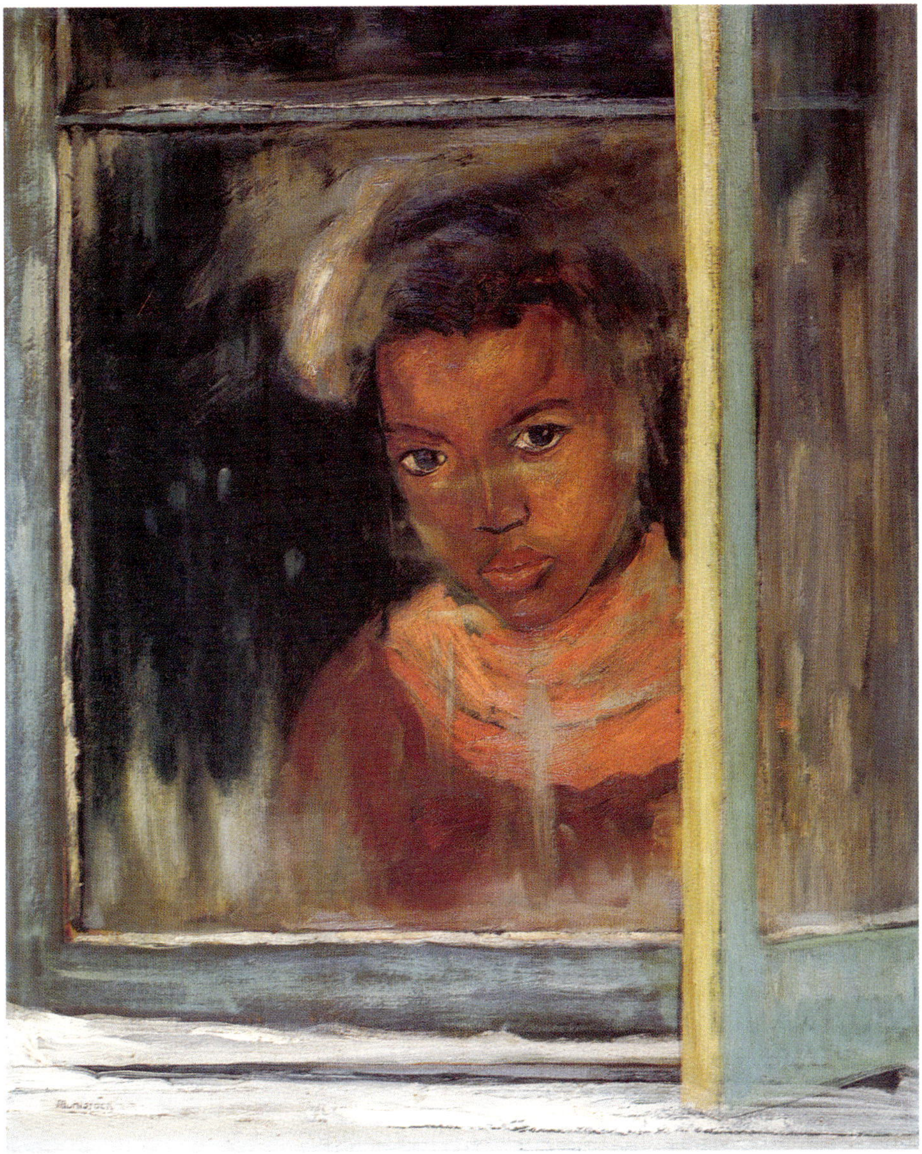

FIGURE 1.11
Louis Muhlstock, *Evelyn Pleasant, Clark Street, Montreal*, 1936, oil on cardboard, 55.1 × 45.8 cm. Private collection.

distrustful of strangers. For example, A.Y. Jackson told the story of how Albert H. Robinson and he had been mistaken for "spies" when they explored the Charlevoix backcountry on snowshoes.[33] It is quite possible that adults' suspicion toward strangers was handed down to the next generation.

This does not seem to apply to little Evelyn Pleasant or the girl in *Clytie*, painted by Prudence Heward,[34] since Black children had nothing to do with the Catholic education of Québécois girls. The one commonality they did share with their sisters in rural Quebec was the extreme poverty in which most were raised. Charlevoix may well have been a paradise for painters, but for large families it offered few opportunities to make a good living, with the result that many children ended up at the orphanage or with adoptive families. The portraits of Jori Smith, for example, show how misery affected many families in the region.[35] The hostility expressed by the children's thin, angular faces was also directed at life itself—the life they had been given without their consent. That the children's portrait would become the occasion of social criticism shows the process of secularization since the seventeenth century. Not only has the religious content has been completely eliminated, but an awareness of the real condition of these children, especially by the painters active in Charlevoix, has been heightened.

Notes

1 Marc Laberge, *Affiquets, matachias et vermillon: Ethnographie illustrée des Algonquiens du nord-est de l'Amérique aux XVIe, XVIIe et XVIIIe siècles* (Montreal: Recherches amérindiennes au Québec, 1998), 95, fig. 78.

2 Reuben G. Thwaites, ed., *The Jesuit Relations and Allied Documents: Travels and Explorations of the Jesuit Missionaries in New France, 1610–1791* (Cleveland, OH: Burrows, 1896–1901), 73 vol. Later, this work will be referred to by its accepted abbreviation, *Jes. Rel.* This quote is from *Jes. Rel.* vol. 44, 292. All quotations are true to the original spellings in the document.

> En France, les hommes & les femmes se font faire des habits assez justes, pour paraître plus lestes; les filles particulièrement se font gloire d'estre menuës. En Canada tout le monde s'habille au large : les hommes & les femmes portent des robes, qu'ils ceignent en deux endroits, au dessous du nombril, & au dessus du ventre, retroussant leurs grandes robes, & les repliant, en sorte qu'ils ont comme un grand sac à l'entour du corps, dans lequel ils fourrent mille choses. Les mères y mettent leurs enfans, pour les caresser, & pour les tenir chaudement.

3 Laberge, *Affiquets*, 129, referring to Joseph-François Lafitau, *Mœurs des sauvages amériquains comparées aux mœurs des premiers temps*. François Maspero, coll. La Découverte, 1983, vol. 1, 171, and to Louis Armand de Lom d'Arce, baron de Lahontan, *Nouveaux voyages de Mr Le baron de Lahontan dans l'Amérique septentrionale....* (La Haye: Frères Honoré, 1704), vol. 2, 95.

4 Conserved at the Thomas Gilcrease Institute of American Art and History, Tulsa, Oklahoma.

5 Lafitau, *Mœurs des sauvages Amériquains comparées aux mœurs des premiers temps* (Paris, 1724), vol. 1, 594–595. Tr. William Nelson Fenton, *Customs of the American Indians Compared with Customs of Primitive Times* (Toronto: Champlain Society, 1974), 357.

> Deux grandes longes d'un cuir fort, qui sortent du berceau par le haut, donnent la facilité aux mères de le porter par – tout avec elles … & de le suspendre à quelque branche d'arbre, où l'enfant est comme bercé, & endormi par le vent, tandis qu'elles travaillent.

6 See J. Russell Harper, *Paul Kane's Frontier* (Toronto: University of Toronto Press, 1971), 246 and 247, figs. 170 and 171.

7 See François-Marc Gagnon, "L'Iconographie classique des saints Martyrs canadiens," in Guy Laflèche, *Les saints martyrs canadiens: Histoire du Mythe* (Montreal: Éditions du Singulier, 1988), vol. 1, 58, fig. 2 for a reproduction of a section of Bressani's map that shows the inset mentioned in the text. The full map is reproduced in pl. 6 at the same place. See also René Latourelle, *François-Joseph Bressani, missionnaire et humaniste* (Montreal: Bellarmin, 1999), 112 for a reproduction of the same map.

8 Samuel de Champlain, *Voyages et decouvertures faites en la Nouvelle France, depuis l'année 1615 jusques à la fin de l'année 1618* (Paris: Claude Collet, 1619), 81 (Ed. Laverdière, 569). Tr. H.H. Langton and W.F. Ganong, *The Works of Samuel de Champlain*, vol. 3 (Toronto: Champlain Society, 1922–1936), 134.

9 Marcel Trudel, *G. Sagard: Le grand voyage du pays des Hurons* (Montreal: HMH, 1976), 134. Tr: George M. Wrong, *Sagard's Long Journey to the Country of the Hurons* (Toronto: Champlain Society, 1939), 144.

> Et en ay veu d'autres qui en portoient encore des brasselets aux bras, et de grandes plaques par devant leur estomach, et d'autres par derriere, accomodez en rond, et comme une carde à carder la laine, attachez à leurs tresses de cheveux.

10 Letter of Father François du Peron of the Society of Jesus to Father Joseph-Imbert du Peron, his Brother, Religious of the Same Society, April 27, 1639. *Jes. Rel.*, vol. 15, 154.

> Ils ne sont couverts que d'une peau de castor, qu'ils mettent sur les deux épaules en forme de manteau; des chausses et souliers en hyver, un sac à petun derrière le dos, le chalumet en main; au col et aux bras, des colliers et brasselets de porcelaine; ils en pendent aussi aux oreilles et au tour de leur moustache.

11 De Champlain, *Voyages*. Ils ont une robbe de mesme fourrure, en forme de couverte, qu'ils portent à la façon Irlandoise ou Aegyptienne, & des manches qui s'attachent avec un cordon par le derriere.

12 H. Provost, "La dévotion à la Sainte Famille en Canada," *La Revue de l'Université Laval*, vol. 18, nos. 5–6 (January–February 1964).

> Le dessein et la fin de cette dévotion est d'honorer la sainte Famille de Jésus, Marie et Joseph, et les saints Anges et de régler les ménages chrétiens sur l'exemple de cette sainte Famille, qui doit être le modèle de toutes les autres ; de sanctifier les mariages et les familles ; d'en exclure le péché, particulièrement celui de l'impureté, cette peste des mariages, qui est la source de tant de maux, et qui peuple la terre et les enfers d'enfants de Satan, qui blasphémeront toute l'éternité leur Créateur ; d'y établir les vertus chrétiennes, particulièrement la chasteté, l'humilité, la douceur, la charité, l'union des cœurs, la patience dans les tribulations et la vraie dévotion.

13 Gabriel Sagard, *Histoire du Canada et voyages que les frères mineurs récollets y ont faicts pour la conversion des infidelles* (Paris: Éd. Tross, 1865), vol. 3, 628–629, quoted in François-Marc Gagnon, *La Conversion par l'image: Un aspect de la mission des jésuites auprès des Indiens du Canada au XVIIe siècle* (Montreal: Les Éditions Bellarmin, 1975), 17 [free translation].

> Tost, tost, mon frere, dit-il à l'un de nos Religieux, ouvrez-moy promptement la porter de vostre chambre, que je voye si Oustachecoucou est dans l'Enfer, car il est mort sans être

baptisé. C'estoit un grand Jugement en taille douce, dans l'Enfer duquel il le pensoit trouver depeint avec les autres damnez, car nos Religieux avoient accoustumé de leur montrer cette image pour leur mieux faire comprendre les fins dernieres de l'homme, la gloire des bienheureux, & la punition des méchants.

14 "The most surprising work of Michel Dessailliant can be found in a detail of *Ange gardien*.... The detail I discussed earlier is the head of this little girl.... It is unforgettable. The oval shape of the face, the nobility of the forehead, the gaze that is both deep and smiling, the thin, delicate lips, even the whimsical bonnet on her head, everything in this portrait is spiritual and kind; it is reminiscent of certain paintings by Marie Laurencin." *La peinture traditionnelle au Canada français* (Ottawa: Le Cercle du livre de France, 1960), 37 [free translation]. He reproduced only this detail in the same book; col. pl. between pp. 8 and 9. In doing this Morisset was isolating the portrait of the girl from its religious context and at the same time transforming it into a "modern" image.

15 Philippe Ariès, *L'enfant et la vie familiale sous l'Ancien Régime* (Paris: Éditions du Seuil, 1973), 212.

16 Erasmus, *Familiarum colloquiorum formulae non tantum ad linguam puerilem expoliandam, verum etiam ad vitam instituendam*, 1522, quoted in Norbert Elias, *The History of Manners* (New York: Pantheon Books, 1978), 173 [free translation].

SOPH.: Fallemus heic oculos Dei?
LUC.: Nequaquam : ille perspicit omnia.
SOPH.: Et angelorum?

17 *Jugements et délibérations ... Conseil Souverain*, vol. 4, 543–553.

18 See Cameron Nish, "Riverin, Denis" in *The Dictionary of Canadian Biography Online*, http://www.biographi.ca/index-e.html (University of Toronto/Université Laval, 2000).

19 Marie-Anne Robinau de Bécancourt was born in 1672 and died at the Ursuline convent in Quebec City on July 26, 1743. She joined the Ursulines in 1689, was ordained in 1691, and took the name Marie-Anne de la Trinité. Cf. *Les Ursulines de Québec*, Quebec City, 1864, vol. 2, 335 and 338.

20 Morisset, *La peinture traditionnelle*, 29; J.R. Harper, *La Peinture au Canada des origines à nos jours* (Quebec: Les Presses de l'Université Laval, 1966), 20–21. However, John R. Porter declared him anonymous in "L'abbé Jean-Antoine Aide-Créquy (1749–1780) et l'essor de la peinture religieuse après la Conquête," *The Journal of Canadian Art History/Annales d'histoire de l'art canadien* 7, no. 1 (1983): 66.

21 On the myth of the School of Arts and Crafts in Saint-Joachim, see Doreen E. Walker, "Instruction pour establir les manufactures: A Key Document in the Art History of New France," *The Journal of Canadian Art History* (1975): 1–18; and F.-M. Gagnon, "L'École des arts et métiers de Saint-Joachim: Un anachronisme?" in my *Premiers peintres de la Nouvelle-France* (Québec: Ministère des Affaires culturelles, 1976, t. II), 133–146.

22 See Madeleine Landry and Robert Derome, *L'Art sacré en Amérique française: Le Trésor de la Côte-de-Beaupré* (Quebec City: Septentrion, 2005), 126 for an excellent colour reproduction.

23 See Jean-Guy Pelletier, "Robinau de Bécancour, René," in *The Dictionary of Canadian Biography Online*.

24 Porter, "L'abbé Jean-Antoine Aide-Créquy," 67 and figs. 10 and 12 implicitly make this point, repeated in Landry and Derome, Robert, *L'Art sacré*, 129 and figs. 144 and 146.

25 Antoine Plamondon, *Louis-Joseph Papineau*, 1836, oil on canvas, 122 × 106.9 cm, National Gallery of Canada, Ottawa. See John R. Porter and Mario Béland, *Antoine Plamondon 1804–1895: Jalons d'un parcours artistique* (Quebec City: Musée National des Beaux-Arts du Québec, 2005), 57, cat. 10, for a colour reproduction of this painting.

26 Antoine Plamondon, *Portrait de Madame Louis-Joseph Papineau, née Julie Bruneau et sa fille Ezilda*, 1836, oil on canvas, 121.8 × 107 cm. National Gallery of Canada, Ottawa. See Porter and Béland, *Antoine Plamondon*, 57, cat. 11, for a colour reproduction of this painting.

27 Porter and Béland, *Antoine Plamondon*, 55, cat. 9; 76, cat. 27; and 86, cat. 33, for colour reproductions.

28 William Berczy, *The Woolsey Family*, 1809, oil on canvas, 59.9 × 86.5 cm, National Gallery of Canada, Ottawa; reproduced in J. Russell Harper, *Painting in Canada: A History* (Toronto: University of Toronto Press, 1966), 66 (detail) and 67 (overview); see also Mary Allodi Macaulay, Peter N. Moogk, and Beate Stock, *Berczy* (Ottawa: National Gallery of Canada, 1991), pl. XI and 218–220, cat. 84, for a commentary.

29 Prudence Heward, *Farmhouse Window*, 1938, oil on canvas, 68.8 × 56.5 cm. Art Gallery of Hamilton; reproduced in Esther Trépanier, "L'émergence de l'art moderne au Québec: Un parcours à travers la collection de l'Art Gallery of Hamilton," in Tobi Bruce et al., *Lasting Impressions: Celebrated Works from the Art Gallery of Hamilton/Images inoubliables Œuvres célèbres de l'Art Gallery of Hamilton* (Hamilton, ON: Art Gallery of Hamilton, 2005), 51, fig. 38. We know that there is a sketch of this painting (oil on canvas, 51.4 × 44.5 cm) in the collection of Laura and Byrne Harper. See Evelyn Walters, *The Women of Beaver Hall: Canadian Modernist Painters* (Toronto: Dundurn Press, c. 2005), 46.

30 *Sisters in Rural Quebec*, 1930, oil on canvas, 157.4 × 106.5 cm. Art Gallery of Windsor; reproduced in Walters, *Women of Beaver Hall*, 42.

31 *Evelyn Pleasant, Clark Street, Montreal*, 1936, oil on cardboard, 55.1 × 45.8 cm. Private collection, Montreal; reproduced in Monique Nadeau-Saumier et al., *Muhlstock* (Quebec: Musée du Québec, 1995), 7, cat. 15, repr. 12.

32 *La Fillette en rouge*, 1941, oil on canvas, 56 × 43 cm. Private collection, Laval; reproduced in Michel Martin, Sandra Grant Marchand, et al., *Alfred Pellan* (Montreal: Musée d'art contemporain, 1993), 90, cat. 40.

33 A.Y. Jackson, *A Painter's Country: The Autobiography of A.Y. Jackson* (Toronto: Clarke, Irwin, 1967), 59.

34 *Clytie*, oil on canvas, 101.8 × 66.6 cm. The Robert McLaughlin Gallery, Oshawa; colour reproduction in Charmaine Nelson, *Through An-Other's Eyes: White Canadian Artists–Black Female Subjects/Le regard de l'Autre: Artistes canadiens blancs–sujets féminins noirs* (Oshawa: Robert McLaughlin Gallery, 1998), 18, cat. 20.

35 Rosalind M. Pepall and Jori Smith, *A Celebration/Une celebration* (Montreal: Leonard & Bina Ellen Art Gallery, Concordia University, 1997).

ABIGAIL A. VAN SLYCK

SHAPING MODERN BOYHOOD

Indian Lore, Child Psychology, and the Cultural Landscape of Camp Ahmek

Lift we our hearts to the home of our dream,
Where beauty of Nature and sky's glory gleam.
Deep in the wildwood set like a gem
Hail to old Ahmek, the maker of men.
—"Spirit of Ahmek"
(lyrics by Dr. Eustace Haydon)

THE FIRST CANADIAN-OWNED PRIVATE SUMMER camp in Ontario's Algonquin Park, Camp Ahmek stands on the shores of Canoe Lake, some three hundred kilometres from Toronto. When it opened in 1921, its built environment was rudimentary indeed. The initial brochure mentioned sleeping tents, a "well-appointed" kitchen, and a "spacious dining hall"—although early photographs reveal this last as a large tent. As with the first generation of North American summer camps established for middle-class boys in the 1890s, the most important components of the camp environment were natural: "a sandy bay,… [proximity to] fifteen hundred lakes and rivers,… forests teeming with wildlife,… [and] lake breezes … impregnated with health-giving fragrance filtered through thousands of acres of pine and balsam."[1]

Within a decade, however, the cultural landscape of Camp Ahmek had been transformed by the construction of an astonishing variety of permanent structures, all recorded on Harold V. Shaw's map of about 1928 (fig. 2.1). Accommodating camper activities were a dining hall cum recreation lodge, a council ring (with nearby totem pole), a cabin built by naturalist Ernest Thompson Seton, a massive log theatre, an Indian village, horse stables, and rings for both riding and boxing. Supporting the camp's administrative functions were an administration building, an infirmary, a medical cabin, a doctor's cottage, and cabins making up the "rest camp." Purely utilitarian structures included a kitchen and its stores, an ice house, a pump house, a water tower,

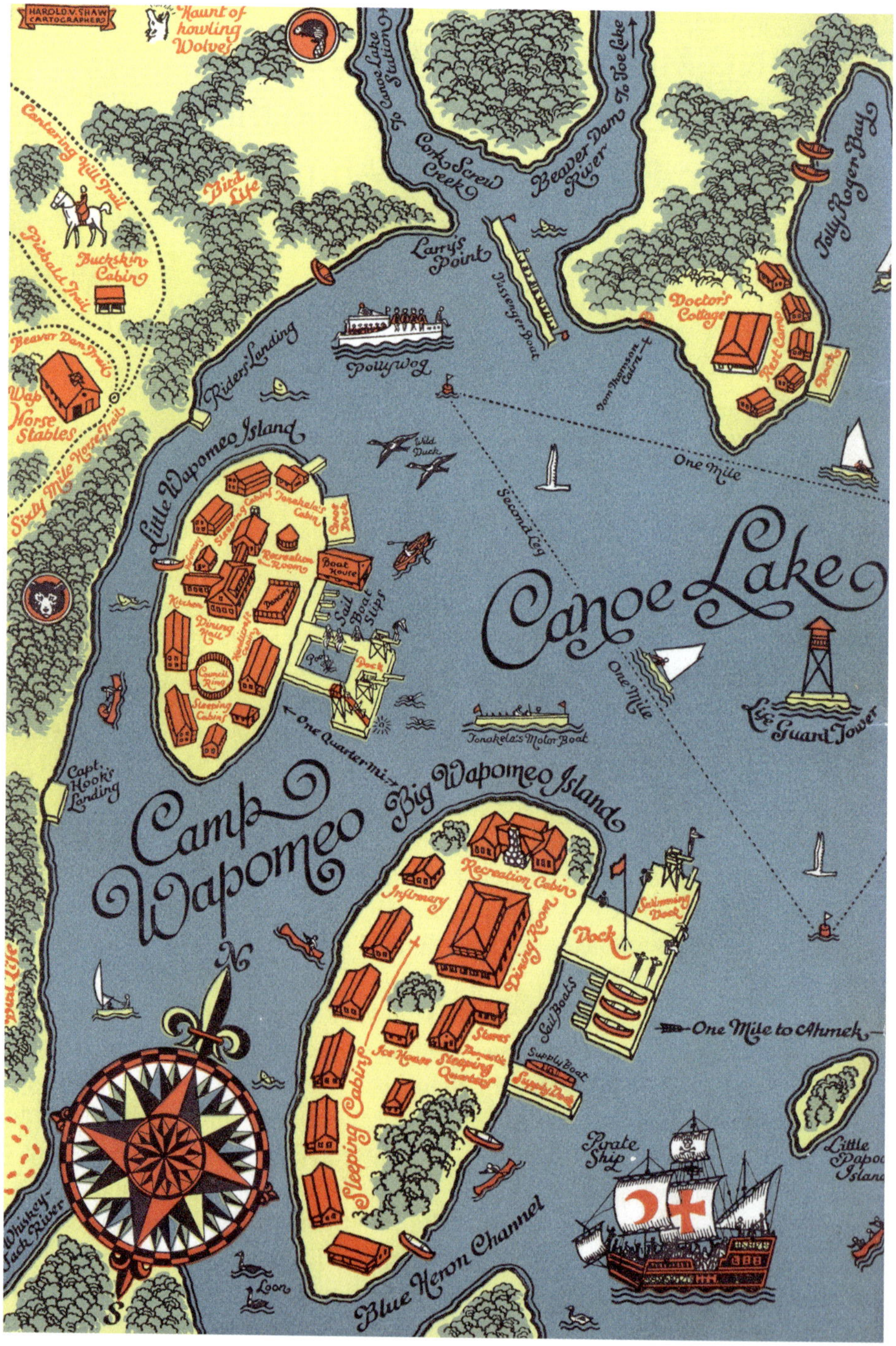
HAROLD V. SHAW CARTOGRAPHERS
Haunt of howling Wolves
Cantering Hill Trail
Bird Life
Buckskin Cabin
Piebald Trail
Beaver Dam Trail
Wap Horse Stables
Sixty Mile Horse Trail
Riders Landing
To Canoe Lake Station
Cork Screw Creek
Beaver Dam River
To Joe Lake
Larry's Point
Passenger Boat
Pollywog
Tom Thomson Cairn
Doctor's Cottage
Rest Camp
Docks
Jolly Roger Bay
Little Wapomeo Island
Wild Duck
One Mile
Second Leg
Sleeping Cabins
Tonakela's Cabin
Canoe Dock
Recreation Room
Boat House
Kitchen
Dining Hall
Sail Boat Slips
Dock
Council Ring
Sleeping Cabins
One Quarter mi.
Canoe Lake
One Mile
Life Guard Tower
Tonakela's Motor Boat
Capt. Hook's Landing
Camp Wapomeo
Big Wapomeo Island
Recreation Cabin
Infirmary
Dining Room
Swimming Dock
Dock
Sail Boats
One Mile to Ahmek
Stores
Ice House
Sleeping Quarters
Supply Boat
Supply Dock
Sleeping Cabins
Pirate Ship
Little Papoose Island
Bird Life
Whiskey-Jack River
Loon
Blue Heron Channel
N
S

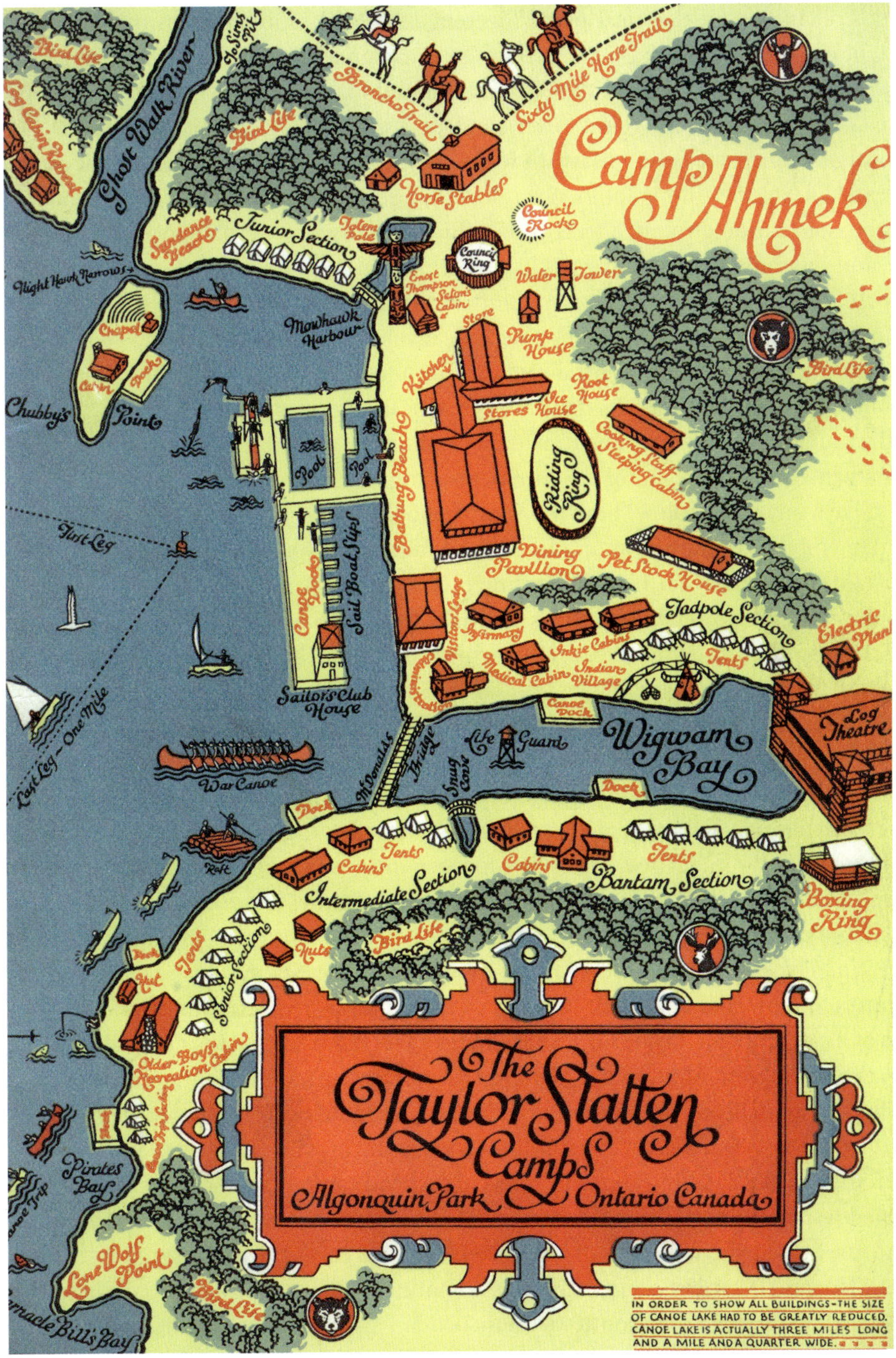

FIGURE 2.1
Map of Camps Ahmek and Wapomeo, Algonquin Provincial Park, Ontario, c. 1928. Drawn by Harold V. Shaw, this map graced the cover of Ahmek brochures in the 1930s. (Courtesy of Taylor Statten Camps)

a root cellar, and an electrical plant. Sleeping tents and cabins for campers, visitors, and the cooking staff were also numerous. The camp landscape extended into Canoe Lake as well, with swimming and boating docks (accommodating, among other craft, a pirate ship and a war canoe), life guard towers, and, on a small island, an open-air chapel. (On two larger islands, the closest of which was a kilometre away, stood Ahmek's sister camp. Founded in 1924, Camp Wapomeo was less fully equipped than Ahmek, but nonetheless boasted a dining room, a recreation cabin, an infirmary, permanent sleeping cabins, and swimming and boating docks on each island.)

At one level, this rapid development is a testament to the ambitions of Ahmek's founder, Taylor Statten, who had first become involved in camping in 1905, when he ran Camp Couchiching for the Central YMCA of Toronto.[2] Thanks in large part to his efforts at Ahmek, Statten became a leader in North American camping circles, serving in 1939 as the founding president of the Canadian Camping Association and in 1941 as the first Canadian elected president of the American Camping Association.[3]

Like many of his fellow "boys' work professionals" (to use the parlance of the time), Statten embraced camping as an ideal way to pursue the spiritual goals at the heart of the YMCA enterprise. Yet he also became increasingly disenchanted with the YMCA's emphasis on religious conversion, as well as with what he came to characterize as the unscientific way camp leaders sought to achieve their aims. Thus, in the 1910s, he helped establish the Tuxis and Trail Ranger programs, using Indian lore and woodcraft (the term used to describe skills required to live in the woods) to enliven the Canadian Standard Efficiency Tests (CSET), a system of points, certificates, and badges awarded to boys who met "objective standards" of development along intellectual, physical, devotional, and social lines. So involved did Statten become with the programs that in 1920 and 1921, he hosted ten-day leader training camps for men involved in the movement; the site for Camp Tuxis was on the shores of Canoe Lake in Algonquin Park, near Little Wapomeo, the island on which Statten and his wife, Ethel, had built a summer cabin in 1916.[4]

When he established Camp Ahmek on the Tuxis site, Statten was eager to put his theories into practice and spent lavishly, some would say recklessly, to ensure the success of his experiment. In late 1924, after Ahmek's fourth season, E. Holt Gurney tendered his resignation from Ahmek's board in protest over Statten's spending thirteen thousand dollars—essentially all the camp's liquidity, much of it "borrowed from people who can't afford to lose it"—on capital improvements during the previous year.[5] Five days later, the board (including Gurney) voted to suspend capital expenditures for 1925 and turned responsibility for all purchasing over to George Chubb, another board member (and one of Statten's creditors) who had been serving as part-time business manager since 1921.[6] Nonetheless, physical improvements continued apace: a pirate ship designed by Woodruff K. Aykroyd of Toronto was launched in 1925. The first permanent dining hall was constructed in time for the 1926 season (although it burned in 1937), and the Log Theatre (a gift of Chrysler Corporation president K.T. Keller) debuted the following summer.[7]

Yet a closer look at this landscape—and particularly at its presentation in marketing brochures aimed primarily at parents—suggests that the physical transformations of the interwar years were also fuelled by dramatic changes in adult perceptions of boyhood. In the early 1920s, Ahmek's landscape had much in common with early twentieth-century camps where leaders sought to immerse youngsters in a wilderness environment in order to counteract the so-called overcivilization of a highly structured modern world, a phenomenon that seemed to threaten the normal, healthy development of boys. By the early 1930s, Ahmek was in the vanguard of innovative attempts to apply modern science—especially child psychology—to the camp program. In addition to remaking the camp landscape, these innovations also introduced a new view of boyhood, one that associated the child's natural state with psychological troubles that could be treated only in a tightly controlled camp environment.

Preserving Childhood's Innate Goodness

When Camp Ahmek opened in 1921, it joined hundreds of other North American camps that had been established since the 1880s in response to adult anxieties about overcivilization, effeminacy, and racial decadence. Of particular concern were doting mothers who enforced good manners in tidy parlours, thus undermining hardy boyhood by prompting their sons to adopt the trappings of civilization too soon and turning them into "sissies." By taking boys out of those feminized homes and installing them in all-male environments set in wilder parts of nature, camp organizers saw themselves as offering a much-needed corrective.[8] Even girls' camps—first established in the early years of the twentieth century—were related at least in part to concerns about boys. After all, the girl who enjoyed life out of doors might develop into a new kind of woman, a boon companion to her future husband and sons. In this sense, camping for girls paralleled the rise of companionate marriages like that of Statten and Ethel Mary Page, who were wed in 1908.[9]

In its early days, Camp Ahmek (like many of its peers) treated buildings and equipment as relatively unimportant to the process of saving modern boyhood. In fact, an overbuilt campsite might fail to satisfy what Ahmek brochures called "that 'lure of the wild' which is strong in every normal boy."[10] If early camp leaders were somewhat blasé about buildings and equipment, they felt strongly that the right kind of leader was essential. As Statten wrote in the brochure for the 1924 season, "Character is contagious. It is caught, not taught. Expose a boy during his leisure time to men of sterling character and he will quickly acquire similar characteristics."[11] Identifying such men, however, was complicated by the widespread tendency to temper Victorian "manliness" (with its emphasis on a self-restraint) with more aggressive behaviours associated with masculinity, itself a new term in the late Victorian period.[12] Thus, the first Ahmek brochure highlighted the involvement of Frank Wood, a high-profile athlete (having won the Canadian Swimming Championship in 1914/1915) who could also claim glamorous military experience (having served overseas with the Royal Air Force). At the same time, characterizations of the ideal leader as "virile, red-blooded and gentlemanly" attest to the amalgam of conflicting qualities that informed this new mode of manhood.[13]

Two things set Camp Ahmek apart from its peers. One was its use of Indian motifs to shape both the camp program and the camp landscape. To be sure, camps established in the late nineteenth and early twentieth centuries often adopted Indian names, like Camp Pasquaney in New Hampshire (one of the first camps for boys, established in 1895) or Camp Mishawaka (founded in 1910 in Minnesota). Yet the practice may have been motivated by the desire to present the camp landscape as a wilderness environment untouched and untamed by white civilization, glossing over the fact that many campsites had recently served productive purposes, such as farming or logging. Camp Pasquaney's site, for instance, had been a hayfield on the farm owned by the director's father. When boys impersonated Indians in these camps, they tended to do so only temporarily in games like White Man and Indian; as described in the 1911 book *Camping for Boys*, the conflict between the two teams was the result of attempts by "natives" (cast in the role of savages) to thwart the "progress" of white settlement.[14]

Statten may have used the name Ahmek (the Ojibwa word for "beaver") to a similar end, disguising the fact that Algonquin Park—described in Ahmek brochures as "a paradise of virgin wilderness"—had once been the locus of intense logging activity.[15] Given that Canada had adopted the beaver as a national symbol and embraced diligence as a particularly Canadian trait, the name may have had added appeal for Statten and for those parents eager to send their children to a Canadian-owned camp. But Statten also adopted a new form of Indian play in which a wide range of Indian motifs—council rings, tipis, birchbark canoes, skin-headed drums—supported prolonged impersonations of First Nations people who embodied qualities Statten admired. Thus, Statten himself adopted the name Gitchiahmek (or "Great Beaver") with its suggestion of industriousness. As director of Camp Wapomeo (translated as "Bluebirds of Happiness"), Ethel Statten took the name Tonakela; the Ojibwa word for "you first," it called attention to Ethel's values and encouraged female campers to aspire to the same kind of selflessness.[16] The difference in these names also confirms the extent to which the camp movement—for all its efforts to reform gender roles—continued to reinforce stereotypes of hard-working men and selfless women.

This newer mode of Indian play was directly informed by the work and writings of naturalist and author Ernest Thompson Seton, whose ideas Statten had used as early as 1905 at Camp Couchiching. Just a few years before, Seton had founded the Woodcraft Indians, a youth organization that encouraged boys to emulate Indian practices—adopting Indian names, donning Indian garb, living in tipis—while learning skills that would allow them to survive in the woods. Informed by antimodernist notions that exposure to primitive life could help men and women counteract the overcivilization of the modern world, Seton's program also resonated with the recapitulation theory of psychologist G. Stanley Hall. Positing that child development repeated (or "recapitulated") human evolution, Hall argued that each child (although he meant each white child) moved through a series of developmental stages from savagery to civilization. According to this theory, white children were not only closer to Indians than they were to white adults, but their development could be derailed if they were forced to adopt too soon the trappings of white civilization.[17]

In the 1910s, a failing alliance with the Boy Scouts prompted Seton to promote Woodcraft activities with renewed vigour: he renamed the organization the Woodcraft League, opened it to girls, and visited summer camps to initiate new Woodcraft tribes.[18] To be sure, these recruiting trips served Seton's interests. Yet Ahmek's history suggests that camp directors eagerly embraced the marketing potential inherent in hosting the famous naturalist. The brochure for Ahmek's initial 1921 season was careful to mention staff members associated with Seton and his Woodcraft organization, notably Stuart Thompson ("a nephew of Ernest Thompson-Seton") and Philip D. Fagans ("of the Woodcraft League of America").[19] The next year, Statten invited the great man himself to visit Ahmek at a salary of twenty dollars per day.[20] In return for his investment, Statten secured years' worth of high-quality brochure copy, including Seton's poetic letter of endorsement reprinted in full in the 1924 brochure.[21]

Seton's sojourn at Ahmek began on August 12, 1922, after an overnight train trip from Toronto. Except for one night at Northway Lodge (another Algonquin Park camp—this one for girls—established in 1908 by Miss Fanny Case, a schoolteacher from Rochester, New York), Seton spent the next nine days at Ahmek, teaching Indian lore, assigning Indian names (dubbing his nephew Stuart Thompson Ashkonib, meaning "Many Fires"), demonstrating Indian dances, and overseeing the construction of a small log cabin (known for decades as the Ernest Thompson Seton cabin) and a large council ring (fig. 2.2). At the council ring, Seton staged grand council fires, elaborate evening events based on an amalgam of First Nations motifs—what he called "the best things of the best Indians."[22] Thanks to Seton's magnetic presence, these grand council fires were the Woodcraft League's most effective recruiting tool. When he left on August 21, Seton was treated like departing royalty. "A guard of

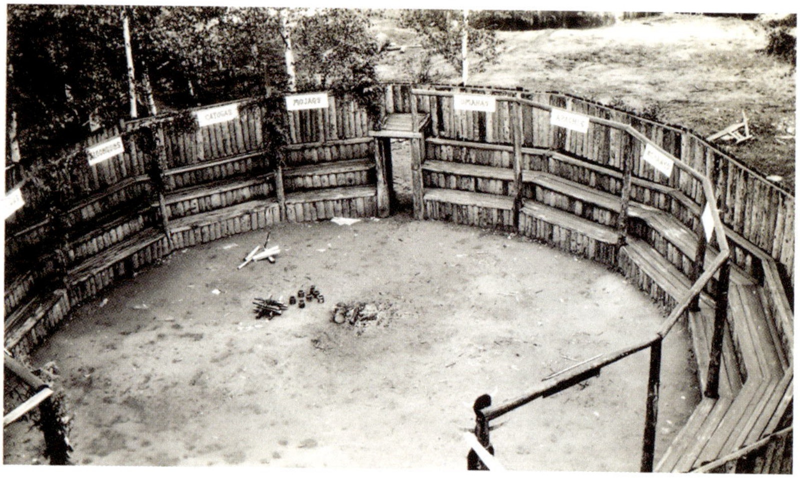

FIG. 2.2
Camp Ahmek council ring, constructed under the supervision of Ernest Thompson Seton in August 1922. The site of weekly ceremonies, the council ring accommodated the entire camp with boys seated with their assigned "tribes." (Courtesy of Taylor Statten Camps)

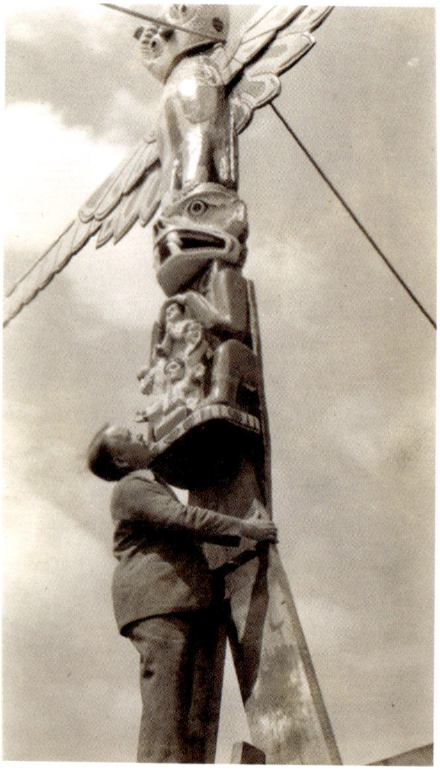

FIG. 2.3
Jack Ridpath with the totem pole he designed and carved for Camp Ahmek in 1922. The central figure is Gitchiahmek, protecting four boys who represent spiritual, physical, intellectual, and social growth, respectively. Translated as Great Beaver, Gitchiahmek was Taylor Statten's name at camp. (Courtesy of Taylor Statten Camps)

twenty full canoes" accompanied him to the train station, where he was photographed holding a beaver.[23]

Seton's visit helped reinforce the importance of Woodcraft activities at Ahmek, where the landscape was soon filled with the physical trappings of Indian culture. Jack Ridpath (of Ridpath's Cabinet Shop in Toronto) designed and carved a totem pole, almost seven metres high, that was installed at the entrance to the council ring (fig. 2.3).[24] The 1924 brochure mentioned four "India [*sic*] Teepees," four large war canoes, and "weird Indian totem poles from British Columbia"; it also featured a photograph of men building "an Indian Sweat Lodge."[25] By 1926, Basil Partridge and Bill Stour from the Algonquin Golden Lake First Nation were teaching campers to construct birchbark canoes.[26]

Within this landscape, the council ring stood out. Most of Seton's council rings—including one he built at his own home in Connecticut (fig. 2.4) and another he described in his 1912 publication, *The Book of Woodcraft*—were simple in form: "a perfectly level circle twenty-four feet [7.3 metres] across … [with] a permanently fixed circle of very low seats" with low backs, and additional rings of progressively higher seats in sufficient numbers to provide a fixed seat for each person in camp.[27] At Ahmek, however, Seton carried out this basic idea in a particularly elaborate way (see fig. 2.2). A palisade of vertical logs—about three metres high for most of its length—defined a rough circle some fifteen to eighteen metres in diameter. Lining the interior of the palisade were three tiers of benches, also supported by vertical logs. Built into the front edge of the bottom tier was a log framework that supported signs bearing the names of Ahmek's "tribes," among them Algonquins [*sic*], Cayugas, Mohags [*sic*], Omahas, Apaches, Iroquois, and Owenokes. This arrangement was interrupted at one side by a tall platform that backed up onto a cliff face. A totem pole in the middle of the platform was aligned on axis with a narrow entryway on the side of the ring that faced Canoe Lake. Seton declared it "the finest Council Ring in North America."[28]

The relative grandeur of this structure attests to the importance Statten placed on the rituals that would take place there, chief among them a ceremony called the council ring. For at least two years after Seton's visit, the council ring was a semi-weekly event held on Wednesday and Saturday evenings, but by 1926 elaborate council rings were held only on Saturday nights.[29] By this time as well, these events followed a common pattern.[30] The Zuni Council call—alone and then punctuating the beat of the tom-tom—signalled the beginning of the event. Draped in "blankets of many colors and patterns," campers took their seats in the council ring with the rest of their tribe. Then came the parade of chiefs of the cabinet, followed by the sachems, and then Statten—known at camp as "the Chief"—dressed in fringed leggings, tunic, and a full feather headdress. After a song, the Chief set light to a neat stack of horizontal logs, an arrangement Seton prescribed for an easily started fire that gave a steady, bright light with little heat. (Seton

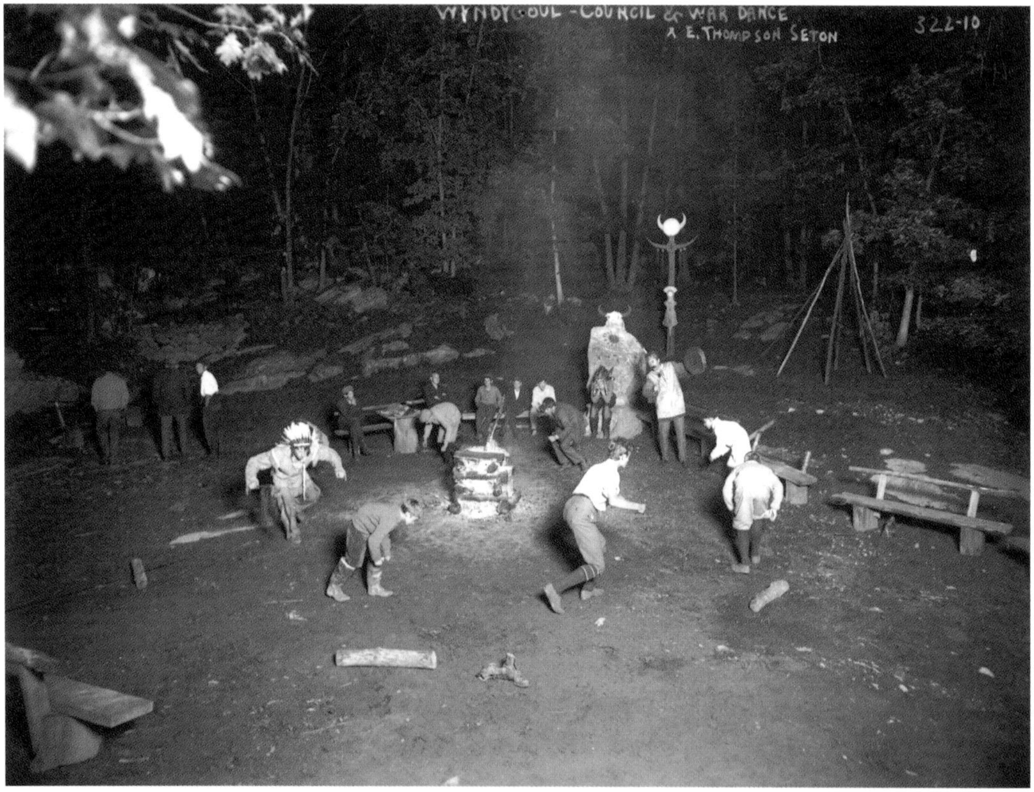

FIGURE 2.4 Ernest Thompson Seton and Woodcraft Indians conducting a council and war dance at Wyndygoul, Seton's estate in Cos Cob, Connecticut, in 1908. (Prints and Photographs Division, Library of Congress)

objected vehemently to the high pyramid used in bonfires, as it "goes off like a flash, roasts everyone, and then goes dead.")[31] Once the fire was ablaze, the evening's program began. Its specific content varied, but it typically included reports of wild animals observed on hikes or canoe trips, camp craft competitions (such as fire-lighting and water-boiling), Indian dances (some invented by the campers themselves), the telling of Indian legends, and sometimes enactments of unspecified "incidents from early American history."[32] A talk by the Chief followed this program and led into the Omaha tribal prayer that brought the ceremony to a close.

The physical and literal focus of this event—the campfire itself—was understood to reconnect campers with the primitive past, before men had been feminized by over-civilization. In this sense, it was integral to the ongoing cultural project of reforming manliness. As Seton explained in *The Book of Woodcraft*, the campfire was closely associated with the very emergence of man:

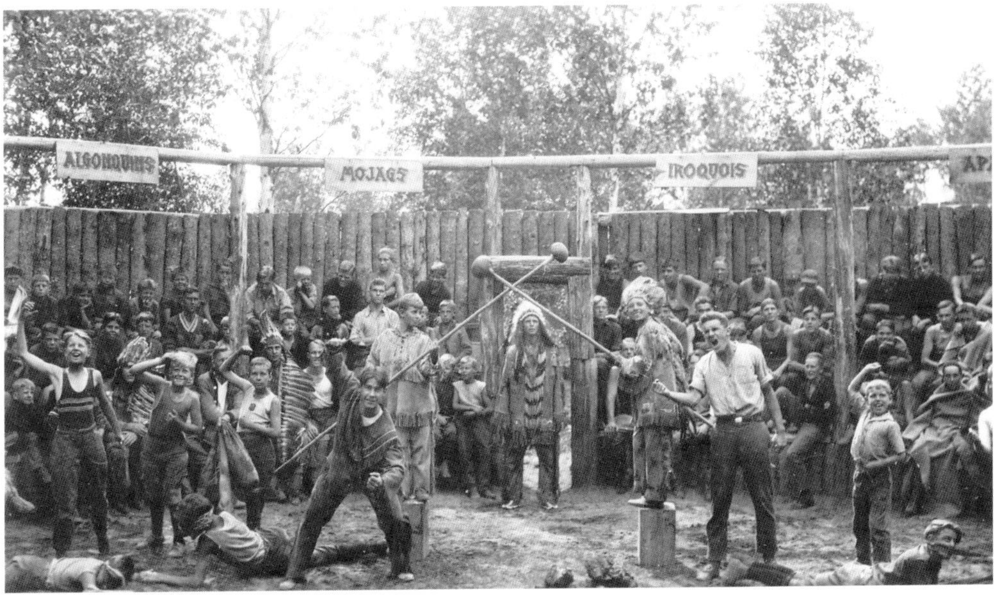

FIGURE 2.5 Jousting tournament at the council ring at Camp Ahmek, c. 1923. Dressed in feather headdress and fringed tunic, Taylor Statten is framed by the entrance to the council ring in the centre of the photograph. (Courtesy of Hugh Statten)

> When first the brutal anthropoid stood up and walked erect—was man, the great event was symbolized and marked by the lighting of the first campfire.
>
> For millions of years our race has seen in this blessed fire, the means and emblem of light, warmth, protection, friendly gathering, council.

For Seton, the campfire was a portal to premodern authenticity that enabled boys to connect with one another. He went on to write:

> Only the ancient sacred fire of wood has power to touch and thrill the chords of primitive remembrance. When men sit together at the campfire they seem to shed all modern form and poise, and hark back to the primitive—to meet as man to man—to show the naked soul.[33]

The campfire not only put individual men in touch with their essential manliness, but it also encouraged close bonds of friendship among them.

Ahmek's council ring clearly was meant to function in the same way. Period photographs reveal that the council ring was often the setting for the performance of more aggressive modes of manliness, whether boxing matches or jousting competitions. During jousting matches, boys in Indian garb stood on what appear to be vegetable crates and used long poles with padded ends to knock one another off their low perches (fig. 2.5). Cheered on by the other members of their "tribes," boys practised the use of physical force that the twentieth century associated with masculinity, while also experiencing loyalty to their group. In many ways, the weekly council ring ceremonies reinforced the same lessons on a larger scale. Evening programs provided a venue for competition among the various tribes, but these competitive events were framed by shared rituals that invoked "the Ahmek spirit" and reinforced the unity of the entire camp.

Statten himself played the lead role at Ahmek's early council rings; friends remember him as a born performer, a quality many believed he shared with his kinsman P.T. Barnum.[34] As former camper Brownlee Haydon recalled in 1959, Ahmek council fires often started with "a restlessness and a bit of boredom." He continued:

> But somehow, the austere and pervading presence of the Chief transformed the play into a realistic re-enactment of all Indian ceremonies of all time. The twentieth century slipped away in the darkness, and all evidences of modern civilization were not only absent, but somehow forgotten as the Chief intoned the tribal prayers and called upon reports from his sachems and braves.... It was a shock, returning from this other world in which we had all been participants—not observing—and the validity of the experience was owing to the magnificent skill of the Chief. He was really *The Chief*—and we were all dedicated to his service. (emphasis original)[35]

In this sense, Ahmek's council fires were particularly potent mechanisms for reinforcing camp loyalty, even as they created what Statten described in the brochure for the 1924 season as "a character-building centre permeated with an atmosphere which would inspire boys to develop the best that is in them."[36]

Correcting Childhood's Inherent Pathologies

Within ten years Statten's attitudes toward boys and their needs had changed dramatically, a shift that is most sharply apparent in his "Personal Note" in the front of the brochure for the 1934 season. It begins:

> All children are conscious of a feeling of inadequacy. They see their parents and others doing so many interesting things that they are unable to do. Their little brains create desires much faster than their physical ability can satisfy them.... The human child suffers and experiences torturing sentiments of inadequacy. The young of no other species is conscious of its own deficiencies in quite the same way.

Statten noted that this inherent sense of inferiority often set children on the wrong path. "Thwarted and frustrated in their efforts" to overcome their feeling of inability, "many adopt modes of conduct which make them unattractive, and even offensive, to other children." Some take to bragging, bullying, using profanity, or stealing, while others become day dreamers, or "Alibi Ikes." Still others throw temper tantrums or "adopt a Pollyanna or sour grapes attitude toward life."[37] In whatever form they expressed their frustrations, these children were a far cry from the boys Statten had imagined in 1924, lads who simply "caught" character from the right role models.

This view of childhood as a stage of life fraught with inherent psychological perils was the result of camp innovations introduced by Hedley S. Dimock, who joined the Ahmek staff as special instructor in religious education in 1924. A professor of education at what came be to called George Williams College (a YMCA training school in Chicago), Dimock was keen to apply the methods of the nascent child-study movement to the camp environment.[38] Ahmek must have seemed like an ideal venue in which to pursue this interest, thanks to Statten's commitment to developing clear and measurable objectives for assessing camp's impact on the boys' character development. Indeed, during the first four seasons at Ahmek, Statten and his staff borrowed the basic idea of the Tuxis program, scoring tent groups on the external behaviours they believed were closely associated with the internal character traits they valued: punctuality at meals, tent tidiness, table etiquette, posture, and camp spirit. Each day, winning groups received small leather "medals" or wild goose feathers (provided by noted bird specialist Jack Miner). In time, silver cups were introduced and the awards system was expanded to cover "almost anything and everything," according to an early staff member. Although the bookkeeping was unwieldy, "the daily tent competition became a recognized institution within the camp."[39]

Dimock convinced Statten that the awards system was deeply flawed. In fact, he argued, once a tent group realized that they had no chance of winning that day, they "lapsed into carelessness and indifference." Statten discontinued the use of cups and awards after the 1924 season, although the Ahmek crest and bars remained. (Akin to a Girl Scout sash, the crest belonged to an individual camper and served as the support for bars indicating achievement in canoeing, swimming, boxing, camp craft, and other camp activities.) He also gave Dimock permission to attempt a scientific evaluation of Ahmek's effectiveness in character building. For the next five years, Dimock and Charles E. Hendry (who had worked with Statten at Camp Tuxis and had been on the Ahmek staff from the beginning) treated the camp something like a child-study laboratory, introducing innovations that would put the traditional character-building mission of camp on a more scientific footing. The results of their study appeared as *Camping and Character: A Camp Experiment in Character Education*, a scholarly book first published in 1929 and reprinted in 1930; a second edition was issued in 1939 and reached its fourth printing in 1947.[40]

At the heart of the assessment process was the direct observation of camper behaviour. Counsellors were given detailed instructions on how to describe their observations

("Avoid giving your own opinion and judgements") and provided with specific suggestions for what to describe. The Behaviour Observation Record offered twenty "suggestive items for description," each one of which had several parts. Item 3, for instance, asked, "Does he have many, few, or no companions or friends? Is he accepted as one of the group? Especially sought after as a friend? Or teased, annoyed, razzed, or bullied? Describe concretely." To be completed for each camper within the first three days of camp, and then once or twice more during the camp stay, this document combined aspects of teachers' reports with those of medical record-keeping. Like those attempts to facilitate the communication of specialized knowledge among professionals, Ahmek records required a substantial commitment of time and effort on the part of the counsellor. Indeed, the instructions recommended that counsellors spend a portion of each evening recording the significant episodes of the day.[41]

Another key tool for assessing the overall effectiveness of camp was the Behaviour Frequency Scale, which asked the counsellor to assess each camper on fifty-four separate forms of behaviour, noting for each whether its occurrence was Never, Seldom, Occasionally, Fairly Often, Frequent, or Extreme. Although some of the behaviours to be observed (such as "Untidy in appearance or tent" or "Practicing bad posture") were the same external signs that had once been the subject of the awards system, most focused more specifically on character traits, and particularly those that facilitated group acceptance. Positive behaviours included "considering others first," making a "friendly approach" to an "unlikable boy," making a "friendly approach to those of his group," making a "friendly approach to those of other social, economic or racial status," "contributing well considered suggestions to the thinking of the group," "showing enthusiasm for group enterprises," and "co-operating readily." Negative behaviours included "disturbing any group meeting," "hogging equipment," "hurting another's feelings," and "considering himself first." While "assuming leadership" and "displaying courage" were valued, these qualities were to be tempered by modesty; "accepting recognition modestly" was specifically articulated as a positive behaviour, while boasting, showing off, and acting superior were listed separately as distinct sins, as was "exercising authority objectionably." Dimock and Hendry also acknowledged camper sexuality, asking counsellors to record if a camper engaged in "irregular sex behaviour"; although the form itself did not specify the meaning of "irregular," a summary of their findings confirms that they—like Horace Bushnell and other nineteenth-century moralists—were primarily concerned about masturbation.[42]

The Behaviour Frequency Scale could be used in two ways. First, it was used to assess the emotional health of individual campers, and in the most extreme cases to identify boys needing consultation with the camp psychologist. (Although Ahmek did not cater to troubled boys, application forms, letters, and personal interviews encouraged parents to think about the behaviour modifications that they would like to see in their sons.) By quantifying camper behaviours at the beginning and end of the camp season and comparing the differences, the Behaviour Frequency Scale allowed Ahmek staff to offer parents what they felt was objective evidence of the camp's effectiveness in shaping and reshaping their sons. Yet Dimock and Hendry were equally interested in compiling behavioural data for the whole camp and using those results to guide improvements in camp program. In the process, Dimock and Hendry became increasingly confident in their abilities to quantify "normal" boy behaviour at each stage of development; their instructions on the Behaviour Frequency Scale, for instance, informed counsellors that "it is not likely that more than 5 per cent of all the boys rated will fall within each of the extreme columns."[43] The sine qua non of the field of child study, such statistical methods provided a scientific basis for the claims to professional expertise that Dimock and Hendry used to launch their own careers.[44]

Some extreme cases were documented in *Camping and Character* as well. Freddy, for instance, had to be the centre of attention: he engaged in boastful talking, he whistled before diving to ensure himself an audience, and overall he displayed "a sad lack of stick-to-it-iveness." The diagnosis emphasized two points. First, Freddy was bright and attractive and tended naturally to assume the central role in any situation; his bragging and showing off were simply shortcuts to satisfying his strong desire for recognition and status. Second, Freddy's father also sought "to achieve recognition and social prestige in rather superficial and ostentatious ways," and he "worshipped" Freddy. Freddy's mother "oscillate[d] between severity as a corrective for the father's doting attitude, and indulgence as a reaction to her own severity." The method of treatment was threefold: Freddy was to stop whistling before he dove; he was to write a letter to his father saying that he was unpopular at camp but would try to overcome it; and his counsellor was to prevent him from starting any new project until he had finished the previous one. Freddy was also moved twice to a new tent during the same summer to allow him to start fresh. The results of the treatment were not completely successful; indeed, Freddy was moved to yet a third tent before the summer was through. The only hope, Dimock concluded, was to deal with Freddy "in an extra-home environment for a considerable length of time."[45]

Other cases also pointed to poor parenting as the root cause of campers' behavioural difficulties. Tom suffered from hysterical homesickness because parental control had been inconsistent. Albert and James, two restless, untidy, irresponsible brothers, came from a family with "four bosses": their mother, a woman of culture who was frequently away; a grandmother, who looked after them in the mother's absence; a housekeeper, who was responsible for the boys at meal time; and their father, a successful stockbroker who returned home only on weekends and lavished on the boys gum, candy, toys, and clothes. Martin, who became enraged upon slight provocation, was "badly pampered in his eating at home." While these case studies made it clear that fathers often had a hand in creating troublesome boys, Dimock and Hendry blamed women for bad parenting. The book's summary chapter, for instance, emphasized "the desirability of getting the boy away from the female when there is evidently too much 'petticoat' government. Housekeepers, maids, and governesses in too great an abundance are not the best means for developing the social abilities and attitudes of the boy."[46]

The highly gendered nature of this discussion is familiar from the earliest years of the camp movement, but with an interesting twist. The needs of boys had always received intense professional scrutiny, perhaps because the perceived crisis of masculinity had greater resonance with the men who dominated the fields of camp directing and child psychology. Likewise, the tendency to blame mothers (or their female surrogates) for children's problems was nothing new. What was new was the tendency to put the psychological state of the child first, instead of assuming—as had camp directors of an earlier era—that a camper's emotional stability would increase with enhanced physical strength. Equally new was the application of scientific child-rearing to the specifics of camp life. Rather than using amorphous concerns about the feminized home as a general rationale for the summer camp, *Camping and Character* suggested that camp could diagnose particular parental failings and prescribe individual remedies. No longer a mere consumer of expert advice on child development, the summer camp could serve as a child-study laboratory, contributing more actively to scientific understandings of childhood.

The Ahmek system required leaders—now called counsellors—to approach their work in new ways. Jack Thompson, who was a seventeen-year-old counsellor-in-training (CIT) in the summer of 1930, later recalled that "every evening after supper there was a counsellors' meeting where we discussed actual problems arising in the camp." Even as a CIT, Thompson read "and received much benefit from" two recommended texts: *Camping and Character* and *Creative Camping* (by Joshua Lieberman). For Thompson (who went on to become a clergyman) the experience was formative: "It was at Ahmek that I got my first taste of applied psychology. My earliest interests in the personalities of men were aroused at Ahmek."[47]

Perhaps more important to the daily life of campers, Ahmek's innovations proposed a new form of camper–counsellor interaction. Earlier in the century, leaders at boys' camps had often been selected for their athletic prowess, and their job performance was defined primarily by their activities on the camp's playing fields or at the waterfront. While they sometimes lived with campers in their tents or cabins, leaders were largely seen as a passive force for good: twenty-four-hour role models of robust manliness that, it was assumed, required little special training or extra effort on their part. This older kind of leader had been on display for campers, who were meant to look at him even as they looked up to him. At Ahmek in the 1930s, the camper became the

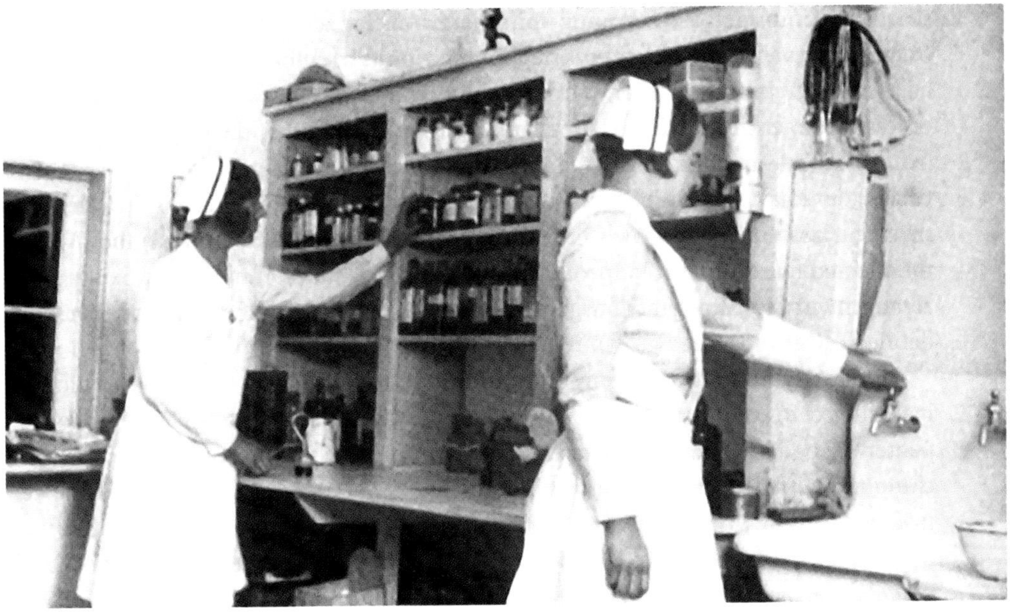

FIGURE 2.6 The medical cabin at Camp Ahmek, as presented in the brochure for the 1931 season. The accompanying caption assured parents that "through the eternal vigilance of our Department of Health, with its adequately equipped and sanitary medical cabin, and a staff of doctors and graduate nurses, we have established an enviable health record." (Courtesy of Taylor Statten Camps)

object of the counsellor's scrutiny. So important was this camper-directed gaze that Dimock and Hendry included it as "one of the major skills of good leadership."[48]

In the 1930s, this emphasis on adult scrutiny of campers carried through other aspects of the Ahmek experience as well, from the presence of a university-trained dietitian responsible for overseeing balanced meals, to the "eternal vigilance" provided by a staff of doctors and graduate nurses.[49] Both the dietitian and the nurses were themselves subject to the camera's scrutiny, as brochures relied ever more heavily on photographic evidence to convince parents they were delivering their children into expert hands (fig. 2.6). In fact, Statten argued that "children are much safer at a good summer camp than they are at home, or at a summer resort with their parents," thanks to "the constant supervision that they receive at camp."[50]

This new understanding of campers and their needs had a number of landscape implications as Statten sought to make Ahmek a place of "joyous freedom," while maintaining "a controlled environment ... stimulating, but at the same time safe and wholesome."[51] In part this control was achieved through the use of what professional camp planners came to call the unit plan.[52] In this decentralized arrangement, the camp was scientifically minded camp leaders could carve out for themselves a central role in the life of every child. When leaders like Statten asserted the therapeutic importance of a tightly controlled and carefully supervised environment, they also sought to give summer camps a seemingly unassailable importance in child development.

Yet Camp Ahmek's cultural landscape reveals additional insights into the construction of modern boyhood, notably that new theories of child development—even ones that enjoyed the support of distinguished scientific experts—did not always drive out existing practices. At Ahmek, the physical traces of seemingly conflicting theories of childhood co-existed and even worked in complimentary ways. It is not just that totem poles and tipis stood next to carefully controlled activity areas where the safety of campers could be monitored and their behaviour observed. Indian motifs also came to play a more active role in the therapeutic environment, helping mask campers' awareness of the extent to which their experience was informed by adult scrutiny and expert guidance. In this sense, Indian motifs and child psychology worked together at Ahmek, "the maker of men."

Notes

My thanks go out to the many people who facilitated my research on the Taylor Statten Camps, especially Taylor C. Statten (who provided access to archival materials in the Toronto office); Kelly McRobie and Sarah Henderson (my guides at Ahmek and Wapomeo); and Vanessa Reid (for her companionship and research assistance in the summer of 1999). Thanks are also due to Loren Lerner, who waited so patiently for this essay, and to Annmarie Adams, who gave an earlier version of this text her usual insightful reading.

1 Camp Ahmek brochure for the 1921 season, n.p. (Taylor Statten Camps Company [TSCC] archives).
2 Today's Camp Couchiching is a different entity operated by the Anglican Church of Canada on the same site, purchased from the YMCA in 1945.
3 The facts of Statten's life story here and elsewhere are drawn from C.A.M. Edwards, *Taylor Statten: A Biography* (Toronto: Ryerson Press, 1960). Camp Couchiching is discussed on pages 28 to 36. His involvement with the American Camping Association (recently renamed the American Camp Association) is mentioned on page 103.
4 Edwards, *Taylor Statten*, 28–49, 65–73.
5 E.H. Gurney, letter to Taylor Statten, December 29, 1924 (TSCC archives).
6 Minutes of the Board of Directors' meeting, January 5, 1925 (TSCC archives).
7 Liz Lundell, ed., *Fires of Friendship: Eighty Years of the Taylor Statten Camps* (Toronto: Taylor Statten Camps, 2000), 44, 50, 53.
8 These concerns about masculinity fuelled a wide range of youth organizations, notably the Boy Scouts, whose founder Robert Baden-Powell blamed working-class mothers for the poor quality of soldiering he had encountered during the Boer War. David Macleod, *Building Character in the American Boy: The Boy Scouts, YMCA, and Their Forerunners, 1870–1920* (Madison: University of Wisconsin Press, 1983), 136–141.
9 Throughout the Stattens' marriage, family life and camp life were closely intertwined. Not only did the couple honeymoon at Camp Couchiching, but Ethel brought their first child to camp when

she was just five weeks old. Christened Adele, this child was known as Couchie, after the camp. In later years, Ethel served as the founding director of Camp Wapomeo. Edwards, *Taylor Statten*, 34–35, 98–99.

10 Camp Ahmek brochure for the 1921 season, n.p. (TSCC archives). Working with a minimum of permanent equipment was common at turn-of-the-century YMCA camps, where the reliance on borrowed land necessitated removing any physical evidence of camp activities at the end of each season. Abigail A. Van Slyck, *A Manufactured Wilderness: Summer Camps and the Shaping of American Youth, 1890–1960* (Minneapolis: University of Minnesota Press, 2006), 14–15.

11 Camp Ahmek brochure for the 1921 season, n.p. (TSCC archives).

12 Gail Bederman, *Manliness and Civilization: A Cultural History of Gender and Race in the United States, 1880–1917* (Chicago: University of Chicago Press, 1995), 16–23.

13 Camp Ahmek brochure for the 1921 season, n.p. (TSCC archives).

14 Van Slyck, *Manufactured Wilderness*, 174–175.

15 Camp Ahmek brochure for the 1921 season, n.p. (TSCC archives).

16 Liz Lundell, Bev Bailey, and John Taylor, *Summer Camp: Great Camps of Algonquin Park* (Toronto: Stoddart, 1994), 10, 28, 34.

17 Not everyone embraced Seton's admiration for the culture of First Nations peoples or Hall's assertion that savagery played a positive role in child development. Daniel Beard, for instance, founded a competing youth organization called the Sons of Daniel Boone which promoted older stereotypes of Indians as bloodthirsty. Van Slyck, *Manufactured Wilderness*, 170–173.

18 In some years, Seton maintained a gruelling travel schedule, as in 1918, when he visited six camps between mid-May and mid-August, three of them in a twelve-day period. Seton diaries, vol. 24, 85–95. Seton's diaries are preserved in the Natural History Museum in New York, although photocopies are also available in the Seton Memorial Library on the Philmont Scout Ranch in Cimarron, New Mexico.

19 Camp Ahmek brochure for the 1921 season, n.p. (TSCC archives).

20 Edwards, *Taylor Statten*, 88.

21 Camp Ahmek brochure for the 1924 season, 23 (TSCC archives).

22 Ernest Thompson Seton, *Trail of an Artist-Naturalist* (New York: Charles Scribner's Sons, 1940), 384.

23 Seton diaries, vol. 25, 154–157.

24 Lundell, *Fires of Friendship*, 24.

25 Camp Ahmek brochure for the 1924 season, 10–11, 19 (TSCC archives).

26 Lundell, *Fires of Friendship*, 25.

27 Ernest Thompson Seton, *The Book of Woodcraft* (1912; repr., Garden City, NY: Garden City Publishing, 1921), 183.

28 Edwards, *Taylor Statten*, 90.

29 Camp Ahmek brochure for the 1924 season, 18; Camp Ahmek brochure for the 1926 season, 12 (TSCC archives).

30 The following characterization of Ahmek council ceremonies is based on three sources: a description published in Hedley S. Dimock and Charles E. Hendry, *Camping and Character: A Camp Experiment in Character Education* (New York: Association Press, 1929), 72–75; a commentary on that description in Lundell, *Fires of Friendship*, 24; and Brownlee Haydon's 1959 reminiscences quoted in Edwards, *Taylor Statten*, 97.

31 Seton, *Book of Woodcraft*, 191.

32 Dimock and Hendry, *Camping and Character*, 73.

33 Seton, *Book of Woodcraft*, 5.

34 Lundell, *Fires of Friendship*, 23.
35 Quoted in Edwards, *Taylor Statten*, 97.
36 Camp Ahmek brochure for the 1924 season, 2 (TSCC archives).
37 Camp Ahmek brochure for the 1934 season, 2 (TSCC archives).
38 The YMCA of Montreal also established a college named for Williams, the organization's founder. Eventually called Sir George Williams University, the Montreal institution merged with Loyola University in 1974 to become Concordia University. Concordia University, "History," http://www.concordia.ca/about/history/ (accessed April 23, 2007).
39 Dimock and Hendry, *Camping and Character*, 96–97.
40 Dimock and Hendry, *Camping and Character*, 99; Edwards, *Taylor Statten*, 100–101.
41 Dimock and Hendry, *Camping and Character*, 153–155.
42 Ibid., 170, 282.
43 Ibid., 357.
44 Dimock and Hendry went on to organize the Institute for Character Education in the Summer Camp, which sponsored at least eight annual meetings before 1937. The report of the eighth meeting is Charles E. Hendry's *Appraising the Summer Camp* (New York: Association Press, 1937). The American Camp Association's Hedley S. Dimock Award ("given to one who contributes to camping through related fields such as outdoor education, conservation, recreation, medicine, education, architecture, or the social sciences") continues to recognize Dimock's importance to the field. American Camp Association, "Hedley S. Dimock Award," http://www.acacamps.org/awards/dimock.php (accessed February 24, 2007).
45 Dimock and Hendry, *Camping and Character*, 188–192.
46 Ibid., 21–22.
47 Lundell, *Fires of Friendship*, 19.
48 Many camp directors with professional aspirations decried these hiring criteria, but their repeated complaints suggest that the practice continued. Dimock and Hendry, *Camping and Character*, 156.
49 Camp Ahmek brochure for the 1934 season, 7 (TSCC archives).
50 Ibid., 3.
51 Ibid., 2–3.
52 In the United States, the unit plan was widely used at camp sites built in Recreational Demonstration Areas developed under the auspices of the New Deal. It was codified in the third volume of *Park and Recreation Structures* by Albert H. Good (Washington, DC: National Park Service, 1938). Van Slyck, *Manufactured Wilderness*, 29–32.
53 Camp Ahmek brochure for the 1921 season, n.p. (TSCC archives).
54 In a memoir published in the *Fires of Friendship*, Bill Piggot (who was at Ahmek from 1955 to 1963, first as a camper and later as a staff member) refers to an event whose history "is shrouded in the mists of Ghost Walk Creek." Rather than describing the appearance of the creek on a particular day, his comment reveals the extent to which he had come to associate the creek with a mysterious atmosphere. It is equally clear that he expected his evocative image of the creek to resonate with generations of Ahmek alumni. Lundell, *Fires of Friendship*, 115.

SHERRY FARRELL RACETTE

HAUNTED
First Nations Children in Residential School Photography

My girl, there is no spirit of the children here in the community, no laughter of children, all that remains on the reserve is us old people and small babies.[1]

IN THE LARGER BODY OF PHOTOGRAPHIC IMAGES OF First Nations people in archival collections, there are comparatively few images of children. Their relative absence begs the obvious question: Where are the children?[2] Why do so few children appear in the photographs Edward Curtis took during his Canadian expeditions in the early twentieth century?[3] The photographs Edmund Morris took during the 1907–1910 fieldwork for his "Indian" portrait series show a similar absence.[4] The stark answer is that pictorial absence reflected physical absence. Very few children were left in the communities they visited. Most had been taken to residential and industrial schools, and it is in this photographic legacy that we must seek their images.

At first glance, many photographs of children in residential schools are indistinguishable from the broader genre of school photography. Children wearing uniforms, arranged in rows, bracketed by stern, authoritative figures are standard compositions. Small group photographs also emulated photographs of students clustered around their teachers at boarding schools such as St. Mary's Academy in Ottawa.[5] However, while some photographs may have borrowed formal poses from the conventions of school photography, the residential and industrial school system implemented in late nineteenth-century Canada was not a branch of the European boarding school tradition. Rather, its roots can be found in the educational institutions established to implement Ulysses S. Grant's American policy of "aggressive civilization."[6] One institution in particular, the Carlisle Industrial School, which used photography as a promotional strategy, was upheld as a model of effectiveness.[7]

Carlisle's origins can be traced to educational experiments conducted by Captain Richard Pratt, the superintendent at Fort Marion, a military prison camp established in

1875 in Florida.[8] Men and women involved in wars of resistance on the American plains were transported from their homelands to Fort Marion, where they were confined as prisoners of the U.S. government. When Fort Marion closed in 1878, Pratt visited the Hampton Normal and Agricultural Institute in Virginia, a school established for recently freed African Americans after the civil war. Hampton had just begun to accept First Nations students, in what was termed the "Indian Experiment," and a group of Fort Marion inmates appeared on the Hampton school roster.[9] The following year, Pratt established the Carlisle Industrial School with a student body that also included individuals transferred from the camp to the school. In 1892 he spoke to the Annual Conference of Charities and Correction in Denver, Colorado, espousing the Carlisle philosophy:

> A great general has said that the only good Indian is a dead one, and that high sanction of his destruction has been an enormous factor in promoting Indian massacres. In a sense, I agree with the sentiment, but only in this: that all the Indian there is in the race should be dead. Kill the Indian in him, and save the man.[10]

"Kill the Indian, save the man" was Carlisle's unofficial slogan, and variations of it were echoed in the policy documents and discourse of Canadian government officials.

In 1879 Nicholas Flood Davin submitted his *Report on Industrial Schools for Indians and Halfbreeds* to the Minister of the Interior. Davin had toured the Hampton Institute, the Manual Labour School in Indian Territory (later the state of Oklahoma), and the boarding school at the White Earth Agency in Minnesota, which opened in 1871.[11] His report enthusiastically endorsed the American strategy. He identified the industrial school as the "principal feature of the policy known as … aggressive civilization."[12] The model of American industrial schools, emerging as they did from the forcible confinement and imprisonment of resistant nations, became the model for industrial and residential schools in Canada. Removal and separation of children and their reconstruction into useful "citizens" were closely woven into an overall policy that envisioned the destruction of collective identities, the assimilation and integration of individuals, and the subsequent acquisition of remaining First Nations lands.[13]

The system developed in Canada built upon an educational foundation begun by missionaries prior to Confederation. The Canadian government decided, on Davin's recommendation, to graft the proposed new system onto the older missionary project. As a result, the residential and industrial school system inherited its Christian zeal and accumulated frustration with a relative lack of success, and the subsequent identification of parents, a love of hunting, and traditional religious practice as the enemies of progress. Davin's report uses the missionary experience to corroborate his evidence from the American strategy, concluding, "if anything is to be done with the Indian, we must catch him very young."[14]

Control over children became an important strategy in policy implementation. The subjugated bodies of children were to be raw clay in the project of transforming independent and resistant nations into a useful class of docile labourers and servants. While this need to control is perhaps more understandable in the late nineteenth-century context of armed resistance on both sides of the Canada–U.S. border, its continuation well into the twentieth century becomes more chilling. Several punitive Canadian policies were put in place in the aftermath of the 1885 Saskatchewan Resistance/s, but the shift to increasingly restrictive policies between 1920 and 1930 corresponds more closely with the global rise of fascism and extreme conservativism. Duncan Campbell Scott, deputy superintendent of Indian Affairs from 1913 to 1932, secured successive pieces of legislation that culminated in the most oppressive period of First Nations history in Canada. In 1920 Scott maintained that the residential school system was an essential component of Canada's policy: "Residential Schools were established to get rid of the Indian problem.... Our objective is to continue until there is not a single Indian in Canada that has not been absorbed into the body politic and there is no more Indian Question and no Indian Department."[15]

As late as 1949, terms such as "liquidating" and "abolition" peppered policy discussions.[16] Most restrictive and controlling policies were part of the Indian Act until 1951, and First Nations people did not receive basic citizenship rights until 1960. However, the apprehension and removal of children continued beyond that date. Government attention consistently focused on children, viewing them as mute bodies to be emptied and erased, and upon that blankness, an appropriate text of modest knowledge inscribed.

Regardless of unchanging government policy, proponents of the residential and industrial school system were engaged in a continual dance to market the project, justify budgetary requirements, wrangle resources, and maintain the schools' perceived role as the "bringers of good society."[17] In her seminal essay "Can the Subaltern Speak?" Gayatri Chakrovorty Spivak used the phrase "white men are saving brown women from brown men" to describe the manner in which both colonial actions and actors can be manipulated to appear brave and noble.[18] In the case of residential schools, white men were saving brown children. Children were repeatedly described as requiring protection from their own people, specifically their parents and grandparents. As Davin proclaimed, "This is not merely a matter of policy.... It is a sacred duty."[19] Their "success" was considerable, given that the system peaked in 1930 with eighty schools and survived across two centuries. The photographic archive from the residential and industrial school period extends roughly over that time period, although there are significant gaps and telling absences. The photographs can be grouped into three general categories: photographs to illustrate government reports and other official publications, those taken by staff and visitors, and a remarkable group of photographs taken by students at the Spanish Indian Residential School. Father William Maurice, who worked at the school between 1952 and 1958, built a darkroom and trained several boys to develop film and print photographs.[20] Students had access to cameras, and these photographs show a remarkable inner view of residential school life. Through the diverse fingers that pressed camera shutters, a considerable body of photographs resulted. However, there is a striking, unsettling similarity to many of them.

Before and After: Promoting the Project

In 1968 James Gladstone's "Indian School Days" marked the emergence of a series of autobiographical works that voiced the experiences of children who attended residential schools.[21] The scholarly histories that followed, accompanied by a growing political movement, culminated in the tangle of public hearings, court actions, and restitution still unfolding today. During this process, out of the hundreds of photographs taken of children, a scant handful has become the iconic representation of the residential school experience. Their staged poses, graphic impact, and dramatic intent have allowed them to be reframed from their original purpose of promoting the project into the visual tools of exposure and denouncement. These are the "before and after" photographs.

Although before and after / savage to civilized images can be found as early as George Catlin's 1837–1839 portrait of a Nakoda man, "Pigeon's Egg Head (The Light) Going to and Returning from Washington," the genre emerged as a photographic strategy with Captain Richard Pratt at Carlisle. The much-published photographs of Thomas Moore at the Regina Industrial School "before and after tuition" (fig. 3.1), first published in the 1896 annual report of the Department of Indian Affairs, are clearly modelled on earlier photographs Pratt used to provide visual evidence of Carlisle's success.[22] Although the earliest of these comparison photographs was taken at Hampton in 1878, students at Carlisle were frequently photographed on their arrival, and their "progress" was documented in a later staged photograph that mimicked the original seating arrangements and poses.[23] Progress was represented by an altered physical appearance.

Throughout the colonial experience, particular aspects of dress and presentations of the self became symbolic of resistance and the subsequent focus of campaigns for change. For First Nations people, these were the blanket, long hair, and hide clothing. For men, long hair and breech clouts were profound signifiers, while the free-flowing hair, uncorsetted bodies, and short dresses of women were similar affronts to colonial sensibilities. The double portrait of Thomas Moore, with a new name to accompany his physical transformation, was clearly borrowed from the Carlisle repertoire. However, there are some elaborations. In the first image, a young boy wearing a fringed trade-cloth tunic embellished with a double row of metal tacks, a beaded breech clout, beaded

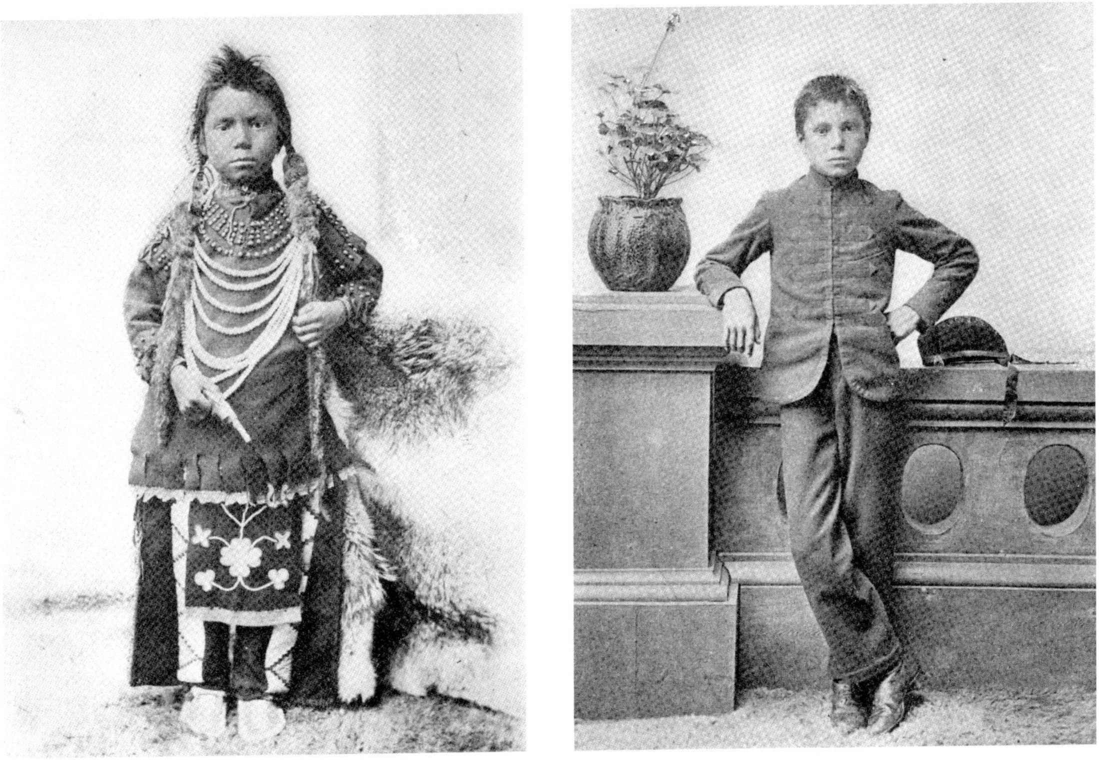

FIGURE 3.1 Thomas Moore, before and after tuition at the Regina Industrial School, 1896. (Saskatchewan Archives Board, R-A8223, 1 & 2)

leggings, and moccasins leans against a large piece of furniture. His hair is worn in two braids wrapped in fur, with a brass bead hair-tie on the right side of his head. To emphasize his "primitive" state, the furniture and floor are covered with fur pelts, and he holds a small toy pistol in his right hand. The soft roundness of his face, his direct gaze, and his slightly pouted mouth indicate, perhaps, a small boy on the verge of tears. The fingers of his left hand are curled protectively inwards. The tentativeness of his body language makes the small pistol an ironic note. In the second photograph, Thomas is older. His legs are longer, his face is slimmer, his hair cropped. He is dressed in a school uniform and leather shoes. He is posed in front of a short wall, leaning against an abutment. As in the earlier photograph, he gazes directly into the camera. His body language is confident. He stands erect, one leg crossed in front of the other, his left fist on his hip, his right hand relaxed with fingers extended.

In addition to the toy pistol in the earlier photograph, the degree to which the photographs were staged needs to be considered. A checked shirt, visible at the neck and wrists, is worn under the trade-cloth tunic. Posed among furs upon his entrance into school, Thomas is later photographed with a potted plant and a glengarry cap resting beside him on the stone wall, which itself appears to be a photographer's prop. These photographs were given considerable thought. Symbolically surrounding Thomas with the signifiers of savagery and civilization provided visual cues for the viewer, supported by the physical transformation of the boy himself. The slight defiance in his gaze, however, indicates that something might be amiss.

Beyond the shallow aspects of borrowed strategy and staging, the Thomas Moore photographs need to be explored within the context of the 1896 Department of Indian Affair's annual report, the site of their initial publication. Between 1895 and 1905, these annual reports were regularly illustrated with a selection of photographs. They were typically organized along a narrative trajectory that began with nostalgic and vaguely affectionate images of elderly people in traditional dress, followed by photographs of active, mature men and women engaged with implements signifying progress, such as farm machinery and sewing machines, new houses, or villages organized in orderly rows. Images of residential school buildings and students engaged in a variety of useful activities accompanied the section on education near the end of the report, providing a visual conclusion that looked ahead to an optimistic future of utility, combined with an appealing docility.

Departing from the age/youth/savage/civilized trajectory, the 1896 annual report begins with Thomas Moore's transformation as full-page illustrations in the frontispiece. Scattered throughout the report are seven other photographs of industrial schools at Regina, Saskatchewan, and High River, Alberta. These appear to be a visual response to threats to government policy, intended to reassure or discourage interrogation. The text describes and repudiates complaints regarding the high costs of educating First Nations children and published reports that unfavourably compare the costs of educating "white" and "Indian" children from the national purse. The text responds to these criticisms by emphasizing the economy practised at industrial schools and the use of student labour to reduce costs. According to the 1896 report, 3861 students were being educated in residential and industrial schools across the country, at a cost of $73.82 per pupil per annum. The report further proclaims that the schools are

> fitting for useful citizenship the youth of a people who one generation past were practically unrestrained savages. These schools are now thoroughly equipped and efficiently managed ... an ultimate measure of success ... with the slow and tedious work of uplifting a savage race and eradicating the nomadic and other inherent tendencies which centuries of a wild and barbarous life have firmly implanted.[24]

Thomas's small self is the visual embodiment of this momentous project.

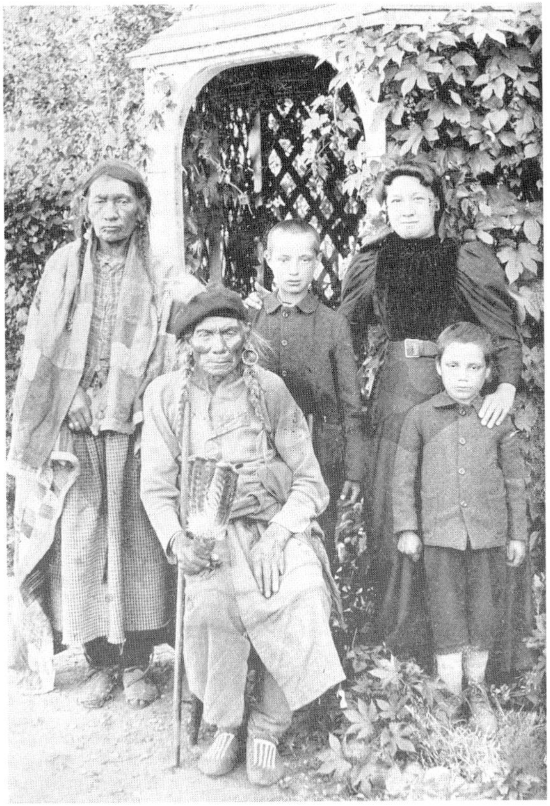

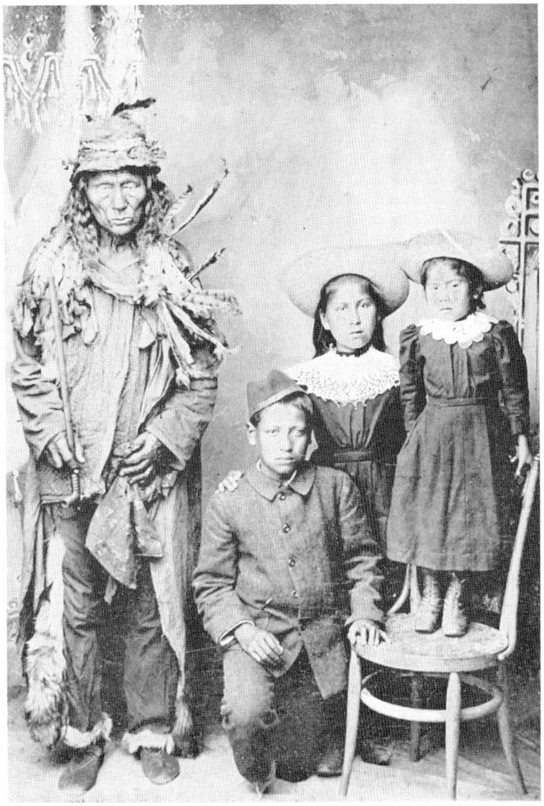

FIGURE 3.2a "Parents and Children Attending Qu'Appelle Industrial School." FIGURE 3.2b "Father and Children Attending Qu'Appelle Industrial School." (*Annual Report of the Department of the Interior for the Year End 30th June 1900*. Ottawa: Government of Canada, 1901, pp. 321 and 337)

Another form of the "before and after" photograph gracing official publications is the photograph of students and their parents. Two such photographs were included in the 1900 annual report.[25] Girls in high-necked dresses and boys in military-style uniforms are posed with their parents, who, through their traditional dress, represent the "wild and barbarous life" the schools were positioned against. In the first photograph (fig. 3.2a), a girl with upswept hair stands with two younger children and her parents. Although the caption reads "Parents and Children Attending Qu'Appelle Industrial School," it seems unlikely that the two younger children are part of the family group. They are more likely the children of staff members or visitors. The parents are quite elderly, wearing fabric clothing of traditional cut, leggings, and beaded moccasins. Their hair is worn in long braids, and their bodies are wrapped in blankets. It is probable that these photographs were also somewhat staged. The father, in addition to his beret, large earrings, and blanket, holds a feather fan. The mother, who stands to the left of the group, wears a patchwork quilt draped over her shoulders instead of the more typical wool trade blanket. The other photograph (fig. 3.2b) also uses props. In "Father and Children Attending Qu'Appelle Industrial School," the elderly man's shoulders are encircled with feathers, and he holds a ceremonial pipe in his right hand. While their humble clothing may reflect the poverty of local reserves, and their long hair and moccasins signify their cultural positioning, it seems unlikely that fathers brought ceremonial regalia and objects on school visits. As visual representations of the frequently stated philosophy, "nothing can be done with the Old Indians," these photographs were structured to illustrate or project the desired alienation between children and their families resulting from the ideological campaign to denigrate traditional beliefs by associating them with poverty and "backwardness." The choice of elderly people to represent the collective body of "parents" also associates the persistence of traditional beliefs with a generation soon to pass away, a visual construction of the desired "vanishing Indian race."

Some photographs of children evoke "before" from the visual memory or stock mental images that the viewer might hold. There is an implied comparison to an uncontained, undisciplined former state, and an assumption that the sight of children in Western dress was a novelty, an indication of "progress." In other photographs, school staff members slip into the vacant space of "parent," reinforcing the status of children as wards of the government. Groups of girls in high-necked dresses, with their hair confined or tucked under matching hats, sit, stand, or walk under the watchful eyes of school matrons and teachers. School instructors and supervisors stand in for the undesired parental figures depicted in other photographs. The "before and after" photographs, whether framing the experiences of an individual child or offering direct and indirect comparisons to parents and community, were created during the initial years of the residential and industrial school project. They were used to solicit public support, silence critics, and illustrate the launch of an ambitious initiative. They served to represent the government as a benevolent, caring agent, the harbinger of progress, entrusted with the "sacred duty" of transforming First Nations children into a class of labourers, tradesmen, and domestic servants.

Roundup: Seizure and Transportation

> *When that truck did come, boy, I tell you. We had a back door and a front door and we bee-lined it. I didn't know exactly where they were going, but when everybody started running, I started to run too and realized that the truck was there. And they literally chased us down.... And the kids that are on the truck they're all bawling because they're seeing us, you know, screaming and yelling.... Of course they're all crying because we're crying and Mum's crying and I can remember [saying], "What did I ever do to you? Why are you sending me away?"*[26]

In 1884 reports of children running away from industrial schools began to appear in the *Regina Leader* and local newspapers across the country. Headlines such as "Four Boys Flee Industrial School at Elkhorn" and "Boy Flees Indian Industrial School" were indications that children were not happy with their surrogate family.[27] In the early years, parents voluntarily sent their children to the schools, hoping to prepare them for adulthood in a vastly different world from the one they had known. School staff were under considerable pressure to recruit and keep students, as continued funding relied on success. Reports of bribery and kidnapping began to appear in Department of Indian Affairs documents, and students such as Dan Kennedy of Carry the Kettle First Nation recalled being "lassoed, roped and taken to the government school."[28] Student enrollment wavered as parents grew alarmed and expressed concerns regarding the treatment of their children, motivated by the stories of homesick children who had fled the premises.

Having made a considerable investment in the construction of residential and industrial schools, and being unwilling to deviate from their chosen course of action, the Department of Indian Affairs responded by obtaining successive amendments to the Indian Act that reduced the rights of First Nations parents and increased the government's power over children. In 1920 the Act mandated school attendance until the age of fifteen and empowered Indian agents and department officials with the right to search homes and call in the police to arrest parents who refused to send their children to school.[29] This latter amendment launched an era of "roundups," where children were forcibly removed from their homes and transported to schools in overcrowded wagons, cattle trucks, and boats. The youngest children were five years old, but there are reports of even younger children being apprehended. Not surprisingly, given the emotionally charged and unpleasant scenes of children being forcibly removed from their homes, few photographs were taken. However, there are notable exceptions, such as the surviving photographs of the crowded cattle truck so vividly remembered by children who attended the Kamloops Indian Residential School.[30] As Mary Anderson recalled:

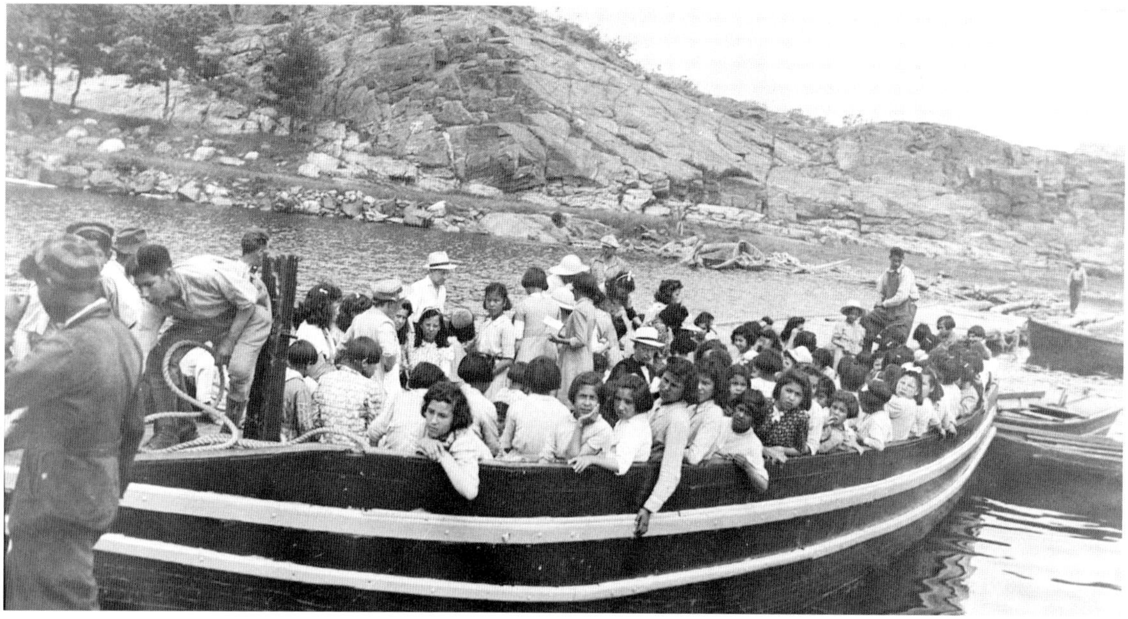

FIGURE 3.3 Girls arriving at Spanish Indian Residential School from Manitoulin Island, c. 1950. (Father William Maurice S.J. Collection, The Shingwauk Project and Residential School Research Archives, Algoma University College)

> It was a flatbed truck with rails around it, like the kind you carry cattle in. It was a big truck and they had already picked up other children along the way so I don't know where their starting point was. They continued to pick up more children along the way.... It was a long trip. The year was 1948 and I was six years old. We rode all bunched up sitting on wooden benches. It was a long tedious, and tiring journey for a six year old. I remember one time it rained and we were wet. There were no rest stops.[31]

Photographs of the boats that transported children from Manitoulin Island to the Spanish Indian Residential School have also survived. The children were separated by gender and loaded into boats that appear to be dangerously overcrowded. In one photograph (fig. 3.3), at least seventy-five girls with supervising adults are crowded into a moderately sized, open boat. Between six and seven girls are seated in each horizontal row, while others line the edge. In another photograph, a crowded boatload of boys is shown pulling up to the dock. The faces of the children are solemn and apprehensive; no one is smiling. Their body language reflects their facial expressions. Many of them are slumped, possibly with exhaustion from trips from communities as far away as Quebec and Manitoba.[32]

Breaking the Individual: Haircuts, Numbers, and Personal Boundaries

> *The farm instructor ... came in with a sheep's shear and cut my four braids off and threw them on the floor. After a while along came a young boy rolling a horse clippers into the room and that horse clippers bounced over my head and gave me a bald head. After he got through, he said, "Now you are no longer an Indian" and he gave me a slap on the head.*[33]

Many residential and industrial schools appear to have developed cruel and often sadistic arrival rituals to mark a child's entry into a world that utterly rejected all their previous experiences. Following the trauma of removal and long journeys to the school, children were stripped of their clothing and scrubbed, had their hair cut or shaved, and were dressed in either uniforms or second-hand clothing donated from missionary societies. Each student was also given a number. In many schools, particularly in western Canada, children were frequently given new names. When Ochankuga'he was captured and taken to the Regina Industrial School in 1886, his hair was cut and he was given a new name: Dan Kennedy. Kennedy recalled the impact of receiving his new name. An interpreter translated the principal's words, "We are going to civilize him, so we will give him a civilized name."[34] His Nakoda name, which translates as "Path Maker," commemorated his grandfather's war record and was a source of great pride to the young boy. Kennedy's memories of the Regina Industrial School can further contextualize Thomas Moore's "before and after" photographs. They were students at the same school at approximately the same time. Who was Thomas Moore before he was renamed? What special name had he carried? In addition, as Dan Kennedy recalled, for boys like himself and Thomas Moore, short hair "was a token of mourning—the closer the relative, the shorter the cut.... I wondered if my mother had died, as they had cut my hair close to the scalp." Panicked, he ran away from school three times. The short hair in residential school photographs is the visual testimony of a deeply symbolic and traumatic gesture enacted on the bodies of children.

Many of the children who arrived at schools in western Canada had never had their hair cut, and the grooming of their hair had been associated with affection. Hair in most First Nations traditions was a rich expression of personal beauty, community aesthetics, and cultural practice. The length, lustre, and often complex styling of hair communicated personal and public information, and the care and dressing of another's hair—particularly a spouse or child—was an expression of love. The ritualized, and often terrifying, haircuts given to children upon arrival provide a context for the very short hair of the youngest boys in large group photographs. The annual report of 1900 included a group photograph of children from St. Joseph's Industrial School in

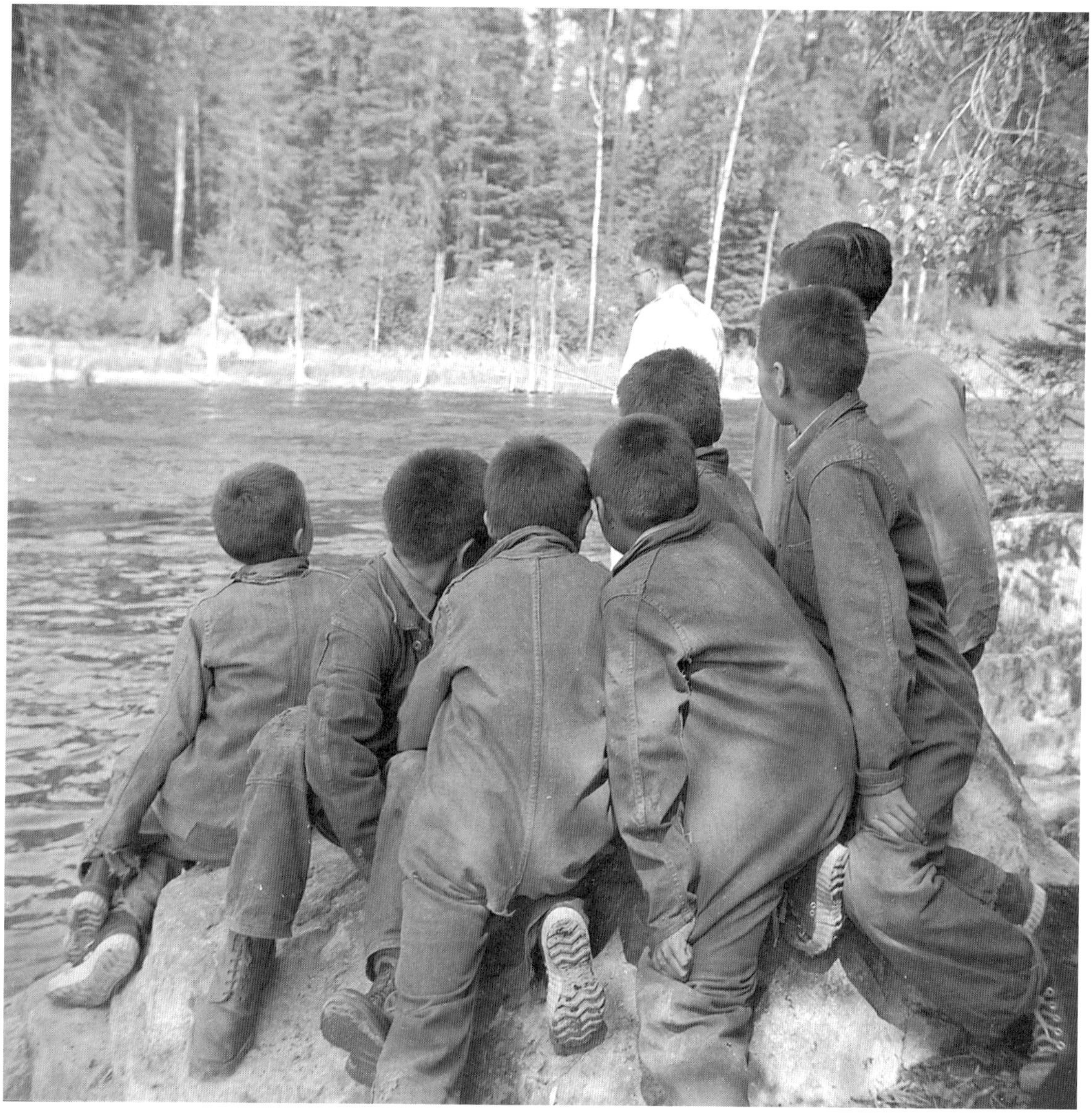

FIGURE 3.5 Students of the Anglican residential school at Pelican Falls, near Sioux Lookout, watching a fisherman. (Photo by John Macfie, 1955. Archives of Ontario, C 330-8-0-0-5)

The Subjugated Body: Discipline, Punishment, and Regimentation

> *The conditions prevailing in these schools are common knowledge throughout the Province. Inferior staffs, inadequate food, constant overwork, military and religious routine, together with genuine cruelty, have caused those who have attended them to term these schools, "Penitentiaries." This is the manner in which the provision of Treaty [promises] re Education has been provided, and it is to such schools that Cree children are compelled to attend FOR THE CRIME OF BEING BORN AN INDIAN.*[39]

In 1940 Malcolm Norris, an Alberta Métis activist and political organizer, reported that residential school graduates used the euphemism "penitentiaries" to describe their schools. In fact, in 1940 many aspects of "being born an Indian" were criminalized, and would remain so for much of the twentieth century. Ceremonies such as the potlatch and sundance had been banned in the late nineteenth century; all forms of traditional dance, and even public appearances in traditional dress, were prohibited in the early twentieth century.[40] Daily life was closely regulated through a series of passes and permits. The law also demanded residential school attendance.

The prison-like nature of residential schools becomes particularly clear when their rhetoric and activities are placed in the context of Michel Foucault's history of the prison, particularly his discussion of the "panopticon."[41] While residential and industrial schools were identified as "schools," the discourse of government and school authorities borrowed heavily from the field of corrections, not educational pedagogy. The schools were a social and political experiment that rested conceptually and structurally between categories. Foucault describes the panopticon as a "laboratory of power" that can take a variety of forms.[42] One possible means for the panopticon to exercise its power is "as a machine to carry out experiments, to alter behaviour, to train or correct."[43] The focus of correction, "the crime of being born an Indian," included language, religious beliefs, cultural persistence, and collective social structures—the "tribalism" so frequently decried. Confinement was one aspect of residential and industrial schools that shifts them conceptually toward the panopticon. Unlike other boarding schools, where children returned home for frequent vacations and parents were encouraged to visit, residential and industrial schools discouraged parents' efforts to maintain connections with their children because they had an "unsettling" effect. As early as 1886, school authorities and government officials discussed strategies to separate children from parents and limit visiting privileges. Further to that, attempts were also made to restrict the freedom of graduates.

The principal of the Regina Industrial School, Reverend A.J. McLeod, advocated every effort to "break up the reservation and tribal system" and lobbied the Department of Indian Affairs that "graduates of Indian schools should not be permitted to return to their reserves."[44] Father Hugonnard of the Qu'Appelle Industrial School freely admitted in his submission to the 1896 annual report that he kept students in school beyond the legislated period.

> The conduct of the pupils is as good as can be expected from such a number, especially as many of them have passed school age. It is to be hoped that later, when the old uncivilized Indians shall have disappeared, it will not be necessary to keep the pupils after school age.[45]

Hugonnard's admission that he kept students beyond the legal age is an indication of the power that had been devolved to school officials and Indian agents. It was published in the annual report of the Department of Indian Affairs and included in the parliamentary sessional papers, and as such was a matter of public record. It was widely known, and generally accepted, that students were being confined in schools "for their own good." In addition, residential and industrial schools frequently received visitors, and photographs of the large institutional buildings were sometimes available as postcards. As time went on, and school practices became more obsolete, residential schools became more isolated and were removed from the consciousness of the average Canadian. They became increasingly enveloped in a secrecy that became essential to their continued exercise of power. As Foucault stated, "Secrecy is imperative, and so too is autonomy, at least in relation to this technique of punishment; it must have its own functioning, its own rules, its own techniques, its own knowledge; it must fix its own norms, decide its own results."[46]

Discipline and punishment were integral and indispensable strategies in institutions with roots in a military prison camp, charged with the responsibility of "civilizing" their young wards. These aspects of the school system recall Foucault's discipline of the panopticon, which "sometimes requires enclosure, the specification of a place heterogeneous to all others and closed in upon itself. It is the protected place of disciplinary monotony."[47] The task of subjugation and transformation required a complex interplay of structure, power, discipline, and the tedium of a rigorous routine that permeated every moment of an individual's life. It also required what Foucault described as a ceaseless inspective function—"The gaze is alert everywhere."[48] The surveillance, hypervigilance, and system of punishments to which students were subjected at residential schools were also more similar to practices in prisons than those in educational institutions.[49]

Discipline was further implicated in the scheme to use student labour to offset the costs of running the schools. At a time when the social movement to restrict child labour was getting underway in the rest of Canada, student labour was critical to school economies. The 1896 annual report that calculated student labour into the financial accounting of educational costs was published six years after the 1889 Royal Commission on the Relation of Labour and Capital, which marked the beginning of Canada's concern with child labour. Across Canada, children worked at residential schools, and in some cases they laboured for the entire day and rarely saw the inside of a classroom. Students cooked, cleaned, farmed, worked in gardens, and did laundry. Their days were highly structured, beginning at 5:30 a.m. and ending with evening prayers at 8:00 or 8:30 p.m. Student work was designated in the daily schedule as "fatigue, trades" or "school, trades" and accounted on average for six hours of the day.[50] Although labour was initially intended to be the priority of schools that followed the industrial model, all residential school students worked, and worked very hard.

Photographs of students working were frequently published in the annual reports to accompany enthusiastic text that identified the volume of work done by students and, not infrequently, the revenue it generated. In 1896 A.J. McLeod, the principal of the Regina Industrial School, reported, "Our farm work is very remunerative and a splendid training ground."[51] The school had fifty-six hectares under cultivation, including a four-hectare garden for school use. The crops were entirely maintained by the boys under the supervision of a farm instructor. The principal of the Washakada Indian Home at Elkhorn, Manitoba, reported that "over $6,000 worth of business was done during the past year in the four shops directly under the management of the school, which means a great deal of labour and is evidence of the progress of the pupils."[52] Two photographs included in the annual report for 1900 were clearly intended to promote student labour. The first, entitled "St. Boniface Industrial School, Ready for Fatigue," shows a group of fifteen boys, posed with seven supervising adults, holding rakes, scythes, lawn mowers, shovels, wheelbarrows, and a saw.[53] The other photograph, "The Indian Boys of the Duck Lake Boarding School Working at the New Addition to Their School" (fig. 3.6), shows thirty-nine boys, some very young, climbing, sitting, and standing on a two-storey structure. Early photographs not only promoted the school program, but when considered with the Department of Indian Affairs' high profile at regional agricultural fairs and exhibitions, were intentional strategies to market the "New Indian" as an asset to the labour pool. The department was clearly attempting to prove that their charges were domesticated and useful.

While photographs of both genders focus on the acquisition of useful skills, images of girls emphasize docility, industry, and neatness. Girls were most often photographed in the sewing room, and less often in the kitchen. They were never photographed in the laundry room or scrubbing floors, which actually constituted the bulk of their work. In 1895 fifteen girls were photographed in the Qu'Appelle Industrial School's sewing room (fig. 3.7).[54] Six girls sit behind Singer sewing machines, five sit in chairs hand sewing, two

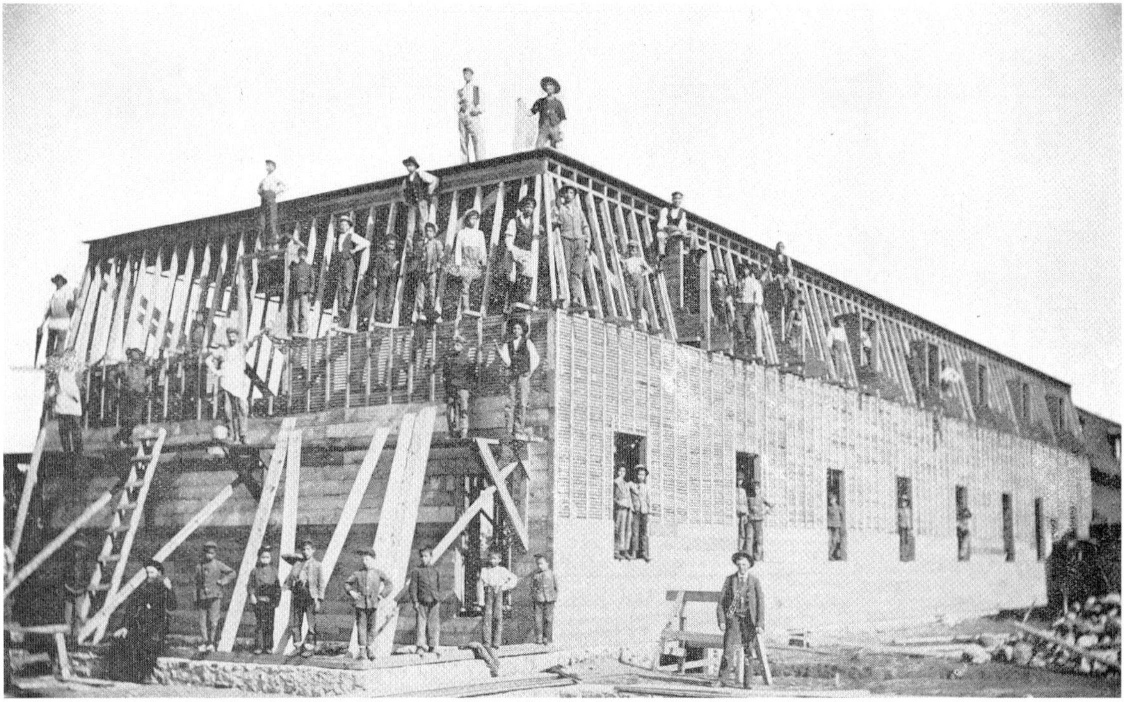

FIGURE 3.6 "The Indian Boys of the Duck Lake Boarding School Working at the New Addition to Their School." (*Annual Report of the Department of the Interior for the Year End 30th June 1900*. Ottawa: Government of Canada, 1901, p. 368)

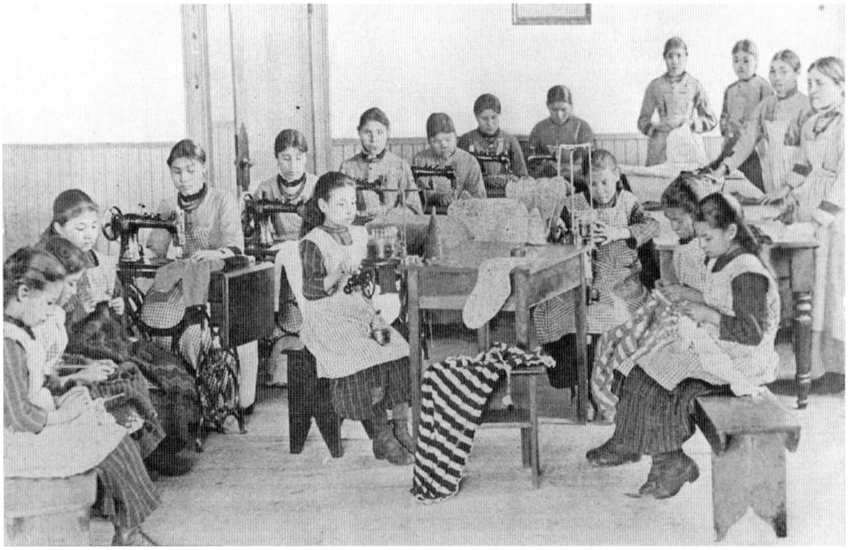

FIGURE 3.7
"Sewing Room," Qu'Appelle Industrial School. (*Annual Report of the Department of the Interior for the Year End 30th June 1895*. Ottawa: Government of Canada, 1896, p. 200. Saskatchewan Archives Board, R-B9)

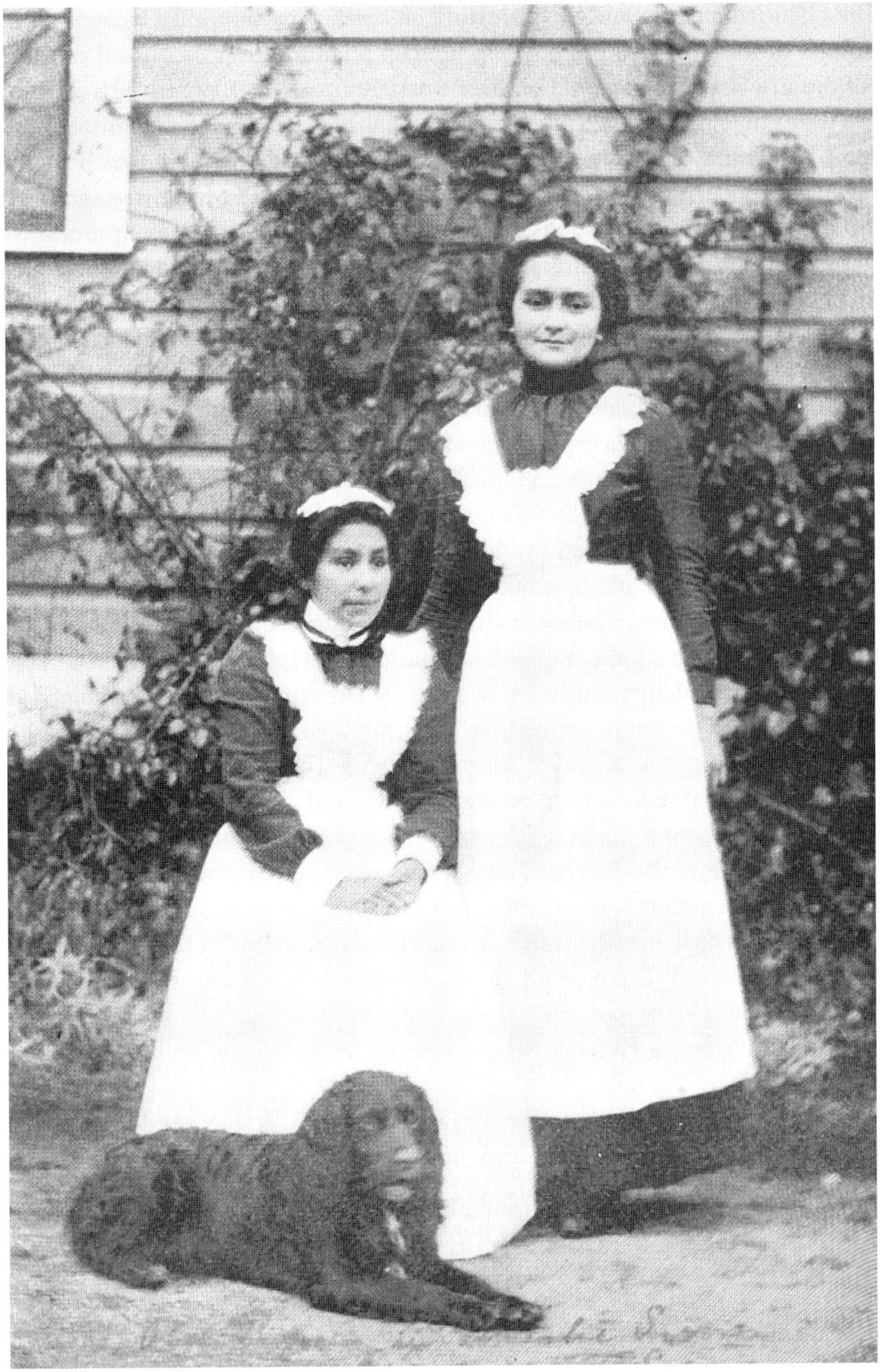

FIGURE 3.8
"Old Pupils of All Hallows' School, Yale B.C., Now in Domestic Service." (*Annual Report of the Department of the Interior for the Year End 30th June 1902*. Ottawa: Government of Canada, 1903, frontispiece)

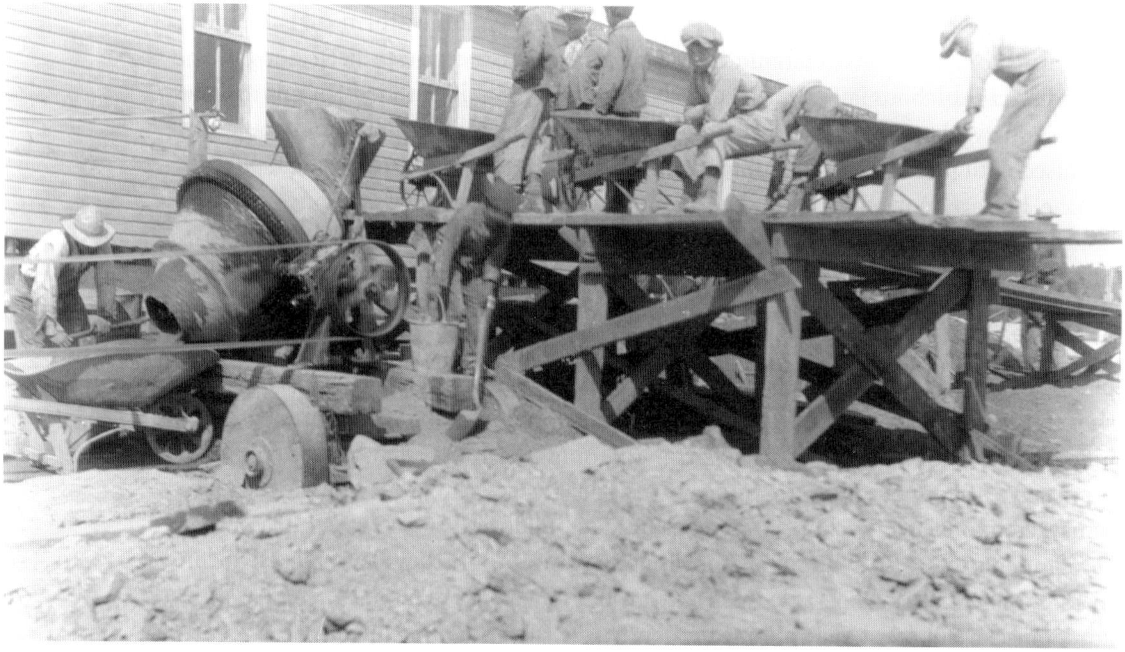

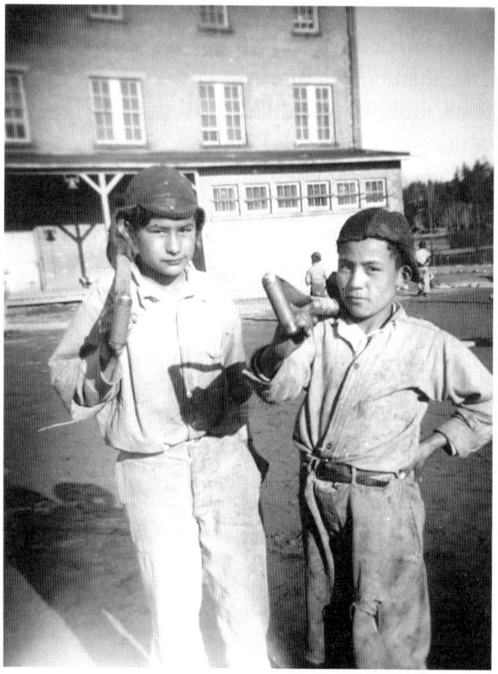

FIGURE 3.9a (above)
Boys working on building construction.

FIGURE 3.9b (left)
Adam Roy and Peter Cooper hoisting their shovels, Spanish Indian Residential School, 1945. (Father William Maurice S.J. Collection, The Shingwauk Project and Residential School Research Archives, Algoma University College)

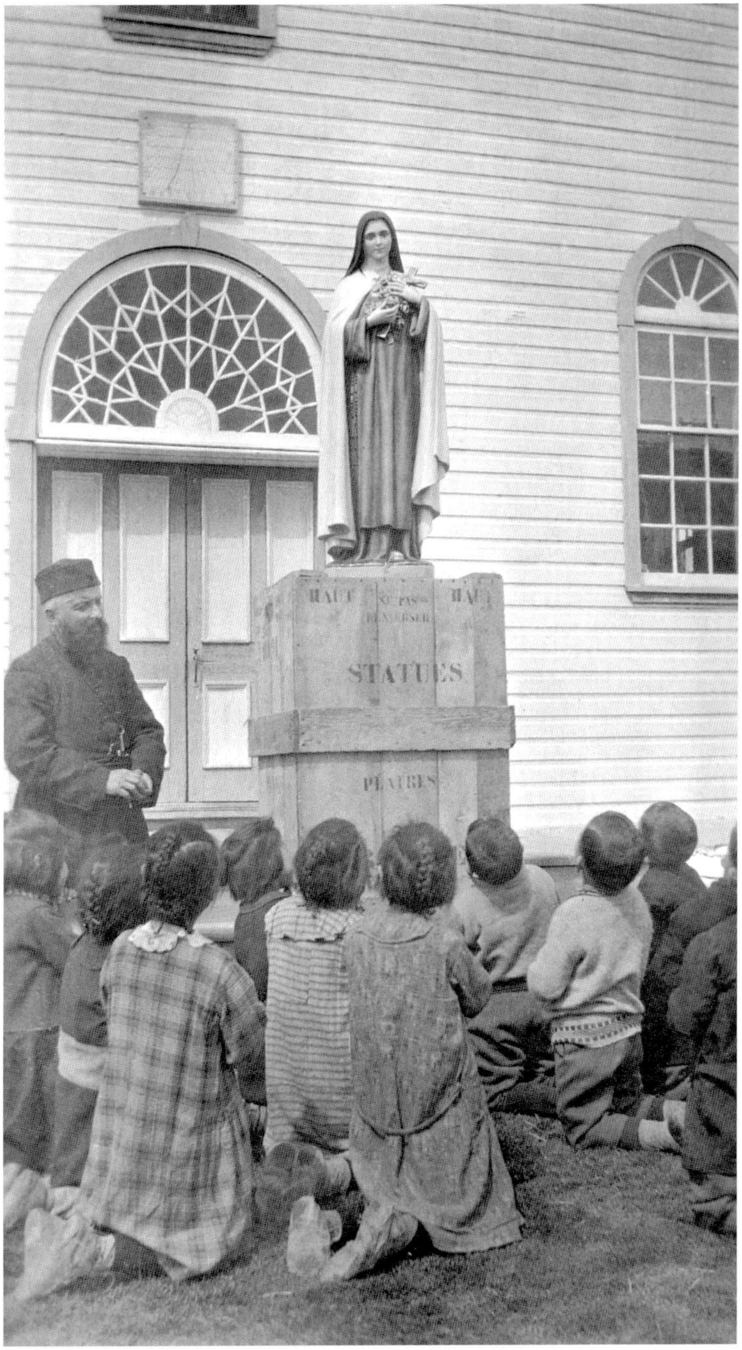

FIGURE 3.10
Children praying to a statue of the Virgin Mary newly arrived from France, Holy Angels Residential School, Fort Chipewyan, Alberta, 1931. (Missionary Oblates, Grandin Collection at the Provincial Archives of Alberta, OB 735)

One of the more disturbing images of children praying is a photograph taken in 1931 at the Holy Angels Residential School, Fort Chipewyan, Alberta (fig. 3.10). A group of children is shown kneeling at the foot of a packing crate, upon which a newly arrived statue of the Virgin Mary has been placed.[66] A priest stands to the right, looking down at them. The children are wearing wrap-around moccasins, and several are poorly dressed. With hands clasped, they look upwards toward the statue, whose surface seems to glow with the resources and concern that should have been invested in their care.

Haunted

The experience ... was a feeling of loneliness, loneliness, terrible loneliness.[67]

In 1904 Dr. Peter H. Bryce, medical inspector for the Department of Indian Affairs, released a shocking report of the death rate of students and recent graduates. The Bryce report created a scandal for the government and the churches in charge of administering the schools, but a close examination of department records clearly indicates that not only had children been dying in residential schools at an alarming rate for years, but they continued to do so. The principle cause of death was tuberculosis. Department officials and school administrators refused the advice of their own medical advisors and continued to subscribe to racial essentialist beliefs that equated First Nations "blood" with genetic weakness. Many department and school officials were adamant that tuberculosis was hereditary and not a contagious disease.

In 1893 Father Hugonnard's annual report for the Qu'Appelle Industrial School stated that "general health has been good," and continued to list "twelve deaths, most of which were from consumption, hereditary in the families of deceased and the germs of which were probably brought from home."[68] He persisted in these views in 1895 when he reported, "nearly every case of death from consumption we have had here has been clearly hereditary."[69] In 1897 the Indian agent deposed Chief White Bear when he refused to send the children of his community to the Qu'Appelle Industrial School. His sons supported their father's position, explaining, "those that had left in the past had died in the Qu'Appelle school, and no one wanted to risk this happening again."[70] Racial essentialism conveniently rationalized the devastating impact of colonization on First Nations communities with notions of the preordained destiny of a weaker race. As late as 1900, Marshall O. Scott, a pioneer in Canadian journalism, inexplicably folded paganism, blood, and health in his article "Pagan Indians in Canada," published in the *Canadian Magazine*.[71] Scott pronounced, "old pagans of inferior blood are dying out faster than men of good race who wish to improve themselves." However, it was not only "old pagans" who were among the dead. In 1907, three years after the release of the Bryce

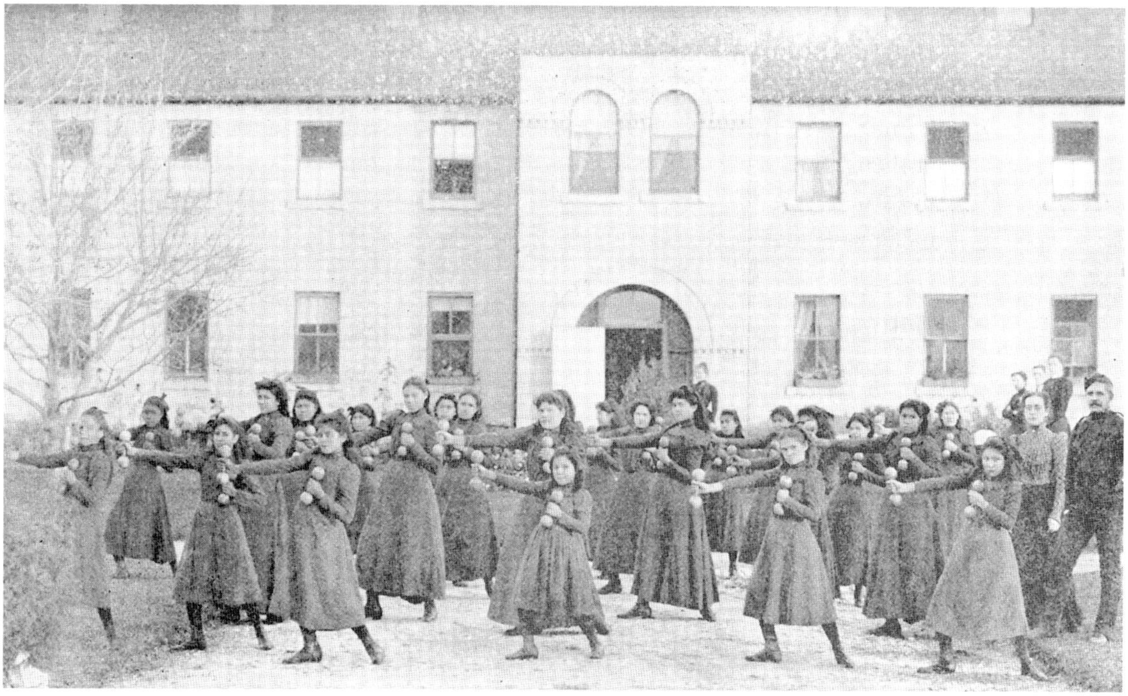

FIGURE 3.11 Girls' Calisthenics Club, St. Paul's Industrial School (near Winnipeg), October 10, 1900. (*Annual Report of the Department of the Interior for the Year End 30th June 1901*. Ottawa: Government of Canada, 1902, p. 128)

report, S. Hume Blake, a Toronto lawyer representing a group of Protestant missionaries, demanded a 50 percent increase in the grants to schools in the west. In his correspondence Blake called upon the department to "take more vigorous steps to reduce the high death rate" and warned that the "Department would be guilty of manslaughter" if steps were not taken to improve living conditions.[72]

Concerns such as these were masked and deflected by photographs designed to undermine or diminish the reports. The 1901 annual report featured a girls' calisthenics class posed in front of the St. Paul's Industrial School in Manitoba (fig. 3.11). Wearing identical plaid dresses and holding a set of small barbells, each girl performs the same choreographed action. Right arms outstretched, left arms held against the chest, the girls have lunged to the right. It seems an awkward pose, and several students have arched their backs to offset the weight of the barbells. Six adults stand on the sidelines watching, two immediately to the right. Clearly staged to represent the school environment as healthful and active, the photograph appears to include every girl in the school. The "club" is located in the school grounds in front of the main entrance. The size of the group, the location, and the number of passive adults in attendance speak to a special demonstration for a specific purpose. Similarly, photographs of smiling children sitting at tables with platters of food and pitchers of milk were visual responses to dismiss and counter the constant complaints from both parents and inspectors about the inadequacy of the diet at most schools.

In 1907 Dr. Peter H. Bryce, chief medical officer for the Department of Indian Affairs, investigated health conditions in fifteen residential schools in western Canada. The shocking death rates he reported revealed that "of a total of 1,537 pupils reported upon nearly 25 per cent are dead, of one school with an absolutely accurate statement, 69 per cent of ex-pupils are dead, and that everywhere the almost invariable cause of death given is tuberculosis."[73] In 1922, alarmed at the department's continuing inaction, Bryce published *A National Crime*, which made the results of his 1907 report public and documented the government's refusal to protect the health of the children in their care.[74] As late as 1937, it was reported that students at the Lac La Ronge Residential School in northern Saskatchewan were underfed, and many students who were ill with tuberculosis slept in the same overcrowded dormitory as other children. Reports on these conditions were continually made by both Indian agents and attending physicians. In addition to illness, other causes of death included accidents, neglect, and suicide. Kuper Island Residential School, located on an island in British Columbia, is a particularly haunted space. Children drowned trying to escape, and former students are adamant that some were murdered.[75]

More recently, residential schools have been exposed as sites of widespread institutionalized physical and sexual abuse. In 1891 School Inspector Macrae was sent to take charge of the Battleford Industrial School and investigate numerous complaints parents had made about the treatment of their children. Macrae himself was to become the subject of a later investigation. It was discovered that he had constructed cells in which boys were confined, and that girls had had their hands tied behind their back for extended periods of time.[76] In one of the more notorious cases of sexual abuse, former students of the Gordon Residential School in Saskatchewan brought charges against William Starr, who sexually abused boys from 1968 to 1984 when he worked as an administrator.[77] Identified as a "monster" in the press coverage of his trial, Starr was found guilty and served prison time. This is the larger context of the photographic legacy of residential schools, and it is this reality that frames many of the images.

In photograph after photograph, the haunted eyes of sombre-faced children speak of profound loneliness or a deeper pain. In an early twentieth-century photograph taken at Duck Lake Residential School in Saskatchewan, two children hold hands and stand in front of the camera (fig. 3.12). The younger child, a girl wearing a white dress with a large white bow in her hair, leans slightly away from the boy who holds her hand.

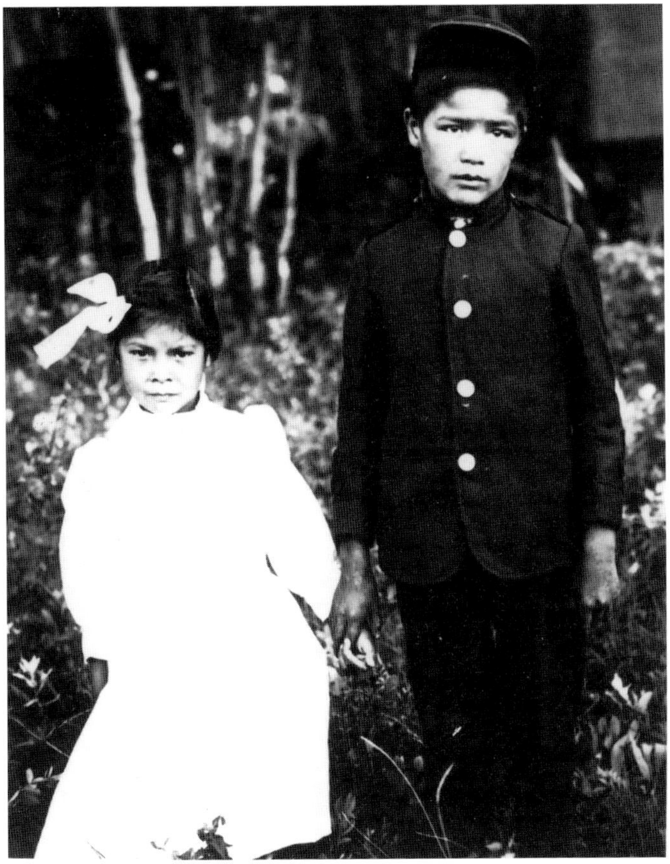

FIGURE 3.12
Boy and girl holding hands, Duck Lake Residential School, c. 1905. (Saskatchewan Archives Board, RA-8292-13)

Her face is serious, her brow slightly furrowed as she looks straight ahead. Her companion is wearing an ill-fitting uniform that is too short in the sleeves and a jaunty cap pushed back on his head. However, there is nothing jaunty about his body language or his facial expression. His shoulders are slumped and his head is slightly turned to the left. His large, troubled eyes provoke speculation. Why is he so sad? What is he looking toward? Does his expression communicate longing or pain? Emotionally, he, unlike the little girl, is not present. She is engaged, perhaps slightly confrontational, while he is preoccupied and distant. Their touch is tentative, their hands loosely enfolded. Although he is holding her hand, it seems more likely that she would lead him if they should walk out of the picture frame.

In other photographs the restraining hands of supervisors are disturbingly intimate. While perhaps not abusive, the hands are invasive and controlling. In 1902, seven boys

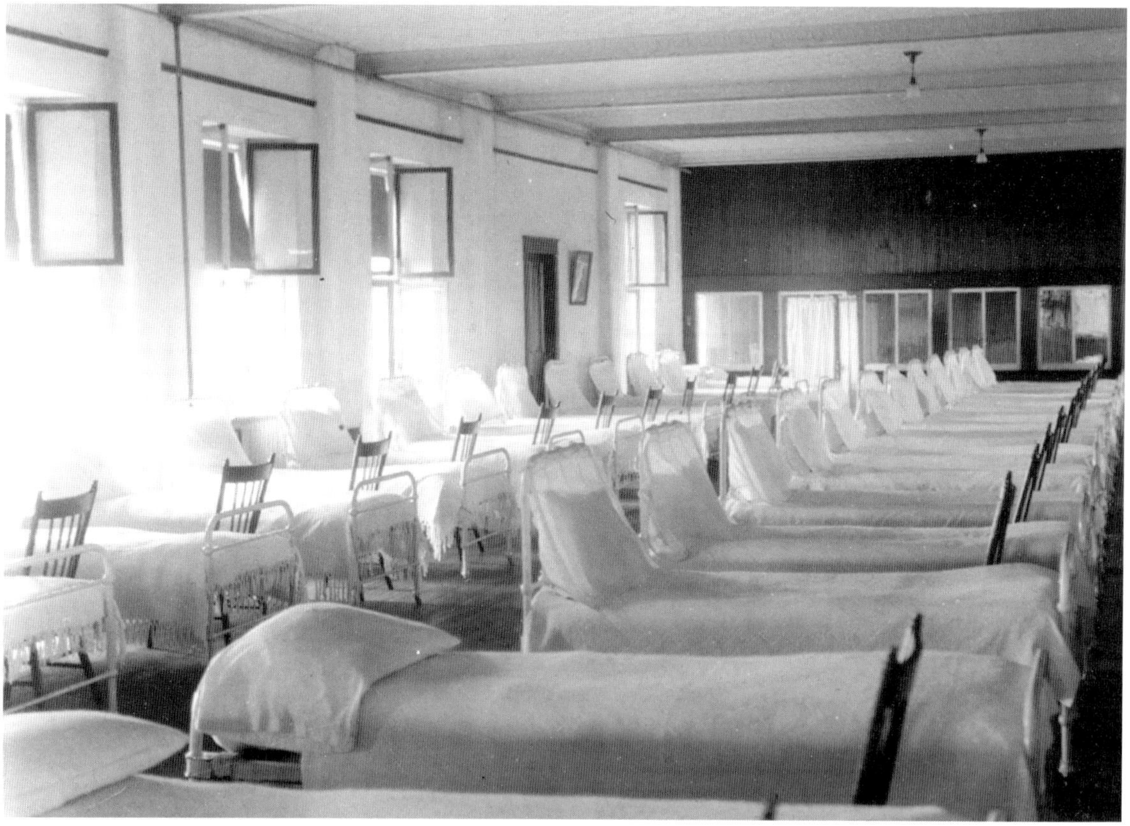

FIGURE 3.13 Empty beds, Spanish Indian Residential School dormitory. (Father William Maurice S.J. Collection, The Shingwauk Project and Residential School Research Archives, Algoma University College)

from the Dunbow Residential School hockey team and their coach were photographed at the Edmonton studio of Charles E. Masse.[78] Their coach was a priest, and also the principal of the school. He sits in the front row with two boys sitting on either side of him. Three other players stand behind them. They are wearing skates and sweaters with the initials of their school, and they hold hockey sticks. The boys show varying degrees of tension and relaxation. The body of the priest is slightly turned toward the young player on his right. The priest's hand holds what appears to be a hockey puck and rests lightly on the young man's upper thigh. The young man gazes steadily into the camera lens, but his left arm rests protectively across his upper thigh and the hand appears slightly clenched. His right arm is relaxed, the hand loosely holding his hockey stick. In the context of what is now known about the darker aspects of the residential school experience, these images are disturbing. In other photographs, the mere representation of a particular place, while devoid of children, triggers a strong response. Photographs of empty beds in the dormitories at the Spanish Indian Residential School are haunted by memory, pain, and fear (fig. 3.13). The crowded rows of ghostlike, little white beds are powerful evocations of the absent children.

Haunted Redux: Resistance, Resilience, and Reframing

> *There was one lovely kind woman who remains so dear to my heart today.*[79]
>
> *They took away everything from me. Everything that was important to me, mother, father, culture. But not my spirit no way.*[80]

The panopticon that was the residential and industrial school system has had a cataclysmic impact on First Nations communities, and the repercussions continue to be felt. However, both memory and photographs attest to the strength and resilience of the children who lived the experience. Despite the powerful totality of the institution, it was unsuccessful in its efforts to destroy the cultural traditions and collective identities of the children confined in its enclosed spaces. Kind staff members, protective friends, and their own courage enabled students to negotiate human spaces in an inhuman, prison-like environment.

Photographs, combined with archival evidence, document the small victories negotiated by parents and community advocates on behalf of children. A close examination of the rows of children photographed at St. Joseph's Industrial School in 1896 (see fig. 3.4) and another photograph taken in 1900 at Blackfoot Crossing reveal the rare sight of five boys whose hair was not cut.[81] Pictured among the shaved heads of their classmates, the long braids of these boys are visual evidence of parents or grandparents with social and political clout who advocated on behalf of their children and whose displeasure residential school authorities were reluctant to provoke. Parents and grandparents were often uncomfortably close to the schools, and school administrators obviously chose to compromise the important and symbolic act of cutting the hair of these boys. The principal at the Piegan Boarding School expressed his frustration with the presence of concerned parents and complained in 1896 that in "the matter of discipline again our proximity to the camp is a great hindrance, and no Indian likes to have his child punished."[82]

School programs and experiences also varied widely, and although the overall policy structure and colonial intent remained unchanged, the quality of a child's experience greatly depended on the character of individual staff members and school administrators. Some schools embarked on a series of initiatives designed to make schools more attractive to children. Music and art programs were implemented with considerable success. Games and sports were introduced, which originally were foreign and novel but became enduringly popular. The recreational program at the Battleford Industrial School had the initial objective of weaning students "from their wild habits and traditions," but students quickly appropriated these games and used them as a means to express individuality.[83] Because school teams participated in tournaments and competitions as "Indian" teams, often wearing uniforms bearing the initials of their schools, their success reinforced, rather than diminished, their collective identity.[84] In 1894 Alfred Betournay, inspector of Roman Catholic Indian Schools, reported, "The boys have distinguished themselves in athletic exercises where public sports have been held.... The junior and senior clubs have already played six or eight matches with outside clubs and have been victorious in most of the games."[85] Photographs of students playing musical instruments, singing, and engaging in team sports were used to generate positive publicity and mask other realities, but they also reveal moments when students could escape into artistic or physical expression.

Parents and community leaders were not the only ones who struggled against the panopticon. Children engaged in their own ongoing battle of wits with supervisors, stealing food and getting into various forms of mischief.[86] Play and mischief were forms of resistance and required courage because they could have serious consequences in terms of discipline and punishment. Students also continued to be children. While very few residential school photographs show children smiling, the photographs taken at Spanish show groups of students crowding in front of the camera with wide grins, small groups of friends, and the family relationships that continued among same-sex siblings and cousins.[87] One photograph taken at the school in Sturgeon Lake, Alberta, in 1946 shows a group of boys playing in the snow (fig. 3.14).[88] The boys are joyously exuberant, revelling in play, with their heads thrown back laughing. It is a visual tribute to the resilient spirits of children. It was this resilient spirit that eroded the power of the panopticon from within, causing the failure of the "laboratory of power."

Residential and industrial school photographs have acquired new significance in recent years. They have been read as historical documents and have been used as admissible evidence by former students seeking restitution through the courts.[89] Several communities have initiated major projects to reclaim silenced voices and reconstruct a lost history. Photographs have played a critical role in these healing projects. Museums, such as the Glenbow Museum, have embarked on naming projects to identify the children in the photographs in their collections.

Photographs are a key component of major projects initiated by the Shingwauk Project and Residential School Research Archives at Algoma University College in Sault Ste. Marie, Ontario, the Secwepemc Cultural and Education Society in British

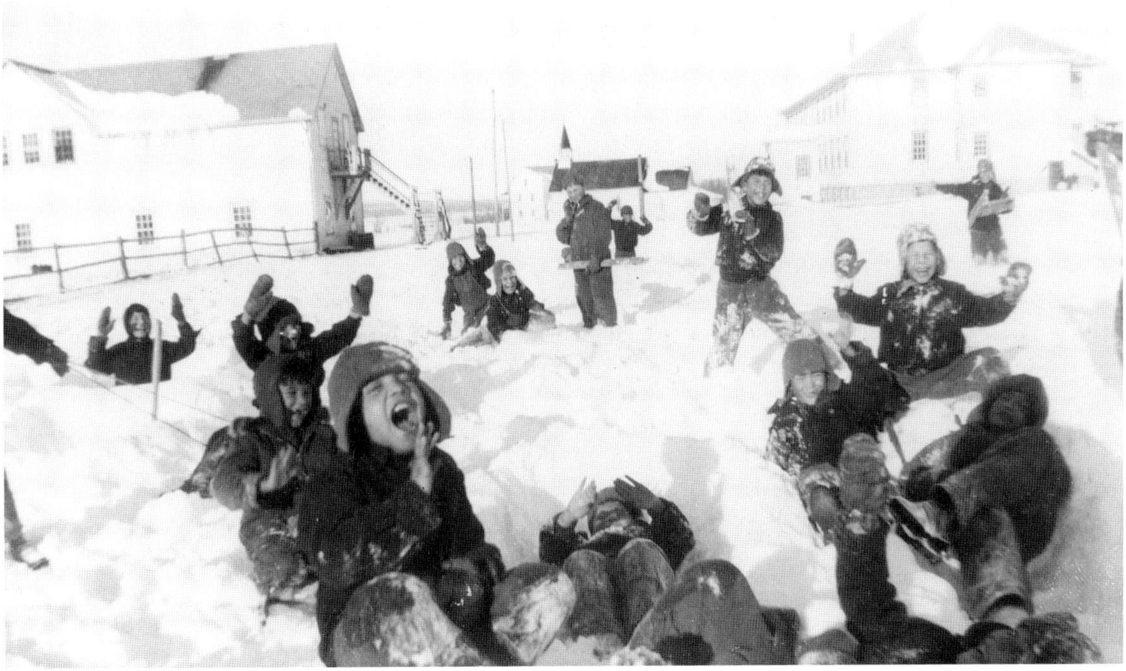

FIGURE 3.14 Cree children playing in the snow at residential school, Sturgeon Lake, Alberta, c. 1946. (Glenbow-Alberta Institute Archives, NA-1954-9)

Columbia, the Aboriginal Healing Foundation, and the Assembly of First Nations. The Long Plain First Nation of Manitoba is in the planning stages of developing the Indian Residential School Museum of Canada and hopes to be the permanent home of the *Where Are the Children* exhibition.

Contemporary artists have also gone to the photographic archive of residential schools, drawn by personal histories and the power of the photographs to evoke memory and provoke emotion. Robert Houle's *Sandy Bay* (1998–1999) uses a ghostlike image of the Sandy Bay Residential School, a small photograph of students, and the gesture of the partial name of the institution. The simple combination of a phrase and faint images crystallize to form a painful history. For his billboard *1885*, Edward Poitras reframed a compelling photograph of Father Hugonnard and a group of children from the Qu'Appelle Residential School.[90] Taken in 1885 by Oliver B. Buell, the official photographer at the trials of Louis Riel, and others involved in the Saskatchewan Resistance/s, the artist researched the context that surrounded the photograph.[91] He discovered that it was partially staged by Hugonnard, who had arranged rows of students along the edge of the valley facing southwest toward Regina, where First Nations and Métis men were tried and Louis Riel was executed. The children were forced to witness events that lay beyond the range of their vision—a cautionary lesson organized and performed for the camera. The image dominates Poitras' billboard with the large text "The Amazon is burning" written across the top, and in smaller print "while you play bingo." The artist explains:

> I used this image in a billboard thus taking the students who appear on that picture into the industrialized world they were being trained to become part of, all dressed in their uniforms. So they may witness the impact of industrial progress on nature. The grass still grows. The sun shines and the water still flows. The trees burn in the Amazon and things move. Like the Buffalo, they come and go. Like waves of change.[92]

Edward Poitras and Robert Houle are not alone in their recognition of the power of these images. Although silent, photographs of First Nations children in residential schools have given voice to children who were forced to participate in a disastrous social experiment, and whose experiences have rocked the Canadian conscience. Collectively, they provide a visual history of children's experiences over four generations, alternately serving to promote, mask, conceal, and reveal the realities that lay behind the doors.

Notes

I would like to recognize the many elders and former students who have shared their stories over the years, particularly the late Beatrice Lavallee, Piapot First Nation, Saskatchewan; the late Alexander Wolfe, Sakimay First Nation, Saskatchewan; the late Josie Courchene, Saugeen First Nation, Manitoba; and the late Albert John Musqua, Cote First Nation. I would also like to acknowledge Francis Fontaine Anaquod, elder and Saulteaux language teacher at Muscowpetung First Nation in Saskatchewan, who, in the court hearings for former residential school students, testified in her first language, forcing the courts to use a Saulteaux interpreter. You are my hero.

1 Ann B. Callahan recalling her father's words in "On Our Way to Healing: Stories from the Oldest Living Generation of File Hills Residential School" (MA thesis, University of Manitoba, 2002), 127.
2 This question formed the title of a recent exhibition of residential school photographs curated by Onondaga photographer Jeff Thomas for the Aboriginal Healing Foundation. *Where Are the Children? Healing the Legacy of the Residential Schools* opened at the National Archives of Canada in 2002 and will tour Canada until 2008.
3 Edward S. Curtis came to Canada in the early twentieth century on three photographic expeditions to the northwest coast, the northern plains, and the Arctic. See Mick Gedley, *Edward S. Curtis and the North American Indian, Incorporated* (Cambridge: Cambridge University Press, 1998).
4 Edmund Morris accompanied the Treaty Number 9 negotiation party in 1906 and between 1907 and 1910 worked on an Indian Portrait series commissioned by the governments of Ontario, Saskatchewan, and Alberta. The photographs he took as part of his fieldwork are in the collection of the Archives of Manitoba.

5 The composition of female students clustered around their teachers at St. Mary's Academy in Ottawa in 1870 (Library and Archives Canada [LAC], PA-032891), and other similar photographs is clearly repeated in the 1896 photograph of girls at the Regina Industrial School with their instructors.

6 Grant's bill to seek a "negotiated peace" with resistant First Nations, rather than continue an aggressive military strategy, passed in the U.S. Congress in 1869. See Robert M. Utley, *The Indian Frontier of the American West, 1846–1890* (Albuquerque: University of New Mexico Press, 1984), 129–130.

7 For a discussion of the Carlisle photographs, see Lonna M. Malmsheimer, "'Imitation White Man': Images of Transformation at the Carlisle Indian School," *Studies in Visual Communication* 11, no. 4 (Fall 1985): 54–75.

8 For a brief history of Carlisle, see David Wallace Adams, *Education for Extinction: American Indians and the Boarding School Experience, 1875–1928* (Lawrence: University Press of Kansas, 1997).

9 The "Indian Experiment" at Hampton Institute lasted from 1878 to 1923.

10 Richard H. Pratt, "The Advantages of Mingling Indians with Whites," in *Americanizing the American Indians: Writings by the "Friends of the Indian" 1880–1900*, ed. Francis Paul Prucha, 260–271 (Cambridge, MA: Harvard University Press, 1973).

11 C.L.B. (a special correspondent), "The New Northwest: An Indian Reservation, White Earth Chippewa Agency, Minnesota," *The New York Times* (July 24, 1873). An Indian agency was a local administrative unit under the authority of a federally appointed Indian agent of the U.S. Office of Indian Affairs.

12 Nicholas Flood Davin, *Report on Industrial Schools for Indians and Halfbreeds* submitted to the Minister of the Interior, Ottawa March 14, 1879, Saskatchewan Archives Board (SAB), 1.

13 The government planned to use education as a means to promote the concept of individual property, which would lead to enfranchisement and the dispersal of collectively held lands and transform "rude savages" into "intelligent and well-behaved Indians." *Annual Report of the Department of the Interior for the Year End 30th June 1874* (Ottawa: Government of Canada, 1876), 5–6.

14 Davin, *Report on Industrial Schools*, 13.

15 Duncan Campbell Scott as cited in Roland Chrisjohn and Sherri Young, *The Circle Game: Shadows and Substance in the Indian Residential School Experience in Canada* (Penticton, BC: Theytus Books, 1997), 42.

16 A special joint parliamentary committee received a paper from anthropologist Diamond Jenness entitled "Plan for Liquidating Canada's Indian Problem within 25 Years," as cited in Celia Haig-Brown, *Resistance and Renewal: Surviving the Indian Residential School* (Vancouver: Tillacum Library, 1988), 32.

17 Gayatri Chakrovorty Spivak used the phrase "imperialism's image as the establisher of the good society" in "Can the Subaltern Speak?" in *Colonial Discourse and Post-Colonial Theory: A Reader*, ed. Patrick Williams and Laura Chrisman, 66–111 (New York: Columbia University Press, 1994), 94.

18 Ibid., 92.

19 Davin, *Report on Industrial Schools*, 13.

20 The Father William Maurice, S.J. Collection is now part of the Shingwauk Project and Residential School Research Archives and Visitors Centre, Algoma University College, Sault Ste. Marie, Ontario. The collection is part of the Remember the Children naming project and is available online at the Shingwauk Project's website (http://www.shingwauk.auc.ca).

21 James Gladstone, "Indian School Days," *Alberta Historical Review* 15, no. 1 (Winter 1967); Louise Moine, *My Life in Residential School* (Regina, SK: Provincial Chapter of I.O.D.E., 1975); Basil Johnstone, *Indian School Days* (Toronto: Key Porter Books, 1988).

22 *Dominion of Canada Annual Report of the Department of Indian Affairs for the Year Ended 30th June 1896* (Ottawa: S. E. Dawson, 1897), iv. The Thomas Moore photographs appear on the covers of Ward Churchill, *"Kill the Indian, Save the Man": The Genocidal Impact of American Indian Residential Schools* (San Francisco: City Lights, 2004) and J.S. Milloy, *A National Crime: The Canadian Government and the Residential School System, 1879–1986* (Winnipeg: University of Manitoba Press, 1999).

23 The 1878 photographs of Ziewie, a Lakota girl from Crow Creek, South Dakota, taken at the Hampton Institute, were not staged to the same extent as Carlisle's "before and after" portraits.

24 *1896 Annual Report*, 186.

25 *Annual Report of the Department of the Interior for the Year End 30th June 1900* (Ottawa: Government of Canada, 1901), 321 and 337.

26 Celia Haig-Brown, *Resistance and Renewal: Surviving the Indian Residential School* (Vancouver: Tillacum Library, 1988), 48.

27 "Four Boys Flee Industrial School at Elkhorn," *Regina Leader* (August 10, 1886), 3 and "Boy Flees Industrial School," *Regina Leader* (February 23, 1893), 8, SAB

28 A 1904 memo to Duncan Campbell Scott and the 1908 inspection report submitted by F.H. Paget included references to bribery and kidnapping. As cited in *The Report of the Royal Commission on Aboriginal Peoples* (RCAP) (Ottawa: Government of Canada, 1991), 30; Dan Kennedy (Ochankuga'he), *Recollections of an Assiniboine Chief* (Toronto: McClelland & Stewart, 1972), 54.

29 It is important to remember that Canadian schools were segregated. First Nations parents did not have the option of sending their children to provincial or municipal schools until the 1960s. Some reserves had day schools, but most did not. Haig-Brown, *Resistance and Renewal*, 31.

30 These photographs are in the collection of the Secwepemux Cultural and Education Society and the Shuswap Nation Tribal Council, Kamloops, British Columbia.

31 Mary Anderson (interviewee) in Agnes Jack, ed., *Behind Closed Doors: Stories from the Kamloops Residential School* (Penticton, BC: Theytus Books, 2006), 33.

32 While many of the children were from the Anishnabek communities of Manitoulin and Walpole islands in Ontario, the student body included Mohawk, Algonquin, Wyandot, and Cree children from Quebec to the east, and the Cree community of Nelson House in northern Manitoba.

33 Former student interviewed by Ann Callahan, "On Our Way to Healing," 40.

34 Kennedy, *Recollections of an Assiniboine Chief*, 54.

35 *1900 Annual Report*, 358.

36 Jack, *Behind Closed Doors*, 15.

37 Correspondence re: Shingwauk Residential School–Sault Ste. Marie Agency, File 469-5, Vol. 6213, Series C-V-4, RG 10, LAC as cited in Donald J. Auger, *Indian Residential Schools in Ontario* (Ottawa: Nishnawbe Aski Nation and the Aboriginal Healing Foundation, 2005).

38 Callahan, *On Our Way to Healing*, 88.

39 Malcolm Norris, *Indian Speaking Leaf* (May/June 1940) as cited in John Milloy, *A National Crime* (Winnipeg: University of Manitoba Press, 1999), 191.

40 Katherine Pettipas, *Severing the Ties that Bind: Government Repression of Indigenous Religious Ceremonies on the Prairies* (Winnipeg: University of Manitoba Press, 1994).

41 Michel Foucault, *Discipline and Punish: The Birth of the Prison* (1977; repr., New York: Vintage Books, 1995), 200.

42 Ibid., 204.

43 Ibid., 203.

44 RG 10, Vol. 3965, File 150000-1, LAC.

45 *1896 Annual Report*, 346.
46 Foucault, *Discipline and Punish*, 129.
47 Ibid., 141.
48 Ibid., 195.
49 Letters were scrutinized and "a strict watchfulness" was kept throughout the day. Some schools developed complex systems of student monitors, student courts, and informants who were rewarded for reporting misdeeds. See *Dominion of Canada Annual Report of the Department of Indian Affairs for the Year Ended 30th June 1883* (Ottawa: S.E. Dawson, 1884), 96; *Dominion of Canada Annual Report of the Department of Indian Affairs for the Year Ended 30th June 1888* (Ottawa: S.E. Dawson, 1889), 22.
50 High River School Schedule, *1887 Annual Report*, 180 and Qu'Appelle School Schedule, *1893 Annual Report*, 173 as cited in Jennifer Lorretta Pettit, "To Christianize and Civilize": Native Industrial Schools in Canada (Ph.D. dissertation, University of Calgary, 1997), 284–285.
51 *1893 Annual Report*, 344.
52 *1896 Annual Report*, 318.
53 *1900 Annual Report*, 352 and 368.
54 *1895 Annual Report*, 200.
55 *1905 Annual Report*, 144a.
56 File 1-1-1, Vol. 6001, RG 10, LAC.
57 Office of the Commissioner of Indian Affairs, North-West Territories, Report from the Battleford and Qu'Appelle Schools, *1895 Annual Report*, 201; "In Domestic Service," *1902 Annual Report*, 1a.
58 *1893 Annual Report*, 177; *1896 Annual Report*, 343.
59 Slides 138-148, EY Spanish Indian Industrial School, Father William Maurice, S.J. Collection: The Shingwauk Project–Algoma University, Sault Ste. Marie, Ontario.
60 Adam Roy and Peter Cooper, Slides 118-119, EY Spanish Indian Industrial School, Father William Maurice, S.J. Collection: The Shingwauk Project–Algoma University, Sault Ste. Marie, Ontario.
61 Max Simon, Slide 120, EY Spanish Indian Industrial School, Father William Maurice, S.J. Collection: The Shingwauk Project–Algoma University, Sault Ste. Marie, Ontario.
62 Bridget Moran, ed., *Stoney Creek Woman: The Story of Mary John* (Vancouver: Tillacum Library, 1988) as cited in Pettit, "To Christianize and Civilize," 247.
63 *1896 Annual Report*, 322.
64 "Father Joncas and Boys in Dormitory 1954," Slide 17, Boys Spanish Indian Residential School, Father William Maurice, S.J. Collection: The Shingwauk Project–Algoma University, Sault Ste. Marie, Ontario.
65 "Girls Dormitory, Old Sun School," NA 4817-22 , "Boys Dormitory, Old Sun School," NA 4817-24, Glenbow-Alberta Institute Archives (GAI), Calgary, Alberta.
66 "Native Children Praying to Statue of the Blessed Virgin Newly Arrived from France," OB 735, Oblate Collection, Provincial Archives of Alberta.
67 Former student interviewed by Ann Callahan, "On Our Way to Healing," 62.
68 *1893 Annual Report*, 88.
69 *1895 Annual Report*, 132.
70 Minutes of November 1897 meeting, White Bear Band, RG 10, Vol. 3940, File 121, 698-13, LAC.
71 Marshall O. Scott, "Pagan Indians in Canada," *Canadian Magazine* 15 (July 1900) as cited in Ronald G. Haycock, *The Image of the Indian: The Canadian Indian as a Subject and a Concept in a Sampling of the Popular National Magazines Read in Canada, 1900–1970* (Waterloo, ON: Wilfrid Laurier University Press, 1973), 1.

72 S.H. Blake correspondence, RG 10, Vol. 4023, File 289,032-1, LAC.

73 P.H. Bryce, *Report on the Indian Schools of Manitoba and the North West Territories* (Ottawa: Government Printing Bureau, 1907), 18; Peter Bryce, M.A., M.D., *The Story of a National Crime: Being an Appeal for Justice to the Indians of Canada; the Wards of the Nation, Our Allies in the Revolutionary War, Our Brothers-in-Arms in the Great War* (Ottawa: James Hope & Sons, 1922).

74 Bryce, *A National Crime*, 129.

75 Suzanne Fournier, "Gathering Marks School's Grim Litany of Death," *Vancouver Province* (June 1996), 4.

76 Following the investigation into Macrae's conduct, he was transferred to Ontario. RG 10, Vol. 3880, File 92, 449, LAC.

77 "When a Monster Finally Says Sorry," *Regina Leader Post* (August 9, 2004), D3.

78 "Dunbow School (St. Joseph's Industrial School) Hockey Team 1902," Charles E. Masse fonds, PR1458, Provincial Archives of Alberta.

79 Callahan, "On Our Way to Healing," 122.

80 E.I. (interviewee) in Jack, *Behind Closed Doors*, 15.

81 Pupils of the St. Joseph's Industrial School, High River, Alberta, *1900 Annual Report*, 358; students and staff of the Blackfoot Crossing Mission School (Crowfoot School), 1900, NA-3482-8, GAI.

82 *1896 Annual Report*, 343.

83 T. P. Wadsworth, inspector of Indian agencies, report on Battleford Industrial School, *1889 Annual Report*, 296.

84 For a discussion of this unexpected outcome of residential school athletic programs see John Bloom, *To Show What an Indian Can Do: Sports at Native American Boarding Schools* (Minneapolis: University of Minnesota Press, 2000).

85 Albert Betournay, inspector Roman Catholic Indian Schools, August 2, 1894, Regina, *1894 Annual Report*, 14.

86 Celia Haig-Brown's interviews with former students of the Kamloops Residential School revealed a complex culture of resistance. See *Resistance and Renewal*, 98–114.

87 Children were divided by gender. Brothers and sisters had very limited contact.

88 Sturgeon Lake Residential School, NA1954-9, GAI.

89 J.R. Miller, "Reading Photographs, Reading Voices: Documenting the History of Native Residential Schools," in *Reflections on Native–Newcomer Relations: Selected Essays*, ed. J.R. Miller, 82–104 (Toronto: University of Toronto Press, 2004).

90 Originally part of Warzones, a billboard project of Presentation House Gallery, Vancouver, in 1999, *1885* was also included in the exhibition and online exhibition site of *Tales of Two Valleys* at the Mendel Gallery, Saskatoon, in 2002.

91 "Father Joseph Hugonnard, Principal, with Staff and Aboriginal Students of the Industrial School 1885," O.B. Buell, PA-118765, Library and Archives Canada.

92 Edward Poitras, artist statement, "Pile of Rocks," *Tales of Two Valleys* online exhibition, http://qu'appelle.mendel.ca/edwardpoitras/pileofrocks.html (accessed May 8, 2007).

CAROL PAYNE

A LAND OF YOUTH

Nationhood and the Image of the Child in the National Film Board of Canada's Still Photography Division

On June 27, 1964, the Still Photography Division of the National Film Board of Canada (NFB) released a photo story entitled "Canada's Future Belongs to Them" (fig. 4.1). Produced and distributed to mark Dominion Day, this pictorial features eight photographs of exuberantly happy children, apparently selected to demonstrate the country's harmonious cultural and geographical diversity. The children are pictured alone or at play in small groups, together forming a youthful and ebullient "imagined community."[1] Reflecting that pictorial optimism, the brief accompanying text announces that, although entering its ninety-eighth year, "Canada is still a land of youth":

> Canada's next generation will have its own special legacy. A wide, rich land of promise, a multi-racial population to nourish the roots of tolerance, a broad foundation of knowledge, wisdom, technology and freedom upon which to build the future and explore the widening avenues of philosophy and adventure. Their heritage will be the natural beauty of vast woodland vistas, the clear waters of millions of lakes, the freshness of wilderness rivers, the ruggedness of mountain ranges and arctic expanse. They will inherit good, rich soil to sustain many people, untold wealth in sub-surface rocks, valuable tools of learning and room to build. This Canada—nearly 100 years old—has a future dependent on the outlook, energy and knowledge of its youngest citizens—the adult Canadians of the world of tomorrow.

In image and text, "Canada's Future Belongs to Them" draws a correspondence between childhood and the nation. Indeed, the scenes of children at play and the textual references to Canada's "good, rich soil" situate children within the country's very earth. These children are presented as markers of Canadian identity, the citizenry as a whole, and the country's aspirations.

There has long been a connection between modern discourses of childhood and the Canadian state. As Neil Sutherland has demonstrated, by the 1870s many reformers

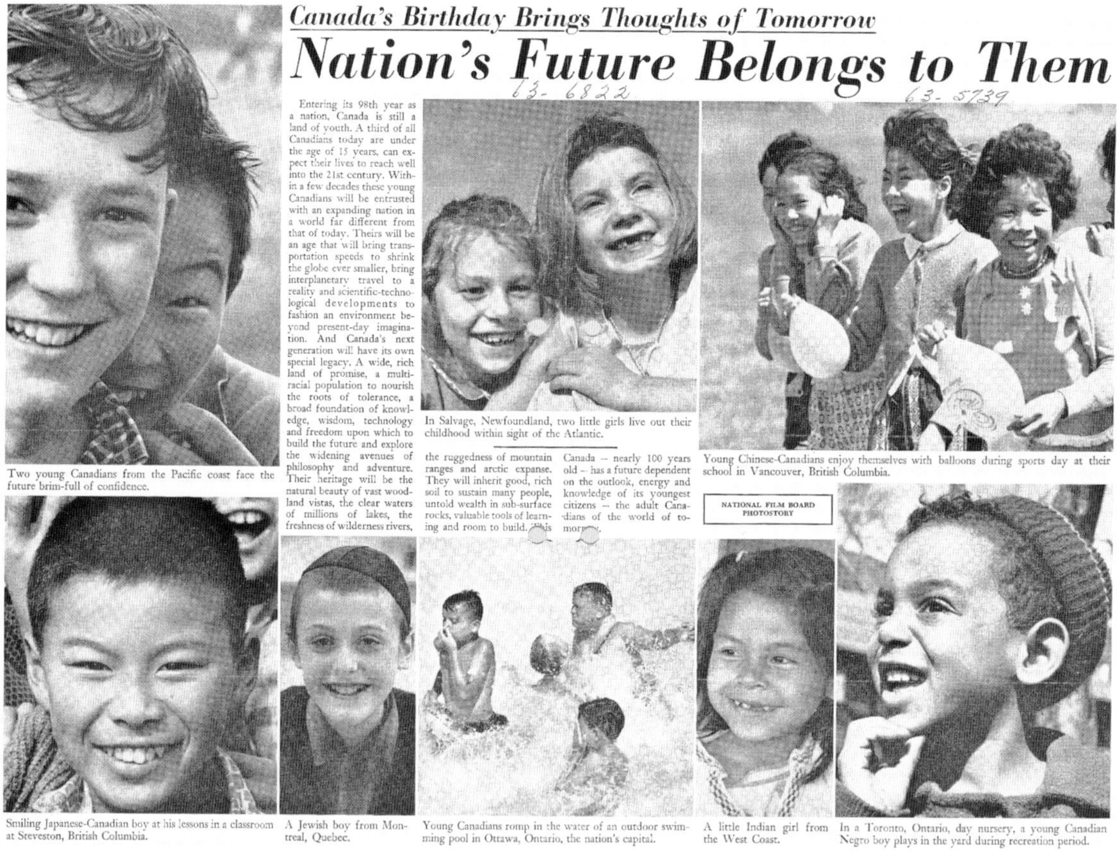

Canada's Birthday Brings Thoughts of Tomorrow

Nation's Future Belongs to Them

Entering its 98th year as a nation, Canada is still a land of youth. A third of all Canadians today are under the age of 15 years, can expect their lives to reach well into the 21st century. Within a few decades these young Canadians will be entrusted with an expanding nation in a world far different from that of today. Theirs will be an age that will bring transportation speeds to shrink the globe ever smaller, bring interplanetary travel to a reality and scientific-technological developments to fashion an environment beyond present-day imagination. And Canada's next generation will have its own special legacy. A wide, rich land of promise, a multi-racial population to nourish the roots of tolerance, a broad foundation of knowledge, wisdom, technology and freedom upon which to build the future and explore the widening avenues of philosophy and adventure. Their heritage will be the natural beauty of vast woodland vistas, the clear waters of millions of lakes, the freshness of wilderness rivers, the ruggedness of mountain ranges and arctic expanse. They will inherit good, rich soil to sustain many people, untold wealth in sub-surface rocks, valuable tools of learning and room to build. This Canada – nearly 100 years old – has a future dependent on the outlook, energy and knowledge of its youngest citizens – the adult Canadians of the world of tomorrow.

Two young Canadians from the Pacific coast face the future brim-full of confidence.

In Salvage, Newfoundland, two little girls live out their childhood within sight of the Atlantic.

Young Chinese-Canadians enjoy themselves with balloons during sports day at their school in Vancouver, British Columbia.

NATIONAL FILM BOARD PHOTOSTORY

Smiling Japanese-Canadian boy at his lessons in a classroom at Steveston, British Columbia.

A Jewish boy from Montreal, Quebec.

Young Canadians romp in the water of an outdoor swimming pool in Ottawa, Ontario, the nation's capital.

A little Indian girl from the West Coast.

In a Toronto, Ontario, day nursery, a young Canadian Negro boy plays in the yard during recreation period.

FIGURE 4.1 National Film Board of Canada, Still Photography Division, "Canada's Future Belongs to Them," Photo Story 367 (June 27, 1964). (Canadian Museum of Contemporary Photography, National Gallery of Canada, Ottawa)

espoused the belief that the well-being of the country as a whole rested with the health and nurturing of young children.[2] In subsequent generations, child welfare became central to government policy. Indeed, the country's first universal social program (the family allowance, which was instituted in the 1940s) was designed specifically to ensure the care of all Canadian children.[3] More recently, the government of Stephen Harper has attempted to implement controversial child-care legislation, which Harper's Conservative Party promoted as a signature policy proposal during the 2006 federal election. But in all these examples, children not only are the concrete subjects of legislative policy, they are also invoked because of the loaded symbolic implications of childhood.

This essay will explore the signification of the image of childhood and how it has been mobilized to serve the project of Canadian nationhood. As a case study I will examine photographs and photo stories dating from the 1950s through the 1960s, such as "Canada's Future Belongs to Them," from the archive of the NFB's Still Photography Division. Over its full history—spanning from 1941 to 1984—the division commissioned and disseminated some 200,000 photographs, as well as lavish pictorial publications, exhibitions, and hundreds of narrativized photo stories. Childhood is a prominent trope within the division's enormous visual archive of the nation. Children appear in pictorials devoted to everything from multiculturalism policies and immigration to tourism, education, and health care, and from scientific research to agriculture and industrial production. I will argue that throughout these promotionals, the division employed the image of the child as a potent sign of Canadian citizenry and national aspirations.

During the course of the period I trace here, strategies for representing children changed dramatically. In the 1950s and early 1960s, images of children reflect facets of expository documentary seen in contemporary, didactic NFB films of the time.[4] Here, images and pictorials are instructional and formalized; in these images, children serve as models of an idealized citizenry. These photographs embody a view of Canadians as malleable beings in need of the paternalistic protection and guidance of government. Yet by the mid-1960s, the style and meanings of division photographs would shift. Many of the photographers supported by the division at this time worked in a manner more closely resembling observational documentary (as seen in direct cinema, or cinéma-vérité). Their work is characterized by a seemingly unobtrusive and spontaneous approach, and in turn the children they depict appear as carefree spirits, rarely seen under adult supervision. In contrast to the earlier depictions of the child as malleable citizen, in these later images, the child becomes a sign of liberal individualism and is particularly useful in promoting Canada's emergent multiculturalism policies, as seen, for example, in "Canada's Future Belongs to Them."

As an examination of the child as sign of citizenry and nationhood, this essay is primarily an inquiry into the semiotics of the photographic image rather than a social historical exploration of childhood in Canada during the 1950s and 1960s. And yet, signification and social experience are always intertwined. Neither feminism, which is foundational to the historical study of childhood, nor the indexical character of the photograph will allow us as viewers to forget that although these representations mediate lived experience and transform it into national symbolism, they nonetheless depict actual lives, actual children.[5] Accordingly, as part of the exploration of childhood as signifier of the nation, this essay will also reference social attitudes and governmental policies about children while considering the symbolic role representations of children play in this "land of youth."

The photo story "Canada's future belongs to them," with its cheery images and jingoistic language, in many ways exemplifies key aspects of the NFB's production and mandate. As noted above, the Still Photography Division was chartered in 1941, two years after the National Film Act had established the National Film Board as a whole.[6] Drafted by John Grierson, the country's first film commissioner in 1939, the Film Act not only was the board's founding legislation but also established its mandate and entrenched key attitudes about Canadian nationalism. Central to this document was an emphasis on Canadian unity. Even in the heat of World War II, anxiety over fragmentation within the country was prioritized over Canada's involvement in the international conflict. As I have noted elsewhere, that emphasis on unity would remain consistent throughout the NFB's history.[7] The 1946–47 NFB annual report lauded, among the "vital" work being done by the board, "creating a better understanding among Canadians by interpreting widely separated communities to each other."[8] By the mid-1950s, this concern for unity would be articulated more succinctly by the mission "to interpret Canada to Canadians and to other nations."[9] For administrators, filmmakers, and photographers at the NFB from the 1940s to the 1960s, offering educational information about Canada's diverse regions and creating visual symbolism of the nation were essential to this goal of creating a cohesive sense of nation.

The NFB's internationally celebrated cinematic productions have long overshadowed its role in producing and disseminating still photographs. Indeed, throughout much of its history, the Still Division was underfunded and little known; it consisted of a skeletal staff of photographers, writers, editors, and other administrators.[10] Yet, despite chronic challenges, the division was prolific. From 1941 until the early 1970s, when it turned its attention primarily toward collecting photography, the division produced about 200,000 images as well as over 550 photo stories and numerous publications and exhibitions.[11]

The division initiated photo shoots and publications itself, but in many cases it filled commissions from various governmental departments. Accordingly, it was more closely tied to the policies of the federal government at the time than were the board's film production units. This distinction between cinematic and still photographic divisions became a fissure in 1955 when the board's film production divisions moved to the greater Montreal area. The Still Division, along with a few other board units, remained behind in Ottawa, cementing its role as a service department for the government.[12] The Still Division, for example, not only produced images on commission for federal agencies but also maintained a library that governmental departments—as well as private industry and publishers—used regularly as a stock library.[13]

The Still Photography Division met the board's mandate of fostering national cohesion largely by creating or reinforcing visual symbolism of the nation. Drawing on

Louis Althusser's influential theorization of ideology, this had the effect of "interpellating" viewers as citizens of the state; that is to say, in responding to photographs and photo stories that seemed to hail or call out to them, viewers identified themselves as Canadian citizens.[14] Division photographs and their accompanying texts were the products of what was in effect group authorship. Photographs were produced in the field, often hundreds or thousands of kilometres from Ottawa; they were then transported to the capital, where, typically with little or no input from the photographers, images were edited and division staff wrote accompanying text.[15] Over the period discussed here, the key means of distributing division images were large-scale picture books, such as the popular centennial publications *Call Them Canadians*, *Ces visages qui sont un pays*, and *Canada: A Year of the Land*, and regularly produced photo stories. Photo stories, like "Canada's Future Belongs to Them," with which I introduced this essay, were publication-ready layouts of between two and nine images with accompanying captions and texts. Produced weekly or bi-weekly by the division, they were circulated extensively through newspapers, magazines, and exhibitions across Canada, as well as to international audiences through the federal Department of External Affairs. The photo story "Canada's Future Belongs to Them," for example, was distributed to at least eight Canadian publications of various sizes, including the Ottawa/Hull newspaper *Le Droit* and the Toronto-based Italian-language paper *Corriere Canadese*; records also show that it was distributed to thirteen Canadian missions abroad, including those in Switzerland, Japan, Pakistan, South Africa, and Spain.[16] At the peak of division activity during the 1950s and 1960s, countless Canadians (and international viewers, including potential immigrants) regularly pored over these images, seeing in them instructive and idealized accounts of what it was to be a Canadian.

The division's renderings of the country resonated with this prime audience partly because of the indexical status of the documentary photograph. Photographic images, like those in "Canada's Future Belongs to Them," seem to offer the viewer a direct, unmediated representation of life and, therefore, effectively naturalize the point of view or specific governmentally endorsed message espoused. In this case, the very real energy and youth of the children depicted, which are enhanced by the dynamic layout, make the text's message about the nation's dynamic economy and future promise of prosperity seem more vivid. Moreover, the subcategory of documentary enhances the photograph's indexical character by stressing the image as a carrier of factual information and thereby delimiting other potential readings.[17] Conceptualizations and forms of documentary are central to the history of the NFB as a whole, including the Still Division. Indeed, it was the NFB's founder, John Grierson, who coined the term "documentary." Grierson famously termed documentary as the "creative treatment of actuality," signalling a dual commitment to social engagement and expression.[18] At the same time, during his tenure at the NFB, he stressed documentary as a tool to serve the state, specifically toward the mission of socially managing the citizenry.[19] Grierson's commitment to realism and visual propaganda provided a foundation for the Still Division's work throughout most of its history, even as the form of its documentary images would change.

In addition to the distinctive power of the documentary image, division photographs were effective in fostering a sense of national cohesion through their development or reinforcement of visual symbols of Canada. Today, the division's archive stands as a pictorial inventory of Canada from the 1940s through the 1960s. Division officials were clearly concerned with geographic representation: images depict virtually all areas of Canada's vast land mass and coasts. Throughout, there is an emphasis on visual symbolism of the nation through what today seem to be pictorial clichés: grain elevators, vast Arctic scenery, rustic fishing villages, snow-covered terrain. And while it doted on individual achievement in the arts and sciences, the division was particularly attentive to what it deemed to be quotidian experience.

The image of childhood holds a notably prominent place in the division archive. Young faces appear, predictably, in shoots devoted to education and leisure activities, as well as those addressing such surprising topics as agriculture and industry. In short, like kids running wild, images of children and youth within the division archive are irrepressible. Sixty-six out of two hundred and fifty photo stories produced between 1955 and 1960, for example, feature children prominently. By 1967, images of children were mainstays in the division's extensive promotions of both the country's centennial celebrations and emergent multiculturalism policies.

As Brian J. Low has demonstrated, a concern with childhood was also central to NFB cinematic productions.[20] He has identified more than seven hundred out of about eight thousand NFB films with significant portrayals of children.[21] From the World War II era to the end of the 1980s, children were both key subjects and targeted audiences for documentary and fiction films. Low convincingly asserts that their portrayals reflect significant changes in attitudes toward child-rearing and education.

In contrast, the Still Photography Division depicted scenes related to children's health, education, and rearing only occasionally. Such topics do appear in individual images and photo stories, providing didactic information about children's literacy, infant care, and mental health. However, these are exceptions within the division archive. More often than not, images of children appear in contexts that do not explicitly address issues relating to what are conventionally deemed to be children's experiences. Indeed, out of the sixty-six photo stories dating from the late 1950s with prominent images of children cited above, only twelve are actually devoted to children's concerns, such as education, children's health care, and leisure for the young. The remaining fifty-four pictorials address an idiosyncratic range of topics, from federal park lands and natural scenery to sugar beet production and fur merchandising. A consideration of their intended audiences provides clues to this distinction between the depiction of children in NFB films and still photographs. According to Low, once television became more widely accessible, beginning in the early 1950s, "the audience for the NFB [film] became largely juvenile" as the NFB increasingly distributed films directly to schools.[22] With children themselves as intended viewers, the subjects of the films focused on their own life concerns. In contrast, the Still Division never explicitly aimed its promotional materials at a juvenile audience. Instead, as noted above, its images and pictorials were distributed to the media and embassies as well as shown in exhibitions. In all these venues, the intended audience was decidedly adult. While, as parents or others engaged with the care of the young, the audience may have been deeply invested in children's lives and welfare, ultimately these concerns were secondary to the symbolism of childhood.

In addition to intended audience, pragmatic and media-related concerns also contributed to the format of division images. As noted above, the division archive served as a stock library for its own publications as well as those of other government agencies and commercial publishers; accordingly, its images, including those of children, were regularly reused in different contexts. The images from "Canada's Future Belongs to Them," for example, were compiled and arranged from the work of various photographers in the division archive.[23] As in any stock library, generic images (photographs not indelibly associated with one temporal or thematic circumstance, thereby allowing for a wider range of applications) were prioritized.[24] As the American photographic theorist Allan Sekula has explained, within a photographic archive, photographic meaning is "liberated" from the context in which the negative was originally taken while other meanings accrue owing to its new placement or ownership.[25] In short, unlike film, still images can be recontextualized readily. While the films featuring children studied by Low, for example, are grounded temporally and by cinematic narrative to specific child-related themes, images of children from the Still Photography Division archive are, within a somewhat limited range, quite pliant. Accordingly, although division images exploit indexicality to authenticate their messages, they, at the same time, serve a symbolic function.

In turn, the particular symbolic role played by these images is informed by broader cultural meanings of childhood. In images from World War II to the early 1960s, I suggest that the division consistently seems to draw on common associations with the "Romantic child," which Anne Higonnet characterizes as the modern conceptualization of childhood as a period characterized by innocence and purity.[26] The division, for example, regularly appears to have exploited perceptions of childlike cuteness, charm, and vulnerability simply—and, perhaps, cynically—as eye-catching devices. But, more pointedly, I suggest that the idealized and innocent Romantic child served a symbolic function in division pictorials, appearing as a marker of the Canadian citizenry and of the aspirations of the nation as a whole. A detailed examination of one photograph of this time illustrates the symbolic potency of the image of childhood within the Still Photography Division archive.

In March 1953, division staff photographer Chris Lund produced a photograph of a young girl stricken with polio (fig. 4.2).[27] Shot frontally, the image is framed by the rails and bars of a ramp designed to teach polio patients to walk with braces. The rails provide orthogonal lines for the sharp perspectival view around which the picture is organized. Centred at the vanishing point is the tiny girl, her hands clutching the rails tightly. A woman in a medical uniform leans over and encourages the tiny patient along. The child's gaze is directed toward both the camera and a doll that has been placed in the foreground at the opposite end of the ramp. The doll is apparently being used as a reward or lure by her adult attendant, but, at the same time, resting on its sturdy little plastic legs, this toy mirrors the child's apparent aspirations for strength, mobility, and independence.

This image addresses perhaps the most emotionally loaded health crisis of the time. In the years before the Salk vaccine was introduced in 1954 and 1955, poliomyelitis afflicted thousands of children annually, including thousands of Canadian children. Today, the disease still has not been eradicated internationally. According to the historian Christopher J. Rutty, in 1953, the year this image was made, the polio virus infected approximately 9 percent of all children in Canada.[28] Polio is an acutely infectious disease that can attack the nerve cells activating muscles, resulting in irreversible paralysis and, in severe cases, death.[29] Largely affecting children under three years of age, before the development of a vaccine, the disease crossed all socio-economic lines.

Lund's image of the tiny polio patient in many respects exemplifies key aspects of social documentary photography or what is sometimes termed "socially concerned photography." It addresses a social theme (polio) not through scientific information but in a highly personalized and sentimentalized fashion. Indeed, the photograph exploits viewer empathy. Those prominent bars, the light from a side window, and the curved back of the child's attendant all lead the viewer's eye inescapably to the child's body and, particularly, to her own gaze. We feel ourselves meeting that gaze, in effect directly encountering this child and her plight. The image might well be considered maudlin, but few would deny that it is effective in eliciting an emotional engagement from the viewer.

The emotional impact of this photograph was self-consciously rendered. Like most photojournalists of the day, Lund made dozens of negatives during a single shoot; this image, for example, was one of thirty-five shot in March 1953 at the Sudbury Polio

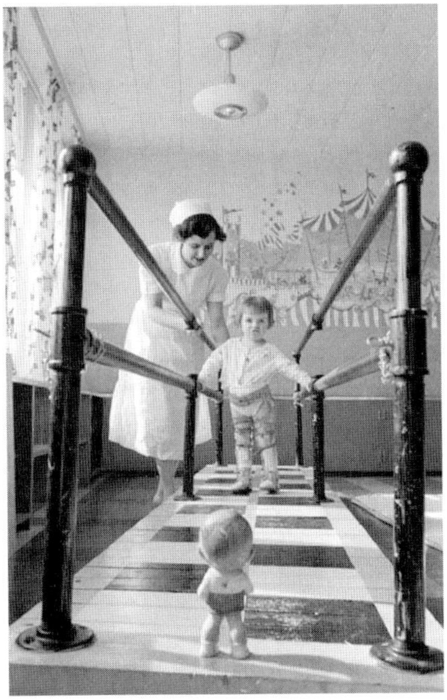

FIGURE 4.2
Mrs. E. Marr, physiotherapist, with Dorothy Gifford, 2½, at the walking bars in the polio clinic, Sudbury General Hospital, Sudbury, Ont. (Photo by Chris Lund, March 1953. Library and Archives Canada, National Film Board of Canada / PA-116675)

Clinic at the Sudbury (Ontario) General Hospital.[30] Notes made by the photographer tell us that the image discussed here depicts "Mrs. E. Marr, physiotherapist, with Dorothy Gifford, 2½, at the walking bars in the polio clinic, Sudbury General Hospital, Sudbury, Ont."[31] In fact, this is one of four extant negatives made showing Dorothy Gifford's struggle to walk. In shooting multiple negatives, Lund was clearly at pains to compose the image precisely. The negative of the image discussed here is annotated with the words "All available of doll in f.g. [foreground]" and two small arches extending the legs of the doll. Written perhaps by Lund himself or a photo editor at the Still Division offices in Ottawa to their printers, the message shows a concern with heightening the composition's emotional impact. In a 1982 audio interview, Lund acknowledged—with audible pride—how he constructed the composition: "It is dramatized with a low angle … I mean, I set this thing up. The converging lines of the bars, the walking bars. You look at this thing, your eye widens and it goes right down to the child and the nurse … helping that child, helping her reach her goal."[32]

If the photographer and photo editors contrived this image, its eventual editorial placements also mediated its meaning. This photograph appeared as the lead image in a March 1955 photo story entitled "Canada Will Start Trials of Polio Vaccine April 18," promoting the Salk vaccine (fig. 4.3).[33] Within this photo story, meaning, already modified by the photographer and the constraints of the photographic medium itself, would shift again. Filling almost half the layout, the image dramatically draws the reader into the story. Two other images, both depicting laboratory scenes, are featured. The image at the lower right depicts two lab technicians at the Connaught Medical Research Laboratories of the University of Toronto, a key facility in the development of the Salk vaccine for North American trials.[34] At the upper right is a small image of a researcher with a monkey used in laboratory experiments. These images were made in separate shoots. The laboratory at the upper right, for example, is apparently unrelated to Salk vaccine research. Dating from January 1950, this photograph depicts a scene at a University of Montreal laboratory that was part of a shoot largely depicting cancer research in Montreal.[35] But viewers in the 1950s would probably not have recognized these inconsistencies. Instead, the images would appear to "fit" seamlessly. Together in the photo story, they dramatize advances in medical efforts to eradicate poliomyelitis within specifically nationalist terms. The title ("Canada Will Start Trials of Polio Vaccine April 18") itself asserts a nationalist reading, while the text emphasizes the financial contributions made by federal and provincial governments. We are told, for example, that an $83,000 federal research grant has funded the work at the Connaught laboratory. Text continues to inform the reader that "these trials, which will see an estimated 500,000 Canadian school children vaccinated, will be arranged and conducted by provincial health departments. Up to $375,000 of national health grant funds, to be matched by an equal amount from the provinces, have been earmarked to ensure an adequate supply of the Salk vaccine for the trials."

If the text stresses a governmental commitment to research in very specific terms, the caption accompanying the image of the polio patient is far more generalized. It states that "treatment centres, like this Rotary-sponsored clinic at Sudbury, are key weapons in the successful rehabilitation of polio sufferers. But medical men look forward to the day when preventive vaccines will make therapy and leg braces unnecessary."

Dorothy Gifford is not presented as a specific individual but as a typology: she stands for all Canadian children battling polio. At the same time, the dramatic photograph of her struggling toward a goal is a metaphor for the research work undertaken in Canadian laboratories. The context provided by words, images, and layout effectively directs or limits readings of this photograph. It has been transformed from an emotionally wrenching photograph of a small girl to a composition around which arguments about Canadian achievements in medical science are marshalled.[36]

The connection between nationalism and children afflicted with polio was, of course, one that the division itself constructed. Interestingly, photographs by Chris Lund of the Sudbury polio clinic were featured in another prominent photo story, which only alluded to the question of nationhood. On October 10, 1953, eleven images of the clinic were published as the photo story "Sudbury's Polio Clinic: A Whole

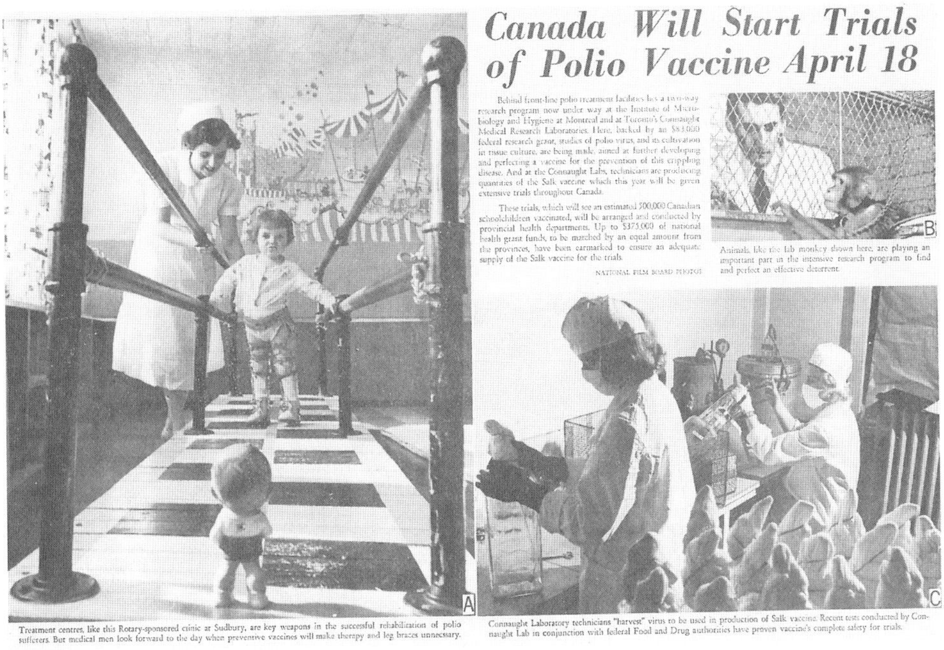

Canada Will Start Trials of Polio Vaccine April 18

Behind front-line polio treatment facilities lies a two-way research program now under way at the Institute of Microbiology and Hygiene at Montreal and at Toronto's Connaught Medical Research Laboratories. Here, backed by an $83,000 federal research grant, studies of polio virus, and its cultivation in tissue culture, are being made, aimed at further developing and perfecting a vaccine for the prevention of this crippling disease. And at the Connaught Labs, technicians are producing quantities of the Salk vaccine which this year will be given extensive trials throughout Canada.

These trials, which will see an estimated 500,000 Canadian schoolchildren vaccinated, will be arranged and conducted by provincial health departments. Up to $375,000 of national health grant funds, to be matched by an equal amount from the provinces, have been earmarked to ensure an adequate supply of the Salk vaccine for the trials.

NATIONAL FILM BOARD PHOTOS

A: Treatment centres, like this Rotary-sponsored clinic at Sudbury, are key weapons in the successful rehabilitation of polio sufferers. But medical men look forward to the day when preventive vaccines will make therapy and leg braces unnecessary.

B: Animals, like the lab monkey shown here, are playing an important part in the intensive research program to find and perfect an effective deterrent.

C: Connaught Laboratory technicians "harvest" virus to be used in production of Salk vaccine. Recent tests conducted by Connaught Lab in conjunction with federal Food and Drug authorities have proven vaccine's complete safety for trials.

FIGURE 4.3 National Film Board of Canada, Still Photography Division, "Canada Will Start Trials of Polio Vaccine April 18," Photo Story 003 (March 1955). (Canadian Museum of Contemporary Photography, National Gallery of Canada, Ottawa)

Community of Volunteers Pitches in to Operate" in *Weekend Magazine*, a pictorial supplement to newspapers across the country.[37] Appearing many months before the introduction of the Salk vaccine, this photo story centres around community involvement in the treatment of polio patients. The selected images all emphasize warm relationships between patients and nurses or physiotherapists. Text announces that until "the day when the dreaded disease will be licked completely ... the fight goes on, a splendid achievement of civic enterprise and community spirit."[38] In short, the key concern here is the "remarkable and heart-warming community" of Sudbury; while additional attention is given to the signs of the disease, it is not framed as a Canadian problem.[39]

In contrast, the Still Division's editorial treatment of the Sudbury polio clinic was wholly nationalistic. Further, the photo story exemplifies the division's treatment of children in the late 1950s and early 1960s. As noted above, children appear in about one-fourth of all photo stories of this time. A minority of pictorials that address children's issues explore childhood literacy, health, and education. The majority cover a divergent range of themes. In some, a predictable correspondence is established between childhood and leisure, at times with religious overtones, as in the December 1957 pictorial "Canada Exports 'Merry Christmas': Yule Tree Industry Boom."[40] In photo stories like "Spring in Canada: A Time of Discovery," the figure of the Romantic child is invoked to promote the Canadian land with particular reference to presumptions about pristine nature.[41] But in most cases from 1955 to the early 1960s, children appear in commercial and institutional contexts. At times, they promote the Canadian economy in, for example, photo stories devoted to agricultural production[42] and, surprisingly, the fur trade.[43] In most division photo stories of the 1950s, children appear in institutional contexts. They are, for example, virtually ubiquitous in stories addressing health care, such as the polio pictorial described above.[44]

But viewed from a distance of several decades, there seems something distinctly, well, un-childlike about most of the children depicted by the division during this time. Tidy and well behaved, they march into dentists' and doctors' offices stoically and listen attentively—even admiringly—to adults. In virtually all these photographs, they possess an aura of poise and self-confidence that few of their elders could match. The playful irreverence and sheer noise most of us associate with childhood have been muted. In short, children are usually not depicted in division images of the late 1950s and early 1960s principally to reference childhood itself; instead, this determined yet obedient group of kids in effect serves a metonymic function, standing for an idealized Canadian citizenry reliant on the paternalistic care of government.

In these images, the message of paternalistic authority is underlined in the compositions and style of the images themselves. In most of them, like the Chris Lund image of Dorothy Gifford, the photographer adopts what is often termed a "fly on the wall" view. Subjects often seem unaware of the photographer's—and by implication, our own—gaze and presence. (When, like little Dorothy, subjects do meet the gaze of the camera, their look suggests a deference to authority.) The all-seeing and all-powerful gaze in such images became a common feature in division photography during the late 1950s and early 1960s. It marked a still photographic equivalent of the "voice of God" narratives so familiar from documentary films produced by the board during the same years.[45]

Although there are pivotal distinctions between cinematic and still photographic images, the correlation with characteristics of NFB film of the time is instructive nevertheless. Images like these, I suggest, relate to what film theorists Bill Nichols and Julianne Burton have termed an "expository mode" of documentary representation. For Nichols and Burton, expository documentary is exemplified by the cinematic productions that John Grierson oversaw at the Empire Marketing Board in England and the National Film Board of Canada. These didactic films directly address the viewer and are organized around the establishment of a solution for a social problem. Audio commentary takes precedence, with images serving to buttress a textual argument. The films typically employ voice-over narratives and editing to retain a sense of rhetorical continuity. And, crucially, they emphasis the notion of unquestioned objectivity.[46]

Division images and photo stories of the late 1950s and early 1960s depicting children, and exemplified by the photo story featuring Dorothy Gifford, translate many of those characteristics into still photographic terms. Organized around a specific social message, the photographs and text offer governmental protection and intervention as a solution to any given problem. The images are carefully edited to support a written text. And, finally, the characteristic of objective authority remains unquestioned and is pivotal to the image. It appears, as I have noted, in the use of an all-seeing vantage point but also in the rhetoric of the accompanying captions and text.

The division's numerous contemporary representations of Aboriginal youngsters underscore childhood as a sign of governmental care of its needy citizens. Explicitly in text and by implication in images, Aboriginal peoples—particularly Inuit—were often infantilized in division pictorials. Accordingly, Aboriginal children were typically portrayed as those in the greatest need of authoritative governmental intervention.[47] Today, in light of current knowledge of governmental and institutional interventions into the lives of Aboriginal children and youth—including residential schools—this emphasis on intervention is ominous.

The expository mode of photographs and photo stories dating from the late 1950s and early 1960s, with their representational reinforcement of institutional authority, reflected a return to "normalcy" in the wake of World War II. With their emphasis on obedience to authority and inflexible gender roles, these images reinforced broader social trends of the time, as discussed by Mona Gleason, Mary Louise Adams, and Valerie Korinek, among others.[48] Division images and pictorials were, to borrow Gleason's phrase, "technologies of normalcy" that constructed a model of the normal Canadian citizen. In doing so, they provided a visual form for the division's own ideological emphasis on the government as a paternalistic caretaker for its citizenry, its needy children. As an agency that effectively served the federal government as a public relations tool, the division pictorially and textually promoted policies during the period in which Canada emerged fully as a Keynesian "welfare state."[49] But while archival records indicate that the division had a close relationship with the federal government and maintained its existence by supporting official policy, division staff also had a great deal of autonomy in their choice of subject matter and modes of representation. It seems clear that while the division in some instances served as handmaid to the government, directly illustrating policy, in others, staff were so fully immersed in notions of the Canadian government as a paternalistic caretaker that they reproduced that construction as a "natural" state. In most of its depictions of the young over these years, there is an implicit message that the government is a trusted caretaker and Canadian citizens are the children of a caring state.

It is hard to imagine the joyful and raucous kids in "Canada's Future Belongs to Them," the 1964 photo story with which I began this essay, at play with Dorothy Gifford or any of her well-behaved and rigidly "normal" contemporaries. Indeed, the obedient and contained child as idealized citizen of the late 1950s and early 1960s has little in common with the division's approach to representing childhood by the mid-1960s. I contend that childhood would continue to serve as a prominent signifier of nationhood and the citizenry during the mid and later 1960s, but notions of what constitutes nation and the citizen would change, just as means of symbolizing these abstract concepts shifted.

Lorraine Monk, who was named the division's executive producer in 1960, reworked the division's direction dramatically. Although photo stories such as "Canada's Future Belongs to Them" would continue to be produced, this format was slowly phased out in favour of ambitious picture books, exhibitions, and small monographic publications. Many of Monk's programs were prompted by the country's lavish centennial celebrations, and, like the spectacles organized around the country, division productions took a decidedly more ambitious tone. Chief among these were four well-known books celebrating the country's centennial,[50] a program of exhibitions in Ottawa, and, during Expo '67, a monumental installation of photographic portraits of Canadians. Each featured the work of a then-young generation of photographers—including Pierre Gaudard, Michel Lambeth, John Max, Nina Raginsky, and Michael Semak. Their work stood in marked contrast to the overtly didactic and staged images made by Chris Lund and his contemporaries. The photographer Michel Lambeth's poetic description of his own best work characterizes production by this entire generation: "photographs which are memorable in that they are, in a way, analogues of terse poetry, images which give up their message very quickly without pretence of gimmick, subterfuge or flippancy."[51]

In short, the photography that Monk and the division began to promote during the 1960s, evident, for example, in "Canada's Future Belongs to Them," presented a seemingly more direct and unvarnished view of the world. These photographers drew in part from precedents in the work of such figures as Robert Frank, Helen Levitt, and those associated with New York's Photo League. Moreover, they—and the division—conceived of photography as, if not as an art form, then at least an expressive medium with a premium placed on the individualistic vision of each photographer. Even when the division was drawing on its own archive of images, as in "Canada's Future Belongs to Them," choice of image and composition replicated the new style of more spontaneous documentary.

Although the look of photography and attitudes toward photographers changed in the division during the 1960s, some of its time-honoured iconography would remain. Childhood, for example, continued to be a prominent trope in division images, publications, and exhibitions of the mid and late 1960s. Indeed, two of the division's major publications of this period—*Call Them Canadians: A Photographic Point of View* and *Ces visages qui sont un pays* (1968)—are organized around a life cycle and, therefore, feature images of children and youth prominently.[52] While these two publications differ, both reflect a cyclical biological model,[53] which opens with infancy then presents childhood, youth, and the stages of adulthood and eventually returns to images of childhood.[54]

Within the biological narrative established in *Call Them Canadians*, for example, children hold a privileged position as the subjects of the publication's key opening and closing images. Accordingly, they reveal changing approaches to representation and, in turn, the symbolic rendering of the nation and citizenship. The first photograph following the title page[55] exemplifies this new representation of the child (fig. 4.4).[56] Created by Toronto-based photographer Michel Lambeth, this work is characteristic of the photographer's ironic images of contemporary society.[57] The picture depicts a teeming crowd, largely consisting of adults, who peer attentively at a public spectacle, perhaps a parade. Yet Lambeth undermines common expectations of such an event: we view the crowd from the back without any visible sign of the event that is captivating their attention. (The ambiguity of the scene is enhanced by Monk's editorial decision to omit photographers' credits, titles, and dates beside the photographs.[58]) Our attention is drawn not to the public spectacle but directly and inescapably to a lone infant, seated in a stroller, who fills the foreground. Image composition suggests that the child has been left behind the throng possibly while her mother lifts a sibling up to see the sights.[59] As we watch the crowd watching, this little person turns her gaze toward us. She does not pose for the camera or enact the performance of childhood cuteness; instead, with one hand clutching the edge of her stroller and her head tilted slightly, she scrutinizes us with what seems to be a sustained and thoughtful concentration.[60]

Clearly, the concept of the gaze is central to this image. It reflects what Catherine A. Lutz and Jane L. Collins have usefully described as a complex "intersection of gazes," which, in anthropological and social documentary photography specifically, at once reveal, enact, and contest power dynamics.[61] The child's gaze, therefore, contrasts with Dorothy Gifford's obedient gaze and the compositional enhancements of it in the Lund photograph discussed above. In the Lambeth image, the child's intelligent gaze and her positioning apart from and unseen by the crowd signal her as a discerning and individualistic presence. Any tendency to visually consume this child as a sweet innocent or typology has been denied by her determined and quizzical gaze. She appears to demand that we see and meet her on her own terms, on equal terms. In short, she is an

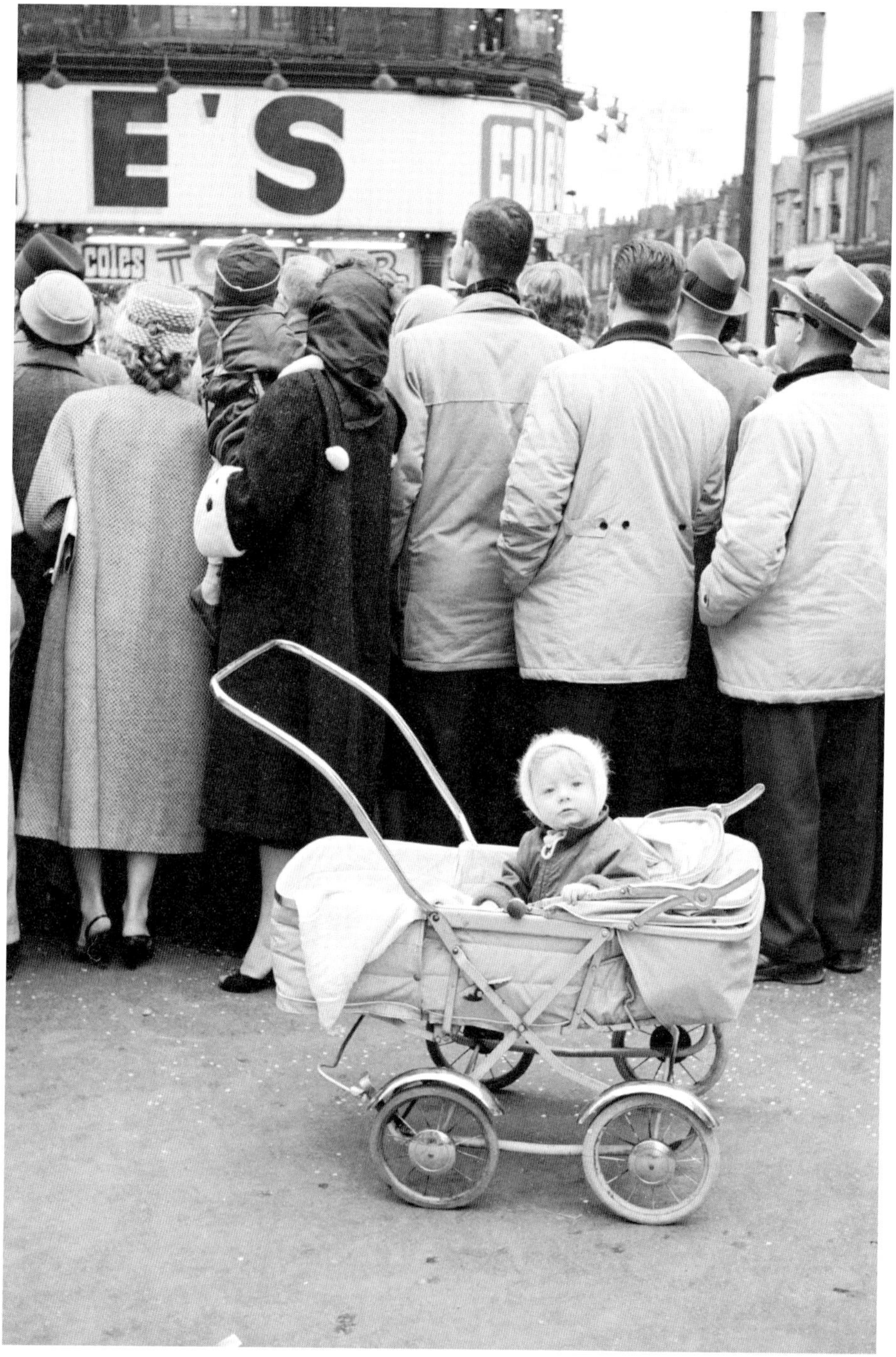

FIGURE 4.4
Child behind crowd at Grey Cup Parade. (Photo by Michel Lambeth, May 1965. National Film Board of Canada, Still Photography Division archive. Canadian Museum of Contemporary Photography, National Gallery of Canada, Ottawa, negative 65-3018)

example of what Anne Higonnet has usefully termed the "knowing child." As Higonnet explains, "Unlike Romantic children who are arranged and presented as a delightful spectacle to be enjoyed, Knowing children are neither available or controllable. They themselves are looking at an inner world of the imaginary, or at the adult world."[62]

Yet like the image of Dorothy Gifford, this photograph, too, serves as a national emblem. Although the Lambeth photograph appears without a prominent photographer credit, it is accompanied by text. Throughout *Call Them Canadians*, poetic verse by Miriam Waddington, which she wrote in response to images selected for the publication by division staff, is paired with selected photographs. The photograph of the infant behind a crowd is accompanied by the following short verse:

> What is a Canadian
> Anyway? A mountain, a maple
> Leaf, a prairie, a Niagara fall,
> A trail beside the Atlantic, a
> Bilingualism, a scarred mosaic,
> A yes-no somehow-or-other maybe
> Might-be should-be could-be
> Glacial shield, grain elevator,
> Empire daughter imperial order of
> Man woman child or what?[63]

Here Waddington echoes the visual irony of Lambeth's image with a satiric litany of national monuments and nationalist identity, while her quizzical voice replicates the child's apparent curiosity. Like the photo story featuring Dorothy Gifford, text imbues image with new layers of meaning. Waddington's verse directs the viewer toward a nationalist reading of the image, though one that acknowledges national identity as a construct. Indeed, Monk presented the publication as a whole, without Waddington's irony, as a portrait of Canada and a visual expression of nationalistic pride.[64]

In the majority of NFB Still Photography Division images depicting children during the mid to late 1960s, not only in *Call Them Canadians*, but throughout the division's production, images of the knowing child replace those of the Romantic child. As already noted, children are no longer confined to institutional settings, as they were a decade earlier; they are often seen only in the company of other children or at least separated from adults and therefore are presented as autonomous. When they are shown in institutional settings, their body language and facial expressions undermine rather than offer deference to authority. In most of these representations, children are seen at play with other children. These communities of children, who seem to live free of much adult supervision, have displaced those institutional-contained children who are always shown under the tutelage of adults even when at play. Stylistically, the images of the mid and later 1960s reflect Michel Lambeth's distaste for "gimmick, subterfuge [and] flippancy."[65] They show us a reality, which, although certainly mediated, seems more direct and spontaneous. Moreover, as in Lambeth's image of the infant and the crowd, the characteristic "god's eye view" of a decade earlier has been supplanted by vantage points that implicate the viewer in the scene chiefly through the use of the gaze. Finally, again as seen in the Lambeth image, text has a less didactic and direct relationship with the image.

If division photography of the later 1950s and early 1960s reflects what Bill Nichols and Julianne Burton have termed an "expository mode" of documentary, we might argue that the images of the mid to late 1960s correlate to what these film theorists have called the "observational mode." Reflecting films termed "cinéma-vérité" by Stephen Mamber and "direct cinema" by Erik Barnouw, the observational mode is exemplified by the films of Jean Rouch and Fred Wiseman. Observational documentary typically offers an exhaustive depiction of the everyday, using editing to replicate "real time" and, according to Nichols, "convey[ing] the sense of unmediated and unfettered access to the world."[66] These characteristics are enhanced by the fact that filmmakers associated with expository cinema typically eschew voice-over narratives. Many Still Photography Division photographs by the mid-1960s translate observational documentary's emphases on the unfettered, spontaneous, and unobtrusive into still photographic terms.

Still Photography Division of the 1960s would continue to use childhood as a loaded signifier of the nation, its aspirations and citizenry. Now, however, the meaning has changed. Many Still Division images, exhibitions, and publications from this time period depict children to signal the promise of the nation. In the mid-1960s the country was not only celebrating the past century of nationhood but also positing Canada as a youthful state just "coming of age." Governmental rhetoric, including that emerging from the Still Division, as seen in "Canada's Future Belongs to Them," promoted Canada as a "land of youth" and promise. The young people depicted in images by the mid-1960s, who are off on their own, unsupervised by adults, at play without responsibility, and utterly unconvinced by institutional authority, are hardly the obedient, orderly children of a decade before. Instead, as "knowing children," they function to embody a sense of autonomy, freedom, and individuality. Again, terms established to define different modes of representation in documentary cinema are helpful in understanding the meanings behind this shift in forms. The observational mode—technically and stylistically reflective of the values of autonomy while still insisting upon the unimpeachable, indexical evidence of the image—provides an ideal means of visually organizing and promoting the notion of individualism.

This new stylistic approach to images, in turn, served as a vehicle for promoting nationalist values and policies during the period leading up to and immediately following the country's centennial. Generally, this approach gave form to liberal individualist values at this key moment in the international Cold War. More specifically, it marked an ideal form to represent and promote the federal government's emergent multiculturalism policies. In centennial publications and exhibitions, as well as photo stories such as "Canada's Future Belongs to Them," this new stylistic form highlighted claims of Canadian cultural pluralism. As Eva Mackey has argued, "In the 1960s Canada, managing and representing forms of difference were central to the creation of national identity, and to the success of the nation-building project."[67] At times and in support of specific governmental agencies, multiculturalism was an explicit subject of the representations and directly promoted governmental programs. In others, Monk, division photographers, and staff were so fully immersed in the rhetoric of Canada as a benevolent, pluralist society that they replicated it visually and textually as a true picture of the country at the time.

For the National Film Board of Canada's Still Photography Division, childhood was a potent and multivalent signifier. Children served as signs of the nation's citizenry, and, in turn, their representations are indicative of the federal government's changing attitudes toward its people. At the same time and within a wide range of contexts, children signified the nation as a whole, suggesting the energy and promise of Canada as a "land of youth." As I have argued, during the 1950s and early 1960s, they embodied a view of Canadians as malleable beings in need of the paternalistic protection and guidance of government. In contrast, a decade later, child became a sign of liberal individualism and, accordingly, reflected wider discourse and governmental policy revolving around multiculturalism.

Notes

Many thanks to Loren Lerner for her editorial acumen. I am also indebted to Katie Cholette, James Opp, and Sarah Stacy for their useful comments on an earlier draft of this essay. Lastly, I want to express my gratitude to Martha Langford for her thoughtful editorial suggestions.

1 National Film Board of Canada, Still Photography Division, "Canada's Future Belongs to Them," Photo Story 367 (June 27, 1964). Photographers are uncredited in the photo story. In fact, the images come from various photographers, including prominent division photographers Chris Lund and Ted Grant. The reference to an "imagined community" is drawn, of course, from Benedict Anderson's seminal study. His concept of nationhood as an imaginary link between peoples informs my larger study on the Still Photography Division. Benedict Anderson, *Imagined Communities: Reflections on the Origins and Spread of Nationalism* (London: Verso, 1991).

2 Neil Sutherland, *Children in English-Canadian Society: Framing the Twentieth-Century Consensus*, 2nd ed. (Waterloo, ON: Wilfrid Laurier University Press, 2000).

3 Alvin Finkel, *Social Policy and Practice in Canada* (Waterloo, ON: Wilfrid Laurier University Press, 2006), 130–135; Dominique Marshall, "Reconstruction Politics, the Canadian Welfare State, and the Ambiguity of Children's Rights, 1940–1950," in *Histories of Canadian Children and Youth*, ed. Nancy Janovicek and Joy Parr, 255–274 (Oxford: Oxford University Press, 2003).

4 The models referenced here are drawn from the work of the film theorists Bill Nichols and Julianne Burton. See Julianne Burton, "Toward a History of Social Documentary in Latin America," in *The Social Documentary in Latin America*, 3–6 (Pittsburgh: University of Pittsburgh Press, 1990); and Bill Nichols, *Representing Reality: Issues and Concepts in Documentary* (Bloomington: Indiana University Press, 1991), 32–75.

5 For regular reminders of this lesson in social engagement, I lovingly thank my wise, wonderful daughters, Meg Collins and Alice Payne.

6 The division attending to still photographic production went under a number of names over the history of the NFB. For the sake of clarity, I refer to it as the Still Photography Division, a title that Lorraine Monk, executive producer of the division during the 1960s, conferred on it.

7 Carol Payne, *A Canadian Document: The National Film Board of Canada's Still Photography Division* (Ottawa: Canadian Museum of Contemporary Photography, 1999).

8 National Film Board of Canada, *1946–47 Annual Report* (Ottawa: National Film Board of Canada, 1946–47), 4; Payne, *A Canadian Document.*

9 National Film Board of Canada, *Annual Report, 1954–55*, 3.

10 Lilly Koltun, interviews with Lorraine Monk. October 20, 1976, to June 15, 1977, National Film Board of Canada Fonds, Library and Archives Canada, Ottawa.

11 For histories of the division, see Carol Payne, *Canadian Document*; Renate Wickens-Feldman, "The National Film Board of Canada's Still Photography Division: The Griersonian Legacy," *History of Photography* 20, no. 3 (Autumn 1996): 271–277; Martha Langford, introduction to *Contemporary Canadian Photography from the Collection of the National Film Board* (Edmonton: Hurtig, 1984), 7–16.

12 National Film Board of Canada, *Annual Report* (1954–55), 22; National Film Board of Canada, *Annual Report* (1955–56), 3–6.

13 Norman Hallendy (NFB Still Photography Division staff member during the 1960s) interview with Carol Payne and Robert Evans, November 2003.

14 Louis Althusser, "Ideology and Ideological State Apparatuses," in *Lenin and Philosophy and Other Essays*), 127–186 (New York: Monthly Review Press, 1971).

15 John Ough and Hélène Proulx-Ough (NFB Still Photography Division staff members during the 1960s), interview with Carol Payne and Robert Evans, November 2003.

16 Distribution records, National Film Board of Canada, Still Photography Division archive, Canadian Museum of Contemporary Photography.

17 Payne, *Canadian Document.*

18 Forsyth Hardy, ed., *Grierson on Documentary* (London: Faber & Faber, 1979), 11.

19 John Grierson, "The Documentary Idea: 1942," Hardy, *Grierson on Documentary*, 113.

20 Brian J. Low, *NFB Kids: Portrayals of Children by the National Film Board of Canada, 1939–1989* (Waterloo, ON: Wilfrid Laurier University Press, 2002).

21 Ibid., 3.

22 Ibid., 77.

23 To cite just one further example, photo story 162-L from June 17, 1958, "English Lessons with Leah," included a photograph of a group of Inuit children in Resolute Bay running toward their young teacher and makeshift school. That photo story lauded an effort by a young woman, Leah

Idlout, to teach English in one of the government's newly settled communities in the High Arctic; the children's eagerness to reach the school suggested the success of the program. The same photograph was reused in photo story 305, titled "Play in the Land of the Long Day," dating from February 20, 1962. To illustrate the theme of this later photo story on leisure in the Arctic, the children's teacher and the schoolhouse have been cropped out. Accordingly, its meaning has been reframed completely. While my discussion here is mainly limited to production and editorial placement made by the division itself, other clients also dramatically recontextualized these images.

24 At the Still Photography Division, for example, staff and freelance photographers were regularly assigned to undertake regional "tours" of the country aimed to amass generic images for the photo library. National Film Board of Canada, Still Photography Division archive, Canadian Museum of Contemporary Photography.

25 Allan Sekula, "Photography Between Labour and Capital," in Leslie Shedden *Mining Photographs and Other Pictures, 1948–1968: A Selection from the Negative Archives of Shedden Studio, Glace Bay, Cape Breton*, ed. Benjamin H.D. Buchloh and Robert Wilkie, 193–268 (Halifax: Press of the Nova Scotia College of Art and Design and the University College of Cape Breton Press, 1983), 194.

26 Anne Higonnet, *Pictures of Innocence: The History and Crisis of Ideal Childhood* (London: Thames & Hudson, 1998), 23.

27 Chris Lund, "Mrs. E. Marr, physiotherapist, with Dorothy Gifford, 2½, at the walking bars in the polio clinic, Sudbury General Hospital, Sudbury, Ont.," negative 65093, copy negative PA 116675 (March 1953). Library and Archives Canada, National Film Board of Canada collection.

28 Rutty cites the rate of infection as almost nine thousand per population of one hundred thousand. Christopher J. Rutty, "The Middle-Class Plague: Epidemic Polio and the Canadian State, 1936–1937," *Canadian Bulletin of Medical History* 13 (1996): 277–314.

29 Public Health Agency of Canada, "Poliomyelitis," http://www.phac-aspc.gc.ca/tmp-pmv/info/polio_e.html (accessed October 15, 2006).

30 Library and Archives Canada, NFB collection, negatives 65081–65115. The other images in this shoot include nurses in training and tending to child patients as well as one sequence of a couple visiting their young son at the clinic.

31 Library and Archives Canada, NFB collection, negative 65093, copy negative PA 116675.

32 *Chris Lund: Words and Images*, audio interview with slide projections. Martha Langford, executive producer, Pierre Dessureault, producer. Ottawa: National Film Board of Canada, 1982.

33 National Film Board of Canada, Still Photography Division, "Canada Will Start Trials of Polio Vaccine April 18," Photo Story 003 (March 1955).

34 Christopher J. Rutty, "40 Years of Polio Prevention! Canada and the Great Salk Vaccine Trial of 1954–1955," http://www.healthheritageresearch.com/salk.htm (accessed October 15, 2006)

35 Library and Archives Canada, NFB collection, negative 51859A. The caption accompanying the negative reads, "Chief technician Bernard Messier, with one of the monkeys used for experiments in medicine at the University of Montreal." The photo story does mention the Institute of Microbiology and Hygiene at Montreal, but this image does not seem to depict that centre.

36 Many NFB Still Division images appear to have been made on assignment for specific governmental agencies and departments. However, in this case, archival records do not indicate who initiated or commissioned Lund's original shoot at the Sudbury Polio Clinic. I thank Sue Lagasi and Tim Campbell of the Canadian Museum of Contemporary Photography for checking this information.

37 "Sudbury's Polio Clinic: A Whole Community of Volunteers Pitches in to Operate," *Weekend Magazine* 3, no. 40A (October 10, 1953): 2–5. I am indebted to Sarah Stacy, Photography Archivist, Library and Archives Canada, for drawing my attention to this photo story.

38 "Sudbury's Polio Clinic," 3.

39 These readings are intended in part to demonstrate the malleability of photographic meaning. Indeed, this photograph continues to be used and reused in a variety of ways. It formerly appeared, for example, on the Health Heritage Research Services website (http://www.healthheritage research.com/PolioHistory.html; accessed October 15, 2006), where the dated styles of clothing and design signal it as an image from an earlier, and in some respects more medically precarious, era.

40 National Film Board of Canada, Still Photography Division, "Canada Exports 'Merry Christmas': Yule Tree Industry Boom," Photo Story 136 (December 17, 1957).

41 National Film Board of Canada, Still Photography Division, "Spring in Canada: A Time of Discovery," Photo Story 283 (April 18, 1961).

42 National Film Board of Canada, Still Photography Division, "Farmers Reap Sweet Harvest: Biggest Crop in History," Photo Story 195 (February 3, 1959); "Rabbit Industry Booms in Lakehead Area," Photo Story 038 (December 27, 1955).

43 National Film Board of Canada, Still Photography Division, "Canadian Mink Reigns Supreme: Where Elegance and Fashion Meat," Photo Story 134 (December 3, 1957); National Film Board of Canada, Still Photography Division, "The Pampered Chinchilla," Photo Story 042 (January 24, 1956).

44 National Film Board of Canada, Still Photography Division, "The Five Year Road to a D.D.S.: 175 Graduate Annually," Photo Story 048 (March 20, 1956); National Film Board of Canada, Still Photography Division, "Montreal's Institute of Cardiology: Designed Exclusively to Serve the Heart," Photo Story 196 (February 10, 1959).

45 Payne, *Canadian Document.*

46 Nichols, *Representing Reality*, 34–38.

47 Carol Payne, "Lessons with Leah: Re-Reading the Photographic Archive of Nation in The National Film Board of Canada's Still Photography Division," *Visual Studies* 21, no. 1 (April 2006): 4–22; Carol Payne, "Through a Canadian Lens: Discourses of Nationalism and Aboriginal Representation in Governmental Photography," in *Canadian Cultural Poesis: An Anthology*, ed. Garry Sherbert, Annie Gérin, and Sheila Petty, 421–442 (Waterloo, ON: Wilfrid Laurier University Press, 2006).

48 Mary Louise Adams, *The Trouble with Normal: Postwar Youth and the Making of Heterosexuality* (Toronto: University of Toronto Press, 1997); Mona Gleason, *Normalizing the Ideal: Psychology, Schooling and Family in Postwar Canada* (Toronto: University of Toronto Press, 1999); Valerie Korinek, *Roughing It in the Suburbs: Reading Chatelaine Magazine in the 1950s and 1960s* (Toronto: University of Toronto Press, 2000).

49 Finkel, *Social Policy*, 149.

50 *Canada / A Year of the Land* (Ottawa: National Film Board of Canada, 1967), *Stones of History: Canada's Houses of Parliament* (Ottawa: National Film Board of Canada, 1967), *Call Them Canadians: A Photographic Point of View*, and *Ces visages qui sont un pays* (Ottawa: National Film Board of Canada, 1968).

51 Michel Lambeth, "Statement on Photography," 1966. Reproduced in Maia-Mari Sutnik, *Michel Lambeth: Photographer* (Toronto: Art Gallery of Ontario, 1998), 29.

52 These two volumes are linguistic variants. Although they use many of the same images, the text—by Miriam Waddington for the English version and Rita Lasnier for the French—and layouts are distinct. Carol Payne, unpublished conference presentation, Universities Art Association of Canada, November 12, 2005.

53 Monk has clearly taken as her model the most popular photographic exhibition and publication of the day, *The Family of Man*, which was also famously organized as the life cycle of a homogenized, international family.

54 Interestingly, old age and references to death are represented in few images and are generally addressed euphemistically by references to organized religion and spiritual contemplation.
55 This is not literally the first image in the book. *Call Them Canadians* announces itself as a picture book through a series of plates appearing before bibliographical information. Nonetheless, as the image appearing immediately after the title page, it signals the opening of the book's pictorial and poetic narrative.
56 According to NFB records, the image was made in May 1965. National Film Board of Canada, Still Photography Division archive, negative 65-3018. Canadian Museum of Contemporary Photography (National Gallery of Canada), Ottawa.
57 Sutnik, *Michel Lambeth*, 11–27; Michael Torosian, *Michel Lambeth: Photographer* (Ottawa: National Archives of Canada, 1986).
58 The volume does close with a list of photographers and page references. However, its position at the end of the book and lack of detailed information still has the effect of limiting extraneous information and remoulding individual images to the overall message of the volume. In fact, according to records in the Still Division archive at the Canadian Museum of Contemporary Photography, the image depicts the Grey Cup Parade in Toronto.
59 To the left of the stroller is a woman hoisting up another child.
60 Lambeth or division staff were clearly aware of the girl's direct gaze and its implications. Division notes state that the "photo shows a little girl watching the photographer as the crowd behind her watches the Grey Cup Parade." Still Division archive, Canadian Museum of Contemporary Photography.
61 See Catherine A. Lutz and Jane L. Collins, "The Photograph as an Intersection of Gazes," chap. 7 in *Reading National Geographic*, 187–216 (Chicago: University of Chicago Press, 1993).
62 Higonnet, *Pictures of Innocence*, 210–211.
63 Miriam Waddington, *Call Them Canadians*, 15.
64 Melissa Rombout, "Imaginary Canada: Photography and the Construction of National Identity," *Views: the Journal of Photography in New England* 12, no. 2 (Spring 1991): 4–9.
65 Michel Lambeth, "Statement on Photography," 1966. Reproduced in Maia-Mari Sutnik, *Michel Lambeth: Photographer* (Toronto: Art Gallery of Ontario, 1998), 29.
66 Nichols, *Representing Reality*, 43.
67 Eva Mackey, *The House of Difference: Cultural Politics and National Identity in Canada* (London: Routledge, 1999), 63.

constant presence and use of the objects to the degree that often they are not even considered to have a history. When interviewing respondents about their artifacts, usually they have little to say about this aspect. By contrast, according to Riggins, connotative information is of a personal nature and concerns individuals' relationships with objects, and interviewees usually have a good amount of detail about this aspect of the artifact. In explaining his use of this term he uses the word "mapping" to suggest how the objects serve as "entry points for the telling of stories about the self and its personal relationships."[5] In conducting autoethnographic fieldwork in his parents' living room, Riggins carefully and systematically photographs (and comments on) the space and the objects (both permanent and ephemeral).

In our analysis of Canadian dolls and doll-play we look at both denotative dimensions (what we refer to as "out of context") and connotative aspects ("in context") or the "storying" involved when interviewing others or ourselves using a "memory-work" method and other autobiographical approaches. The first section provides a historical overview of dolls in Canada in relation to Canadian girls by using and problematizing the question "What is a Canadian doll?" in terms of considering aspects such as the nationality of the producers, the consumers, and the users of the artifact. Our particular focus in the first part is on the methodological issues related to the materiality of dolls in doll-play. Within the framework of viewing museum collections, we provide examples of dolls that are unique in terms of their "Canadianness," such as the Eaton's Beauty doll, the Maggie Muggins doll, the Barbara Ann Scott doll, and the Anne of Green Gables doll, as well as others that do not possess the same national signification. In the second part of the essay we extend the discussion of "What is a Canadian doll?" from the artifacts to the players to examine how we might use techniques of memory-work as tools for studying both the doll and the players. Here, we draw on the gendered memory-work studies of Haug et al., Mitchell and Reid-Walsh, and Mitchell and Weber to look at several types of personal meanings:[6] memories of Barbie-play, memories of Eaton's catalogue play as constructing homemade paper dolls from the pages of the catalogue, and memories of doll-play organized according to the physical features of the dolls. In the third section of the essay we consider some of the contemporary work on commodification and the "gendered object"[7] and offer examples of how this kind of methodological work on childhood could contribute to a new girlhood (and boyhood) studies "play construction" agenda within Canadian collections, such as the doll and toy collection housed at the McCord Museum in Montreal, virtual collections such as the Canadian Doll history site sponsored by the Museum of Civilization in Ottawa, or the construction toy collection at the Canadian Centre for Architecture in Montreal.

What Is a Canadian Doll? Describing Dolls "Out of Context" in Collections

The question of trying to define what is Canadian in respect to doll history is in some ways parallel to the ongoing project of studying the history of Canadian children's literature. This question of what is Canadian troubled Sheila Egoff in her groundbreaking bibliographic work, *Canadian Children's Books, 1799–1939* (1992), which defined Canadian children's literature as a distinct field in its own right, and is highlighted in recent issues of the journal *Canadian Children's Literature (CCL)*. In each case, recurring questions arise: Is the label "Canadian" defined by national boundaries? For example, is the key criterion the place of manufacture, as it is for curators,[8] the nationality of the character depicted in the book or artifact, or the nationality of the child reader/player/owner, or the geographical location of the stored artifact? This question lies in the background of the material and virtual collections and available resources for doll research in Canada. Often, this question is not specifically articulated, although Evelyn Robson Strahlendorf does raise the point with regard to whether the Shirley Temple doll can be considered Canadian, for although it was manufactured in Canada during the 1930s, it depicts an American icon.[9] On the other hand, when looking at a European-made doll preserved over multiple generations by a family and then bequeathed to a Canadian museum, can the doll not be considered Canadian? When analyzing more recent dolls, Barbie poses a similar question. In the late 1950s Ruth Handler adapted the doll from a German adult doll,[10] but Barbie is considered the epitome of an American icon. But girls in Canada have played with her for almost fifty years, as in many other countries, and she exists in several textual forms (such as in magazines, comics, and websites and on Barbie trading cards that apparently were manufactured only in Canada during the 1990s).[11] Can these Barbie dolls or these representations of Barbie then be considered Canadian? In practice, as will be seen in the following discussion of dolls located in various museum collections, and in an authoritative Canadian doll history, it would seem the definition of Canadian shifts among all three criteria in a fluid manner.

When approaching dolls as instances of material culture, it is important to heed the advice of material culture theorist Daniel Miller, who warns that researchers need to consider the object under study initially as a thing that is apprehended by the senses before interpreting it as a socially constructed text. He reminds researchers that "an artifact exists as a physical object, apart from any person's mental conception of it."[12] He notes that paradoxically, the physical presence of an object, or its "visibility," often causes difficulties for researchers who make it "invisible" in their rush to textualize or interpret.[13] He insists on the importance of examining the objects in their specificity, in their ordinary sensual and material aspects, before beginning to "unpick" the more subtle links between the object and cultural life. In his own ongoing work on Coca-Cola, for instance, he insists on describing it as a sweet, fizzy drink in a glass bottle before addressing it as an icon in the context of Trinidadian culture.[14] Often, researchers jump over the object itself and rush immediately to "reading" material objects as texts, overlooking the significance of the artifact itself in their social analysis.

Any account of dolls then has to begin with an encounter with them as constructed objects or artifacts in their own right apart from any play use brought to them by their players. In the case of early dolls, they are usually taken out of their original contexts and preserved for safekeeping in museum collections. In order for the unspecialized viewer to make sense of the artifacts, though, some perspective needs to be brought to bear. In order to organize the description of dolls in Canada, we use a historical approach combined with a modified genre approach that is employed in the classification process. The following discussion stems from an examination of three resources publicly available for historians of Canadian dolls: the material collection of Canadian dolls at the McCord Museum in Montreal; the online collection of the Museum of Civilization called "Timeless Treasures: The Story of Dolls in Canada"; and scholarly published work, such as that of Evelyn Strahlendorf.[15]

In comparison to European doll history, such as that outlined for collectors by Caroline Goodfellow or A.F. Robertson, it seems that a history of Canadian dolls is fairly inclusive in terms of the types of dolls available, how the dolls are made, and the implied players of the dolls.[16] Dolls from Aboriginal communities in Canada follow a historical trajectory from home or individual manufacture to commercial manufacture, through the early settlement days to the present, similar to that noted by Miriam Forman-Brunell in terms of her historical research on American girls and their dolls from the nineteenth century to the early mid-twentieth century.[17] Likewise, as in the United States, a marked contrast exists between the stereotypical representation of black dolls and the apparently benign images of white dolls. Forman-Brunell points out, though, that the soft dolls, especially the soft black "Dinah" dolls, were very popular with girls in the early twentieth century, likely owing to the popularity of the black nanny in affluent white households.[18] As Strahlendorf points out, in Canada a "Dinah" doll was manufactured in 1904[19] and a "Topsy" doll was manufactured in 1940.[20] In Canada, however, the shift of place of manufacture from home to factory is heavily inflected by the ethnicity of the maker and of the human depicted in the object—for example, Inuit dolls carved from wood or bone continue to be made in the traditional way, but today they are not playthings for children of the community but rather artifacts for adult collectors. First Nations dolls are no longer made in the traditional way for children in the community but instead are manufactured as inexpensive plastic replicas intended for tourists.[21] This is not to say all twentieth-century dolls were commercially produced. For example, during World War II, there were both commercial and homemade dolls constructed by women representing men who belonged to the army, air force and navy.[22]

Elaborate dolls for Canadian girls have been largely imported from Germany, France, Britain, and the United States, beginning with imports from Europe in 1839.[23] Ironically, it was only during the periods of the two world wars that a Canadian doll industry was able to emerge. This was particularly the case during World War I, since up until then Germany had been the leading manufacturer of dolls and toys generally. Boycotts made these dolls unavailable and a Canadian doll industry viable.[24] Strahlendorf notes that the history of Canadian doll manufacture can be seen in miniature in the pages of the Eaton's catalogues devoted to dolls. The Eaton's Beauty doll, produced from 1900 to 1994, is the most obvious example, but from the catalogue of 1888–89 onwards, catalogues for most years displayed ads for a variety of dolls at different prices. Less expensive dolls were included alongside the expensive ones, usually on the same page. Strahlendorf considers the role of the Eaton's catalogue to be crucial in the history of Canadian dolls in that it initiated the fashion for imported dolls owing to its universal, free access in most Canadian homes. She goes so far as to state that the catalogue precipitated the demise of the fledgling Canadian doll-manufacturing industry that was not overturned until World War I.[25]

The range of types of dolls available to Canadian girls (as noted by Forman-Brunell about American dolls) seems to have always been diverse: unlike those in Europe and Britain, Canadian dolls do not seem to have switched from the shapely lady doll of early centuries to dolls representing children, and then to baby dolls in the mid-nineteenth century, and later to the shapely (teen) female body in the mid-twentieth century.[26] Multiple types of dolls from different materials (rag, wood, paper, etc.) were produced at home in the earliest white settlements. The shapely Georgian doll, or later the Victorian lady doll, was one type of doll available but limited to very affluent children. These dolls existed in a landscape of dolls of different shapes and genders that were manufactured individually. When commercially manufactured dolls became dominant in the twentieth century, these factory-produced dolls represented different ages of child, different sexes of children, and to a degree different ethnicities of children.

Throughout the history of commercial Canadian doll manufacture, well-known dolls have been produced that are unique in terms of their "Canadianness," such as the Eaton's Beauty doll (1900–1994), the Maggie Muggins doll (1947), the Barbara Ann Scott doll (1948–1954), and the Anne of Green Gables doll (1972–). It is intriguing that these dolls are defined by a company, an Olympic hero, and two icons of Canadian children's literature for girls. These enduring dolls should be considered in relation to others that were more ephemeral. Scanning the material and digital repositories makes it apparent that some dolls focus on sport celebrities, such as Marilyn Bell, the teenaged swimmer who crossed Lake Ontario in 1954, or male hockey stars,[27] and others focus on key Canadian icons, including the Royal Canadian Mounted Police (1936) and the First Nations poet Pauline Johnson;[28] all these dolls were manufactured in Canada. Some dolls devoted to Canadian celebrities have even been manufactured in the United States, such as those depicting the Dionne quintuplets (1934).[29] During the two world wars, patriotic dolls were produced commercially, including the Tipperary doll in World War I (1915) and nursing sister dolls for each of the armed forces, which were produced by Reliable Toys during World War II and are presently housed at the Canadian War Museum in Ottawa.[30] Black nurse dolls were not manufactured until the 1960s.[31] There have been specifically Quebec dolls, as well, such as nun dolls[32] and priest dolls that were intended to urge Quebec children to enter religious vocations. The McCord Museum even holds in its collection a doll house fashioned as the mother house of a religious order.

As with any artifact, these three-dimensional dolls need to be situated within a contextual "landscape" composed of other relevant information from the environment.[33] In terms of the material environment, three-dimensional dolls need to be studied in the context of two-dimensional dolls: paper dolls and other flat dolls, whether composed of cardboard, paper, felt, or other materials.[34] In Canada, paper dolls were first fairly widely available in the pages of the *Canadian Home Journal* from the late 1920s and 1930s.[35] Flat dolls of different materials exist in the McCord collection, beginning with paper dolls from the late nineteenth century; through the Canadian-manufactured magnetic "magic dolls" of the 1930s that were based on the royal princesses Elizabeth and Margaret; and on to paper doll books from the 1950s that were manufactured in the United States but owned by Canadian girls. This landscape of three-dimensional and two-dimensional dolls has continued to the present. A plethora of different types of paper doll books are available for purchase in chain bookstores, often as tie-ins to physical dolls or stories, such as the American Girl, Barbie, and Anne of Green Gables paper dolls. Paper dolls are also available "for free" (except for the cost of the paper) to be printed from websites for girls such as Dollmaker.[36] Virtual paper doll sites abound, where girls play dress-up with virtual dolls. Again, these are usually tie-ins to pop culture dolls such as Barbie and more recent dolls such as Polly Pocket or Bratz.

Doll-Play "in Context": Exploring the Personal Meanings of Doll-Play within Canadian Girlhood

In applying Riggins's idea of the connotative reading or mapping to explore objects and spaces, we draw on the rich body of literature on memory-work. While, as Riggins points out, people tend to be much more focused on remembering and explaining personal meanings, a socio-semiotic reading can include denotative details as well. In his own memories of his parents' living room, for example, he also describes something of the history of the television set (and not just what it meant to the family). As we have explored elsewhere, memory-work can be a useful tool and entry point to studying the play and materiality of childhood. Ranging from studies of early memories of playing school,[37] cowgirl-play,[38] Barbie-play,[39] and catalogue-play,[40] we have tested out a variety of approaches to using memory in childhood studies. These have included working with photographs and objects to study such phenomena as playing school[41] and digital images to study websites.[42] As part of the same work, we have also set up memory-work projects that make use of what Patricia Hampl refers to as "first draft" and "second draft" memory writing.[43] In this approach to memory, which also draws on the work on collective memory of Frigga Haug, June Crawford, et al., the point is to move from unselfconsciously mediated remembering (free recall–first-draft memory) to working back in a systematic way that interrogates memory (second-draft memory): Why do we remember X and not Y? What might be left out of the memory?[44] We have also been interested in the ideas around "staging" that Jo Spence and Rosy Martin developed in their research a few years ago to interrogate memory, class, and childhood. For example, as part of their projects on girlhood, they dress up, as adults, in school uniforms. Each holding a cigarette, they re-examine girlhood, using both body representations (dressing up in schoolgirl clothing) and the visual (the actual photographs taken).[45]

In our various memory-work projects, our focus has been on the act of deliberate remembering as opposed to solely accidental remembering, with the idea that working with the past can serve as a useful feminist tool for contesting (and sometimes recovering) the past. Thus, when we were studying the "afterlife" of children's popular culture for our book, *Researching Children's Popular Culture*, we each decided to engage in deliberate remembering around cowgirl-play. Drawing on published accounts of other women's memories, such as those found in the work of bell hooks, we each wrote first- and second-draft memories of growing up in the 1950s and early 1960s. As part of the same project, we also did a cultural reading of Jessie, the cowgirl doll in the animated feature *Toy Story 2*, a film that we argue can be regarded as a cultural reading on memory and various components of child's play in and of itself, including a study of girls' relationships with objects such as a specific doll.[46]

Applied more specifically to doll-play, we offer here several examples of working with the personal meanings attached to doll-play: (1) our mothers' and other relatives' memories of creative catalogue play related to Eaton's catalogues; (2) Claudia's recollections of doll-play organized according to the physical aspects of the doll; and (3) a summary of several women's memories of Barbie-play. In the context of our discussion in the previous section about what constitutes Canadianness in doll-play, one might regard all three as examples of Canadian doll-play, even though cut-outs from the Eaton's catalogue, while specifically Canadian, may not typically be regarded as dolls (though of course the Eaton's Beauty doll is), an analysis of memories based on the physical aspects of dolls is not unique to Canada, and Barbie is not of Canadian manufacture (although played with by Canadian girls since 1959). Nonetheless, we believe all three examples work toward mapping out the broader agenda of examining the tools of study that will enhance our understanding of Canadian girlhood.

Creative Catalogue Play: The Eaton's Catalogue as a "Text of Desire"

Applying Riggins's method of denotative and connotative analysis to the Eaton's Beauty doll, what can we learn about Canadian girlhood and material culture? As noted in the first section of this essay, Eaton's Beauty dolls were especially associated with the Eaton's catalogue in the players' minds. Beginning in 1900, the doll was featured in the company's fall/ winter catalogue. While the doll initially represented a young woman, by 1904 she resembled more a young girl. The doll always had a red ribbon with gold lettering identifying it as an Eaton's Beauty. During the World War I, European dolls were not available, so in 1915 and 1916 the Eaton's Beauty doll was made by the Dominion Toy Manufacturing Company of Toronto. During World War II, the doll was once again made in Canada, this time by the Reliable Toy Company of Toronto. In the 1950s and 1960s, the Eaton's Beauty was an ordinary vinyl play doll. By the late 1970s, the company offered limited editions of bisque dolls for the benefit of collectors.[47]

Doll collector Judy Tomlinson Ross provides a detailed description of the doll in terms of dates, materials of the head and body, clothing, hair, and so on, along with numerous photographs. She notes that in keeping with Eaton's policy to attract as wide a range of customers as possible, the price for the smallest doll was one dollar from 1900 to 1916, and under two dollars until 1943. Throughout their manufacturing, the dolls were formed of different materials. In the first four years they had a bisque shoulderhead with a leather body. The body changed to papier mâché in 1906, then to composition around 1912, latex in 1954, plastic between 1960 and 1965, back to composition in 1977, and then bisque in 1983, when it was a collector's item costing four hundred and fifty dollars. The head changed materials as well, from bisque (1900–1914) to composition (1915–1916), bisque (1924–1940), composition (1940–1943), vinyl (1954–1965), and back to bisque (1977). The doll was initially sold undressed, but after 1908, she was wearing a chemise. Between 1940 and 1943, one could buy extra outfits, while from 1954 onwards she was sold fully dressed.[48]

There are several ways of looking at the connotative meanings of the Eaton's Beauty doll. It is interesting to note, for example, that the Ontario Archives project has

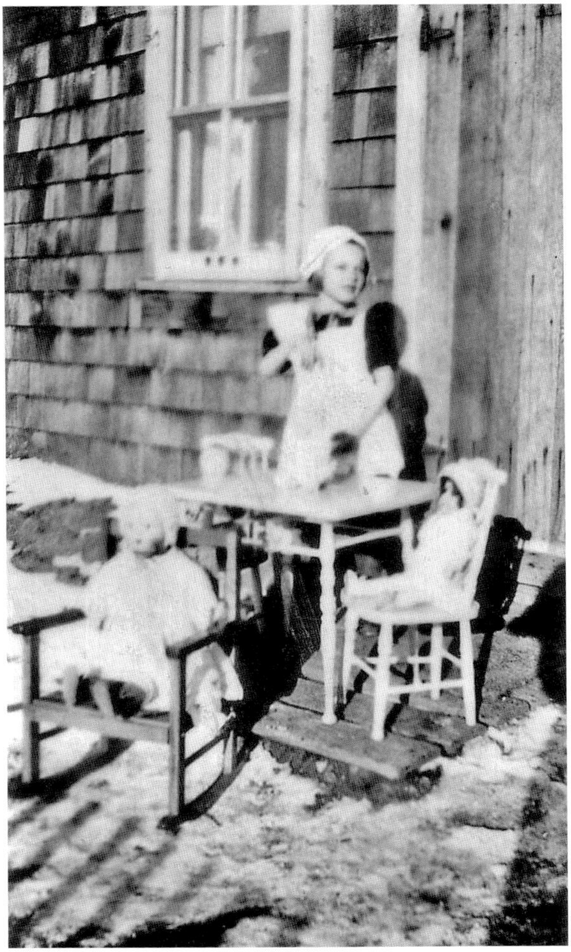

FIGURE 5.1
Joan with her Eaton's Beauty doll, Christmas, 1939. (Photographer unknown. Private collection)

established an Eaton's Christmas Memory site, where people now in their fifties, sixties, and seventies recall Santa Claus parades and specific Eaton's toys, including such objects as the Eaton's Beauty and Punkinhead, the Eaton's bear. Respondents have been asked to offer their personal recollections of Eaton's at Christmas. What is interesting is the way in which Eaton's now sits as its own nostalgia piece in terms of the Eaton's Beauty doll and other Eaton's-produced toys, such as Punkinhead, but also as a recurring "text of desire" (a phrase coined by Linda Christian-Smith to refer to girls' fashion magazines)[49] in terms of the catalogue through which the doll could be purchased. As Fredelle Maynard recalls in her memoir of growing up on the Canadian Prairies, *Raisins and Almonds*:

> Though for many country families Eaton's [mail-order catalogue] was a chief source of goods, in our house the catalogue served no such practical purpose. I don't recall that we ever sent off a single order.... The catalogue was a book to dream over, and the fact [that] I was not getting a new Eaton's Beauty doll took nothing from my pleasure in studying her rosy smile and fringy lashes.[50]

Claudia Mitchell recalls hearing stories from a favourite aunt and a cousin who both grew up in the 1930s and had an Eaton's Beauty doll. Years later, when various relatives would refer to the dolls, there would always be a type of astonishment and awe: "Remember Viv and her Eaton's Beauty doll." Recently, when Claudia spoke with her cousin Joan about her Eaton's Beauty doll, all these years later she still showed amazement that she had ever received such a doll. Joan even found a picture of her five-year-old self with the Eaton's Beauty doll at Christmas 1939 (fig. 5.1). She recalls how special she felt, saying, "I must have been really spoiled. It would have cost a lot for Mum and Dad to get me that doll." Interestingly, an account by another woman posted on a website and looking back at growing up in the 1930s says more or less the same thing:

> The other Christmas gift that impressed me was an "Eaton's Beauty" doll, which I knew, from having seen it in the catalogue, had cost a whole dollar. I was tremendously impressed—imagine my parents caring enough about me to spend a whole dollar on a toy I wanted! And Mother had dressed it in an exact copy of a dress of my sister's—white striped with green, with a sailor collar and a four-in-hand tie that really untied, and which I had to learn how to tie myself.[51]

When we interviewed our own mothers, both of whom grew up on the Prairies in the 1920s, about their recollections of the Eaton's catalogue, we were struck by their ingenious "making do" improvisation of creating paper dolls and fictional families from cutouts from the catalogue. Again, however, we were also struck by the place of the catalogue in their memories:

> In the summer of 2006 Jacqui's mother, Irene, who was 93, was recovering from a slight stroke in hospital. When they were talking, Jacqui mentioned her continuing interest in dolls and paper dolls. They discussed how years ago when working on a catalogue project with Claudia, both she and Claudia's mother had talked about the Eaton's catalogue as a wish book, and its role in rural western households in the early decades of the twentieth century. Irene said their family never had an Eaton's Beauty doll, but that she and her sisters cut out figures from the catalogue and used them as paper dolls. Jacqui and Irene talked about the memory again, and Irene said that she got the idea from her cousin's mother, who had a magazine with paper dolls in it. In a later telephone conversation, Jacqui mentioned that in the reference book *Dolls of Canada*, there are paper dolls in the magazine to cut out that were included in the *Canadian Home Journal* from the 1920s and 30s, and Irene said she thought it might have been the

> Ladies Home Journal. Irene, who was about five or six at the time, her three sisters, and her cousin who lived with them all played with these homemade paper dolls together. She recounted an incident when she had wanted to wash the dolls and had taken them to the trough and became quite upset when their heads washed off! They laughed, and Jacqui told her how elsewhere, she and Claudia had written about other forms of doll "destruction," but clearly Irene's had been unintentional![52]

As can be seen through the ingenuity of the girl players themselves, the medium for the representation and marketing of three-dimensional dolls in turn became the artistic medium for making dolls for paper doll–play. In these cases, at the individual level, the girls' actual play practices or "(mis) use-value" subverts the commercial project of the images, which the Eaton's company intended to be used to sell the dolls pictured in the catalogue.[53]

"Curatorial" Doll-Play: Doll-Play Organized by Physical Genres of Dolls

Another way of studying personal meaning is to apply Riggins's categories to dolls categorized according to physical genres, as opposed to specific dolls such as the Eaton's Beauty, the Maggie Muggins doll, or the Barbara Ann Scott doll. There are a variety of ways of looking at physicality. For example, in her study of porcelain collector dolls (PCDs), Robertson categorizes dolls according to physical age categories: infant (up to one year and usually prone, held, or propped up); toddler (up to one to three years and often sitting, with the soles of their feet typically turned inward); child (over three years to puberty); and adult (past puberty and including brides).[54] Here, we look at the dolls that Claudia played with in the 1950s according to the primary material used in their construction: the rubber doll, the composition doll, the hard plastic bride doll, and the vinyl doll. As we note, each of these genres has its own denotative meaning (albeit a taken-for-granted aspect of dolls to a little girl growing up on a farm in western Canada in the 1950s), which flows into the connotative meanings that she now attaches to the specific dolls within each genre. Claudia recalls the following memories:

> Playing with a rubber doll is probably my earliest doll memory, and in the accompanying photograph (fig. 5.2) I am about four years old and wheeling my rubber doll around in a doll carriage. She was a "wet-ums" type doll, one of those dolls that had a hole for her mouth so she could drink from a small baby bottle and then also pee. As near as I can determine from an Internet search, my rubber doll was probably one of the dolls made by Sun Rubber between 1919 and the early 1950s.
>
> Then came my composition dolls.[55] I recall having two of these dolls: Peggy, who was fairly small (about twelve to fourteen inches) and had a cloth body and what my brothers and I always referred to as a wooden head. Her hair was painted on and there was a raised loop built right into her head so that you could tie on a ribbon. Her eyes

opened and closed, and she made a sound if you tipped her over. Someone in the family had knitted her what must surely be one of the ugliest dresses in history: dark brown knit with a bit of orange trim. When I first read *Anne of Green Gables* and encountered those serviceable dresses that Marilla created for Anne, I could so understand Anne's dismay. Peggy always had to be sort of my "work doll"—as well as a weapon. I recall, for example, hitting my brother over the head with Peggy. Within the same era I received Dallas. Dallas was definitely not Canadian. My grandmother brought me the doll from a trip she took to Dallas, Texas. I was so intrigued by the name of the place I immediately took it for my doll. Dallas was my first big doll—probably more than twenty-four inches tall. She came with a dark wig in the form of pigtail style, which eventually came off. Underneath she had a slightly moulded hair style. She also came with a very lovely satin-like yellow and white frock.

Somewhere in my doll-play I managed to acquire a bride doll. This hard plastic, fourteen-inch bride doll (now selling on eBay for $129) still exists in the family, though her head now is attached to her neck with surgical tape. I am not quite sure when I received the bride doll, though like the Eaton's Beauty doll of my aunt Viv and cousin Joan, she existed within a state of awe and amazement, spending most of her life (at least during my childhood) in a plain cardboard box with a cellophane window in our linen closet, to be taken out only on special occasions. In some ways she might be taken as a precursor to Barbie in that she was shapely, with slight breasts. She came dressed in an off-white satin gown; satin underpants, which to this day have never been removed; tiny white leather shoes; and mesh white socks. With her beautiful shock of thick, dark hair, I always thought she looked like my aunt Joyce in her wedding photo. To the best of my knowledge there was never a photo of me taken with my bride doll, and she never had a name. She was just "my bride doll." In the accompanying photo (fig. 5.3), we see that she did eventually leave the cellophane box—and is now the worse for wear.

Then came my vinyl doll. Vinyl dolls first made an appearance around the mid-1950s. I think my grandmother bought Joanne for me, and she managed to stay in the family into the early eighties—until Rebecca and Sarah, my two daughters, were about seven and ten. She was, as the adults around me described her, "Claudia's last doll." There must have been some sense that I was getting too old for dolls. Joanne had thick, rooted, blonde hair, blue eyes that opened and closed. Her body, I seem to recall, had a certain stiffness to it (perhaps as a result of some sort of internal wire system) so that it was easy to get her legs to bend so she could sit well on her own. The thing I remember particularly vividly about Joanne was her smell. There was a beautiful new-vinyl smell that I think she kept over the years. Having read an essay by Heather Hendershot about the smell of dolls (particularly the Strawberry Shortcake phenomenon),[56] I think the vinyl smell is significant, as I don't remember the smell of any of my other dolls. Notwithstanding Joanne's lovely scent, however, Joanne's soft vinyl was her downfall, as my daughter Sarah wrote on her face with black indelible marker, which bled into the vinyl, and Joanne was thrown out in one of our moves.

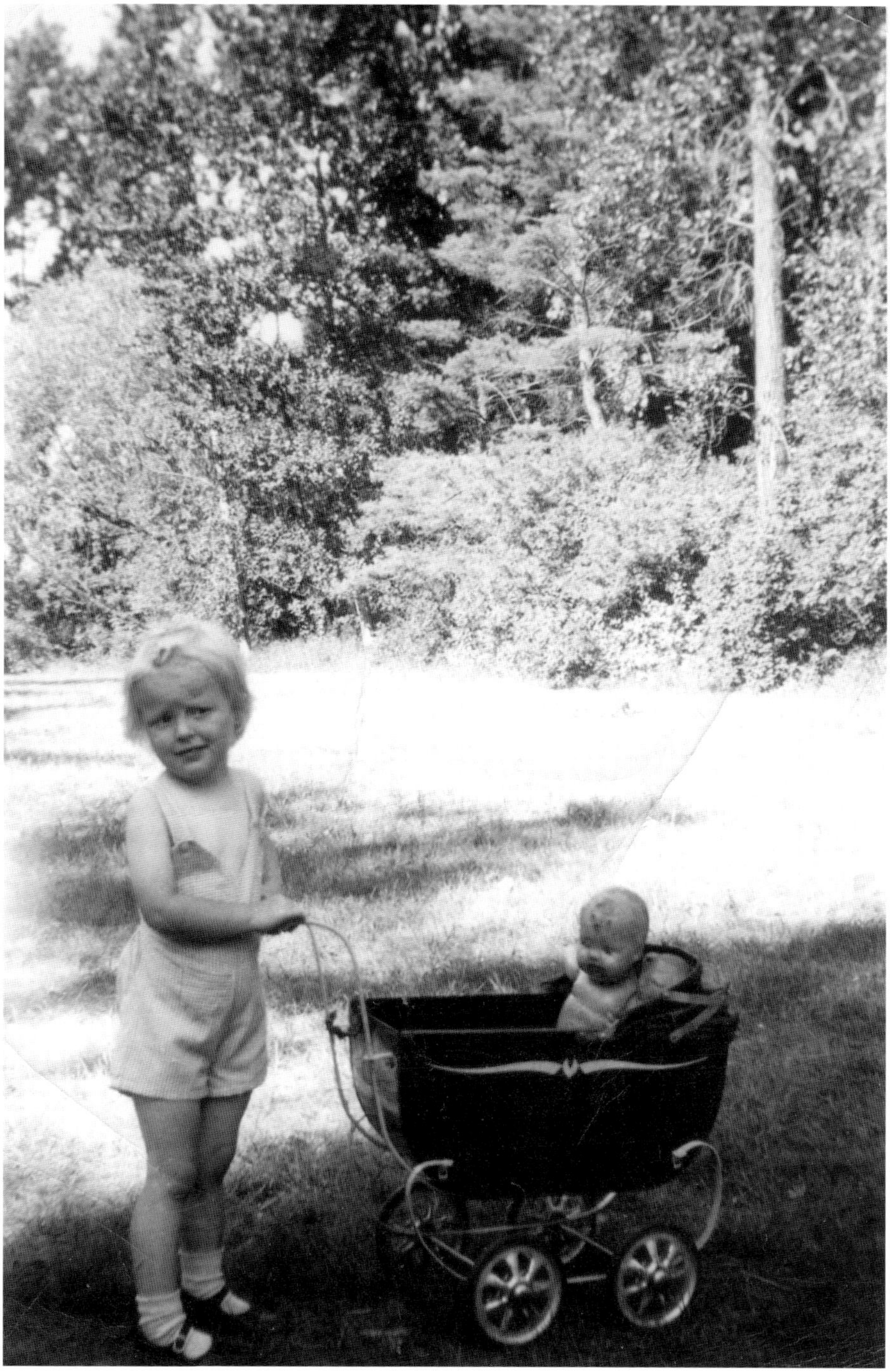

FIGURE 5.2
Claudia with her rubber "wet-ums" doll in carriage. (Photographer unknown. International Visual Methodologies collection, McGill University)

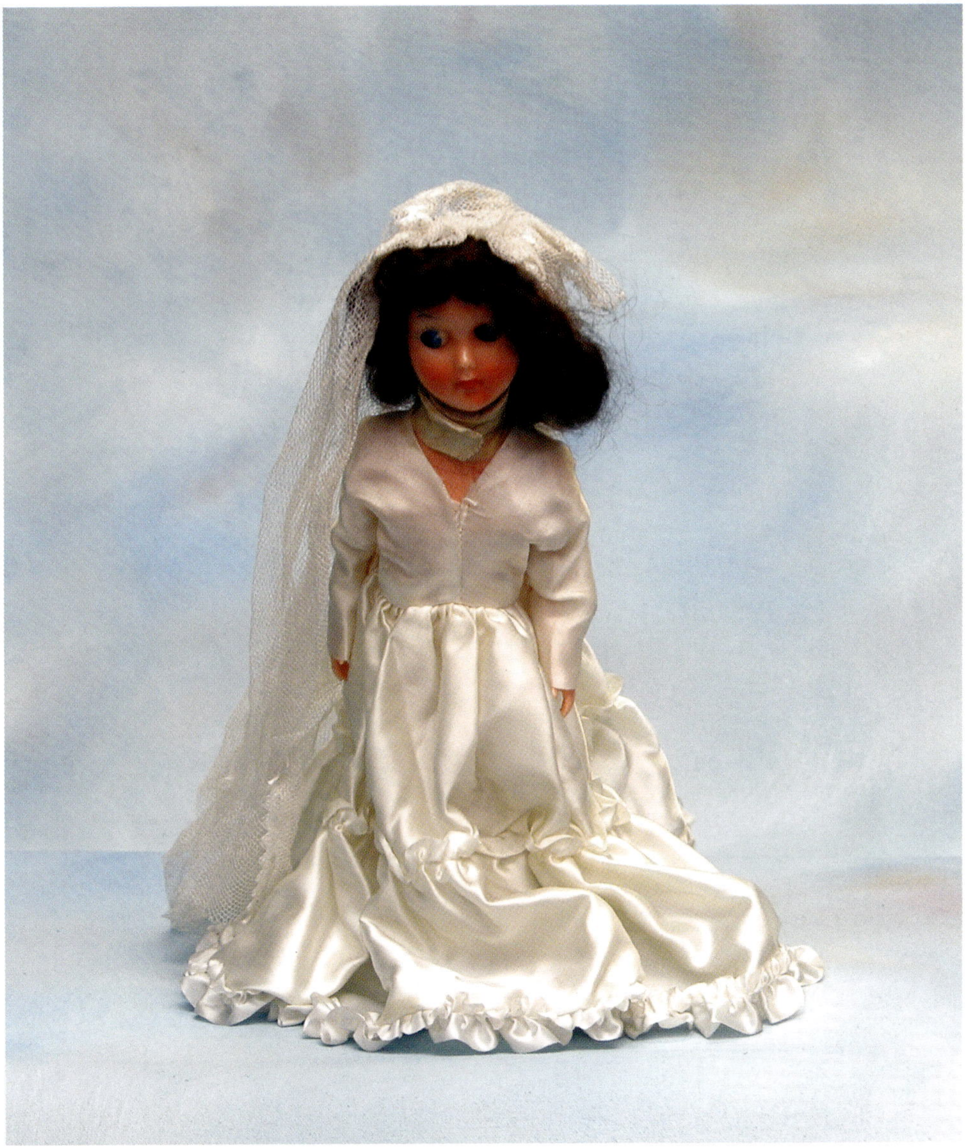

FIGURE 5.3 Bride doll. (Photographer Lewis Wosu. From the private collection of Claudia Mitchell)

Barbie-Play: Getting Dressed Up and Going Out

For some time we have been particularly interested in the ways in which Barbie might be remembered and possibly interpreted somewhat differently from the more typical moral panic narratives with which she has been associated over the years. Some women, we have discovered, recall that Barbie was the first doll they played with where they weren't obliged to practise "women's work" of changing diapers, cooking (with an Easy-Bake oven), or cleaning (with a Little Sweeper). Rather, through Barbie they "got dressed up and went out." As we describe elsewhere,[57] Annmarie Adams, now a professor of architecture at McGill University, recalls that one of her early design projects as a twelve- or thirteen-year-old girl was to create and build her own Barbie dream house. Ingrid, a computer consultant in Montreal, recalls that as a girl she became tired of the flimsy Barbie apartments she had constructed. Accordingly, she constructed her own Barbie house out of scraps of gyproc left over from her parents' remodelling efforts. She became even more ambitious in her finishing touches. As she writes:

> Then I got even more creative. Inspired by the 160-in-one electronic project kit, I installed a security system in the doll house. When Barbie inserted a magnet into a slot cut in the side of the door, she could enter the house without making a sound. If she forgot to use the magnet, Christmas lights would flash and a little buzzer would sound. It wasn't that I was an electronic wizard, but I wanted to keep my Barbies away from my younger sister. The system did exactly that and won me second prize in the school science fair.

Another woman, Nadine, now a school teacher, remembers using Barbie in constructing "teacher Barbie" scripts, before Mattel devised such a type of doll. Following is an excerpt from a lengthy description of how she devised elaborate scenarios. Notably, she used an improvisational approach to the materials she needed, adapting a similar "making do" philosophy as the older women we interviewed who engaged in catalogue play:

> Up to the age of eleven, I remember (especially around nine years old) we played Barbie dolls a lot and often we tried to create the house, churches, stores, etc., that our dolls lived or worked in. We had a room (made of a cardboard box decorated with doll furniture, if we had them, leftover fabrics, scraps from catalogues and the hardware store samples, or anything else we could scrounge up) for each "setting" we play-acted our dolls in. I remember one of these cardboard rooms was a school room. I had a Skipper as well as a Barbie, as did my young sister, who was my major playmate. The Skippers were the students and usually my Barbie was the teacher. My sister's Barbie was usually the mother to whom the Skippers would return to at the "home" box when my Barbie dismissed class. What I remember most is making sure my Barbie was dressed

> well—always neatly but nothing for a party. The Skippers wore nice dresses but not their "Sunday Best."

Nadine also refers to how Barbie and school play created a type of levelling in terms of class and ethnicity among the children: "School was one thing we all had in common, so it was easy for us to pick roles and we all seemed to know what each of us should do." We consider this levelling idea important in the context of Barbie-play owing to the attacks against Barbie for her "culturally imperialist" positioning.[58] In the case of Nadine, by contrast, play with Barbie formed a kind of "common ground" crossing over ethnic, economic and cultural differences amongst the children.[59]

WHAT ALL THESE NARRATIVES SUGGEST IS THE significance of going beyond studies of dolls "out of context" primarily geared toward historians, collectors, and connoisseurs, to look at what Attfield describes as "toys in the dynamic context of mass consumption at the stage in which they are transformed from commodity to material culture."[60] The three kinds of memory accounts suggest the variety of ways in which people remember their toys: the first narrative situates the speaker within a creative "make do" culture that could be seen as subverting the catalogue's aim as advertising toys for purchase. The second narrative is an account of meta-play, where the child is playing at being a curator, for the adult Claudia's account shows how as a child she was categorizing her dolls by type (both by composition and by theme) as seen in curator's accounts and in books for collectors. The third set of accounts seem deterministic in that the women remembering their Barbie-play prefigured their present occupations in their kinds of Barbie-play. Throughout all, it is apparent that working with memory accounts supports Attfield's challenge by providing both denotative and connotative accounts of dolls "in context" of various girls' lives. In the above cases, we have drawn on the memories of doll-play of several Canadian women whose lives as girls span the first half of the twentieth century.

Discussion

In the sections above, we have offered some methodological approaches to looking at Canadian doll-play, and in so doing, we have attempted to highlight some of the rich historical and cultural meanings attached to dolls and hence their place within girlhood studies more broadly. At the same time, in comparison to the relatively benign memory space of boys' toys, we do not wish to give the impression that dolls, or any other gendered object, particularly those associated with girls, occupy a neutral space. As Canadian researcher Suzanne de Castell, for example, points out in her essay with Mary Bryson on the dystopias of gendered play:

> I remember I cried the first Christmas I got a doll, a baby doll, from my parents. When they asked me why I was crying I remember telling them I was "just so happy," when I was terrified and appalled at the realization that this was what I was supposed—biologically supposed—to like. To love, even. How on earth to play with this diapered apparition into which you squeezed water on one end and mopped it up at the other? Unlike my friends (who had Barbies) I never abused "Baby Wet-ums," who in time, after what I must have imagined would be a respectable period of intense maternal guardianships, lay dusty on her flannel-sheeted metal bed.[61]

Within the bigger picture of childhood studies internationally, studying the materiality of a Canadian childhood approached, say, in terms of types of toys, gender, age, ethnicity, and geographical location could have something substantial to contribute. This project could build on researchers' existing work on Canadian children and their toys. Notably, this research includes books by communications theorist Stephen Kline, who outlines his groundbreaking study of children, commercial toys, and marketing in *Out of the Garden: Toys and Children's Culture in the Age of TV Marketing* (1993), and by historian Neil Sutherland, who creates a revisionary historiography of the education of Canadian children in *Growing Up: Childhood in English Canada from the Great War to the Age of Television* (1997).[62] We might also look to the historical collections of specific toys, such as construction toys like Lego, Meccano, dream houses, and other architectural toys at the Canadian Centre for Architecture in Montreal, and particularly Douglas Coupland's autobiographically based installation and exhibition called *Super City*, composed of Lego and similar construction toys.[63]

At the same time, we see that the kinds of denotative and connotative meanings of dolls and doll-play that we have assembled here really only scratch the surface of the social and historical meanings attached to growing up as a Canadian girl. Interestingly, a few months ago, when a group of graduate students studying childhood as a cultural space in the Faculty of Education at McGill toured an exhibition called *Growing Up in Montréal* at the McCord Museum, some of the most provocative comments related to presence and absence and whose childhoods were preserved and whose, by virtue of class, geographic location, religion, ethnicity, gender, and so on, had a more ephemeral quality. What this discussion opened up, though, more than anything, was the recognition of the unique features of Canadian childhoods that should be preserved and studied by future scholars across a wide range of disciplines.[64] We believe that it is important for this kind of methodological work on Canadian childhoods to be undertaken within existing Canadian collections of toys in order to contribute to a new girlhood (and boyhood) studies agenda.

Notes

1 Miriam Forman-Brunell, *Made to Play House: Dolls and the Commercialization of American Girlhood, 1830–1930* (New Haven, CT: Yale University Press, 1993).
2 Here, for example, we are thinking of such studies on Barbie as Mary Lord, *Forever Barbie* (New York: William Morrow & Co., 1994); Ann Ducille, "Dyes and Dolls: The Merchandizing of Difference," *differences* 6, no. 1 (1994): 231–247; Erica Rand, *Barbie's Queer Accessories* (Durham, NC: Duke University Press, 1995); Mary Rogers, *Barbie Culture* (Thousand Oaks, CA: Sage, 1999); as well as more recent studies, such as R.S. Hegle, "Global Makeovers and Maneuvers: Barbie's Presence in India," *Feminist Media Studies* 1, no. 1 (2001): 129–133; and Catherine Driscoll, "Girl-Doll: Barbie as Puberty Manual," in *Seven Going on Seventeen: Tween Studies in the Culture of Girlhood*, ed. Claudia Mitchell and Jacqueline Reid-Walsh, 224–241 (New York: Peter Land Associates, 2005). We are also thinking of historians of doll-play such as Karen Calvert, *Children in the House: The Material Culture of Early Childhood, 1600–1900* (Hanover, NH: Northeastern University Press, 1992); Forman-Brunell, *Made to Play House*; Frances Armstrong, "The Dollhouse as Ludic Space," *Children's Literature* 24 (1996): 23–55; and Claudia Mitchell and Jacqueline Reid-Walsh, *Researching Children's Popular Culture* (London: Routledge Taylor Francis, 2002).
3 Pat Kirkham, *The Gendered Object* (Manchester: Manchester University Press, 1996).
4 Stephen H. Riggins, "Fieldwork in the Living Room: An Autoethnographic Essay," in *The Socialness of Things: Essays on the Socio-Semiotics of Objects*, ed. Stephen H. Riggins, 109 (Berlin: Mouton de Gruyer, 1994). In our own previous work, we have adapted his ideas to an analysis of children's bedrooms: Claudia Mitchell and Jacqueline Reid-Walsh, *Researching Children's Popular Culture* (London: Routledge, 2002).
5 Riggins, "Fieldwork," 109.
6 Frigga Haug et al., *Female Sexualisation: A Collective Work of Memory* (London: Verso, 1987); Mitchell and Reid-Walsh, *Researching Children's Popular Culture*; Claudia Mitchell and Sandra Weber, *Reinventing Ourselves as Teachers: Beyond Nostalgia* (London: Falmer Press, 1999).
7 Judy Attfield, "Barbie and Action Man: Adult Toys for Girls and Boys, 1959–93," in *The Gendered Object*, ed. Pat Kirkham, 80–89 (Manchester: Manchester University Press, 1996).
8 Conrad Graham, curator, Decorative Arts, McCord Museum of Canadian History, Montreal, in telephone conversation with J. Reid-Walsh, March 28, 2007.
9 Evelyn Robson Strahlendorf, *Dolls of Canada: A Reference Guide* (Ottawa: Booklore, 1986), 86.
10 Carl Schneider, *Children's Television* (Chicago: NTC Books, 1987), 26.
11 Please see our "And I Want to Thank You Barbie: Barbie as a Site of Cultural Interrogation," in *Education and Cultural Studies: Towards a Performative Practice*, ed. Henry Giroux with Patrick Shannon, 103–116 (New York: Routledge, 1997). Here, we propose that Barbie is a "cumulative culture text" that needs to be analyzed in all her numerous material and textual forms.
12 Daniel Miller, *Material Culture and Mass Consumption* (London: Basil Blackwell, 1987), 98.
13 Ibid., 108.
14 Daniel Miller, ed. *Material Cultures: Why Some Things Matter* (London: UCL Press, 1998), 9–10.
15 McCord Museum of Canadian History, *Decorative Arts: Dolls* (permanent collection) (Montreal: McCord Museum of Canadian History, 2006); Evelyn Robson Strahlendorf and Peter E. Rider, curators, "Timeless Treasures: The Story of Dolls in Canada," Canadian Museum of Civilization, http://www.civilisations.ca/cmc/exhibitions/hist/dolls/dointo1e.shtml; Strahlendorf, *Dolls of Canada*.

16 Caroline Goodfellow, *The Ultimate Doll Book* (Montreal: Reader's Digest, 1993); A.F. Robertson, *Life-like Dolls: The Collector Doll Phenomenon and the Lives of the Women Who Love Them* (London: Routledge, 2004).
17 Forman-Brunell, *Made to Play House.*
18 Ibid., 28.
19 Strahlendorf, *Dolls of Canada*, 38.
20 Ibid., 266.
21 Ibid, chap. 2 and 3.
22 Strahlendorf, *Dolls of Canada*, 43; McCord Museum, *Decorative Arts: Dolls.*
23 Strahlendorf, *Dolls of Canada*, 33.
24 Ibid., 117.
25 Ibid., 34.
26 See note 8.
27 Strahlendorf, *Dolls of Canada*, 92–93.
28 Ibid., 94, 260.
29 Ibid, 86–90.
30 Ibid, 168, 270.
31 Ibid, 265.
32 Ibid., 98.
33 Ann Smart Martin and J. Richie Garrison, eds., *American Material Culture: The Shape of the Field* (Winterthur, DE: Winterthur Museum, 1997), 14–15.
34 See note 8.
35 Strahlendorf, *Dolls of Canada*, 111.
36 "Dress Up Games for Girls Online," Doll Palace, http://www.thedollpalace.com/doll-maker/dress-up-games.php (accessed January 8, 2007).
37 Mitchell and Weber, *Reinventing Ourselves as Teachers.*
38 Mitchell and Reid-Walsh, *Researching Children's Popular Culture.*
39 Jacqueline Reid-Walsh and Claudia Mitchell, "Just a Doll?": 'Liberating' Accounts of Barbie-Play," *Review of Education / Pedagogy / Cultural Studies* 22, no. 2 (2000): 175–190.
40 Claudia Mitchell and Jacqueline Reid-Walsh, "Mail-Order Memory-Work: Towards a Methodology of Uncovering the Experiences of Covering Over," *Review of Education / Pedagogy / Cultural Studies* 20, no. 1 (1998): 57–75.
41 Mitchell and Weber, *Reinventing Ourselves as Teachers.*
42 Jacqueline Reid-Walsh and Krista Walsh, "Tween Girl in a Technology Household: Interpreting the Digital Building Blocks of a Tween Girl's Web-Site." Presentation at Transforming Spaces: Girlhood, Agency and Power, Concordia University, Montreal, November 21–23, 2003.
43 Patricia Hampl, "Memory and Imagination," in *The Anatomy of Memory: An Anthology*, ed. James McConkey, 201–211 (New York: Oxford University Press, 1996).
44 Frigga Haug et al., *Female Sexualisation*; June Crawford et al., eds., *Emotion and Gender: Constructing Meaning from Memory* (London: Sage, 1992); Patricia Hampl, "Memory and Imagination."
45 J.R. Martin, "Phototherapy: The School Photograph (Happy Days Are Here Again)," in *Photography/Politics: Two*, ed. Patricia Holland, Jo Spence, and Simon Watney, 40–42 (London: Comedia / Photography Workshop, 1986). See also Mitchell and Weber, *Reinventing Ourselves as Teachers.*
46 See Mitchell and Reid-Walsh, *Researching Children's Popular Culture*, 47–78.
47 Canadian Museum of Civilization, "Eaton's Beauty Dolls 1900–1994," Timeless Treasures: The Story of Dolls in Canada, http://www.civilization.ca/hist/dolls/doeat01e.html (accessed January 12, 2007).

48 Strahlendorf, *Dolls of Canada*, 57.

49 Linda Christian-Smith, *Becoming a Woman through Romance* (New York: Routledge, 1990).

50 Fredelle Maynard, *Raisins and Almonds* (Toronto: Doubleday, 1972).

51 Winifred Wallace Sankey, "An Eastern Township's Childhood," http://www.sankey.ws/childhood.html (accessed November 17, 2008).

52 Irene Reid, in conversation with J. Reid-Walsh, July 28, 2006, and November 20, 2006.

53 Bill Brown, "How to Do Things with Things (A Toy Story)," *Critical Inquiry* 24 (1998): 935–964.

54 A.F. Robertson, *Life-like Dolls.*

55 Composition, as described by Denise Van Patten, "is generally a mixture of glue mixed with sawdust. Heavier and denser than paper mache, composition is easily molded and is thus an excellent material to make doll heads. Composition was used to make doll bodies for many years, from approximately the late 1870s, long before it was widely used to make doll heads. Since the material a doll head is made from determines the type of doll, only dolls with heads made of composition are referred to as composition dolls.... Composition dolls overtook the market for bisque dolls in the early 20th Century. Hailed by American dollmaking companies as unbreakable compared to bisque (also often called porcelain) dolls, the novelty of the new material for doll heads, coupled with World War I, helped to bring down the once mighty German dollmaking industry, and helped to make America the premier dollmaking country of the early to mid 20th Century." Denise Van Patten, "Composition Dolls," About.com: Doll Collection, the New York Times Company, http://collectdolls.about.com/od/dollprofiles/p/compositiondoll.htm (accessed November 18, 2008).

56 Heather Hendershot, "Dolls: Odour, Disgust, Femininity, and Toy Design," in *The Gendered Object*, ed. Pat Kirkham, 90–102 (Manchester: Manchester University Press, 1996).

57 Mitchell and Reid-Walsh, *Researching Children's Popular Culture.*

58 Shirley Steinberg "The Bitch Who Has Everything," in *Kinderculture: The Corporate Construction of Childhood*, ed. Shirley Steinberg and Joe Kincheloe, 212–215 (Boulder, CO: Westview Press, 1997).

59 Adapted from Jacqueline Reid-Walsh and Claudia Mitchell, "Just a Doll? 'Liberating' Accounts of Barbie-Play," *Review of Education / Pedagogy / Cultural Studies* 22, no. 2 (2000): 180–182. In Mitchell and Weber's *Reinventing Ourselves as Teachers*, Nadine's account is analyzed in terms of memories of playing school.

60 Attfield, "Barbie and Action Man," 81.

61 Suzanne de Castell and Mary Bryson, "Retooling Play: Dystopia, Dysphoria and Difference," in *From Barbie to Mortal Combat: Gender and Computer Games*, ed. Justine Cassell and Henry Jenkins, 232–261 (Cambridge: MIT Press, 1998), 232.

62 Stephen Kline, *Out of the Garden: Toys and Children's Culture in the Age of TV Marketing* (Toronto: Garamond, 1993); Neil Sutherland, *Growing Up: Childhood in English Canada from the Great War to the Age of Television* (Toronto: University of Toronto Press, 1997).

63 Alice T. Friedman and Rosemary Haddad, eds., *Maisons de Rêve, Maisons Jouets / Dream Houses, Toy Homes* (Montreal: Dimédia, 1995), published in conjunction with the exhibition *Dream Houses, Toy Homes* shown at the Canadian Centre for Architecture in Montreal; Peter Smithson and Cammie McAtee, eds., *Ville En Jeux / Toy Town* (Montreal: Dimédia, 1997), published in conjunction with the exhibition *Toy Town* shown at the Canadian Centre for Architecture in Montreal; Douglas Coupland, ed., *Super City* (Montreal: Canadian Centre for Architecture, 2005), published in conjunction with the exhibition *Super City* shown at the Canadian Centre for Architecture in Montreal.

64 Here we are thinking of an analogy to recent work on Soviet childhood, toys, and material culture, such as the 2002 exhibit in Moscow *Thank You Comrade Stalin, for Our Happy Childhood* and Lisa A. Kirschenblaum's *Small Comrades: Revolutionizing Childhood in Soviet Russia, 1917–1932* (London: Routledge, 2001).

OTHERS AND OUTSIDERS

ALENA M. BUIS

THE RAW MATERIALS OF EMPIRE BUILDING
Depicting Canada's Home Children

THE TERM "ARTISTIC FICTION"[1] IS OFTEN USED to discuss the creative licence child welfare agencies employed to dramatize promotional imagery circulated in Great Britain during the late nineteenth and early twentieth centuries. More commonly, this term refers to the subtle alterations and theatrical staging used to form emotionally charged, highly symbolic photographs that functioned as both documentation and advertising for philanthropic organizations. Reflecting not only the goals of the child welfare movement but also larger imperialistic aspirations, a wide variety of literature, composed of descriptive imagery and powerful metaphors, was used to paint a picture of the destitute child. R.M. Ballantyne's children's adventure novel *Dusty Diamonds Cut and Polished: A Tale of City-Arab Life and Adventure* is an excellent example of the ways in which both visual and literary imagery and fact and fiction combined in the cultural consciousness of the time. The "artistic fiction" used to depict the transformation of Great Britain's "orphans, waifs, and strays" to Canada's home children extends beyond the use of creative contextualization to reveal how children were actively imagined as the raw materials of empire building.

Between 1869 and 1930, over one hundred thousand children were "rescued" from the orphanages, workhouses, and streets of London, Glasgow, Manchester, and other industrialized cities to be shipped off to start a better life in Canada. Initiated by philanthropists such Maria Susan Rye (1829–1903) and Annie Macpherson (1825–1904), and soon adopted by many organizations such as the National Children's Home and Orphanage of London, the Orphan Homes of Scotland, the Church of England Waifs and Strays Society, Fegan Homes, and Barnardo Homes, the mass emigration of orphaned and destitute children was viewed as a rather simple solution to social, economic, and moral problems that had developed in overcrowded urban areas.

Initially, the development of child emigration programs functioned as "a safety valve to tide over the troubles"[2] within Great Britain. Rapid industrialization and urban expansion had resulted in congested cities and overburdened government agencies. It became far more cost efficient to "export" the children that had accumulated in workhouses and children's homes than to support them as dependants of the state. Once sent to the colonies, the "British home children," as they were called, were either adopted or apprenticed as labourers. According to many organizations, their mandate was simple:

> We permanently save the children from relapsing into the misery of their former lot. We relieve our own overcrowded population, where the struggle for existence grows fiercer every day. We supply our own colony with her greatest need, healthy honest labor.[3]

As child emigration increased, images and language appeared that reflected colonial aspirations and epitomized notions of "imperial philanthropy."[4]

Almost completely dependent on public donations and community support, child welfare organizations actively promoted child emigration schemes as an ideal solution to a wide variety of social ills perceived to have been created by poverty. Children of lower-class families were forced to work as chimney sweeps, scavengers, rag pickers, beggars, and miners, for long hours and under horrendous conditions. Orphans and runaways were not protected from the elements or from the dangers of life on the streets. Faced with the "inadequate and sometimes inhuman methods" developed in the wake of reforms to laws dealing with the poor, many philanthropists were responsible for adapting rather radical alternative solutions for destitute, homeless, and orphaned children.[5] In 1869 Rye, one of the first facilitators of organized child emigration, wrote a letter to the *London Times* publicizing her organization, Maria Rye's Emigration Home for Destitute Little Girls, by asking the British public, "Why not take the 'gutter children' of London, Manchester, Birmingham, Bristol and Liverpool and emigrate them to Canada and the Western States of America?"[6] Outspoken leaders of organizations, such as Thomas Bowman Stephenson (1839–1912), John Throgmorton Middlemore (1844–1924), William Quarrier (1829–1903), and Thomas John Barnardo (1845–1905), relentlessly published their accounts of child rescues and emigration success stories to garner community support on both sides of the Atlantic. Editorials, magazines, leaflets, and photographs that appealed for donations from the wealthy and for co-operation from the middle class went beyond fundraising to reveal a greater public fascination with the caricatures presented of the poor. The outpouring of philanthropic literature published by child welfare organizations reflected "the ubiquity of ragged children in the urban landscape and their centrality in the Victorian moral imagination."[7]

Although other evangelical agents such as Stephenson, Macpherson, and Fegan also used photography to both document and promote their work, Barnardo was most prolific and controversial. In May of 1874, Barnardo established a photographic studio at his boys' home at 18–26 Stepney Causeway in London, England, that would go on to produce over fifty thousand images. Using conventions recently developed by asylums and prisons to explore the physiognomic characteristics of their charges, Barnardo's photographer, Thomas Barnes, systematically documented children upon their admission to the homes. These photographs, combined with information on the child, were used to create "history" sheets that were collected in albums to show curious visitors, potential donors, investigating police officers, or parents in search of lost children. Most of the photographs are "perfunctory portrayals" showing children in the same poses;[8] however, on occasion more dramatic scenes were re-enacted. The photographs produced by Barnardo and his colleagues of the children they were rescuing reveal how photography of the time was "capable not only of recording facts, but also of representing fiction."[9]

Although Barnardo was accused by George Reynolds (1842–1909), a Baptist minister also in the child rescue business, of exaggerating the condition of children for photographs used to promote the Barnardo homes, the "staging" of photographs was common practice during the Victorian era. In fact, during the early years, large, cumbersome cameras and long exposure times requiring sitters to remain still for extended periods of time created technical limitations that meant all photographs were staged to a certain degree.[10] These conditions allowed photographers, under the guidance of their philanthropic patrons, to construct images that contributed to the contemporary consciousness surrounding poverty. In an essay entitled "The Directorial Mode: Notes toward a Definition," photography critic A.D. Coleman suggests that photographers working in a "directorial mode" at the turn of the century approached their subjects "*rather as raw material to be itself manipulated as much as desired prior to the exposure of the negative*" (emphasis in the original).[11]

When accused of manipulating the condition of children to create more sympathetic imagery, Barnardo insisted that his dramatic rescue of street children often occurred at night, forcing him to re-create the condition of the child upon admission in later photo sessions. When called on the "authenticity" of these works, he defended his intentions by emphasizing that the photographs were constructed to convey a certain "class" of children.[12] The image of orphans, waifs, and strays in both visual and textual descriptions had become so expertly constructed by philanthropists that readers could no longer distinguish between journalism and the didactic literature churned out by the organizations.[13]

To legitimize their evangelical missions, publicly active agents such as Barnardo and Rye used vivid imagery of orphans, waifs, and strays to construct in the Victorian imagination a compelling portrait of poverty. Descriptions are so vivid that the reader can almost see, hear, and smell life in the slums. One beggar's "frock was made of rotten-looking brown material," and another urchin's "bony shanks were thrust in to large boots that squelched and made sucking noises."[14] The resulting imagery reveals a distinct characterization of the "waifs," "guttersnipes," "street-Arabs," and "beggars" who were all "dehumanized by physical wretchedness."[15] Quite often the language and images philanthropic organizations used to justify emigration reduced the children to objects—potentially valuable objects, but objects nonetheless. One of the most popular metaphors used in this objectification was the child as crude matter that with philanthropic intervention could be moulded into a potentially valuable national resource.

One particularly vivid example of the construction of children as a precious commodity comes from one of Barnardo's highly symbolic "artistic fictions." The photograph "The Raw Material as We Find It" (n.d.; fig. 6.1) depicting a group of boys being "discovered" by Barnardo's assistant Edward Fitzgerald employs elements often found in staged photographs of the time. Such an image also represents Barnardo's awareness of contemporary debates as to whether photographs were "objective documents of social reality or subjective works of art." For Barnardo, each of these dichotomies could be used to promote his philanthropic work, for documentary photography could be used to depict genuine orphans, waifs, or strays, while more embellished imagery would still appeal to a particular audience adept at "reading" symbolic imagery.[16]

"The Raw Material as We Find It" satisfies both a desire for authenticity and more sophisticated means of representation. The children depicted are most likely "street urchins," but the scene is carefully constructed. With such sentimental subject matter and theatrical composition, the image would have been easily understood at the time, and Barnardo's intentions decoded through the iconography present. Despite the daylight, Fitzgerald holds a lantern, an object that was symbolic not only of Christian salvation but also associated with the rescuing missions of child welfare organizations which often dramatically took place at night. The arched framing of the photograph and the pile of rubble upon which the boys are placed resemble ruins, alluding to the classical past of the British Empire.[17] Drawing heavily upon many of the artistic conventions used by child welfare agencies at the time, this image is emblematic of the ways in which publicity materials illustrated destitute children as raw materials suitable for empire building.

Powerfully demonstrated by Barnardo's image, orphans, waifs, and strays as potentially valuable resources became a predominant theme in the "artistic fictions" of child emigration philanthropy. In promotions, both the imagery and the language used in discussing the creation of home children reflect an industrial process that very much echoes the advancements in technology that had allowed for Great Britain's emergence as a powerful world nation. Child welfare agencies were responsible for "mining" their subjects from the streets and "refining" them before "exportation." Once "shipped" to Canada, the "precious freight"[18] of children were held in "distributing houses" until

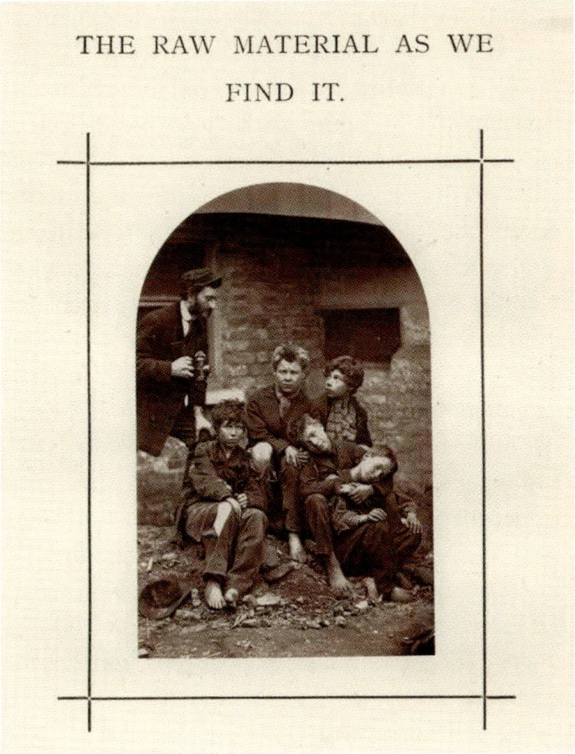

FIGURE 6.1
"The Raw Material as We Find It." (Photo by Thomas Barnes [?], n.d. Barnardo's Photographic Archive)

they could be placed with foster families or apprenticed out. The innumerable metaphors for the moulding and shaping of poor children through the emigration process to Canada allowed philanthropic organizations endless possibilities for visually appealing promotion of their community interventions.

The Canadian landscape provided not only a practical but also a powerful symbolic backdrop for the reformers' goals. When Barnardo declared, "What was needed in order to give them the opportunity they had missed was in every real sense a new heaven and a new earth, the fresh conditions of a colonial life,"[19] Canada was exactly what he had in mind. Canada was a relatively close and inexpensive destination for Great Britain's home children. Desperate for labourers, the government of Canada paid the emigrating organization two dollars per child imported, as well as subsidizing the transportation costs. With over 75 percent of Canada's population living in rural, agricultural communities, children as a form of cheap labour were literally and figuratively a valuable resource during the scramble to expand the young nation. Foundations that participated in child emigration could easily glorify the "dignity of labour"[20] by imagining

Canada as an ideal destination for the "Sons of the soil ... who cultivated millions of overseas acres."[21]

Depicted as a vast, untouched land, Canada provided a perfect foil for the corruption from which the children were being removed. In contrast to the "twice breathed air"[22] and squalor in British urban areas, Canada was "where the prospects [were] as bright as the flame that glows on the maple leaf in fall."[23] Ripe with an array of symbolic potential, Canada became an ideal destination for the Victorian imagination. Similar to the artistic licence used to create a dramatic image of children in need of rescue, philanthropic literature presented the colonies in a contrived manner. Imagery circulated by emigration organizations reinforced connections made in the public consciousness between the youthful nation of Canada and the impressionable immigrants. Canada as a nation served as an analogy for the children; youthful and wild, it could be transformed into a valuable, hardworking member of the dominion's family.

Simultaneously, Canada was easily personified as a surrogate mother for Great Britain's children: "the nation that opened its great fertile spaces to their forbearers who came as frightened children trembling into the bountiful arms of the New World."[24] Because as few as one-third of the children emigrated were actually orphans, a great deal of the fictionalization that occurred served to justify the separation of the children from their families. Mothers and fathers were demonized as drunks, prostitutes, or the morally depraved, and by removing them from the family, organizations were seen as rescuing the children not only from a life of poverty but also from being burdens to the state.[25] When the children were placed in Canada, their adopted home provided both physical and psychological distance between the reborn children and the evils associated with urban industrialism. As part of the construction of the "orphan," philanthropists formulated their own paternal and maternal images. Barnardo became known as "The Father of Nobody's Children." Similarly, a cartoon in *The Canadian Illustrated News* (fig. 6.2) from 1870, depicting "The Situation" of immigration in Canada, perfectly illustrates the manifestation of child rescue ideology by presenting a matronly figure like Rye or Macpherson welcoming "the homeless of Europe" in from the cold. The accompanying article announces that "Miss Canada feeling the responsibility delegated to her by old Britannia, extends towards the coy little minx" her protecting arms. A reference to the shivering waif as "Miss Winnie Peg" further alludes to the thousands of children sent to Manitoba to labour on farms.[26]

Although many of the organizations were nondenominational, the height of child emigration occurred during a time when Victorian public policy and Christian missionary endeavours were so closely enmeshed that religious salvation became a key component in philanthropic work.[27] As a result of the transparent evangelical drive of child welfare organizations, the visual and literary imagery produced was filled with Christ-

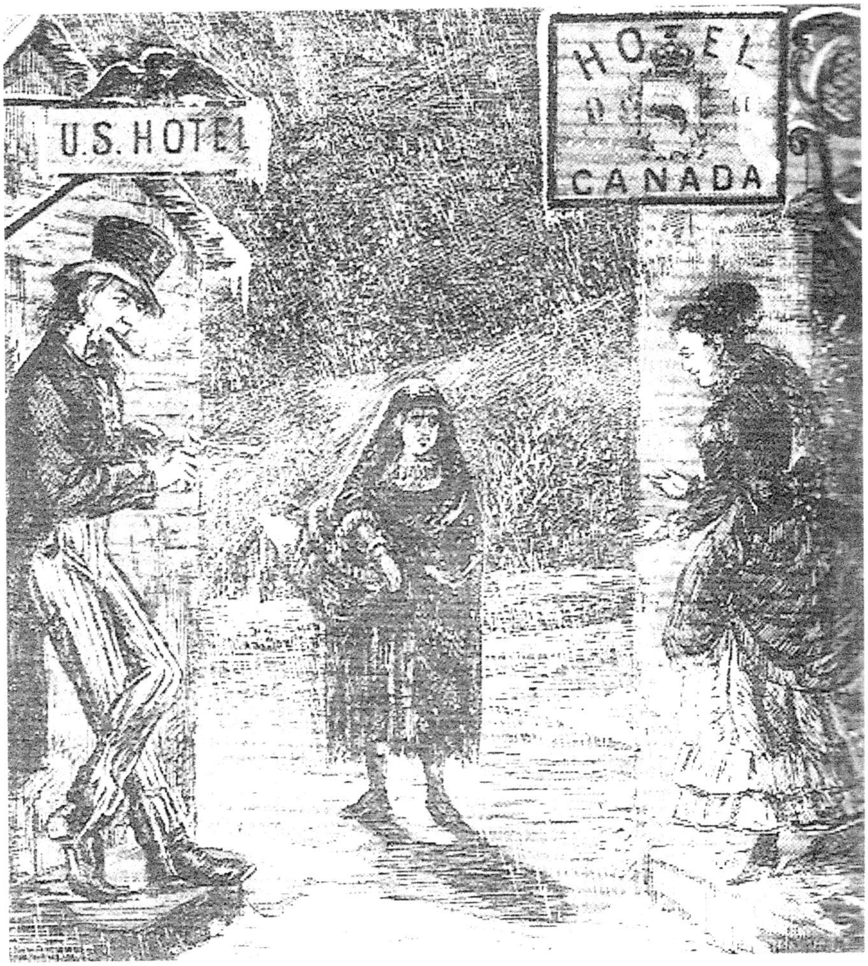

FIGURE 6.2
"The Situation." Illustrator unknown. *Canadian Illustrated News* 1, no. 13 (January 29, 1870): 193.

ian symbolism. Religious iconography was drawn upon to appeal to the virtues of charity, forgiveness, and redemption. Each act in the saving of the destitute souls became significant; bathing their filthy charges implied not only a physical cleansing but also a spiritual baptism. The journey to Canada was framed as a religious pilgrimage that would transform the souls of the children. The Canadian setting also was key to a spiritual rebirth, for it removed the little emigrants from their previous sinful environment. As an agricultural society, the young country of Canada was viewed as more pious and temperate than the eroding morals that had manifested as a result of industrialization in Great Britain.[28]

For children, the raw materials "from which the 'dangerous' classes were formed,"[29] the transformation process involved in emigration had a distinct moralistic agenda closely linked to the spiritual conversion facilitated by emigration. Reflecting dominant Protestant convictions of the child welfare movement, the instillment of a distinct work ethic was viewed as the solution to moral depravity. Throughout the promotional imagery created, labour, particularly agricultural work, was glorified as the ultimate path to salvation.[30] Imbued with religious symbolism, difficult labour was necessary in the physically demanding settlement of Canada and was considered integral to a proper upbringing. To avoid the temptations of idleness, Canadians were noted for "putting children to work at a very early age."[31] Through hard work and a newly endowed civic responsibility, the basis of physical, moral, and spiritual well-being was instilled in orphans, waifs, and strays.

The agricultural nature of home children's labour also provided vivid imagery for publicity. In drastic contrast to the dismal corruption of urban slums, in Canada children would be engaged in wholesome outdoor activities, "free to roam the fields, explore the woods, pick wildflowers, chase rabbits, chipmunks and squirrels."[32] The outdoors provided a fitting contrast to the cramped, urban areas from which they were being removed. Founder of the Orphan Homes of Scotland, Quarrier saw as his role to "care for the little mites and fragments of humanity ... picked up from the great desert of human need, and planted in the paradise of God's manifested care."[33] In promotional imagery, children are often shown in lush Arcadian settings, providing for analogies between the children and the bountifulness of plants and trees. Canada offered new possibilities and opportunities to blossom; Macpherson described emigration as "spring transplanting."[34] A popular indicator of public consciousness, *Punch* magazine published a cartoon with the caption, "Teaching promotes the vigor of the seed, and a right training hearts of oak will breed."[35]

Whether children were trained in workshops before being emigrated or apprenticed with a Canadian family, their training was integral to the transformation process initiated by child welfare organizations. During the late nineteenth century, the increasingly undesirable side effects of urbanization and industrialization had created a romanticized view of preindustrial labour. Child welfare reformers had made part of the rehabilitation process an education in "wholesome" skills to be practised outside the city limits, in contrast to the sinfulness of the city. Emphasis was placed on craftsmanship that would encourage a sense of pride in the children and an investment in their production that was missing in the alienation of mass-produced factory work. Unfortunately, many of the skills that were instilled in the children were trades that were being made obsolete by the very industrialization that had contributed to the present labour situation. Although trades such as carpentry, blacksmithing, cobbling, and farming often had mythological and religious symbolism, these skills were no longer considered necessary in Great Britain. However, in Canada there was a high demand for skilled workers trained in trades that would be useful to agricultural development. Not only was Canada a symbolically loaded destination, it also provided an answer to some of the logistical oversights created by the misguided training of the children in workhouses and orphanages.

Initially the goal was to reform the "moral depravity" of the children through training practical skills, for the dual values of domesticity and productivity were key aspects of British citizenship.[36] However, these mandates quickly expanded to include a more international focus on "imperial citizenship" throughout Great Britain's colonies.[37] Ironically, it was the emigration process that often re-established many of the home children's identities as British citizens. Part of the dramatic imagining of the poor was the distinct "othering" that led them to be depicted as "wild 'Arabs' separate from the civilized English population."[38] Orphans, waifs, and strays, were initially portrayed as being distinctly un-British and likened to an entirely different ethnicity. Throughout Victorian media, the poor became characterized as a "nomadic race" separate from the rest of English society.[39] Child welfare reformers were concerned that without their direct intervention, children who had been allowed to run wild, as a result of parental absence or incompentency, would morally corrupt the entire lower classes and threaten social stability. To emphasize the risk they posed to social order, nomadic children were constructed as a racialized other[40] and commonly described as "street-Arabs." In direct consequence of this overt "othering," poor children within the cities made ideal targets for the civilizing missions of child welfare groups that echoed colonial aspirations throughout the empire.

One of the most motivational images in child philanthropy was the transformation from savage to civilized. The process reflected the belief that

> education not only in books, but in work, transforms with astonishing rapidity and completeness even the facial and bodily characteristics of the street-Arabs.... In this metamorphosis we have a promise for the future. An addition of energy to the national life, an improvement of the physical type of the race, rescue of thousands from a life of squalor and dependence.[41]

Literally and figuratively, the moral and spiritual rehabilitation process administered by the organizations cleansed the children, allowing them to become "white" again and completing the transformation from "street-Arab" to functioning British citizen.[42] Upon their transformation, the children were reborn as ideal representatives of Britain destined to flourish throughout the empire.

Juvenile emigration schemes were a way of maintaining the purity of the Anglo-Saxon race throughout the empire. During this time of imperial expansion, children were viewed not only as a means of keeping the bloodlines of the dominion pure, but also as a strategic way of developing the British Empire.[43] Groups such as the Church of England Waifs and Strays Society advertised home children as "Links of Empire: Welded by the Church of England Waifs and Stray Society" with "More Links Fresh from the Forge."[44] The increasing need for strong connections to colonies became apparent after "uprisings" such as the Boer War in South Africa in 1899. By strategically placing children in colonial countries such as Canada, child emigration schemes ensured populations that would be sympathetic to British concerns. Philanthropists were applauded for their efforts, as Prime Minister Lord Rosebery (1847–1929) declared:

> An empire such as ours requires as its first condition an imperial race—a race vigorous and industrious and intrepid ...remember that where you promote health and arrest disease, where you convert an unhealthy citizen into a healthy one ... you, in doing your duty, are working for the empire.[45]

Pamphlets depicting "before and after" images of the moral, spiritual, and physical transformations initiated by the organizations were extremely valuable methods of publicity. Promotional pamphlets and educational articles were filled with very romantic, melodramatic imagery typical of the Victorian era that encouraged binary oppositions in which notions of good and evil, lazy and industrious, rich and poor, and urban and rural were dichotomized.[46] By emphasizing the visual oppositions in their extremely popular "before and after" images, child welfare organizations were able to showcase results of their interventions. Although Barnardo is most well known for his "artistic fictions," others, such as Quarrier, "the Orphans' Friend," used striking visuals depicting those before, "needing help," and after, "helped." Dirty, ratty, wild-looking children were shown "as received" and then later as clean, civilized, and productive members of society.[47] Like many other Victorian conversion narratives, "before and after" photographs, combined with promotional literature, became an extremely popular method for child welfare agencies to convey their evangelical aspirations to a wide audience.[48] Not only did these images serve as advertisements, but they also now serve as valuable visual records of a segment of society that "had been virtually ignored by the camera."[49] Many examples of photography produced by child-emigrating philanthropic agencies occupy a unique genre somewhere between the "art photography" of Oscar Gustav Rejlander (1813–1875) and Henry Peach Robinson (1830–1901) and what was perceived by the public as more "documentary" accounts by investigative photographers such as Lewis W. Hine (1874–1940).

"E.E.J.M. Home for Working & Destitute Lads" (fig. 6.3) is a typical example of the pairing of two complementary photographs for pamphlets and *cartes de visite* that

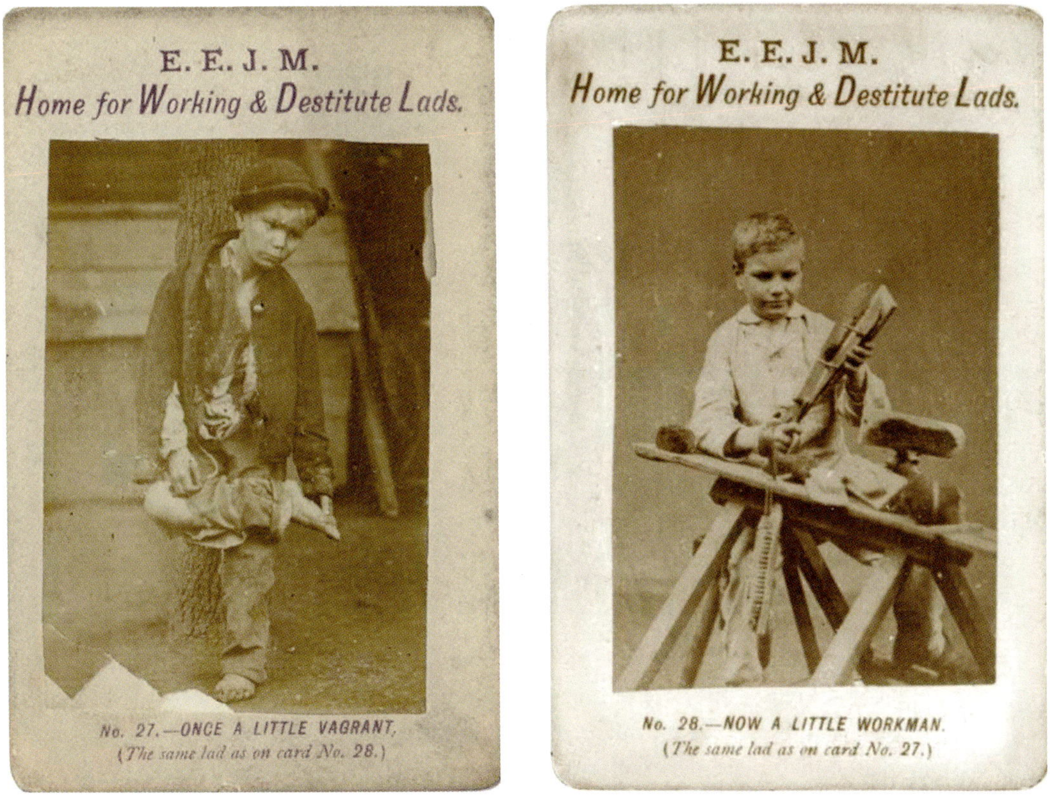

FIGURE 6.3 "E.E.J.M. Home for Working & Destitute Lads." (Photo by Thomas Barnes [?], n.d. Barnardo's Photographic Archive)

Barnardo began publishing in the early 1870s. In the first image, a rescued urchin is shown as "Once a Little Vagrant," barefoot and in ragged clothes and looking mournfully away from the viewer. In the second image, he appears again, "Now a Little Workman," reformed in neat, clean clothing and concentrating on his newly acquired skill. The boy's "physical and moral transformation" is symbolically indicated by his healthy appearance and proper clothing, conveying an "industrious appearance."[50] The same children shown previously as ragged and later "scrubbed and shining and training to do an honest day's work"[51] overtly conveys the values that philanthropic groups were attempting to instill in their charges. Although these contrasting photographs are meant to convey the dramatic transformation process initiated by the agency, these two photos were in fact taken on the same day,[52] revealing just how prevalent and masterful the staging of images was at the time.

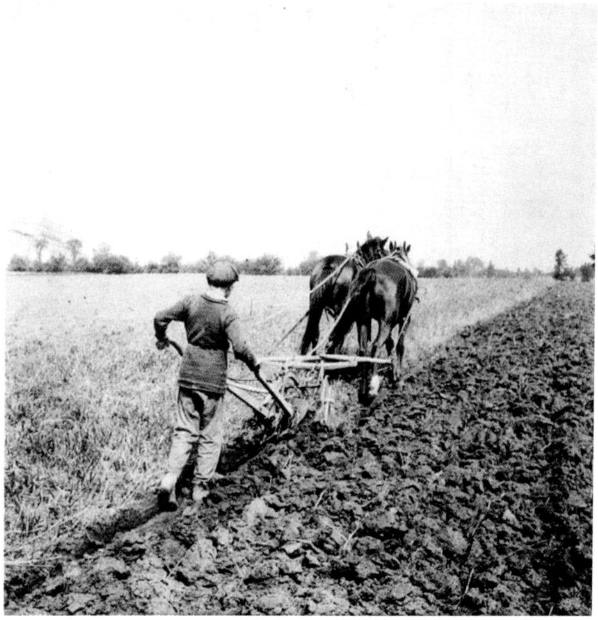

FIGURE 6.4
"A Boy Ploughing at Dr. Barnardo's Industrial Farm," Russell, Manitoba, c. 1900. (Photographer unknown. Library and Archives Canada, copy negative PA-117285)

Compared to the careful documentation of children processed by the Barnardo homes and other philanthropic agencies in Britain, very few images exist of home children after their placement with rural Canadian families. Some institutions such as Rye's took photographs of smiling children smartly turned out in the set of clothes issued to them upon their arrival in the new country. However, once placed with a family in a rural setting, the children were once again part of a demographic of people that was seldom photographed. The images that do exist of home children transplanted in Canada are often carefully contrived extensions of the "after" images.

At some point after the turn of the century, it appears that the Barnardo farm, in Russell, Manitoba, hired the "Davidson Brothers" to document the agricultural training that child immigrants received. One of the few remaining images, possibly by the Davidson Brothers, "A Boy Ploughing at Dr. Barnardo's Industrial Farm" (fig. 6.4), can be read as replicating common "artistic fiction" that marketed children as commodities. The sheer logistics of hiring a photographer and setting up the camera and equipment, combined with the careful composition of the image, suggest that like many photographs of the time, it was less a candid action shot and more of a posed event similar to the precedent in Barnardo's photographic production back in England. The boy is shown from behind, anonymous, symbolic of the labouring resources churned out by the emigration organizations. Like the horses echoing his form, he is a worker, a beast of burden. At his feet, the rich, fertile Canadian soil is being tilled, undergoing a process of cultivation similar to the one he has experienced under the protection of child welfare reformation. In the following essay, Margaret McNay provides a further analysis of "Boy Ploughing" that contributes to an understanding of the issues surrounding the life and work of home children in Canada. As in other "artistic fictions," this image is ripe with the symbolism of Barnardo's other promotional imagery.

"Boy Ploughing" can be viewed as engaging with centuries of Anglo-Saxon iconography associated with ideas of farming. Resonating with the social preoccupations of the time, the image of the boy ploughing supports the suggestion that "actions and objects which are crucial to the well-being of society are laden with symbolic significance."[53] Agriculture was a crucial element in the development of Canada at the turn of the century, but it also resonated with philanthropists' idealization of preindustrial labour. Biblical archetypes of the ploughman further emphasize the theme of religious salvation within emigration schemes. "Boy Ploughing" is the embodiment of 1 Corinthians 9:10 promise that "he that ploweth should plow in hope."[54] As well as providing powerful imagery of the "good Christian" produced, the notion of farming provided a sense of agency, easily glorified in the agricultural work of home children. In parallel narratives present in Christian literature, the work of child welfare agencies can be viewed in the cultivation of children as ideal British citizens, with similar biblical references such as "On the wild field amid the ruins of evil lordship and capital, we shall drive our plough, and gather a good harvest of happiness for the whole working people."[55]

A similar unidentified photograph, "T.B. with a Young Steer" (fig. 6.5), displays the same conventions used in "Boy Ploughing." As in other examples, there is no indication of the negative implications of indentured labour, but rather only the hope and glory of hard work. The road behind the boy disappears into the horizon, a reminder of the distance he has come as well as his bright future. Posing with a strong young steer, the boy is showcased as a wholesome product of the farm, living the good life in the dominions. "Placid, gentle, and known to be a source of wholesome dairy and meat products," the steer, as in other images of cattle popular at the time, "symbolized the virtues of an agrarian life, which seemed increasingly to represent the antithesis of the hectic speed, questionable ethics and constant change of modern urban life."[56] In contrast to the "characteristic physical type of town dweller; stunted narrow-chested, easily weary,"[57] labour has transformed this boy to a sturdy, vivacious Briton "fit to be a strength and not a burden to the nation."[58]

In both these images what is most important, as in many Canadian images depicting home children, is the outdoor setting. Contrary to "after" photographs taken in England against ambiguous studio backdrops, child emigration schemes were so dependent on the romantic imagining of the hope and possibilities of overseas destinations that

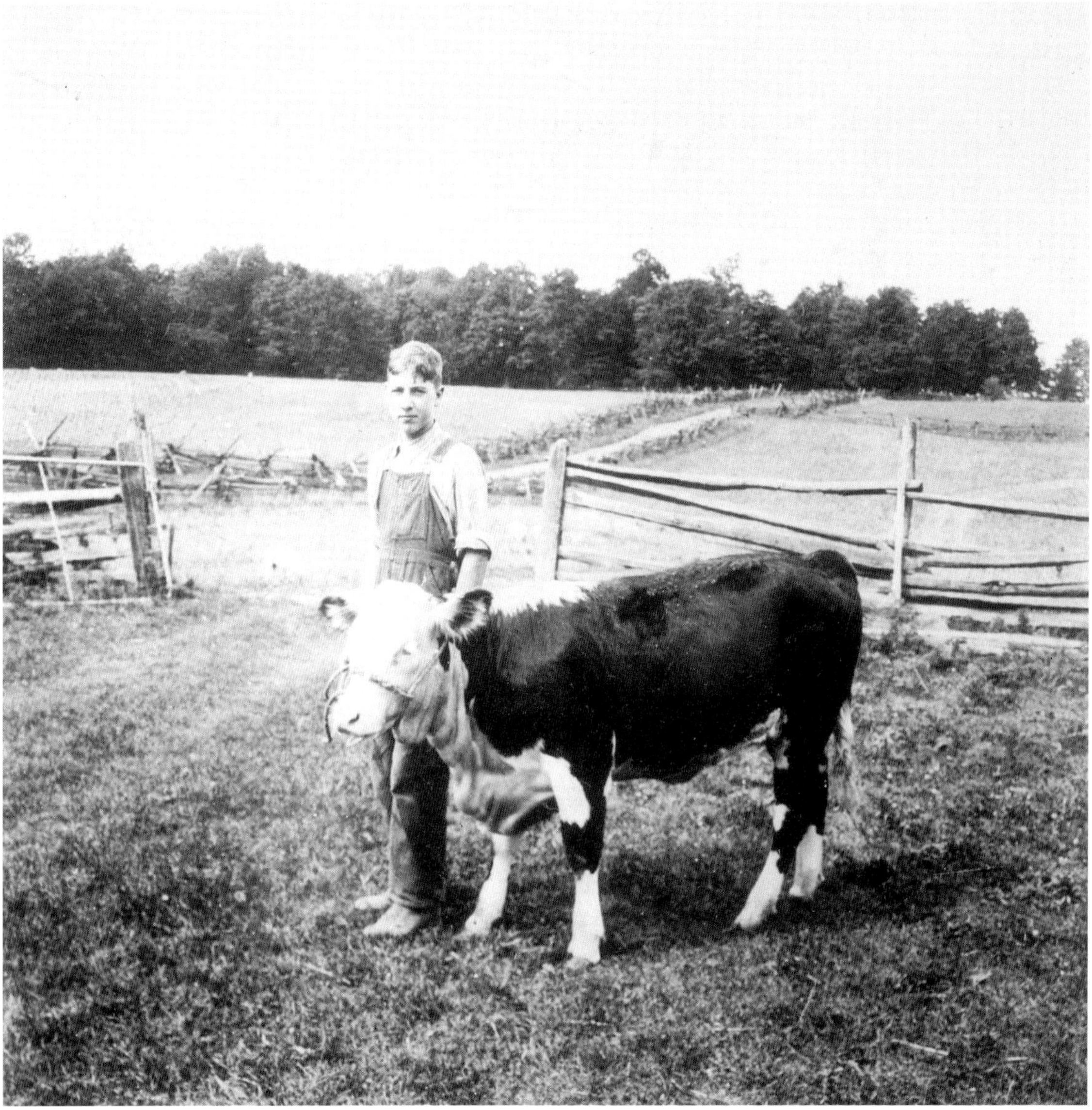

FIGURE 6.5 "T.B. with a Young Steer" (1915). (Photographer unknown. Library and Archives Canada PA-117284)

such settings became a requirement in highly symbolic photographs. The bright, open expanse of land is in drastic contrast to the dark, cramped, close, flat images of dirty street life that had been planted in the viewers' imagination, and from which the young men had been rescued. The depth of the picture plane emphasizes the room available to breathe; in Canada, unlike Great Britain, there was room to grow and prosper. This belief catered to common conceptions of Canada in the Victorian imagination but was also closely linked to ideas of poverty. Popular beliefs surrounding the "indoor poor" greatly influenced the depiction of children in visual culture. Turn-of-the-century social welfare work reveals that there was a general distinction made between the "indoor poor," supported entirely by the state, and the "outdoor poor," who were temporarily down on their luck but had the potential to be productive members of society.[59]

Perhaps the best example of the ways in which the convoluted realities and mythologies surrounding child emigration entered the Victorian cultural consciousness is presented in the children's novel *Dusty Diamonds Cut and Polished: A Tale of City-Arab Life and Adventure.* Written in 1884 by Robert Michael Ballantyne (1825–1894), an author of popular children's imperialistic adventures, the story illustrates the cohesion between visual and textual imagery resulting from philanthropic projections. Like Ballantyne's other stories, such as *The Settler and the Savage* (1877), *The Young Fur Traders* (1856), and *Ungava: A Tale of Esquimaux-Land* (1858), *Dusty Diamonds*' distinct Christian and civilizing forces are outlined as European power is exercised through the experience of the protagonist.[60]

Described by the author as "founded on well-authenticated facts,"[61] most notably nonfictional reports by Barnardo and other child rescue agencies, *Dusty Diamonds* not only weaves in moralistic anecdotes to a dramatic adventure story, but more importantly incorporates statistical information and key figures from the height of the child emigration movement into the tale. Early in the story, while discussing a city Arab, claiming that "to a Londoner any description of this boy, would be superfluous," Ballantyne provides detailed statistics, noting that specifically 11,835 children were lost on the streets of London, and 23 were never to be found.[62] The work of all the major child welfare agencies is also included, providing a fascinating crossover between fact and fiction echoing the layers of public consciousness also present in photography of the time. Macpherson is noted as "the lady ... who sends out so many rescued waifs and strays to Canada, and spends all her time in caring for the poorest of the poor in the East-End and in preaching the gospel to them."[63] Similarly, "there is that noble work carried on by Miss Rye of the Emigration Home for Destitute Little Girls, at the Avenue House, Peckham, from which a stream of destitute little ones continually flows to Canada."[64] Ballantyne also introduces Barnardo,

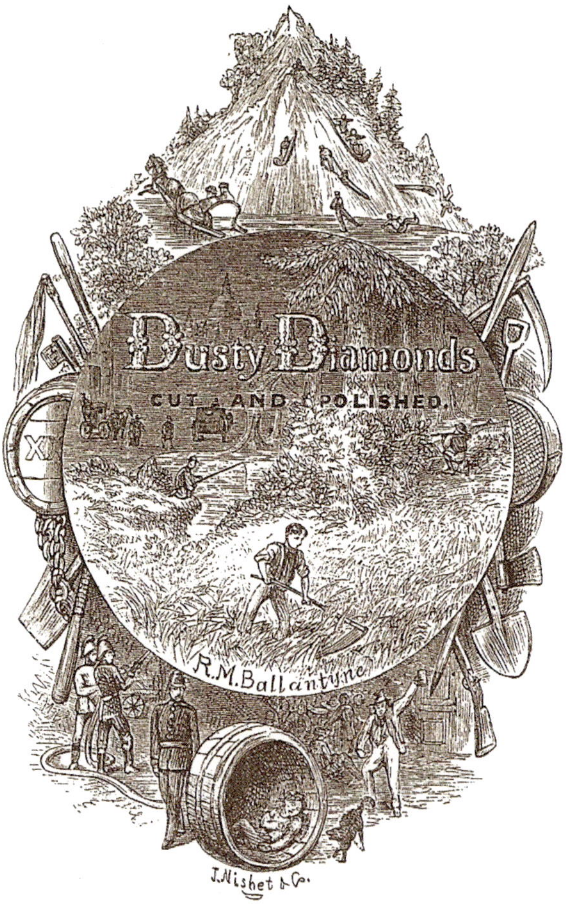

FIGURE 6.6
Frontispiece to R.M. Ballantyne, *Dusty Diamonds Cut and Polished: A Tale of City-Arab Life and Adventure* (London: J. Nisbet, 1884).

> whose Home for Working and Destitute Boys, in Stepney Causeway, is a shelter from which thousands of rescued little ones go forth to labour as honest and useful members of society, instead of dying miserably in the slums of London, or growing up to recruit the ranks of our criminal classes.[65]

The epic adventure follows the rehabilitation of two "city-Arabs" and their blossoming in the wilderness of Canada, facilitated by Macpherson's philanthropic intervention. The tale picks up on the themes of refinement through Canadian apprenticeship by describing a pauper as a "diamond from the London diggings, who had been imported the year before … was undergoing the process of being polished, and gave promise of soon becoming a very valuable gem."[66] *Dusty Diamonds* is an excellent example of how "artistic fictions" very much based in facts expanded beyond the use of embellished imagery to enforce and explain social responses to poverty.

Ironically, very few if any home children would have read Ballantyne's accounts of the home child's experience. However, his narrative overtly fulfills an adult agenda, ultimately conveying popular attitudes and values that had shaped philanthropists' motivations. This story would have appealed to the children of the upper middle class, a demographic that ultimately dictated the dominant societal values and implemented child emigration schemes. The message Ballantyne projects to a young audience attempts to instill very specific Victorian value systems and imperial identity. During the peak of child emigration, an array of literature was produced specifically to morally educate children.[67]

Just as Ballantyne's fictional account of a home child echoes expository journalism of the time, the frontispiece illustration displays much of the same carefully constructed symbolism that appears in photographs of children presented by child welfare organizations. The frontispiece illustration (fig. 6.6) epitomizes the iconographical language used to represent the plight of "street-Arabs" of the time. At the bottom of the image, the protagonist is shown sleeping in a barrel, cowering in the dark. He is no better than the mangy dog that barks at him. Echoing the round framing of the barrel, the boy is depicted again in a large circle after his transformative pilgrimage to the New World. He is strong and upright; threshing hay, he is now an active participant in his environment. This image glorifies preindustrial labour by employing the traditional agricultural vocabulary of manuscript illuminations, particularly those found in a book of hours.[68] In contrast to the dark, shadowy underworld of the boy's former life, a pristine white mountain teaming with robust, healthy pioneers thrusts heavenward. Surrounding the central tondo are rifles, axes, shovels, scythes, and other masculine tools of empire building.

Taken directly from the promotional literature of philanthropic organizations of the time, Ballantyne's richly symbolic transformation of the "the little gem that had been dug out of the London mines"[69] can be viewed as a curious combination of fact and fiction reflecting popular metaphors for the refinement process instituted by child welfare agencies. Vivid imaginings reveal powerful manipulations of fact that were used to represent distinct contemporary social and spiritual truths.[70] During the height of Britain's imperial aspirations, numerous child welfare agencies actively participated in reforming destitute children into productive members of the empire. Advertising, photographs, cartoons, editorials, and children's literature all reveal how text and images formed an "artistic fiction" of the orphans, waifs, and strays that were to become Canada's home children.

Notes

1 Seth Koven, *Slumming: Sexual and Social Politics in Victorian London* (Princeton: Princeton University Press, 2004), 88.
2 Joy Parr, *Labouring Children: British Immigrant Apprentices to Canada, 1869–1924* (Montreal: McGill-Queen's University Press, 1980), 33.
3 "Twenty-Seventh Annual Report of the Manchester and Salford Boys and Girls Refuge for the Year Ending December 31, 1896," quoted in Brian Raychaba, "Generally In Order to Get Cheap Labour: British Child Workers in Canada," *Mirror* 10 (1989): 79.
4 Gillian Wagner, *Children of the Empire* (London: Weidenfeld & Nicholson, 1982), xv.
5 Marjorie Kohli, *The Golden Bridge: Young Immigrants to Canada, 1833–1939* (Toronto: Natural Heritage Books, 2003), 9.
6 Maria Rye, quoted in Wagner, *Children of the Empire*, 41.
7 Koven, *Slumming*, 133.
8 Valerie Lloyd, "The Camera and Dr. Barnardo," in Thomas John Barnardo, *The Camera and Dr. Barnardo*, 11–17 (London: National Portrait Gallery, 1974), 15.
9 Marta Wiess, "Staged Photography in the Victorian Album," in *Acting the Part: Photography as Theatre*, ed. Lori Pauli, 99–132 (New York: Merrell, 2006), 81.
10 Lori Pauli, "Setting the Scene," *Acting the Part: Photography as Theatre* (New York: Merrell, 2006), 16.
11 A.D. Coleman, "The Directorial Mode: Notes Toward a Definition," in *Light Readings: A Photography Critic's Writings 1968–1978* (New York: Oxford University Press, 1979), 252.
12 Lloyd, "The Camera and Dr. Barnardo," 12.
13 Koven, *Slumming*, 93.
14 Evelyn Sharp, quoted in Lionel Rose, *The Erosion of Childhood: Child Oppression in Britain, 1860–1918* (London: Routledge, 1991), 82.
15 Rose, *Erosion of Childhood*, 82.
16 Koven, *Slumming*, 116.
17 Ibid., 107.
18 Parr, *Labouring Children*, 142.
19 Thomas J. Barnardo, quoted in Gail H. Corbett, *Barnardo Children in Canada* (Peterborough, ON: Woodland, 1981), 20.
20 Neil Sutherland, *Children in English-Canadian Society: Framing the Twentieth-Century Consensus* (Toronto: University of Toronto Press, 1976), 10.
21 J. Wesley Beady, *Doctor Barnardo: Physician, Pioneer, Prophet* (London: George Allen, 1930), 217.
22 Raychaba, "Generally in Order to Get Cheap Labour," 83.
23 Ibid., 81.
24 Corbett, *Barnardo Children in Canada*, 76.
25 Parr, *Labouring Children*, 33.
26 "The Situation," *The Canadian Illustrated News* 1, no. 13 (January 29, 1870): 193.
27 Parr, *Labouring Children*, 27.
28 Ibid., 46.
29 Ibid., 33.
30 Lydia Murdoch, *Imagined Orphans: Poor Families, Child Welfare and Contested Citizenship in London* (London: Rutgers University Press, 2006), 125.
31 Sutherland, *Children in English-Canadian Society*, 10.
32 Corbett, *Barnardo Children in Canada*, 54.

33 John Climie, *William Quarrier: The Orphan's Friend* (Glasgow: Pickering & Inglis, 1905), 12.
34 Parr, *Labouring Children*, 46.
35 *Punch*, 1876, quoted in Murdoch, *Imagined Orphans*, 120.
36 Murdoch, *Imagined Orphans*, 26.
37 Ibid., 131.
38 Ibid., 26.
39 Ibid., 25.
40 Koven, *Slumming*, 131.
41 Murdoch, *Imagined Orphans*, 120.
42 Ibid., 141.
43 Raychaba, "Generally in Order to Get Cheap Labour," 83.
44 Philip Bean and Joy Melville, *Lost Children of the Empire* (London: Unwin Hymen, 1989), 146.
45 Quoted in Wagner, *Children of the Empire*, 120.
46 Rohan McWilliam, quoted in Murdoch, *Imagined Orphans*, 15.
47 Climie, *William Quarrier*, 11.
48 Murdoch, *Imagined Orphans*, 36.
49 Lloyd, "The Camera and Dr. Barnardo," 11.
50 Murdoch, *Imagined Orphans*, 36.
51 Lloyd, "The Camera and Dr. Barnardo," 12.
52 Ibid., 20.
53 Michael Camille, "Labouring for the Lord: The Ploughman and the Social Order in the Luttrell Psalter," *Art History* 10, no. 4 (December 1987): 430.
54 Ibid., 430.
55 Ibid., 448.
56 Annette Stott, *Holland Mania: The Unknown Dutch Period in American Art and Culture* (Woodstock, NY: Overlook Press, 1998), 55.
57 Parr, *Labouring Children*, 142.
58 Raychaba, "Generally in Order to Get Cheap Labour," 83.
59 Octave Thanet, "The Indoor Pauper: A Study," *The Atlantic Monthly* 47, no. 284 (June 1881): n.p.
60 Stuart Hannabuss, "Ballantyne's Message of Empire," in *Imperialism and Juvenile Literature*, ed. Jeffery Richards, 53–71 (Manchester: Manchester University Press, 1989), 54.
61 R.M. Ballantyne, *Dusty Diamonds Cut and Polished: A Tale of City-Arab Life and Adventure* (London: J. Nisbet, 1884), iii.
62 Ibid., 40.
63 Ibid., 92.
64 Ibid., 66.
65 Ibid., 120.
66 Ibid., 267.
67 Rose, *Erosion of Childhood*, 84.
68 Camille, "Labouring for the Lord," 431.
69 Ballantyne, *Dusty Diamonds Cut and Polished*, 121.
70 Koven, *Slumming*, 96.

MARGARET MCNAY

IMMIGRANTS, LABOURERS, "OTHERS"
Canada's Home Children

MY FATHER NEVER TALKED ABOUT HIS *childhood or family. He disclosed little more about his past than that he had been born in Glasgow and farmed in Ontario. I gathered he had come to Canada when still of school age and I assumed he had immigrated with his family but if I asked about his parents or whether he had brothers or sisters he became silent and turned away. When he was ready to claim a pension, I thought it strange he had no proof of his age, and stranger still that, after he wrote to the Scottish Record Office in Edinburgh for a copy of the registration of his birth, the document that arrived showed he had been born in Ayrshire, not Glasgow, and that he was three years older than he had thought. He offered no explanation and my mother said only, "Your dad had a hard life." He died in 1983, never having revealed to his daughters the stories of his childhood and youth.*

Then one day my mother, almost inadvertently, disclosed the secret she had helped my father keep for the forty years of their marriage—the secret she had kept for the fifteen years since he had died and that I believe she had meant to keep forever: "Your Dad was a home child, you know," she said, nothing more, and never spoke about it again. Indeed, my father had been one of tens of thousands of children between the ages of three and fourteen who in the late nineteenth and early twentieth centuries had been placed in rescue and orphan homes in Great Britain and subsequently emigrated to Canada. Some such children had been orphaned or abandoned; others, my father and his siblings among them, had been surrendered into care when their families could no longer provide for them. Between 1869 and 1933, an estimated 80,000 children—including in 1920 the boy just turned thirteen who would eventually become my father—were sent to Canada.

I accepted my parents' silence about my father's life, but with a certain sense of loss and, yes, guilt. Somehow it seemed wrong, uncaring, even disrespectful, that a daughter should know so little about her father's history. Perhaps I also felt, on the one hand, that his silence was somehow a fault on my part, and, on the other, that I was being denied something to which I was entitled. The rich heritage of my mother's family, the narratives of her life, were set in my mind against the void that was my father's life. Thus I lived with a certain emptiness, an incomplete narrative inheritance,[1] *an absent memory,*[2] *and perhaps it was inevitable that one day I should search out my father's story and write about it.*[3] *The task of mourning, and of honouring his life, seemed impossible to finish until I did so. As well, suggests Goodall, "What we inherit narratively from our forebears provides us with a framework for understanding our identity through theirs."*[4]

Beginning with the publication of four books between 1979 and 1981—Kenneth Bagnell's best-seller, *The Little Immigrants*,[5] Gail Corbett's *Barnardo Children in Canada*,[6] Phyllis Harrison's *The Home Children: Their Personal Stories*,[7] and Joy Parr's meticulously researched *Labouring Children: British Immigrant Apprentices to Canada, 1869–1924*[8]—the phenomenon of child migration and the stories of the children's lives, individually and collectively, began to be recounted for the first time. In the 1990s, child emigration to Australia was the subject of an exposé by Margaret Humphreys[9] and a special investigation by the British parliament,[10] and, in the new century, an international conference.[11] Websites such as Home Children Canada[12] and Quarrier's Canadian Family[13] have helped thousands of Canadians find the child immigrants in their family histories, and documentaries such as the National Film Board of Canada's *Welcome Home*[14] and Lockwood Film's more recent production, *Nobody's Child: Canada's Home Children*[15] have made the story available to television audiences. Over the past twenty-five years, British child emigration has been researched and theorized by scholars from a variety of disciplines.[16] The saga of the home children is part of the history of Canada and the British Empire; part of the history of immigration, settlement, and agriculture in Canada; part of the history of childhood, child labour, and social welfare; and part of the history of who we are as Canadians. As well, it is part of the personal history of Canadians such as I who have discovered, often belatedly, a link with a still somewhat little known past.

Among thousands of photographs of children in archives, museums, and libraries across Canada are a relative few, scattered under subject headings such as "Immigration and Colonization," "Health and Welfare," and "Agriculture," that identify their subjects as "home children." The provenance of most of these photographs is linked to one of the major nineteenth-century children's emigration homes—to, for example, the Barnardo, Quarrier, Macpherson, Stephenson, or Fegan homes, or the homes of the Church of England's Waifs and Strays Society. The Barnardo organization, in particular, made extensive use of the camera,[17] and today maintains a rich photographic archive.[18] Photographs of home children also survive in historical documents, books, and other publications, and in private collections and family albums. Here I present seven photographs—two of children sponsored by Thomas Barnardo, one of a group of girls associated with Annie Macpherson, and four of children from William Quarrier's homes.

Without an understanding of the British child emigration movement and the context of the photographs, one would have difficulty reading them. Meaning, like memory, is constructed in the mind of a viewer:

> Memories evoked by a photo do not simply spring out of the image itself, but are generated in a network, an intertext of discourses that shift between past and present, spectator and image, and between all these and cultural contexts, historical moments. In this network, the image itself figures largely as a trace, a clue: necessary but not sufficient, to the activity of meaning making; always pointing somewhere else.[19]

I begin below, therefore, with a brief recounting of the circumstances surrounding child immigration to Canada, and then turn to the photographs themselves, each of which depicts child immigrants *in* Canada or, in the case of figure 7.1, on a ship bound for Canada. I have chosen photographs that symbolize three themes in home children's lives: their status as immigrants, as labourers, and as "others." Of course, I am also seeking memories—the memories that my father repressed, that my mother kept secret, that were absent from my life—that now I might create for the first time.

The Background

British child emigration began in the seventeenth century and continued for 350 years. The first child emigrants were sent to Virginia Colony in 1618 and the last, nine boys, to Australia in 1967. The peak of the movement occurred between 1869 and 1933 when an estimated 150,000 children were sent to Canada, Australia, New Zealand, and South Africa. Today, 11.5 percent of Canadians are thought to be descended from the more than 80,000 children who made the journey to this country.[20]

Child emigration was a way for Britain to deal with widespread poverty and enormous numbers of orphaned or otherwise destitute children. Two complementary beliefs, one based in fear, the other in hope, helped to rationalize the scheme. The fear was that orphaned and destitute children would, if left "untreated," become "'foul sewage' stagnating beneath [Great Britain's] 'social fabric.'"[21] The hope was that countries such as Canada could offer a future to children who otherwise had none. Rural settings, which could provide fresh air and outdoor work, seemed to romantic Victorian minds to represent all that was moral and good, and family life all that was civilizing. Farm life in the new country would, it was thought, enable children to grow into healthy, hard-working, independent adults.

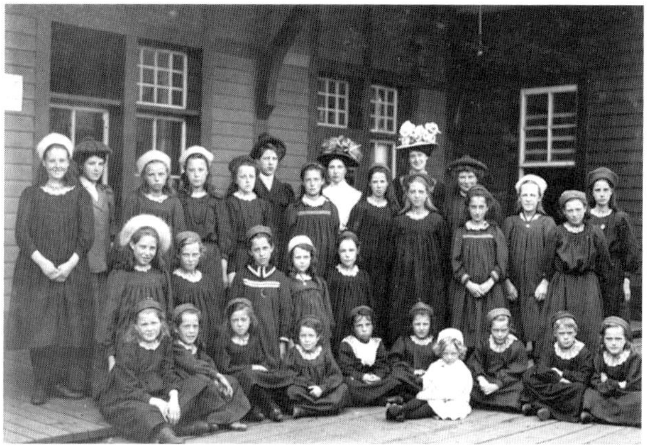

FIGURE 7.2
Group of immigrant girls en route to a home at Stratford, Ontario, 1908. (Photographer unknown. Library and Archives Canada, negative PA-020906)

Upon arriving in Canada, usually in Halifax, Saint John, Quebec City, or Montreal, child immigrants travelled by train to a local orphanage or distributing home. Depending on the sending institution, they might go to a Barnardo home such as Hazelbrae in Peterborough, Ontario, or to a Barnardo farm in Manitoba or New Brunswick. Or they might go to a home in Ontario associated with Annie Macpherson—Blair Athol in Galt, Marchmont in Belleville, or the Macpherson Home in Stratford—or to William Quarrier's home, Fairknowe, in Brockville, Ontario; to John T. Middlemore's home, Guthrie House, in London, Ontario; or to still other distributing homes in other cities and towns across the country. Figure 7.2 shows a group of twenty-eight girls en route to one of the best-known distributing homes, the Macpherson home in Stratford, Ontario.

The "group of immigrant girls" pictured in figure 7.2 poses with three chaperones (back row) on the platform of a train station. Except for the girl on the far left who is smiling broadly, most of the girls are frowning. Perhaps they are squinting in the light, but one can imagine they may also be tired and irritable. The smallest child, particularly noticeable in her light-coloured dress and hat, sits in front. Might she be five or six? The other girls appear to range in age to their mid or late teens. They are dressed similarly, the younger girls in yoked dresses, a few older girls in dresses with waists, and most with lace collars. One of the chaperones wears a particularly large, elaborately adorned hat, much in the style of the period. The hat, and her broad smile, distinguish her from the other chaperones and perhaps signify her higher status in the group, or her desire for status. Two girls who appear to be the oldest in the group wear Scottish tams, and one (second from left in the back row) wears a suit rather than a dress—perhaps she is a helper to the chaperones rather than

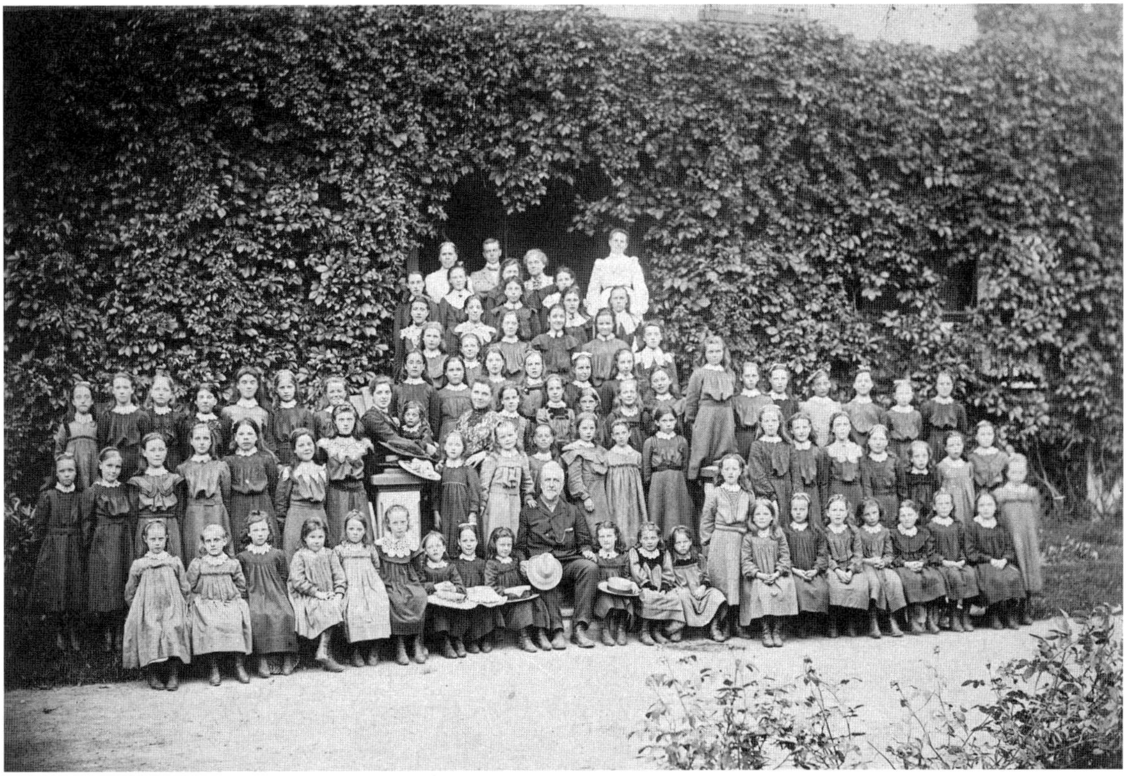

FIGURE 7.3 "Party of 84 girls from Bridge-of-Weir, Scotland. Reached Fairknowe Home, Brockville, Ont., 18th July 1905." (Photographer unknown. John Joseph Kelso/Library and Archives Canada, copy negative C-086392)

an immigrant. Several girls wear white or light-coloured hats with turned-up brims; others wear straw pillbox hats.

Few symbols evoke a sense of travel and impermanence more strongly than do trains and train stations. The stationhouse at which these girls wait appears well built and strong, promising them shelter and protection. They, nevertheless, wait outside. This is a temporary place, a place for passing through, not a place for staying, and it is, perhaps, symbolic of the impermanence and transitions the girls have experienced and have yet to experience in their lives.

Figure 7.3, taken in 1905, shows a group of eighty-four girls who have travelled from Quarrier's homes in Scotland to the Fairknowe home in Brockville, Ontario. It was only the third group of children, and the first party of girls, to be emigrated from the Orphan Homes of Scotland since Quarrier, insulted and angered by new legislation in Ontario that placed child immigrants under official control and required all immigration homes to be licensed, had stubbornly discontinued emigration work in 1897.[24] One is struck not only by the large number of children but by how young some of them are, perhaps as young as five or six. As do the girls in figure 7.2, the younger girls wear yoked dresses, the older girls wear dresses with waists, and most wear lace collars. Quarrier believed in recognizing children's individuality; thus, the girls' dresses differ in details of style and colour rather more than do the dresses of the girls in figure 7.2.

Children who came through Fairknowe were photographed at the front entrance to the house, which here is almost completely hidden behind a lush growth of vines that screen the verandah. The pillars that stand on either side of the bottom step are visible, and close examination shows evidence of porch railings, a front door, a window on the far right, and lattice work near the ground. The bearded man seated in the front row is David Jack Findlay, pastor of a Glasgow church and one of Quarrier's sons-in-law, who, with his wife, Isabella Quarrier Findlay, conducted many groups of children to Canada. He rests his hat on his knee and holds a hand of each of the girls on either side of him, girls who look enough alike to be identical twins. Another girl standing just behind him rests her hand on his shoulder and smiles serenely. Further to the left stand two women, one leaning against a pillar and holding a young child, her arms, like the pillar, strong and secure. The other woman rests both her hands on the shoulders of the girl standing in front of her. Their faces, and that of the bearded man, appear gentle and kind, and the manner in which they make physical contact with the children seems to reflect a desire to protect them. Although only a few of the eighty-four girls are clearly smiling, there is a sense here of contentment and safety.

In a photograph taken at the Fairknowe home sixteen years later (fig. 7.4, taken in 1921), four girls and forty-six brushed and polished boys smile for the camera. The vines that covered the verandah in 1905 have disappeared, and one can read a symbolic welcome in the open front door. Many of the boys are not only smiling, but smiling broadly—to an extent rarely seen in photographs of child immigrants. One suspects the photographer has amused them. The boys wear three-piece suits, ties, and well-polished boots. Each boy's hair is neatly trimmed and brushed, and two in the front row whose jackets are open (far left and sixth from left) appear to be wearing watch chains. The girls wear light-coloured dresses and each has a ribbon in her hair. All have been turned out for this photograph looking their very best.

One of the striking features of this photograph, in contrast to the older photographs in figures 7.1 to 7.3, is the absence of very young children. The four girls and most of the boys appear easily to be fourteen, and none of the children look younger than perhaps ten or eleven. Indeed, by the beginning of the twentieth century, both British and Canadian governments had started more stringently to enforce the guidelines governing child migration, particularly those requiring children to be sent to school for a full

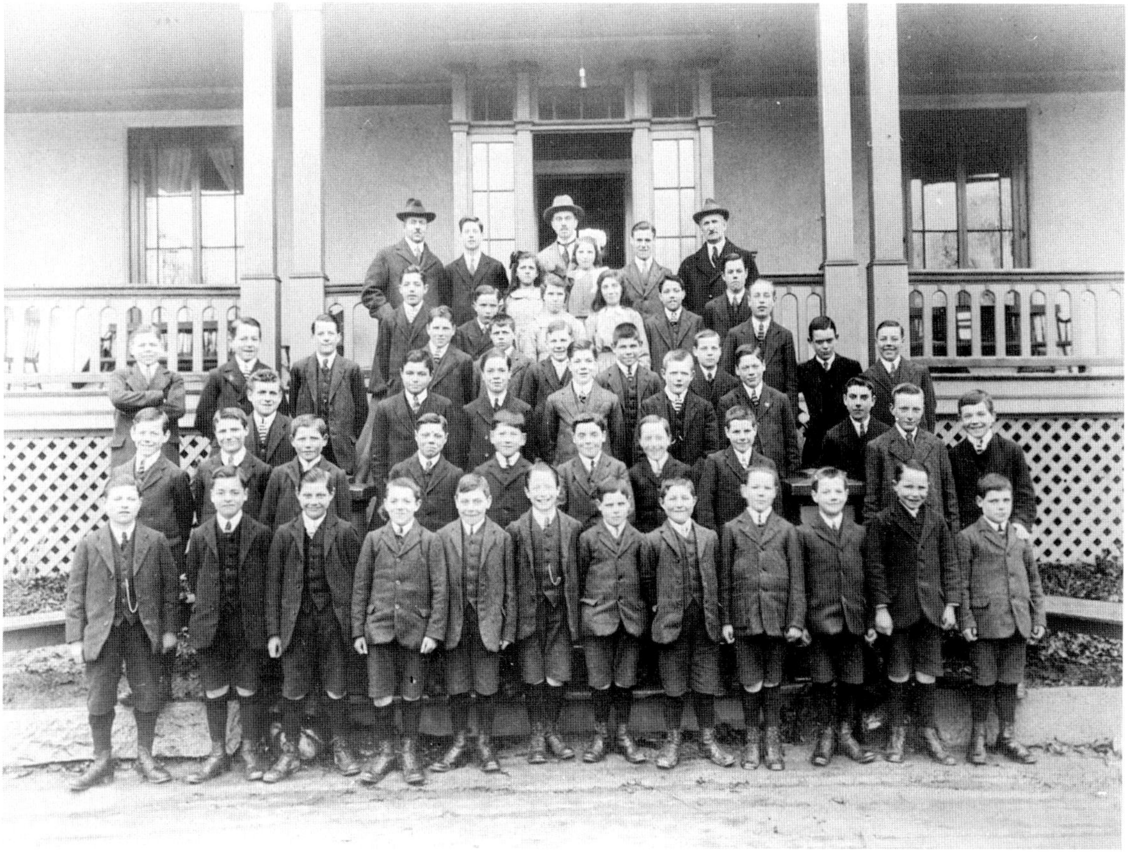

FIGURE 7.4 Group of immigrant boys and girls from Scotland arriving in Canada, 1921. (Photographer unknown. Library and Archives Canada, copy negative PA-041418)

nine months each year until they were fourteen; thus, the number of farm homes willing to take children under that age had begun to decline. Farmers wanted children who could work, not children they had to send to school.

The boy at the far left in the third row is fifteen-year-old William Young.[25] He stands with his arms folded across his chest, a posture perhaps suggested by the photographer but also indicative of a sense of vulnerability. Indeed, several boys, especially the smaller ones, look somewhat anxious. Three men stand in the back row, their hats, overcoats, and moustaches distinguishing them from the older boys. On the left is William Douglas,[26] who escorted many groups of boys from Quarrier's to Canada; in the middle is Claude Winters,[27] the Canadian-born manager of the Fairknowe home from 1912 until it closed in 1934. The third man is unidentified. The men's hats and overcoats suggest their travelling is not yet done, and their sombre faces that perhaps they know something of which the smiling boys are as yet unaware. Child immigrants usually spent no more than a few days at a distributing home before being sent to the farms where they would live and work. The term "distributing home" itself makes clear that the children's journey is not yet finished and the children are not yet home.

Labourers

All that is known about the "boy ploughing" (fig. 7.5) is that he was a "Barnardo boy" and a resident of Barnardo's Industrial Farm in Russell, Manitoba, around the turn of the last century. No records have survived that might tell us his name, age, or history.

The photographic plane is divided more or less in half by the horizon and comprises almost as much sky as land, thus evoking the flatness and openness of the Canadian prairies and the eight thousand–acre Barnardo farm. The ground already ploughed and the expanse of grassland yet to be worked point to the enormous labour involved in farming the Canadian prairie. The subject of the photograph—a boy with a plough and a team of horses—does not appear as small and lonely in this broad expanse of prairie as he might have done had the photographer been farther away or taken the photograph from a different angle. Nevertheless, the field being ploughed seems immense, and the work to be done too heavy for a boy so slight of frame. The plough seems too big for him, requiring him to keep his arms somewhat raised and making it impossible for him to use efficiently whatever strength he might have in his back and shoulders. His fine-knit sweater suggests he has not purposely dressed for a day's ploughing, or even for spending a day *learning* to plough. Indeed, it is quite possible he has been posed with the plough—because farm work was what he had been sent to Canada to do, and Barnardo in particular took pains to preserve a photographic record. While one might like to think this photograph was taken in pride for a boy's willingness to attempt a man's job, it was more likely taken to provide documentation—photographic evidence that Barnardo institutions trained boys to farm, and that their boys could and did do heavy labour.

There is a striking though probably accidental geometry in this photograph. Two strong lines separate the picture plane into three spaces. The horizon line creates the two rectangles of sky and land, a diagonal line divides the land into congruent triangles of ploughed and unploughed earth, and the two lines converge in a single vanishing point on the extreme right. The minimalist structure and content of the photograph, however, belie symbolic richness. Child rescuers believed that children from the notoriously crowded, dirty, and disease-ridden slums of British cities deserved a chance at a better

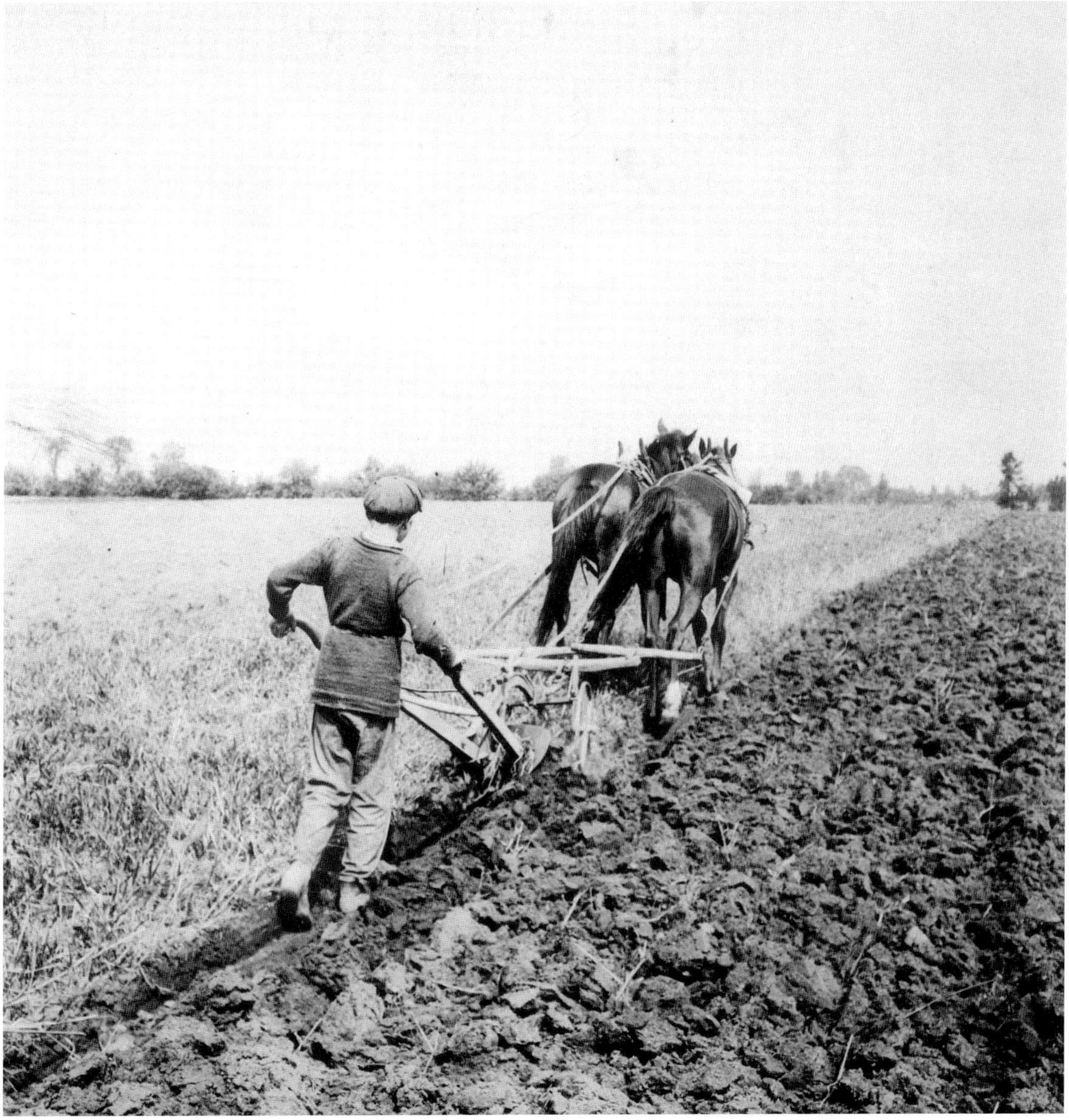

FIGURE 7.5 "A Boy Ploughing at Dr. Barnardo's Industrial Farm," Russell, Manitoba, c. 1900. (Photographer unknown. Library and Archives Canada, copy negative PA-117285)

life, and that the cleanliness, sunshine, fresh air, training, and hard work to be had on Canadian farms would be their salvation, literally and figuratively. Although the vanishing point future in this photograph is unclear, unknowable, and almost infinitely distant, it promises that with continuing hard work—and *only* with continuing hard work—the boy might approach it. The boy's physical location between earth and sky, between ploughed and unploughed land, between what has been done and what remains to be done, between accomplishment and potential, can be read as a metaphor for his location in life.

"Others"

School photographs have been a custom in Canadian schools almost from the time photography was invented. Itinerant photographers made it possible even for rural schools to participate in the annual ritual of posing children and teachers together for a group portrait. "Four Barnardo Children" (fig. 7.6) may have been taken on one of those traditional "school picture" days.

The schoolhouse dominates the background. Fifteen children stand casually on the porch, with two larger figures in the doorway behind. One of these is a woman, almost certainly the teacher. The other, hidden more deeply in the shadows, is probably an older student or a helper in the classroom. Four girls in the centre of the group stand out because of their light-coloured dresses; three are wearing their hair up and two have ribbons in their hair, a likely sign they expected to have their pictures taken today. Except for one boy who stands to the right, slightly apart from the group and arms akimbo while he chats with a smaller boy, all are looking toward the camera, watching as the photographer focuses on four children—three girls and a boy—who have been separated out.

The four are identified only as Barnardo children, and the caption to the photograph makes it clear they have been photographed separately precisely *because* they are Barnardo children. The girls are dressed plainly, without the ruffles and ribbons that decorate the dresses and hair of some of the girls in the background. All four are barefoot, either because the families with whom they live have not provided them with shoes, at least not for the summer, or because the children simply prefer not to wear shoes in warm weather; quite possibly, some of the other children in the school are barefoot, too. The girl on the far left wears eyeglasses, more likely provided for her by the Barnardo home from which she came than by the family with whom she was living. She and the boy standing next to her have hints of a smile on their faces, but the tallest girl looks sad, and the girl on the far right angry.

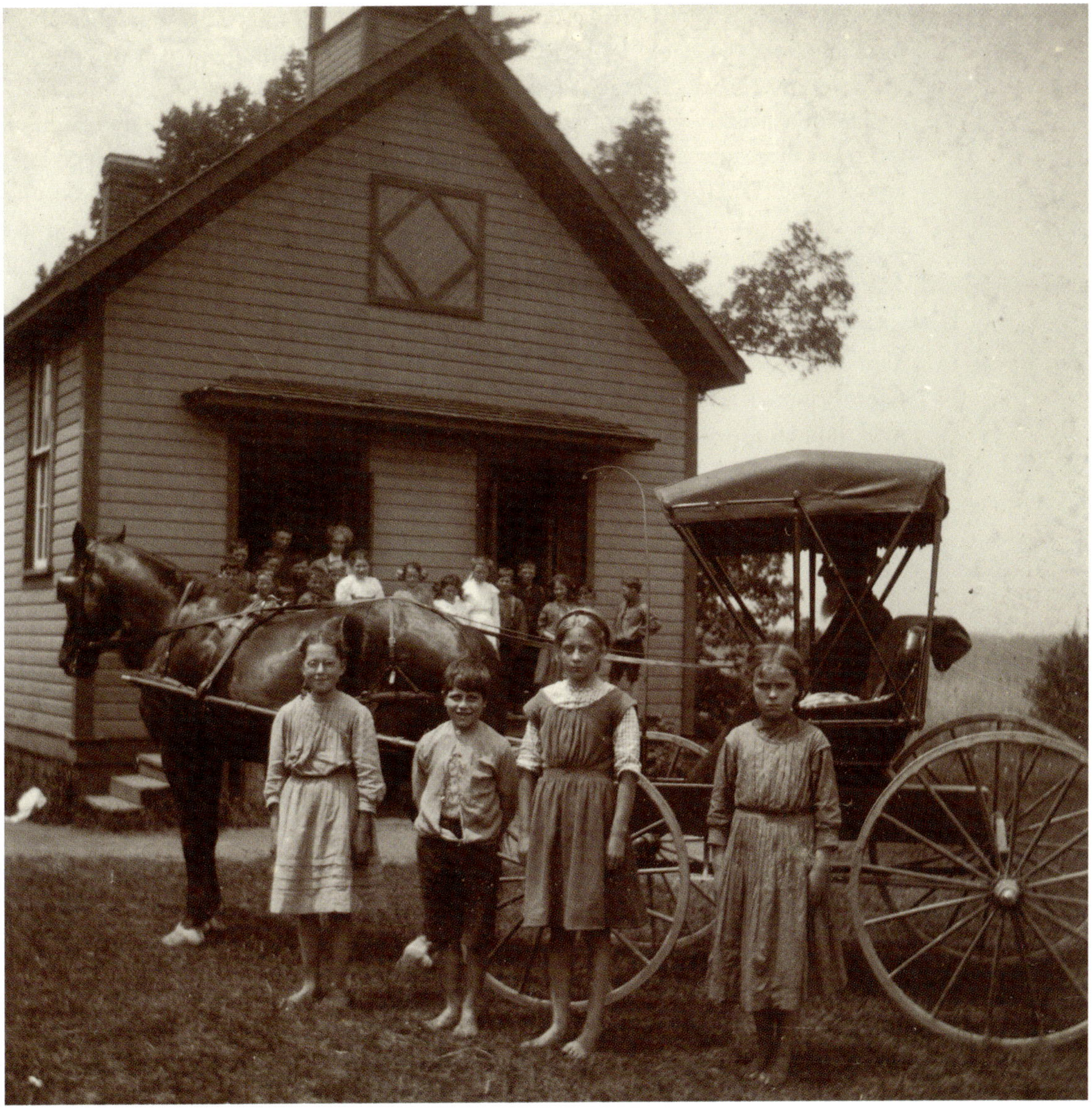

FIGURE 7.6 "Four Barnardo Children," in front of their Canadian classmates at Cavan School, Durham County, Ontario, 1912. (Photographer unknown. Barnardo's Photographic Archive)

One wonders why a small group of home children should be photographed apart from the rest of the school. Was it to provide documentation for the Barnardo home that the children were being sent to school? If indeed this is school picture day, the more likely explanation is that someone—the teacher, the other children, or the photographer himself—saw these four as different, and thought it appropriate to photograph them separately. One fears these four may not have appeared in a picture with the rest of the school. Many former home children recall being verbally abused, excluded, and mistreated by other children.[28] Said one, "You're just in a class. You're an orphan.... You counted as dirt. You were a nobody."[29] By the late nineteenth and early twentieth centuries, more and more Canadians were expressing concern about the effects on Canadian communities of so many immigrants from the lower and "dangerous" classes of Great Britain, fearing that child immigration might be turning Canada into "a dumping ground for the refuse of the highways, byways and vice haunts of the great cities."[30] Canadian children, overhearing such talk among their parents and being admonished, as many were, not to play with home children, found home children an easy target for taunts about their slum origins, dependence on charity, and unfamiliar accents and mannerisms. One can only too readily imagine school children making derisive remarks and, with the full force of childhood cruelty, declaring as they got ready to be photographed, "I'm not standing next to her!" "Who wants to stand next to an orphan?" or "They've had their picture taken; they don't need to be in ours." Perhaps the teacher was disapproving of home children, or resentful because they increased her workload and required attention she might have preferred to give to Canadian-born children. It was the stigma attached to the label, "home child," and the treatment it engendered that caused so many home children to keep the story of their childhoods a secret even when they were grown and even from their families.

The placement and symbolism of the horse and buggy in this photograph are striking. As a means of transportation, the rig reminds us that these children, young as they are, have already travelled great distances and have further to go. Spanning the frame from one side almost to the other, the rig not only separates the children from the rest of the school but seems partially to bar their way back. Indeed, many home children were moved from one location to another throughout all or part of their childhood, many were sent sporadically to school or not at all, and many had to struggle for any small advantage they might gain in life. A bearded man, recognizable as such only in silhouette, sits in the buggy holding the reins. Perhaps he is a government inspector, an inspector from a Barnardo home, or a driver for the photographer. Whatever his role, his presence in the photograph can surely be taken symbolically to represent all those figures behind the scenes in the lives of home children—men such as Thomas Barnardo and William Quarrier, women such as Annie Macpherson, and hundreds of others—who rescued, transported, and placed children; who made decisions for them; and who, essentially, held the reins that controlled the directions their lives would take.

The presence of a photographer, of the teacher and children gathered on the porch, and of girls wearing ruffles and ribbons suggest this is indeed school picture day. Whether or not the four home children were included in another photograph *with* the other children, the act of separating and photographing them while everyone else watched was just the sort of act that contributed to constructing, confirming, and reifying them as different, not us, *other*.

Narrative Inheritance, Absent Memory

Finally, I examine one last photograph (fig. 7.7), reproduced from William Quarrier's annual report[31] for 1920—a group of fifty-nine boys at the entrance to the Fairknowe home in Brockville, Ontario, the home we have already seen in figures 7.3 and 7.4 above. There is the wide verandah with its vines, and the front door open in welcome. On the left stands Claude Winters, manager of the home, and on the right, William Douglas, who had escorted the boys from Scotland. There are few smiles among them, but these boys are undoubtedly as brushed and polished as those in the 1921 photograph. It is April 1920, and one of these boys is James McNay, my father, at age thirteen.

Having never seen a depiction of my father as a child, I at first despaired of distinguishing him from the other boys in the photograph. Archival records tell me, however, that he was one of the youngest in this group, and when I look more closely at the smallest boys I find something startlingly familiar in the shape of the face and the thick brown hair of the boy seated second from left in the front row. Here, I am sure, is the boy for whom I am looking, the boy with unruly hair (fig. 7.7 inset) who was photographed some years later farming with his brother, the boy whose childhood is no longer a hole in memory, the boy whose narrative I have, belatedly, inherited.

The camera has captured a moment in my father's childhood, a moment during his first day or two in Canada. As do some of the other boys, he sits with his arms crossed and seems not to be looking directly at the camera. Is it because I think I know him that I sense he is anxious and restless? What can be going through his mind? Did he come to Canada because it seemed likely to be a great adventure? Is he hoping to find his two older brothers and the sister who immigrated before the war? Does he have any friends among the other boys, and what will the next few years bring for him?

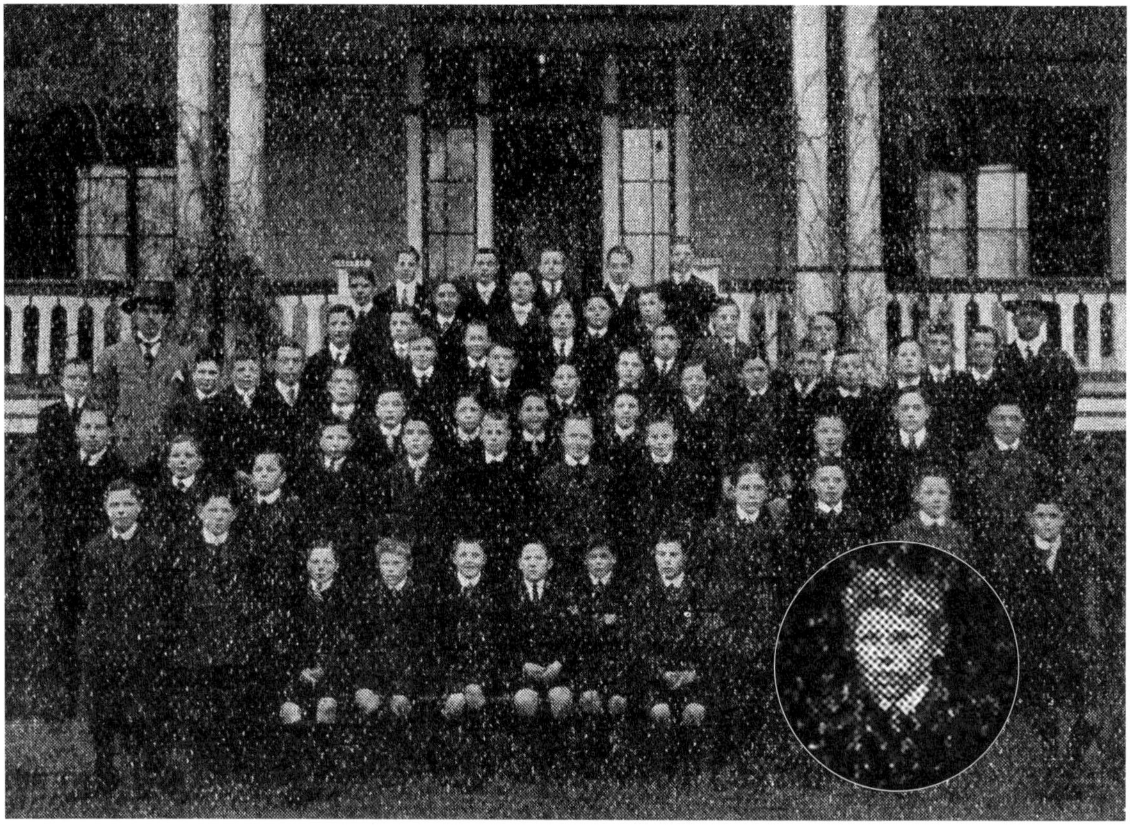

FIGURE 7.7 Boys' Canadian party at Fairknowe, 1920. (Photographer unknown. Reproduced from William Quarrier, *A Narrative of Facts Relative to Work Done for Christ in Connection with the Orphan and Destitute Children's Emigration Homes*, Glasgow: George Gallie & Son, 1905, p. 12). Inset: James McNay, c. 1925. (Photograph unknown. Private collection)

Discussion

The photographs reproduced here are a few among hundreds, perhaps thousands, of extant photographs that depict Canadian home children. Here we see at least 285 children, the symbols and accoutrements of travel surrounding them, a tiny fraction of the tens of thousands of "little immigrants" who came to Canada. How easy it must have been to feel invisible or lost in the crowd. How ironic that the poor quality of the photograph in figure 7.1 makes the children almost faceless, and that the single photograph that shows only one child (fig. 7.4) does *not* show his face. How debilitating to one's sense of self to be identified only as "a Barnardo boy" or one of four "Barnardo children." Using electronic processes to magnify the more highly resolved photographs—figures 7.2, 7.3, and 7.5—one can look more closely at some of the faces. One is both fascinated and moved in doing so—fascinated by each one's uniqueness and individuality, moved by speculation about each one's courage and vulnerability.

But who took these photographs, and why? Although Thomas Barnardo for a number of years employed a photographer on his staff in London, England, the photographers of Canada's home children are otherwise unknown. *Why* the photographs were taken, however, is apparent in the uses to which they were put: the photographs provided documentation of the work the homes were doing, evidence that the children fared well, and, above all, a means of publicizing child rescue and emigration among people and groups who might be moved to support the work. The brushed and polished appearance of the boys in figure 7.4, for example, and the tidy, modest dresses and hats of the girls in figures 7.1, 7.2, and 7.3, would have helped to assure the public that child rescue and emigration was an eminently successful and beneficial undertaking. Photographs of children who were well dressed and well groomed, orderly, and apparently obedient and respectful would have helped to allay the public's fears that the children might have been "tainted" by the poverty of their former lives. These are children of whom anyone among the late nineteenth- and early twentieth-century middle classes would have been proud.

"It is from those who have suffered the sentence of history," wrote Bhabha, "subjugation, domination, diaspora, displacement—that we learn our most enduring lessons."[32] Forced into an orphanage or rescue home by poverty and circumstance, emigrated far from their homes and families without passports, visas, or birth certificates, indentured to labour until they were eighteen, and widely treated as "others," there can be little argument that, as a group, home children "suffered the sentence of history." Despite a felt loss of identity and personhood, and a lifelong sense of dislocation and disconnection, however, many home children grew up to accept Canada unconditionally as their home and to find steady jobs, marry, raise children, and live more or less normal—even distinguished—lives. Many have said they are grateful to the homes that took them in, and for having been sent to Canada, despite the rejection, loneliness, and pain they experienced in the process. Are there, then, "enduring lessons" to be learned from the saga of the home children?

One lesson, so obvious to us now it is difficult to imagine how little it was credited in the early decades of the twentieth century, is that children can suffer loneliness, homesickness, fear, and humiliation even when their physical requirements are adequately met, that they have feelings and an emotional life, and require compassion as well as discipline. Another lesson, illustrated here as in so many other times and places over the course of history, concerns the amazing strength and resilience with which children often meet difficulty, even tragedy, faring well despite the scarring caused by "barbaric"[33] treatment. Other lessons in the home child saga, too complex to rehearse here, have to do with the evolution of policies and practices concerning child labour, education, and children's welfare, and with how readily governments, institutions, well-meaning individuals, and the general public accepted a social policy that, its successes notwithstanding, was expedient, opportunistic, misguided, and flawed.[34]

Epilogue

"Your dad had a hard life," my mother had said, thereby in her mind both explaining and forgiving his chronic anxiety, low-grade depression, and sometimes difficult temperament. I once asked her what it was about his life that had been so much harder than her own or than that of so many others who had lived through the Great Depression and two world wars. Of course, she refused to answer. I know now she was referring to his having been abandoned by his mother, surrendered to an orphanage, and sent to Canada to labour for strangers; to the loneliness, homesickness, and insecurity he suffered throughout his childhood; and, probably worse than anything else, to the shame engendered by the label "home child."

"A narrative inheritance," writes Goodall, "touches everything, one way or another, in our lives."[35] *Having discovered my father's story—and I will never know all of it—I have come to understand that his experiences of poverty, the orphanage, emigration, indentured labour, and a life of unskilled, poorly paid jobs shaped his character and, ultimately, a legacy for me. My own identity has been deeply influenced by the working-class values he embodied*[36]*—respect for honest labour and a job well done, commitment to an honest day's work for an honest day's pay, belief in self-sufficiency, and faith in the potential of education to improve one's life. My choice in recent years to commit part of my professional scholarship to researching the life of William Quarrier and the education he provided the children in his homes derives from my attempts to understand more fully my newly discovered narrative inheritance. Even my choice many years ago to become a teacher, and my promise to myself that if I did nothing else in the classroom I would make sure I never shamed or embarrassed a child, seems likely to have had some of its roots in my father's sense of fairness, and in the effects his absent memory had on me as I was growing up.*

I find nothing toxic about the secret my parents kept from me, as Goodall does about the secret his parents kept from him.[37] *I am not embarrassed by it or angry that the truth was so long untold, and I believe that had I known my father's story when I was a child I would have thought it exciting and adventuresome and certainly nothing shameful. And that is how I think about it now. Depending upon how, exactly, he had presented his past, things might have been very different. Probably he felt he was protecting me with his silence. Nevertheless, I am glad to know his story at last; I am glad to know.*

Notes

Nancy Johnson of Lockwood Films, London, Ontario, first called my attention to Loren Lerner's project, *Depicting Canada's Children*, and to the possibility of writing about photographs of Canada's home children. In generously sharing with me her extensive research for Lockwood Films' 2005 production, *Nobody's Child: Canada's Home Children*, she has assisted enormously in this project.

1 H.L. Goodall, "Narrative Inheritance: A Nuclear Family with Toxic Secrets," *Qualitative Inquiry* 11 (2005): 492–513. Narrative inheritance consists of "stories given to children by and about family members" (492).

2 Susan Rubin Suleiman, "Reflections on Memory at the Millennium," *Comparative Literature* 51 (1999): v–xiii. Absent memory occurs in situations in which "the normal transmission of cultural or collective memory has been blocked by the radical disappearance of the older generation, or else by their traumatized silence" (xi).

3 Margaret McNay, "The Home Child: A Daughter's Search" (presentation to the annual meeting of the International Society for Educational Biography, Chicago, April 2001); Margaret McNay, "'Your Father Was a Home Child, You Know': Discovering the Story of Canada's Home Children" (lecture, Museum London, ON, June 2005); Margaret McNay, "British Child Emigration to Canada, 1869–1933," *Vitae Scholastica* 21 (2004): 49–62.

4 Goodall, "Narrative Inheritance," 497.

5 Kenneth Bagnell, *The Little Immigrants: The Orphans Who Came to Canada* (Toronto: Macmillan, 1980).

6 Gail Corbett, *Barnardo Children in Canada* (Peterborough, ON: Woodland, 1981).

7 Phyllis Harrison, ed., *The Home Children: Their Personal Stories* (Winnipeg: Watson and Dwyer, 1979).

8 Joy Parr, *Labouring Children: British Immigrant Apprentices to Canada, 1869–1924* (London: Croom Helm, 1980).

9 Margaret Humphreys, *Empty Cradles* (London: Doubleday, 1994).

10 Select Committee on Health, House of Commons, United Kingdom Parliament. "The Welfare of Former British Child Migrants," Third Report, July 30, 1998, http://www.parliament.the-stationery-office.co.uk/pa/cm199798/cmselect/cmhealth/755/75502.htm

11 First International Congress on Child Migration, New Orleans, October 27–31, 2002.

12 Home Children Canada, http://www.orphantrainriders.com/HomeChild/HomeIndex.html

13 Quarrier's Canadian Family, http://www.quarrierscanadianfamily.com/history.html

`14 *Welcome Home* (Cue Films, 1990). Produced in association with the Canadian Broadcasting Corporation, National Film Board of Canada, P.A.F.P.S. Program (Ontario Centre) TVOntario.

15 Nancy Johnson, *Nobody's Child: Canada's Home Children*, videorecording (Lockwood Films, 2005).

16 For example, P. Bean and J. Melville, *Lost Children of the Empire* (London: Unwin Hyman, 1989); John Eekelaar, "'The Chief Glory': The Export of Children from the United Kingdom," *Journal of Law and Society* 21 (1994): 487–504. Julie Grier, "Voluntary Rights and Statutory Wrongs: The Case of Child Migration, 1948–67," *History of Education* 31 (2002): 262–380; Michelle Langfield, "Voluntarism, Salvation, and Rescue: British Juvenile Migration to Australia and Canada, 1890 to 1939," *The Journal of Imperial and Commonwealth History* 32 (2004): 86–114; Frederick McEvoy, "'These Treasures of the Church of God': Catholic Child Immigration to Canada," *Historical Studies* 65 (1999): 50–70, 127; Patricia Rooke and R.L. Schnell, "The 'King's Children' in English Canada: A Psychohistorical Study of Abandonment, Rejection, and Colonial Response (1869–1930),"

Journal of Psychohistory 8 (1981): 387–420; Geoffrey Sherrington, "'Suffer Little Children': British Child Migration as a Study of Journeyings between Centre and Periphery," *History of Education* 32 (2003): 461–476; Neil Sutherland, *Children in English-Canadian Society: Framing the Twentieth-Century Consensus* (Toronto: University of Toronto Press, 1976); Gillian Wagner, *Children of the Empire* (London: Weidenfeld & Nicolson, 1982).

17 Gillian Wagner and Valerie Lloyd, *The Camera and Dr. Barnardo* (exhibition catalogue) (London: National Portrait Gallery, July–November 1974).

18 "The Barnardo Photographic Archive," *Library Review* 44 (1995): 34–39. The Barnardo Archive is located at Barnardo's headquarters in Tanners Lane, Barkingside, Essex IG6 1QG, UK.

19 Annette Kuhn, *Family Secrets: Acts of Memory and Imagination*, new ed. (London: Verso, 2002).

20 Home Children Canada, http://www.orphantrainriders.com/HomeChild/HomeIndex.html

21 Parr, *Labouring Children*, 33.

22 See, for example, Bagnell, *The Little Immigrants*; Bean and Melville, *Lost Children of the Empire*; Wagner, *Children of the Empire.*

23 Ibid.

24 After Quarrier died in 1903, his heirs re-evaluated and then re-established the practice.

25 "William Westwood Young's Life," http://www3.sympatico.ca/turbod/wwyhistory/page8.html (accessed December 23, 2006).

26 Ibid.

27 Ibid.

28 See, for example, Bagnell, *Little Immigrants;* Bean and Melville, *Lost Children of the Empire*; Corbett, *Barnardo Children in Canada*; Harrison, *The Home Children.*

29 Quoted in S. Lightstone and K. Bagnell, "'Flower of the Flock' (Barnardo Home Children: William Price and Ada Allan)," *This Country Canada* 5 (Spring 1994): 56–65.

30 Rooke and Schnell, "The 'King's Children,'" 387.

31 William Quarrier, *A Narrative of Facts Relative to Work Done for Christ in Connection with the Orphan and Destitute Children's Emigration Homes, Glasgow* (Glasgow: George Gallie & Son, 1920).

32 Homi K. Bhabha, "Postcolonial criticism," in *Redrawing the Boundaries*, ed. Stephen Greenblatt and Giles Gunn, 437–465 (New York: The Modern Language Association of America, 1992).

33 Select Committee on Health, House of Commons, United Kingdom Parliament, "Welfare of Former British Child Migrants."

34 Margaret McNay, "Expedient, Opportunistic, Misguided, and Flawed: Late 19th and Early 20th Century British Child Emigration to the Colonies" (presentation to the History Department, University of Western Ontario, March 19, 2003).

35 Goodall, "Narrative Inheritance," 503.

36 My mother, of course, played an equally important part in my formation. She, too, bore strong working-class values and a narrative inheritance that helped to define my identity.

37 Goodall, "Narrative Inheritance," 492.

ELSPETH TULLOCH

RE-VISIONING THE GIRL'S NARRATIVE FOR THE 1980S

The Case of the Short Story "Jack of Hearts" and Its Film Adaptation

GIRLHOOD IS CHARACTERIZED BY THE PRESSURES of social adaptation, a process that becomes conflicted, even anguished, when the girl does not fit the dominant mould. Observes the young female narrator of Alice Munro's frequently anthologized "Boys and Girls":

> The word *girl* had formerly seemed to me innocent and unburdened, like the word *child*; now it appeared that it was no such thing. A girl was not, as I had supposed, simply what I was; it was what I had to become. It was a definition, always touched with emphasis, with reproach and disappointment. Also it was a joke on me.[1]

Girls growing up in twentieth-century Canada who were nontraditional in some way often found themselves forced to deal with what society considered their social failings as females and forced to decide whether to conform or reassert their own ways of being.

A complex aesthetic situation arises when this type of narrative of fraught, failing, or failed social adaptation and concomitant lack of social acceptance intersects with the process of film adaptation, for two, at times interacting, acts of adapting become implicated. One involves the story of a girl reacting to socially imposed gender roles, and the other a filmmaker modifying the narrative containing that struggle with social adaptation to fit a new medium and new social pressures. Adaptation for the female character may involve adjusting to or bucking socio-environmental pressures, while for the filmmaker it may involve making changes arising from these or other intrinsic or extrinsic factors to the female character or other aspects of the text. What happens, then, when a short story about a girl who fails to fit the mould and who is forced (temporarily) into another one is adapted to film? What is adapted? How does the depiction of the girl fare?[2]

The case of the film adaptation of Isabel Huggan's short story "Jack of Hearts" provides an interesting case in point. First published in 1980, then integrated into the Bildungsroman short story cycle *The Elizabeth Stories* in 1984, it was adapted to the screen in 1986 by director Cynthia Scott (best known for her later feature film *The Company of Strangers*, 1990) and by scriptwriting team Jack Blum and Sharon Corder for a series co-produced by Atlantis Films Limited and the National Film Board of Canada (NFB).[3] Thus, both the source text and the adaptation were conceived during a period when concerns about the socialization of girls were high on the public agenda.

Adapting a Source Text to the Screen: The Forces of Change at Play

Before delving into the particulars, it needs to be noted that film adaptation implies modification. Fidelity to the source text, in the way that this goal is still understood and often advocated by the popular press and general audiences, has been out of favour for some time as an evaluative stance among many scholars in the field. As Robert Stam explains, "Th[e] shift, in adaptation, from a single-track, uniquely verbal medium such as the novel to a multitrack medium like film, which can play not only with words (written and spoken) but also with music, sound effects, and moving photographic images, explains the unlikelihood, and I would suggest even the undesirability, of literal fidelity."[4] Different technical, material, and semiotic ways of conveying meaning may lead to different emphases, even different messages. Cinematic conventions associated with narrative length frequently require condensing, simplifying, and pruning lengthy and involved source plots. Additionally, different modes of production may affect content as creation moves from a very limited generative site, generally involving a single author aided by an editor or editors, to the multiple-role realm of filmmaking, involving any number of people as the film proceeds from pre-production through to post-production. Possible factors in altering content include budgetary constraints as well as implicit and explicit censorship. Moreover, as Brian McFarlane points out, "conditions within the film industry ... [including] a studio's 'house style' ... or the prevailing parameters of cinematic practice" may affect choices made in the involved process of adaptation.[5] These particular conditions relate to what Stam calls "aesthetic mainstreaming," in which "adaptation is seen as a kind of purge. In the name of mass-audience legibility, the novel is 'cleansed' of moral ambiguity, narrative interruption, and reflexive meditation."[6] As numerous specialists in the field remind us, an adaptation is simply one more reading of the source text among many. One spectator's memory of a precursor text cannot provide the ultimate interpretation of that text or the ultimate evaluation of its cinematically reworked one. In rereading the source text, the adapters may, for instance, focus on unexpected but pre-existing narrative elements. For example, as Kamilla Elliott points out, "a subtext may become the main text of a reading at the expense of the whole.... Some apparently total departures from the novel by an adaptation [actually] serve to fulfill the disappointed hopes and desires of its characters."[7]

In the view of many, then, infidelity is not to be lamented but recognized as an intrinsic, often revealing, and sometimes even misapprehended part of the process. Peter Dickinson demonstrates that "questions of *infidelity* ... often provide ... productive starting points for adaptation studies," while Julie Sanders argues that "it is usually at the very point of infidelity that the most creative acts of adaptation ... take place."[8] Already, twenty-odd years ago, Christopher Orr, in his influential review of several adaptation studies, was calling for an examination of "lapses of fidelity ... as they provide clues to the ideology embedded in the [film] text."[9] Certainly in the breakages with as well as the erasures and the reworking of the source text one may discover, in part, what, as Linda Hutcheon observes, are "the political ... intentions of ... adapters [which] are potentially relevant to the audience's interpretation [and which] are often recoverable,... their traces ... visible in the text."[10] As she and numerous others have pointed out, changes may be made in adapting a text to the screen that either add to, reorient, downplay, or elide the source text's political critique. This type of transformation belongs to what Elliott calls "the trumping concept of adaptation [under which] the novel's signs lose representational authority in the name of a signified that the novel 'meant to' or 'tried to' or 'should have' represented when the adapting film is perceived to have represented it better."[11]

Thus, adapters with feminist interests, of concern to this case study, may read the source text for feminist critique, for a feminist agenda, or for a feminist aesthetic of some sort, whether explicit or implicit, correcting for any or all of these when and in ways they think necessary.[12] A small but significant of body of research has begun to delineate these varied feminist readings, most particularly in feature length film.[13] The response to feminist and other political, ideological, social, and cultural content is often related to the climate of the times.

Recognizing that "adaptation is primarily a phenomenon of *recontextualization of the text*" (emphasis in the original), Francesco Casetti offers a method for conceptualizing the precursor influences on the adaptation.[14] His method allows us to isolate social, political, biographical, and aesthetic factors that together may, as he states, "bend the [source] text one way or another" as it is adapted.[15] It is too complex to deal with all four of his factors in one reading. What interests me here is what he calls the "intertextual frame," which he defines as "a series of background discourses."[16] Recognizing these intertexts allows us to consider not only the source text but also other social discourses shaping the creation of the adaptation. Even when the adaptation is made in the same era as the source text, as in the case of *Jack of Hearts*, the adapters may be affected by other discourses than the source author or may consider these other discourses differently.

Adapting Images of Girls and Women: Responding to Social Discourse on Sex-Role Stereotyping

Jack of Hearts was made in the years immediately following the release of *Images of Women* (1982), the influential report of the Task Force on Sex-Role Stereotyping in the Broadcast Media struck in 1979 by the Canada Radio-television and Telecommunications Commission (CRTC).[17] This report now serves as a barometer of the times, given the size of the task force and the extent of its research and consultations. It identified specific types of limitative or derogatory images of women as they were manifested in advertising and programming for adults and children and made numerous recommendations to the CRTC, the federal government, the advertising industry, and public and private broadcasters, as well as the general public.

The second wave of feminism, to which the report was responding, had raised intense concerns about and spawned numerous studies on what was then termed "sex-role stereotyping" in the media. One of the perceived problems was the lack of diverse, positive role models for girls and the possibility of deleterious effects on their development as a result.[18] During this period, feminists had increasingly criticized the use of biological sex as a factor in limiting access to social and professional roles and in anticipating, categorizing, shaping, or evaluating intellectual and physical ability, as well as emotional behaviour. One of the suggested solutions was to improve and broaden the representation of girls and women by tackling aspects of sex-role stereotyping in images, activities, and behaviours portrayed by the media—to create so-called positive images. Issues included, but were not limited to, socialization and femininity; body image; female role models for girls; and sex-role or gender coding as reflected in social, professional, and familial roles, in behaviour (especially passive and obedient behaviour), and even in colours and toys.

Distilling ten years of research on the topic in conjunction with information gleaned from public hearings and submissions, the task force called for de-objectifying, diversifying, and otherwise improving the general images of women; broadening the range of their particular portrayals in professional, social, and familial roles; varying the form and constellation of familial and interpersonal relationships, to make them, among other things, less patriarchal; removing derogatory and sexist language; and creating female characters with more positive personal qualities and personality types (as expressed through their motivations and needs, their character traits, and their intellectual abilities). While the representation of adult women was the primary focus of the report, that of girls was also encompassed, as the task force stated that its general concerns and suggested solutions also applied to dramatic and children's programming.

During this period of attempted redress, Atlantis Films and the NFB co-produced, with the participation of the Global Television Network and Telefilm Canada, the series of twenty-five half-hour adaptations of Canadian short stories (1984–1986), including *Jack of Hearts*. The films were aimed initially for telecast to a general audience and then for subsequent use in Canadian schools as part of the Canadian Short Story Video Series (CSSVS).[19] Although not directly subject to the recommendations of the CRTC task force, Atlantis Films and the NFB were indirectly affected, since they were seeking to have the adaptations aired by a private broadcaster who was implicated via the recommendations that the task force made to the Canadian Association of Broadcasters. In any case, gender stereotyping was enough a topic of public discourse at the time that those involved in film and cultural production could hardly have been unaware of it. Indeed, on other occasions separate from the CSSV series, Atlantis Films and the NFB had responded to the widespread consideration given to the representation of girls and women and concomitant social themes.

To ascertain the degree to which the adaptation *Jack of Hearts* was responding to this social climate, it is germane to establish generally how the films in the series reflect the type of recommendations found in the CRTC task force report, particularly those films focusing on female characters. In spite of the politicized tenor of the times and the specific recommendation of the task force that females and males be equally represented onscreen, one of the cornerstones of the task force's corrective measures, the producers of the CSSV series collectively demonstrated little sensitivity to rectifying the under-representation of female protagonists. Only seven of the twenty-five source stories retained for what was to become the CSSVS boast a female in the leading role.[20] This statistic runs counter to "the ascension to leading roles" by girls and women that Brian Low observes in NFB documentaries of the period.[21] Of these seven films, five are concerned with girls or young women, and only two with adult women, reflecting a marked response to the intense public focus on issues related to the development of girls.[22]

Beginning with the adaptation of Lois Simmie's "Red Shoes" (short story collection 1982, film version 1986), which shows two sisters of around seven and nine dealing in the mid-twentieth century with the trauma of parental discord, these five films with girl protagonists chronologically trace events that trigger the process of emotional maturation in females from childhood through adolescence to near adulthood. The adaptation of Margaret Laurence's "To Set Our House in Order" (short story collection 1970, film version 1985) examines a ten-year-old girl's grappling with the reality of mortality in the 1930s as she faces the possibility of her mother dying in childbirth along with her newborn son; the adaptation of Isabel Huggan's "Jack of Hearts" (short story collection

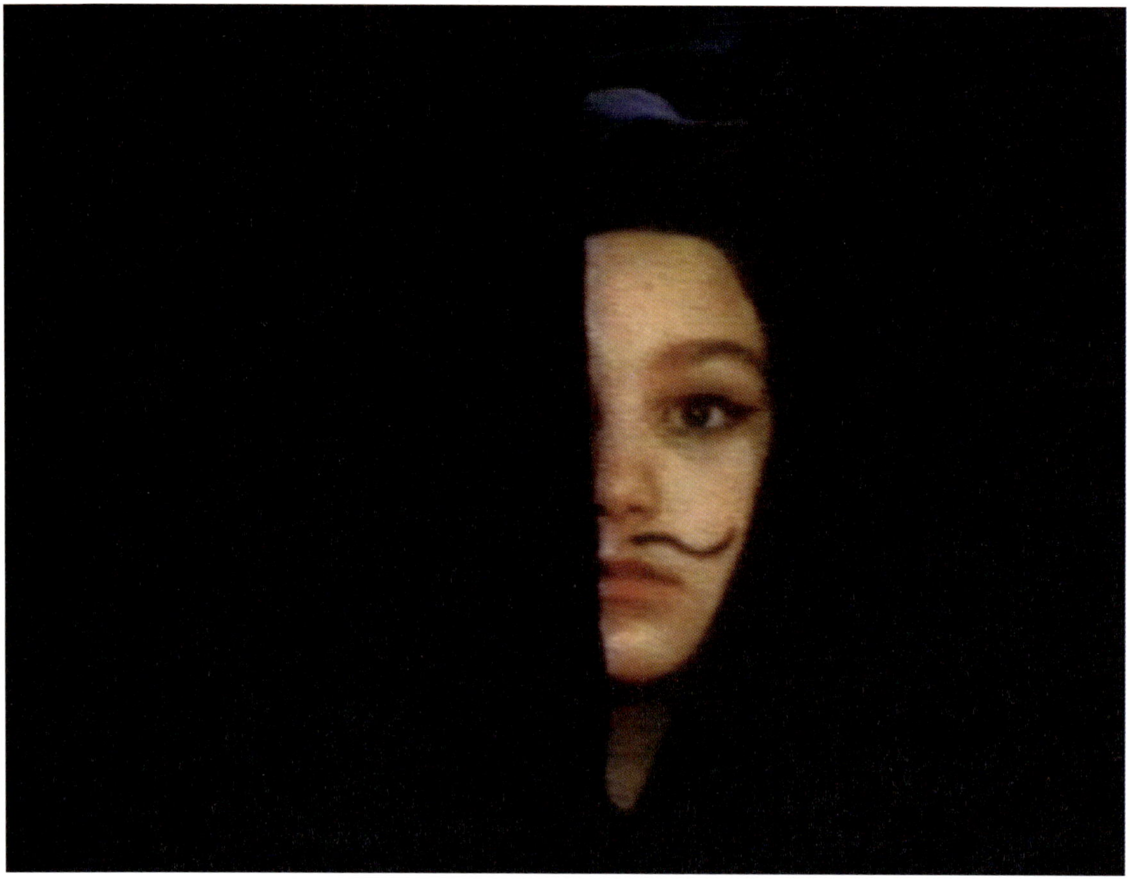

FIGURE 8.1 The young protagonist, Elizabeth Kessler (Renée Gersovitz), peers out at the audience prior to going on stage as the male lead of her ballet recital in *Jack of Hearts*. Elizabeth's half-shrouded face, seen through the vulval form of the curtain opening, intimates the social repression of her female identity, and the painted-on moustache is emblematic of her socially imposed masculinity. VHS frame grab. *Jack of Hearts*. Courtesy of Alliance Films Inc.

1984, film version 1986) explores a masculine-looking eleven-year-old girl's struggle with gender identity when she is assigned a male role in the early 1950s (fig. 8.1); the adaptation of Linda Svendsen's "Esso" (short story collection 1980, film version 1985) presents a young teenaged girl who, working as an assistant in the male-dominated environment of her uncle's garage in the 1960s, strives for emotional independence as she wrestles with her confusion over her first relationship with a boy, her grandmother's dying, and her mother's traditional femininity; and the adaptation of Thomas H. Raddall's "The Trumpeter" (short story collection 1947, film version 1986) chronicles the spunky and unexpected way an independent-minded young woman, who is operating a small, hand-drawn ferry in eighteenth-century Nova Scotia, finds a husband with whom she can enjoy a working partnership.

Taken collectively, and regardless of the range in their historical and regional settings, the five adaptations present a relatively homogenous image of girls in Canada. As such, the films run counter to the spirit of the task force report, whose first general recommendation specifically proposed diversifying age, ethnicity, and physique when depicting female characters. Although the girls' ages do vary,[23] the girls display no ethnic variegation (they are all of European descent),[24] and only minor, generally age-related physical differences. The art of adaptation would have given the filmmakers some liberties in these areas with these texts, and alternative source texts would also have offered somewhat wider choices. Nevertheless, the adapters do show a tendency to cast female leads who stand outside traditional norms of girlish pulchritude, acknowledging the suitability of the plain or less conventionally attractive girl for starring roles, and this regardless of the lack of physical description in some of the stories. On this point the adapters fall in line with the task force's suggestions to avoid overemphasizing images of and obsessions with female beauty.

The task force recommended varying the depictions of families to reflect the growing social reality of less conventional family groupings and of widening gender roles for parents and children. Low's research has since found that family constellations were increasingly varied, and traditional familial hierarchies were "democratizing" in NFB documentaries of this period.[25] Nevertheless, the girl principals in these adaptations are, for the most part, shown being socialized within traditional familial models, and no conflict arises as a result of young daughters being at odds with that model. Tensions may brew and occasionally flare up because of latent, intergenerational differences on traditional values governing gender in social roles, comportment, or identity, as in *Jack of Hearts*, *Esso*, or *To Set Our House in Order*, but not because of filial rejection of the traditional family model itself.

However, the adaptations do reflect a common and abiding concern with the task force's second general recommendation on diversifying images of girls and women, that of broadening the range of female characters' activities. Specifically, the films show the young female protagonists in a variety of undertakings inside and outside the home, with four of the five placing the girls in social, leisure, or work situations that explicitly or at least implicitly challenge traditional conceptions of female roles (*Red Shoes*, *Esso*, *Jack of Hearts*, and *The Trumpeter*). In the case of the adaptations of Simmie's, Svendsen's and Raddall's stories, the girls' tasks and pastimes are, to varying degrees, masculinized compared to the source texts. In *Red Shoes*, the elder sister, Meg, becomes mildly tomboyish, unlike in the story, repeatedly wearing blue and once climbing a tree; Valerie, the female adolescent gas station worker in *Esso*, takes on more male duties than in the precursor narrative; and Thankful, the young female ferry operator in *The Trumpeter*, whose ability to fend for herself by chopping wood is merely hinted at in the story, is specifically shown wielding the axe in the film. In the fifth adaptation, that of the story "To Set Our House in Order," the young girl, Vanessa, assumes a more assertive stance than in the original story in relation to her domineering grandmother. These modifications jibe with one of the predominant aims of the mainstream feminist movement of the time: to open doors for girls to so-called masculine occupations and to encourage girls to become more physically active, self-reliant, outspoken, and confident.

Although all the adaptations engage at least implicitly with gender issues, *Jack of Hearts* stands out from the rest, as it explicitly and principally deals with the issues of extending the depictions of female activity beyond the feminine and of portraying less normative female physique, making these aspects of female role and female image overtly central to narrative conflict and, more significantly, to an investigation of the struggle with gender identity. As such, the film merits particular consideration. Moreover, its narrative explores the emotional implications of these questions, giving psychological substance to the more surface-based changes proposed by the task force report. However, a close reading of this adaptation shows a mixed result.[26] In seeking to modify the source text in ways that incorporate so-called desirable female images, the adapters also introduce regressive elements that undermine the superficially positive thrust of some of the surficial changes. They mirror the ambivalence of the period toward feminists' demands for change as reflected in the range of social intervention found in cinematic adaptations of the time, from non-feminist or anti-feminist to varying degrees of feminist.[27]

Complicating the analysis of this adaptation is the fact that the official corrective measures of the mainstream feminist movement, as reflected in the task force report, were largely inspired by content-based approaches that lagged behind more sophisticated methodologies emerging since the mid-1970s for analyzing female representation in the cinema and for deploying more substantive ways of addressing problematic aspects of that representation. British feminist film critics, such as Annette Kuhn in *Women's Pictures* (1982), had begun to advocate examining the underlying elements of cinematic narrative and the formal features of cinematic technique, both separately and as they interrelate with narrative, character, and image.[28] Using psychoanalytical analysis, Laura Mulvey had introduced her seminal and highly debated concept of the male gaze by 1975, raising what were to become long-standing questions among feminist scholars about female spectatorship and desire. Indeed, even the quest for so-called positive images, as outlined, for example, in Linda Artel and Susan Wengraf's *Positive Images: Non-Sexist Films for Young People* (1976), was not without its critics during this period. They charged, for example, that proponents of this cosmetic tack were seeking the dissemination of wished-for, ideal, or idealized images rather than realistic ones.[29] Nevertheless, the adapters, themselves, were versed in cinematic technique and thus well able to engage, if they chose, in more sophisticated responses to the concerns about female representation, regardless of the official methods suggested by public agencies. This study will thus take into account not only some of the veneered revisions this particular adaptation makes to its source but also their interrelationship with underlying narrative structure or with cinematic codes (particularly costuming) to determine how the adapters were responding to the climate of concern about female representation. This more comprehensive approach recognizes the complex of signifying practices within filmmaking, as advocated by numerous theorists of cinematic adaptation. It also acknowledges the ideological significance that changes found in the adaptation may express. To isolate differences based on extrinsic factors, notably those reflecting the circulating discourse on sex-role stereotyping, I focus on aspects of the source narrative that are related to gender representation and that are least subject to change because of the transfer to the new media (e.g., dialogue, basic character traits, colours, filmable scenes, maintainable plot points).[30]

"Jack of Hearts" and Its Film Adaptation: Challenging the Traditional Image of the Girl

Although the short story "Jack of Hearts" is set in the 1950s, it speaks indirectly but compellingly to the discomfort surrounding gender that the call for nontraditional occupations caused some girls and young women in the early 1980s, the period in which the story was published. Well received in Canada, the short story cycle *The Elizabeth Stories* in which the story then appeared was reprinted in Britain and the United States in 1987, earning two American literary awards.[31] The 1986 film version of the story also resonated with audiences and juries, receiving second prize in the live-action film category (for shorts under thirty minutes) at the International Children's Film Festival in Chicago in the same year and an honourable mention in the literary adaptations (elementary) category at the National Educational Media Network Competition awards in Oakland in 1987.

Boyishly built—tall and big-boned—the protagonist, Elizabeth Kessler, to her great humiliation, is assigned the only male role, that of the heartbreaker knave, in her ballet class's recital. The narrative thus chronicles an eleven-year-old girl's crisis in femininity, asking why a masculine-looking girl cannot be accepted as female by her milieu. As such, the source story and its adaptation offer a twist on one of the period's gender-related quandaries that the call to broaden personal and career choices posed for some girls: How do young women who assume so-called masculine roles or who display such traits retain their sense of femininity or even femaleness? Oppressed by the strict norms of gendered appearance adhered to by her mid-twentieth-century, small, conservative hometown, the fictional Garten, Ontario, Elizabeth is distressed at being perceived as too hefty to play a part reflecting her biological sexual identity (fig. 8.2).[32] Forced to acknowledge that her body type does not conform to that of the delicate ballerina and thus disallows her from projecting the epitomic image of traditional femininity, Elizabeth feels she has hit "a hidden switch that suddenly made visible, as far as my eye could see, limits and lines and boundaries over which one could not transgress without great danger and pain. There it was for the first time; the minefield of sex."[33] She encounters the age-old conundrum of what it means to be "woman"—whether it is an essential or constructed identity—and what it means to have society accept or reject various physical versions of it. She instinctively begins seeking a way out of these gendered limitations, a process Huggan shows to be fraught with pitfalls, given the limited number of constructive forms of female rebellion. In a bid to avoid playing the inauthentic male, Elizabeth acts out in ways traditionally associated with pathological feminine behaviour: melodramatically feigning illness and indulging in fantasies of self-injury. Paradoxically, her bid to find her own particular, perhaps unconventional, more masculine form of femaleness is in the end encouraged by a brazenly feminine woman, the "flamboyant," "flashy," and very fashionable friend of her mother's, Aunt Eadie, a never-married executive secretary to a stock broker, whose "loose" social and sexual mores send Elizabeth's conservative father into tirades.[34] This extravagantly feminine woman flirts with vice as a means of circumventing stultifying codes of conduct.

The adapters include all the pivotal points in the narrative, the "cardinal functions" that McFarlane argues are transferred from source text to film when the filmmaker is "bent" on remaining faithful to the original narrative.[35] Changes both to and within these cardinal points may reflect progressive or regressive ideological alterations to the source text or may bespeak a neutral stance. In this particular case, the adapters adhere to all the basic story elements related to Elizabeth's gender crisis and subsequent quest for identity, reflecting their decision to tackle the story's timely and ideologically engaged theme. As such, the film shows (with only minor modifications) the assignment of the male role to Elizabeth; the lack of parental understanding of her distress; the dress rehearsal in which she initially dons the knave costume; the purchase of her constricting first bra by her mother; the theatrical attempts Elizabeth makes to avoid performing; the humiliating recital, at the end of which she defiantly shouts, "I'm really a girl"; the mortification of her parents at her display of "hysteria," as her father labels it; and the arrival of Aunt Eadie, who conveys the notions of risk taking and nearly limitless possibility by teaching Elizabeth poker as well as the ideas of diversity and performance in assuming identity by giving her a "box of discarded costume jewelry."[36]

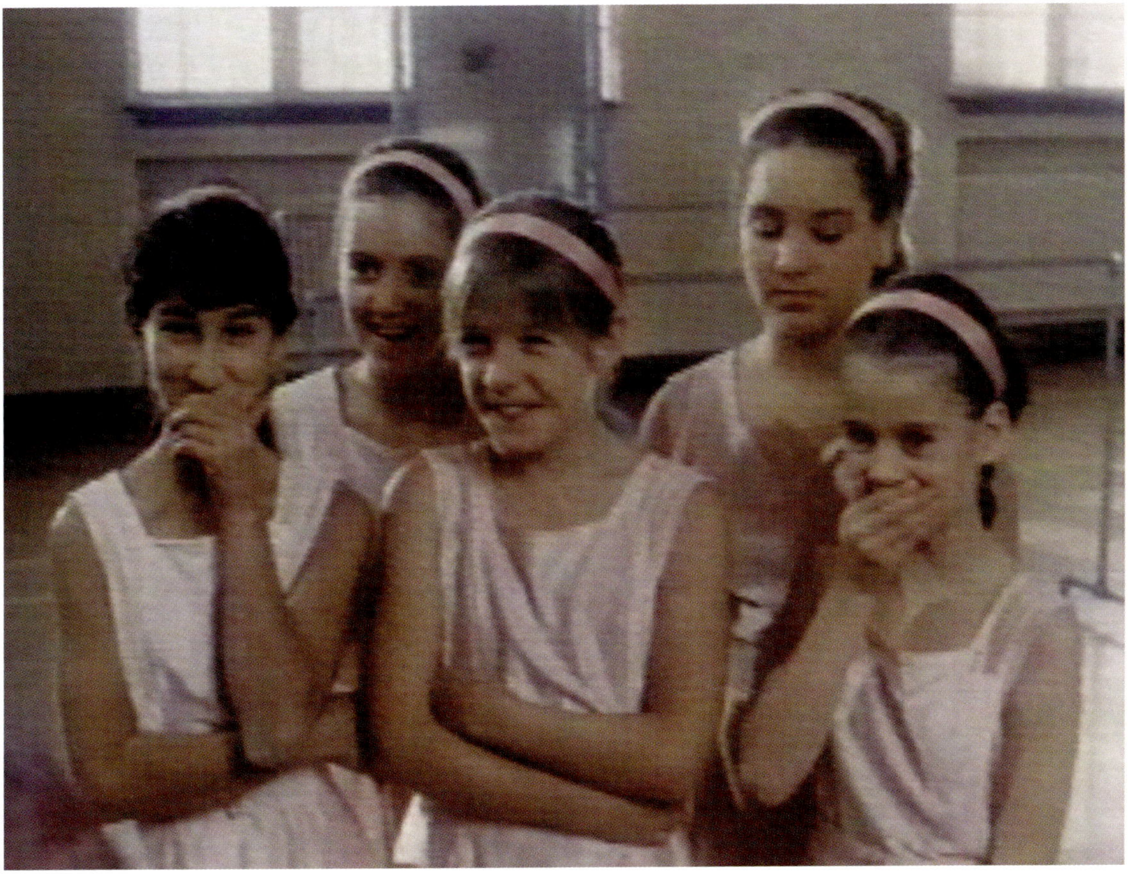

FIGURE 8.2 Elizabeth looks downcast as her fine-boned peers titter when she is informed in ballet class that she will play the male lead in the upcoming ballet recital. VHS frame grab. *Jack of Hearts*. Courtesy of Alliance Films Inc. All rights reserved.

However, subtle changes in plotting, dialogue, and costuming revise Elizabeth's and her mentor's characterization, making them more conservative than one would expect if the adapters were heeding the calls for less traditional portrayals of girls and the women from whom they learn about gender. Although the film addresses in a superficially positive way some of the task force's suggestions for broadening the image and role assignment of girls, it also partially, if unintentionally, undermines others concerned with the intellectual abilities and the emotional tendencies of girls and their female mentors.

One of the most significant differences in the narrative order is in the timing of Aunt Eadie's actual arrival at the Kesslers', a change that ultimately weakens Elizabeth as an agent capable of reflecting even instinctively on the factors shaping her own development. In the source text, Aunt Eadie arrives near the end, only after the weekend of the fateful recital; she does not witness Elizabeth's disgraceful "hysteria."[37] By contrast, in the film, she arrives near the beginning of the story, not long after Elizabeth has learned that she must play the male lead and has unsuccessfully sought her parents' sympathy. The screen version of Aunt Eadie thus witnesses not only Elizabeth's on-stage rebellion but also her subsequent chastisement by her father, a sequence of events that changes Aunt Eadie's rapport with Elizabeth, recuperating Aunt Eadie for a more traditional, empathetic, and nurturing role. Unlike in the source story's denouement, in which her primary motivation for playing poker with Elizabeth is self-serving—to fulfill a personal need to break temporarily with stifling social rules—in the film her primary motivation is altruistic. While in the film she revels in her vices (smoking, drinking, and card playing), she also, if not mostly, seeks to distract Elizabeth from her woes by having her engage in unconventional female leisure activity. The poker lesson leads to a conversation not found in the source text on the acceptability of being different. Seeking to bolster Elizabeth's sense of self-worth, Aunt Eadie avows her own fearlessness at not conforming to conservative social values (symbolized by Elizabeth's disapproving, small-town banker father). Implicitly offering herself as a role model, Aunt Eadie encourages Elizabeth to accept her own form of difference—her unconventionally feminine body. The adaptation thus accords Aunt Eadie an actively didactic role as conveyer of "life lessons," as they are overtly termed in the film (fig. 8.3). They are not formulated as such in the source story. This new role for the adult character perhaps increases the irony of her assumption of such a function, given her outcast status, but nevertheless recasts her within a more respectably maternal relationship with her temporary female charge.

In contrast, in the story, Aunt Eadie's mentorship role is more implicit, with the young girl, Elizabeth, the one extrapolating insights from the poker lesson and from the pace and drama of the game itself. Aunt Eadie does no more than teach the "solace of rules ... the thrill of tampering with chance" and then affirm Elizabeth's abilities and worth after Elizabeth wins the pot: "You're good.... You're going to be okay."[38] Ascertaining the significance of the card game through observation and self-reflection, the young Elizabeth in the source text exhibits more agency and psychological independence than she does in the film, in which she apprehends the game's meaning through the explicit teaching of an adult, and Huggan exhibits more faith in her adult readers' interpretative abilities than the film adapters do in that of their youthful spectators. In tempering Elizabeth's capacity to begin working things through for herself, the adapters reduce her power to broach the decision-making process, a skill reflecting intellectual competence, which the task force report had also advocated amplifying in female characterizations. In reverting to the simplistic approach of ensuring a more positive, in this case less self-indulgent, image of an adult woman, the adapters show little faith in the young

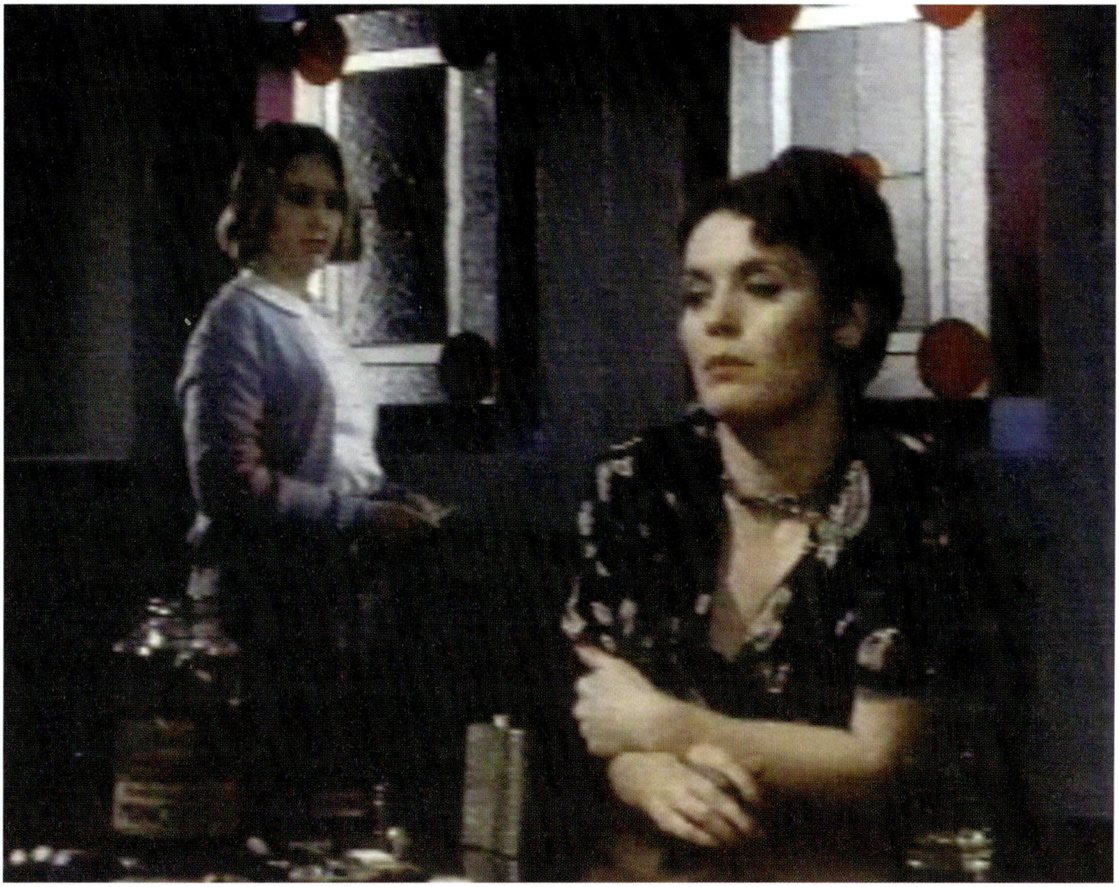

FIGURE 8.3 Aunt Eadie (Patricia Phillips), an atypical, flashy, and flamboyant role model, gives Elizabeth life lessons, telling her that Trudy, Elizabeth's delicate dance partner and chief taunter, along with those of Trudy's ilk, do not have "a thing on" Elizabeth. VHS frame grab. *Jack of Hearts*. Courtesy of Alliance Films Inc. All rights reserved.

audience's ability to think critically about the thematic significance of this particular adult character's interaction with the young girl. Early critics of the positive images approach had argued for just that type of critically engaged interaction as a necessary pedagogical exercise when using film in school to teach awareness about sex-role stereotyping.[39] As this case reveals, both girl character and girl spectator are relegated to a more passive relationship within the now more evidently hierarchal adult world, one in which the adult instructs and the child learns.

Not only do the source story and its adaptation suggest the importance of adult women in helping girls deal with the emotional challenges of not conforming to gender norms, but they explore the nature and construction of gender identity, glossed over in the task force's call for a wider range of roles and relationships for girls and women. The fundamentally performative nature of gender is a central theme of both the source story and its film adaptation, relayed through the metaphoric use of the ballet motif as well as the repeated references to costuming, notably in the depictions of the young girls' outfits for their dance routines and the adult women's everyday attire. Elizabeth's costume fitting at the dress rehearsal underlines the elaborate preparation required to carry off a gendered performance as well as its potentially fundamental inauthenticity. Elizabeth's wearing of the comparatively loose knave's costume over her confining first bra suggests the constructed, conflicting, and layered nature of this type of performance. In addition, the source story, unlike the film, overtly reveals the mother's role in imparting to her daughter the ways of presenting femininity in larger society, underscoring the socialization process in engendering the girl. Mrs. Kessler explains to Elizabeth "the importance of appearance,"[40] training her to assume a conservative form of femininity by encouraging her to admire Aunt Eadie's sense of classy fashion, while discouraging the imitation of her more gaudy tastes.

In the story, Elizabeth ponders the seemingly familiar "conventions of dressing up," asking, "What did it *mean* to be a girl or a boy, and why did I feel like such a failure?"[41] However, in the film, after being assigned the male role, Elizabeth's drolly toned voice-over simply laments, "Could no one understand what I was feeling? A boy! To play a boy! I knew it would expose what a disaster I was as a girl," and in the next scene, she complains in a line not remotely similar to anything in the story, "Everyone else gets to wear beautiful dresses. I have to dress up like a stupid boy!"[42] Her instinctive questioning of the larger issue of gendered performance in the source text is narrowed and personalized in the film to merely her distress over not being able to preen prettily. The insertion of this line points to the underlying stereotypical aspiration to be an object of beauty, the precursor to the sex object, something that the task force report specifically sought to reduce in media representations of girls and women. The adapters may be recognizing the phenomenon of young girls instinctively playing up to an "internalized … male gaze," a reality Emma Renold reviews in her study *Girls, Boys and Junior Sexualities*.[43] If anything, the film subtly accentuates this emerging desire by creating a scene, nonexistent in the story, in which Elizabeth, hidden in her closet, tearfully dreams of being a ballerina held up by a male dancer (fig. 8.4). She admires a picture of a ballet couple, tracing her finger along the ballerina's slender, graceful arm.

In the source story, Elizabeth does manifest a yen for dressing up, but not because it makes her feel or look attractive or because it may pair her with a supportive boy.[44] She remembers becoming enamoured of costuming because it offers opportunities for ephemeral escape from social strictures:

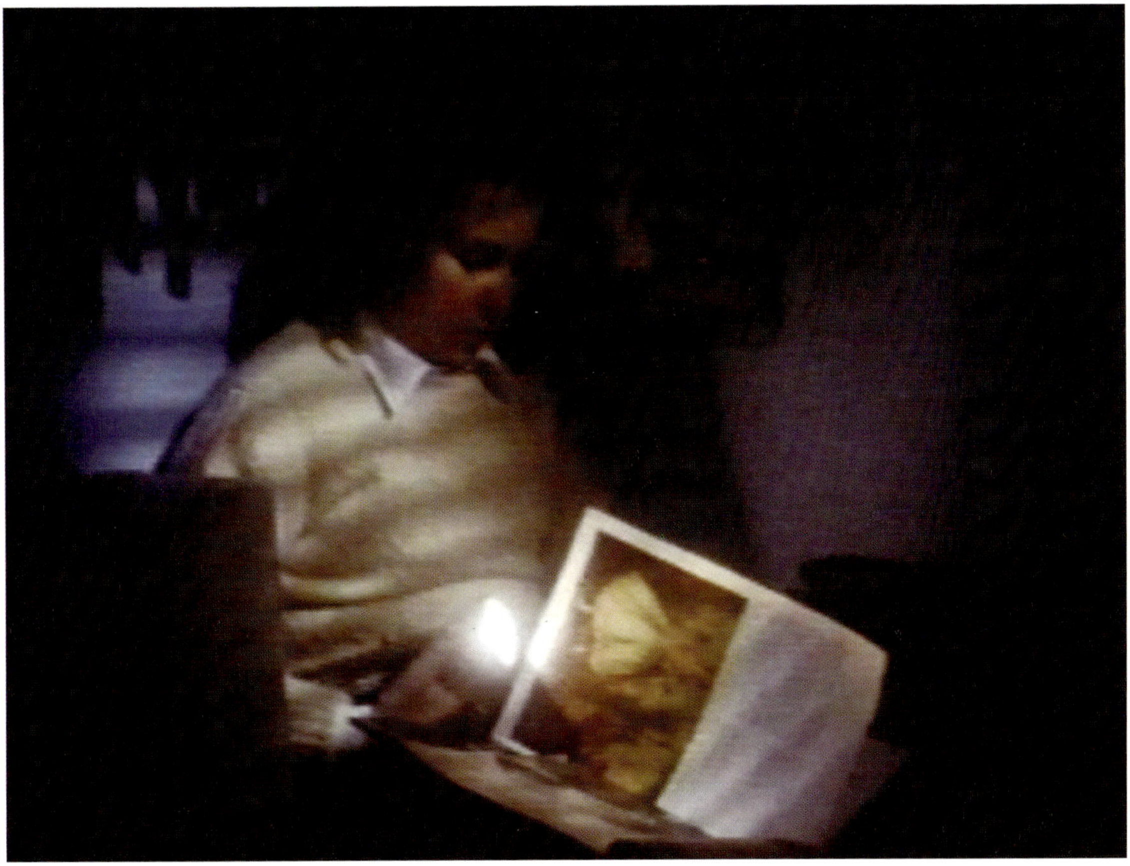

FIGURE 8.4 Elizabeth hides in her closet, tearfully leafing through images of ballerinas she dreams of emulating.VHS frame grab. *Jack of Hearts*. Courtesy of Alliance Films Inc. All rights reserved.

> Even in the early years of our own recitals, when the junior classes only got to dress up as tulips or bunnies, I felt my heart would burst with excitement once I was zipped and buttoned into a new being. I would become, for the duration of that dance, whatever my costume dictated and thus discovered a release from the confines of Garten, transient but intense.[45]

In addition, Elizabeth's need for recognition and acceptance by her peers is expressed in the precursor text in her one reverie about her upcoming costumed performance. Before she is told in the source story that she has been assigned the male lead, she fantasizes that she is being trained for the starring female role, "fore[seeing] something for … [her]self in glistening white satin and tulle. The other girls … [serving as her] handmaidens, circling around."[46] An inelegant, only child, rejected by the other girls in her ballet class, she craves—for once—to be the centre of her dainty peers' attention and admiration. The whiteness and sheerness of her outfit connote the innocence, fragility, and illusionary quality of her dream in this world ordered by stereotypes, where she bitterly comes to realize that she is considered "too ugly to be a girl."[47] She can be only the object of her petty peers' "mockery and teasing."[48]

In both source story and its film version, the large Elizabeth becomes an object of public derision through the antics of her dance partner, the petite Trudy, at the recital. At the end of their dance number in the source text, she "suddenly [and] unrehearsed ... jumps up and perches on ... [Elizabeth's] extended knee and fluffs her skirt, and Mr. Willis [the local newspaper's photographer] springs up and snaps a picture."[49] Humiliated at being made the butt of an apparently newsworthy joke that denies her sexual identity and, implicitly, her as yet unexpressed sexual orientation, the young and sensitive Elizabeth shouts three times out at the startled audience, "I'm really a girl."[50] The only people who the readers learn for certain are embarrassed by her outburst are her parents. The film adds to this scene by having Trudy sassily kiss the discomfited Elizabeth twice on the cheek, implicitly ridiculing her heterosexual desirability, while lampooning her as a poor parody of a boy and underscoring her raison d'être as a mere prop for Trudy's own attention-getting shenanigans (fig. 8.5). The audience, which begins laughing when Trudy poses on Elizabeth's knee, roars even louder when Trudy begins kissing Elizabeth. As in the story, the confused and upset protagonist attempts to reassert her sexual identity; however, the adapters have her begin her yelled affirmations about being a girl with one about not being a boy, which is then reinserted twice more in her brief but impassioned monologue. They also have her incorporate twice within it the rhetorical question "Can't you see?"[51] The overt reiteration that she is not a boy reflects a need some girls expressed in the gender-bending period in which the adaptation was made to expressly distinguish themselves from boys, even when they took on so-called male roles. The repeated nature of the affirmations suggests a near phobia about being wrongly perceived, a theme played upon by the motifs of seeing built into the scene through repeated cuts to the watching recital audience and to the photographer, with his sizable camera and its enormous, firing flash, and then mirrored in the implicit existence of the watching film audience itself. Elizabeth's second assertion about not being a boy is accompanied by a close-up of her with her painted-on moustache, which then cuts to a young adult man in the audience looking askance. He is no doubt as taken aback as the rest of the audience by her lack of feminine decorum. However, his facial expression, not clearly replicated by his female companion, also suggests the difficulty the heterosexual males in the audience have in perceiving Elizabeth as anything but masculine and therefore ever attractive or one day sexually desirable. The adult Elizabeth's

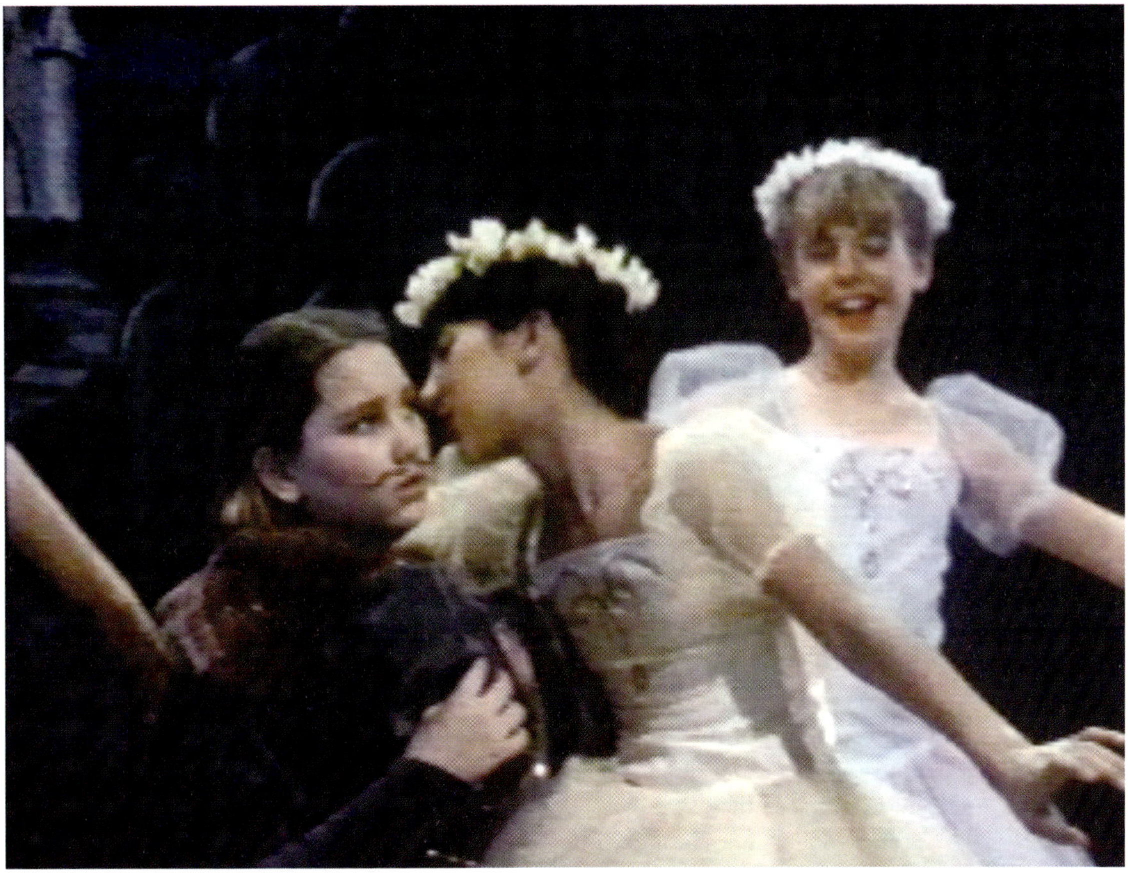

FIGURE 8.5 Trudy (Michelle Polak), perched on Elizabeth's knee, kisses Elizabeth as they take their bows after completing their dance. A third girl in the background joins the audience and the other ballerinas on stage in laughing at Trudy's antics. VHS frame grab. *Jack of Hearts*. Courtesy of Alliance Films Inc. All rights reserved.

voice-over reveals her pained self-consciousness about her body, unarticulated at this moment in the source text: "They were laughing at me.... I was large and ugly."[52] Through these various additions, the adapters show more forthrightly than Huggan in her text the anguish of nonacceptance that gender variance may bring to developing heterosexual girls of masculine build in a traditionally gendered, appearance-driven society.[53] The scene in the adaptation is reminiscent of a noted one in Dorothy Arzner's *Dance, Girl, Dance* (1940), studied by feminist film critics in particular in the latter part of the twentieth century, in which a nonerotic, young dance-hall woman, who plays the stooge to a sexy and glamorous principal, turns on her audience, berating them with her view of their cruelly amused perception of her. While, as Pam Cook argues, the Arzner film critiques "the ideology of woman as spectacle, object of [male] desire,"[54] the adaptation of "Jack of Hearts" critiques the tyranny of delicate femininity as the sum total of what is socially acceptable for girls. This set of modifications, building on notions suggested by the source text, allows the adaptation to delve beyond the mere broadening of images recommended by the task force report, revealing not only a progressive questioning of femininity but an aesthetics informed by feminist film history and concomitant theory.

Given its capacity for visual presentation, the film conveys the idea of gender as a costumed performance more overtly and consistently than the source text, adding, of cinematic necessity, depictions of costume even when they are not described in the source text. However, some of the costume's gender coding is also altered in the adaptation in ways that elide the social critique of gender confinement. One of the notable changes relates to the colour of the bra that Elizabeth's mother, embarrassed by the bounce of her daughter's prepubescent breasts during the dress rehearsal, buys Elizabeth just prior to the recital. In the source story, the brassiere finally foisted on her is "blue satin,"[55] and she states clearly that it uncomfortably restrains and warms her active body. She explicitly bewails the discomfort it causes her during the recital: "cut[ting] and bind[ing] along … [her] midriff and under [her] arms."[56] The undergarment's blue colour, twice repeated for emphasis, suggests the hidden patriarchal codes that constrain the blossoming young woman. Over her concealed underwear fits the male costume that further "weight[s] [her] down."[57] Elizabeth's negative comments about the inner and outer layers of her gender-making costumes (she refers to the blue bra as "costume-like") make it clear that her femaleness is being oppressed by male-defined gender codes in both the most outwardly public and most intimately private spheres.[58]

The film is less explicit. The bra is white, suggestive of virginal innocence, of a pre-gendered state, and Elizabeth's voice-over during the recital laments only that her "costume [her knave outfit, not her undergarment] boiled and ripped at … [her] as … [she] repeated the steps blindly."[59] Only the external layer of masculine social codes creates discomfort. Gesture in the film does not suggest the digging of the bra straps into her shoulders, which she describes experiencing in the story when raising her arms. The whitewashing of the undergarment's colour-coding refocuses the theme of oppression solely on Elizabeth being made to look like a boy; the more hidden constraints of patriarchy, symbolized by the biting blue bra, are not suggested. Nevertheless, in the film scene in which the mother purchases the bra, Mrs. Kessler and the saleswoman both wear blue, while in the source text the mother wears a more neutral and fashionable black and the saleswoman's clothes are not described. Also in the film, Mrs. Kessler utters a reworked version of the saleswoman's words in the story, telling the protesting Elizabeth that she will "get used to" the pointy bra cups.[60] The mother, flanked by the saleswoman, is thus more obviously aligned in the film's version of this scene with the prevailing masculine social codes, an alignment she displays in other ways in other scenes in the source story. Thus, the conditions under which Elizabeth acquires the bra in the adaptation do hint at patriarchy subtly functioning through acquiescing women who socialize their daughters into circumscribed, unnatural roles. However, since the bra's direct effects on Elizabeth, together with their symbolic meaning, remain unsuggested in the adaptation, her instinctive, subtextual objections to the limiting social system are excised. Moreover, her ultimate immurement behind a hidden but confining version of the feminine is left unintimated in the adaptation, as the dressing room's pink curtain, behind which she tries on the bra in the source story, is neutralized to brown and yellow in film.

While Elizabeth's mother initiates her into the fundamental and anchoring constraints of femininity, her ballet entourage excludes her from its public version. Her shunning from the normative female community is emphasized in the adaptation through an expanded use of gendered colour-coding in costuming. Specifically, the adaptation extends the coding of her ballet teacher's dress beyond what it is in the source story and contrasts it with Elizabeth's costumes to reveal tensions between masculine and feminine codes and Elizabeth's placement within them. In the story, only once is the colour of Mrs. Verser's clothing mentioned: during the dress rehearsal, when it is described as "sapphire silk,"[61] suggesting the coordinating role of male social codes behind the scenes. In the film, by virtue of its presentational power, her costuming is documented throughout the narrative. Her attire shifts from a floral purple blouse and flowing orange skirt in the ballet class scene, in which she assigns the pink-clad Elizabeth the male role, to a fussy aquamarine gown at the dress rehearsal, during which Elizabeth glumly tries out the dark male costume, to a formal, light rose outfit at the actual recital, at which Elizabeth unhappily performs the male lead. The gendered colour-coding of Mrs. Verser's garments thus alternates between the feminine (ballet class at the beginning and ballet recital near the end) and the masculine (ballet rehearsal in the middle), underscoring the fluctuation between the two gender codes. The central thematic tension between the two is hinted at midway through the film by the main characteristics of her blue gown, its hue connoting the masculine and its soft form, sheer sleeves, and satin ribbon trim, the feminine. That the ballet teacher's final dress colour is soft pink in a recital dominated by budding ballerinas in tutus of various girlish pastels (lilacs, pinks, salmons, apricots, turquoises, and baby blues) emphasizes that the performance of the feminine is the teacher's and her students' ultimate goal, the culmination of weeks of practice. This predominance of the "frothy" feminine, as it is characterized in the source text,[62] underscores Elizabeth's gendered exclusion as the more drably attired, chunky, masculine female (fig. 8.6).

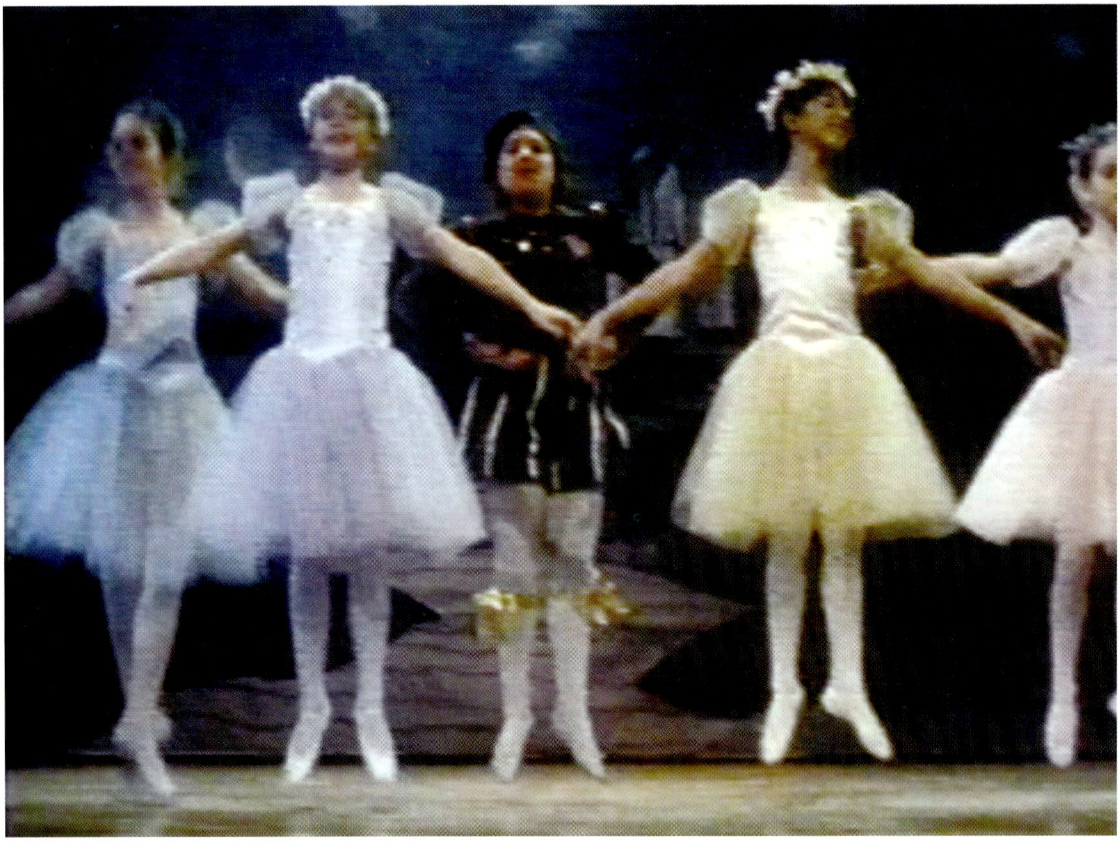

FIGURE 8.6 Several shots show Elizabeth set apart from the other girls. In this example, Elizabeth springs with her ballerina peers during the ballet recital, while the arms of the tutu-clad girls in front reinforce her exclusion from their feminine line. Trudy is on the right. VHS frame grab. *Jack of Hearts*. Courtesy of Alliance Films Inc.

This visual tracking of Elizabeth's gendered position through the coding of costuming focuses the film narrative almost exclusively around her struggle for female identity, largely censoring a concomitant theme found in the source text of learning by adulthood to play hardball in the risky, male-run game of gendered power relations after being temporarily quashed as a young girl by her father at story's end. Having clearly set up the main conflict of the film as solely Elizabeth's identity crisis, the adapters have the narrative conclude more optimistically than the source story, suggesting an easier path and a more immediately positive outcome for Elizabeth. Specifically, in both versions, Aunt Eadie gives Elizabeth her old costume jewellery, implicitly affirming Elizabeth's right, regardless of her body type, to flashy feminine apparel (should she wish to wear it) and more implicitly nurturing Elizabeth's need to try out new identities. The story's final reference to costuming is, however, ambiguous. After Elizabeth's father apparently forces Aunt Eadie's departure, he, supported by Elizabeth's acquiescent mother, orders Elizabeth to remove the trashy rhinestone ring she received from Aunt Eadie. We are not told how Elizabeth reacts, although we infer that she will at some point disobey her parents, since she reveals that in the coming years she will play poker with Aunt Eadie many times again.[63] Thus the young girl, whose mother admonishes to be "good," to obey her father by removing Aunt Eadie's meretricious ring, becomes, ironically, "good at poker"—a game for so-called bad girls.[64] In beginning to master Aunt Eadie's survival skills, symbolized by the card game, Elizabeth assumes the rebelliousness of the female outsider. Like Aunt Eadie, she will excel at taking risks, at conning her way out of bad situations, at going beyond social boundaries and gender limitations, exemplified by eventually learning to bluff men to the poker pot without compunction.[65] She will project a harsher, less decorous, less passively feminine image as she matures. She will become adept at playing the male game in adulthood through ruse, sham, and show, flirting with the myriad possibilities that life has to offer, as symbolized by the countless poker hands she begins contemplating. The refining of those acts and characteristics lie in her future, though. At the very end of the actual story, the eleven-year-old Elizabeth remains caught in a dull, restrictive, identity-stifling environment. She hides in her closet, dealing out cards, "figuring out all the possibilities," capable only of "dreaming of face-cards"—her alternative identities—at night.[66] Her bid to consider other identities remains, for the time being, concealed, any overt attempts at trying out and trying on crushed by her father.

The adaptation, in contrast, changes the ending of the source story to lessen any doubt that, as the narrative closes in childhood, Elizabeth is "going to make it after all," to borrow the phrase from the popular Mary Tyler Moore sitcom of the 1970s. Here, the adapters are reading the source text for Elizabeth's future hopes, as Elliott suggests not infrequently happens in adaptations, in this case Elizabeth's desire to eventually succeed as a woman. Simultaneously, the film erases the allusions to her stray from feminine propriety as an adult. The film does make it clear that Elizabeth is actively seeking to forge her own version of female identity thanks to Aunt Eadie's identity-fashioning gift of baubles. However, the scene in the story in which Mr. Kessler orders his daughter to remove Aunt Eadie's discarded ring is substituted for an invented one in the film in which Elizabeth, alone in her bedroom, tries on necklace after necklace, her grown-up voice-over affirming in a progressive, didactic tone: "Finally, I felt like someone. I had a glimpse of who I was becoming, not Eadie, not Trudy, not mother, but me, Elizabeth. The next morning I would use the word individual for the very first time." This overt summation of her maturation process is not in the source story.

Since Elizabeth affirms that she is becoming *unlike* her immediate models, who do not remotely tend to the masculine or otherwise different, running the gamut from the matronly (her mother) to versions of the ultrafeminine (Aunt Eadie and Trudy), spectators infer that Elizabeth may succeed in differentiating herself from them. However, her trying on identities using highly feminine jewellery raises conflicting questions about how free she really is to construct her own identity as an unconventionally feminine young woman. On the one hand, her actions affirm her interest, as a more masculine girl, in donning feminine accessories—and her right to do so. On the other, her actions suggest an attempt at projecting a feminine exterior, at compensating for masculine traits. To a certain extent her actions in the film mimic the situation developed in the story, in which Elizabeth leans to Aunt Eadie's ways. The film's necklaces serve as substitutes for the source story's ring, although they are less garish, less tarty, not referring as strongly to Aunt Eadie's shadier side, as did her gaudy, "spectacular" ring, whose "red enamel" evoked her flashing "painted nails."[67] However, in downplaying Elizabeth's secret emulation of Aunt Eadie, the film remains ambiguous on how broadly it is embracing diversified female images. The masculine girl cannot be glaringly provocative.

Indeed, the adapters play on the notion of ambiguity rather than female variance by suggesting Elizabeth's androgyny rather than a more audacious, even wily, form of masculine femininity. Building on the hybrid shading of her knave costume—which is neither black nor white but grey in both source text and film, suggesting the blurring of gender codes—the adapters also mark Elizabeth's décor and clothing as dual-gendered, something unspecified in the precursor text. When Aunt Eadie comes to fetch Elizabeth to play poker, the young girl is dressed in a pink and blue plaid skirt. Ultimately, we understand her true identity to be androgynous, as her bedroom, in which she tries on her necklaces in the final scene, also has a gender-mixed décor: blue walls and pink furniture. Here she assertively begins playing with this blended identity. No longer hidden in her closet, as in the source text, Elizabeth sits more openly on her bed and faces the audience directly. Her act of putting on the necklaces is framed by her resolutely dealing out cards, suggesting that she will deal her way out of her confused, confusing situation once she assumes her bipartite identity.[68] More confident and less obviously oppressed by her paternally controlled milieu, Elizabeth is facing the future—and us, her audience, her perceivers—with a metaphorically stronger hand than in the source story. Cleaned up for a grade-school audience, the film makes no allusions to her card-playing adulthood—notably to her less than decorous, deceptive methods for beating her male competitors. Didacticism prevails as the source text, originally aimed at adults, is edited, the girl's future in the dicey world of patriarchy sanitized and unproblematized.[69]

On a superficial level, then, the adaptations with girl protagonists in the Canadian Short Story Video Series attempt to depict a broader range of opportunities for girls, refashioning on screen elements from the source texts to respond to the generalized call for more positive images that was circulating during the period in which the films were produced. However, as the close comparison of the short story "Jack of Hearts" and its film adaptation reveals, the revisions make for both regressive and progressive outcomes, at times simplifying or eliding the complexities and conflicts associated with gendered roles and representations, at others echoing or engaging with feminist concerns of the period. Ultimately, adapters opt to idealize possibilities for girls rather than grapple, as fully as the texts or reality itself might dictate, with the challenges that maturation posed for young women in late twentieth-century Canada, when conventions surrounding gender were being questioned.

Notes

I would like to thank my research assistants, Isabelle Guy and Nachammai Raman.

1 Alice Munro, "Boys and Girls," in *Dance of the Happy Shades* (Toronto: Ryerson Press, 1968), 119.

2 The study of the adaptations of Canadian short stories remains largely unstudied. See Peter Dickinson, *Screening Gender, Framing Genre: Canadian Literature into Film* (Toronto: University of Toronto Press, 2007), 11.

3 *Jack of Hearts*, VHS, directed by Cynthia Scott. Co-produced by the National Film Board of Canada and Atlantis Films Ltd. (Montreal: National Film Board of Canada, 1996). First released in 1986.

I will be referring to those involved in the adaptation as "the adapters." Although the various contributors to the three phases of film production have specific roles, a number of those contributors may, in one way or another, influence the adaptation. As Monique Carcaud-Macaire and Jeanne-Marie Clerc argue, the process of adaptation is a dynamic form of mediation. Ultimately, those involved in the process act as a collective interpreter. See their article "Pour une approche sociocritique de l'adaptation cinématographique: L'exemple de *Mort à Venise*," in *La Transécriture: Pour une théorie de l'adaptation*, ed. André Gaudreault and Thierry Groensteen, 151–176 (Quebec: Éditions Nota bene, 1998), 152–153.

4 Robert Stam, "Introduction: The Theory and Practice of Adaptation," in *Literature and Film: A Guide to the Theory and Practice of Film Adaptation*, ed. Robert Stam and Alessandra Raengo (Oxford: Blackwell, 2005), 17. He is far from the first to make such claims, as similar ideas go back, in one form or another, to at least George Bluestone's *Novels into Film* (1957).

5 Brian McFarlane, *Novel to Film: An Introduction to the Theory of Adaptation* (Oxford: Clarendon Press, 1996), 21–22.

6 Stam, "Introduction: The Theory and Practice of Adaptation," 43.

7 Kamilla Elliott, "Literary Film Adaptation and the Form/Content Dilemma," in *Narrative across Media: The Languages of Storytelling*, ed. Marie-Laure Ryan, 220–243 (Lincoln: University of Nebraska Press, 2004), 234.

8 Dickinson, *Screening Gender*, 211; Julie Sanders, *Adaptation and Appropriation* (London: Routledge, 2006), 20.

9 Christopher Orr, "The Discourse on Adaptation," *Wide Angle* 6, no. 2 (1984): 72–76, p. 73.

10 After decades of near abrogation in literary studies, authorial intention, or perhaps more accurately re-intention in the case of adaptation, has been rehabilitated by Linda Hutcheon as a legitimate concern. See her *A Theory of Adaptation* (London: Routledge, 2006). See 107 for the quotation and 105–111 for her discussion of this particular issue.

11 Elliott, "Literary Film Adaptation," 238.

12 Some of these strategies are discussed in Lisa Jeanne Weckerle, "Revisioning Narratives: Feminist Adaptation Strategies on Stage and Screen" (PhD diss., University of Texas at Austin, 1999).

13 Although case studies have documented the prevalence of adaptations depoliticizing source texts with explicit or implicit feminist critique, others have observed the opposite phenomenon. For a cross-section of these various studies see, for example, Molly Hite, "Romance, Marginality, and Matrilineage: *The Color Purple* and *Their Eyes Were Watching God*," in *Reading Black, Reading Feminist,* ed. Henry Louis Gates, Jr., 431–453 (New York: Penguin Meridian, 1990); Benjamin Lefebvre, "Stand by Your Man: Adapting L.M. Montgomery's *Anne of Green Gables*," *Essays on Canadian Writing* 76 (Spring 2002): 149–167; Kim A. Loudermilk, *Fictional Feminism: How American Bestsellers Affect the Movement for Women's Equality* (London: Routledge, 2004); Barbara Tepa Lupack, ed., *Vision/Re-Vision: Adapting Contemporary American Fiction by Women to Film* (Bowling Green, OH: Bowling Green State University Popular Press, 1996); Lee Parpart, "Adapting Emotions: Notes on the Transformation of Affect and Ideology from 'We So Seldom Look on Love' to *Kissed*," *Essays on Canadian Writing* 76 (Spring 2002): 51–82; Thelma J. Shinn, "Gender Images and Patterns from Novel to Film," *Gender, I-deology: Essays on Theory, Fiction and Film*, ed. Chantal Cornut-Gentille D'Arcy and José Ángel García, 451–459 (Atlanta: Rodopi Landa, 1996); and Sue Sorensen, "'Damnable Feminization'? The Merchant Ivory Film Adaptation of Henry James's *The Bostonians*," *Film/Literature Quarterly* 25, no. 3 (1997): 231–235.

14 Francesco Casetti, "Adaptation and Mis-adaptations: Film, Literature, and Social Discourses," in *A Companion to Literature and Film*, ed. Robert Stam and Alessandra Raengo, 81–91 (Oxford: Blackwell, 2004), 83.

15 Ibid., 84.

16 Ibid.

17 Canada Radio-television and Telecommunications Commission—Task Force on Sex-Role Stereotyping in the Broadcast Media, *Images of Women: Report of the Task Force on Sex-Role Stereotyping in the Broadcast Media* (Ottawa: Department of Supply and Services Canada, 1982).

18 For a review of the literature of this type of research, see Nancy Signorielli, "Television's Gender Role Images and Contribution to Stereotyping: Past, Present, Future," in *Handbook of Children and the Media*, ed. Dorothy G. Singer and Jerome L. Singer, 341–358 (London: Sage, 2001).

19 The NFB originally called the series the Canadian Short Story Film Series. Three other films were considered for the series, for a total of twenty-eight. Two were part of Atlantis Films' original roster—*Fred,* which had an adolescent girl protagonist, and *Game Plan*, which had two elderly gentlemen as main characters—but these films did not make it into the distribution agreement with the NFB. A third, *Capital*, which also had male lead characters, was initially made by the NFB, recut in co-production with Atlantis Films, then excluded from the series. Both its versions are currently distributed by the NFB but separately from the series. Twenty of the twenty-five films that were included in the series are still available for sale through the NFB, including all those discussed in this study.

20 At 28 percent, this result is similar to the 30 percent of starring roles that were filled by women on prime-time adult American television programs between 1953 and 1977 (Joseph R. Dominick, "The Portrayal of Women in Prime Time, 1953–1977," *Sex Roles* 5, no. 4 [1979]: 405–411, specifically

p. 408) and is better than the total nonexistence of female lead characters observed in a random sampling of American educational programming for children of the era (Rita Dohrmann, "The Effects of Television on Children and Adolescents: A Gender Profile of Children's Educational TV," *Journal of Communication* 25, no. 4 [1975]: 56–65, specifically Table 1, p. 58 and p. 60). Similarly, the CRTC reported in *The Portrayal of Gender in Canadian Broadcasting: Summary Report 1984–1988* (Ottawa: Minister of Supply and Services Canada, December 1990), pp. 20 and 28, that in 1984, 26 percent of characters in Canadian television dramas and 25 percent of characters in Canadian children's programs were female.

21 Brian J. Low, *NFB Kids: Portrayals of Children by the National Film Board of Canada, 1939–1989* (Waterloo, ON: Wilfrid Laurier University Press, 2002), 21.

22 The two films with adult female protagonists are out of the scope of this study. One is based on Alice Munro's short story "Connection," and the other on Sinclair Ross's "The Painted Door."

23 This interest in depicting female characters of different ages continues with the films about adult women, with *Connection* and *Painted Door* portraying women at somewhat different stages of marital breakdown.

24 This fact contrasts with the 12 percent of female characters in Canadian dramas who were from visible minorities in 1988, which was the first time the later commissioned CRTC benchmark study reported on this variable in *The Portrayal of Gender in Canadian Broadcasting*, 27.

25 Low, *NFB Kids*, 21, 159, 196–197.

26 Close reading is a productive method for this type of comparative work, as Erica Sheen suggests in her introduction to *The Classic Novel: From Page to Screen*, ed. Robert Giddings and Erica Sheen (Manchester: Manchester University Press, 2000), 11.

27 See the previously cited references to studies in this area.

28 Annette Kuhn, *Women's Pictures: Feminism and Cinema* (London: Verso, 1993), 5–8.

29 See, for example, Diane Waldman, in "There's More to a Positive Image than Meets the Eye," *Issues in Feminist Film Criticism*, ed. Patricia Erens, 13–18 (Bloomington: Indiana University Press, 1990), 14. Waldman's appraisal was first published in *Jump Cut* 18 (1978) in reaction to Linda Artel and Susan Wengraf's *Positive Images: Non-Sexist Film for Young People* (San Francisco: Bootlegger Press, 1976).

30 Brian McFarlane argues that one must distinguish between what can be transferred from one narrative medium to another and what requires actual adaptation through the use of cinematic equivalences (when they exist). See his *Novel to Film*, p. 13. I am focusing on some of the transferable elements.

31 In 1987 Huggan was awarded the New Voice of the Year Award by the Quality Paperback Book Club, indicating the popular encouragement critics felt her work merited, and the Alan Swallow Award for Fiction through the *Denver Quarterly*, reflecting the positive critical reception of her work. This acclaim was also voiced in reviews in the likes of the *New York Times*.

32 In Huggan's story, Elizabeth thinks others see her as too ugly (p. 41) and too tall (p. 42) to play the part, and once dressed for it, describes herself as "look[ing] like a big fat boy" (p. 44). In the film, her mother is more charitable, telling her, "It's probably because you're big for your age" (Atlantis Films, transcript of the film, p. 2). The pretty face of Renée Gersovitz, the young girl cast as Elizabeth, further downplays the character's masculinity in the film.

33 Isabel Huggan, "Jack of Hearts," in *The Elizabeth Stories* (Ottawa: Oberon, 1984), 43.

34 The cited adjectives are from Huggan, "Jack of Hearts," 35.

35 McFarlane, *Novel to Film*, 14.

36 Huggan, "Jack of Hearts," 52.

DEREK FOSTER

LOCATING CHILDREN IN THE DISCOURSE OF SQUEEGEE KIDS

In the late 1990s, the Ontario provincial government became concerned by the issue of squeegeeing (motorists being approached while stopped at intersections and asked if they would like to have their windshields cleaned, with the expectation of a donation in recognition of this brief labour). This issue arose after Ontario (specifically Toronto, its biggest city) became inundated with "squeegee kids" who were driven out of other provincial jurisdictions by targeted anti-squeegee laws. Squeegeeing became a lightning rod for widespread moralizing, and verbal and visual depictions of squeegee kids were marked by both concern and condemnation. Squeegeeing in the streets was a dramatic spectacle. But it was the public rhetoric of pro-squeegee activists and anti-squeegee advocates that communicated the issue to the public and dramatized it in the public imagination.

Notably, this rhetoric was both verbal and visual. If rhetoric is understood, broadly, to mean "an art of adjusting ideas to people and people to ideas,"[1] and visual rhetoric can be seen as "the study of the use of visual symbols to influence and manage meanings,"[2] then analysts of popular culture and the sometimes divisive discourses that inform it ought to pay attention to the variety of ways in which public arguments are constructed. For this particular analysis, I will focus on the rhetorical power of a comic strip, taking up the call for the application of rhetorical theory beyond the traditional approach to discrete texts such as speeches or other forms of public address.[3]

While verbal claims-making in newspapers labelled these windshield washers as "squeegee brats"[4] and "real terrorists,"[5] visual claims-makers used rhetorical platforms such as cartoons to communicate (or, in some cases, contest) such messages. This analysis will focus on a specific political cartoon strip, *Weltschmerz*, the creation of Gareth Lind. This cartoon was featured in several free, advertiser-supported weekly newspapers for more than a decade. As John Oswald noted (in a letter to the editor published in Toronto's *Eye Weekly* on April 5, 2007, when the cartoon ended its eleven-year run in that publication), "Gareth Lind's *Weltschmerz* is the most consistently and subversively clever socio-political cartoon printed in North America." While it was Toronto- and Ontario-centric (both in its publication and in its subject matter), the cartoon was also published in Alberta and focused on issues of national and international significance. Horst and Celia were the cartoon's main characters, and between 1995 and 2008 Lind used their lives and interactions as a platform to comment on topical political issues.

However, some specific cartoons did not follow the character-driven narrative and focused solely on politicians and the issues of the day. This is the case with the cartoons I examine, which deployed caricatured representations of Mel Lastman, then mayor of Toronto, and Mike Harris, the premier of Ontario at the time. Since this analysis does not depend on a strict understanding of the chronological development of the social issue of squeegeeing, the four cartoons I focus upon are not presented in their order of publication. Rather, they are used to demonstrate how cartoons can function as visual rhetoric and how cartoons can depict contemporary Canadian "children." *Weltschmerz* was not used to persuade audiences that kids should be seen in a certain light, but it does encourage audiences to identify with kids and against politicians who use kids as ballast for their political platforms.

Starting in 1997, both the mayor of Toronto and the premier of Ontario seemed particularly anxious that the fate of their shared urban spaces, cities, and communities would be rendered impure because of the presence of impure children and youth. Yet, as I will demonstrate, Lind's visual depictions of squeegee kids also had to depict the spectacular aspects of squeegee kids in order to characterize the political response to squeegee kids as extreme. Consequently, even as they attempted to subvert these politicians' rhetoric, these comics also made a visual argument about what it meant to be a kid in Lastman's Toronto and Harris's Ontario and on the receiving end of their proclamations and policies. In this sense, the use of squeegee kids as inventional topoi in the *Weltschmerz* comic is an excellent example of visual rhetoric.

Since the 1970s, the study of rhetoric has been broadened to include the nondiscursive and the nonverbal as well as the discursive and the verbal, and now any object can be interrogated as rhetoric if it is intended to modify attention, perceptions, attitudes, or behaviour.[6] Subsequently, it is not unreasonable to suggest that, given the amount of visual imagery surrounding us, "the study of verbal discourse alone is limiting because it includes only a minute portion of the symbols that affect us daily."[7] Thus, when seeking to understand how public claims-makers strategically construct their symbolic inducements in order to influence the thought and behaviour of others, we must not only examine words and speeches but also images and sometimes uncharitable or uncivil graphical discourse such as political cartoons. Visual rhetoric goes beyond semiotics. The point is not to ask what these cartoons mean. Indeed, the most important question is not "What do they symbolize?" but "What difference do they make?" Political cartoons can be entertaining, but they do more than divert people's attention from the news of the day. In fact, political cartoons can raise awareness of newsworthy items by shining a particular kind of light on these items. Political cartoons are usually one-sided and sometimes offensive, but they have the ability to reflect if not influence public opinion. In this capacity, cartoons are rhetorical devices.

Political cartoons can be highly persuasive appeals, but this is by no means the extent of their impact. Importantly, "rhetoric is more than efforts at persuasion. Through rhetorical practices, people construct, perpetuate, and transform identities, discourses, cultures, and worldviews."[8] Cartoons do just this. As DeSousa and Medhurst indicate:

> The power of the political cartoon lies not in the specific artist's intent or success at fostering change but in the degree to which, and the manner by which, the cartoonist taps the collective consciousness of readers and thereby reaffirms cultural values and individual interpretation of those values.[9]

The cartoon relies greatly on visual elements for its impact. In many ways, the visual depiction of political events and political controversies can communicate messages more directly than strictly verbal accounts. For one thing, cartoons typically use caricature, which is a device that allows audiences with limited time or passing interest to still catch the intended meaning of characters and events that are portrayed. Even if the image itself does not present a specific argument, "the image functions as visual topos"—a visual reference point that forms the basis of arguments about a variety of themes and subjects.[10] I cannot confirm how audiences for these cartoons used them to reinforce their sense of self, others, and society in general. I am most interested in how these cartoons helped to define the issue of squeegeeing and how, as a sort of snapshot of the politics of the time, they helped frame the larger issue of "kids" in that political climate. Such an investigation is important as visual rhetoric gives us "concrete images to anchor more abstract claims about childhood and the family."[11] Whether the object of inquiry is a series of images of children used to underscore the larger rhetorical purposes of public claims-making or, even more powerfully, image-based claims such as cartoons, visual rhetoric grants us insight into how Canadian children are depicted. In turn, we can recognize and reconstitute the contours of our public culture in which the contemporary child is such a contested object.

Editorial cartoons and political cartoons are often treated as synonyms within the rhetorical literature on cartoons, in part because most analyses focus on single-frame cartoons on the editorial pages that are used as a vehicle for social and political commentary. These cartoons I discuss are not the typical editorial cartoon that has been defined as "a graphic presentation typically designed in a one-panel, non-continuing format to make an independent statement or observation on political events or social policy."[12] *Weltschmerz* depends on multiple panels, a continuing format, and many words to supplement the visual representations. However, even the words are graphics that are often depicted in a manner that humorously points out shortcomings or hypocrisies within the political system. It is an explicitly "political" cartoon strip. This does not mean the ideological politics of the cartoonist follow clear-cut political party lines. But they tend to be inimical to those in power and to skewer those ripe for satire or burlesque. In this capacity, *Weltschmerz* functions like all political cartoons "to make a point through ridicule, sarcasm, or pathos. The fundamental nature of the political cartoon is to simplify and reduce complex personalities [and issues] to easily identifiable labels and caricatures."[13]

In the mid to late nineties, *Weltschmerz* tended to focus on local issues that would be immediately relevant to the readers of the papers in which the cartoons appeared. These papers most often were free weekly "alternative" publications in Ontario. Thus, Ontario premier Mike Harris and his Conservative Party's "Common Sense Revolution" plan for the province formed the frequent backdrop for Lind's comics. Law and order policies were a crucial component of this plan and serve as an example of what Medhurst and DeSousa call the "political commonplaces … [that] are the raison d'être of political cartoons in the sense that one cannot create a political cartoon without focusing reader attention, at least momentarily, on some agreed upon component of politics."[14] The Conservative Party's law and order platform depended on the common sense idea that society was too lenient with its criminal offenders. Young offenders and nuisance issues were targeted and tougher penalties recommended. This phenomenon was observed by Schissel:

> Whether Canadians like to admit it or not, Canada's war on crime is increasingly becoming a war against youth. From varying proposals to reintroduce the death penalty for young killers to the implementation of boot camps for all young offenders, Canadian society is embarking on a crusade to increase punishment for children.[15]

As figure 9.1 demonstrates, squeegee kids were a major part of this "war" in Ontario. As skewered by Lind, squeegeeing was a visible nuisance conducted by nonconforming kids, kids who needed to be properly disciplined just as those who had dropped out of school, those who were on welfare, or those who resorted to begging or panhandling on the streets. Without the more beneficent guidance of institutions such as the family, schools, or government agencies, discipline came in the form of boot camps for wayward or errant youth. In this climate, even nuisance behaviour became criminalized as the Ontario government introduced the Safe Streets Act to outlaw squeegeeing and aggressive panhandling. As figure 9.1 seems to suggest, squeegee kids (and disruptive kids in

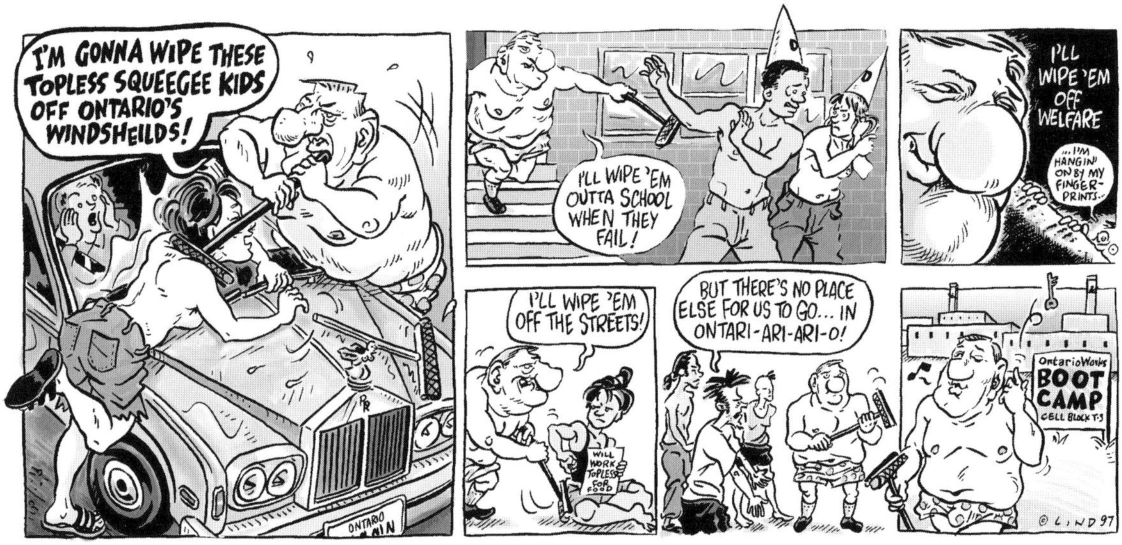

FIGURE 9.1 Squeegee kids ("I'm gonna wipe these topless squeegee kids ...") in *Weltschmerz. Eye Weekly*, June 26, 1997. (Photo: Gareth Lind / Weltschmerz / http://www.lindtoons.com)

general) were like so much dirt to be cleaned off windshields. By making spectacles of themselves, they marked themselves as targets to be metaphorically and literally cleansed from the streets. Thus, while squeegee kids were a curious spectacle for some and a minor nuisance for others, for many they were an irritant and a perceived threat. As calls for action increased to a near fever pitch in 1999, the issue had become an object of concern for every level of government, and many government officials insisted that squeegee kids constituted a problem that demanded a solution. Lind's comics, with their liberal use of caricature, were the graphic response to the following scene:

> To the Gulliver observing our media, the fight over the nation's windshields might easily be mistaken for our civilization's last stand against the Nazi hordes. Whole squadrons of newspaper columnists have taken to their keyboards with the passion of Spitfire pilots scrambling to meet the Hun, while Mel Lastman, our very own Churchill with hair plugs, exhorts us not to surrender a loonie to the green-haired enemy. Never in the field of human conflict was so much said by so many about so little.[16]

The interesting thing about the squeegee phenomenon was its framing as activity conducted by "kids." Whereas New York suffered from the blight of "squeegee men," in Toronto, "it's the youthfulness of the squeegeers that unsettles the city's pundits."[17] One letter writer acknowledged this situation: "Perhaps it's the connotation of kids that evokes some sympathy for this segment of society, as though they are some poor pre-adolescent waifs."[18] But for that letter writer (as for many others), the allusion to "children" contained in the label "squeegee kids" had no resonance, given the number of older squeegeers in the streets. As the spectacle of squeegeeing grew, those who were irritated by it tended to deny that youth was a factor in the phenomenon. A report by the Community Social Planning Council of Toronto underscored the widespread nature of this belief. Of the city's street youth surveyed, "two-thirds were under 21 years of age; only 10 per cent were over 25," yet "the myth persists that these are mostly squeegee men plying a lucrative trade."[19]

Obviously, these were not children, in the strictest sense of the word, confronting drivers with their weapons of choice. Yet they were identified as "kids" because of their surly glances, unkempt and dirty appearances, and general disposition with squeegees wielded as ever-ready "weapons." When someone is called a "squeegee kid," the very label calls forth a plentitude of cultural references, such as developing bodies, dissidence, passionate arguments, and alienated social groups. Squeegee kids are children insofar as they are "kids," though this suggests the problematic category of "youth" that spans the gap between childhood and adulthood. Informed by discourses of youth, talk about squeegee kids became part of the process by which social norms about troublesome young people were produced and circulated. Yet the problem of squeegeeing was never framed as one of "squeegee youth" but rather as the spectre of "squeegee kids"—and, as one commentary in *Canadian Dimension* magazine noted, a government's choice to target and scapegoat children seems, at first glance, to be counterintuitive since children carry with them connotations of bucolic innocence.[20] Lind emphasizes this innocence when he depicts kids as victims of symbolic violence at the hands of the Ontario government, victimized rather than victimizing (fig. 9.1). Also, "typical" boys and girls are used to ironically comment on the government's policies toward youth (fig. 9.2). Lind does not explicitly tell his readers that kids are innocent and not dangerous but rather shows readers how random and misplaced the inference of violence can be. However, the gap between those who mock such political platforms and those who flock to them is not clearly defined. As Saunders suggests, "Contemporary culture is characterized by a strong ambivalence toward children."[21] On the one hand, children can be innocent, vulnerable, uncontaminated, and threatened by others. On the other hand, children are also increasingly perceived as a threat to the rest of us, violent, antisocial, uncontrollable, and in need of control.[22]

To wit, an early reference that sensitized readers to this new phenomenon began with an image of infestation: "The kids pour off the curb, descending on the stopped car like a plague of locusts."[23] This article contained fewer descriptions of confused and annoyed drivers than reports of the enterprising spirit of street kids. Even though the term

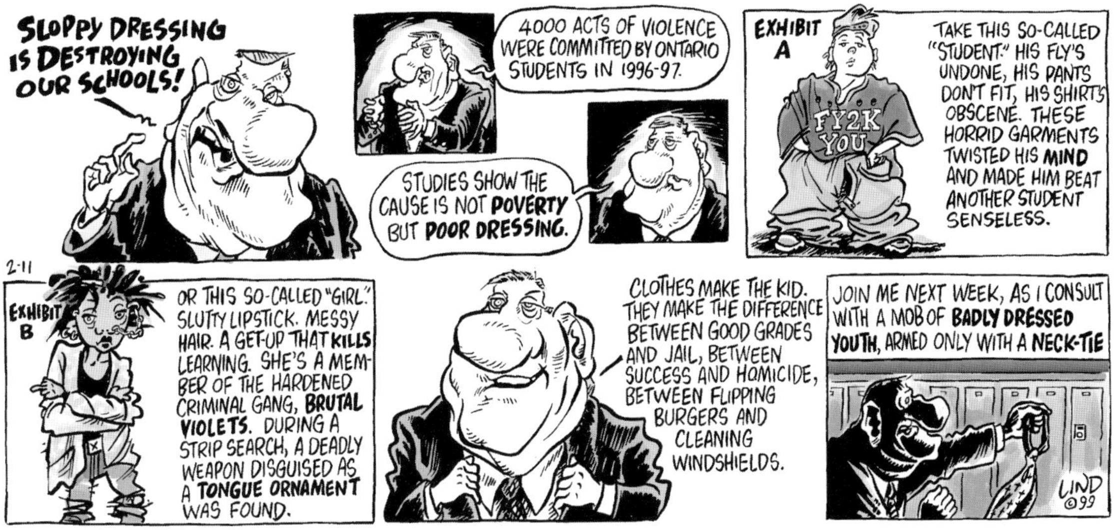

FIGURE 9.2 Sloppy dressing in *Weltschmerz*. *Eye Weekly*, February 11, 1999. (Photo: Gareth Lind / Weltschmerz / http://www.lindtoons.com)

"squeegee kid" is never used, the practice is identified as "barely a week old, it's the latest trend among street kids," and no one over the age of seventeen is quoted. Squeegeeing is described as "a lucrative new twist on begging." Quickly, though, as an increasing number of kids participated in this new practice, squeegeeing became a sign of disorder, and "freedom, usually a celebrated aspect of childhood, [was] seen as dangerous, and the children as feral, even vermin, playing strange, dangerous games."[24] Yet why did the Ontario Conservatives list squeegeeing (and aggressive panhandling under the rubric of "Safe Streets" legislation) as one of their top three priorities (along with tax cuts and a balanced budget) after being re-elected in 1999? Surely there were other youthful, arguably comparable, sites of public anxiety, such as skateboarding, graffiti, and rave parties. Why did these not become the source of legislation and the subject of political cartoons as squeegee kids did? In part, we can blame the "look" of squeegee kids. As people looked at squeegee kids, their appearance (in addition to what they were saying or maybe even doing) reinforced the public image of kids as more troubling than in trouble.

Figure 9.2 helps to contextualize the public image of kids and situate squeegee kids as products of bad decisions, those kids who have gone down the wrong path (the windshield cleaners mentioned in the second-last frame). In fact, though it is tongue-in-cheek, the cartoon can be seen to blame kids' appearances for their actions. This graphic portrayal of kids reinforces the verbal discourse about squeegee kids in which their appearances were nearly always described in accounts of squeegee activity and they were invariably depicted as adopting a punk aesthetic. From the 1970s on, such markers of street-wise sensibility have served as a shortcut to signify youthful rebellion. Squeegee kids' adoption of this fusion of downtroddenness and vituperation encouraged onlookers to label them as "gutter punks," a 1990s reinvention of punk's "sartorial terrorism" and attitude among itinerant street youth.[25] Playful performativity and a culture of conspicuous display distinguished squeegee kids from mainstream, adult culture. However, there is nothing particularly distinct about squeegee kids' appropriation of this culture. As one letter writer observed, this symbolism of youth versus adults expressed a "symbolic language as old as the human race."[26]

With this in mind, we can see how public knowledge of squeegee kids (and hence the ability to decipher the codes within the political cartoons) depended on a pre-existing "public image" of kids. This is "a cluster of impressions, themes and quasi-explanations ... a kind of composite description-*cum*-explanation ... [that] tend[s] to appear *in place of analysis*."[27] Thus, for many audiences, squeegee kids generally confirmed how kids' fashion sense distinguishes those "normal," well-behaved children from transgressive kids, unruly children whose precociousness has turned disruptive and whose choices demand punitive measures. As one columnist noted, "in the language of clothing, street kids' message is clear: fishnet stockings and post-nuclear makeup symbolise rejection of society."[28] These widespread cultural associations did not have to be explained each time squeegee kids were graphically depicted. One merely had to represent them with the correct "uniform."

Thus, even as cartoonists sought to challenge the legitimacy of Harris and Lastman's rhetoric of kiddie- and poor-bashing, the images made sense only in the context of ongoing anxieties over the undisciplined nature of young people, central to the social order throughout modern times.[29] Like other visual arguments, then, the audience had to fill in the missing premise while processing the cartoons. This form of argument is known as an enthymeme, when "the arguer deliberately leaves unstated a premise that is essential to its reasoning. Doing so has the effect of drawing the audience to participate in its own persuasion by filling in that unexpressed premise."[30] Cartoons show their readers that squeegee kids look like punks. They don't say that punks are disruptive. They don't have to. The cartoon "works" because the cartoonist knows that most potential audience members are familiar with the themes being emphasized. In this way, "graphic rhetoric, like its oral counterpart, relies to a great degree on the enthymematic form. The artist must know and utilize the beliefs, values, and attitudes of his audience if he or she is to be an effective persuader."[31]

Enthymematic form highlights the audience's active role in constructing meanings out of messages constructed specifically for them by the rhetor in question. Lind, for instance, would likely not have been able to take such liberties if he knew his audience was constituted strictly of *Globe and Mail* readers. Instead of just poking fun at squeegee kids, Lind could poke fun at Harris and, knowing his audience, be relatively confident that most readers would supply the necessary warrant to move from data to conclusion.[32] These comics present an argument in visual form and "function as part of a larger public controversy."[33] By using squeegee kids as a platform for larger social commentary about the Harris government, these comics do more than present stylized representations of victims and victimizers. These comics demonstrate how visual depictions of squeegee kids became a common means by which the downtrodden nature of the city and its occupants (confronted as they were by the threat of these kids) were represented. As such, they contribute to a larger debate about kids and their role in the contemporary public sphere.

Like all visual rhetoric, then, Lind's (graphic) messages depended on audiences' familiarity with the idea of children/youth as potentially polluting agents that can threaten a scene of social stability. Older, familiar images of disruptive young people combined with newer ideas and images of squeegee kids at intersections in order to make the social issue of squeegeeing meaningful. Of course, this "uniform" of squeegeeing was not fixed. For instance, Lind depicts a shirtless premier literally cleaning the streets of nonconforming kids (fig. 9.1). In this case, the squeegeeing kid is a topless female. Here, for the cartoon to be successful, the audience must be aware of the "idiosyncratic and transient situations which appear unexpectedly,"[34] in this case, topless squeegeeing. On June 11, 1997, with rising temperatures and a late 1996 ruling by the Ontario Court of Appeal that made toplessness legal, Attorney General Charles Harnick announced that squeegee kids should not use that ruling as a marketing tool. This prompted the following editorial comment:

> Premier Mike is suddenly feeling faint about Metro's mini-boom in "in-your-face" bare breasts. And Police Chief Dave is sweating, well, bullets about the squeegee kids who are sprouting like weird, pierced rhubarb on traffic-clogged street corners. And both are having a meltdown over that ultimate challenge to Toronto the Good: Bare-bosomed squeegee kids![35]

Thus, the youthful rebellion and playful nonconformity of squeegee kids provided an affront to some (but not all) adult sensibilities. Lind took this rebellion and nonconformity and used it as an opportunity for a graphic indictment of those who demonstrated little tolerance for childlike behaviour. This cartoon also demonstrates how political cartoons depend on personal character traits and situational themes to make their point.[36] They depend on the audience cluing in to "the exaggeration of amplification of physionomical features (caricature, in the narrow sense)." Such depictions are

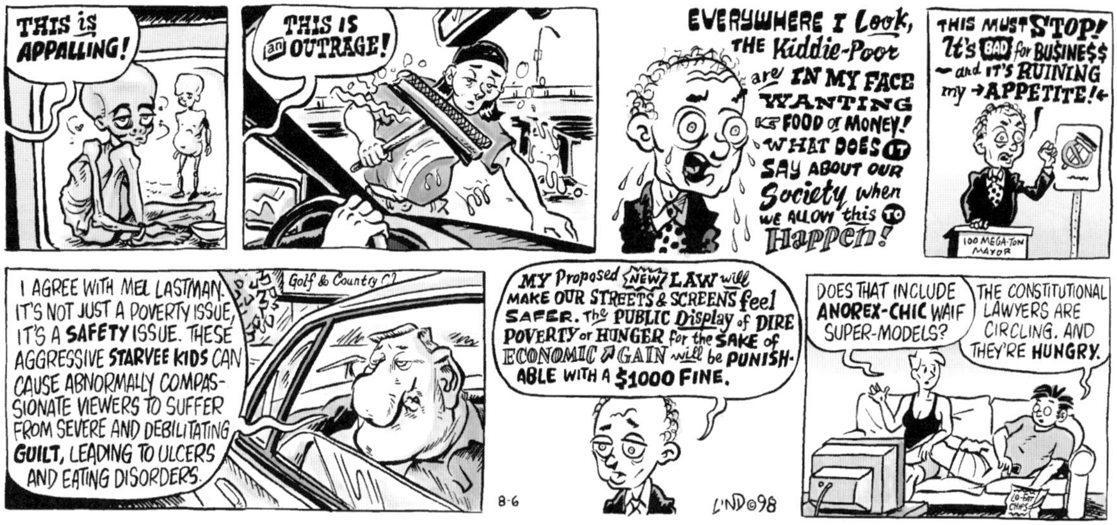

FIGURE 9.4 Starvee kids ("This is appalling …") in *Weltschmerz*. *Eye Weekly*, August 6, 1998. (Photo: Gareth Lind / Weltschmerz / http://www.lindtoons.com)

longer just bad youth polluting city streets with their particular brand of slacker hedonism; they are outsiders who are "at risk" and therefore also present a risk—both to themselves and to others. Concerns *for* young people blend with concerns *about* young people as the circumstances of "at-risk" kids threaten to affect others' lives as well. Unruly kids become human pollution in this vision of a salubrious city defined by law and order and civil behaviour toward one another. Hence, the political cartoon lampoons the idea that squeegee kids can be so bad for business that they sully the image of "Toronto the good" and threaten to turn Toronto into the equivalent of a Third World country.

This cartoon also demonstrates how even the text in a cartoon is part of the overall graphic discourse. As Kenney and Scott suggest, the Greek alphabet, Egyptian hieroglyphs, and Chinese ideographs all encode speech using symbols for sounds: "The full scope of human history shows pictures, not alphabetic words, as the primary mode of discourse."[42] Indeed, even Lind's depiction of alphabetic words is symbolic. In figure 9.4, for instance, the hyperbolic rhetoric of Toronto mayor Mel Lastman is symbolized through the use of hyperstylized fonts. As Foss notes, these constitute part of the "presented elements" of visual rhetoric, the physical features of the image, such as the size and shape of the fonts, that are the strategic, purposeful choices of the cartoonist-rhetor. These are then decoded as "suggested elements" by a knowing audience who is familiar with the codes of representations and likely to infer certain shared concepts, ideas, and allusions.[43] Through the carnival barkeresque style of Lastman's speech-as-graphic, the disproportionateness of governments' reaction to squeegee kids is communicated to *Weltschmerz*'s readers. If one cannot infer the message that Mike Harris is a bully or Mel Lastman is a fool from Lind's physionomical renderings, then additional visual elements such as the cartoons' texts should reinforce this picture. Through this graphic depiction of Lastman's rhetoric, Lind provides a further explanation of the meaning of the images of starving children and squeegeeing children, cementing the connection with the epithet "kiddie-poor." He also manages to reveal his "truth" about the politicians and the controversy in question to his readers. In this capacity, we can see how "the texts of political cartoons function simultaneously as commentary, explanation, and revelation."[44]

The power of these cartoons does not come exclusively from the artist's drawing skill but also from their ability to evoke foundational ideas in our culture about children and out-of-control kids. We can see, then, how "cartoons enable deep-seated culturally grounded beliefs to be expressed visually, re-entrenching cultural ideals."[45] Thus, even though the comics pilloried politicians more than squeegee kids, they perpetuated and contributed to the larger socio-cultural discourse whereby young people were seen as more adult-like since their actions seemed to contradict much of what was assumed about properly behaved children.

As the cartoons demonstrate, the debate over squeegee kids occurred at the same time as other discourses about child- and youth-based criminality, about children and the nuisances that they can pose and the more serious disruption that they can augur. Debates about unions, air pollution, and other problems seemingly unrelated to youth were also attached to squeegee kids in these cartoons, further reinforcing how kids, in general, can be problematic and the source of public lamentation and condemnation. Depictions of squeegee kids, then, operated as a synecdoche insofar as they were the part that stood for the whole ideology that kids need to be disciplined, controlled, condemned, or, at the very least, understood and managed better. These comics hinted at widespread public attitudes and invited readers to contemplate how a variety of factors conspire to disadvantage children. For instance, kids were depicted as threatened by dangers as varied as poverty, economic disenfranchisement through tax cuts and welfare policies, and criminality both in and outside schools. In addition, they were exploited as political targets, when kids' dual identity as "at risk" and "the risk" encouraged "common sense" campaigns that tied concern for and about kids to concerns over public safety.

Thus, to understand the phenomenon of Canadian squeegee kids is not an exercise in understanding Canadian children, per se. It is, rather, an attempt to understand the power of mobilizing the label of childhood in a particular Canadian context. At the end of the twentieth century and the beginning of the twenty-first, what does it mean to speak of Canadian "kids" in this manner? With imprecise demographics, squeegee kids are often not "kids" in the strictest sense. But by publicly conducting activity that can be read as youthful and undisciplined, these individuals can be seen as "still growing," extending the psychological—if not the physiological—development of childhood and its sometimes uncomfortable transition to adolescence. With this in mind, the public image of unruly Canadian squeegee kids can be contrasted with children whose conduct is more benign, whose rebellion is less taxing for a culture that needs to discipline out-of-bounds behaviour and uncontrolled activity.

In an earlier era, youthful refusal to be tamed was consistent with hale and healthy individualism. An attitude of accepting the childishness of children coincided with the dream of future strength and stability. Here, prosperity came to be embodied in the promise of a generation moving forward. Today, however, the refusal to be tamed is seen as a tacit challenge to the legitimacy of cultural norms. It is for many, then, an explicit cause of concern instead of an encouraging sign of future generations' nascent development of their own independent capacities. Both metaphorically and literally, Lind's cartoons are a graphic depiction of this contemporary condition.

Seen together, these cartoons indicate how the political cartoonist's work can act as depictive rhetoric: "strategic pictures, verbal or nonverbal visualizations, that linger in the collective memory of audiences as representative of their subjects when rhetoric has been successful."[46] The cartoons by Lind were strategic depictions of politicians and the political problems they faced and/or constructed. They depicted this subject matter in a fashion that both relied on and contributed to a public image of squeegee kids in particular and kids in general. Lind's depictions not only presented the cartoonist's view. Rather, they can be seen as "images used strategically in the public sphere [that] reflect not only beliefs, attitudes and values of their creators, but those of the society at large."[47] They helped construct a public imagining of what (certain) kids were capable of, what they looked like, and how they could (or could not) be blamed for their actions. Through the depictions of kids in this fashion, public attitudes were focused and intensified. Audiences were given another opportunity to identify with the main object of ridicule (the politicians) or against them, and hence identify with the only slightly less ridiculed object of the cartoons, kids whose unruly activity spurred the focus in the first place.

Cartoons are one way that rhetorical actors in the public sphere can depict a particular version of an ongoing political reality and invite readers to share this worldview. In the case of *Weltschmerz*, the comic reader's attention was drawn to key elements of what it meant to be a kid in Ontario at the end of the twentieth century via Lind's parodied representations of squeegee kids and burlesque representations of politicians. Whether one laughs at Premier Mike Harris or at the squeegee kids' condition as victims/scapegoats as a result of the premier's policies, these "cartoons present politicized contexts that, through satire, irony, and parody, motivate differing senses of community."[48] Through these depictions of (squeegee) kids, audiences were encouraged to reaffirm their own identities and political priorities. How much would they tolerate? Whose side do they take?

Admittedly, cartoon images distort the way in which one might view political issues and politicians through an objective lens. However, as the cartoonist Jeff MacNelly argues, even though "political cartoonists violate every rule of ethical journalism—they misquote, trifle with the truth, make science fiction out of politics,... when the smoke clears, the political cartoonist has been getting closer to the truth than the guys who write political opinions."[49] This "truth" about squeegee kids is, in fact, rhetorical. "To the degree that meaning is indeed shared between the cartoonist and his readers, it occurs as a result of the juxtaposition of the visual elements on the page (artistic truth) and the interpretation of that juxtaposition in the mind of the reader (rhetorical truth or conviction)."[50]

These cartoons demonstrate how visual artifacts can function as rhetorical interventions in the public sphere that help define and construct the reality of that public sphere. Through his burlesque representations, Lind seeks to produce a knowing and sadly ironic pleasure in his readers, who might also be amazed that kids could provoke such a response in the first place. Seen in this light, the comics told the "truth" about squeegee kids in a way that editorials, even those driven by satire, could not. Thus, the truth about squeegee kids, one particular form of contemporary Canadian childhood, can be communicated via political cartoons. This truth is not the product of objective understanding or some kind of scientific knowing, but of the negotiated understanding that lies in the dialogue between a comic's creators and its readers, between those who recommend tolerance of kids' youthfulness and those who interpret such tolerance as irresponsible. It is an understanding of kids that is not either true or false, but simply negotiated. These comics help constitute the landscape of meanings by which we come to understand squeegee kids, and by extension, how kids in general can come to be known. We should not view them as accurate or false based on how they correspond to the "reality" of squeegeeing, or view them as powerful based on how closely they correspond to our own values or provoke oppositional letters to the editor. Rather, one should interrogate how such visual artifacts invite readers to construct their own meanings and how they encourage different readings and new understandings to develop.

SUSAN HART

A CHILD'S PLACE IN OTTAWA'S COMMEMORATIVE LANDSCAPE

IN 1857 QUEEN VICTORIA CHOSE OTTAWA AS THE capital city of what was then the Province of Canada. In 1867 Canada became an independent nation when Queen Victoria signed the British North America Act. Thirty-one years later, the Hon. J.D. Edgar, Speaker of the Commons of Canada, observed in his 1898 publication *Canada and Its Capital*: "When a country is young, and its history is not yet told in monuments nor typified in ancient architecture, its capital should be adorned in other ways."[1] Indeed, in the years between 1867 and 1898, Canadians were busy adorning Ottawa and inscribing their capital city with meaning and identity. By the turn of the twentieth century, commemorative monuments had begun to narrate the young country's history. In 1885 a statue of Sir George-Étienne Cartier by Louis-Philippe Hébert was the first monument to be unveiled on Parliament Hill. It was soon joined by statues of Sir John A. Macdonald (Louis-Philippe Hébert, 1895) and Queen Victoria (Louis-Philippe Hébert, 1897). In the one hundred years since Edgar pointed out Ottawa's lack of monuments, many more commemorations have been placed on Parliament Hill and at other strategic locations in the capital, adding to the unfolding narrative of imagined national identity they help to create.[2] Until recently, that narrative has been dominated by male figures, many political, some military. However, with the new millennium, Ottawa's commemorative landscape has started to become more diverse and inclusive, offering new representations of First Nations people, women, and for the first time, children. Unveiled on September 28, 2003, the *Monument to Canadian Fallen* (sculptor Yoo Young Mun, concept Vincent R. Courtenay, fig. 10.1),[3] in Confederation Park is the first commemorative monument in the heart of Ottawa to seemingly acknowledge children as part of the national narrative. However, on closer consideration and analysis, a more complex picture starts to develop. The children represented are not Canadian children; thus they are not truly representations of the child in the nation. Rather, I would argue, these are representations of the child as (o)the(r) nation—abstract symbols of countries or nations that have not yet reached the maturity that Canada imagines it has.

In Canada, the National Capital Commission (NCC) is the agency responsible for the development of Ottawa as the capital city. As a national capital, Ottawa must create and project a distinctive image of Canada and Canadians to those who live in this country and to those who visit from elsewhere. National identity building involves a complex interweaving of many aspects of urban planning and design, such as architecture and landscape, ceremonies and celebrations, historic sites and monuments. The NCC's 1988 publication *Capital Commemoration: An Urban Design Study for Memorials in the Core of the National Capital* underscores the important role of "commemorative installations of national importance" and demonstrates how "memorials can be organized to reinforce the emerging structure of the centre of the National Capital, with particular reference to Confederation Boulevard and Parliament Hill."[4] Parliament Hill refers to the fenced-in area on Wellington Street, bounded by the Ottawa River to the north, the Rideau Canal to the east, and the Supreme Court of Canada to the west, while Confederation Boulevard refers to a system of ceremonial routes intended to unify and link the central areas of Gatineau and Ottawa. Many of Canada's most important institutions, such as Parliament, the Supreme Court, the National Archives, and the National Gallery, are found on Confederation Boulevard, as well as heritage sites, works of art, and monuments such as the *Monument to Canadian Fallen* (also referred to as the Korean War Memorial). The above urban design study recognizes the value of commemorations as permanent emblems and reminders of shared Canadian values and achievements.

The notion that commemorations are an effective means for cities and nations to develop and communicate a strong sense of collective identity is not new. Since before Roman times, civilizations have recognized the importance of monuments as markers and makers of a nation's history and identity. It is not surprising therefore that increasingly scholars are turning to public monuments in an attempt to unravel the ways in which various identities and communities are being, and have been, imagined. In the introductory essay for the anthology *Commemorations: The Politics of National Identity*, editor and author John Gillis suggests that monuments are "very effective in concentrating time in space, in providing many people with a sense of common identity no matter how dispersed they may be by class, region, gender, religion, or race."[5] In the same anthology, John Bodnar writes that historians have seldom examined the subject of publicly constructed memory in modern America. Bodnar offers a case study of public commemoration in Cleveland over the past century to demonstrate that the city moved through three distinct stages of commemoration marked by a shifting balance of power between official and vernacular cultural interests.[6] In her 1995 case study of the Parnell monument in Dublin, Nuala Johnson agrees that monuments are an underused

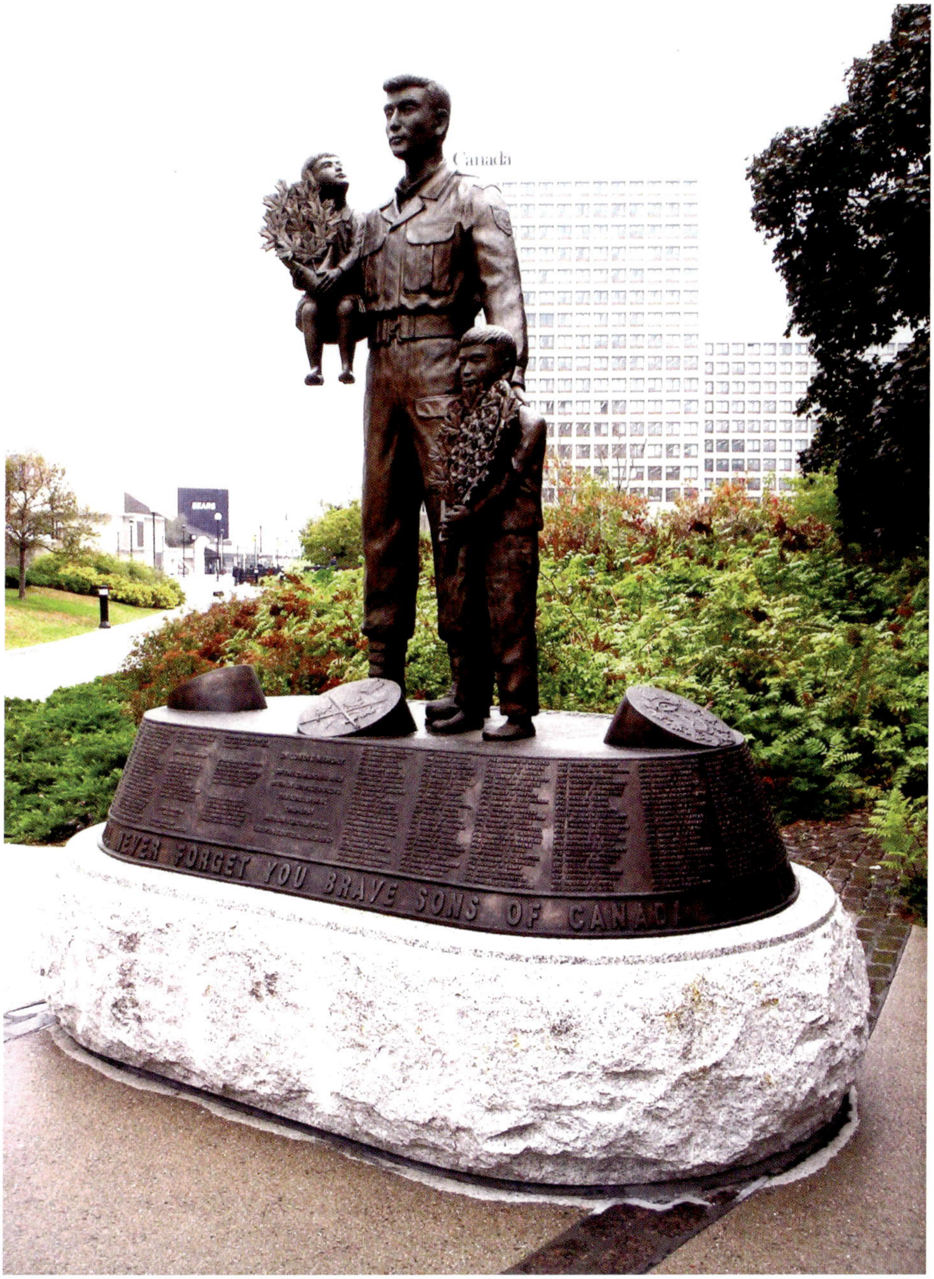

FIGURE 10.1 Yoo Young Mun, *Monument to Canadian Fallen* (Korean War Memorial), inauguration 2002, life-size bronze figures on granite base. Confederation Park, Ottawa. (Photo: Author)

resource in the study of how national identity is imagined and structured symbolically.[7] Within a Canadian context, cultural geographer Brian S. Osborne considers the issue of national identity in a number of journal articles, including his 1998 essay "Constructing Landscapes of Power: The George Etienne Cartier Monument, Montreal," in which he explores how the Cartier monument complex has become a "dynamic site of meaning" since its erection in 1919.[8] Also writing about Quebec, Denis Martin's essay for the 2001 *Louis-Philippe Hébert* exhibition catalogue examines how the commemorative statues that adorn the façade of the Hôtel du Parlement in Quebec City were conceived as "secular saints" in order to exploit French Canadian collective memory for patriotic and religious purposes, while Alan Gordon's 2001 publication *Making Public Pasts: The Contested Terrain of Montréal's Public Memories, 1891–1930* covers a whole spectrum of collective memory or identity-makers such as customs, celebrations, historic sites, and monuments.[9] Clearly, commemorations have been and continue to be an important element of the identity-building process, and critical analysis of commemorations such as Ottawa's *Monument to Canadian Fallen* offers a way to explore the nationalist imaginings represented by them.

The *Monument to Canadian Fallen* came about through the initiative and efforts of Vince R. Courtenay, a Canadian Korean War veteran who conceived of and designed the monument that was sculpted by Korean sculptor Yoo Young Mun.[10] Two identical monuments exist, one in Ottawa and the other in the United Nations Memorial Cemetery in Busan, Korea (dedicated in 2002). The Ottawa monument, according to the nearby NCC interpretive panel, has been situated in Confederation Park so that the Canadian volunteer soldier depicted on it faces toward its twin in Busan, South Korea's largest harbour city and staging area for UN troops during the Korean War (1950–1953).[11] The panel also informs the viewer that Canadian veterans from across Canada contributed funds and that the project received support from the people of Canada and the government of the Republic of Korea. While awaiting permanent installation in Ottawa, the Canadian monument was displayed for a period of ten months in Vince Courtenay's hometown of Windsor, Ontario. The monument was unveiled in Ottawa in 2003 in time to mark the fiftieth anniversary of the Korean War Armistice.[12]

The *Monument to Canadian Fallen* is composed of three bronze figures set on a low oval base. The three figures include a male soldier and two children, a boy and a girl. The standing soldier is shown holding a female child on the crook of his right arm. His left arm is extended downward behind the back of a young boy who stands at his side. The soldier, although dressed in military uniform, is hatless and carries no weapons. In fact, there are no symbols of war present on the monument. Both children hold bouquets. According to the interpretative panel, the girl holds a bouquet of maple leaves, symbol of Canada, and the boy holds a bouquet of maple leaves and roses of Sharon, the national flower of Korea. The girl appears to be wearing a dress-like item of clothing, as her legs are bare, while the boy wears a loose-fitting shirt and trousers. Both children wear simple, slip-on type shoes. The female gazes up at the face of the soldier, while both male figures stare straight ahead. There is a static quality to the life-size figures, both in posture and in emotion, when compared to the nearby National War Memorial (formally titled *The Response*, Vernon March, 1939) (fig. 10.2), on which the dynamic and dramatic, larger-than-life-size figures evoke a sense of urgent forward movement. The figures on the *Monument to Canadian Fallen* stand on a low, two-part oval base composed of a bronze pedestal atop a low granite plinth. The upper bronze portion is inscribed with the names of the 516 Canadians who lost their lives in Korea. A bilingual inscribed band runs around the bottom of the bronze pedestal stating, "We will never forget you brave sons of Canada." The bronze part is set on an equally squat, rough-hewn granite plinth provided by the Government of the Republic of Korea. The low base and short static figures do not offer the monument a particularly notable profile on the skyline, and from a distance the monument almost disappears against the backdrop of trees and shrubs. Despite the monument's quiet presence in the commemorative landscape, it does speak loudly about notions of imagined Canadian identity and the place children hold in it.

Images of children have been used on commemorative monuments over the centuries. Indeed, cherubs, cupids, and angels have adorned monuments for millennia, although these winged infants are mythological rather than human figures.[13] Human children have also appeared on commemorative monuments over time, with Roman sculpture providing numerous examples. For instance, the Ara Pacis Augustae (13–9 BCE, marble) features relief portraits of specific children in the imperial family at the time, while Trajan's Column (113 CE, marble) and the Arch of Constantine (312–315 CE, marble) include nonspecific "Roman" and "non-Roman" children in their narrative panel imagery. In her book *Children in the Visual Arts of Imperial Rome*, Jeannine Diddle Uzzi observes that "the sheer number of child images demonstrates the visibility of Roman children in public, and the visual evidence shows that children played an active role in public life."[14] It has been suggested that images of these types are used to indicate the future adult social status of the child and that often, although not always, the child is of an aristocratic or royal family.[15] Indeed, Roman emperors were skilled at using monuments such as these to visually communicate their own status and authority while at the same time disseminating a sense of shared Roman identity throughout the empire.

The ability of national monuments to communicate a sense of shared identity is also explored by Katharine Kennedy, who examines how German elementary school texts at the turn of the twentieth century used images of the Niederwald Monument (completed 1883, based on a design by Johann Schilling, located near Rüdesheim, Germany)

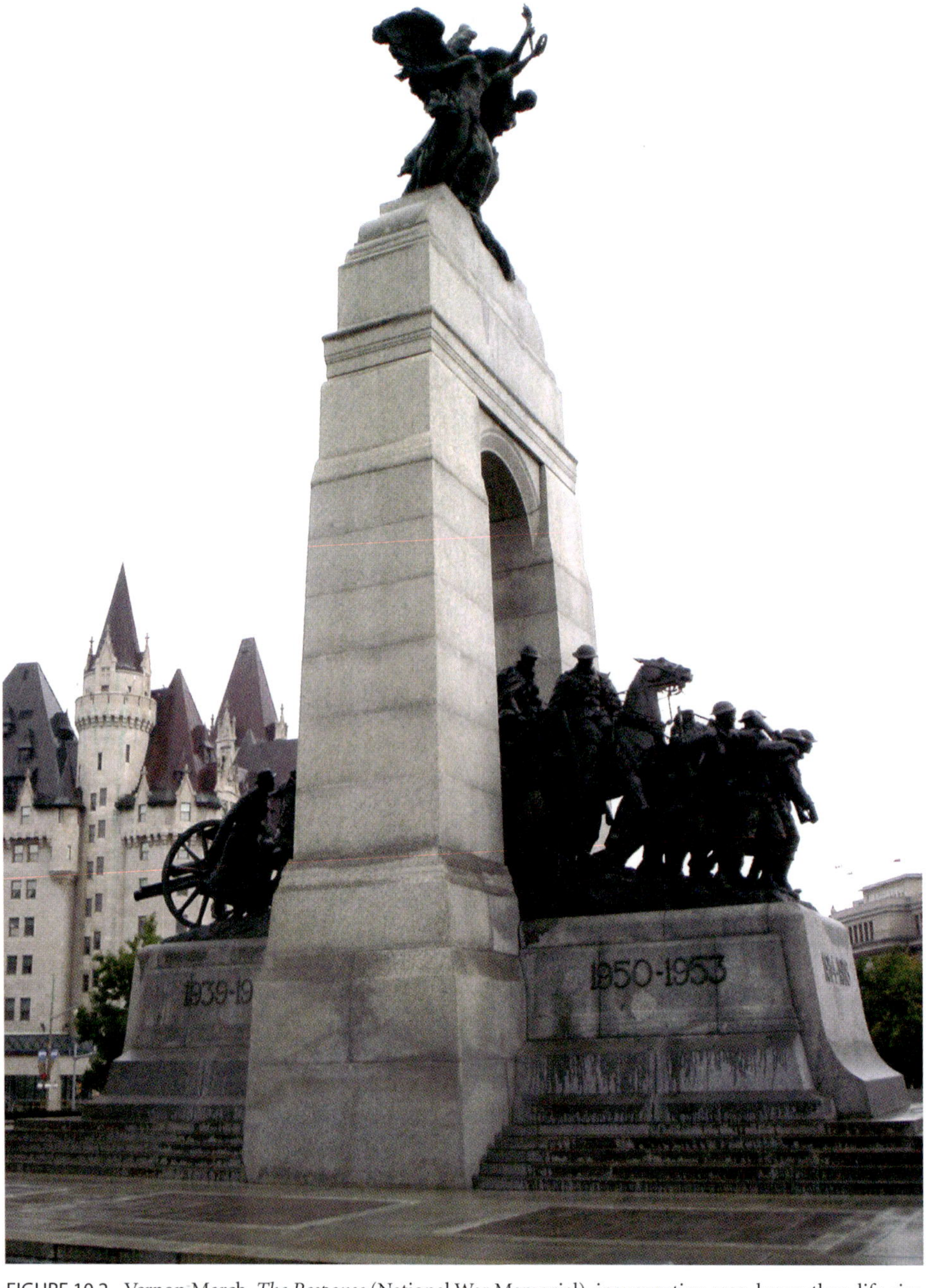

FIGURE 10.2 Vernon March, *The Response* (National War Memorial), inauguration 1939, larger-than-life-size bronze figures on granite base. Confederation Square, Ottawa. (Photo: Author)

to reconcile local, regional, and national identities while promoting and instilling a shared picture of the nation in young children.[16] The inclusion of children on one of the relief panels on the base of the Niederwald Monument explicitly extends the message to children and enables them to imagine themselves in the unfolding narrative.[17] The panel, which depicts soldiers leaving for war surrounded by weeping women and clinging children, also acknowledges the importance of children in the family unit and as future adults in the nation. While the meaning of the monument has almost certainly changed over the years, it did for a time and may still offer Germans from diverse backgrounds and regions a sense of shared national identity. Similarly, the *Monument to Canadian Fallen* offers a reading of how children fit into the Canadian narrative at the beginning of a new millennium.

As with the Niederwald Monument, the presence of children on the *Monument to Canadian Fallen* signals the importance of children in the national narrative—they are, after all, the future of any nation. On a basic level, the children signal and support the naturalized gender roles embodied by patriarchal Western culture. This role is manifest in the binary oppositions at work in the posture and gaze of the two children. The boy stands on his own, whereas the girl is held on the arm of the soldier. He is free to move about, while her movement is restricted. Hence, the male figure is active and the female figure is passive. The figures' gazes also support distinct gender roles. The boy, like the adult male soldier, stares straight ahead. The two male figures look out at and return the gaze of the monument viewer. Both males possess the controlling gaze. Alternatively, the girl gazes up intently at the soldier's face, thus presenting her profile to the monument viewer. She is on display. The children reflect the power inequalities between men and women and hint at their future unequal access to power in the nation. In relation to each other the male child is the subject and the female child is the object, yet in relation to the soldier figure both children become the object in the national narrative, thus bringing the discussion to another level of meaning.

Clearly, the soldier is the subject of the monument and the children are meant to act as foils to his character. As such, the Korean children reflect the Canadian soldier's father-figure status. The soldier is represented as strong and protective in the way he holds the young girl on the crook of his arm. He acts as a role model for the young boy who stands by his side mimicking the manly posture. As well, he offers gentle guidance as suggested by the placement of his left arm behind the boy. Who is he? *He* is the nation. He represents how Canada has come to imagine itself as a nation on the international stage—mature, caring, giving; willing to fight but preferring the peaceful approach. The children are a metaphor for Korea, the "immature" nation that requires protection and guidance. He is the West: they are the East. He is the subject of the nation: they are the object or the other.

This reading is supported by the iconography of *Refuge—Mother and Child* (Pham Thế Trung, 1995, fig. 10.3).[18] Located on the southwest corner of Preston and Somerset on the edge of Ottawa's Asian community, *Refuge—Mother and Child* is not truly a part of the narrative constructed by the monuments on Confederation Boulevard, but it may be seen as a mediator between the National War Memorial and the Korean War Memorial, as it helps to explain the shift in imagined national identity over the years that separate these last two war memorials, which, it is important to note here, *Refuge—Mother and Child* is not. Still, comparison of the National War Memorial and *Refuge* reveals a number of similarities and differences that contribute to an understanding of the iconography of all three monuments. Perhaps the most noticeable similarity is the impression of urgent forward movement conveyed by the figures on both monuments. Although both sculptors use a long stride to impart a sense of dynamic movement to their figures, the message expressed by each monument is quite different. While the multiple military figures on the National War Memorial eagerly rush forward to prove themselves in war, the civilian figure on *Refuge* clearly flees from the reality of war. The opposing messages reflect the opposing functions and names of the two monuments. While *The Response* is meant to commemorate those who lost their lives serving their country, *Refuge* commemorates "those who lost their lives in their quest for freedom."[19]

An obvious difference between the two monuments is in the number of figures on each. Whereas the National War Memorial offers images of numerous adult male and female figures, *Refuge* is composed of only two figures—a woman and a child. Yet both monuments (re)present women in a similar stereotyped caregiver role as either nurse or mother. These are not specific women; rather, they are abstract symbols of an idea of *woman*, allegorical figures much like the two winged females atop the National War Memorial who represent peace and liberty. Thus, the fleeing woman with child on *Refuge* may be seen as a symbol of the reality of war and the future hope of the nation. *She* is not responsible for producing the nation but rather for reproducing the nation. The woman/child duo on *Refuge* clearly illustrates Anne McClintock's statement that "women are typically constructed as the symbolic bearers of the nation but are denied any direct relation to national agency."[20] The woman and child are a symbol of Vietnam. Like the children on the *Monument to Canadian Fallen*, they are the object of the nation: they are other.

Through the mediation of *Refuge*, the shift in symbolism and imagined identity from the earlier National War Memorial to the more recent *Monument to Canadian Fallen* becomes clearer. The eager, young military figures on the earlier monument give way to a single solemn, unarmed soldier on the more recent monument, reflecting a shift in Canada's youthful enthusiasm to prove itself on the battlefield to a more recent image of itself as international peacekeeper.[21] The new soldier figure incorporates the masculine and feminine qualities of the figures on the National War Memorial—he is

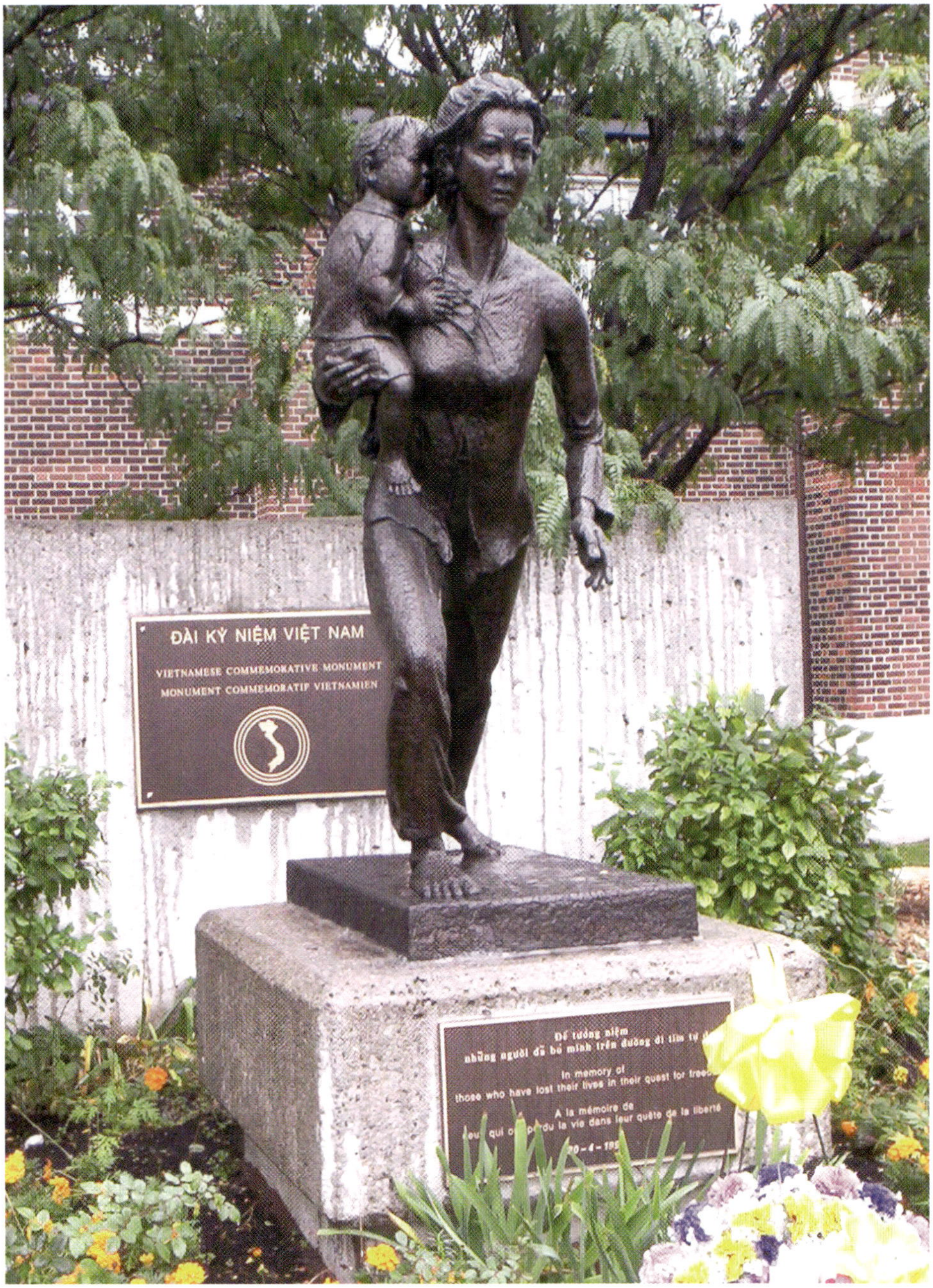

FIGURE 10.3 *Refuge—Mother and Child* (Vietnamese Commemorative Monument), Pham Thế Trung, inauguration 1995, life-size bronze figures on granite base, Somerset and Preston Sts., Ottawa. (Photo: Author)

both soldier and caregiver. The females on the National War Memorial give way to children as a sign of otherness. The female/child role on these monuments is metaphoric or symbolic, whereas the male role is metonymic.[22] Men are contiguous with the nation—men are the nation, whereas women and children stand in for the nation but are not really part of the nationalist imaginings represented by these commemorations. Yes, children have entered the unfolding narrative of imagined national identity created by Ottawa's commemorative monuments, but it appears they have merely joined or perhaps replaced women as allegorical figures in it.

Notes

1 J.D. Edgar, *Canada and Its Capital: With Sketches of Political and Social Life in Ottawa* (Toronto: Morang, 1898), 2.

2 This paper proceeds from the notion that a nation is an "imagined community," as proposed by Benedict Anderson in *Imagined Communities: Reflections on the Origins and Spread of Nationalism*, 2nd ed. (London: Verso, 1991).

3 According to government publications, the monument was proposed and designed by Korean War veteran Vince Courtenay and sculpted by Korean artist Yoo Young Mun (birthdate unavailable). See, for instance, the National Capital Commission's yearly publication *Street Smart/Promenart*, a free tourist guide handout available at various locations in Ottawa, or the website of the Ministère du patrimoine canadien/Department of Canadian Heritage (http://www.pch.gc.ca/newsroom/index_e.cfm) for its September 28, 2003, article, "Dedication of Korean War Monument to Canadian Fallen."

4 *Capital Commemoration: An Urban Design Study for Memorials in the Core of the National Capital* (Ottawa: National Capital Commission, 1988), i.

5 John Gillis, "Memory and Identity: The History of a Relationship," in *Commemorations: The Politics of National Identity* (Princeton: Princeton University Press, 1994), 14.

6 John Bodnar, "Public Memory in an American City: Commemoration in Cleveland," in Gillis, *Commemorations*, 74–89.

7 Nuala Johnson, "Cast in Stone: Monuments, Geography, and Nationalism," *Society and Space* 13, no. 1 (1995): 51–65.

8 Brian S. Osborne, "Constructing Landscapes of Power: The George Etienne Cartier Monument, Montreal," *Journal of Historical Geography* 24, no. 4 (1998): 431–458.

9 Denis Martin, "Les héros de la patrie: La façade de l'Hôtel du Parlement," *Louis-Philippe Hébert*, 216–241 (Quebec: Musée du Québec, 2001); Alan Gordon, *Making Public Pasts: The Contested Terrain of Montréal's Public Memories, 1891–1930* (Montreal and Kingston: McGill-Queen's University Press, 2001).

10 For further information, see Les Peate, "About Memorials," *Esprit de Corps* 10, no. 10 (August 2003): 17–18.

11 In Busan the echo copy of the monument is located in the United Nations Cemetery, where it is the only life-sized statue and where it serves "as a symbolic sentinel over the graves of 378 Canadians killed in the war." See Ray Dick, "Uneasy Lies the Country," *Legion Magazine* (November/December 2003), available in archived articles at http://www.legionmagazine.com under "Memoirs & Pilgramages."

12 Newspaper articles appearing in the *Windsor Star* and the *Ottawa Citizen* at the time of the monument unveilings offered nonjudgmental descriptions of the monument figures. One *Ottawa Citizen* editorial criticized the soldier figure as "a sentimental image of soldiers as uniformed child minders or, perhaps, school-zone crossing guards" (October 1, 2003, B4). Subsequent letters to the editor both agreed and disagreed with this opinion.

13 See Jeannine Diddle Uzzi, *Children in the Visual Arts of Imperial Rome* (New York: Cambridge University Press, 2005), pp. 30–31, for a brief discussion about distinctions between representations of real children and mythological children. As well, see Anne Higonnet, *Pictures of Innocence: The History and Crisis of Ideal Childhood* (London: Thames & Hudson, 1998), pp. 17–19, for a discussion about images of winged babies and the Christ Child. Religious monuments that commemorate the birth of Christ, such as the Madonna and Child statue atop Notre-Dame Basilica on Sussex Drive in Ottawa, are not considered here as commemorative monuments are more generally understood to express secular and political ideas.

14 Uzzi, *Children in the Visual Arts*, 33.

15 Ibid., 56. "It is likely that the children pictured here [on a coin] are symbols of the future Roman populace." Also Higonnet, *Pictures of Innocence*, 17.

16 Katharine D. Kennedy, "Visual Representation and National Identity in the Elementary Schoolbooks of Imperial Germany," *Paedagogica Historia* 36, no. 1 (2000): 225–245.

17 Ibid., 230.

18 In 1990 a working group known as the Vietnamese Commemorative Monument was formed in order to fund and erect a monument to commemorate the Vietnamese community in Ottawa. The monument commission was won by Pham Thế Trung (born in 1955), a Vietnamese "boat person" who escaped Vietnam in 1980 and currently lives in Toronto.

19 The bronze plaque affixed to the base of the monument reads: "In memory of those who have lost their lives in their quest for freedom."

20 Anne McClintock, "'No Longer in a Future Heaven': Gender, Race and Nationalism," in *Dangerous Liaisons: Gender, Nation, and Postcolonial Perspectives*, ed. Anne McClintock, Aamir Mufti, and Ella Shohat (Minneapolis: University of Minnesota Press, 1997), 90.

21 For perspective on this view, see the editorial in *The Ottawa Citizen* (October 1, 2003), B4.

22 See Elleke Boehmer, "Stories of Women and Mothers: Gender and Nationalism in the Early Fiction of Flora Nwapa," in *Motherlands: Black Women's Writing from Africa, the Caribbean and South Asia*, ed. Susheila Nasta, 3–23 (New Brunswick, NJ: Rutgers University Press, 1992).

SHARON MURRAY

FROCKS AND BANGLES
The Photographic Conversion of Two Indian Girls

IN 2004 I INHERITED AN ALBUM OF PHOTOGRAPHS from the late 1890s, assembled and captioned by a distant relative, Miss Amanda Jefferson (1860–1947). Born Amanda Marie Stronach, she was orphaned at the age of eight and adopted by her mother's sister—the Jefferson family of Berwick, Nova Scotia. On completion of her schooling in Berwick, Jefferson trained to be a teacher at the Truro Normal College and then attended the Northfield Seminary in Massachusetts for one year. For reasons unrecorded, Jefferson moved to New York sometime in the mid-1880s, where she worked for seven years at the New York City Mission. There she met her lifelong companion, Miss Emily Terry Minor (1857–1938), an American from Connecticut and a graduate of the Mount Holyoke Seminary. In 1891 both Jefferson and Minor were appointed to western India as foreign missionaries for the Board of Foreign Missions of the Presbyterian Church of the United States of America (PCUSA). They sailed out of New York on September 5 that same year, arriving at the main, western India station in Kolhapur—approximately 320 kilometres southeast of Bombay—later that fall. In the first months of 1892, Jefferson and Minor moved to Ratnagiri, India, their permanent station and their "home."[1]

England was the first to popularize foreign missionary work in the 1790s. They were joined soon after by the United States, followed by British North America, later known as Canada. The impetus of this "great era" of foreign missionary work was primarily the zeal of evangelical Protestants backed by scripture, the Gospel: Jesus Christ's command to "Go ye into all the world and preach the Gospel to every Creature" (Matthew 28:19). Some Christians believed that they were "called" to convert those of other faiths—that it was their duty as servants of their Lord.

In 1852, under the direction of the American Board of Commissioners of Foreign Missions, Rev. R.G. Wilder and his family established the Kolhapur mission. The mission was adopted by PCUSA in 1870. In time, and with the addition of new missionaries to the station, the western India mission expanded to include surrounding villages and towns—Panhala, Sangli, Ratnagiri, and Miraj. The Ratnagiri station, northwest of Kolhapur, was founded in 1873 by Rev. W.P. Barker, although the presence of missionaries there remained relatively small until 1892, when Jefferson, Minor, Rev. and Mrs. W.H. Hannum, and Miss Jennie Sherman were posted to that station. Jefferson was part of the "golden age of missionary expansion" that began in 1880 and lasted until 1920 when the outbreak of World War I initiated the decline.[2] In the years of Jefferson's stay, the missionaries at Ratnagiri established a church, Sunday schools, many small schools for local girls and boys, and an orphanage. Jefferson and Minor were also known for their visits with women and children in surrounding villages and homes, the home for widows, and the leper asylum. Their work was known as "woman's work for woman" and aimed to "educate" Indian women and children about the "true religion" of Christianity and "the benefits [of] our western civilization."[3] With the exception of their three, one-year furloughs to Canada and the United States, Jefferson and Minor worked in Ratnagiri and surrounding areas until 1931, when they retired and together returned to North America. In fact, according to the issue of *Western Indian Notes* in the year of Minor's death, Minor and Jefferson were apart from each other only on the occasion of their furloughs, which they took "at different times, so that each might aid in carrying on the other's work."[4]

Jefferson's album is a hardbound book with a gold-coloured cover and red trim. It contains fifty-one photographs, one to a page, fifty of which are roughly the same size (11 × 16 centimetres), and one considerably larger (25 × 19 centimetres). Each image has been carefully centred on the page and captioned with one or two descriptive lines. The first forty-three photographs are dated 1892 and mainly depict Kolhapur, India, where Jefferson was posted for her first three months of service. The last eight images in the album range in dates from 1893 to 1898 and picture Jefferson's permanent posting at Ratnagiri, where, as Emily Minor observed, "antagonism, prejudice, hostility, and ignorance prevailed."[5] No provenance is given for any of the album's photographs, although those from 1892 are tentatively attributed to Dr. William James Wanless (1865–1933), a medical missionary who worked alongside Jefferson and Minor.[6] Attached to the last page of the album is Jefferson's letter of 1892 explaining that she intended to send the album to the United States to her friends Mr. and Mrs. Parker of New York. Her hope was that it would "be of service in interesting others in the needs of this great field." This letter also indicates that Jefferson owned her own camera and hoped to take "views" of the Ratnagiri station at a later date, once she was "feeling more settled." It seems likely that Jefferson took some of the last eight photographs in the album.

The last photograph in the album pictures two Indian girls dressed in Western frocks (fig. 11.1). Jefferson's caption reads: "Muktie [and] Savitni, 1898. Little Hindoo Girls adopted by Miss Minor & Miss Jefferson." Two handwritten words at the bottom of the photograph—possibly their names—have been scratched out. The girls stand closely together, Muktie, the elder, with her hand resting on Savitni's shoulder. Savitni cradles a doll in her left arm. The two are barefoot. Both girls have their hair tied up neatly, parted in the centre. They wear different patterned dresses, Muktie's principally pale in colour and Savitni's plaid. The dresses fit loosely. The way Savitni's skirt hangs suggests that her stomach is distended. The girls stand in front of a potted shrub backed by a white wall. Palm leaves reach into the right of the frame.

It is difficult to say whether Jefferson's album and the photographs therein reflect any kind of norm for missionary photography during the late nineteenth and early twentieth centuries. Photographs taken by missionaries have largely evaded visual study; missionary history is a recent topic of scholarly interest, although few have chosen to use photographs for anything other than visual reinforcement of historical facts—as data. The lack of attention to this aspect of Western visual culture has resulted in a fragmented visual history, especially that which predates 1900. This is not to say that photographs like Jefferson's are rare. Evidence suggests that missionaries used their cameras quite readily on the mission field, and many of their photographs have been well preserved in seminary and denominational archives. One need look no further than the Basel Mission Picture Archive and its online collection of over 28,000 mission photographs of Africa, India, China, and Hong Kong.[7] It alone attests to the number of pictures generated by foreign missionaries—to the significance of photography to missions. Sheer numbers notwithstanding, the lack of scholarship on missionary photography as a *category* (although arguably a subset of colonial and ethnographic photographies) means that little can be said definitively about the missionary's understanding of the role of photography in his or her mission. Furthermore, prior to 1900, intercontinental circulation of photographs was limited, meaning that few of the photographs taken by missionaries in the latter part of the nineteenth century would have been seen by Western eyes. If Jefferson did send her album to North America, the images in this book might have provided some Westerners with their first comprehensive view of everyday life in an Indian village.

As a result, my study of Jefferson's use of photography serves as a case study in unpacking the meaning of photographs generated by missionaries—the meaning for Jefferson and other Western Christians in her time, and the meaning gained through a contemporary and theoretical reading. The challenge in this is that the information available on Jefferson and her work in Ratnagiri is limited to what the Board of Foreign Missions chose to record and archive. In fact, this album tells me more about Jefferson's life in Ratnagiri than her entire personnel file in the Presbyterian Historical Society's archives. Furthermore, nothing other than this photograph remains of Muktie and Savitni and their

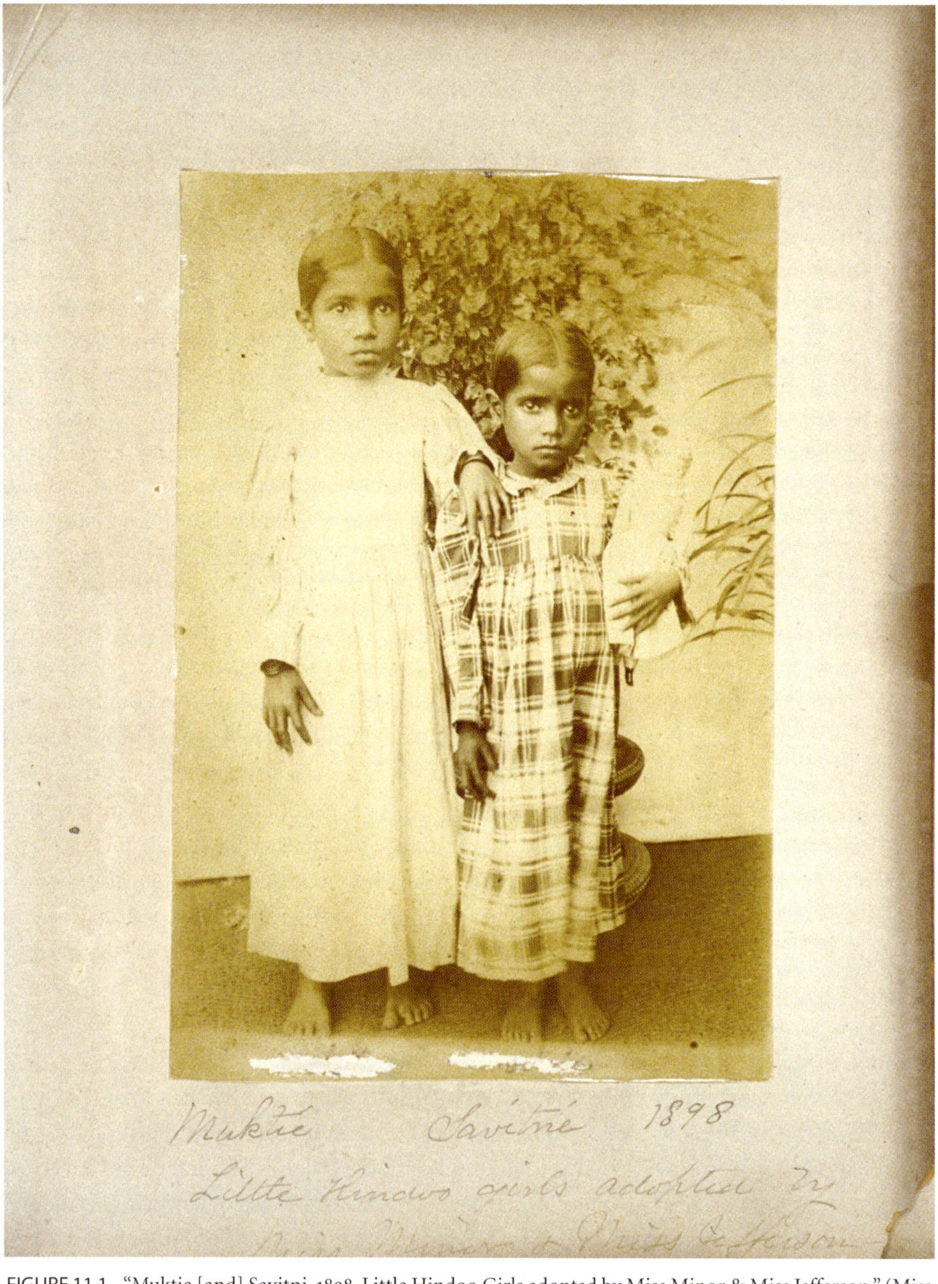

FIGURE 11.1 "Muktie [and] Savitni, 1898. Little Hindoo Girls adopted by Miss Minor & Miss Jefferson." (Miss Amanda Jefferson's photograph album, 1892–1898, private collection)

relationship to this Canadian woman missionary. This photograph provides a rare look into an intimate relationship between the missionary and the "heathen," similarity and difference in the late nineteenth century.

There is no way of knowing whether Muktie and Savitni understood the conversion they were about to face—a presumed requirement of their adoption. Likewise, there is no way of knowing whether these girls ever saw this image or, if they did, whether they were able to comprehend the significance of their visual transformation, the identities constructed for them with the camera, and the resulting photograph's placement within Jefferson's album. What can be addressed in this paper is how this photograph generates the *image* of conversion for Muktie and Savitni: how the photograph can be read within its context; how it generated meaning for Jefferson, its creator; how it produced meaning for its intended receivers. There is more at stake than the fate of Muktie and Savitni. Complicating the story is the photograph's reinforcement of Jefferson's position as a Canadian missionary, her missionary zeal and newfound authority as a "new woman." This photograph pictures a cultural conversion as much as a religious one: the photograph adopts Muktie and Savitni as naturalized, Christian citizens of Jefferson's home culture, regardless of the actuality of their circumstances at the moment the image was created. Like the album itself, this image serves as a means to communicate the agency and successes of Jefferson's life work; it *missionizes* these two Indian girls and, at the same time, missionizes the very medium that generated their image. By means of this photograph, Muktie and Savitni come into contact with white, Western, Christian values, which both produce and define their difference. Photography serves as a *contact zone*[8] between Muktie and Savitni and their new cultural identities, while it simultaneously constructs these very things for the girls—cultural identities that have meaning for the readers of the image, if not necessarily for the adopted daughters who were meant to live them.

The Album as Homemaker

Jefferson's 1892 photographs can be categorized under four themes. The first five pages of the album depict the missionaries and the Indian-Christian, or "Native Christians" according to the captions, at the Kolhapur station: for example, "Some of the Native Christians of the Kolhapur Mission, 1892" and "Native Christian Teachers." The following nineteen pages contain photographs of scenes from around the compound: tradespeople at work, and servants performing domestic tasks such as "Sewing Man," "Water carrier," and "Washerman carrying the clothes to be washed." The images of the second group represent tropes of Indian life, while the Christian subjects of the second group are granted a degree of subjectivity. The next fifteen photographs picture various bungalows, hospitals, schools, and sites in and around Kolhapur, concluding with images of a "Native Whiskey Shop" and a "Hindu Temple." The last four of the 1892 photographs depict scenes from Panhala, a nearby town, including an image of a tower under which "a nauleh girl (Dancing girl) was buried alive" and the queen's summer palace, in which "Human sacrifices were once offered." Jefferson's captions are not without moral judgment.

As Jefferson's letter indicates, she intended the 1892 album for a Western audience to whom India would have been foreign. This part of the album was constructed for such people, an inexperienced, possibly naive audience. To communicate, the album was patterned after what the audience knew, what was familiar to them, versus the India she saw around her every day. It therefore acts as a kind of cultural translator, organizing and classifying India (or the India that was available to Jefferson in the form of photographs) into categories and codes familiar to a Western audience. A narrative is established through the resulting organization of the 1892 images. The first image in the album, dated January 1892, is a group photograph of the missionaries on the Kolhapur compound. This photograph establishes the subject position of the album's author. It pictures Jefferson's mission family and defines a set of visual codes for inclusion—a template for reading the remainder of the album. These missionaries sit and stand together in posed and formal rows, none smiling, all dressed in Western-style clothing, and behind them is a tree and a stone building, probably a bungalow (fig. 11.2). This is the picture of "us" or those who naturally belong to the accepted culture and community established within Jefferson's album. This image is followed by four group photographs of "Native Christians" who worked alongside the missionaries. These images adhere to the visual codes established within the first photograph: all four depict organized and posed groups of people named as Christian standing in front of a bungalow, wall, or tree (fig. 11.3, for example). The visible difference in these images is that all of the "Native Christians" are in native dress—the women in saris and the men in kurta pyjama, some with turbans. These are naturalized citizens who have retained some of their native features, yet conform to the visual and religious standards laid out by the first photograph and the captions.

Following these five images of "us" are sixteen photographs depicting local Indians performing daily tasks. The "Sewing Man" (fig. 11.4) is pictured on page ten of the album, and the "Indian Mode of Sawing Wood" is on page twelve (fig. 11.5). In contrast to the first five photographs in the album, these sixteen images reinforce tropes of Indian life that confirm the "inferiority of third world cultures."[9] Furthermore, in juxtaposition to the previous images of Indian-Christians, these visual tropes appear as

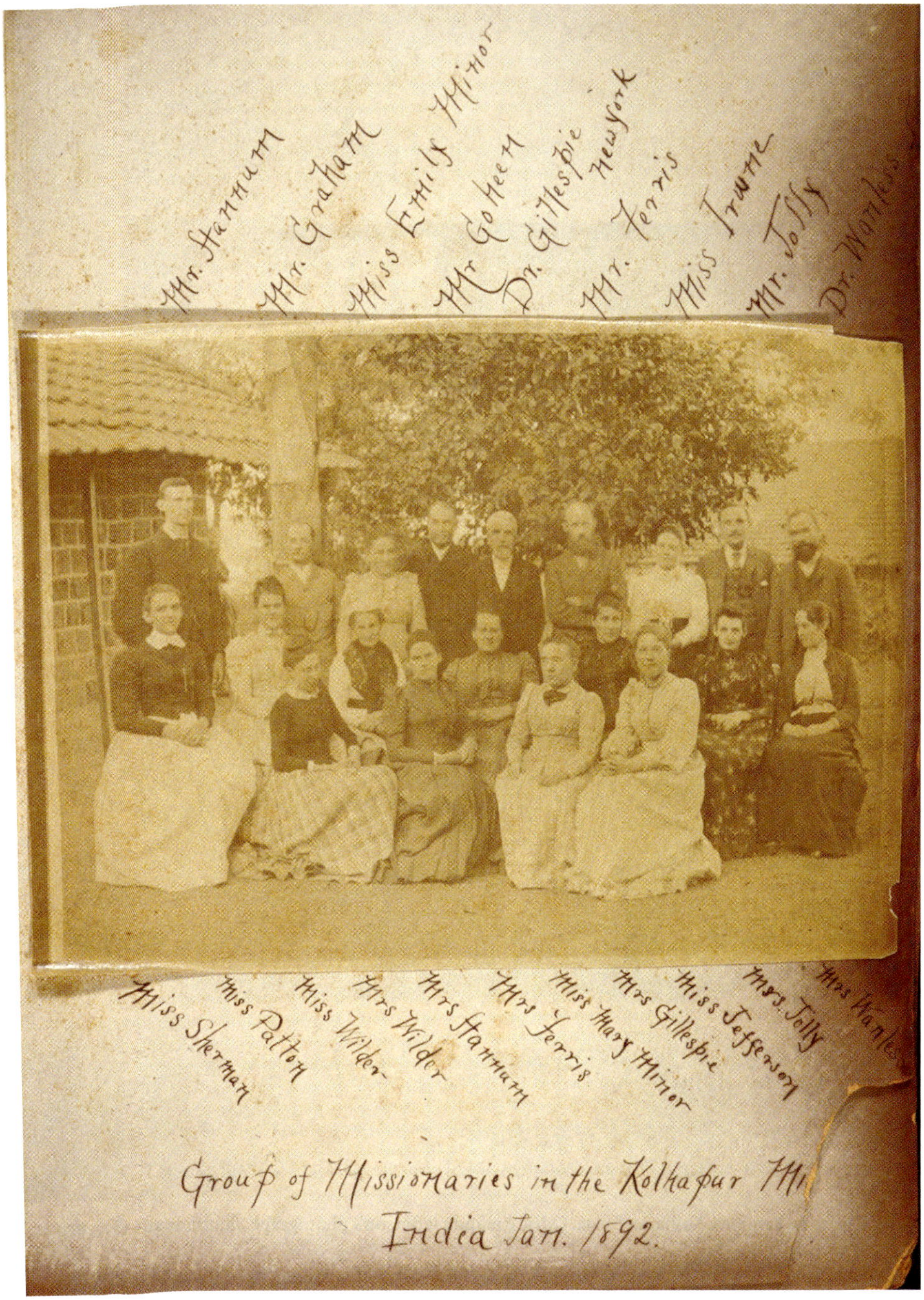

FIGURE 11.2 "Group of Missionaries in the Kolhapur M[ission], India, Jan. 1892." (Miss Amanda Jefferson's photograph album, 1892–1898, private collection)

"repertoire of photographic types includ[ing] persons, objects, places, and occurrences. A vast composite array opens up under the umbrella of daily life, photographs of people whose portraits are cast in the familiar light of habits, hobbies, and mundane affairs."[14] Jefferson's fellow missionaries and the Christian community are depicted in her album—a record of their presence in the field, of her new family. Furthermore, the photographs from 1892 are largely domestic in content—images of homes, hospitals, schools, churches, merchants, labourers, and servants whose work revolves around the home. The Indians pictured are by no means family, but the depiction of these domestic sites and tasks are silently placed in juxtaposition to Western daily life, or what might have been considered "mundane," particularly for women. Jefferson's album produces India for its viewers, an India to be consumed visually and understood within the context of Jefferson's home culture and value system.

Daughters of Difference

Within an album that was intended for a white, Western, Christian viewer, Muktie and Savitni are pictured as belonging to the missionary community and culture Jefferson depicts in her album. This community is bound by the appearance of a common system of values, one that functions and is defined in contrast to images of "heathen" India. The resulting binaries established in and by Jefferson's album—Christian versus "Hindoo," cultured versus uncivilized, educated versus uneducated, West versus East—melt into one another in the last photograph in the album: the image of Muktie and Savitni. This photograph confirms the "global universals" that motivated missionary work and were prevalent in nineteenth-century missionary discourse. In "Beyond Cultural Imperialism: Cultural Theory, Christian Missions, and Global Modernity," Ryan Dunch suggests that missionaries played a significant role in establishing and disseminating the belief in universal truths during the development of the modern order. This belief in the normative, however, tended to produce cultural difference, despite the missionary's aim to bring humanity together under the auspices of the Christian God. Dunch asks, "Might there be ways in which missionaries generated cultural differentiation within and between societies, whether through appropriations of parts of their message or through reactions against them?"[15] The portrait of Muktie and Savitni embodies this friction between normative and difference. The girls are pictured as naturalized citizens adopted into a family of Western women, a Christian community, and Jefferson's Canadian culture while being labelled as other, as "Hindoo." In the terms elucidated by Michael Taussig in *Mimesis and Alterity: A Particular History of the Senses*, Muktie and Savitni are caught within the "insoluble paradox of the distinction between essence and appearance."[16] They are both altered and left unchanged by this image: their "inner *substance*" remains Indian, yet they appear converted.[17] By means of this photograph, Muktie and Savitni are both produced and defined by their difference, yet they are "saved" with this image, twice born, their new identity constructed by mimesis and alterity. This image and their naturalized identities are a new "social currency" for Muktie and Savitni.[18]

Despite my search through the Jefferson letters and records held at the Presbyterian Historical Society of the United States, I have turned up no information that explains the image of Muktie and Savitni. The conditions of their adoption remain a mystery. According to my relatives, however, Jefferson spoke of these girls to her Canadian family during one of her frequent trips to Nova Scotia from her retirement home in Dorset, Vermont.[19] The presence of this photograph in Jefferson's album suggests that Muktie and Savitni were of some importance to Jefferson. Considering that the album's last eight images are reminiscent of a private album and thus heavily coded, Jefferson's choice to include the photograph of Muktie and Savitni, to preserve their image, to document their adoption in her album, indicates that her relationship with these girls was meaningful. The image is attached to the last page of an album that was initially assembled for public viewing, meaning that this photograph acts as punctuation for the 1892 visual narrative. As a travelogue on the path to Jefferson's acceptance of the "heathens" of India and the confirmation of her purpose, this image marks the journey's end. It gives the album a kind of closure while raising many questions in the mind of the modern viewer: Who are these girls? Why were they adopted by Jefferson and Minor? What did "adoption" mean in this context?

New Mothers

The 1890s was the "boom" for single women: they could lead independent, adventurous, and somewhat glamorous lives in comparison to the prior constraints of the private sphere.[20] No longer were women restricted to the private realm of the household, nor did they need to forsake their "womanhood" in order to have a public life.[21] New career opportunities available to single women facilitated independence from men financially and physically.[22] Long-term, domestic relationships between single women were generally accepted as a substitute for marriage and were not uncommon for late nineteenth-century spinsters.[23] According to the 1938 issue of *Western India Notes*, however, the longevity of Jefferson and Minor's relationship and companionship was unusual for the mission field: their partnership was described as a "unique feature in their missionary life."[24] Jefferson and Minor retired from missionary service and settled together in a manor for retired missionary women in Dorset, Vermont. From there they made regular trips to Nova Scotia to visit Jefferson's family and to the Columbia Bible College in

South Carolina. After Minor's death in 1938, Jefferson wrote in memory of Minor that theirs was an "intimate relationship for over half a century" and that she owed to Minor "more than mere words can tell."[25] They were life partners, and the adoption of Muktie and Savitni meant that they became a family.

Jefferson and Minor were part of the "golden age of missionary expansion," which saw numerous North Americans enter the mission field, the majority of them women. "Through foreign missionary service ... even respectable women could become adventurers, and even ordinary women heroines."[26] Missionary work was believed to appeal to the single woman's "capacity for self-denial [and] to her innate desire to relieve suffering."[27] Furthermore, it offered opportunities for higher education, travel, and a certain amount of public recognition that was not regularly granted to women.[28] Like their adopted mothers, Muktie and Savitni were enabled by Christianity. Foreign mission work offered "new women" like Jefferson and Minor independence from men, both financially and physically.[29] As this photograph suggests, Muktie and Savitni's adoption gave them a certain "upward" mobility—from the heathen "Hindoo" to civilized Christian. On the surface they are converted, freed of the depravity and ignorance of their origins, but tucked underneath their rigid pose, cotton dresses, and photographic likeness is their "inner *substance*."[30]

Most missionaries new to the field faced significant culture shock and a sometimes long period of adjustment to their new surroundings—the sights, the smells, the sounds. According to Sherrie A. Inness in her article on Mount Holyoke missionaries, women were often ill prepared for the adjustments to the culture and the environment: they often felt isolated, they encountered drought, disease and hostile people, and some never integrated into their new society.[31] As Frederick J. Heuser writes in *Culture, Feminism, and the Gospel*, possibly the biggest challenge for these missionaries, however, was learning to accept the culture and people of the foreign land. Furthermore, the lack of training and access to "accurate" depictions of foreign cultures meant that missionaries arrived burdened with opinions and biases about the host country and people. As a result, correspondence from new missionaries in the field often reproduced the idea of the "depraved, ignorant heathen in need of salvation."[32] This kind of essentializing of non-Christian Indians is visible in Jefferson's album. Many of the 1892 photographs are "domestic images," according to Laura Wexler in *Tender Violence: Domestic Visions in an Age of U.S. Imperialism*, or "complex, multivalent signs whose symbolic meanings are determined by their insertion into underlying cultural and political patterns. Their codes cannot be understood separately from the entire system of signification that encompasses them."[33] They are "active, difference-producing mechanisms."[34] To get hold of a likeness of Muktie and Savitni, the "orality" of Jefferson's album must be revealed—how Jefferson names India in the photographs through

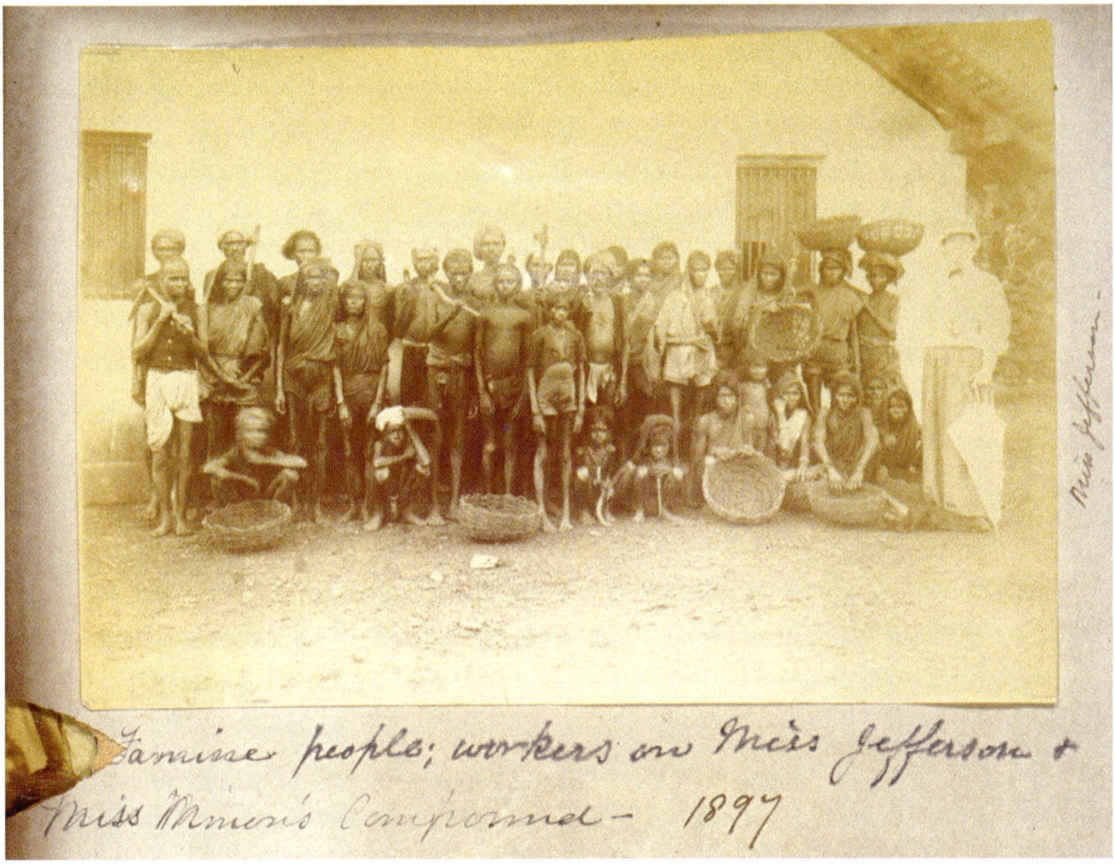

FIGURE 11.6 "Famine people; workers on Miss Jefferson & Miss Minor's Compound, 1897." (Miss Amanda Jefferson's photograph album, 1892–1898, private collection)

selection, organization, captioning, and presentation.[35] Jefferson directs the viewer's interpretation using late nineteenth-century, Western, Christian codes of viewing—the same system of signification that naturalizes the image of Muktie and Savitni within the context of this album.

The western part of India was subject to a number of droughts and famines in the late nineteenth and early twentieth centuries, as the second-to-last photograph in the album indicates: the "Famine people" on Jefferson's compound in 1897 (fig. 11.6). Furthermore, records suggest that other missionaries at Ratnagiri took Indian orphans under their care—"adopted" them. Robert Hannum (1892–1974), the eldest son of William and Annabel Hannum, writes in his autobiography:

> On the day of my birth, May 16, 1892, Father found a newly born boy deserted by the road and brought him home to my mother. "Now we have a dark son and a white son," he told her. My parents adopted Vitthu Ragu and he was my early companion. He was cared for by a nursemaid in a bungalow next to our home.[36]

According to Ruth Compton Brouwer in *New Women for God: Canadian Presbyterian Women and India Missions, 1876-1914*, the famines of 1897 and 1900 prompted many missions in India to rescue orphaned children and homeless widows—relief efforts that were not without evangelism, as the missionaries recognized that these orphans and women had the potential to become the "back-bone" of the growth of their Christian institutions.[37] Dr. Margaret (Maggie) O'Hara, who worked as a medical missionary to central India for the Presbyterian Church in Canada, informally adopted three girls—a teenaged mother and her two infants. O'Hara had a great affection for all three girls, affording them a good education with hopes that they might take her place once she retired.[38] Brouwer suggests that for single women like O'Hara, the care of orphaned children helped to sustain them in the face of the despair they might have felt without a family life.[39]

The care Jefferson and Minor gave Muktie and Savitni must have saved them from a certain amount of hardship. In the late nineteenth century, Indian women were still wholly reliant on men for support. Fathers were the providers for the family—they arranged marriages and supplied the dowries for their daughters—and husbands took over where fathers left off. Without a father to perform this role, Muktie and Savitni's future would have been the responsibility of the orphanage and likely very bleak. In some missionary-run girls' schools, missionaries took on the paternal role for the girls, but this was not the norm.[40] It was in the interest of the mission, however, to wed the girls with Christian boys in order to continue the Christianization of India. This also served to modernize Indian women, "saving" them from a life of gruelling labour and child marriage.[41] Whether or not Muktie and Savitni's adoption conformed to current standards of adoption, it was within the missionizing interests of Jefferson and Minor to see to the care, education, and proper marriage of these Indian daughters.

Despite the fact that there is no way these girls were born of Jefferson and Minor, this image of the girls taps into the tradition of photographic demonstrations of lineage. According to Langford, the family album is known as a forum for visual genealogy but also of identity. A photograph of the Hannum children is a good example of this—it demonstrates the Hannum line and their ability to maintain their Western identity even when surrounded by the "heathen" culture of India (the middle sections of the album).[42] The image of Muktie and Savitni is a family photograph: a family of two Indians, headed by two Caucasians, all four women. With the gender, race, class, religion, and nationality of the Jefferson-Minor family, this photograph both explodes and conforms to nineteenth-century ideals of the Western family. It tells the viewer of the album that Muktie and Savitni will be raised in the likeness of their parents—progressive women who will rise above the limitations of their culture and time. Despite Muktie and Savitni's Indian or "Hindoo" origins, this photograph signifies a means for Jefferson and Minor to continue their work and identities as independent Christian women. The photograph demonstrates that these girls will continue the Jefferson-Minor line not in appearance, not even in name, but in their values and culture.

Dressing the Part

The 1898 photograph of Muktie and Savitni stands as a symbol and description of their adoption. This image is a contact zone between these girls and their soon-to-be adoptive parents, culture, religion, and place within the context of Jefferson's album. This image demonstrates what Taussig calls the merging of "copy and contact."[43] The likeness of Muktie and Savitni is "sensuous knowledge," particularly a "knowing" through the visual and haptic senses. As a result, their likeness is affected by this contact, by what is other than them.

The dresses Muktie and Savitni are pictured wearing were not typical of late nineteenth-century Indian girls' clothing. Their garments are clearly Western-style frocks, most likely hand-me-downs from one or two Western families. These dresses are simple in both detailing and construction—they are made of common, pattered fabrics with little to no ornamentation. The sleeves have a bit of the fullness associated with American girls' garments from the 1890s, but the skirts are longer than what was typical for young girls like Muktie and Savitni.[44] These dresses are not high fashion—they are practical and inexpensive frocks for everyday use, typical of work or play dresses in both rural and urban North America in the late nineteenth century.[45] According to Taussig, the mere act of putting on Western-style clothing meant these girls were coming into physical contact with the West—"the touch, the feel, like putting on a skin."[46] Furthermore, during the height of British colonial rule, it was the men, not the women, who adopted European fashion.[47] As Taussig states, women were the "bearers of the appearance of tradition and … the embodiment of the Nation."[48] Muktie and Savitni are altered by this act of dress-up: their "inner *substance*"[49] covered up, their "Hindoo" identity disguised. But there are cracks in the veneer: their bare feet, the bangles peeking out from underneath the sleeves of their frocks.

In the process of being photographed, Muktie and Savitni encountered another kind of physical contact with their adoptive culture. Compare this photograph to the 1896 photograph of Mary and Robert Hannum on page fifty-five of the album (fig. 11.7). These children of missionaries are dressed in formal clothing—probably their Sunday best. The elder child, Robert, stands slightly behind his younger sister, Mary, with his hand on her these two identities—the naturalized citizen and the depraved heathen—creates a kind of "before" and "after" photograph rolled into one. As Wexler writes about a nineteenth-century "after" photograph of three First Nations girls, they "replicate exactly the ideal image of Victorian girlhood. The only contradiction is the darkness of their skin."[51] In the case of the photograph of Muktie and Savitni, there are many more contradictions than just their skin. Their bare feet play against their formal pose, the bangles against their frocks. It is as if this present-based photograph is invested with powers of clairvoyance. Taken at the point of transition, it predicts Muktie and Savitni's future conversion to Christianity, their rise in social status from orphan girls to daughters of missionaries, their salvation.

The portrait of Muktie and Savitni represents the liminal space between being one thing and being another. It is beyond the simple photographic cut from time; this image is a cut from Muktie and Savitni's cultural identities and their origins. In her article on contemporary adoption narratives and trauma theory, Margaret Homans writes that a child's pre-adoption story is "unclaimed experience."[52] Particularly in the case of transnational or interracial adoptions, Homans suggests that the task is to integrate this past into the adoptee's life, rather than "inventing helpful fictions about the irretrievable historical moments."[53] The adoptee and adopter's construction of an unknown and unattainable history for the child is the focus of Homans's article, along with the resulting "adoptive self-fabrication" that occurs when the adoptee is cut from his or her origins.[54] Homans calls this being "twice-born," a term she borrows from one of the narratives she examines in her text. Adoption is like a rebirth of identity—the new identity is seen as constructed, whereas the birth identity is viewed as natural or given, "carv[ing] out a new self distinction from the one society assigned."[55] This idea of the adoption marking a separation from the adoptee's origins is echoed by Barbara Yngvesson in her article "Going 'Home': Adoption, Loss of Bearings, and the Mythology of Roots." She writes:

> The clean break separates the child from everything that constitutes her grounds for belonging to *this* family and *this* nation, while establishing her transferability to *that* family and *that* nation. With a past that has been cut away—an old identity that no longer exists—the child can be reembedded in a new place, almost as though he or she never moved at all.[56]

Although Muktie and Savitni were not transplanted to Canada, these contemporary perspectives on transnational adoptions offer an interesting view of this image of Jefferson and Minor's adopted daughters. The photograph marks the cut from the girls' origins and the fabrication of their new Christian, Westernized identities. The construction of identity here is twofold: first, their Hindu identity is only partially concealed by their imperfect mimicry of Victorian girlhood, their new "civilized" identities juxtaposed with their "heathen" past. Second, their supposed future identities as Christian, Westernized girls are visually constructed within this photograph, their naturalized citizenship put on display. They wear this new identity, their rebirth, in this image, although the caption alludes to their origins. This is an intriguing reversal of Homans's notion of "self-fabrication." The primary "self-fabrication" here is about Muktie and Savitni's future, not their unknown past. Their origins are lumped together with the other visual tropes in the album—the simple, uncivilized, albeit exotic heathen—which is the unseen, forcefully implied "before" image of these girls. The focus in this image is on their new and fabricated identities that are described to the viewer with the girls' clothing, posture, and the photographic style. Although this image is not meant to picture Muktie and Savitni as available for adoption, it does ask the intended audience of the album to accept them into their hearts and homes despite the girls' origins, history, and first births. As Lisa Cartwright writes about contemporary transnational adoption photographs, or images of "waiting children":

> [The adoptees'] looks might mystify or intrigue Western clients when they are not unambiguously marked with familiar attributes of European looks, Caucasian looks, Asian looks. These children are thus classified in ways that may not match local understandings of cultural identity, or their apparently ambiguous or unfixed identities may make them more easily viewed by agencies, clients, and human rights advocates as essentially stateless.[57]

To follow Cartwright is to understand the fate of Muktie and Savitni as determined by the meanings assigned to this image—meanings contributed by viewers invested in the girls' conversion, naturalization, and adoption. This photograph determines their fate as the adopted daughters of missionary women, and good Christian girls of Canadian and American mothers. Their citizenship is therefore fixed in this photograph—by placing this photograph in her album, Jefferson declared Muktie and Savitni as her children and therefore Canada's as well. And as this album was handed down to Jefferson's Canadian relatives, the girls' photographic citizenship was reinforced by each set of eyes that discovered this page.

Photographic Conversion

According to the viewpoint of the "dear friends" for whom Jefferson compiled this album, this photograph of Muktie and Savitni may have been of service to her mission field—presuming that it was meant to be a supplement to the 1892 series of images intended for a more public audience. The ambiguous relationship of the last eight photographs to the forty-three images from 1892 is just one of many binaries the album establishes—public versus private, personal content versus a political agenda. The binaries culminate in the final, punctuating image of Muktie and Savitni. By means of the girls' portrait, viewers of the album were, in fact, encountering a reproduction of white, middle-class, Christian ideals and values in a depiction of Indian girls. The captioned photograph of Muktie and Savitni photographically reveals acculturated citizens of Jefferson's home, their belonging based on the appearance of conforming to a specific set of visual codes that symbolize the values of the album's author. Hidden beneath the surface, however, is what is "other"—two Indian girls wearing an uncomfortable identity, a skin that is not their own. Savitni stares into the camera as if she knows what this moment amounts to. She sees that she is being looked at, perhaps she senses the alteration in the brief moment that the shutter is open. The creation of this image is the creation of an identity for these girls, not an identity that they necessarily chose, but rather one that has been given to them. It is an adopted identity, one they may wear only in appearance or only for the camera—they have dressed for the photographer. What is captured by this likeness is not only "mimesis and alterity" but also the soul—Muktie's and Savitni's souls are at stake here. As Taussig writes, the photograph brings "spirit, soul, and image, into the one constellation"[58] It establishes a tension between past and the future, what is and what will become, predicting their inevitable conversion and adoption of a system of beliefs. Muktie and Savitni's portrait also predicts the reception of this image by Jefferson's "dear friends" and their adoption of these girls as belonging to their white, middle-class, Christian community. But the future state of Muktie and Savitni's souls is of little consequence; rather, they have already been brought into the fold, "saved" by means of their likeness.

Notes

1 Amanda Jefferson, "Emily Minor of Ratnagiri," *Western India Notes* 19, no. 2 (1938): 31. From Record Group 360, Miss Emily T. Minor's Personnel File, Presbyterian Historical Society, Philadelphia, PA.

2 Patricia R. Hill, *The World Their Household: The American Woman's Foreign Mission Movement and Cultural Transformation, 1870–1920* (Ann Arbor: University of Michigan Press, 1985), 8; Peter Williams, "'The Missing Link': The Recruitment of Women Missionaries in Some English Evangelical Missionary Societies in the Nineteenth Century," in *Women and Missions: Past and Present—Anthropological and Historical Perceptions*, ed. F. Bowie, D. Kirkwood, and S. Ardener, 43–69 (Rhode Island: Berg, 1993), 43.

3 *Historical Sketches of the India Missions of the Presbyterian Church in the United States of America known as the Lodiana, the Farrukhabad, and the Kolhapur Missions; From the beginning of the work, in 1834, To the time of its fiftieth Anniversary, in 1884* (Allahabad: Allahabad Mission Press, 1886). From Record Group 360, Miss Emily T. Minor's Personnel File, Presbyterian Historical Society, Philadelphia, PA.

4 A. Adelaide Browne, "An Appreciation of Miss Emily T. Minor," *Western India Notes* (April 1928): 4. From Record Group 360, Miss Emily T. Minor's Personnel File, Presbyterian Historical Society, Philadelphia, PA.

5 Document dated February 21, 1938, from Record Group 360, Miss Emily T. Minor's Personnel File, Presbyterian Historical Society, Philadelphia, PA.

6 The archives of the Presbyterian Historical Society in Philadelphia house the majority of the historical documents pertaining to the Presbyterian mission to Western India. Among the documents of Dr. William James Wanless (1865–1933), the primary doctor in Kolhapur, is a photograph album bearing the title "Photo Album Miraj, India, 1890–1915." This album is identical to Miss Jefferson's, although the cover is a different colour. The photographs inside provide a detailed visual record of the construction of the hospital in Miraj, the hospital life once built, a number of photographs in and around the Kolhapur mission station, and images of Dr. Wanless's home and personal life. Many of the photographs of Kolhapur are found in Jefferson's album. Based on the similarity in size, print, and paper quality between the images in the Wanless and Jefferson albums, it is my assumption that Jefferson obtained the photographs in her album from Dr. Wanless. Further to this, considering the nature of some of the more personal photographs in the Wanless album—images of the interior of his bedroom in Miraj, he and his family on the porch of their cottage in India—I expect that Dr. Wanless took these images or hired a photographer to take them under his direction. Regardless, I attribute the authorship of the 1892 photographs in the Jefferson album to Dr. Wanless.

7 See the Basel Mission Picture Archive, http://www.bmpix.org/index.html.

8 See Mary Louise Pratt's *Imperial Eyes: Travel Writing and Transculturation* (London: Routledge, 1992), 6. Specifically, in her introduction, Pratt defines the "contact zone" as "the spatial and temporal copresence of subjects previously separated by geographical and historical disjunctures, and whose trajectories now intersect.... A 'contact' perspective emphasizes how subjects are constituted in and by their relations to each other. [It stresses] copresence, interaction, interlocking understandings and practices, often within radically asymmetrical relations of power" (6–7).

9 Frederick J. Heuser, *Culture, Feminism, and the Gospel: American Presbyterian Women and Foreign Missions, 1870–1923* (Ph.D. diss., Temple University, 1991), 127.

10 Micheal Taussig, *Mimesis and Alterity: A Particular History of the Senses* (New York: Routledge, 1993), 136.

11 Marilyn F. Motz, "Visual Autobiography: Photograph Albums of Turn-of-the-Century Midwestern Women," *American Quarterly* 41, no. 1 (1989): 72.

12 Ibid., 63.

13 Martha Langford, *Suspended Conversations: The Afterlife of Memory in Photographic Albums* (Montreal and Kingston: McGill-Queen's University Press, 2001), 87.

14 Ibid., 130.

15 Ryan Dunch, "Beyond Cultural Imperialism: Cultural Theory, Christian Missions, and Global Modernity," *History and Theory* 41 (2002): 319.

16 Taussig, *Mimesis and Alterity*, 176.

17 Ibid., 136.

18 Laura Wexler, *Tender Violence: Domestic Visions in an Age of U.S. Imperialism* (Chapel Hill: University of North Carolina Press, 2000), 87.

19 Annetta Neaves, conversation with the author, May 19, 2006.

20 R. Freeman and P. Klaus, "Blessed or Not? The New Spinster in England and the United States in the Late Nineteenth and Early Twentieth Centuries," *Journal of Family History* 9, no. 4 (1984): 409.
21 Jean Bethke Elshtain, "Moral Women and Immoral Man: A Consideration of the Public–Private Split and Its Political Ramifications," *Politics and Society* 4, no. 4 (1974): 455 and 460.
22 Freeman and Klaus, "Blessed or Not?" 403.
23 Motz, "Visual Autobiography," 85.
24 Browne, "An Appreciation of Miss Emily T. Minor," 4.
25 Jefferson, "Emily Minor," 31.
26 Ruth C. Brouwer, *New Women for God* (Toronto: University of Toronto Press, 1990), 192.
27 Hill, *The World Their Household*, 50.
28 Sherrie A. Inness, "'Repulsive as the multitudes by whome I am surrounded': Constructing the Contact Zone in the Writings of Mount Holyoke Missionaries, 1830–1890," *Women Studies* 23, no. 4 (1994): 378.
29 Freeman and Klaus, "Blessed or Not?" 403.
30 Taussig, *Mimesis and Alterity*, 136.
31 Inness, "Repulsive as the multitudes," 375–379.
32 Heuser, *Culture, Feminism, and the Gospel*, 129.
33 Wexler, *Tender Violence*, 21.
34 Ibid., 22.
35 Langford, *Suspended Conversations*, 122.
36 Robert Henry Hannum, "The Autobiography of Robert Henry Hannum, 1892–1974" (unpublished autobiography, Presbyterian Historical Society archives, Philadelphia, 1974), 3.
37 Brouwer, *New Women for God*, 119–120.
38 Ibid., 172.
39 Ibid., 169.
40 Eliza F. Kent, *Converting Women: Gender and Protestant Christianity in Colonial South India* (New York: Oxford University Press, 2004), 168.
41 Ibid., 10.
42 Langford, *Suspended Conversations*, 95.
43 Taussig, *Mimesis and Alterity*, 21.
44 Estelle Ansley Worrell, *Children's Costume in America 1607–1910* (New York: Charles Scribner's Sons, 1980), 188. Worrell writes that "a girl's skirt length was determined by her age," meaning that as a girl grew into a woman, her skirt lengthened according to what was considered "proper" at the time (129).
45 Ibid., 164–165.
46 Taussig, *Mimesis and Alterity*, 191.
47 Emily Tarlo, *Clothing Matters: Dress and Identity in India* (Chicago: University of Chicago Press, 1996), 25.
48 Taussig, *Mimesis and Alterity*, 177.
49 Ibid., 136.
50 Wexler, *Tender Violence*, 112.
51 Ibid., 111.
52 Margaret Homans, "Adoption Narratives, Trauma, and Origins," *Narrative* 14, no. 1 (2006): 7.
53 Ibid., 9–10.
54 Ibid., 12.

55 Ibid.
56 Barbara Yngvesson, "Going 'Home': Adoption, Loss of Bearings, and the Mythology of Roots," *Social Text* 74, no. 1 (2003): 7.
57 Lisa Cartwright, "Photographs of 'Waiting Children': The Transnational Adoption Market," *Social Text* 74, no. 1 (2003): 85–86.
58 Taussig, *Mimesis and Alterity*, 176.

ANNMARIE ADAMS
DAVID THEODORE
PATRICIA MCKEEVER

PICTURES OF HEALTH
Sick Kids Exposed

TWO TYPES OF PHOTOGRAPHS HAUNT THE history of North American children's hospitals. The first, a therapeutic type, depicts the hospital as a place where heroic physicians use technology to heal children, exposing young patients as frail and helpless beneficiaries of healthcare expertise. Passive children displayed unconscious during surgery are particularly good examples of this genre. In these images young doctors and nurses typically loom over still and vulnerable bodies on tables or beds, surrounded by gleaming medical equipment. The second type, images of playfulness, promotes the institution as a place of socializing and fun. These more positive images of hospital life portray sick children actively defying the seriousness of their circumstances, despite the fear and anxiety associated with illness, through friendship and recreation. This type underlines the role of distraction as a coping mechanism in dealing with illness and treatment. Examples include photographs of young tuberculosis patients laughing outside in bed (even during the winter), or gown-clad children playing games together in hospital playrooms and wards. William Notman's 1893 photograph of the children's ward in Montreal's Royal Victoria Hospital—where sick girls play "tea party" as if they are in a grand home or hotel—is an outstanding model of this type (fig. 12.1). Such images present the hospital as a welcoming place for children, and also as an everyday, ordinary institution—like a school—with little indication of the medical technology, illness, or sense of mortality that characterize the therapeutic pictures.

This interdisciplinary paper surveys the history of these two parallel trends in depicting sick children, with examples drawn from Montreal and Toronto institutions.[1] There are abundant photographs indicative of these two types taken in general hospitals, such as the Royal Victoria tea party, but the archives of paediatric institutions are especially rich, including the Children's Memorial Hospital (later known as the

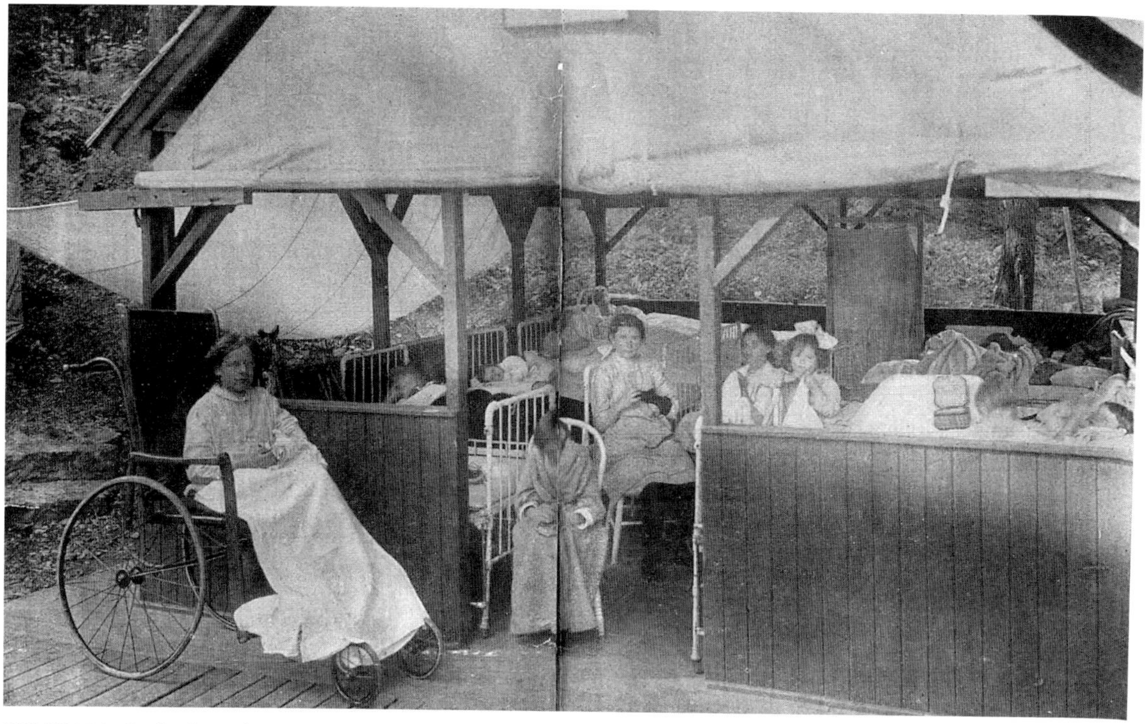

FIGURE 12.8 Sewing hour, from CMH 1912 annual report. (Photo: Montreal Children's Hospital)

simultaneously appreciating the joys of nature. It masks the medical reasons for the children to be exposed (that is, fresh air as a medical treatment) and instead connects childhood to nature's ability to distract and regenerate.

Close-up, somewhat voyeuristic portraits of sick children at the CMH document in remarkable detail how children managed to sew and conduct other handiwork while bedridden. A boy draws illustrations to accompany his own writing (fig. 12.9), again outside amidst the trees, in a white metal bed. The pillow serves as an ad hoc easel, propped up against the headboard. The bed beside the boy is vacant; the nearby dresser has a pitcher of water and a stopper-topped glass bottle. A washcloth is folded on the bed's lower rungs, while a wheelchair and regular chair sit empty in the adjacent space. Flimsy screen-like partitions, like those shown in the sewing image, form the backdrop of the photo. Near the patient's head, a pocket watch hangs between the bars of the bed, and a little further, just within reach, a pile of books sits on a small bookshelf. In short, there is no trace of the boy as a subject of medical control. The photograph transports a sick boy in bed outside to a desk or a table at school. Drawing in bed is a hospital activ-

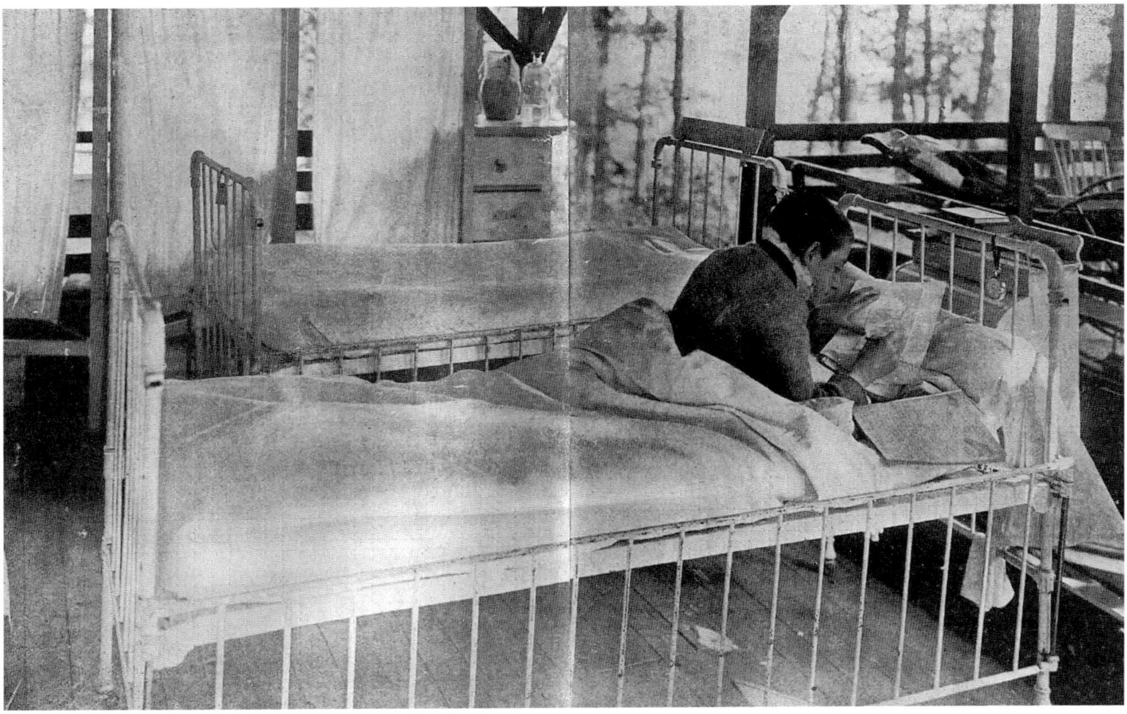

FIGURE 12.9 Boy drawing in bed, CMH 1912 annual report. (Photo: Montreal Children's Hospital)

ity that helps pass the time (borne out by the presence of the watch), but the photograph's content and composition make it a school activity, blurring the distinctions between educational and medical environments.

Another type of leisure photograph comprises images of the modern hospital as a setting for human drama. In the early twentieth century, hospitals regularly promulgated photographs that depict special, sometimes annual, but often unique events such as Christmas parties, visits from entertainers and royalty, or opening day ceremonies. Hospital administrators carefully staged and documented these festivities, promoting an image of the hospital as a humane, social place, and helping to manage powerful, intimate dramas in an increasingly impersonal institution. While some hospitals invested in specialized spaces such as theatres, playgrounds or playrooms, swimming pools, and games rooms, it was actually the activity that mattered more, turning mundane locations like a hospital bed or a hallway into an opportunity for adventure and fun.

Holiday parties, theatrical performances, reading in bed, sewing lessons, and other events or activities were all intended as coping mechanisms during times of sickness. For instance, Notman's photograph of the tea party in the Royal Victoria children's ward (see fig. 12.1), decorated with potted houseplants and rocking chairs, presents life in the hospital as a palimpsest of life in a middle-class Victorian home. It is important to underline the role of these hospitals as charitable institutions; poor kids came here and stayed a long time, especially when compared to today's hospital stays. This may have blurred the lines between home and hospital.[7] Anne Cornfield, hospitalized with scarlet fever at the age of seven, came from a poor home. Her daughter recalls the impact of the event on her mother's life seventy-six years later: "She loved the hospital, the clean and quiet environment, the tranquil routine, the attentive nurses. This was her first encounter with middle-class living. She cherished these memories into adulthood, when she created her own family home."[8] A well-known example from Quebec literature is a scene from Gabrielle Roy's 1947 novel, *The Tin Flute*. Rose-Anna visits her son Daniel Lacasse at the Children's Memorial Hospital and remarks on the "gleaming whiteness" of the ward, the "unfailing patience" of the nurse, and the plenitude of toys—including the namesake tin flute, "such as he had always yearned to have":[9]

> Here he was in a world designed for children.... He could lie at his ease here at last, for he had a bed that need not be closed up and put away every morning. For the first time in his life he had several things of his own. Above all he had never been in a room with so many windows and so much sunlight.[10]

In all these images documenting urban paediatric hospitals in Canada, the sick children are active figures; they sometimes appear even blissful, participating and even enjoying themselves, despite the circumstances that have brought them to the hospital. At the hospital they were exposed to activities and luxuries unavailable to them at home: perhaps sewing, drawing, or bird watching, but especially healthy food, clean linens, and the clean air of Mount Royal. Capturing such activities in photographs for broad distribution in annual reports and fundraising brochures was a way to normalize the hospital environment.

Type 3: SickKids Today

While it may be possible to use institution-sanctioned photographs to help adults retrieve memories of children's hospitals, contemporary photographs can reveal aspects of children's experiences of hospitalization today. For our investigation of children as agents of architectural knowledge, photo-elicitation was used as a research interview technique to form a visual record of how children view the eight-storey atrium at SickKids Hospital in Toronto.[11] Research assistants conducted walking tours of the atrium with forty-five outpatients visiting hospital clinics and thirty-five inpatients whose rooms overlooked the public lobby. The children were interviewed as they walked and used a digital camera to photograph the atrium's architecture.

It is especially important to understand how the atrium typology became the preferred form for the late twentieth-century hospital, as its association with children may not be obvious. It is our contention that the atrium-centred hospital is part of a larger trend by which many building types have come to adopt the multi-storey, naturally illuminated lobby as an ordering device. The now-familiar typology began with hotels, particularly Hyatt hotels associated with the Atlanta-based architectural firm of John Portman & Associates. Portman's twenty-two-storey Hyatt Regency Atlanta of 1967 is generally considered to be the first atrium-based hotel. Exposed, fast-moving elevators (a key element in the SickKids Atrium addition) and the rooftop rotating restaurant are the signature aspects of this daring, much-imitated structure.[12]

The designers of urban shopping malls soon used atriums too. In Canada, it is perhaps no coincidence that the two most important atrium hospitals, Zeidler Partnership Architects' (ZPA) Walter C. Mackenzie Health Sciences Centre in Edmonton and Toronto's SickKids, are not far from the country's best-known malls: the West Edmonton Mall (1981–1986) and the Toronto Eaton Centre (also designed by ZPA, 1977). The Alberta mall boasts a number of Disney-inspired attractions obviously aimed at children (the model of Columbus's *Santa Maria*, zoo, golf course, 270 video games, ten-acre water park with beach and waves). "West Edmonton Mall is like turning on all the channels of the TV at the same time," said a reporter in 1985.[13] The Eaton Centre, however, like the ultra-serious Hyatt hotels, is not as obviously intended as a space for young users, but has self-evident links to leisure, escape, and consumption.

Atriums are used in children's hospitals because many planners (architects, administrators, and healthcare professionals) have internalized contemporary discursive ideals reflecting adult ideas about "the child" and "childhood." Whereas traditional paediatric hospitals contained windowless, maze-like corridors, and unfamiliar routines and smells, contemporary paediatric hospital architects attempt to "de-emphasize connotations associated with institutionalised medicine … [and] normalize the place for children."[14] Like their shopping mall counterparts, atriums include design features that purport to promote a nonthreatening and therapeutic "elsewhere" based on fantasy.[15] The atrium at SickKids is full of supposedly child-friendly features, including potted plants, pastoral wall murals, exposed elevators, and giant, cartoonish figures. The director of planning for the addition enthused in an interview shortly after it opened that "kids walk in and say, 'Wow! This looks like fun.'"[16] This international postmodern design strategy of deliberately disguising a visit to a hospital is borne out by Sir Jonathan Michael in describing the aims for Britain's recent paediatric hospital: "We wanted the new Evelina Children's Hospital to be much more than a landmark building on a landmark site. Our aim has been to create a hospital that does not feel like a hospital by involving children, their families and our staff in every stage of the design process." Non-hospital features at the Evelina are fantasy-based and wide-ranging: "Bright red rocket lifts, clearly visible from inside and outside the hospital, carry people to a four-storey central conservatory. Throughout the hospital, lively artwork … creates a welcoming, friendly atmosphere, whilst each floor of the hospital has been given a colour and a symbol taken from the natural world—from Ocean and Beach through to Savannah and Sky." Window washers at the new hospital even dress as Spiderman![17]

Our study tested whether child patients could reveal their architectural experience of SickKids' atrium through photographs. In the course of a walking tour, children were asked to capture aspects of the atrium's architecture that interested them. To protect patient and staff confidentiality, the children were asked not to photograph people. Like the happy and active children pictured in the second genre of historic photographs, our young photographers exposed aspects of the atrium that seem to reflect their desire to be elsewhere. Many took photographs by directing the camera away from the atrium to capture outdoor cityscapes; others focused on the atrium's confining details; still others captured its imaginary and playful features. In this hospital many children are too sick to play, and those who are well and ambulatory spend time in the atrium's mall-like shopping and fast food eating areas. However, children pictured the desire to be transported elsewhere, whether by looking outside or through fantasy "play." For example, an eight-year-old girl liked the atrium's artificial palm trees because they reminded her of swimming (January 31, 2006, interview #231, 8 yr, girl). Another child said she would like to redecorate the atrium using a Disney theme: "Like you know it's not real but you let yourself feel it is and you just have fun with it. So I think things to distract and just to take your mind off what you're worrying about" (January 23, 2006, interview #226, 16 yr, girl).

Cityscapes

Although sometimes drawn to the natural elements within the atrium, such as the fountain and palm trees, young patients commonly directed the camera to the outside world, making windows very significant. Children liked to look outside to see what was happening or to watch for visiting friends and family. An eight-year-old girl noted that when gazing through the skylight, "[it] feels like we're outside … like there's no roof … I like the wind" (October 5, 2005, interview #107, 8 yr, girl). Others talked about the importance of seeing nature outside: "If it was just closed in … if you just had regular yellow lights it would be depressing and boring.… It's nice to look out even when there are storms" (November 2, 2005, interview #245, 17 yr, boy).

Many patients took photographs from the public area on the eighth floor, where floor-to-ceiling windows face eastward to reveal a dense urban landscape of commercial and

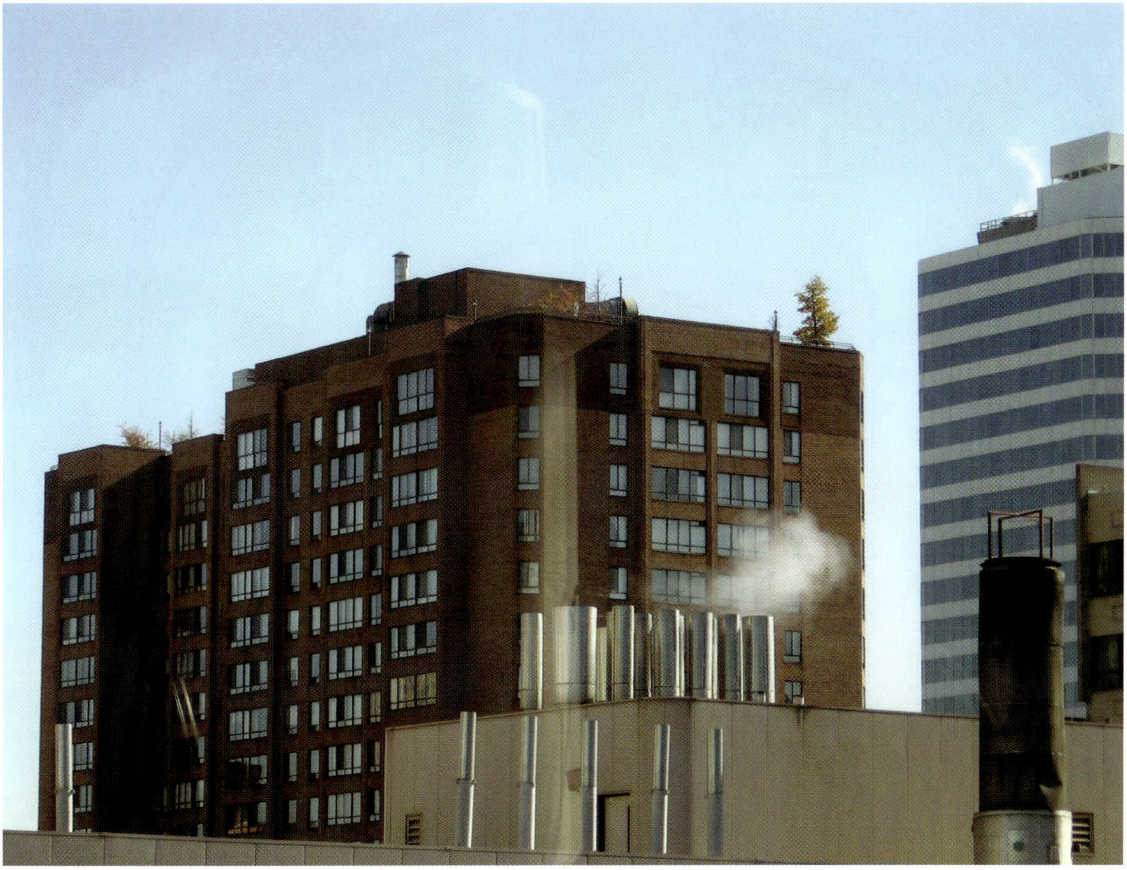

FIGURE 12.10 Toronto cityscape from inside SickKids, photographed by a seventeen-year-old boy. (Photo: 245-003)

residential buildings. One example (fig. 12.10) features a red brick, twenty-seven-storey condominium tower with shops and restaurants on street level, located at the northeast corner of Edward and Bay streets, one block northwest of the Eaton Centre shopping mall. It is striking that this hospitalized child chose to capture the solitary tree on this otherwise mundane rooftop. The chance to see natural sunlight, the sky, the weather, and what was happening outside were important to him, as they were to other children. He chose this viewpoint because "it's just open and it's one of the few places where you can actually see, like, I don't know, out far and it's *something* to look at" (November 2, 2005, interview #245, 17 yr, boy). He described visiting this spot three or four times a day, and even turning the bench around in order to look at the tree on the building and listen to music through earphones.

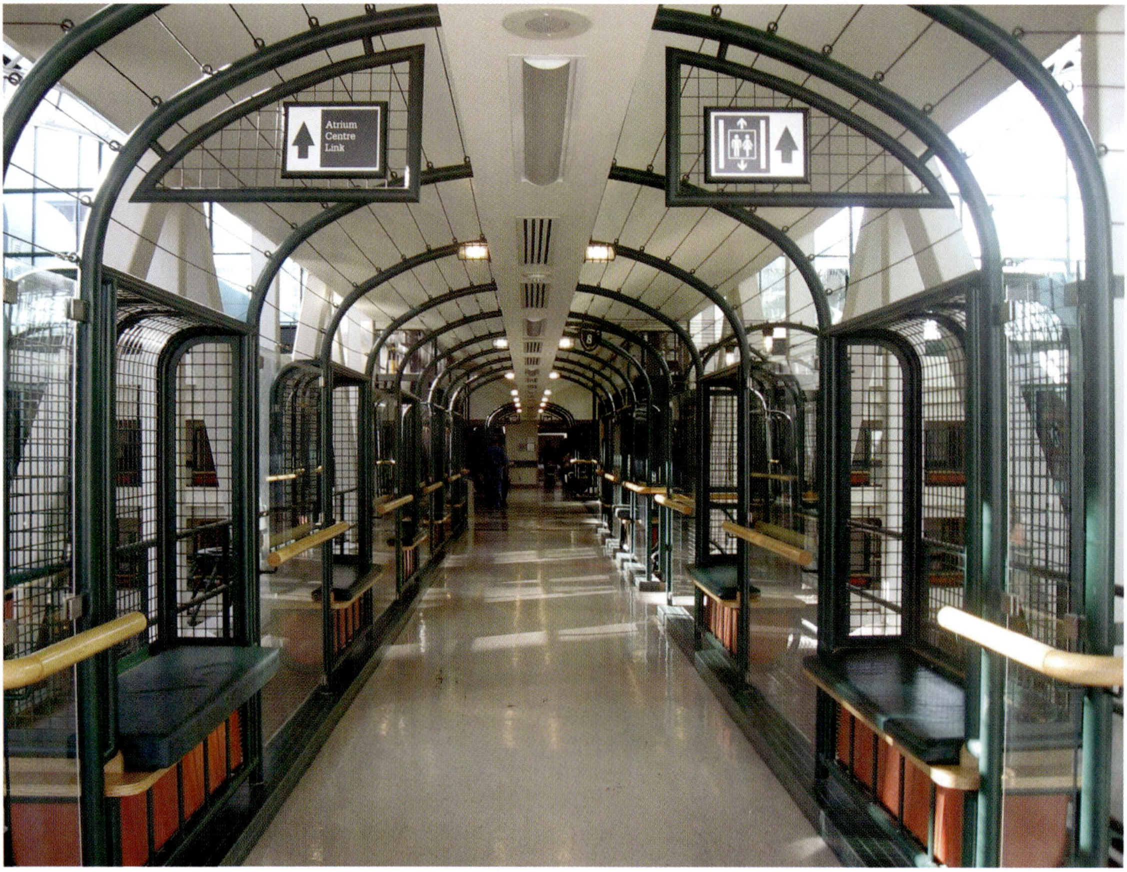

FIGURE 12.11 Tunnel-like image of SickKids by a sixteen-year-old girl, emphasizing the hospital as a site of confinement. (Photo: 226-009)

Places of Confinement

In sharp contrast to the trend of photographing outside views, many young photographers captured the hospital as a place of confinement, emphasizing its sense of enclosure. In one example (fig. 12.11) taken on the eighth floor, facing west, cantilevered benches and the bank of elevators are visible. At the end of the hall is a perpendicular circulation space, while the open atrium lies just beyond the edges of the image. The tunnel-like perspective of this photograph shows the hospital as a closed-in space, reinforced by the grates and repetitive arches. The photographer described the image as follows: "Yeah, I think it's interesting and it's neat to look at, but I find it a little bit intimidating because you're just like, what's going on?... I think for a little kid it would be kinda

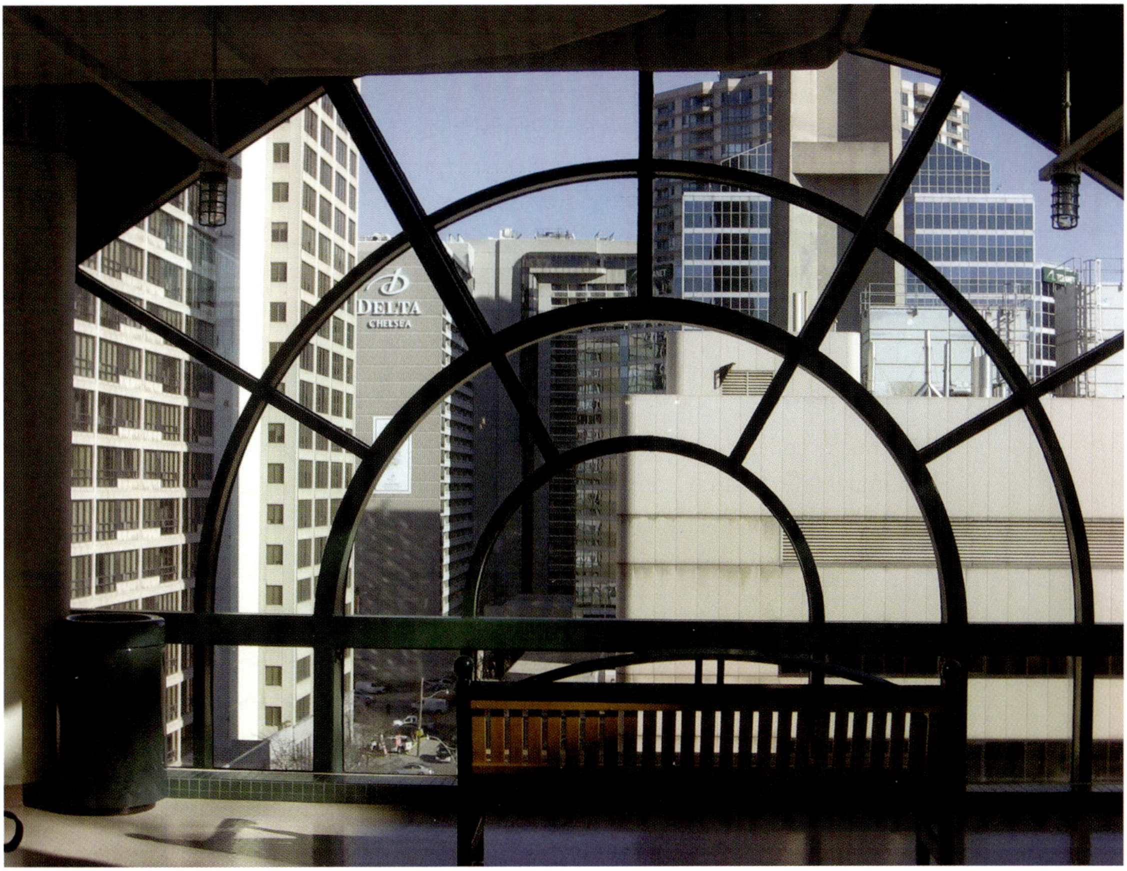

FIGURE 12.12 View outside the hospital by the same sixteen-year-old girl. (Photo: 226-008)

scary because of the wires … it just feels, not really unsafe, it just feels, I don't know how to describe it, it's just a little bit scary, it reminds me of a spider net or something. And like all of the cages, I know they're there for safety but it's just not very appealing, it looks a little scary" (January 26, 2006, #226, 16 yr, girl).

If the earlier photographs from the Children's Memorial Hospital, then, established the outdoors as part of the hospital's physical cure, these patients-photographers look to nature as a solace and psychological cure, helping them to relieve anxiety and stress. Just prior to taking the tunnel-like image, the sixteen-year-old girl photographed the view eastward looking outside the hospital (fig. 12.12). Then she turned around and took the view of the hall facing west. She described her choice to take the outside view: "I think it's just a really pretty view and like it's open, you get windows to look in, so you have lots of natural light coming in and that's really important just because I don't know, if you're stuck in a hospital all day you don't get to see outside so it's really good to have this spot where you can come and just look, there is an outdoors and that you can enjoy it" (January 26, 2006, #226, 16 yr, girl). This feeling of not wanting to be trapped was echoed by other patients. A twelve-year-old girl, referring to the atrium's "glass ceiling," liked the wide-open feeling: "You're not closed up ... so that kids don't get as scared of being trapped" (November 7, 2005, #126, 12 yr, girl). Many of the photographs reflect a disquieting ambivalence. The hospital remains a place of safe enclosure, confinement, and longing, despite the atrium's openness and the child-friendly décor.

Conclusion

The images collected by young photographers at SickKids stand apart from the historical images of children's hospitals mainly because of differing intentions. On the one hand, the historic photographs strive to present the hospital as therapeutically efficient or socially joyous, attitudes that made the images useful for fundraising and hospital promotion. On the other hand, the contemporary children's photographs denote feelings of safety, protection, longing, and confinement. Thus if the earlier photos provide a particular reading of the history of children's hospitals, the later ones taken by children suggest a way of reinterpreting that history, and of connecting the historical photos to contemporary concerns about the character of childhood and hospitalization. The suggestion that historic photographs show distraction as a way of coping with hospitalization, for instance, is both reinforced and contrasted in the contemporary photos: some of today's patients used the camera not to portray enjoyment but rather to make imaginary escapes through the architectural elements in the atrium. These photographs allow us to understand more comprehensively the situation of children in healthcare settings throughout the last century. In the future, family albums or perhaps even video footage may add to the information gleaned from promotional photos and child-centred images. We can supplement the passive bodies and smiling faces of the historic photographs—images of children blissfully unaware of their precarious conditions—with images of the hospital itself, created by self-reflective agents seeking to go beyond its visual and material limits. Coming to terms with images both of and by sick children means coming to terms with children as active agents of architectural knowledge.

Notes

The authors gratefully acknowledge the time, effort, and thoughtfulness of the children and adolescents who participated in "The Paediatric Hospital Atrium: Designers' Intentions versus Children's Experiences" project (short title: "Kids in the Atrium"), which was funded by the Canadian Institutes of Health Research (CIHR: FRN# 74457). Support for the proposal development was provided by an Interdisciplinary Capacity Enhancement Grant from the Health Care, Technology and Place, CIHR Strategic Training Program at the University of Toronto. The project benefited greatly from the generous input of SickKids Children Council. Thanks to research assistance from François-Xavier Caron, Julia Tischer, Cora McLaren, and especially Ellie Goldenberg, who also contributed to the writing of this paper. We thank, as well, the institutions and their staff members who provided access to their buildings and photographs: Hôpital Ste-Justine, Montreal Chest Institute, Montreal Children's Hospital (Jack Charters), Royal Victoria Hospital, and SickKids. We are grateful to Loren Lerner for insightful comments on an earlier version of this work.

1 For a history of the architecture of children's hospitals in Montreal and Toronto, see Annmarie Adams and David Theodore, "The Architecture of Children's Hospitals in Toronto and Montreal, 1875–2010," in *Children's Health Issues in Historical Perspective*, ed. Cheryl Krasnick Warsh and Veronica Strong-Boag, 439–478 (Waterloo, ON: Wilfrid Laurier University Press, 2005).

2 Jesse Boyd Scriver, *The Montreal Children's Hospital: Years of Growth* (Montreal: Montreal Children's Hospital and McGill-Queen's University Press, 1979); Max Braithwaite, *Sick Kids: The Story of the Hospital for Sick Children in Toronto* (Toronto: McClelland & Stewart, 1974).

3 A growing body of literature in architectural history explores places for children and childhood. See Abigail A. Van Slyck, *A Manufactured Wilderness: Summer Camps and the Shaping of American Youth, 1890–1960* (Minneapolis: University of Minnesota Press, 2006); Marta Gutman and Ning de Coninck-Smith, eds., *Designing Modern Childhoods: History, Space, and the Material Culture of Children* (New Brunswick, NJ: Rutgers University Press, 2008). The rise in popularity of children's architecture may be related to the popularity of children as a subject for museum exhibits: Abigail A. Van Slyck, "Kid Size: The Material World of Childhood," *Winterthur Portfolio* 39 (2004): 69–78.

4 A focused analysis of this photograph is undertaken in Annmarie Adams and Kevin Schwartzman, "Pneumothorax Then and Now," *Space and Culture* 8, no. 4 (November 2005): 435–448. For more on the relationship between tuberculosis therapies and place, see Annmarie Adams, Kevin Schwartzman, and David Theodore, "Collapse and Expand: Architecture and Tuberculosis Therapy in Montreal, 1909, 1933, 1954," *Technology and Culture* 49, no. 4 (2008): 908–942.

5 Joel D. Howell, "Machines and Medicine: Technology Transforms the American Hospital," in *The American General Hospital: Communities and Social Contexts*, ed. Diana Elizabeth Long and Janet Golden, 109–134 (Ithaca: Cornell University Press, 1989).

6 On the history of the CMH, see Scriver, *Years of Growth*, and Adams and Theodore, "The Architecture of Children's Hospitals," 447–451.

7 David Charles Sloane, "'Not Designed Merely to Heal': Progressive Reformers and Children's Hospitals," *Journal of the Gilded Age and Progressive Era* 4, no. 4 (October 2005): 331–354.

8 Personal correspondence from Loren Lerner to Annmarie Adams, February 14, 2007.

9 Gabrielle Roy, *The Tin Flute*, trans. Hannah Josephson (New York: Reynal & Hitchcock, 1947), 178–179. Denise Lemieux, in *Une culture de la nostalgie: L'enfant dans le roman québecois de ses origines à nos jours* (Montreal: Boréal Express, 1984), writes of a "myth" of childhood that develops in Quebec literature between the wars, often centred on nostalgia and a romanticized folkloric past (p. 12).

10 Roy, *The Tin Flute*, 184.

11 On photo-elicitation techniques, see Marisol Clark-Ibáñez, "Framing the Social World with Photo Elicitation Interviews," *American Behavioral Scientist* 47, no. 12 (2004): 1507–1527; Philip Darbyshire, Colin MacDougall, and Wendy Schiller, "Multiple Methods in Qualitative Research with Children: More Insight or Just More?" *Qualitative Research* 5, no. 4 (2005): 417–436; Douglas Harper, "Talking about Pictures: A Case for Photo Elicitation," *Visual Studies* 17, no. 1 (2002): 13–26; Robin Riley and Elizabeth Manias, "Snap-Shots of Live Theatre: The Use of Photography to Research Governance in Operating Room Nursing," *Nursing Inquiry* 10 (2003): 81–90.

12 For studies of the relationship of shopping mall design and architecture, see Howard Gillette Jr., "The Evolution of the Planned Shopping Center in Suburb and City," *Journal of American Planning Association* 51 (1985): 449–460; Michael Sorkin, ed., *Variations on a Theme Park: The New American City and the End of Public Space* (New York: Hill & Wang, 1992); Timothy Davis, "The Miracle Mile Revisited: Recycling, Renovation, and Simulation along the Commercial Strip," in *Exploring Everyday Landscapes: Perspectives in Vernacular Architecture 7*, ed. Annmarie Adams and Sally McMurry, 93–114 (Knoxville: University of Tennessee Press, 1997); Robert Venturi, Denise Scott Brown, and Steven Izenour, *Learning from Las Vegas* (Cambridge, MA: MIT Press, 1972).

13 Ian Brown, "8th Wonder of the World?" *Globe and Mail* (June 22, 1985): 10.

14 Robin A. Kearns and J. Ross Barnett, "'Happy Meals' in the Starship Enterprise: Interpreting a Moral Geography of Health Care Consumption," *Health & Place* 6 (2000): 81–93. For more on the stress of contemporary hospitals, see James W. Varni and Ernest R. Katz, "Stress, Social Support, and Negative Affectivity in Children with Newly Diagnosed Cancer: A Prospective Transactional Analysis," *Psychological Oncology* 6 (1997): 267–278.

15 Jeffrey S.P. Hopkins, "West Edmonton Mall: Landscape of Myths and Elsewhereness," *Canadian Geographer* 34, no. 1 (1990): 2–17.

16 Matthew D. Pavelich, "Why the New Hospital for Sick Children Was Built: An Interview with Anne Marie Christian," *Leadership in Health Services* 2, no. 5 (1993): 15.

17 Evelina Hospital, "Evelina Children's Hospital in 2005," http://www.thegarret.org.uk/evelinaNow.htm (accessed February 5, 2007).

ANDREA N. WALSH

HEALTHY BODIES, STRONG CITIZENS
Okanagan Children's Drawings and the Canadian Junior Red Cross

Research about First Nations children's agency and identity has rarely addressed their production of contemporary culture, rather than merely their reception of it. Even more rare are examples of critical analyses of Aboriginal children's and youth visual culture. I seek to make such inquiry by critically thinking about production, circulation, and consumption of drawings created by Okanagan students at the Inkameep Day School near Oliver, British Columbia, published in the *Canadian Red Cross Junior* magazine in 1938 and 1939. The drawings, produced by youth approximately aged ten to seventeen, interpret the "Twelve Health Rules" taught to youth members of the Canadian Red Cross as part of its public health mandate. I believe these images provide visual evidence of how Osoyoos Indian Band youth actively used their understanding and experience of Okanagan culture to negotiate dominant paradigms of health and models for citizenship promoted by both the provincial government and the Canadian Red Cross. The *Canadian Red Cross Junior* magazine was created as part of the Canadian Red Cross peace program as a means to facilitate the organization's mandate to promote health, citizenship, and service in an engaging manner to its youth membership. I suggest that rather than deliver and enforce the Red Cross's message about the relationship between personal and public health and the welfare of the nation, the Inkameep students' drawings interrupt the Red Cross's dominant narrative of health and citizenship by providing embodied evidence of the impossibility of a healthy "universal" childhood.

I begin the following with a discussion about the creation of the Junior Red Cross in Canada and the correlation between its mandate and the content of the organization's journal, the *Canadian Red Cross Junior* (CRCJ). I take examples from Red Cross records and the CRCJ to demonstrate how standards of good health for Canadian children were based on dominant paradigms around hygiene and sanitation that were in turn buttressed by scientific claims of the day. Good health practices were created by white, middle-class, male professionals. Mona Gleason argues these practices were "organized along defensive lines, dependent on surveillance of the public ... and thoroughly developed along racial lines."[1] Good health was linked directly to social acceptance.[2] The CRCJ sutured the responsibility of good personal health to patriotic duty for its youth membership.

I then provide an overview of the local context in which the Inkameep health rule drawings were produced. By examining school life on the Osoyoos reserve against larger political processes of educational reform and emerging narratives of citizenship and national identity, one bears witness to the agency of the Osoyoos youth at a time when many of their peers' voices were silenced by the disciplinary regimes of residential schools. Admittedly, one cannot deny the multiplicity of ways in which the disciplinary gaze of governmental authorities played a role in daily life at the Inkameep school. Yet, critically examining the Inkameep health drawings for the purpose of seeking out childhood voices and perspectives exposes how Osoyoos Indian Band youth resisted in some ways total assimilation into dominant society. The drawings allow for a glimpse into the realities of these Aboriginal youth who were living their lives in the midst of opposing beliefs held by dominant society about Aboriginal childhood, during the interwar era and years of World War II in Canada.

The Canadian Red Cross and the Junior Red Cross

In 1919 Canadian Parliament set forth new and additional purposes for the Canadian Red Cross Society's peacetime mandate: the organization would act as an auxiliary to the government in its public health reform efforts. The society's nationwide membership was a valuable asset. Chief executive of the Canadian Red Cross Dr. James W. Robertson said the society could "do much to assist the official health authorities to influence multitudes of individuals to understand and advocate the continuous improvement of personal hygiene, wholesome sanitary environment, adequate Public Health Medical and Nursing Service, and all these measures and services which under modern conditions are so necessary and desirable."[3] As a voluntary auxiliary, the Red Cross was given three principal duties: (a) to stimulate and maintain interest in public health work, (b) to support and if needed supplement the work of government agencies, and (c) to disseminate useful knowledge concerning health through demonstration, education, and other methods.[4]

Public health became a principal issue to the agendas of both provincial and federal governments in Canada at the end of the Great War. From this time onward, health reform on a sweeping scale was envisioned through strategic campaigns aimed at educating the masses about the correlation between personal hygiene and public health and welfare. The Red Cross played a major role in this "health crusade." Though educational campaigns were delivered broadly to diverse communities, they often targeted children in particular.

James W. Robertson stated in his 1921 annual campaign address to Red Cross members, "Every child born in Canada should have an opportunity of starting a life in sound physical health, of growing to maturity in and through the healthful exercise of its powers and then of continuing to live in good health under wholesome conditions until the full course of life is run."[5] Robertson attributed the primary challenges to such a universal outcome for the children's health and welfare to ignorance and cultural difference:

> Most children are born with the possession of good health; the problem is to conserve that precious heritage. In backward civilizations a slow and continued waste of that priceless gift of nature begins from the time the baby is weaned; and scarcely any attempt is made to arrest the wastage ... recent investigations fill us with surprise and anxiety.... An essential part of any national health policy is the instruction in the principles and practice of hygiene of the great mass of the people. In this as in other spheres of human affairs ignorance is the chief curse. We are only now, as knowledge grows, becoming aware of the immeasurable part played by ignorance in the realm of disease.[6]

As part of its peacetime focus on children and youth, the Central Council of the Red Cross Society adopted resolutions in 1919 to create a Junior Red Cross Membership category. The Junior Red Cross would suitably instruct children and youth by promoting interesting activities that endorsed "good health." The resolution stated that the Canadian Red Cross would support the work of Junior members in the following ways:

1. By calling the attention of each Provincial Branch to the importance and necessity of this movement;
2. By the organization of National Junior Membership Campaigns to be conducted annually at the same time as the campaign for Senior members;
3. By the issuing of special Junior Red Cross Membership badges and certificates to which each child shall be entitled on the payment of a membership fee of twenty-five cents;
4. By the publication of a matter of such a character as to attract and interest children and young people, and to be of service to teachers and organizers of Junior work and that special study as to the interests and needs of children should be made in connection with this publication.[7]

A threefold ideal of health, citizenship, and service became the mandate for the Junior Red Cross in Canada. This mandate was carried out through the creation of "Twelve Rules of Health." The rules were used as platform for promoting health education; producing a plan for caring for others, such as crippled children and shut-ins;

and building understanding of local history and international relations through the interchange of portfolios (these contained artwork, writing, and photographs about the Junior group and its locality) with Juniors in other countries. By 1922 all nine provinces in Canada had Junior programs in operation, and a monthly national journal for youth was launched. The journal was initially titled the *Red Cross Junior* and later the *Canadian Red Cross Junior.*[8] The journal published information on the Health Rules and also the portfolio exchanges. Pages were filled with arts and crafts ideas, games and activities, as well as Red Cross reports, stories, news and letters of other Juniors from abroad, and tales from faraway lands, or educational stories about Canada.

The Health Focus of the Canadian Red Cross

A primary focus of the CRCJ was to deliver information to the youth membership of the Red Cross that educated them about the correlation between good personal health and public welfare. A principal teaching tool for this purpose were the "Twelve Rules of Health." These health rules were listed and illustrated on charts and small cards that were distributed for use and display in classrooms where Junior groups met after school (fig. 13.1).

Periodically between the late 1920s and early 1940s, the journal published essays that discussed particular health rules. Each essay explains how the rule supports the virtue of good health. Early in the timeline of these essays, good health is equated foremost with upstanding morality and intelligence. These qualities are linked to being a good Christian and citizen of Canada.[9] One such essay declares, "Our natural tendency is to abuse our bodies,"[10] implying that intelligent people will follow the health rules. It continues, "By doing these things they will be strong and healthy men and women, able to enjoy life at its best, and able to be useful citizens and able to continue to live up to the ideals of Junior Red Cross until it shall please God to call them."[11] Such a statement echoes the words of James Robertson in his 1921 annual address quoted above about universal healthcare for Canadian children.

The act of breaking or disobeying the health rules is described in criminal terms that range from misdemeanours to major crimes. For example, if one ignored rule #9 (washing hands), that individual would be seen as "offensive in appearance and a serious breach of good manners."[12] A more serious offence is a contravention of rule #12 (not spitting). In the case of breaking rule #12, the essay proclaims "spitting until recently was almost universal" and that it wasn't until scientists "began to understand that diseases were being spread by the spitters … spitters with tuberculosis, spitters with influenza, spitters with 'colds' and so on." It is noted that science has proven the dangers of "something

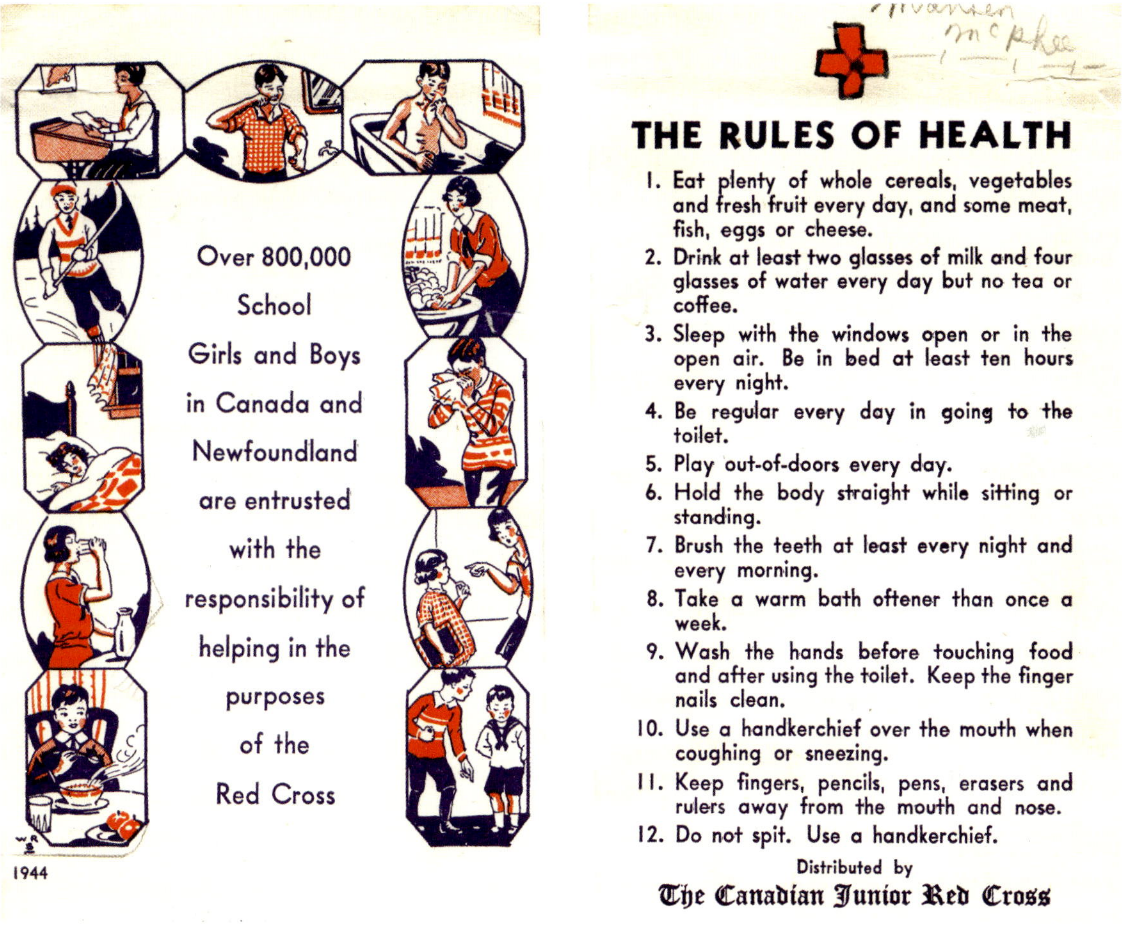

THE RULES OF HEALTH

1. Eat plenty of whole cereals, vegetables and fresh fruit every day, and some meat, fish, eggs or cheese.
2. Drink at least two glasses of milk and four glasses of water every day but no tea or coffee.
3. Sleep with the windows open or in the open air. Be in bed at least ten hours every night.
4. Be regular every day in going to the toilet.
5. Play out-of-doors every day.
6. Hold the body straight while sitting or standing.
7. Brush the teeth at least every night and every morning.
8. Take a warm bath oftener than once a week.
9. Wash the hands before touching food and after using the toilet. Keep the finger nails clean.
10. Use a handkerchief over the mouth when coughing or sneezing.
11. Keep fingers, pencils, pens, erasers and rulers away from the mouth and nose.
12. Do not spit. Use a handkerchief.

Distributed by
The Canadian Junior Red Cross

FIGURE 13.1 Front and reverse sides of a card illustrating and listing the twelve health rules distributed by the Canadian Red Cross, 1944.

disgusting" and deservedly illegal, so Juniors should not participate in this activity, unless they "wish to be looked upon as disgusting barbarians."[13] Language linking progress with cultural evolution is used to enforce rule #6 about posture. An essay states that humans' superiority is claimed by their ability to stand erect, and those children who slouch express inferiority.

Links between dominant practices and beliefs about health and social acceptance reveal the social construction of ideal bodily behaviour. As standards to be achieved, the health rules also served to legitimize existing power relations and reinforced social boundaries.[14] By directly linking ideal practices of health to social acceptance, the Red

Cross situated those who didn't practise or subscribe to the dominant paradigm as deviants and regarded them as spreading contagion. Speaking of school medical inspections in British Columbia in the early twentieth century, Mona Gleason notes that "race was an integral part of the discourse on public health from its earliest days," and protecting "public health revolved around a paradox: it meant excluding and demonizing a particular portion of that public."[15] The rule against spitting targeted Asian communities in which the practice of spitting or expelling fluid through the nose was in fact considered a way of ridding one's body of unhealthy fluids and was considered a practice of personal hygiene. The health rule lessons in the journal reinforced the British Columbia provincial government agenda's of creating and maintaining a dominant health paradigm.

Creating Links Between Good Health and Strong Citizenship

In March 1930 the editors write, "Health is not something we enjoy 'naturally' and now we know that we have to seek after and work for health just as we have to seek after and work for knowledge, wealth or power."[16] Health is something to be "secured and preserved," and diseases are described as "sins against bodily welfare." These sins are repeatedly described as being created through "wrong and foolish" acts and general "foolishness."[17] In the late 1930s, the concept of building the "House of Health" emerged. This teaching tool about citizenship was directly related to the health rules about good eating and nutrition.[18]

In March 1940 a grade seven student from Toronto submitted an essay titled "How Children Can Save the Empire." In it the student writes:

> Building a strong body is one of the most essential things in life. This also is very necessary in serving your Empire. The twelve Health Rules, if followed regularly, are the source of good health. There are many different ways in which you can assist by having a strong body. The most important is that your children and grand children will inherit sturdy bodies, in this way helping to build stronger and healthier future generations.

By 1941 the health rules would move away from a base of morality and religion to being entrenched as a personal obligation of children in the war effort as citizens of Canada. The editors write, "Young people who cannot take up arms for their country's defense can do one great service—they can build up their own health and help to protect other people's. If all the pupils and students in Canada undertook this task they would be exemplifying practical patriotism of the very best quality."[19] In sum, it was children's duty as citizens of Canada to create and maintain healthy bodies.

In February 1921 *The Globe* reported that the Red Cross Society's peacetime mandate was to include special attention to pubic health issues and education. It noted that "one revelation of the war was the shockingly poor condition of the men of the British Empire"[20] and that in Canada, medical examinations found that about half of the draftees for military service were "physically unfit for full service in the field. The disabilities were not the result of active disease, but evidently in most cases the consequence of poor nutrition, neglect of personal hygiene and unsanitary conditions of working and living."[21]

In the late 1930s two series of essays appeared in the CRCJ titled "On the Hilltops of Citizenship" and "Am I a Good Canadian." "On the Hilltops" chronicles the lives of several children as they act inappropriately (being dirty, being impolite, acting unfriendly to new Canadians, stealing, and being unreliable) and then learn to act as good citizens. In fact, the editors turn these morals into play as they encourage children to "play the citizenship game" with one another. Notably, many of the stories are about children who must learn to act responsibly in the absence of fathers who are at war or dead from the war. Children are told that there are certain kinds of citizens that they should strive never to be: the *poor citizen* (exemplified as the criminal who is interested only in money and resents paying taxes), the *indifferent citizen* (exemplified as women who don't vote or belong to community or religious organizations), the *prejudiced citizen* (exemplified as people intolerant of new Canadians), the *dangerous citizen* (exemplified as the political agitator who endeavours to break down existing society without offering any thing better in its stead, the more clever, and the more dangerous), and the *sick citizen* (exemplified as the pitiful drifter who is a burden and expense to society and who was as a child dull and lazy).

During the years of World War II, images circulated in the CRCJ that emphasized the relationship between personal health and the nation at war. Images of military personnel were featured on the front covers of the journal, and advertisements for baby formula used the war as a backdrop for their products. In one instance, a knight with a javelin seated on a rearing horse is shadowed behind a baby boy, with the phrase "He shall not go naked into battle" placed under the images of the child and soldier.

Red Cross Juniors were encouraged, if not mandated, to personally invest in the health of their nation by caring for their own bodies and monitoring their social behaviour. Such measures emphasized the role of youth in building a healthy, strong country. Though still subjects of the British Empire, children were metaphorically linked by their early stage of development and potential to that of their young nation of Canada.[22] Drawing on the work of Yuval Davis, Jane Helleiner has remarked in her work on the representation of children in Canadian postwar political discourse that settler nations, like Canada, that do not have a common past create a bond between citizens by emphasizing narratives of futurity.[23] For children in Canada, health was both a duty and a privilege associated with citizenship. Aboriginal children, like those students who attended the Inkameep Day School, lived their lives largely outside of this health–citizenship equation. These children, as well as their parents, were not considered citizens of Canada, unlike their non-Aboriginal peers. Rather, they lived their lives under the legislation of the federal government's Indian Act. Segregated onto reserves, or separated from their communities while attending residential schools, Aboriginal children's lives exposed fissures of inequality and diversity in the narratives of universal health, childhood, and citizenship in Canada.

The Representation of Aboriginal People/Bodies in the Canadian Red Cross Junior

Almost all representation of Aboriginal peoples in the CRCJ is presented as historical. Most references to Aboriginal culture occur within pseudo-ethnographic essays under the heading "Canadian Arts and Crafts." These essays feature material culture of Aboriginal peoples from across Canada. CRCJ content about Aboriginal peoples also includes step-by-step instructions about how to do an "Indian Dance" that matches the measures of a musical score to dancers' actions. At the end of the dance students are instructed to give a "war cry." Another example is an essay about the famous "Grey Owl." By framing Aboriginal people and their cultures as historical and omitting information that positioned Aboriginal peoples in Canada as contemporaries of the Red Cross Junior membership, the CRCJ effectively excluded Aboriginal children from the narratives of "futurity" in Canada that the magazine aimed to promote.

Twice, however, in the period under consideration, Aboriginal people are worked into the CRCJ foci on health and citizenship. The first example is found within a discussion of health rule #6, where a sculpture of an Aboriginal man riding a horse is used as an example of exemplary posture. The second example is the first essay for the series "Am I a Good Canadian." The essay begins with a discussion of what it means to be a good Canadian. The essay is written by a CRCJ editor who is responding to a Junior's request to know more about "the early days of Canada and how it developed into such a wonderful civilization as it is today."[24] The editor begins her answer by writing, "We're going to start with Canada itself and think of our country as it was several hundred years ago, and of her first citizens, the Indians." She proceeds to describe Native peoples and their cultures as exemplary "citizens" of Canada. She begins her essay in the Atlantic region, and notes first and foremost that all Indian children played in their youth and then learned survival skills "without complaining." The Algonkian tribes are praised for their industriousness, having "lived almost entirely by hunting and fishing." Generalizing about Aboriginal subsistence, she carries on that "everything the Indian needed for living he had to obtain from the woods and waters around him." The Iroquois are noted for their ability to co-exist, as multiple families lived in longhouses. Iroquoian people were also noted as having had excellent government structure and systems. Continuing across Canada, she notes that the Plains Indians, like the Algonkians, were nomads "or wanderers ... but they had a good deal of system about their moving." She writes, "They could make or break camp with great speed because in camping or traveling, we are told, they had a place for everything and everything was always in its place." She asks, "I wonder if anyone could write that of us?" Plains camps are described as "one continual picnic" with outdoor family meals, stories, and children running and playing. The Plains people also celebrated with the Sun-Dance, "a festival held to offer thanks to the Great Spirit, which was their name for God." Making it to the west coast, she notes the exemplary carpentry and architectural skills of the west coast people, and claims their deep sense of respect for the dead and understanding of history play a large part in the display of totem poles. The editor concludes by quoting what she says is a Thompson tribe lesson for children: "It is bad to steal, to lie, to be lazy, to boast, to be cowardly, to be inhospitable or stingy, to be quarrelsome. It is good to be pure and cleanly, to be honest, truthful and faithful; to be brave, industrious and grateful; to be hospitable, liberal and friendly; to be modest and sociable." She concludes that left out of that list was the quality of loyalty and states that Indians "loved their country and were loyal to it."

The Junior Red Cross in Schools

The CRCJ was circulated to Junior members through their schools where Junior Red Cross chapters met as an extracurricular activity. Through the 1920s and 1930s, public education in Canada broadened to include a focus upon health. During this era, "child-savers and public health reformers sided with new educators to use the school to improve the health of children and the nation."[25] During the 1930s, in particular, child-centred, activity-based learning was paramount to progressive philosophies of education and curriculum instruction. There was also a call to make schooling "more practical and more relevant" by "teaching skills needed in the workplace."[26] This progressive movement combined health and social activities as a way of educating the "whole child," while simultaneously promoting democratic citizenship.[27] Educators' focus on democracy through health and social activity complemented the mandate of the Red Cross, which moved away from a focus on political rights toward public health education. Social *reform*, however, was not a part of the peacetime agenda for public education or the Red Cross.

Junior Red Cross meetings were typically held after school hours. These meetings were conducted almost entirely by the youth, with their teacher acting solely as an advisor/facilitator to the group. Committees were struck by election for the purpose of presenting information and monitoring Junior activities in the areas of personal hygiene, safety, and health rules. Through the use of parliamentary rules and democratic voting / majority decision making, the Junior Red Cross was "organized and administered by the children" and was a "first hand lesson in civics."[28]

Though always on the periphery of the main curriculum, there were direct advantages and benefits to having the Junior Red Cross as part of a classroom. First, the Red Cross curriculum complemented and supported what Sheehan has identified as the "two strands of new education," which were: (1) humane, child-centred, and development oriented, and (2) more practical, more relevant, and skill oriented.[29] Second, Junior Red Cross chapters received free educational materials for use in their classrooms free, and the administering of the program required no additional skills on the part of the teacher or additional space within the school. As Sheehan notes, "charts, materials, curricular ideas and magazines ... were a boon to most classes, but especially to rural schools and schools in poorer areas."[30]

The Red Cross curriculum was based upon project-oriented learning and child-centered activities. The local community in which the Juniors lived was the base for most of their projects. Education about health was geared directly to the local population; children monitored one another's well-being and hygiene practices as part of their personal and local duty to the protection of public health and the nation. Education related to citizenship involved both local activities, such as fundraising for the Red Cross, and international exchanges of portfolios with Red Cross Juniors from other countries. These portfolios contained Junior members' writing and art that expressed their knowledge of their local community's history and present-day character. Juniors interacted with other Canadian Juniors through poster and story contests and essay competitions. Top submissions were published in the CRCJ.

The Junior Red Cross at the Inkameep Day School

Junior Red Cross projects and activities were a prominent part of the curriculum at the Inkameep Day School. Evidence of the ways by which the watchwords of health, citizenship, and service were a part of the students' education is spread widely across a diverse array of sources that range from personal memories of Okanagan elders who attended Inkameep[31] to archival government documents, photographs, newspaper articles, and children's drawings. Direct evidence of the Red Cross health curriculum at the Inkameep school is seen in two rare photographs. The first is published as part of a 1935 *Public Health Nurse Bulletin*.[32] The photograph shows twelve Inkameep students outside their school, all brushing their teeth. The caption for the photograph reads: "tooth-brushing drill, Inkameep Indian Day School." The second photograph is taken in about 1940 and records the interior of the schoolhouse. A line of individually hung towels and drinking cups is seen next to the door of the classroom. Viewing this photograph prompted Okanagan elders to recall their regular school routine of washing their hands and faces, brushing their hair, and using their own drinking cups.

A news article appearing in the *Mail and Empire* quotes a letter written to the Canadian Red Cross by Inkameep student and Red Cross Junior Ernest Baptiste. In his letter, Baptiste comments on how he and other Junior members at Inkameep have started to drink milk and cod liver oil during the winter months, and as a result they have all gained the proper weight.[33] This comment by Baptiste about proper weight indicates that a health rules chart was likely a feature in the classroom; the chart cited information about "proper" healthy weights and heights for children based on age groups.

In the same letter, Baptiste cites how he and other Juniors practise their good behaviour during sporting games. He writes, "I always try to win but I do not get mad if I lose, because if I did I would spoil the game for the other players."[34] Such a comment brings forth lessons of social graces as part of group activities. Elders recalled how citizenship lessons were incorporated into life at Inkameep when they viewed a picture of themselves with their peers and their teacher standing outside the school. They noted the Union Jack flag on its pole next to the building and commented on how it was raised at the beginning of each school day and lowered at its end. Such patriotic activities were a part of general education during the interwar years in Canada. A shift in emphasis from imperialism to nationalism as it related to citizenship in Canada was mirrored in Junior Red Cross activities. Sheehan notes that "the influx of immigrants, the Canadian successes in WWI and the interest in a more practical role for the school helped to develop a more pro-Canadian spirit."[35]

At Inkameep the foci on citizenship and service are evident through students' participation in international portfolio exchanges with other Juniors and in their fundraising efforts for the benefit of local Red Cross branches.[36] The CRCJ identifies Inkameep students as "Canadian" Red Cross Juniors. However, the art and writing produced for their portfolios and the plays they performed for Red Cross fundraisers were based upon the Inkameep students' lives, identities, and cultural knowledge as Okanagan First Nations peoples. It is here, between the *content* of Inkameep students' projects and activities and the *context* of the operations/mandate of the Junior Red Cross, that a significant fissure is exposed within dominant paradigms of health and citizenship. Here, too, narratives of universal Canadian childhoods are interrupted in the midst of opposing conceptualizations and realities of Aboriginal childhoods held by government and school authorities.

In order to explore how such negotiations and interruptions might occur through Inkameep art, it is important to understand something of the context in which the art was made at the Inkameep school, and the teacher who led the classroom of Okanagan students. The Inkameep school was not a residential school but a day school on the Osoyoos Indian reserve that taught a secularized curriculum; it was not operated under the authority of the Oblates. The school was built as a result of the initiative of the chief of the reserve, Batiste George. Earliest records show that in 1913 he wrote to the Department of Indian Affairs requesting a school be placed on the Osoyoos reserve. In 1915 the Osoyoos Indian Band hired the first teacher for the Inkameep Day School on its own accord. Over the years the school was operated out of temporary facilities on the reserve and was opened and closed at different points during the year, depending on the availability of a teacher willing to teach in an isolated location.

In 1931 an Irish immigrant teacher by the name of Anthony Walsh came to teach at the Inkameep School, which by then operated out of a permanent, one-room schoolhouse. For ten years Walsh taught at the school, living in conditions of near poverty in the small one-room teacherage attached to the schoolhouse. During Walsh's residency at the school, he created both a practice and a philosophy of teaching and learning through artistic endeavour that worked together with the progressive child-centred education movement. In an essay titled "An Art Experiment among Indian Children," Walsh described how art became a core element of the curriculum at Inkameep. He wrote, "This does not mean that other subjects were neglected, rather they were enhanced, for you cannot have vigorous discussions about art without making use of the English language. Compositions which had always been unpopular become acceptable when brightened by the addition of pen and ink sketches. *Tables and health rules were more easily remembered by painting birds and animals clad in gay and fantastic human attire*" (emphasis added).[37] Interviews conducted during his tenure at Inkameep and Walsh's memoir writing demonstrate his belief that racial tolerance and democracy could be achieved through the production and exchange of artistic efforts. The art and drama that Walsh encouraged his students to produce honoured and used traditional Okanagan culture. However, he recognized that the children's knowledge and identity were also being shaped by their increasingly Westernized lifestyles. His support of the youths' complexly layered identities is evident in his encouragement of the youth to sign their art with either or both their Indian and Western names. The principal areas in which the students worked were two-dimensional drawing and painting, some ceramic art, singing, dancing, and theatre.

The art program at the school began around 1934. This was after Walsh spent his initial years gaining the trust of the students' parents regarding his commitment to their children's education. Early on in his tenure, Walsh recognized that the Okanagan peoples had a rich visual history. The Inkameep reserve was surrounded by hills on which the evidence of early rock paintings was found. "There were days," wrote Walsh, "after the closing of the school when pupils and myself would ride off and sketches would be made of these designs, and then transferred to the top of the blackboards of the school. Then further sketches were made of the designs on bags and moccasins."[38] Walsh and the students eventually turned a small garage building near the school into an outdoor studio. It was there after school and at breaks during the day that the students would work on various individual and group art and drama projects.

Inkameep art was sent to national exhibitions and competitions in Edmonton, Winnipeg, Ottawa, Montreal, and Toronto.[39] In British Columbia their drawings were seen throughout the Okanagan region in Summerland, Penticton, Oliver, and Kelowna, and on the coast in Vancouver and Victoria. Through Walsh's efforts, the Inkameep students' artwork was also exhibited in Dublin and Glasgow. Inkameep art toured with Red Cross art exhibitions to Paris, Vienna, and Prague during the late 1930s.[40]

It was soon after Walsh arrived at Inkameep that he signed the children up to be members of the Canadian Junior Red Cross.[41] As part of their membership they received the CRCJ. The national ranks of the Canadian Red Cross Juniors did include a small number of Aboriginal chapters. The CRCJ specifically mentions four such groups during the interwar years. Yet, the Inkameep youth appear to be one of the most active Aboriginal Junior groups if one accounts for this by the number of times their activities are mentioned in the CRCJ magazine. The Inkameep Juniors and/or their art appear in no less than fourteen articles between 1934 and 1942.

Okanagan Drawings of the Twelve Health Rules

In May 1938 and January 1939, the CRCJ published drawings created by Inkameep students that depicted their Okanagan versions of the twelve health rules.[42] The images were originally assembled in a frieze; their positioning in the journal is out of numeric order as they were rearranged to fit onto the printed page. Of the twelve rules, eleven appear in the journal in the two issues. In the 1938 issue rules 1, 2, 3, 5, and 7 are illustrated. In 1939 rules 8 through 12 are published. The text surrounding the drawings does not comment on the images, but acknowledges the names of the artists (Mary Baptiste, Francis Baptiste, Johnnie Stalkia, and Netty Kruger).[43]

The health rule drawings depict mostly native animals of the Okanagan (rabbit, bear, deer, badger, coyote, and skunk); however, one drawing includes pigs. Inkameep students would have encountered all of these animals regularly through their time on the land, or working on the ranches that many Osoyoos Indian Band families operated. The animals are shown both in built houses and in the landscape of the rolling hills of the Okanagan Valley. They are dressed in attire that was likely *de rigueur* on the reserve: caps, pants, shirts, and sweaters for the men, and dresses and aprons for the women. Some drawings, however, depict the animals in fashions such as waistcoats with ties and fancy shoes. The drawings do not make clear which animals might be "adults" or "children."

Unlike the images presented earlier that depict a universal human family entering the Kingdom of Health (fig. 13.2), or the health rules card (fig. 13.1) that depicts universal children practising the health rules, the Inkameep interpretations of the health rules reflect and incorporate each artist's personal knowledge and experience as an Okanagan person (figs. 13.3 and 13.4). This personal interpretation is particularly evident in the depiction of rule #8, which is about hygiene and bathing. Here, one does not see a child seated in a bathtub, as in the Red Cross card illustration of rule #8; rather, a lodge and lake are depicted with animals swimming in the refreshing water after their cleansing sweat. The Red Cross illustrations of the health rules were created *for* children; the Inkameep illustrations were created *by* children.

Placing the Inkameep health drawings within the wider context of the art program at Inkameep allows a more in-depth reading of these images. As mentioned before, Inkameep students were encouraged by their teacher to learn and speak their language and to know their history. With Mr. Walsh's support and with assistance from the children's elders and parents, Inkameep students created dramas that were modern versions of Okanagan stories of relationships between human and animals. Inkameep students often illustrated scenes from these dramas as part of their art program (fig. 13.5). Surviving photographs depict the children in costume rehearsing their plays (fig. 13.6). These photographs document the same event as the children's drawings of the dramas. Importantly, the information available in the drawings is based upon the experience of the child, *both as actor and as artist.* Student drawings of drama scenes (such as in fig. 13.5) document their embodied experience of the dramas as events—as individual *persons* and as individual *animals.*

This last point acknowledges the role that traditional knowledge about transformation between human and animal worlds plays throughout many Aboriginal cultures, the Okanagan people included. The belief held by Okanagan people that humans and animals could change shape to be a part of one another's worlds is paramount to our contemporary witnessing of Inkameep students' agency expressed through art and drama. By considering cultural beliefs around transformation that the children likely held, one can look deeper than the surface of the drawings to reveal invisible aspects of the health drawings. I argue that the drawings by Inkameep students discussed here are equally about students' agency and traditional knowledge as they are about visually recording particular events. What we see in figure 13.5 as animal characters from the play may be in fact drawings of particular children *in animal form.*[44] If one accepts this reading of the drawings associated with the animal dramas, it can be hypothesized that the animals depicted in the health rules drawings are not just fanciful images from a child artist's

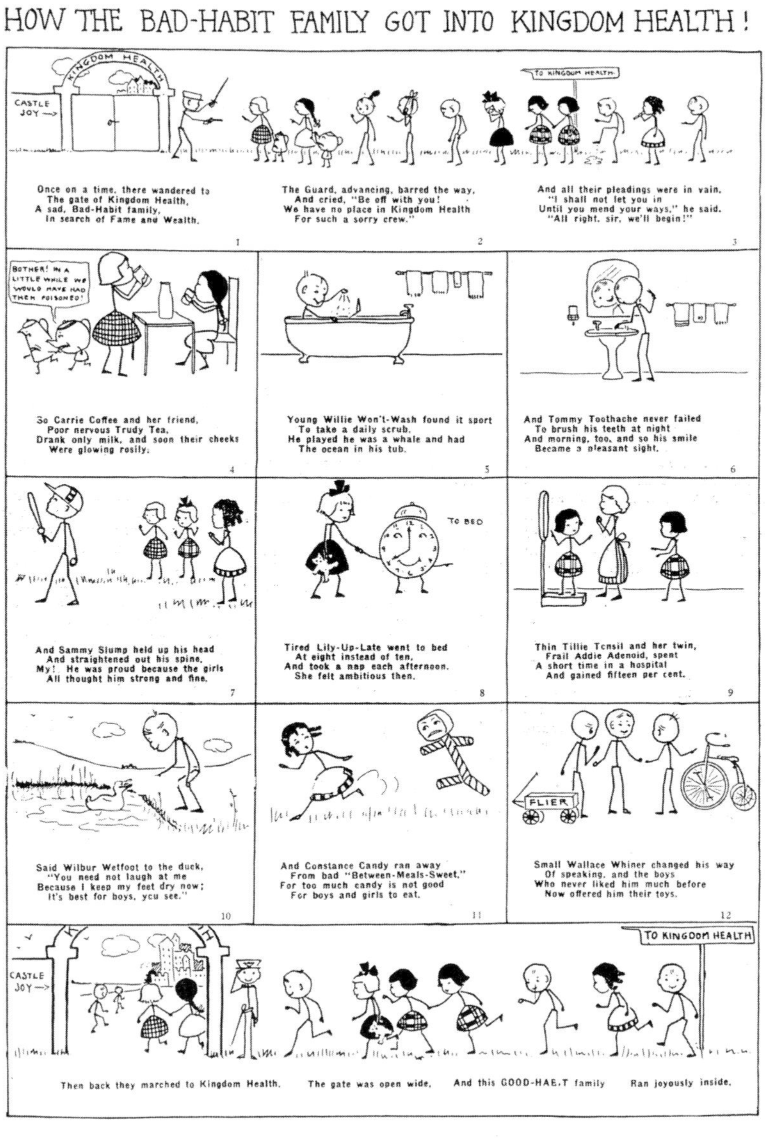

FIGURE 13.2
Stick figures illustrate the story of how one family entered the Kingdom of Health, allowing a universal reading of the bodies of the individuals.

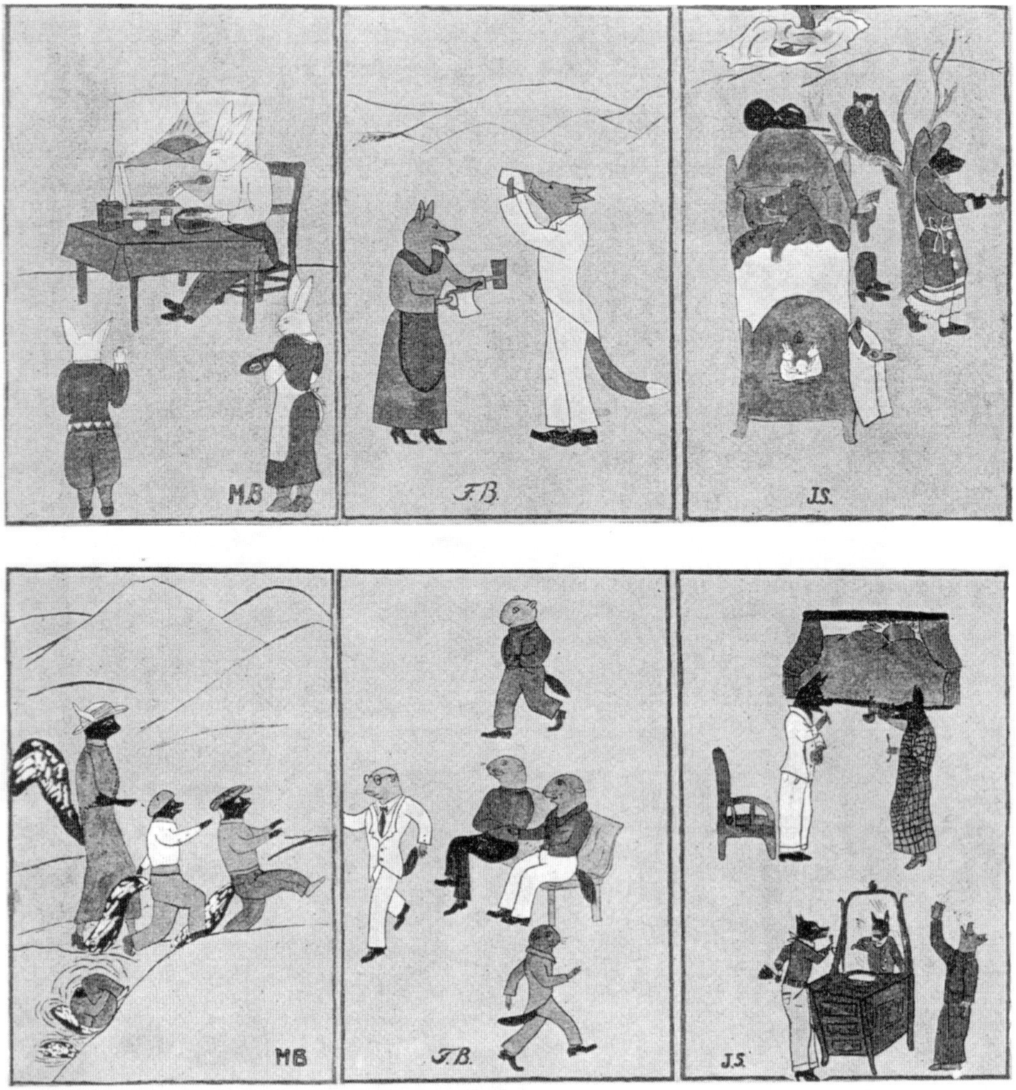

FIGURE 13.3
Inkameep health rule drawings that appeared in a 1938 issue of the *Canadian Red Cross Junior*.

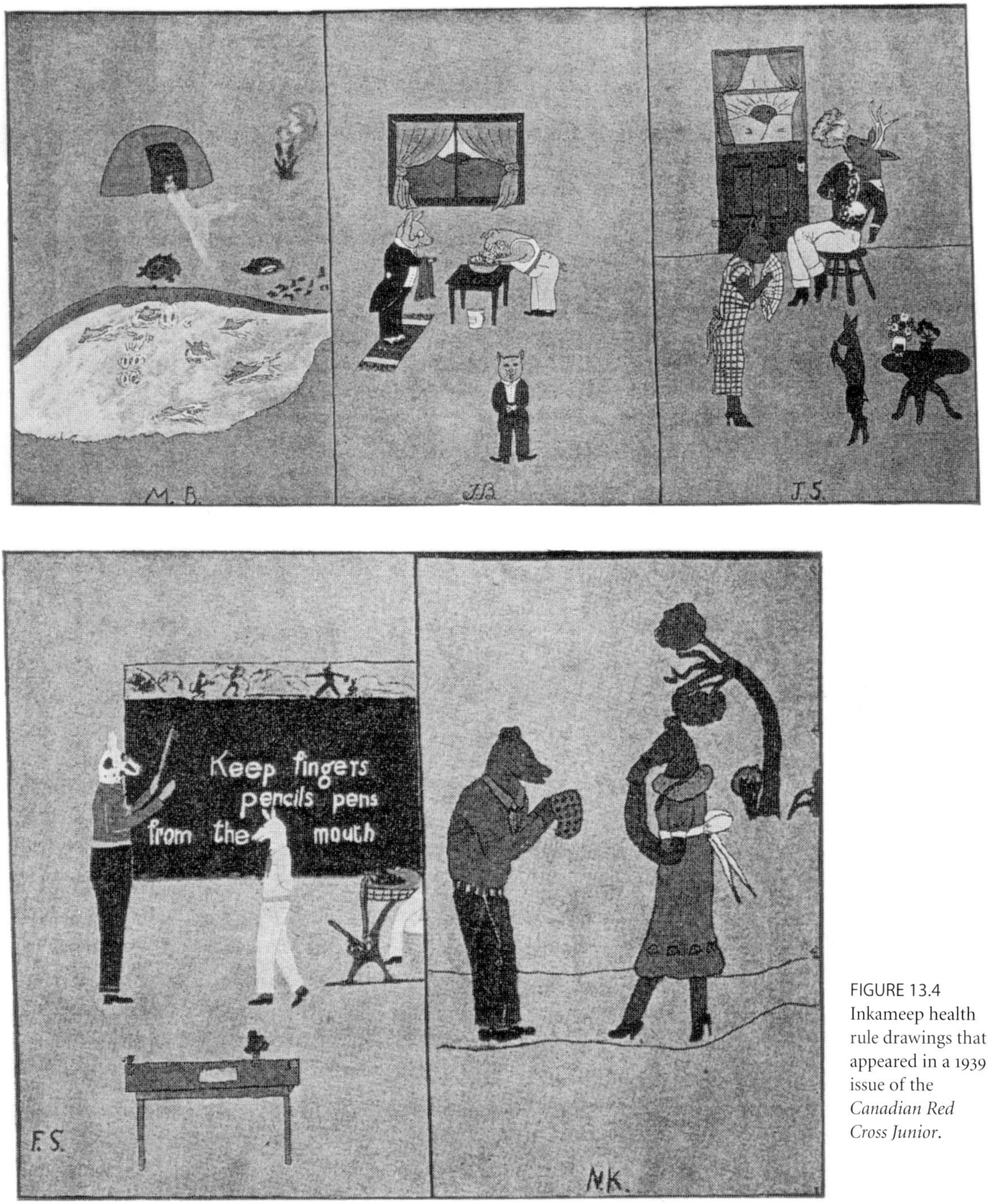

FIGURE 13.4
Inkameep health rule drawings that appeared in a 1939 issue of the *Canadian Red Cross Junior*.

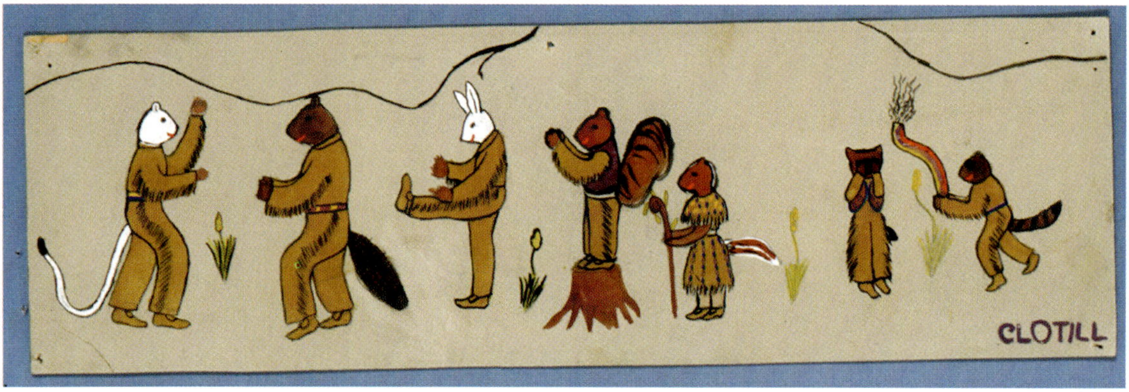

FIGURE 13.5 Scene or rehearsal of an Inkameep drama recorded by an Inkameep student drawing. (Courtesy of the Osoyoos Museum Society, Acc#1963-113-5029)

imagination—they could be of the children themselves practising good health measures, in a transformed state of being.

At the outset of this chapter, I identified how the Red Cross acted as an auxiliary to government medical programs. In this role, the organization sought to improve the welfare of children by providing extracurricular health and society programs to schools. These programs were based on the assumption that white, upper-class practices around personal hygiene and sanitation were superior to those based upon other cultures' knowledge and health practices. In turn, the superiority of Western models of health were buoyed by the high value placed upon scientific evidence in the crusade for health and disease prevention.

The efforts made by the Canadian Red Cross within schools were cached within a larger mandate and framework of surveillance regarding national health that was carried out by public health nurses and doctors, and in the lives of Aboriginal peoples, Federal Indian Agents. For students attending the Inkameep Day School, interaction with health professionals took place mainly during a visit from a travelling public health nurse. The school nurse who wrote a 1935 report on the health conditions at Inkameep noted, "Health lessons are necessarily very elemental when one remembers that most of the children have previously never seen a toothbrush, a bathtub was unheard of, and a balanced diet beyond the limits of imagination.... Surely our chief aim in this special branch of our work is to help develop the Indian into a healthy, respectable, self-supporting citizen."[45]

School medical inspections were a primary tool for enabling the surveillance of those students whose race, class, and location challenged the maintenance of health standards set out by the provincial and federal governments. Writing about school inspections in British Columbia, Gleason states:

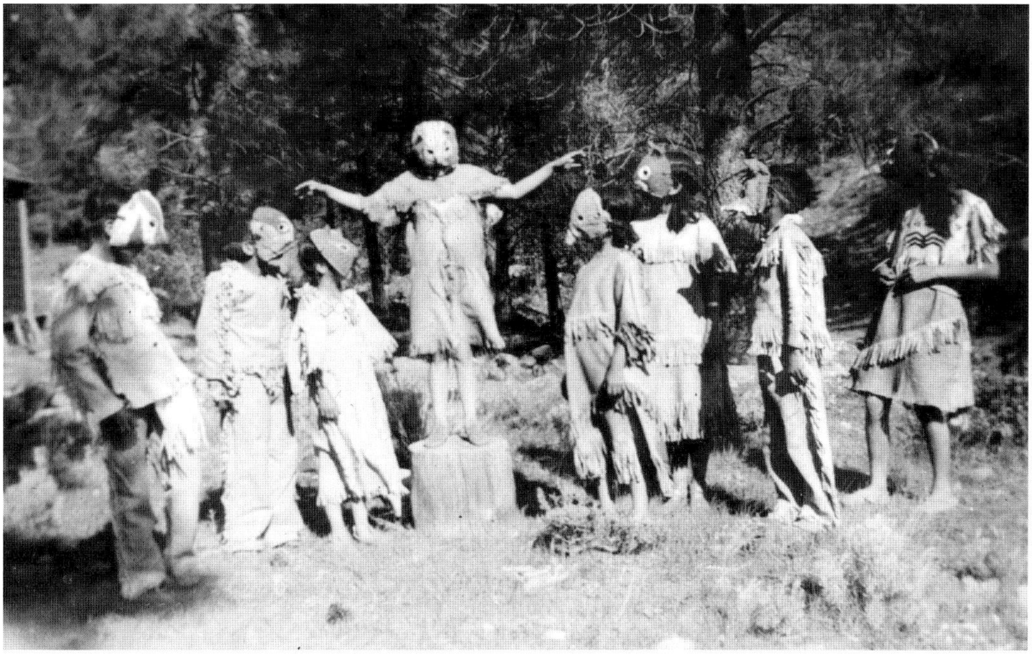

FIGURE 13.6 Inkameep students, in costume, rehearsing one of their dramas, c. 1941. (Photograph courtesy of the Osoyoos Museum Society, Acc#0099)

> The interest of public health reformers in shaping attitudes towards healthy children was inextricably bound up in concerns about racial and class "contagion." School medical inspection, and its considerable capabilities of social surveillance and discipline, enabled White middle-class professionals, primarily but not exclusively male, to infuse notions of "health" with the values and priorities of White middle-class and urban British Columbia.[46]

Educators and administrators in schools sought to standardize education for children; this curriculum included lessons in "proper" healthcare and socialization. In effect, a primary goal of schooling was to "Canadianize" students.[47] The mandate of public education to strengthen the nation through the promotion of health and social standards[48] worked symbiotically with the Red Cross's mandate to create a universal childhood and bodies onto which those *Canadian* values and practices might be scribed.

In her work about the disciplinary aspects of schooling between 1930 and 1960, Gleason draws upon Foucault's contention that "the body is the inscribed surface of events," and in the case of schooling, student bodies "bore witness to the school's role as a forceful instrument of the dominant culture in Canada."[49] "The body acted," writes

Gleason, "as a crucial site upon and within which the seemingly contradictory impulses of compliance with the dictates of others (such as teachers, administrators, and peers) and individual identity were played out."[50]

At the time the Inkameep health drawings were created, many traditional remedies and medicines were regularly used. It would have been far more likely that medicine people were consulted regarding injury or illness than a medical doctor. The knowledge and practices of these trained people would not have fit into the narrative of public health based upon scientific evidence circulated by the Red Cross. Indeed, their work might well have fed into Robertson's criticism of "backward civilization's" practices being one of the principal problems toward a universal healthy child. The Red Cross health rules were about Canadianizing the bodies of students via "proper" health practices aimed at creating a universal health standard for children and youth. Bodies that lay at the outskirts of boundaries of social acceptance were often the targets for strict forms of discipline.

During the residential school era, Aboriginal students' bodies were alarming sites of contagion to governing authorities. Accordingly, the abolishment of Aboriginal cultural practices that resisted or contradicted dominant health paradigms was a principal goal in the federal government's agenda to assimilate Aboriginal people into being full Canadian citizens. The Inkameep drawings interrupt narratives that correlated health and citizenship by resisting the inscription of Canadianness onto the students' bodies, or their visual representations. By presenting student bodies in animal form, students demonstrated their willingness to engage "other ways of knowing" the body and self. By illustrating these "other" bodies practising "other" healthy acts (sweats), they demonstrated a will and knowledge to participate in activities that challenged the ideal or universal practice of health. The students' connection to these fundamental Okanagan ways of knowing and being challenges the notion that their schooling was fully achieving the desired result of their assimilation or standardization toward being a Canadian citizen.

Inkameep drawings of the health rules appear in issues of the CRCJ twenty-two years prior to when Aboriginal people would be given Canadian citizenship with voting privileges by the federal government. Therefore, the Inkameep students' relationship to the nation of Canada was fundamentally different from that of other Juniors who were engaged in Red Cross programs that linked health and citizenship. The Inkameep Juniors in all respects were ideal role models for the Red Cross; they learned and practised their health rules, they raised money for the Red Cross for its humanitarian causes through the sale of their drawings and collection of donations at their dramatic play productions, and they promoted international goodwill by exchanging portfolios with other Juniors around the world.

Despite these ways in which the Inkameep Juniors' activities fall into line with the mandate of the Junior Red Cross, the publication of their drawings in the journal and inclusion of articles about their activities point to the ambivalence toward Aboriginal children and youth felt by authorities at the head of the nation-building project. There was a strong desire on the part of the journal's editors to include the Aboriginal students as part of its collective. In so doing, they hoped to realize the ideal that children from all "races" could make up a collective that represents the universal Canadian child. The text that accompanies the Inkameep drawings in the 1938 journal states, "The Canadian Junior Red Cross is indeed fortunate in having among its members such talented artists. Their generosity in supplying illustrations for the magazine is very much appreciated by the Editor, and indeed by all the readers. Their work is known and admired not only in Canada but in other countries to which our magazine goes."[51] The editor's praise extended to individual Inkameep artists about their further training as artists, and their citizenship activities as Juniors denotes an underlying desire to educate and Canadianize the students.

The contest over representation and participation of Aboriginal children in the CRCJ is evident through the juxtaposition of generalizing, stereotypical narratives and images of Aboriginal peoples, with the specific images created by Inkameep students. Through their essays, the editors position Aboriginal peoples' cultural knowledge and history outside of the nation's modern history and identity, yet they identify images by contemporary Inkameep students practising their culture as Canadian. The slippery and ambiguous nature of the representation in the CRCJ merely hints at the ways by which Inkameep students lived their lives between socially constructed historical narratives of the nation and their everyday realities as Osoyoos Indian Band youth.

Why would the teacher of the school encourage the participation of the Inkameep students in the Junior Red Cross? And, why promote their art to the society in light of its assimilationist agenda? I believe that Walsh disagreed with the assimilation of Aboriginal peoples into Canadian society. His writings and memoirs indicate a belief that Aboriginal peoples and their cultures had much to contribute to the country of Canada, but that those contributions were not dependent upon the surrender of their status as members of a First Nation, nor of their cultural knowledge and practices. This model of co-existence and different governance would precede modern treaty discussions of retention of distinct nation status for Indigenous people in Canada by decades. Participating in Junior Red Cross activities that promoted the health and well-being of Canada, but through Okanagan means of art and drama, was what Walsh himself termed "an experiment."

My analysis of the Inkameep health rules drawings as evidence of children and youth's agency responds to Jane Helleiner's critical examination of the roles children and childhood have played in the development of modern nation-states and nationalist projects. As Helleiner has noted in her work on racialized childhood in postwar Canada, children are seen as assets of the nation and as such move to the centre of the political agenda in terms of health and education mandates. The site of the school was paramount in the creation of patriotic citizens, and this too was differently experienced based on racial identity, and for Aboriginal children, this often meant residential schooling.

Building on Tuen van Dijk's work on elite discourse and racism,[52] Helleiner argues convincingly for critical attention to be paid toward the disproportionate influence of discourse by Canadian federal politicians on the lives of children in postwar Canada; however, this analysis remains at the level of adult circulation and consumption. How might we understand the consequences of politics on historical children's lives from their perspectives? In a precautionary note about investigating historical childhoods, Mona Gleason draws on Neil Sutherland's warning that adults' recollection of the past is often riddled with contemporary politics: "If we are ever to get 'inside' childhood experiences, then we must ask adults to recall how they though about, felt, and experienced their growing up."[53] My analysis of the content and context of Osoyoos children's and youth visual culture positions their drawings as *visual quotes* from this era, through which I have sutured a particular story. I fully acknowledge that my argument presented here is but one story the drawings may serve to tell. By critically discussing the production and circulation of Inkameep children's drawings published in the *Canadian Red Cross Junior*, I hope to have brought a new line to bear on the circulation of interwar and World War II agendas around health and citizenship for children's consumption. Importantly, the Inkameep health drawings allow contemporary viewers to more fully understand the effect of these adult agendas by looking at fissures in their narratives, brought to our attention by children themselves.

Notes

I would like to thank and gratefully acknowledge the generosity and knowledge of the members of the Osoyoos Indian Band who have supported and participated in our collaborative research project about the Inkameep Day School. In particular, I would like to thank the Baptiste family, Ms. Jane Stelkia, and Mrs. Irene Bryson for their kind sharing of childhood memories that contributed to this chapter. I would like to thank the board of directors and curators Leslie Plaskett and Gayle Cornish of the Osoyoos Museum for openly sharing their collection and archives of the Inkameep Day School. I acknowledge and thank the National Red Cross Archives in Ottawa for facilitating my use of their collections and providing copies of the Junior Red Cross journals used for illustration in this chapter. This research was in part funded by a Standard Research Grant from the Social Sciences and Humanities Research Council, the Osoyoos Indian Band, the Osoyoos Museum Society, and the Centre for Religion and Society at the University of Victoria.

1 Mona Gleason, "Race, Class, and Health: School Medical Inspection and 'Healthy' Children in British Columbia, 1890–1930," *Canadian Bulletin of Medical History/Bulletin canadien d'histoire de la medicine (CBMH/BCHM)* 19 (2002): 98.
2 Ibid., 95.
3 James W. Robertson, *The Crusade for Good Health* (Toronto: Canadian Red Cross Society, 1921), 5.
4 Ibid.
5 Ibid., 14.
6 Ibid., 5, 14.
7 James W. Robertson, *Peace-Time Policy and Programme of the Canadian Red Cross Society* (Toronto: The Canadian Red Cross Society, 1920), 1.
8 According to a 1944 Red Cross Health Rules card, the Junior membership in Canada by that time was 800,000 members strong.
9 *Canadian Red Cross Junior* 9, no. 1 (January 1930): 18.
10 *Canadian Red Cross Junior* 9, no. 3 (March 1930): 4.
11 Ibid.
12 *Canadian Red Cross Junior* 20, no. 2 (February 1941): 8.
13 *Canadian Red Cross Junior* 9, no. 2 (February 1930): 16.
14 Mona Gleason, "Disciplining the Student Body: Schooling and the Construction of Canadian Children's Bodies, 1930–1960," *History of Education Quarterly* 41, no. 2 (2001): 189–215.
15 Gleason, "Race, Class and Health," 27.
16 *Canadian Red Cross Junior* 9, no. 3 (March 1930): 4.
17 Ibid.
18 For a case study look at narratives of health and the Junior Red Cross in the United States, see John F. Hutchinson, "The Junior Red Cross Goes to Healthland," *American Journal of Public Health* 87, no. 11 (1997): 1816–1823.
19 *Canadian Red Cross Junior* 20, no. 1 (January 1941): 3.
20 *The Globe* (February 25, 1921).
21 Ibid.
22 The 1946 Canadian Citizenship Act defined citizens for the first time not as British subjects but as Canadians.
23 Jane Helleiner, "'The Right Kind of Children': Childhood, Gender and 'Race' in Canadian Postwar Political Discourse," *Anthropologica* 2 (2001): 146.
24 *Canadian Red Cross Junior* 14, no. 7 (September 1940): 12.

25 Nancy Sheehan, "Junior Red Cross in the Schools: An International Movement, a Voluntary Agency, and Curriculum Change," *Curriculum Inquiry* 17, no. 3 (1987): 255.

26 Ibid., 253.

27 Ibid., 254.

28 Ibid., 251.

29 Ibid., 255.

30 Ibid., 260.

31 These elders are Ms. Jane Stelkia and Mrs. Irene Bryson. Both women attended the Inkameep Day School as youth and were students of Mr. Anthony Walsh.

32 Rita M. Mahon, "Inkameep Indian Reserve—Oliver District," *Public Health Nurses Bulletin* 2, no. 2 (1935): 11–14.

33 *The Mail and Empire* (May 1, 1936).

34 Ibid.

35 Sheehan, "Junior Red Cross in the Schools," 256.

36 Inkameep students performed their dramas for the purpose of raising funds for the Red Cross in Penticton, B.C., on May 31, 1940, and on April 17, 1940 in Oliver, B.C. At both events, the presidents of the local Red Cross addressed the audience.

37 Anthony Walsh, "The Inkameep School," in *The Thirty-Eighth Annual Report of the Okanagan Historical Society*, 14–19 (Kelowna: Okanagan Historical Society 1974): 14.

38 Ibid.

39 Thirty-three pieces of their art was part of a display of Junior work at the national headquarters of the Canadian Red Cross in Toronto during May 1935.

40 The children also raised money toward the purchase of a Spitfire plane on behalf of the B.C. Indian Spitfire fund that had been established by B.C. Indian chiefs in the province, and they sent their works to London, England, to be auctioned off for the war effort (raising in one instance eight hundred dollars). From 1936 to 1942 Walsh entered the drawings done by his pupils at the school in the Wartime Drawing competition for children held by the Royal Drawing Society of London, at which Inkameep students' work competed against art by thousands of other children of the Empire. Many of his students won awards of high honour in this competition. Notably, in 1938 Sis-hu-lk (Francis Baptiste) won a silver star and Thith-hak-key (Johnnie Stelkia) won two bronze stars for their drawn and painted works. That year, Sis-hu-lk's drawing on buckskin was viewed by Queen Elizabeth and purchased for Buckingham Palace's King Edward and Queen Alexandra Memorial Collection. This drawing was the first "Canadian" piece purchased for this collection. In 1941 the Inkameep youth began corresponding with Walt Disney about their interest in art. His return correspondence to the youth is recorded in a Christmas card of that same year, as well as a letter thanking them for their Christmas card that depicted their version of the Seven Dwarfs. The Inkameep students performed a selection of their plays in 1941, too, for the opening of Thunderbird Park in Victoria at the Provincial Museum.

41 Exact date is unknown, but would be between 1931 and 1934, when the first mention of the Inkameep Juniors is made in the CRCJ.

42 *Canadian Red Cross Junior* 17, no. 5 (May 1938): 24; *Canadian Red Cross Junior* 18, no. 1 (January 1939): 24.

43 In addition to naming the artists who created the health rule drawings, the editor of the journal gives praise to Francis Baptiste, a prolific artist at Inkameep, for furthering his education in the southwest United States at the School for Indian Art at Santa Fe. In the text surrounding the 1938 images, the editor of the CRCJ acknowledges that the paintings (originally in frieze format) from

the Inkameep Juniors were given as a Christmas present to the editor. She also notes that the Juniors would be creating paintings of the other health rules for future viewing. The text accompanying the 1939 published images states that Walsh exhibited the images in cities throughout England and continental Europe, where they received much attention.

44 In interviews conducted with Jane Stelkia of the Osoyoos Indian Band, she would often cite the names of students with whom she went to school upon looking at drawings of the animal plays. She stated it was as if she were looking at a photograph of the children themselves.

45 Quoted in Gleason, "Race, Class and Health," 95.

46 Gleason, "Race, Class and Health," 105.

47 Gleason, "Disciplining the Student Body," 190.

48 Ibid., 194.

49 Ibid., 190.

50 Ibid., 194.

51 *Canadian Red Cross Junior* 17, no. 5 (May 1938): 24.

52 Tuen van Dijk, *Elite Discourse and Racism* (Newbury Park, CA: Sage, 1993).

53 Gleason, "Disciplining the Student Body," 194.

KAI WOOD MAH

CHILDREN AND SCHOOL INTERIORS
The User-Material Culture-Environment Nexus in Late Nineteenth-Century Toronto

RENOVATION IS A COMMON PRACTICE FOR transforming buildings to suit everyday use. Increasing floor area, providing fire exits, and integrating new mechanical technologies renew the life of buildings. Changes made to buildings update current codes, regulations, and space requirements, or introduce completely different functions. These are the most basic purposes. An overview of the physical transformations, however, underlines the intimate relationship between the built environment and the users. Fundamentally reactive, renovations enable people to change buildings to the way they want them to be. Renovations leave physical traces of how users settled into their spaces, recording the consensual acceptance of the established human and material relationships, which I refer to as the user-material culture-environment nexus. For the purpose of this anthology, the physical history of this nexus is a rich arena for excavating experience of the cultural landscapes of education.

In this chapter, I explore the historical construction of the children-material culture-environment nexus in the nineteenth century, probing the physical changes at Wellesley Street School in Toronto for everyday experience. George Hodgins, William Caniff, W.M. Oldright, and Ada Marean participated in the process of creating the modern school interior, assisting, to various degrees, in defining children's places in public buildings. In writing a social history of this process, I gathered materials from disparate archives: architectural drawings, photographs, and handbooks, along with textual sources, to situate Wellesley Street School in space and time.[1] How did the modern school interior come into existence? What were the circumstances and situations in this historical process? What was the experience of melding the physical environment and children in designing schools?

From a historical perspective, this children-material culture-environment nexus was (re)conceptualized through a century and a half of educational reform and technological

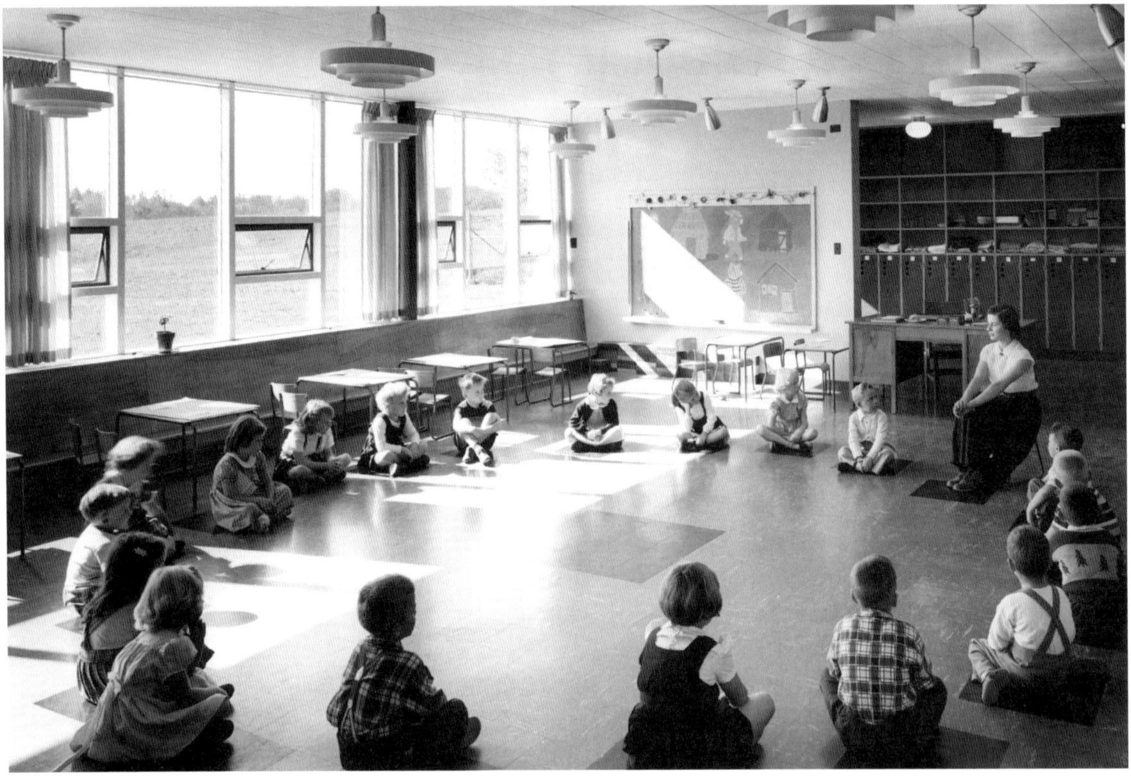

FIGURE 14.1 Georgetown School, 1953. (Canadian Architectural Archives, University of Calgary, PAN 53783)

change in North America, beginning in the mid-nineteenth century, when public schools were first established.[2] I suggest that identifying this historical context is an important step toward a critique of the social implications of design, pointing to the ways schools are compartmentalized, specialized, gendered, or imagined as healthy and safe. Interior photography helps us to visualize the relationships, presenting the links between the material and the occupants illegible in architectural plans. The following reading of a photograph demonstrates this potential.

The 1953 photograph (fig. 14.1) provides a rich visual description of a modern classroom, as defined by material culture. The children and teacher sit for the photographer, in the kindergarten room at Georgetown School in Georgetown, Ontario. Ample natural light from large windows uninterrupted by pilasters or columns floods the spacious classroom. Fresh air enters through operable windows, which also frame a pastoral setting. Inches above the floor along the side wall below the windows are thermostat-controlled radiators, for a consistent room temperature. Healthy-looking children sit on square mats, legs crossed, on a linoleum floor, forming a perfect circle. Behind them are small-scale tables and chairs, and along the far wall is a line of lockers for outdoor clothes, easy for little hands to reach. Imbued with beliefs and social convictions about health, safety, comfort, and learning environments, the photograph showcases the material contents of a typical mid-twentieth-century classroom—the physical features and arrangement, including children and teacher, form the material armature that defines the modern school interior. Perhaps, such interior environments are of particular urgency in times of change and social instability because of their implied stable imagery. This photograph typifies a genre of images taken in the World War II and postwar years from, for example, Crow Island School in Winnetka, Illinois, designed by Eliel Saarinen and Chicago firm Perkins and Will (1940), and Sunnylea Public School in Etobicoke, Ontario, designed by J.B. Parkin (1941). Other historical social issues, including population growth, immigration, and gender and class values, as well as concerns such as contagious disease and fire safety in the second half of the nineteenth century had inspired similar arrangements of school interiors.[3]

The 1898 photograph of the model kindergarten at the Toronto Normal School in Toronto (fig. 14.2) is an example from this earlier time period.[4] The children sit calmly next to one another in rows of three, feet on the floor, at special tables and in chairs designed for them. Attended by a model teacher, a different object-lesson is being demonstrated at each table—paper folding, Froebel blocks, illustrated picture cards, and ball-and-stick building sets—to the women spectators observing at the far end of the room. Walls decorated in floral wallpaper and framed paintings and photographs recall the drawing room of a Victorian middle-class home. A woman plays a piano at one end; a rabbit in a cage and several potted plants occupy the room, and close to the lower left corner of the picture frame is a toy castle.[5] As in the first example, this nineteenth-century photograph depicts architectural space that is furnished and arranged with thoughtful features to enhance the spatial quality and comfort of its inhabitants: the orderly arrangement of children and furniture through geometry (circular lines in the first and straight lines in the second); the purpose-designed objects for children and educational apparatuses; the conspicuous display of middle-class culture through clothing and interior finishes; and children's occupation of learning through playful activities. This image of the interior landscape disseminated the interrelated spatial, visual, and material ideals of education. The photographic images are visual fragments of a complex nexus of children-material culture-environment, embedded in the general school plan.

School interiors and children have not attracted scholarly attention, despite a recent stream of studies on the architecture of education.[6] However, designers have contributed much to a more nuanced understanding of the relationship between

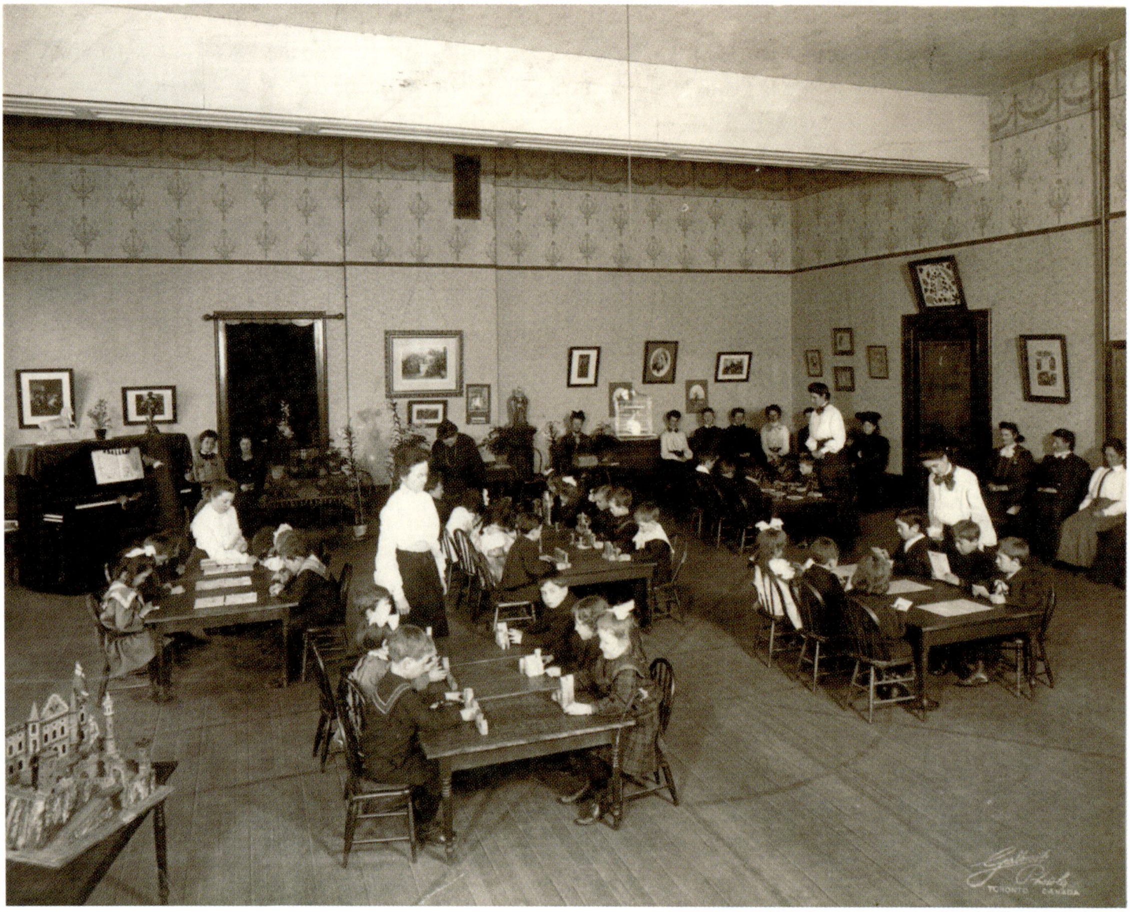

FIGURE 14.2 Student teachers practise teaching kindergarten at the Toronto Normal School, c. 1898. (Archives of Ontario, RG 2-257)

children and interior space. For example, a recent United Kingdom project, "Classroom of the Future," has proposed the concept of "classroom landscape" in designing schools.[7] Conceived as an alternative way of conceptualizing educational environments, the classroom landscape encourages the consideration of educational spaces as evolving spaces of use and adaptive reuse through improvisation and alterations. Buildings perceived as such emphasize the spatial relationship between the physical environment and children's everyday use, a connection that might seem obvious.[8] However, the completeness of the inhabited school interior in the two photographs we have explored is markedly contrasted by the disturbing absence of children in photographer Peter Polidori's fractured image of a Chernobyl classroom—in which furniture and school equipment are postnuclear waste.[9] In history, the link between school interior and children melded gradually through decades of physical transformations, as the following examination of Wellesley Street School demonstrates.

Wellesley Street School was for Toronto a symbol of urbanity, especially from the street (fig. 14.3). Indeed, like other social institutions, schools were material and visual indices of a modern city, especially in relation to other buildings.[10] Designed by William G. Storm (1826–1892), the architect of several important commissions for the City of Toronto at the time, Osgoode Hall and its Convocation Hall (1875) and the New St. Andrew's Presbyterian Church (1875), to name a few, Wellesley Street School was an important addition to Toronto's urban landscape. In 1873 public school administrators described it as the "most handsome and best furnished" of the thirteen public schools in Toronto, and it was the first school to accommodate all grades of primary education.[11] Torontonians were impressed by Wellesley Street School's bell tower as they turned the corner of St. Vincent Street and St. Albans Street. The elevation was a long stretch of stone and brick, composed of various colours and fenestrated with eclectically detailed, arched windows. Seeing the building at a distance from the fence and separated by a lawn added to the visual effect of its scale on passersby. The Gothic profile of the school roof adorned with cast-iron details along its edges would have drawn in observers. Indeed, Wellesley was unlike other schools in the city.

Despite form and exterior articulations, Wellesley Street School (fig. 14.4) was essentially a modern school building. It was a two-storey wood structure with masonry cladding and topped with a wood-truss roof. Originally designed without a basement, it was supported on a strip foundation. Wood wainscotting wrapped the interior walls, with a height below the window sill. It had an L-shaped plan, formed by two large, rectangular classrooms and two entrance lobbies with interior stairs. A description in J. George Hodgins's *School House* (1876) is helpful to contextualize Wellesley Street School as "modern," compared to the "old-fashioned school-houses." The "old, shattered, broken-down school-houses" had no "play-ground attached to it, and weeds grow rank and luxuriantly around it." Moreover, the old "comfortless" interiors had poor ventilation, and walls were "without maps, or charts, or pictures." As a contrast, reformed school buildings like Wellesley Street School had five major features, which Hodgins has pointed out as defining modern: school site, climate control and ventilation, interior arrangements (furniture), and school apparatus. The school site provided sufficient area in the front and back for setbacks from the street and ample space for separate boys' and girls' playgrounds in the back with playground equipment. The classroom interiors were ventilated and warmed, providing comfort and fresh air. Modern classrooms were also furnished with desks and furniture and teaching apparatuses such as maps, globes, and other object lessons.[12]

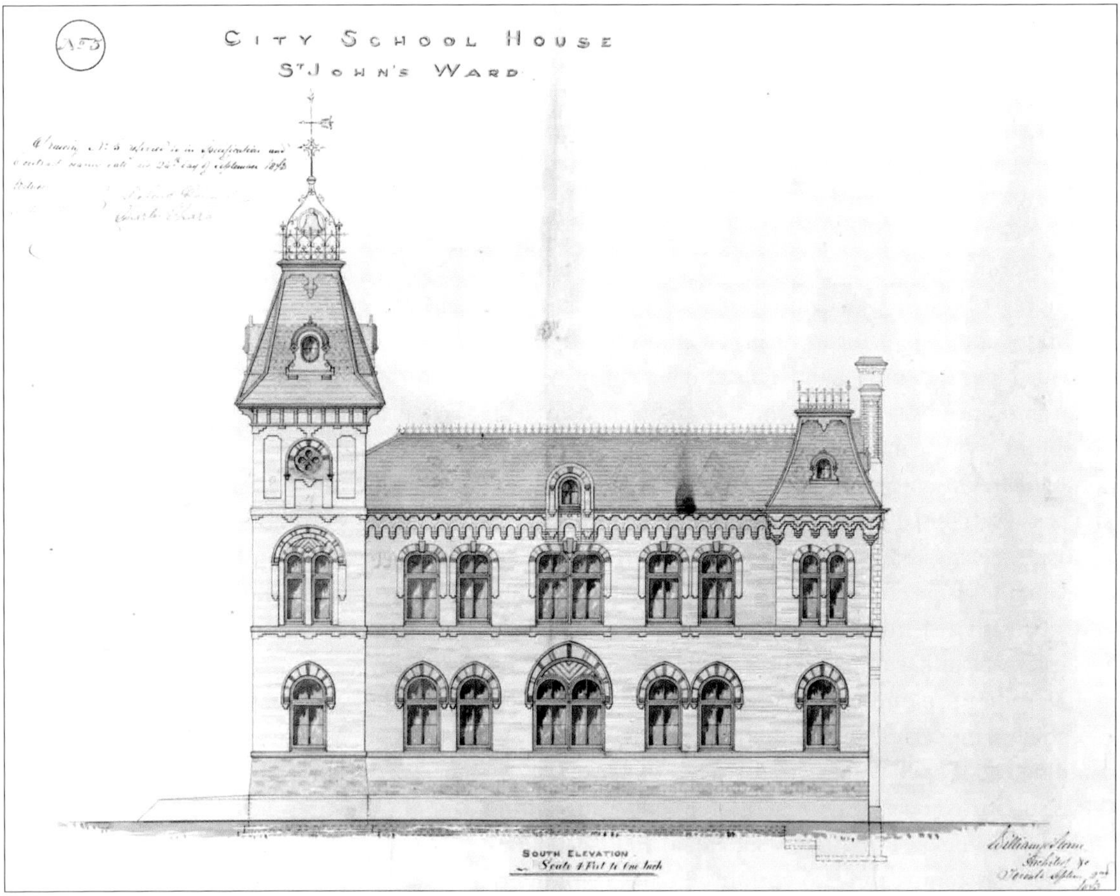

FIGURE 14.3 Wellesley Street School, 1873. (Archives of Ontario, C11-709-0-1)

Compared to St. Lawrence Ward School, a contemporary public school in the city, Wellesley Street School differed in building form and exterior but not in modern building features. Although a much more modest building, St. Lawrence Ward School also had Hodgins's prescriptions for a modern school building. Like Wellesley Street School, it had a setback of more than forty feet from the street, away from the "dust" of the street (figs. 14.5 and 14.6). The one-room plan also observed the interior environmental qualities of ventilation and heating with windows and vents. Both schools had modern features. In addition, if the furniture, educational apparatuses, and equipment furnished a modern school building, it's arguable that Wellesley differed because of its exterior form and ornamentation.

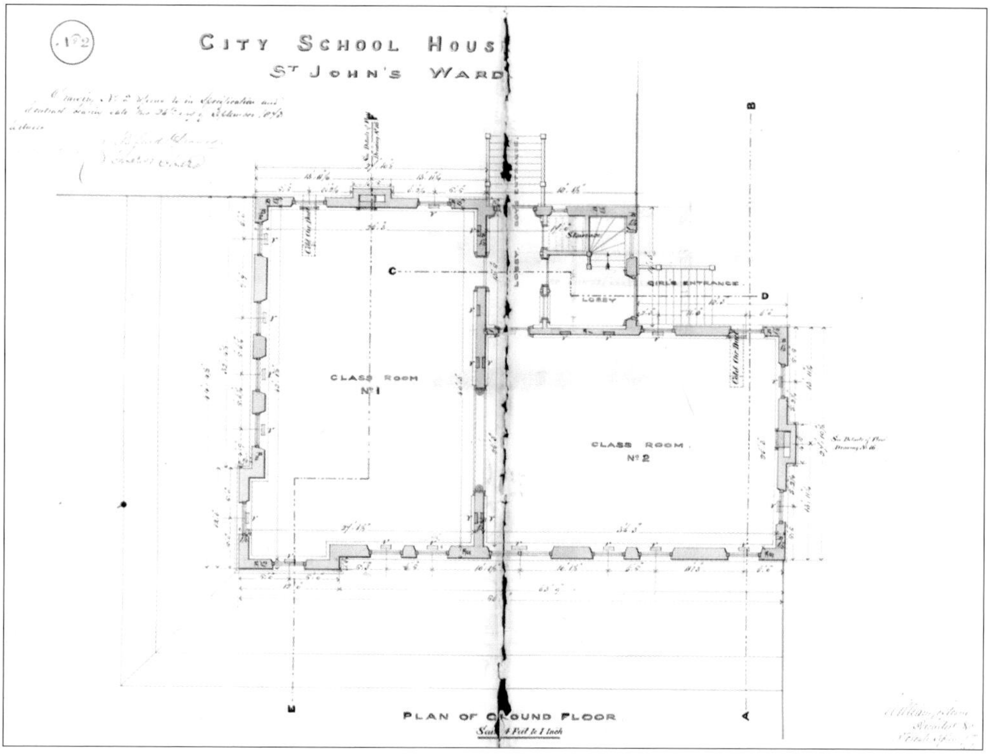

FIGURE 14.4 William G. Storm, Wellesley Street School, 1873, ground floor plan. (Archives of Ontario, C11-709-0-1)

The emphasis on Wellesley's form can also tell us about the social significance of material difference as expressed in Toronto's urban landscape and how it influenced the lived experience of the users. Two noteworthy points are the specificity of location and the differing intentions between the building exterior and interior. An illustrative example is to look at Wellesley's surroundings in St. John's Ward and how its exterior blended fittingly in the urban landscape. A block to the west of Wellesley Street School was the expansive lawn of Queen's Park, a park opened by Edward, Prince of Wales, graced with the quadrangle of University of Toronto buildings. At the north edge of the park was Baptist College, a private religious college. North of it, across St. Joseph Street, was St. Basil's College and grounds, an elite institution of higher education. Wellesley Street School's form was impressive only in comparison to other ordinary public school buildings such as St. Lawrence Ward School, but not so to its immediate neighbours. Through Wellesley Street School's material distinction, Toronto participated in the performance of middle-class gentility and urbanity.

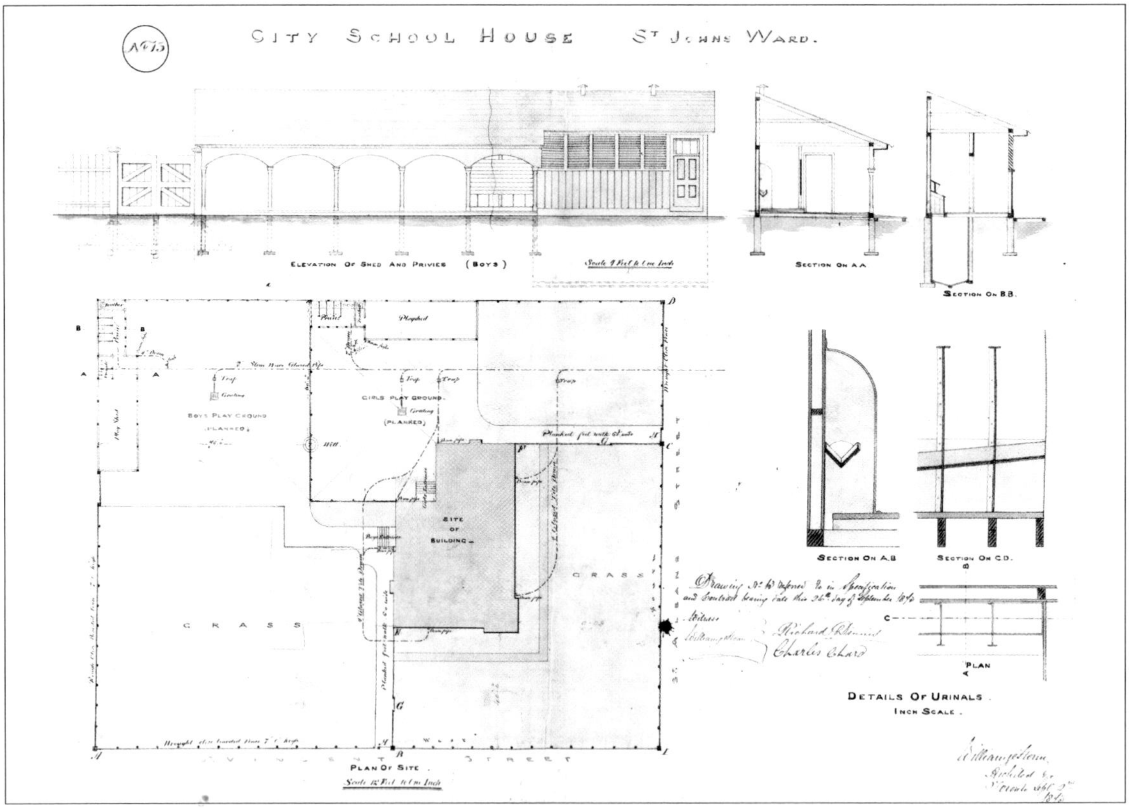

FIGURE 14.5 William G. Storm, Wellesley Street School, 1873, showing site plan, play sheds, and privies. (Archives of Ontario, C11-709-0-1)

The tension between performance of urbanity and actual practice is underlined by the inconsistency of gender separation of Wellesley Street School's exterior and interior. For example, the site plan (fig. 14.5) maintained strict physical barriers between boys and girls; girls entered the building from St. Alban Street and boys entered from St. Vincent Street. The playgrounds were also separated by a fence into sections for boys and girls, along with the outdoor privies and connected play sheds, but the interior functioned differently. Note that the ground plan (fig. 14.4) has a window and door connecting the two neighbouring lobbies, providing a less gender restrictive plan. In a later renovation (fig. 14.7), a stricter spatial separation was imposed, dividing the plan into two separate spheres, without any internal connections. Why the sudden change in attitudes toward segregation? This shift coincided with a general change in the design of schools during the 1880s, when school interiors became the main focus, which was preoccupied with healthy, safe learning environments.

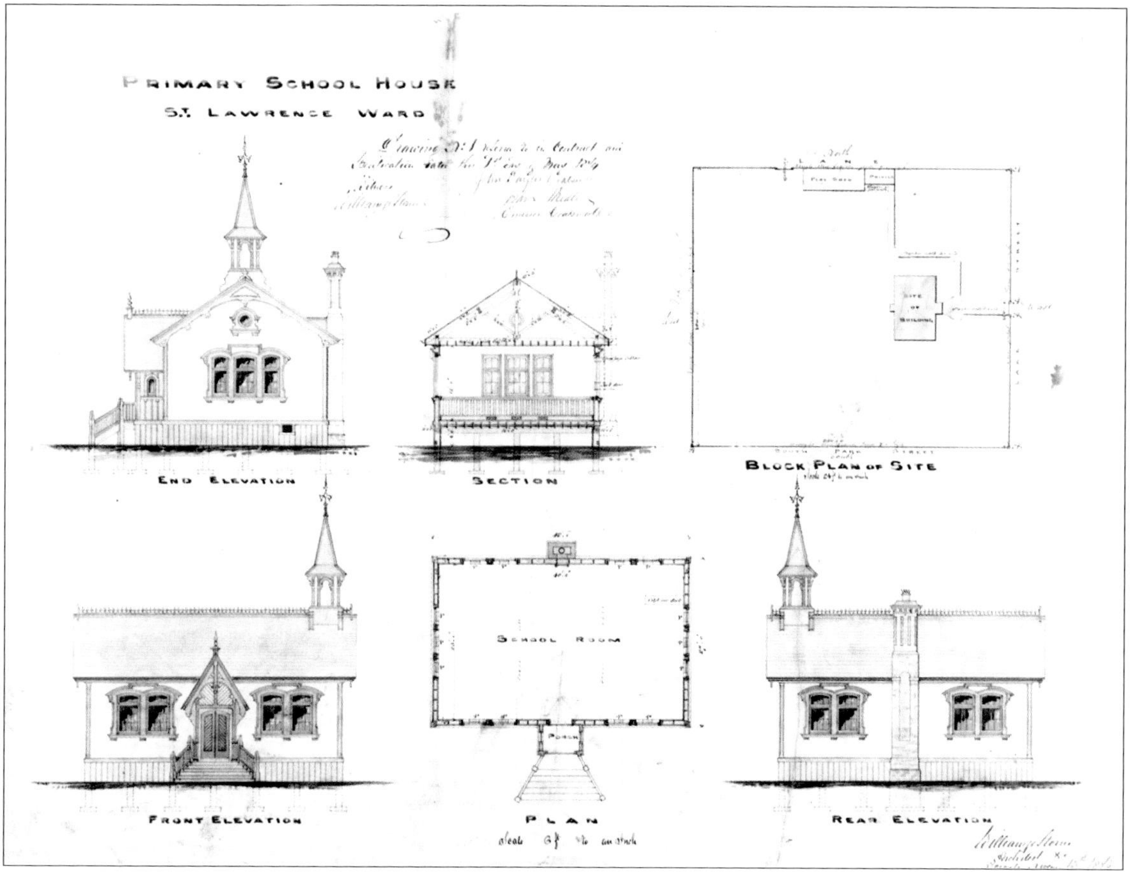

FIGURE 14.6 William G. Storm, St. Lawrence Ward School, 1873. (Archives of Ontario, C11-753)

With this shift came an emphasis on efficient plans. Hodgins's *Hints and Suggestions on School Architecture and Hygiene*, published in 1886, explains this change:

> It is in this matter of interior arrangement that the greatest difficulty arises. As the exterior of a school house, that is a matter of taste and of expense; but the constantly arising demands on School Boards, for increased and improved school accommodation, renders it necessary that the greatest care should be exercised in the planning of the interior of the school building. Economy, convenience, and health have to be consulted, and it is with a view to aid trustees in this difficult and responsible part of their duty, that I have selected, with the approval of the Minister, and inserted in this book, so many plans of the *interiors* of school houses and but few *exteriors*.[13] (emphasis in the original)

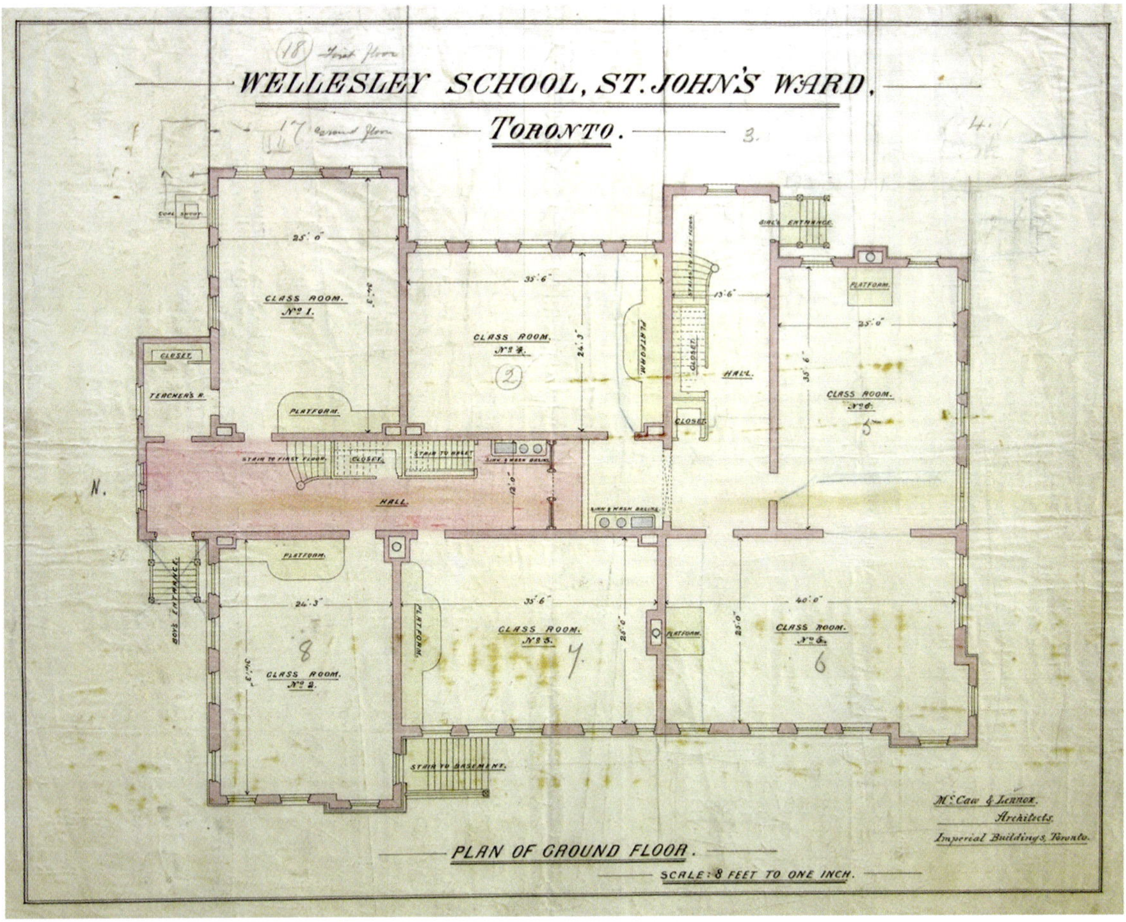

FIGURE 14.7 Wellesley School, St. John's Ward, plan of ground floor. (Sesquicentennial Museum and Archives, Toronto District School Board)

This sudden focus on interior arrangements was a major step toward modernizing schools. Other ordinary institutions—such as hospitals—privileged function over form in the process of modernization in the early twentieth century.[14] This shift had profound implications on children, leading to physical alterations for healthy and safe interiors.

In less than a decade, Wellesley Street School was considered to be too small and unsafe. The archival materials and the building renovations show that in the 1880s, children were thought to be in danger of the undesirable environments of the 1870s. Noxious airborne substances and fire hazards threatened children's safety in public spaces.

Torontonians became more conscientious about designing educational facilities, as the following solutions demonstrate. Indeed, developments such as the germ theory, ventilation technologies, and the establishment of a bacteriology laboratory in Toronto helped the modernization movement. Unsafe schools were a citywide problem. The provincial government issued its first Public Health Act in 1884, and in the same year, Toronto appointed the city's first medical officer, William Caniff, a former dean of Victoria Medical School. Caniff inaugurated his first medical inspection of public education with a visit to thirty-six schools, reporting on heating, drainage, privies, and building adjacencies. Like many of his contemporaries, he was concerned about sanitary reform, mainly environmental pollution and sanitation problems, and their removal in preventing the spread of disease in the city, as his 1889 letter to the Toronto School Board concerning the provision for adequate ventilation indicates.[15]

Caniff's sympathetic letter to the Toronto Department of Education recognized the difficulty of supplying sufficient accommodations for city children. Indeed, the sanitary problems were beyond the responsibility of the school board; the city as a whole struggled to supply proper infrastructure for an expanding city. "An examination of a sample of this water shows it to be, to say the least, unsafe to drink. I therefore would ask that the City water be at once provided."[16] Supplying water, roads, and sewage systems were among the many challenges of modernizing Toronto, and schools were an important part of this scheme.

Of great concern was the transmission of the highly acute, contagious *bacillus Corynebacterium diphtheriae*, commonly known as diphtheria, which produces a mucous membrane in the throat. Diphtheria was thought to be spread from outdoor privy pits, as was detected with a test issued by the bacteriology lab and, indeed, by the noxious smell exacerbated by the summer heat. At a meeting of the local Board of Health on August 20, 1887, "it was ordered that the Public School Board be requested to do away at once with all privy pits in connection with the school buildings in the City, and to replace them with properly trapped water closets and urinals, the order to be imperative."[17] In the same year the report was filed, Alderman Carlyle reported an "alarming" case of diphtheria in the St. Andrew Ward at the Phoebe Street School, where there were fourteen cases of diphtheria and "four deaths had occurred within about ten days." Upon his inspection, Carlyle observed, "While it could not be declared that the disease originated in the building, it was very plain that children attending the school were exposed to effluvia which would favor the development of the diphtheritic poison."[18]

The actions taken to eradicate the problem can be seen at Wellesley Street School. W.M. Oldright, on September 26, 1891, wrote to E.F. Clarke, the Major of Toronto, regarding the horrible stench at Wellesley Street School:

> It is so difficult to understand how any well-informed person in this last decade of the nineteenth century can defend these disgusting relics of barbarism [privies] that I hardly know what points to take up in a letter which must necessarily be brief. In one block in St. John's Ward 67 × 200 yards, a physiological calculation shows that there are deposited annually from 14 to 18 tons of solid excreta. What must be the condition of the soil?[19]

Oldright was referring to the odour emanating from the Wellesley Street School construction site, a by-product of the "filth spreading from a row of school privies on the east side of the site towards a well at the south-west angle of it, about 50 feet distant."[20] The renovation of Wellesley Street School's basement (fig. 14.8) was part of the mandate for healthy and safe schools. Replacing the outdoor privies with indoor water closets was the topmost priority of changes, as the basement plan illustrates. On the right of the plan, the "girls play room" is adjacent to the "water closet room." For the boys, this same situation is located on the left. Like today, the water closets were in individual stalls, separated by partitions, and fitted with new windows for fresh air flow.

Safety was another social and technical concern that prompted school builders to focus on school interiors. Fear sparks public attention. Middle-class families would read frightening columns about their children's schools in the morning newspaper. "Imperfect Ventilation and Overcrowding at the Victoria Street School," "A Wretchedly Seated Room," "Many Children Awaiting Admission," broadcast *The Globe*.[21] A journalist criticized parents for sending children "too early in age" to schools, pointing out the "evils" of such practices on their hygiene and the worsening of consequences by "overcrowding." The local newspaper *The Globe* explains:

> It certainly is a hardship for parents who are taxed heavily for school purposes to find that they cannot get their children into any of the city schools.... It may be questioned whether the children who are kept away from school to grow up in health and ignorance are not after all better off than those who have their little bodies packed into almost any of the junior 10th divisions in the city.[22]

By 1901 the population of Toronto was 208,040, a 240 percent increase from 1880 (86,415) and 144 percent from 1890 (144,023).[23] As a result of this unprecedented growth, the scale of schools increased dramatically. In the case of Wellesley Street School, the size problem was addressed through building additions. Taller, bigger buildings and numerous additions accommodated the increasing population; Storm's Borden Street School is another good example. But, the sheer size and low quality of the architecture were a cause for criticism. A writer in *The Canadian Architect and Builder* pointed out that "erecting barn-like structures" and caretakers' residences on school lots looking a lot like "dog-kennels ... is doubtless [a result of] the insufficiency of the funds at the disposal

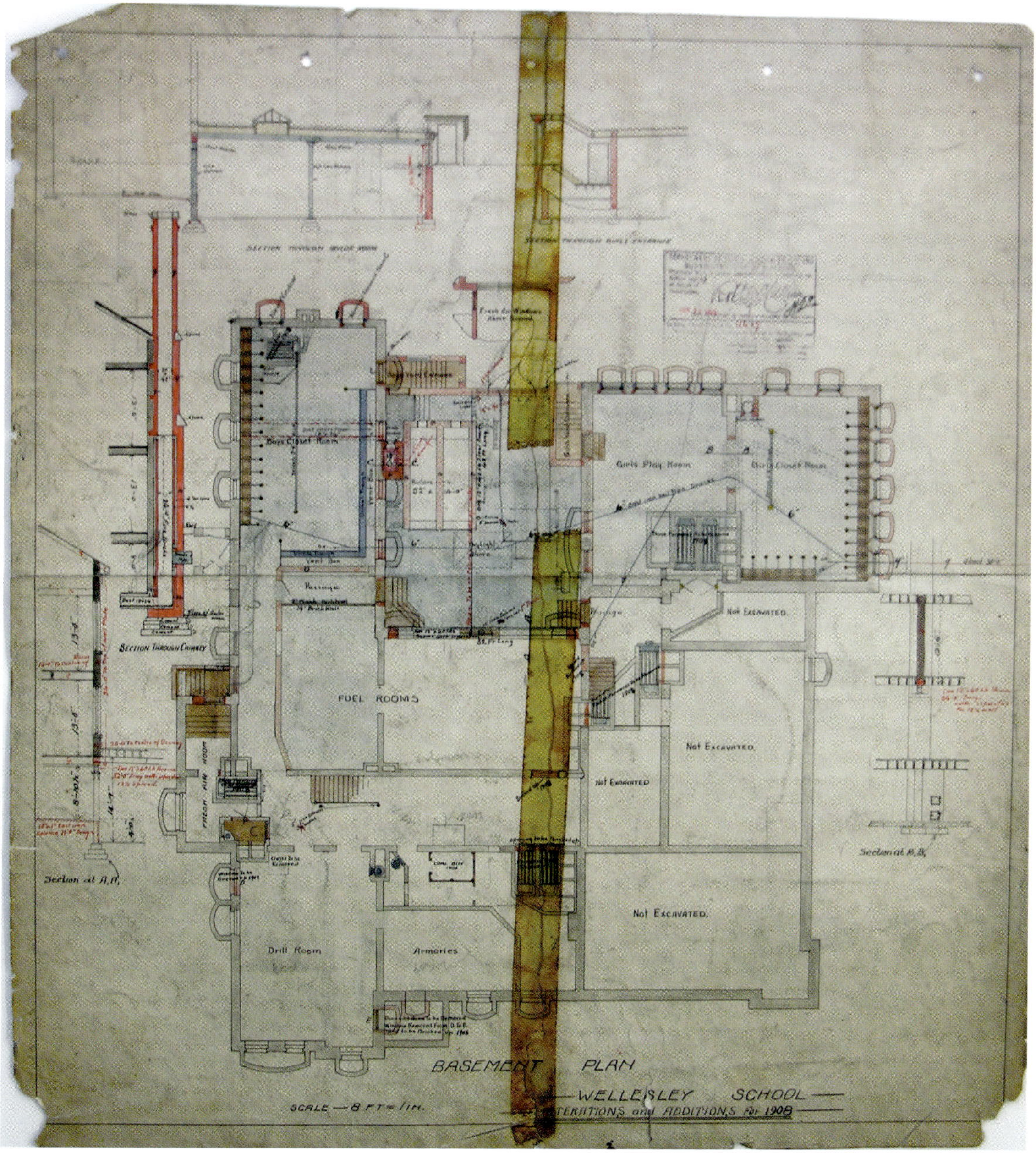

FIGURE 14.8 Basement plan of Wellesley School. (Sesquicentennial Museum and Archives, Toronto District School Board)

of the School Board."[24] The writer continues that "it seems a matter for regret that the children should be compelled to spend so much of their lives in contemplation of these cheap and nasty structures."[25]

School safety was rated according to the successful arrangement of the interior. A reporter compared schools in a local newspaper after a fire at the new Hope Street School on July 8, 1884:

> Thanks entirely to the fact that yesterday afternoon's fire did not occur at the Church Street School instead of Hope Street, we have to chronicle merely a light loss instead of an awful catastrophe. The Hope Street building is a new and excellently arranged one, and consequently on the alarm being given the teachers were able to put the fire drill at once in practice, and the three storeys were emptied in a few seconds of their crowds of little ones. What if such a fire had occurred in Church Street School? What if even an alarm were given? As our reporter showed lately, the children would probably not get out of the clumsily contrived building quickly enough to prevent a panic occurring. Ill-equipped as that building is with means of egress, even a false alarm of fire might cause loss of life which it is dreadful to think upon. Now, what is the School Board going to do about it?[26]

Designing for the children also included changes made to the circulation spaces—stairs and hallways—widening and rearranging them for easy egress in the event of a fire. As can be seen in the ground floor plan of Wellesley Street School's renovation (fig. 14.7), the architects maximized egress with the addition of new classrooms. In total, three exit points led directly to the outside, avoiding dead-end corridors.

Gender separation was also an issue of safety. For example, home economics and workshop spaces were created among other specialized end-of-the-century educational spaces. The basement plan (fig. 14.8) shows how recreation spaces for boys and girls were transformed. The boys' section of the school was connected by stairs to the basement, which contained a drill room and armories. In the girls' section, next to the girls' closet was a play room. Drill was introduced into the Toronto school system in the late 1870s as a way of constructing male masculinity. This same trend corresponded to other gender-defining institutions, including summer camps, as Abigail Van Slyck has shown.[27]

Once the school interiors were deemed healthy and safe, educationists experimented with educational matters.[28] Most expressive of learning interiors was the design of the kindergarten room. By the early 1880s, the introduction of the kindergarten into the public school system in Toronto was underway. In 1881 the Toronto Public School Board sent teacher Ada Marean to St. Louis, Missouri, for instructions in the kindergarten system. In his *Annual Report* for 1882, Superintendent James L. Hughes recommended that the internationally renowned kindergarten teachers Susan E. Blow,

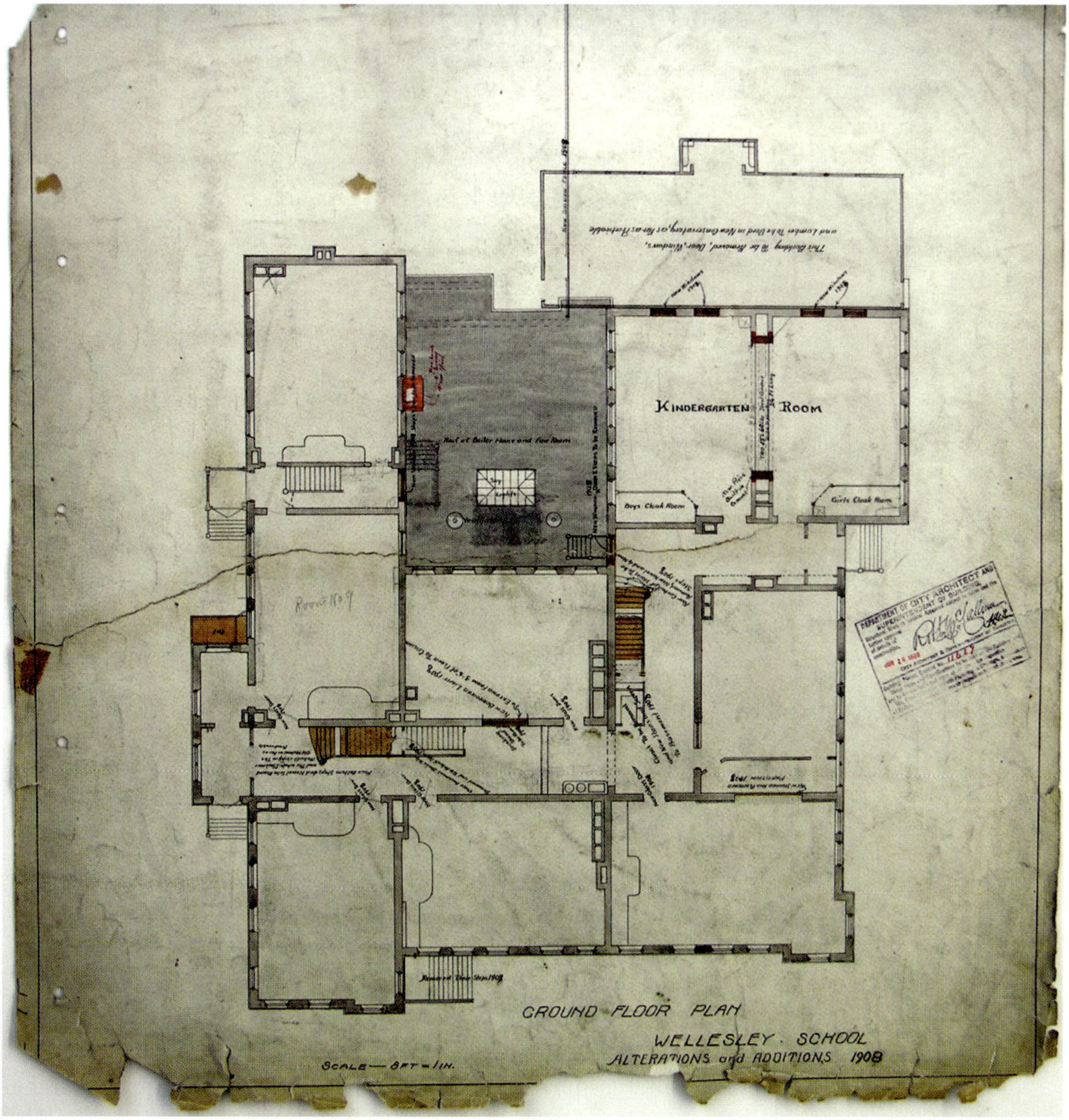

FIGURE 14.9 Wellesley School, alterations and additions, ground floor plan, 1908. (Sesquicentennial Museum and Archives, Toronto District School Board)

who established the first kindergarten in the United States, and Clara B. Hubbard of St. Louis be invited to Toronto to deliver lectures on the principles and methods of the kindergarten system. Other sources were available to Canadians on the inspirational Friedrich Froebel's theory of the kindergarten, or children garden in the United States, such as the translation by Milton Bradley (manufacturer of the Kindergarten Gifts, the designed objects used for Froebel's object lessons) of Froebel's book *Paradise of Childhood* (1869), and later Blow's publications on the subject. The excitement about kindergartens was palpable; the 1876 Philadelphia Centennial Exposition, for instance, had a full-size kindergarten in the Women's Pavilion.[29] Documents also show activities of building kindergartens in the city. The *School Management Report* for 1883 records payments made out to G.R. Hay and Company for $158.50 for kindergarten furniture, $85.00 for kindergarten supplies to James Bain and Son, and $15.00 for hiring of a piano to Mason and Risch.[30] However, the kindergarten at Victoria School in 1882 was simply a room fitted for kindergarten practice. Only in the 1890s was the kindergarten room strategically located at Winchester Street School, where it faced the hall and the main entrance.[31] Queen Alexandra Public School, Hughes Public School, Brown Public School, King Edward School, and Broadview Avenue School had similar arrangements, with the kindergarten as the special feature.

Like other changes throughout the decades, Wellesley's renovation (fig. 14.9) included the addition of a kindergarten, a large, rectangular room located beside the St. Albans Street entrance. The room contained boys' and girls' cloakrooms, and a moveable partition that could separate the space into two classrooms. The location of the kindergarten room in the girls' section of Wellesley Street School underlined the increasing social and cultural responsibility of children as women's labour. The same relationship was displayed at the Chicago World's Fair, where the model kindergarten was located in the Women's Pavilion, adjacent to the main building's entrance. The children-material culture-environment nexus was omnipresent, defining spatial relationships from the scale of a classroom to the school plan in the cultural landscapes of education.

Where are we in school design today? Conceptualizing school environments as landscapes is a good start. It recognizes that the modern classroom and school concept, along with the ossified children-material culture-environment nexus, continue to frame the way we think about school design. Hodgins, Caniff, Oldright, and Marean understood the health, safety, and educational imperatives in designing schools and had clear intentions in reforming children's educational spaces for the nineteenth-century world. Their experiences offer valuable lessons for us to consider a new educational landscape for the twenty-first century.

Notes

I am indebted to Greg McKinnon, David Sowerbutts, and Marie Passerino at the TDSB Sesquicentennial Museum and Archives for their tireless help and generosity. Thanks go to Annmarie Adams, Emmanuel Jannasch, and Ned Shantz, whose valuable comments put this paper into shape.

1 The Ontario Department of Education at the provincial level of laws and legislation, the Toronto School Board at the local level, and people (architects, builders, educationists, doctors, sanitarians, and city officials) are among those influential in the process.

2 For general history of the Ontario Department of Education, see J. Wilson, Robert M. Stamp, and Louis-Phillippe Audet, ed., *Canadian Education: A History*, (Scarborough: Prentice Hall, 1970); and R.M. Stamp, *The Schools of Ontario, 1876–1976* (Toronto: University of Toronto Press, 1982).

3 P. Horn, *The Victorian and Edwardian Schoolchild* (Gloucester: Alan Sutton, 1989).

4 For examples of nineteenth-century British photographs of schools, see Horn, *The Victorian and Edwardian Schoolchild*. For general introduction to using photographs of classrooms as historical evidence, see Ian Grosvenor, "On Visualing Past Classrooms," in *Silences and Images: The Social History of the Classroom*, ed. Ian Grosvenor, Martin Lawn, and Kate Rousmaniere, 85–104 (New York: Peter Lang, 1999).

5 For the location of the room at the Toronto Normal School Building, see Kai Wood Mah, "Classified Landscapes of Education: The Ontario Educational Exhibition of 1876," *Visual Studies* 22, no. 1 (April 2007).

6 For a general introduction, see Abigail A. Van Slyck's entry "School" in *The Encyclopedia of Twentieth-Century Architecture*, 1179–1181. For the most recent monograph on schools of Ohio, see Virginia E. McCormick, *Educational Architecture in Ohio: From One-Room Schools and Carnegie Libraries to Community Education Villages* (New York: Princeton Architectural Press, 2001).

7 Prue Chiles, "The Classroom as an Evolving Landscape," in *Children's Spaces*, ed. Mark Dudek, 101–113 (Amsterdam: Architectural Press, 2005). Also visit the website (www.teachernet.gov.uk/management/resourcesfinanceandbuilding/schoolbuildings/sbschoolsforthefuture/futureclassrooms/tef) for details on the research, including recent building codes, design issues, and materials. The UK firm Sall, Cullinan and Buck Architects (SCABAL) imagines an inclusive school as a collection of spread-out programmatic spaces informally integrated into the urban fabric. The firm was commissioned to produce design guidelines for the Department of Education and Employment, London, England.

8 For a landscape approach to studying the historical significations of educational spaces, see Dell Upton, "Lancasterian Schools, Republican Citizenship, and the Spatial Imagination in Early Nineteenth-Century America," *The Journal of the Society of Architectural Historian*, 55, no. 3 (September 1996): 238–253; and Abigail Van Slyck, *A Manufactured Wilderness: Summer Camps and the Shaping of American Youth, 1890–1960* (Minneapolis: University of Minnesota Press, 2006).

9 Robert Polidori, *Stern Fotografie*, no. 41 (Hamburg: Stern Gruner & Jahr AG & Co, 2006).

10 Toronto's transformation from a commercial town into a city occurred in the second half of the nineteenth century; see Donald Campbell Masters, *The Rise of Toronto, 1850–1890* (Toronto: University of Toronto Press, 1947).

11 The secretary's valuation of school property estimated a total cost of $16,500. Schools in the St. Lawrence Ward cost $4,000 and $9,000, in the financial statements for 1875. Quote from the inspector's report for 1874 in the *Sixteenth Annual Report of the Inspector of the Public Schools of the City of Toronto* (T. Hill & Son, Caxton Press: Toronto, 1975).

12 J. George Hodgins, *The School House* (Toronto: Copp, Clark, 1876), 14–15.

13 J. George Hodgins, *Hints and Suggestions on School Architecture and Hygiene* (Toronto: The Education Department, 1886), 115–117.

14 For a study of the neoclassical exterior and the modern interior of hospitals, see Annmarie Adams, "Modernism and Medicine: The Hospitals of Stevens and Lee, 1916–1932," *The Journal of the Society of Architectural Historian* 58, no. 1 (March 1999): 42–61.

15 William Caniff was the first medical officer (1883–1890), followed by Charles Sheard (1893–1910) and Charles Hastings (1910–1929). See Caniff's *Annual Report of the Local Board of Health, Showing the Sanitary work done during the year, and the Sanitary condition of the City of Toronto, including herein the Annual Report of the Medical Health Officer* of 1888, at the City of Toronto Archives. For a cultural history of the Department of Health, see Heather MacDougall, *Activists and Advocates: Toronto's Health Department, 1883–1983* (Toronto: Dundurn Press, 1990). Caniff's letter is in *Annual Report of the Health Board of 1889*, at the City of Toronto Archives.

16 Quoted from Caniff's letter.

17 *Annual Report of the Local Board of Health* of 1887, at the City of Toronto Archives.

18 Ibid.

19 Letter to E.F. Clarke, Esq., M.P.P., Major of Toronto, from W.M. Oldright on September 26th, 1891, in Norman Allen, *Report on the Sanitary Condition of the City of Toronto. Also an Account of the Operations of the Board of Health and the Vital Statistics for the Year 1891* (Toronto: J.Y. Reid, 1892), p. 23, at City of Toronto Archives, 1891 RG 11 Reports Box 109.

20 Ibid.

21 See "Imperfect Ventilation and Overcrowding at the Victoria Street School," *The Globe* (November 28, 1883).

22 "The State of the Public School," *The Globe* (December 5, 1883).

23 Of the 208,040 people in the city, 94,021 were of English origin and 96,070 were of Scottish or Irish descent. See Peter G. Goheen, *Victorian Toronto 1850 to 1900* (Chicago: University of Chicago, 1970).

24 Articles on school design in trade journals of the time criticized the school board architects' work. We start to see a competition between school board architects versus professional architects, with often the latter criticizing the poor work of the former. See *The Canadian Architect and Builder* 3, no. 9 (September 1890): 98.

25 Ibid.

26 Other schools show these changes. McCaul Street School of 1890 is typical. The Huron Street School employed the same type: the width of the hall and the pair of stairs on both sides made exiting easier than the previous design at Dewson, with one set of interior stairs and a narrow corridor. However, the additional windows on two sides of the classrooms and shorter circulation space made the McCaul-type plan difficult to enlarge, and thus it was short lived for practical reasons.

27 Summer camp culture began around the same time as manual training in public schools. See Van Slyck, *Manufactured Wilderness*.

28 Philosopher and writer John Dewey wrote extensively on children and pedagogy. See, for example, *The Child and the Curriculum* (Chicago: University of Chicago Press, 1956).

29 Mark Dudek, *Kindergarten Architecture: Space for the Imagination* (London: E& FN Spon, 1996).

30 Public School Board, *Minutes for 1883*, Appendix.

31 The report prepared by the Bureau of Municipal Research provides a summary of the plans of school buildings. *Interim Reports of the Toronto School Survey: I. The Physical Plant of the Toronto Public Schools. II. The Building Department of the Toronto Board of Education* (Toronto: Bureau of Municipal Research, 1920).

INNER VISIONS

LOREN LERNER

GEORGE REID'S PAINTINGS AS NARRATIVES OF A CHILD NATION

For the Canadian artist George Reid (1860–1947), fostering a national spirit through his art was of utmost importance. Reid's objective was to produce work that was distinctly Canadian with its own well-defined characteristics and expression of native sentiments.[1] In turn, his images were intended to evoke an emotional response in his fellow citizens, who would see themselves in his work. At the same time, they played the much larger role of manifesting values and qualities of life deemed meaningful for the Canadian nation. Relating to contemporary literary, social, and political life, his paintings were innately understood by Canadians who could extend his narrative with their own memories of childhood. What was created, ultimately, was a shared vision of nationhood.

The wellspring of Reid's creative inspiration was his boyhood on an Ontario farm. His memories of family life, and rural living in general, informed his personal narrative and significantly influenced his vision of the Canadian nation. Reid's story of his development as an artist can be understood in terms of Jerome Bruner's theory of the social construction of reality through narration.[2] Bruner believes that people "make sense" of their lives by organizing all images, sounds, and other sensory experiences into "stories" that link who they are in the present to their past and future actions. For Bruner, stories are not just situation-specific events that have meaning only for the people who experience them; rather, they are part of the process of "narrative accrual,"[3] which is the telling and retelling of analogous stories by many people. The result is a narrative that encapsulates tradition, history, and culture.

The main source of information on Reid's childhood is his official biography, which he commissioned in January 1940 at the age of eighty.[4] The writer was well-respected biographer Muriel Miller, who had considerable input from Reid and ready access to his personal papers during the two years she devoted to researching and writing the book.

The text reads like an autobiography, with recollections and anecdotes that closely interweave Reid's memories of people and events with his art practice. Reid relayed his life to Miller in a narrative account that, according to Bruner, sees Reid as "a Self acting more or less purposefully in a social world."[5] Due to the scarcity of paper during World War II, *G.A. Reid, Canadian Artist* was not published until 1946. It was revised in 1987 to include a catalogue of Reid's paintings, at which time it was also given a new title, *George Reid: A Biography*.

The revised edition begins with a section titled "From Farm to Easel" that describes Reid's early childhood on his parents' farm in Wingham County, Ontario. Reid's father in particular encouraged his son's education at school, at church, and at home. In fact, Adam Reid was instrumental in organizing a tour by a travelling library, which was housed in different area schools and farmhouses for a few months at a time. It was from the paintings reproduced in these books and magazines that young George learned about art, and at the age of eleven he firmly announced his intention of becoming an artist. While Reid's father believed in the intellectual development of the child through reading, he considered art an impractical and frivolous activity. He refused to acknowledge George's pictures and the prizes he won at local fairs for his drawings of animals. He believed, besides submitting to a divine will, that the proper life for a child was the physical activity of working a farm.[6]

As Reid explained to Miller, Adam insisted that his son become a farmer, a "nation builder" who would contribute to the foundation of Canada by cultivating its land. He had immigrated to Canada from Ireland at the age of twenty-four, and after working on a farm near Weston, Ontario, he staked his claim on an upland tract near Wingham, cleared the land for farming, and built a log house he called "The Homestead." It was very clear that Reid and his brothers were expected to follow his example and build their own homesteads.

Nonetheless, when Reid finished school in the spring of 1875 he decided it was time to go to Toronto to study art. Fate intervened when his brother Tom, who was doing the heavy work on the farm, crushed his hand in a straw cutter, and his other brother, John, busy running the adjoining farm to bring in cash for much-needed mortgage payments, forced Reid to postpone his departure. A year later, learning that an art school had been recently opened by the Ontario Society of Artists, he made plans to escape, which he kept secret because of his father's opposition. When his mother suddenly fell ill a second postponement became inevitable, and again his father had his own plans for his son. First he would put Reid to work building a new house for the family, and then he would apprentice him for three years to a local architect—his father had the legal right to apprentice him because he was underage, and in any event, he would learn a useful trade. When the architect's planing mill failed in the spring of 1878, Reid was released from the agreement, and his father gave him the proceeds from a load of wheat, some twenty-six dollars, to pay for his trip to Toronto and sustain him until he found a job.

BY JANUARY 1879 REID WAS ATTENDING EVENING CLASSES with the Ontario Society of Artists and working during the day in a machine shop at the Toronto Foundry. He stayed for four years, studying under Robert Harris (1849–1919), then spent three years in Philadelphia at the Academy of Fine Arts learning with Thomas Eakins (1844–1916). In 1885 he married the artist Mary Heister (1854–1921), and shortly after they set off on a study tour of England, France, Spain, and Italy. Following their trip they settled in Toronto, where Reid opened a studio, exhibited locally, and taught art classes. In 1888, he and his wife returned to Europe, and the next year Reid began twelve months of study at the Académie Julian in Paris.

Reid's desire to make his living as an artist was synonymous with his need to escape becoming a farmer, but his early artworks show that the ideals of rural life and the heroic efforts demanded by pioneer farming were central to his sense of identity. Reid's early sketches and studies described every facet of farm work, including *The Apple-Paring Bee*, *Maple Sugar Making*, *Threshing with a Flail*, *Mowing*, *Carrying Hod*, *Sowing*, *Milking*, *Logging*, *Making Straw Hats*, *Going to Church*, *Spinning*, *Shingle-Making*, and *Sugar-Making*.[7] Upon his return to Toronto from Paris in 1889, he announced his arrival as an artist with three epic paintings of farm life based on childhood memories, *The Story*, 1890 (fig. 15.1), *The Other Side of the Question*, 1890 (fig. 15.2), and *Mortgaging the Homestead*, 1890 (fig. 15.3). Working with sketches, he then made the backdrops for these large-scale works in his city studio, building the hayloft in a barn for *The Story*, part of a town council chamber for *The Other Side of the Question*, and the parlour of a farmhouse for *Mortgaging the Homestead*.

Painting the everyday life of rural Canadians made sense to Reid, who knew that genre painting was at its peak in Canada during the 1890s.[8] For example, Franklin Brownell's (1857–1946) paintings included *School Days*, c. 1890s, a picture of boys learning at a country school, and *Lamplight*, 1892, which showed a mother teaching her young child to read in the evening at home. William Brymner's (1885–1925) subject was pretty young girls in country settings, as can be seen in *A Wreath of Flowers*, 1884, and *Four Girls in a Meadow, Baie-Saint-Paul*, 1885. Frederick Sproston Challener's (1869–1959) paintings included a child at play, as in *Boy Fishing*, 1890, and a girl at domestic work, in *A Sewing Lesson*, 1896.

Admirers of images that focused on Canadian family subjects included urban Canadians with social aspirations and the intelligentsia. In 1894 the artist and art critic W.A.

Sherwood affirmed the place of genre in his essay "A National Spirit in Art," published in *Canadian Magazine*. "*Genré* pictures," he asserted, "awaken a love for the humbler walks of life, and a consequent respect for those therein depicted. We are touched by their sorrows and we are cheered by their joys, as we enter with unfeigned affection into the spirit of rural life."[9] Reid's genre paintings similarly convey a democratic view of human experience through the recounting of the everyday events of country living.

The Story depicts four boys sitting in a hayloft listening to a story being told by a fifth boy who is older. The sun shining through the barn window casts light on the face of the storyteller, whose gesticulating hands suggest he is in the midst of describing a dramatic scene. The younger boys are engrossed, and their response to the dramatic tale is recorded in facial expressions and postures. The oldest of the listeners, wearing a hat, listens pensively with his hand resting on his chin, while the youngest, seated almost in the shadows, has a look of intense concentration. The boy with his back to the viewer sits up straight, alert, unaware of his companion to the right, who stares at the storyteller, completely absorbed.

Following the conventions of genre painting, *The Story* reflects the Victorian mode of realist representation. The viewer is convinced of the genuineness of the narrative because of the artist's excessive attention to detail.[10] In *The Story* Reid emphasizes the individual facial features of the boys, the sheen on their clothing, the grainy texture of the hay, the roughness of the wooden planks around the window, and the makeshift quality of the wooden ladder. The painting's specificity suggests the artist's recalling of an event. The viewer takes part in the painting's reality, on some level aware that a space has been set aside for him (as a boy) to sit down next to the storyteller. In the process of viewing, he creates an imaginary story about the boys and the tale that is being told. The viewer becomes involved both in deciphering the painting and as an imagined part of the picture.

While the viewer interprets the story based on his own experiences, it is also necessary that other stories and pictures drawn from the surrounding culture confirm his interpretation. Furthermore, Reid assumes that the viewer will know immediately what type of story is being told. The meaning of the painting is, in Bruner's words, "so socially conventional, so well known in keeping with the canon, that we can assign it to some well rehearsed and virtually automatic interpretive routine."[11]

The interpretive activity evoked by *The Story* relies on a general knowledge of the art of storytelling and the kinds of stories that are of interest to boys. In the late nineteenth century it was common for families and friends to gather together and tell stories as a form of education and entertainment. Adventure tales were particularly appealing to male listeners and readers, in the books written by well-known Canadian authors such as Sir Charles G.D. Roberts (1860–1943) and Ernest Thompson Seton

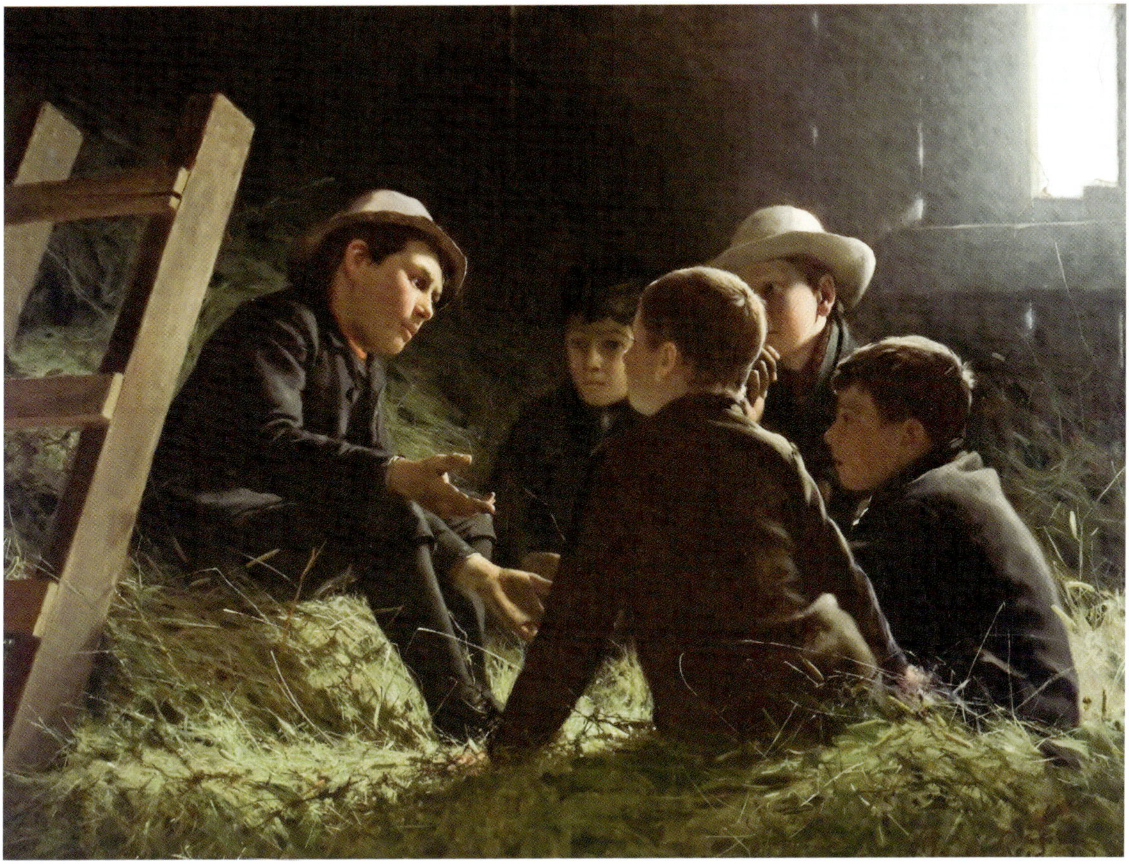

FIGURE 15.1 Untitled (*The Story*), 1890, oil on canvas, 123 × 164.3 cm. Winnipeg Art Gallery, gift from the Hugh F. Osler Estate.

(1860–1946).[12] Writing about Reid's *The Story* in 1895 in *The Monthly Illustrator*, Hjalmar Hjorth Boyesen assumes that the boys are holding a "secret rendezvous in the hayloft."[13] Away from "the actual routine of life, under the senseless compulsion of elders," the boys "harrow each other with gruesome tales of battle, murder, and sudden death." There is "nothing more enviable," Boyesen writes, "than the utterly self-oblivious enchantment of the listeners as they swallow greedily every preposterous detail of the gory plot."

Reid's painting of boys sitting together in a hayloft captures a country spirit very far from the confines of city living. In many respects, *The Story* is pure fiction. It negates the hardships of Reid's years on the farm to create instead the notion of an idyllic boyhood. In fact, the boys posing for the picture were not country boys at all but poor children from the city, one of them a fourteen-year-old orphan by the name of Owen Thomas Sullivan who lived in the St. Nicholas Working Boys Home on Lombard Street. Sullivan remembers wandering onto Yonge Street one day and hearing Reid call out to him to ask if he would model for the picture for ten cents an hour.[14] Reid presents an imagined reality that invites the viewer to participate in the illusion. Reid's audience was happy to comply. At the time Canadians were moving in large numbers to the city,[15] and many of Reid's contemporaries, fresh from the countryside, were nostalgic for country living. As Castell Hopkins, the editor of *Canada: An Encyclopaedia of the Country* wrote in 1900, "Up to within a decade or so Canadians have been emphatically an agricultural people, and it would seem that the vast unsettled lands of the country should maintain them in that condition … restlessness and ambition amongst the young … have tended to drive the young men from the plough."[16] The country boy took on a canonic status in expressions of the ideal of rural life. In "Back on the Farm," for example, a poem written in 1897 by Jean Blewett, a boy's memories of his youth on the farm are celebrated.[17] It ends with this verse:

> A longin' takes me on these days
> When all the world gets warm,
> A-longin' just to be a boy—
> A boy back on the farm.

The man in Blewett's poem longs to be a boy again, when springtime meant life and freedom. Similarly, the boys in *The Story* awaken in the viewer a yearning to break away from the stresses of the urban present and return to an ideal pastoral past, free from adult obligations. The boys, however, are not simply a reminder of childhood; they also embody a set of middle-class values about boyhood, nature, tradition, national spirit, and citizenship. This notion of imposing adult values on children had its origins in the writings of Jean-Jacques Rousseau, whose concept of an ideal education for boys could be found in his 1762 publication *Emile: or, On Education*.[18] Rousseau demonstrates that an education, which begins with a boy's interaction with the physical world, leads to the nourishment and maturation of his mental faculties. Training in nature is the first step in training men to be free citizens of a democratic nation.[19]

The Rousseauian concept of boyhood was popular in North America in the nineteenth century and found frequent expression in the paintings of boys by the American artists Eastman Johnson (1834–1906), Winslow Homer (1836–1910), and John George Brown (1831–1913).[20] The subject matter symbolized the quintessential country boy whose self-reliance, love of adventure, and harmony with nature forecasted the conduct of male citizenry.[21] Johnson's series of barn interiors, *The Quiet Hour*, *Children in the Barn*, and *Barn Swallows*, painted in the late 1870s, could be a precedent for Reid's *The Story*.[22] While Reid's painting suggests the visual image of the country boy by these

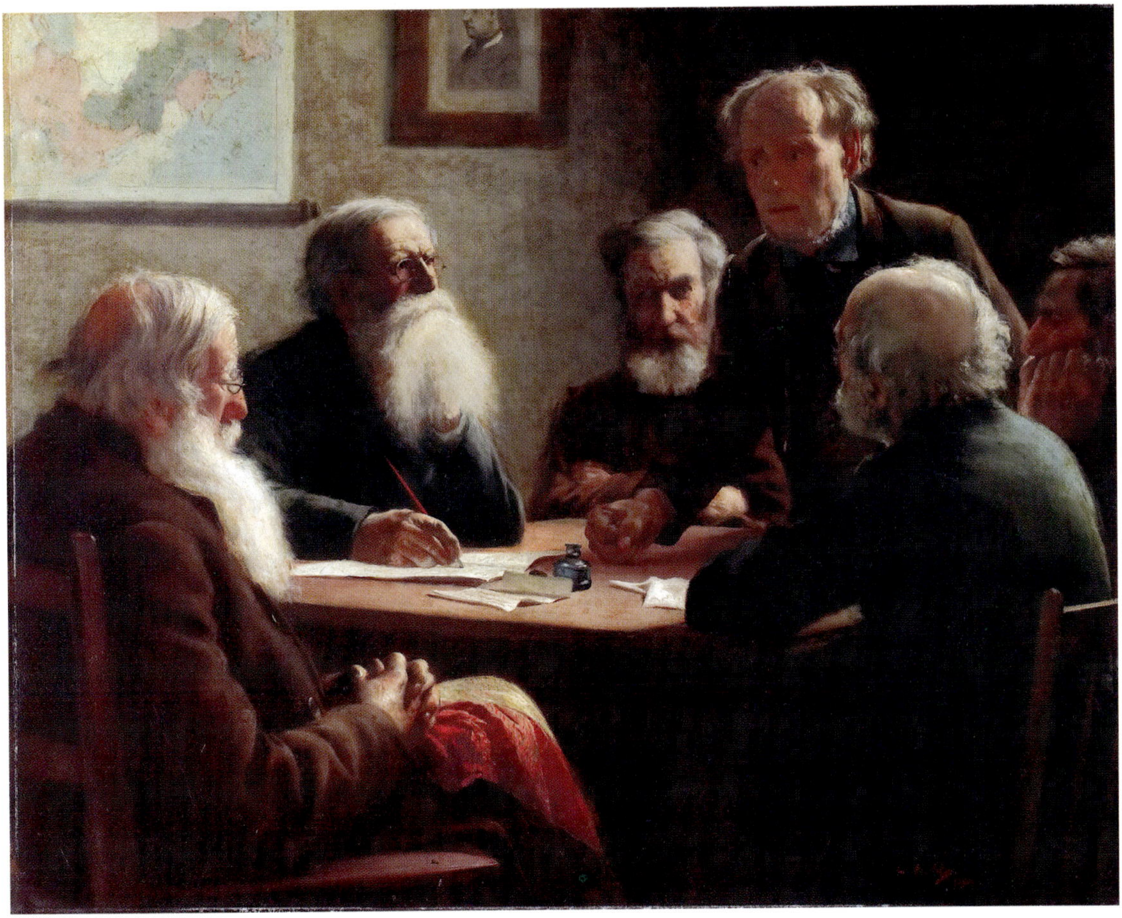

FIGURE 15.2 *The Other Side of the Question*, 1890, oil on canvas, 104.0 × 132.5 cm. Art Gallery of Ontario, purchase 1985.

American artists, he transformed the context to suit a Canadian concept of boyhood and the men the boys would become.

Reid's idea of citizenship is imbedded both in the depiction of the boys in *The Story* and in how this work relates to *The Other Side of the Question*, the second of the three paintings he made in 1890. The representation of male leaders at a town council meeting was described by an art critic in 1893 as "a number of old men evidently discussing some knotty point, some of the faces eager and excited, all interested we know, even the back of a head shows that."[23] The plots of the two paintings seem to be very different, but by connecting the episode of *The Story* to that of *The Other Side of the Question* in Bruner's process of narrative accrual, they become one coherent story about how the experience of being a Canadian boy relates to manhood. The boys in *The Story* can be seen as either the forerunners or offspring of the men at the council. Their free spirit, imagination, and camaraderie typify fundamental values that lead to good governance as exemplified by this sage group of men. The contemporary map of Canada and the print of Queen Victoria on the wall emphasize that the narrative takes place in Canada and that the picture is imbued with the virtues of Canadian life.

The similarities in the composition of the two works also encourage the idea that they are associated. Like the boys in *The Story*, the farmers in *The Other Side of the Question* are gathered in a circle as they listen to someone speak. A space in the forefront of the painting recalls the space in *The Story* that invites the viewer, presumably a male (again), to enter into the scene. In *The Other Side of the Question* the person talking is not the oldest male, but the youngest, and he obviously has a different opinion. His fist pounding on the table indicates his agitation in contrast to the composed manners of his older colleagues, who are listening to this other point of view. The attentiveness that characterizes the boys at play in *The Story* has progressed to the seriousness, responsibility, and much more complex personal relationships that mark male leadership. The connection between father and son is evoked by the connection between the two paintings. Not surprisingly, the man sitting next to the dissenting male looks like Reid's father, Adam, whose portrait he painted in 1886.[24]

The Other Side of the Question validates the idea that the farmer who cultivates the land is the political and moral bedrock of the nation. In fact, the earliest concept of citizenry in Canada identified the citizen as a farmer. In 1894 William K. McNaught, president of the National Club in Toronto, wrote that Canada's farming pioneers "were rough and perhaps uncouth" but an "honest and light-hearted" people who understood the concept of community. Dependent on their neighbours for assistance, they "willingly shared of their plenty with those who were less fortunate.... Nothing binds people more closely together than common hardships and common efforts to surmount them."[25] McNaught was only pointing out what was widely believed. Farming life cultivated virtue.[26] It was also believed that farmers would inculcate these values in their children and could be relied upon to recognize educated and intelligent leaders in their own community. Reid's *The Other Side of the Question* presupposes a solid citizenry that thrives in a culture where the democratic values that nourish nationhood can accommodate the airing of different views and change.

While Reid's *The Story* is reminiscent of the paintings of Eastman Johnson, *The Other Side of the Question* owes a debt to the Canadian artist Robert Harris, who was Reid's teacher at the Ontario Society of Artists. Harris's painting *A Meeting of the School Trustees* from 1885 shows a young woman schoolteacher defending educational reform

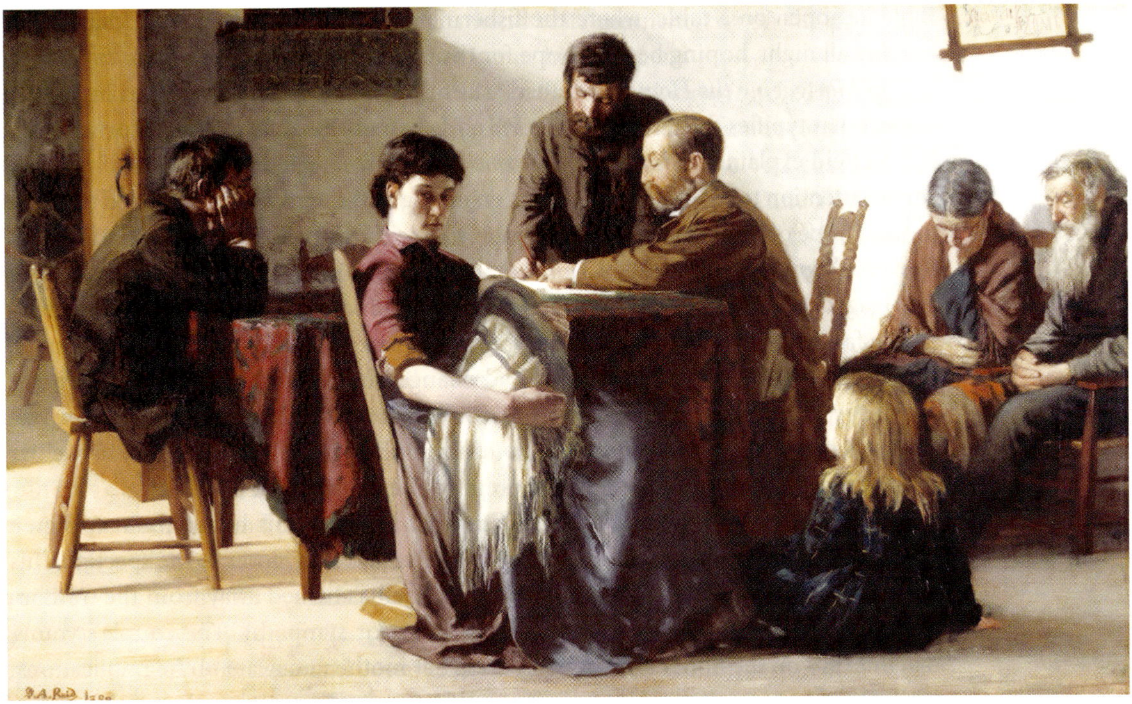

FIGURE 15.3 *Mortgaging the Homestead*, 1890, oil on canvas, 128.3 × 212.1 cm. National Gallery of Canada, Royal Canadian Academy of Arts Diploma Work, deposited 1890.

to a group of older men seated around a table. This is the leitmotif that Reid appropriated for *The Other Side of the Question*. In contrast, the third painting, *Mortgaging the Homestead*, introduces a very different kind of story and source of inspiration.

Of the three paintings done in 1890, *Mortgaging the Homestead* comes closest to the circumstances that motivated Reid to become an artist. Reid's earliest contact with art was through the illustrations in British books and magazines, a part of the lending library that sustained his creative imagination during his youth. British genre art often favoured the country cottage motif, those depictions of family rural life that took place in the modest interior of the home. Canadians were accustomed to seeing this kind of picture, in the form of published illustrations and as reproductions of paintings by the many artists who specialized in this subject matter. Well-known English artists such as Samuel Luke Fildes (1844–1927) and Frank Bramley (1857–1915) more often than not emphasized the tragedies of family life. For example, in Fildes's *The Doctor*, 1891, a little boy lies on two mismatched chairs in a humble cottage, watched over by a doctor by his side, his parents hovering in the shadows. In *A Hopeless Dawn* by Bramley, 1888, a large modes of presentation of *The Story* and *Mortgaging the Homestead*. An example of his work during this period is *Forbidden Fruit*, 1890, which depicts a country youth lying in a hayloft devouring a book. The youngster, who looks like the older boy in *The Story*, is Reid's memory of himself reading *Arabian Nights*, a tale of erotic fantasy that he had to read in secret to avoid his father's disapproval. Another painting from this time is *Family Prayer*, 1890, which is a more hopeful version of *Mortgaging the Homestead*. It portrays a family gathered in prayer before breakfast. The father's torn shirt suggests a life of poverty and hard work. Nonetheless, he leads the family in prayer, his face raised to the light shining through the window, evoking the piety and devotion that keeps a family such as this together.

Reid's paintings of families and children were grounded in the commonly held idea that farming families act according to a collective set of beliefs and desires. These depictions of rural society, in showing both acceptable and unacceptable ways to behave, had an important purpose in the mind of the artist. As he would often say in interviews and public lectures, he did not believe in art for art's sake. A painting should also serve a "utilitarian" principle. For Reid, "morals and aesthetics in the highest sense cannot be separated. No true touch of the artist's hand can be given without relation to the fitness of things."[35] The family values Reid grew up with determined his view of his role as an artist. According to Reid, an artist should "express himself for the sake of his devotion to the beautiful, for his love of truth, for his desire that life should be made to develop all its noblest possibilities."[36] Narrative paintings centred on the rural life of the child and the family were a means to accomplishing this end.

Reid continued to assert his beliefs and values in the paintings he submitted to the World's Columbian Exposition in Chicago in 1893.[37] In the Canadian section of the exposition, among the portraits, landscapes, still lifes, and genre paintings of fellow Canadian artists, he exhibited three works devoted to rural life: *The Visit of the Clockmaker*, c. 1892, *Lullaby*, 1892, and *The Foreclosure of the Mortgage*, 1893 (fig. 15.4). *The Visit of the Clockmaker* was painted in memory of Joseph Shuter, a clock cleaner and distant cousin who had spent a winter at the homestead when Reid was a boy. In the painting some boys gaze appreciably at the aged craftsman at work, his artisan skills rare in the new era of industrial production. As a grandfatherly figure, he seems like a holdover from the past and at the same time a reminder of the tenuous relationship of older people with the changing community. *Lullaby* shows a young mother caressing her child, an image that suggests the simple country life and the mother's centrality to the well-being of her family. *The Foreclosure of the Mortgage* revisits the narrative of *Mortgaging the Homestead*, but this time more directly depicts a tragic ending to the story. The effect of the mortgage on the family's welfare is no longer simply dread; the mortgage cannot be paid, and the family is being thrown out of their home and off the land by the callous sheriff

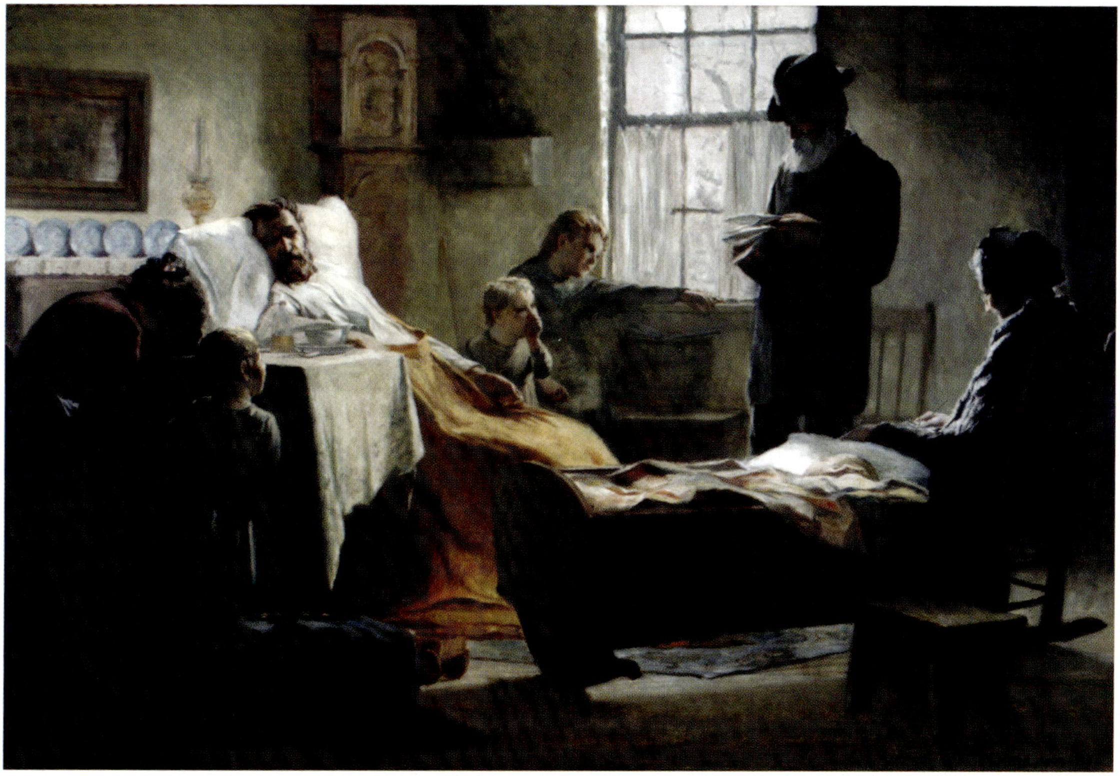

FIGURE 15.4 *The Foreclosure of the Mortgage*, 1934 (replica of original canvas dated 1893, destroyed in fire in 1919), oil on canvas, 180.3 × 276.9 cm. Government of Ontario Art Collection, Archives of Ontario, Toronto.

who stands in front of the dying father. The positioning of the family members and the banker brings to mind the theatrical setting of a dramatic performance. The father and his children are on one side of the painting, illuminated by the light from the window, while the banker on the opposite side stands apart reading the verdict. The farmer looks sadly toward the viewer while his wife and mother, consumed by grief, sit in relative darkness at the margins of the scene.

The passionate outcry of *The Foreclosure of the Mortgage* contributed to its resounding success at the exposition, where it was awarded a bronze medal. A critical factor in its reception was Reid's portrayal of the family's children. The correspondent for *The Montreal Weekly Witness* reported on the reactions of viewers who wanted nothing more than to protect them from harm.[38] One said, "It almost seems to me that I could put my hand on that child's hand by the table." Another declared, "What a pity to have these dear little children homeless."

Compassion, tenderness, sympathy, and indignation were some of the moral values aroused by the children's natural beauty and innocent expressions. The *Witness* also emphasized the children when describing the work: "Seated on the bench beside the pail is a graceful girl in simple attire. One hand lies in her lap, the other is reaching out on the window sill. Her eyes are downcast and her whole attitude is that of quiet suspense." Directly in front of the father, who is lying on his death bed, is "the heirloom—the old wooden cradle—and in it lies a sleeping infant with its face toward the window. The flushed and rounded cheek, the noble brow, the peaceful sleep, the easy position as it lies tucked with a home-made coloured blanket, and the wonderful effect of the light on the child, cover, cradle and rug show the genius of the artist." To the left, "we see leaning in the elder sister's knee a little girl with her thumb in her mouth looking up inquiringly into the man's face.... Opposite him [the dying father] on the front side of the table, with his face towards the window, stands a chubby, two-year old boy. He has left his little cart and is on tiptoe trying to peer over the corner of the table at the man." The critic's reaction is determined by the age of each child, from the unknowing infant in its cradle, to the little boy and girl who are curiously surveying the scene, to the older girl by the window who is fully aware of what is taking place. It is clear that in this "wondrous story of human endeavour, defeat, submission and love," the child serves the ideological function of propagating values based on the love of family and tradition and the hope for a better future.[39]

The Foreclosure of the Mortgage, however, was not without its critics. Months before the painting's enthusiastic reception at the Chicago Exposition, a negative review had appeared in *Arcadia*, a Canadian magazine specializing in art and cultural affairs. The editor's remarks after seeing *The Foreclosure of the Mortgage* at the annual exhibition of the Royal Canadian Academy of Arts expressed the growing dislike for narrative art as an outmoded type of representation. He wrote, "It is a style that always has numerous admirers among spectators. We must confess that such a mournful tale has little charm for us. The sentiment in a subject of that kind should be suggestive, rather than forced on the mind by cumulated appropriateness of detail."[40] The criticism was directed at the painting's overt realism and its melodramatic mood.

Although this kind of negative review was rare, Reid was quickly becoming disillusioned with his paintings of the everyday life of rural Canadians. In fact, he had begun to believe that genre pictures were inadequate for expressing Canada's national spirit. In 1892, during a visit to Paris, he studied the mural decorations of Puvis de Chavannes (1824–1898) that decorated the Hotel de Ville, Pantheon, and Sorbonne.[41] He wanted to determine how the artist expressed the ideals of the French nation with representations influenced by classicism and Italian Renaissance art.[42] At the Chicago Exposition, Reid saw that architects, painters, sculptors, and decorators had collaborated to produce a uniquely American art espousing national ideals, and that these also originated in Greek and Roman sources.[43] For example, in the *Columbian Fountain* by Frederick MacMonnies (1863–1937), the female Barge of State was guided by Feminine Fame and propelled by eight female allegorical figures, including Music, Architecture, Sculpture, Painting, Agriculture, Science, Industry, and Commerce. On the inside of the dome of the Manufacturers and Liberal Arts Building, Edwin Blashfield (1848–1936) had depicted the arts of the goldsmith, the ironworker, the maker of armour, and the worker in bronze as allegorical women. In Marie Cassatt's (1844–1926) mural *Modern Woman*, on display in the Woman's Building, the artist had created a modern parable where women and girls pluck the fruits of knowledge and science in a contemporary version of an Arcadian garden.

Reid's newfound belief in the importance of mural decoration for the expression of Canadian nationhood was thwarted by the lack of opportunity and funding to paint murals in public buildings. Despite this lack of support, he became widely known in Canada for his persistence in promoting mural painting. Given the positions he held at various important institutions and societies—he was a founding member of the Toronto Guild of Civic Art in 1897 and the Canadian Society of Applied Art in 1901, and was principal of the Central Ontario School of Art and Design (now the Ontario College of Art and Design) from 1901 to 1929, president of the Ontario Society of Artists between 1897 and 1902, and president of the Royal Canadian Academy of Arts (RCA) from 1906 to 1907—he had various venues to promote his message. In April 1904, a pivotal moment for Reid's new ambition occurred when Canadian prime minister Sir Wilfrid Laurier responded encouragingly to a letter written by Reid and signed by the members of the executive of the RCA proposing a scheme of mural paintings for the entrance hall of the Parliament Buildings in Ottawa.[44] The scheme, initially called *Canada Receiving the Homage of Her Faithful Sons* but later revised to *Canada Receiving the Homage of Her Children*, was described in the letter as "a pageant of brilliant colour with a centre where a figure symbolical of Canada, supported by figures representing the Provinces, and pages bearing the coats of arms, receives with acclaim the homage of her children." It was not surprising that Reid picked the theme *Canada Receiving the Homage of Her Children*, wherein a procession of families would represent the Canadian people. Emphasizing children both symbolically as the nation's progeny and realistically by depicting actual children made good sense to Reid because it would remind the public of his previous paintings of children, which had been so successful.

Despite Reid's tenacious attempts from 1904 to 1907 to move the project forward, the mural scheme failed to receive government support. Only two preparatory murals were created as a result of the proposal, *Hail Dominion* (1906) by Gustav Hahn (1866–1962) and Reid's *Ave Canada* (1907–1918), both including children and painted on the artists' own initiative. In Hahn's *Hail Dominion*, the nation is allegorized in the grouping of Mother Canada and her nine provincial "daughters." In Reid's *Ave Canada*, the central symbolic image of Canada is a queen mother, with the Canadian provinces depicted as princesses. A young knight stands to the side of "Canada" carrying the Canadian flag. Two winged female figures represent Britain and France, and each holds a scroll signifying the code of law of the founding nation as they crown the personification of Canada with a wreath. Infants representing Canada's progeny cuddle with the "provinces," while children at the forefront of the composition offer the country's harvest of fruits and vegetables. Family groupings on both sides of the painting depict the civic, industrial, rural, and artistic occupations of Canadians and offer homage to a new sovereignty envisioned as an extended royal family. The pageant takes place in a landscape setting where the serenity of the forest, lake, hills, and sky complements the dignity of the people who are gathered in the meadow. In this way, the landscape allegorizes the nation as a rural family nurtured by the fecundity of the land.

With *Ave Canada*, Reid attempted to release himself from the predictable conventions of genre art to construct another form of narrative, an allegory, that expanded the meaning of his stock of family characters. As well, he was generating imaginative associations with the Canadian landscape to stimulate the viewer to see a new and expanded national sentiment. There is more than one way of telling a story, Bruner explains; innovations occur not only "in the content of the imagination but in its modus operandi."[45] Reid's *Ave Canada*, however, failed to garner public support because it was not a narrative that Canadians cared to understand. As Margaret Fairbairn wrote in her article on Reid in the November 1907 issue of *Canadian Magazine*, since the 1890s, "after two lengthy trips abroad" and "due in part to foreign influence," all of Reid's art "has been confined to mural decoration." She continues, "Not a few of the artist's admirers, have expressed a wish that he would return to his earlier manner."[46] In Bruner's terms, Reid's allegorical painting lacked "context sensitivity and negotiability," ingredients that are key if others are to comprehend and assimilate a narrative on their own terms.[47] As early as 1894, James Mavor had questioned the use of classical imagery in mural art, recommending that dense allegorical themes be replaced with straightforward contemporary subjects:

> A laboured attempt to illustrate a recondite allusion or to express in paint that which is probably not susceptible on any terms of being so expressed is apt to miss its point so far as concerns the average observer, while the story which is so simply told on canvas as to be intelligible to a child may also be the most interesting to the cultivated intelligence.[48]

Like many of the intellectual leaders of his time, Mavor was convinced that art's main objective should be the education of Canada's youth. William A. Sherwood agreed. When writing about the "national spirit in art" and the role of genre painting in pursuing this end, Sherwood emphasized the education of the young person, starting with the very young child: "In the nursery and in the schoolroom, during our very impressionable period of child-life, it is indeed, no easy task to determine the influences which are at work moulding the youthful mind. The silent language of pictures must, upon the very earliest dawn of intelligence, communicate its simple stories to the child."[49] Mavor and Sherwood expressed the opinion of the majority of Canadians, that art should not be an esoteric medium but a vehicle to guide Canada's youth. This is also what Reid intended, but perhaps he had gone too far in the complex allegorical references to child and nation of *Ave Canada*.

According to what Reid told his biographer Muriel Miller, his upbringing on the farm and his early contact with art were the guiding forces that remained with him his whole life. In his paintings, Canada's youth were often a central force in communicating his ideas about Canadian society, because he recognized that his viewers' life stories were similar to his own. More than likely Reid ceased painting realistic depictions of farm children because he recognized that the agrarian foundation he knew as a child was no longer a foundational force for many Canadians. The British homesteaders who arrived in Canada between 1896 and 1914 were different from his grandparents and parents in that they had great difficulties adjusting to the frontier environment and quickly moved to the city.[50] Furthermore, the country's rural population was being transformed by Ukrainians, Hungarians, Icelanders, Mennonites, Doukhobors, and Hutterites who travelled to western Canada in large numbers and established tight-knit communities that retained many Old World customs.[51] *Ave Canada* was Reid's attempt to sustain his ideal of the English rural family, bound to traditional values and a love of nature, in the face of the transformation taking place in Canada's farming communities.

Reid stayed the course, adhering in his art and actions to a core narrative that focused on Canada's children. At least two examples from his later years demonstrate that the child continued to play a role in his construction of reality. The first is a series of murals he painted on the walls of the auditorium of a high school in Toronto, Jarvis Collegiate Institute, between 1928 and 1929.[52] The works are part of a World War I war memorial. In the mural titled *Sacrifice*, cadets guard the cenotaph and hold the drooping flags of Great Britain and Canada, while a Girl Guide kneels and places a wreath at its base. Other cadets and Boy Scouts stand at attention on either side as family groups, students, educators, artists, national leaders, and children approach the monument bearing flowers and wreaths expressing homage to the memory of the dead. In the second large mural, *Patriotism* (fig. 15.5) Canada is a female figure standing on a raised dais.

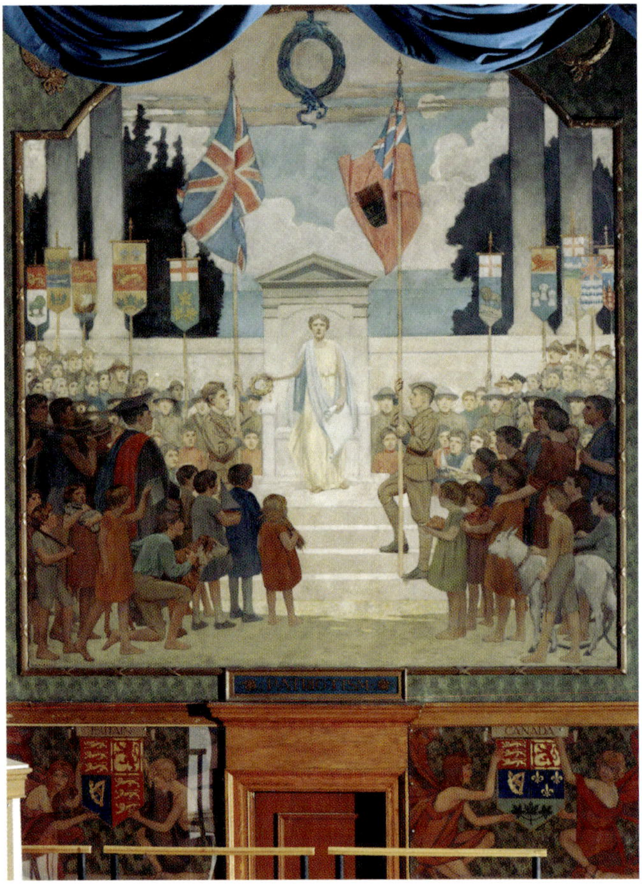

FIGURE 15.5
Patriotism, 1929, oil on canvas, 411.48 × 457.2 cm. Auditorium, Jarvis Collegiate Institute, Toronto. (Photo: Isaac Applebaum)

Gathered around the figure of Canada are groups representing the family, law, education, labour, government, and defence, each expressing homage to the nation. School cadets bear the flags of Great Britain and Canada, while in the near background soldiers and Boy Scouts fill the width of the composition. At Jarvis, the depiction of Canada allegorically through the imagery of its children references the students who attended the school, including the cadets and Boy Scouts who occupy the central spaces of the paintings as the nation's future defenders.

The second example also relates to Reid's interest in the education of Canada's youth. In 1944 Reid bequeathed his collection of 459 paintings to the government of Ontario's Department of Education.[53] The larger canvases were to be placed in the Parliament Buildings, the medium-sized canvases were to be sent on permanent loan to teacher-training institutions, and the collection of small paintings were to form travelling exhibitions that would be made available to the province's schools. With titles like *Black Spruces*, *Agawa Valley*, *Trout Brook*, and *The Dark Canyon*, these landscapes, a subject he had begun painting in the 1920s, were empty of children. Importantly, though, his intention was for the paintings to be seen by children at school; even if the children were living in towns and cities, the landscapes would, he hoped, promote their connection to Canada and a love of Canada's land. Furthermore, the idea of circulating the paintings to schools across the province was reminiscent of the lending library of Reid's youth, where he first encountered reproductions of art in books and magazines. Not having seen a painting until he was eighteen years old,[54] perhaps Reid wanted to give these children what he had lacked in his own education.

In accordance with Bruner's concept of narration, Reid was a storyteller who linked his own personal experiences as a child with his vision of the Canadian nation. Thus, the boys in *The Story* and *Forbidden Fruit* became the children of *Ave Canada*, *Sacrifice*, and *Patriotism*. They were "tokens" of a story that connected the memories of Reid's youth with an idealization of Canada's potential as a nation. As Bruner also observes, a cornerstone of narrative theory is the assumption that there are basic social contracts that, when violated, must be explained and rectified.[55] For example, stories present a problem and describe the characters' response to that problem, after which they usually provide a solution. From the forceful persuasion of *Mortgaging the Homestead* and *The Foreclosure of the Mortgage* to the gentle spirit of *The Visit of the Clockmaker* and *Lullaby*, Reid's story begins with genre paintings that postulate that society has a moral contract, in the sense of implying rights, duties, privileges, and responsibilities, to protect the child, the family, and the agrarian way of life. When the contract is not respected, the whole nation is put at risk.

Although *Ave Canada*, *Sacrifice*, and *Patriotism* are different from these earlier paintings in that they are allegories, the message is the same, though somewhat extended. The premise is that children, if they are to become good citizens and the guardians of future generations, must learn the meaning of family. They must also undertake the duties and obligations of being Canadian, including the giving of one's life to protect the nation. Finally, they must recognize the importance of Canada's natural environment. As such, Reid's significant donation to Canadian school children demonstrates his ongoing belief that he could positively influence the acceptance of those values that would foster a robust national spirit and a strong Canada.

Notes

1 John George Bourniot, "National Sentiment in Canada," *University Quarterly Review* 1, no. 1 (February 1890): 3–23.
2 Jerome Bruner, "The Narrative Construction of Reality," *Critical Inquiry* 18 (Autumn 1991): 1–21.
3 Ibid., 8.
4 Muriel Miller, *George Reid: A Biography* (Toronto: Summerhill Press, 1987). First edition published under the name Muriel Miller Miner and title *G.A. Reid, Canadian Artist* (Toronto: Ryerson Press, 1946).
5 Bruner, "Narrative Construction," 8.
6 Neil Sutherland, *Children in English-Canadian Society: Framing the Twentieth-Century Consensus* (Toronto: University of Toronto Press, 1976), 10.
7 Miller, *George Reid*, 49.
8 Gabriel P. Weisberg and Petra Ten-Doesschate Chu, *Redefining Genre: French and American Painting 1850–1900* (Seattle: University of Washington Press, 1995).
9 W.A. Sherwood, "A National Spirit in Art," *Canadian Magazine* 3, no. 6 (October 1894): 499.
10 Julia Thomas, *Victorian Narrative Painting* (London: Tate, 2000).
11 Bruner, "Narrative Construction," 9.
12 Spanning the late nineteenth and early twentieth centuries, Ernest Thompson Seton and Sir Charles G.D. Roberts wrote books about the Canadian wilderness for and about children. Examples include *Wild Animals I Have Known*, *The Trail of the Sandhill Stag*, and *Lives of the Hunted* by Seton and *The Heart of the Ancient Wood*, *The Kindred of the Wild*, and *The Watchers of the Trails* by Roberts.
13 Hjalmar Hjorth Boyesen, "Boyhood and Girlhood," *The Monthly Illustrator* 4, no. 12 (April 1895): 6.
14 Lotta Dempsey, "A Sell-Out for Carol," *Toronto Daily Star* (January 30, 1967): 38-News.
15 Sutherland, *Children in English-Canadian Society*, 24–25: "Despite the great growth in agriculture and other rural activities, the percentage of the population that lived in urban areas more than doubled over forty years, going from 23.3 per cent in 1881 to 29.8 in 1891, 34.9 in 1901, 41.8 in 1911, and 47.4 in 1921."
16 J. Castell Hopkins, "The Canadian People and Political Parties," in *Canada: An Encylopaedia of the Country*, vol. 6, ed. J. Castell Hopkins, 195 (Toronto: Linscott, 1900).
17 Jean Blewett, *The Heart Songs* (Toronto: G. Morang, 1897; repr., CIHM no. 00143, http://www.canadiana.org), 165–167.
18 Jean-Jacques Rousseau, *Emile: or, On Education*, introd., trans., and notes by Allan Bloom (New York: Basic Books, 1979).
19 Leslie F. Claydon, ed. and introd., *Rousseau on Education* (London: Collier-Macmillan, 1969).
20 Elizabeth Johns, *American Genre Painting: The Politics of Everyday Life* (New Haven, CT: Yale University Press, 1991).
21 Sarah Burns, "The Barefoot Boys and Other Country Children: Sentiment and Ideology in Nineteenth-century American Art," *American Art Journal* 20, no. 1 (1988): 24–50.
22 Patricia Hills, *The Genre Painting of Eastman Johnson: The Sources and Development of His Style and Themes* (New York: Garland, 1977).
23 Anon. "The Study and Work of Mr. G.A. Reid," *The Lake Magazine* (Toronto) 1, no. 7 (February 1893): 427.
24 See reproduction of Adam Reid portrait, Christine Boyanoski, *Sympathetic Realism: George A. Reid and the Academic Tradition* (Toronto: Art Gallery of Ontario, 1986), 59.

25 William K. McNaught, "Pioneers of the Canadian Farm," in *Canada: An Encylopaedia of the Country*, vol. 5, ed. Castell Hopkins, 23 (Toronto: Linscott, 1900).
26 Carl Berger, *The Sense of Power* (Toronto: University of Toronto Press, 1970), 175: "One of the fundamental features of Canadian imperialist social thought was an idealized conception of agriculture and a tendency to regard it as the most healthy foundation of national life."
27 G.A. Reid, "The Evolution of Two of My Pictures," *Massey's Magazine* 1, no. 1 (January 1896): 14.
28 A.L.O.M., *The Brock Family* (Toronto: W. Briggs, c. 1890; repr., CIHM no. 30197, http://www.canadiana.org), 17.
29 Ibid., 18.
30 Joanna E. Wood, *The Untempered Wind* (New York: J.S. Tait, c. 1894; repr. CIHM no. 26048, http://www.canadiana.org), 49.
31 Ibid., 57.
32 *Official Report of the Debates of the House of Commons of Canada; First Session, Seventh Parliament ... Comprising the Period from the Tenth Day of July to the Twentieth Day of August, Inclusive* (Ottawa: B. Chamberlin, 1891, scanned from the microfiche held by Micromedia, Colonial Government Journals, http://www.canadiana.org), 2096.
33 *Official Report of the Debates of the House of Commons of Canada; First Session, Seventh Parliament ... Comprising the Period from the Twenty-first Day of August to the Thirtieth Day of September, Inclusive* (Ottawa: B. Chamberlin, 1891, scanned from the microfiche held by Micromedia, Colonial Government Journals, http://www.canadiana.org), 4893.
34 Bruner, "Narrative Construction," 15.
35 Reid, "The Evolution of Two of My Pictures," 11.
36 Ibid., 14.
37 Canadian Department of Fine Art. *World's Columbian Exposition, 1893, Catalogue of Paintings* (Toronto: C.B. Robinson, 1893).
38 Anon, "Canadian Art in the Art Palace of the White City (Special Correspondence of 'Witness')," *The Montreal Weekly Witness* (August 30, 1893): 10.
39 Julia Thomas, *Pictorial Victorians: The Inscription of Values in Word and Image* (Athens: Ohio University Press, 2004).
40 Anon. *Arcadia* [Review of the Annual Exhibition of the Royal Canadian Academy of Arts] 1, no. 21 (March 1, 1893): 49.
41 Rosalind Pepall, "The Murals in the Toronto Municipal Buildings: George Reid's Debt to Puvis de Chavannes," *The Journal of Canadian Art History* 9, no. 2 (1986): 142–161.
42 Claudine Mitchell, "Time and Idea of Patriarchy in the Pastorals of Puvis de Chavannes," *Art History* 10, no. 2 (June 1987): 188–202; Jennifer L. Shaw, "Imagining the Motherland: Puvis de Chavannes, Modernism and the Fantasy of France," *Art Bulletin* 79, no. 6 (December 1997): 586–610.
43 Howard Mumford Jones, "The Renaissance and American Origins," *Ideas in America* (Cambridge: Harvard University Press, 1944), 140–151; Erika Doss, *Twentieth-Century American Art* (New York: Oxford University Press, 2002), 19–33.
44 George A. Reid et al., Letter to The Right Honourable Sir Wilfrid Laurier, Ottawa, April 1904 (Ottawa: National Archives of Canada, Prime Ministers' Fond, Wilfrid Laurier), 225911-13.
45 Bruner, "Narrative Construction," 15.
46 Margaret L. Fairbairn, "The Art of George A. Reid," *Canadian Magazine* 22, no. 1 (November 1903): 6.
47 Bruner, "Narrative Construction," 116.

48 James Mavor, *Notes on the Objects of the Toronto Guild of Civic Art and on the Exhibition of Prints of Mural Paintings with Condensed Catalogue* (Toronto: Rowsell & Hutchison, 1898), 6.
49 Sherwood, "National Spirit in Art," 498.
50 R.G. Moyles and Doug Owram, "'A Farm of One's Own': The British Emigrant's View of Western Canada," in *Imperial Dreams and Colonial Realities* (Toronto: University of Toronto Press, 1988), 115–139.
51 Roger Riendeau, *A Brief History of Canada* (Markham: Fitzhenry & Whiteside, 2000), 179–181.
52 George Reid, *Descriptive Notes of Mural Decorations. Designed and Painted by G.A. Reid, R.C.A., O.S.A., assisted by Lorna Claire, A.O.C.A.* (Toronto: Jarvis Collegiate Institute Auditorium, undated); L.G. McKerracher, "Our Canadian Art Section: Jarvis Collegiate Murals," *Teachers' Bulletin* (Ontario Secondary School Teachers' Federation Bulletin) 2, no. 2 (April 1931): 39–42.
53 Miller, *George Reid*, 151; Fern Bayer, "The 'Ontario Collection' and the Ontario Society of Artists Policy and Purchases, 1873–1914," *RACAR* 8, no. 1 (1981): 32–54; Fern Bayer, *The Ontario Collection* (Toronto: Published for the Ontario Heritage Foundation by Fitzhenry & Whiteside, 1984).
54 J.L.R., "George Agnew Reid: An Interview," *Acta Victoriana* (Christmas and Book Number 1906): 121.
55 Bruner, "Narrative Construction," 7–11.

SANDRA PAIKOWSKY

JAMES WILSON MORRICE'S *RETURN FROM SCHOOL*
A Modernist Image of Quebec Children

Born in Montreal in 1865, James Wilson Morrice spent little time in Canada after leaving for Europe in 1889 and settling in Paris three years later. Although he would keep a studio in the French capital until his death in 1924, Morrice was a constant traveller; as his friend Henri Matisse remarked, "He was always over hill and dale, a little like a migrating bird but without any very fixed landing place."[1] Despite his self-imposed exile, Morrice made almost annual visits to Quebec until the time of his parents' deaths in 1914, but such trips would become increasingly rare in the years that followed. As a result, Morrice's images of Quebec constitute a limited portion of his total production. The majority of his Canadian work reflects his voyages home at the end of the nineteenth century and the first few years of the twentieth century. Views of Montreal and Quebec City are joined by images of rural Côte-de-Beaupré, northeast of the provincial capital on the upper shore of the St. Lawrence River, and are usually associated with his visit to Canada from December 1896 to late April 1897. He would then return in the winter of 1900 and again the following year.[2] It was the result of his time in the area of Beaupré that Morrice produced one of his rare paintings of Canadian children: *Return from School* (fig. 16.1), now in the collection of the Art Gallery of Ontario (AGO),[3] which also holds the oil study (fig. 16.2) for the larger canvas.[4] His image of five young women making their way along a country road in the grey days of winter encapsulates both Morrice's modernist distillation of the momentary and Quebec's traditional preservation of the past.

There is still a great deal of mystery surrounding Morrice's life, and even the details of his trips home to Canada are not fully known. He left few letters and no personal diaries; fortunately, the Musée des beaux-arts de Montréal / Montreal Museum of Fine Arts has the majority of his known sketchbooks, and these provide an invaluable glimpse into his private world and the ideas for his images. Morrice's paintings and drawings can be associated with general periods in his life because of the changes in his

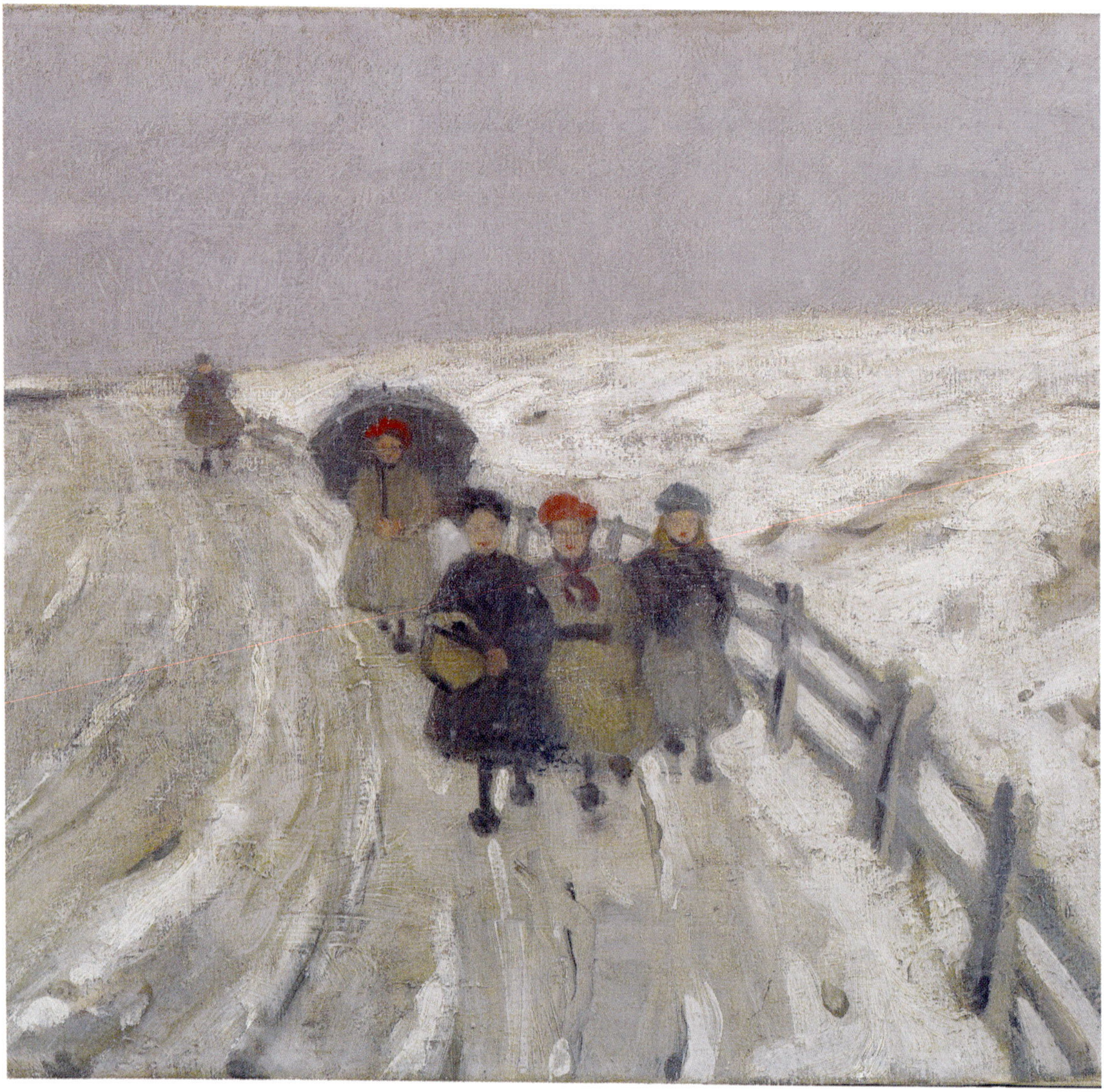

FIGURE 16.1 James Wilson Morrice, *Return from School* (detail), c. 1901, oil on canvas, 44.5 × 73.7 cm. Art Gallery of Ontario, gift from the Reuben and Kate Leonard Canadian Fund, 1948 (47/1).

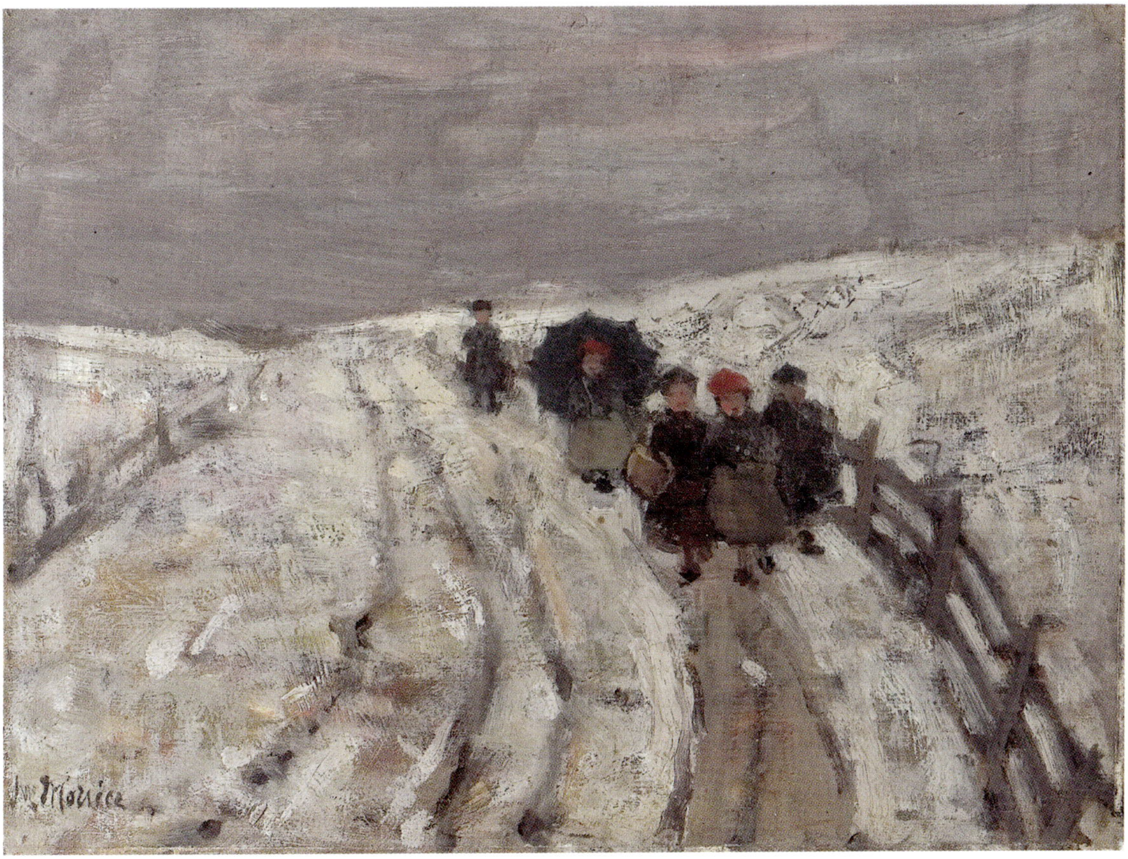

FIGURE 16.2 James Wilson Morrice, *Sketch for "Return from School,"* c. 1897–1901, oil on canvas on pressed board, 23.2 × 31.4 cm. Art Gallery of Ontario, gift from the Estate of R. Fraser Elliott, 2005 (2005/161).

pictorial language and choice of subject matter. However, it is often difficult to determine the sequence of his production within each phase of his career. This situation is further complicated by the fact that a painting was sometimes based on a study done a few years earlier and in a different painting place. Also, works were often exhibited and critically reviewed under different titles, even during his lifetime. This is much the case with *Return from School*.

The large painting was probably produced around 1901 in his Paris studio, using the smaller panel as its model. There are no known drawings that can be linked to *Return from School*, but on a list of seventeen works in his c. 1901 National Gallery sketchbook (7419, 61 recto) is the title *Retour de l'école, Canada*.[5] The work is numbered "16" and the title is followed by the number "25" (although Morrice has drawn a line through the whole notation); "25" follows about half of the titles on the list and likely refers to a size code that was similar to the formula Matisse used in his consignments to his Parisian dealer.[6] The number would signify the French system for canvas sizes and was also used as a means of determining the selling price of a painting. If Morrice followed suit, *Retour de l'école, Canada* closely approximates the size of the AGO's large canvas.

On the following page of the sketchbook, Morrice gives another but shorter list of paintings that includes the title *Enfants—Canada*, followed by the size of 73 × 46 cm; one can safely assume this is also the same painting because of the similar measurements. As well, there is no other known (to me) example of a Morrice painting of Canada that depicts children rather than a single child. There is no obvious explanation for why Morrice retitled the picture, although it was not unusual for him to do so. Equally important, Morrice's other notations on these sketchbook pages imply that he completed the painting before he went to Venice in the summer of 1901.[7] However, this does not preclude the possibility that the smaller version was painted during his 1897 visit to the Côte-de-Beaupré. The AGO painting was exhibited and reproduced under various titles but was recorded as *Return from School* in Donald Buchanan's biographical study of Morrice in 1936, thus finally "returning" the work to its original name.[8] Nevertheless, such archival findings are always secondary to the paintings themselves, for it is Morrice's visual vocabulary that speaks most clearly to his ongoing and revitalized preoccupations with the pictorial possibilities of modernism.

Return from School is an unusual work for Morrice on several counts. First and perhaps most significantly, the principal theme of the image is a group of young women, a rare subject for Morrice despite its widespread popularity among modern painters. The girls' identity remains a mystery, as there is no indication if there is any familial relationship between them or whether they were friends or just acquaintances. This lack of specificity only reinforces the ambiguity that is intrinsic to modernist narratives. As well, it is unusual (except for his World War I paintings) for Morrice to show a desolate rural landscape. His paintings of the area around the Côte-de-Beaupré usually focus on the Quebec village, with its distinctive architecture and horse-drawn sleighs. Of his Canadian paintings of the period, only his substantially smaller painting *On the Road* (Montreal Museum of Fine Arts)[9] suggests similar barren surroundings, with its solitary male figure and darkened farm buildings. In *Return from School*, the sole reference to country architecture is the simple building, presumably a schoolhouse, positioned at the horizon. Neither painting suggests the layered intimate landscape with its boisterous figure wrapped in the joyous winter sunlight of *Logging, Beaupré*, 1896 (Art Gallery of Hamilton) by Maurice Cullen, who was his companion at Ste-Anne in early 1897.

The region of Beaupré attracted various other Quebec artists at the time, but William Brymner, Marc-Aurèle Suzor-Coté, Clarence Gagnon, and most famously

Horatio Walker were often more interested in romantic summer views of rural life, and each idealized the world of the *habitant* in their own way.[10] In many of their paintings, there is an emphasis on physical labour and young people are often shown totally engaged in the essential rituals of subsistence farming. Walker wrote of his images of nearby Île d'Orléans, such as *Ploughing—The First Gleam at Dawn*, 1900 (Musée national des beaux-arts du Québec), that he tried to paint "the poetry, the easy joys, the hard daily work of rural life, the sylvan beauty in which is spent the peaceable life of the habitant ... the daily tasks of the farmyard, all the activity which goes on from morning to evening, in the neighborhood of the barn."[11]

This is emphatically not the vision of rural Quebec in James Wilson Morrice's painting, and there is nothing nostalgic about his view of adolescents in their own habitat. *Return from School* represents the landscape of the range (*rang*), the network of individual lots of land near a road or river and demarcated by a grid of perpendicular roads. The range system was a descendant of the original seigneurial settlements and determined the geography of the countryside as the *rang* "formed one of the basic units of Quebec society."[12] Morrice's design of a spare landscape was perhaps an unintentional reminder of the geometrization of rural Quebec during the *ancien régime*. Moving ahead to the late nineteenth century, his gutted roadway symbolizes the economic problems of Quebec agriculture largely resulting from the poor rural road system. The principal means of transporting goods and people were the range roads, and their neglected condition clearly exacerbated the difficulties of farming, which employed the majority of Quebecers.

While the province exclaimed that agriculture was "the calling" of its people, the life of farmers and day labourers was as hard-worn as Morrice's landscape suggests. Although agriculturalist promoters, especially the Roman Catholic clergy, saw the land as symbolizing an ideal way of life that enabled direct communication with God and nature, such thinking rejected any ideas of modernity and did little to ease the difficult and highly structured conditions in rural areas. It also did little to slow migration to Quebec City and Montreal or to the United States. The dominant ethos was the concept of the *terroir* and the ideology of conservation in which "colonization [clearing and farming] of the land fulfilled a national duty by strengthening the French presence in Quebec and in Canada, and also a Roman Catholic duty by helping to ensure the maintenance of moral values and ancestral virtues."[13] Certainly, Morrice's upbringing within the wealthy, anglophone Protestant community of Montreal would have sheltered him from the larger realities of Quebec life. However, he was undoubtedly aware of the deep divisions within the province that were grounded in language and religion and permeated every aspect of daily existence. Nevertheless, his representation of rural Quebec suggests neither approval nor disapproval but rather a modernist and distanced acceptance of the conditions of the country.

Terroir ideology would also be a major factor in determining the societal conditions of the young women in *Return from School*. The realities for rural girls were quite a different matter from their city sisters.[14] Provincial governmental reforms in the areas of public education and child labour laws meant positive gains for the Protestant urban child. The same was not equally true for Catholic city children, as their welfare remained under the domination of the church, which accorded them few advantages. Church control over rural Catholic children was even more restrictive and oppressive, as they were the least affected by government attempts to improve their lives. This disadvantage was particularly exemplified by the enormous problems in the schooling of young people living in the country.[15]

Secular education had not been a priority within Catholic Quebec, but in 1897, when Morrice likely painted the study for *Return from School*, the newly elected Liberal government attempted major reforms by re-establishing the Department of Public Instruction, which would have independent school inspectors and teachers who had earned a certificate of competence. However, the proposal was unsuccessful, owing largely to the interference of the province's bishops and the power of clerical-nationalist *terroir* ideology. The conservative Legislative Assembly continued to oversee public schooling until a Ministry of Education was created in 1964. While compulsory education had been debated in the provincial legislature since the late 1870s, the first steps were taken only in early 1901 when a bill was tabled (but not passed) in the National Assembly obliging adults under penalty of fines to send their children to school from the age of eight to thirteen for a minimum of sixteen weeks out of the school year. Despite such positive intentions by the government, laws concerning compulsory schooling for children younger than fourteen were, in fact, enacted in Quebec only in 1943. This ruling followed decades of struggle between and within both the church and the state, even though there had been some increase in the number and variety of educational institutions within the province. Compulsory education was steadfastly rejected by Quebec Catholic clergy even when it was condoned by the Vatican.

It is impossible to determine how many children from the area of the Côte-de-Beaupré attended classes. While there is statistical information on Quebec school registration, it does not indicate whether the pupils actually came for their lessons. Rural schools in Quebec villages and the ranges were typically small buildings (fig. 16.3), where classes were often taught by a young girl, sometimes no more than seventeen years old, who had little education herself. These female instructors were rarely certified to teach and received their training on the job. The situation was slightly better in those *rang* schools run by male teachers who had attended Catholic seminaries.

In rural areas, children were first and foremost responsible to the needs of their family and were expected to contribute fully to such seasonal work as planting and

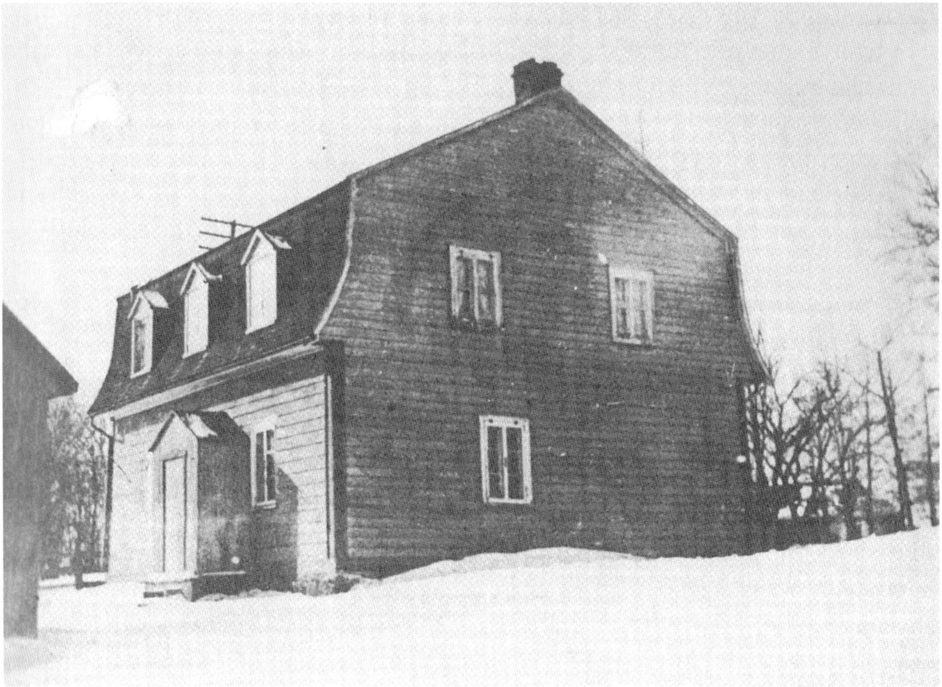

FIGURE 16.3 A country school in 1915. Archives nationales du Québec.

harvesting, as well as to the daily responsibilities in an agricultural community. The time spent in school by rural children (if they attended at all) was a matter of individual family necessity and circumstance, as each member played an essential participatory role in its economic welfare. Education was not free in Quebec, and parents were responsible for half of the amount spent by the state on education. This was a widespread hardship and would have been especially difficult for most rural families. The payment of fees also might help explain why the majority of Catholic children (town and country) left school at the time of their first Communion, which was usually around age ten, and why over 90 percent of Catholic children went to the sixth grade at best, even until the mid-1920s. These factors all contributed to the unfortunate statistic that when Morrice painted *Return from School*, Quebec had the highest illiteracy rate in Canada.

Women in Quebec rural society were defined entirely by their roles as wives and mothers, and childhood was considered merely as a training period for their adult responsibilities. It has been argued that "there was a division of labour based on sex, but since the family was the unit of production, the subordinate position of [rural] women was not as pronounced as it was in urban areas."[16] However, as urban industrialization increased, more young country women than men came to the city in the hope of better opportunities for employment. Unfortunately, little is still known about specific living and working conditions in rural Quebec, but it is certain that children were essential to the productivity of the farm from an early age, and schooling was considered more of a luxury than a necessity. Because winter was a slack time, the young girls in *Return from School* might well have had some relief from the heavy demands of rural life and could spend more time in the classroom; or perhaps the image was just a matter of Morrice's imagination.

Despite the complexities of rural Quebec society, *Return from School* is a deceptively simple composition. The snow-clad *côte* is divided into three wedge-shaped areas separated by the post fences that demarcate the girls' route, and the entire countryside is bounded by a trapezoidal, leaden sky. Morrice's segmentation of the image into a series of interlocking geometrical areas was not unusual in his work at the time and is found in his paintings of France and Italy as well as Quebec, such as *The Ferry*, 1907 (National Gallery of Canada),[17] and *Wharf on the St. Lawrence*, c. 1900 (private collection). The overall tectonic construction of *Return from School* differs little, albeit importantly from the study, and his subtle changes give the larger painting a more acute tension and succinct rhythm than is found in the earlier version. In the final canvas, Morrice has brought the group of four young women closer to the foreground and to our attention. While the first three walk in unison in their bowling ball–shaped boots, they are individualized by the details of their costume and especially their hats. The girl at the right is a step behind, and she is slightly taller and thinner. The rhythm of the round forms of their bodies is reinforced by the wicker basket of the figure at the left and the shape of the tilted umbrella of the fourth child, who is now slightly farther away than in the study. In the larger painting, Morrice has further individualized the foreground figures and shaped the space between their upper bodies by including a glimpse of the fence rails. At the same time, the encompassing silhouette of their bodies creates an abstract rectangular shape that is much more cohesive than in his earlier study.

Bundled up in their ordinary winter clothing, which could be worn by country or city girls, there is no room for any of the erotic subtext thought to underlie many depictions of children at that time. Similarly, the girls' plain costumes also have little to do with the tattered dress of pious poverty often seen in paintings by some other Quebec painters of the period. Instead, their solid bodies accommodate artificial notions of healthy and well-fed rural women in comparison to their poorly nourished, working-class city sisters. While the painting may project, to some degree, the constructed ideal of childhood innocence so prevalent in the Victorian era, Morrice's girls do not symbolize objectified feminine beauty often associated with such representations of young women.[18]

A significant compositional change in the final version is the position of the fifth girl, who is now much closer to the horizon line, creating a more open and clearly measured distance between her and her companions. Her placement near the centre of the painting gives the image a new focus and spatial tension, even as the figure itself becomes less distinct. Although the young women occupy a small proportion of their rural environment, their bodies are carefully anchored in place and contoured by the landscape. Morrice designs the composition so that they have an equal relationship with their surroundings, rather than being imposed upon it as so often happens in the work of other Quebec artists. The comfortable integration of the figures to the place suggests a community of women who share similar experiences and know similar truths.

In the final painting, the fence to the left has a more lazily extended curve that melds with the silhouette of the hill at the right. The wide roadway also now bends more gently to the right and vanishes at a more central and precise point than in the study. Most strikingly, the road is much flatter than in the smaller work and no longer moves upwards, thus performing more in terms of the figures than the adjacent landscape. At the same time that Morrice crops the road in the foreground, he reworks the lines of the fence to extend the space toward the horizon. The packed snow rather than the fence determines the left boundary of the road, which is further articulated by the verticality of the posts.

In evolving the image of the landscape, Morrice has also flattened and softened the contour of the hills along the horizon. The fields have become slightly larger, which also allows for a smaller and more geometrically shaped sky. As part of these refinements, he has slightly increased the size of the schoolhouse to punctuate the horizon line more strongly. By moving the building slightly to the left, it functions as a greater foil to the girls walking along the right side of the road. The colour of the building, which has a dark roof and light walls in the study, is now reversed. This change more clearly separates the isolated architecture from the natural environment, even as the snow-capped roof reiterates the shapes of the fallow fields. Morrice's landscape has obvious affinities with the Impressionists' winter images classified as *effet de neige*, a title that he himself sometimes used. Their privileging of a simplified landscape to heighten the subtleties of winter light and colour is adopted in *Return from School* and reinforces the particular atmosphere of the wintry Quebec countryside.

Other subtle changes in the figures, the fences, and the fields can be attributed to Morrice's more specific working out of the nuances of the compositional design. It is these finely tuned adjustments and refinements in the play of weights and measures, shapes and spaces that ensure the quiet resonance of *Return from School*. The unwavering unity of the image is, as always in Morrice's work, a matter of his nuanced tonal harmonies and carefully modulated light. The sensitive play of colour by the painter with the "delicate eye," as Matisse would later describe him, was recognized just a few years after *Return from School* was completed:

> In his studies around Ste. Anne de Beaupré, Quebec, the various plays of light and shadow are exceedingly subtle. One consciously feels the atmosphere inhaled by the little school children as they plod dutifully on to that village in New France where shrines are not unknown and beliefs are always simple. Follow the same little ones up the hill to the church [schoolhouse] beyond the way, and then look back upon the road as it winds tortuously through the snow.... The lights are warm, even if the shadows are cold.[19]

The presence of a young woman or a child in Morrice's painting is a common thread in his European paintings and occurs frequently in his images of Canada. In fact, it is around the turn of the century that the female figure appears most often, and interestingly, this coincides with the early years of his relationship with the young Lea Cadoret, who was the subject of several works. There are, however, only a few images where a single female child is the primary theme, and she is often shown absorbed in sewing or knitting within a placid summer landscape, oblivious to the fact that she is the object of observation. His European paintings, such as the seated figure in *Girl Knitting (near St-Malo, Brittany)* or the standing child of *Girl Wearing Clogs* (fig. 16.4), both dated c. 1896 and both at the National Gallery of Canada, are studies in stillness, which is reiterated by the self-containment of the children's pose and gesture and the rapt attention they pay to their work.

One Canadian example is a portrait of his sister from c. 1895 (private collection). Annie Mather Morrice (later Mrs. Alan Gilmour Law) was born in 1879 and was considerably younger than her brother. This small interior view of Annie in profile at about age sixteen also describes her total attention to her needlework. The close-up view emphasizes both the intimacy of the relationship between the siblings and the close scrutiny that is essential to Morrice's modernist vision. Learning domestic handiwork was part of the expected education of young women; in the case of less-privileged girls, such skills might help them earn a living.

Only a few Morrice images display the individual rural Quebec child. The farm girl in *Towards Evening Beaupré*, c. 1900 (private collection) solemnly carries out her daily chores, but her stopped movement and aura of quietude have little to do with the glorification of physical labour in Horatio Walker's images of country children at work. Morrice's study for *Sugar Bush*, c. 1897 (private collection), is a rare example of his representing a young man. Here, the slightly awkward boy stands on guard among the trees in front of the sugar shack, looking suspiciously at the viewer (and Morrice) as he protects his precious enterprise. In the larger painting, dated c. 1897–1898,

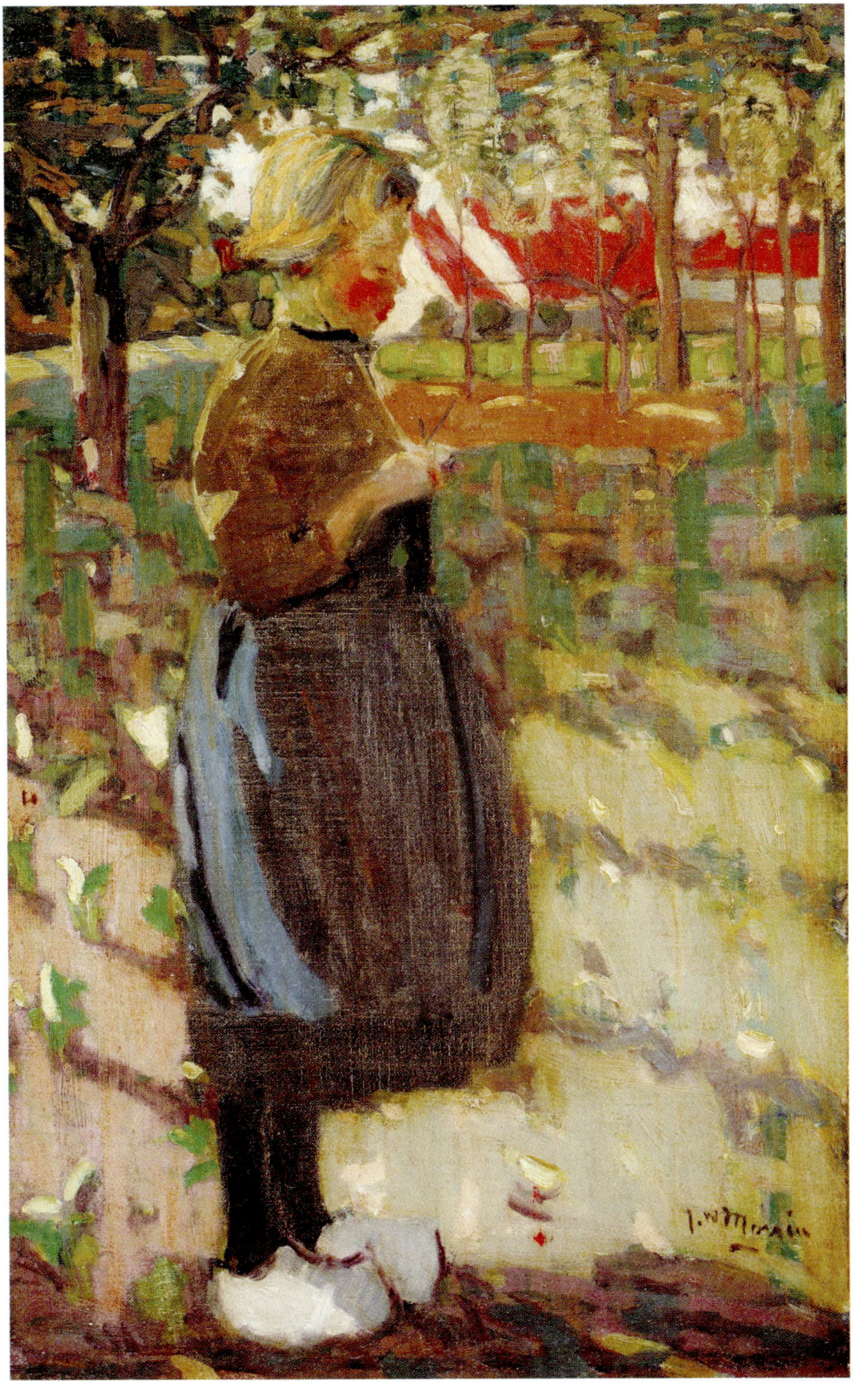

FIGURE 16.4
James Wilson Morrice, *Girl Wearing Clogs*, c. 1896–1898, oil on canvas, 55.5 × 35.5 cm. National Gallery of Canada, Gift of G. Blair Laing, Toronto, 1969 (30470).

(fig. 16.5), the image seems like the next moment in the narrative, as the boy has retreated inside the shack and shyly looks out the doorway, just as wary of intruders but much less visible.

A recurring motif in Morrice's paintings is the urban female child in the company of her mother or caretaker, navigating a city street or a park. Curiously, in many of these images, the older female is shown in profile while the child is frontally posed and stares directly out at the viewer, such as in *La Communiante*, 1899 (Musée national des beaux-arts du Québec) (fig. 16.6). Of course, she might also have been looking at Morrice, who was known for working in a seated position while outdoors, and this would physically position him within the purview of the child (Morrice was not a tall man). In those pictures using this motif, the young girl takes on a more distinct personality and presence than the older woman. The child in *The Barber Shop*, c. 1905 (private collection), confidently walks away from her companion toward the artist as though she is as inquisitive about him as he is of her. Compared to the standard visual representations of children and their elders at the time, Morrice has reversed the expected order of the active adult and the passive child. The motif of the child moving toward the viewer (and Morrice) is echoed in the movement of the girls in *Return from School* and signifies its pictorial narrative.

Many of Morrice's images of young women share the theme of walking, and it is the essential subject of *Return from School*. The representation of walking was often intrinsic to modernist urban images of the nineteenth century and became a recurring motif in many of Morrice's European paintings, as well in his Canadian works. Because the act of walking is part of everyday experience, whether in the city or the country, it has been considered a way of encountering and experiencing the world. The movement of the walking body becomes a metaphor of the passage through life. As Nancy Forgione has written of late nineteenth-century Parisian painting, to depict walking was to thematize motion by the "attempt to incorporate the lived experience of walking into the pictorial structure in any of the variety of ways that serve to register the traces of discursive movement through the depicted urban space."[20] While Morrice's walking women do appear most frequently in the context of the city, he adapts the area of the Côte-de-Beaupré as an equally appropriate site for his five young pedestrians. They transcribe themselves onto the landscape and articulate the site in the same way that his female figures navigate the streets in his images of the Quai des Grands-Augustins in Paris or the Riva degli Schiavoni in Venice.

In the countryside, the girls in *Return from School* enjoy an unencumbered, expansive setting that is not found in his paintings of the city. The adolescents share a rhythmic walk that has its counterpoint in the curve of the snow-tracked road and the tilted fence posts, which align their bodies to the landscape. However, the horizontality of the

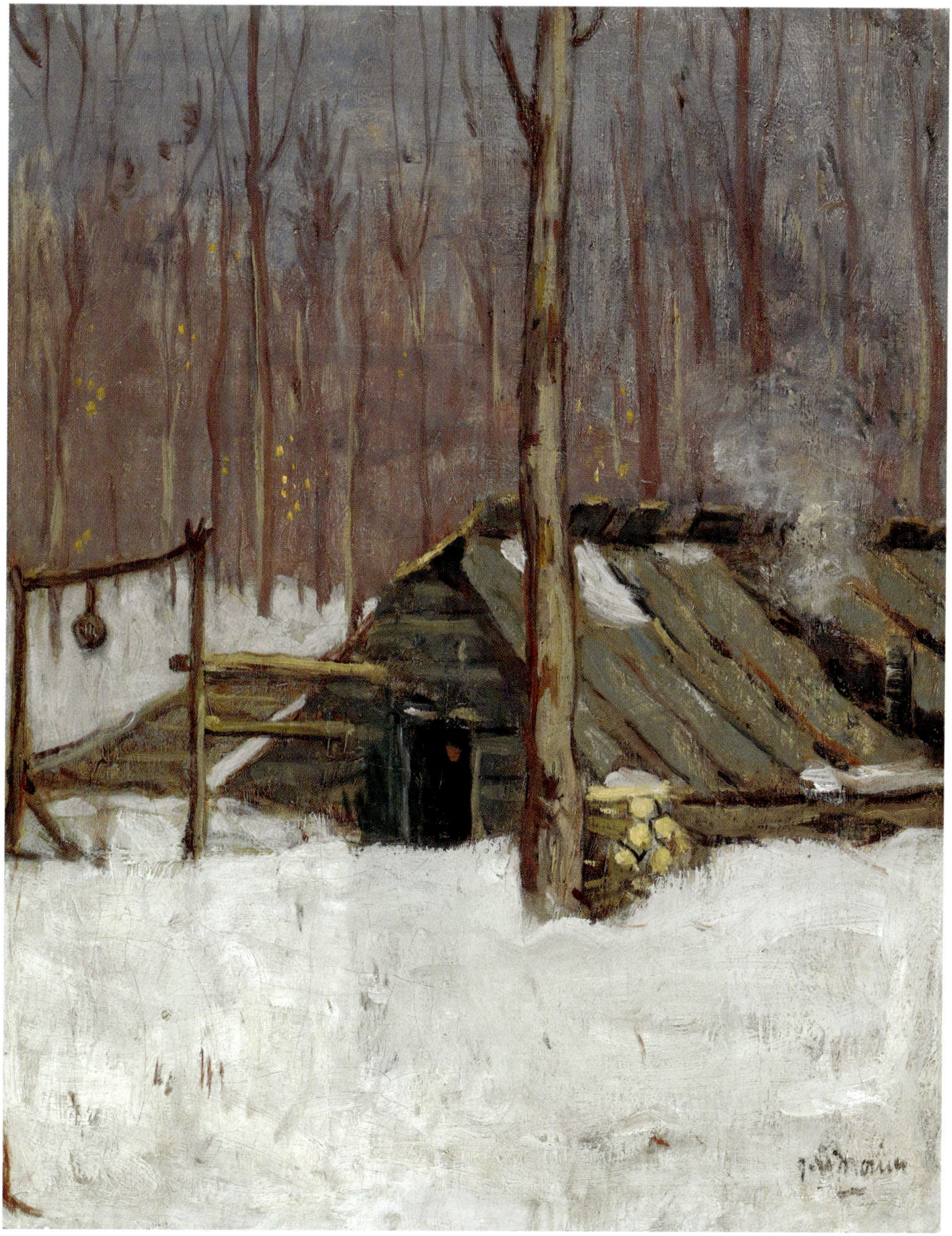

FIGURE 16.5 James Wilson Morrice, *Sugar Bush*, c. 1897–1898, oil on canvas, 51.6 × 41.1 cm. National Gallery of Canada.

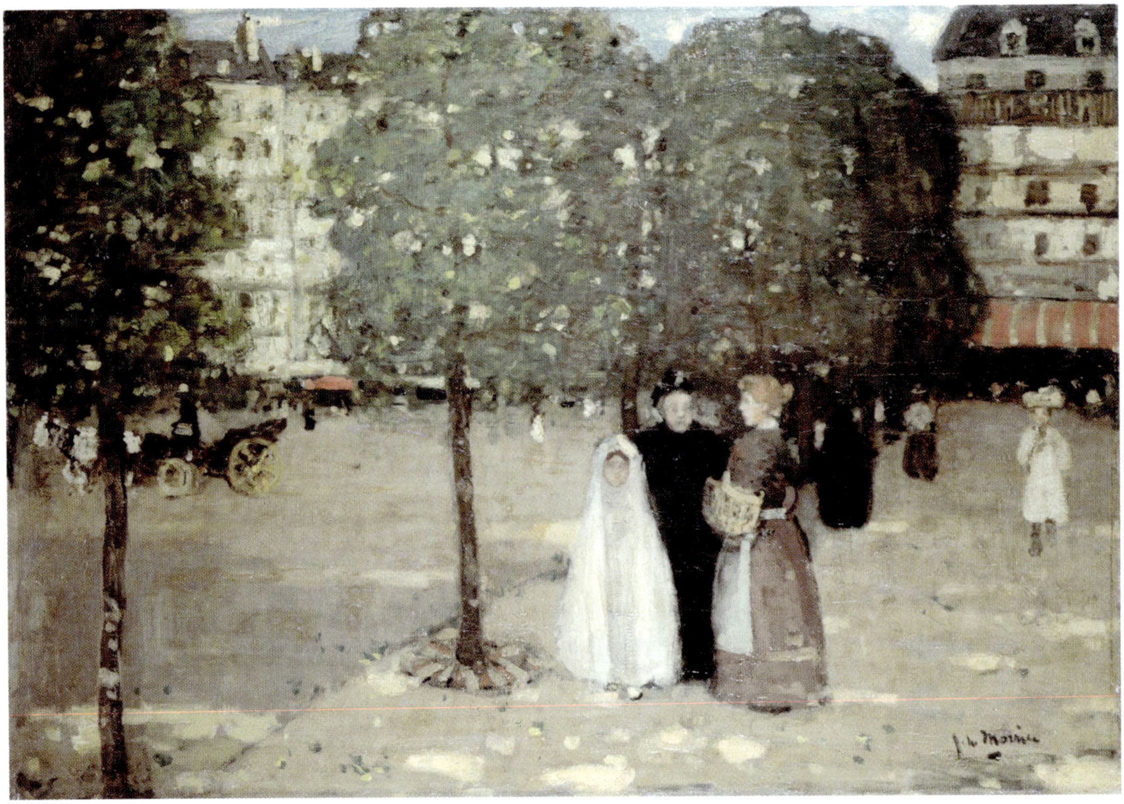

FIGURE 16.6 James Wilson Morrice, *La Communiante*, 1899, oil on canvas, 83 × 118 cm. Musée national des beaux-arts du Québec (78.98). (Photo: Jean-Guy Kérouac)

landscape seems to temper the speed of their movement forward along the route. While the title of the painting suggests that the children have practical reasons for appearing together on the road, they maintain a leisurely pace that one associates (correctly or incorrectly) with the slower tempo of rural life. At the same time, the fact that all the figures move forward in casual procession heightens the sensation of motion and the intensity of their walking. The informal pace of their stride down the road is further suggested by the sequential but irregular positioning of the figures from one end of the route to the other. Because the girls' legs are clearly evident, the stride of their bodies and the similarity of their gait give further clarity to the visualizing of thematic walking. As Ann Hollander has commented, "The actual physical size of a human body is made apparently larger by its movements, and if its movements are what constitute its essential visual reality, they must be what gives it its visual substance."[21]

The lack of architectural structures or any sign of the urban grid that would usually measure the distance of their walk and mark their progress through the city increases the sense of the encapsulated moment in *Return from School*. The girls' placement in the unbounded landscape also separates them from the pictorial convention of women occupying the enclosed territory of a domestic interior, a gated garden, or even the farmyard of rural images. In *Return from School*, the lyrical compositional design reiterates the motion of walking for pleasure, and the flow of the girls' movements suggests the tempo of a leisurely stroll. As well, their relaxed pose and modest appearance add to the sense of freedom and familiarity that is often associated more with photographs of the period than paintings and is rare for Morrice.[22]

The concept of thematized motion is also suggested by Morrice's approach to painting. His repertoire of undisguised, discrete gestures and marks gives the sensation that the picture was "painted quickly" in the mode established decades earlier by the Impressionists. As Richard Brettell has shown, the impression convention was intended only to give the *appearance* that the image was quickly painted as a means to suggest a moment in time, but it has nothing to do with the time involved in making the painting.[23] Their modernist perception that nature and its inhabitants were in a state of motion is also made manifest by Morrice's compositional strategies. The sensation of the girls' continuous movement through the schematized landscape derives from the rhythm of the brush in tandem with the flow of the surface design. *Return from School* suggests some of the visual concerns of "painting quickly," and it disguises his lengthy method of working from the study and the fact that he could "spend three days on a surface hardly bigger than a medium-sized envelope."[24] In Brettell's terms, *Return from School* is a conflation of the represented time of his painting process and the representation of time through the theme of walking.

Morrice's thematized motion is substantially different in *On the Road*, of a similar time and place. Supported by his cane, the elderly male farmer walks at a snail's pace. Looking down at the ground and making his way in measured steps, this solitary pedestrian has only the landscape of the Côte-de-Beaupré in common with the adolescents in *Return from School*. While the figure is carefully positioned in relation to the distant building and the fence, they now seem to support his body metaphorically in its slow movement along the snowy road. The relaxed interplay of the young women who walk down the (possibly) same country road is in stark contrast to the solitariness of the farmer. That he is in profile while the children are presented in frontal view makes him all the more emotionally distant and isolated. The theme of motion displayed in *On the Road* reflects the theory that the act of walking can be a metaphor of an individual's interior life, where the walker is lost within his own thoughts as he moves through a familiar landscape without paying it any attention. While the girls of *Return from School* may well be occupied with their own thoughts, Morrice does not deny us the pleasure of their company. But his sensitivity to both generations of Quebec country people and their shared habitat is fully evident and gives the pictures their enduring appeal.

Morrice's responsiveness to the site and its inhabitants provides the ultimate meaning of the picture. His contemplation of the subject from close proximity and his implied viewpoint near the front curve of the road metaphorically places Morrice in the company of his young women. Their gaze in the direction of the viewer also symbolically falls on the painter. He becomes the invisible companion in their walk through the countryside, and the centrality of his vantage point also suggests that he is the unseen counterpart of the fifth girl positioned nearest the horizon. Morrice spent his career wandering from one place to another, and the young women's journey to an unspecified destination could be a metaphor for his own life. While he still maintains some of the character of the Baudelairean *flâneur* associated with his European urban images, there are no encroaching buildings, busy pedestrians, or traffic-filled streets to attract his roving gaze. Instead, this empty section of the Côte-de-Beaupré and its lazy procession of schoolgirls provide Morrice with a quiet and unencumbered reality that lays bare his commitment to looking and seeing.

In an undated letter from the Impressionist painter Alfred Sisley to a friend, he makes a comment that easily defines the intention of *Return from School*: "The spectator should be led along the road that the painter indicates to him, and from the first be made to notice what the artist himself has felt. Every picture shows a spot with which the artist has fallen in love."[25] Morrice's affection for the rural landscape of Quebec and his empathy with its children are equally evident in *Return from School*.

Notes

This text is dedicated to my husband, John Fox (1927–2008).

1 Donald W. Buchanan, *James Wilson Morrice* (Toronto: Ryerson, 1936), 111.

2 For a chronology of his visits to Canada, see Nicole Cloutier, *James Wilson Morrice 1865–1924* (Montreal: Musée des beaux-arts de Montréal / Montreal Museum of Fine Arts, 1985). Lucie Dorais, *J.W. Morrice* (Ottawa: National Gallery of Canada, 1985), 20, dates his last trip to Canada from late 1920 to early 1921.

3 *Return from School*, oil on canvas, 44.5 × 73.7 cm, Art Gallery of Ontario, Gift from the Reuben and Kate Leonard Canadian Fund, 1948 (47/1). The AGO dates it c. 1901. The work was presumably first purchased by Col. James W. Woods of Ottawa, who owned it by the time of the 1925 Morrice *Memorial Exhibition*; it went to the Stevens Art Gallery in Montreal by the early 1940s and then to the Watson Art Galleries by 1948. I wish to thank Allan Zigayer for his help in this research.

4 *Sketch for "Return from School,"* oil on canvas on pressed board, 23.2 × 31.4 cm, Gift from the Estate of R. Fraser Elliott, 2005 (2005/161). It had earlier been at the Heaton and the Klinkoff galleries in Montreal. The AGO dates the painting c. 1901, although it was probably produced earlier. I wish to thank Dennis Reid and Gregory Humeniuk at the AGO for their assistance.

5 This title has not been noted in previous citations of the painting. For a discussion of the National Gallery of Canada sketchbooks, see Lucie Dorais, "Deux moments dans la vie et l'œuvre de James Wilson Morrice," *Bulletin 30/177*, National Gallery of Canada, 1978: 19–35.

6 See Alfred H. Barr Jr., *Matisse: His Art and His Public* (New York: MOMA, 1951), 553: "Appendix C: Contracts between Matisse and Bernheim-Jeune, between 1909 and 1926."

7 On page 60 verso of the National Gallery of Canada sketchbook (opposite to where *Retour de l'école, Canada* is noted), Morrice lists paintings by Tintoretto in four churches in Venice, suggesting that he made these notes prior to his visit that summer. On page 62 recto, he notes two other Venetian churches and a *scuola grande*, as well an article on an Italian spa from the *New York Herald* of May 25, 1901.

8 Buchanan, *James Wilson Morrice*, 154. One of the earliest reproductions of the painting is in William H. Ingram, "Canadian Artists Abroad," *Canadian Magazine* 28, no. 3 (January 1907): 220, as *Canadian Pastoral*. For references to the work, see *Art Gallery of Ontario: The Canadian Collection* (Toronto: McGraw Hill, 1970), 316–317.

9 *On the Road* (*Sur La Route*), c. 1897–1901, oil on canvas, 38.7 × 56.2 cm, Musée des beaux-arts de Montréal / Montreal Museum of Fine Arts (943.786), Bequest of William J. Morrice.

10 Ontario artists Edmund Morris, William Cruikshank, and Curtis Williamson, among others, also painted in the region.

11 Quoted in J. Russell Harper, *Painting in Canada: A History* (Toronto: University of Toronto Press, 1977), 204.

12 Paul-André Linteau, René Durocher, and Jean-Claude Robert, *Quebec: A History 1867–1929* (Toronto: James Lorimer & Co., 1983), 13. The authors' discussion of rural Quebec forms the basis of my discussion on the conditions of the province. Their important analysis of the power of the Catholic Church provides the context for the anticlerical anger of Paul-Émile Borduas' *Refus global*.

13 Ibid., 105.

14 For discussions of childhood in Quebec during this period, see among many others, Renée Joyal, *Les enfants, la société et l'État au Québec, 1608–1989* (Montreal: Éditions Hurtubise HMH, 1989); Bettina Bradbury, *Working Families: Age, Gender, and Daily Survival in Industrializing Montreal* (Toronto: McClelland & Stewart, 1993); Linteau et al., *Quebec: A History*.

15 Among the many discussions of Quebec education, see Philippe Audet, *Histoire de l'enseignement au Québec*, 2 vols. (Montreal: Holt, Reinhart & Winston, 1971) and his other publications. The differing histories of the education of Catholic, Protestant, and Jewish children (who were considered as part of the Protestant school system) in Quebec from the late nineteenth to the early twentieth century are well documented and will not be elaborated upon here.

16 Linteau et al., *Quebec: A History*, 189.

17 Charles C. Hill, *Morrice: A Gift to the Nation. The G. Blair Laing Collection* (Ottawa: National Gallery of Canada, 1992), 50, dates the study of *The Ferry* from 1879. Hill provides important analyses of Morrice's Quebec work.

18 For a recent discussion and bibliography of the image of the child, see Marilyn Brown, ed., *Picturing Children: Constructions of Childhood between Rousseau and Freud* (Aldershot, Hants, England: Ashgate, 2002).

19 Ingram, "Canadian Artists Abroad," 221.

20 Nancy Forgione, "Everyday Life in Motion: The Art of Walking in Late Nineteenth-Century Paris," *Art Bulletin* 87, no. 4 (December 2005): 664. Her excellent article is also an important source for writings on the theory of walking.

21 Anne Hollander, *Seeing Through Clothes* (New York: Avon Books, 1980), 154–155.
22 There is nothing to suggest that Morrice, unlike many of his Parisian counterparts, was interested in photography or used a camera.
23 See Richard Brettell, *Impressionism: Painting Quickly in France 1860–1890* (New Haven, CT: Yale University Press, 2000).
24 Muriel Ciolkowska, "Memories of Morrice," *Canadian Forum* 6, no. 62 (November 1925): 52–53.
25 Quoted in Robert Goldwater and Marco Treves, eds., *Artists on Art* (New York: Pantheon Books, 1972), 309.

JOHANNE SLOAN

SOMETHING RESEMBLING CHILDHOOD
Artworks by Jack Chambers, Daniel Barrow, and Rodney Graham

IN THE 1972 PAINTING BY JACK CHAMBERS (1931–1978) entitled *Diego Asleep* (fig. 17.1), a small child lies sleeping on a sofa in a modern-looking living room. A few articles of clothing lie casually draped over the furniture, and some toys are strewn around. The toy that stands out is a King Kong figure, and it looks as if this pop-culture icon is striding across the floor, away from the sleeping boy and directly toward the viewer. All of this ordinary childish stuff is painted in an impressively realistic and even "photographic" manner, as if this were a snapshot glimpse of a domestic environment. But while *Diego Asleep* describes the surface appearance of things, I want to argue that this painting also makes evident how images of childhood are linked to memory, pop culture, and the psychodynamics of family life. Although the boy in the picture is not in a conscious state, the artist has turned this to his advantage, by presenting an imaginative forcefield surrounding the sleeping child, as something that threatens to undermine the very logic of realistic representation. This interpretation of Chambers's painting leads to how childhood (or the memory of childhood) is represented in some recent art practices. In a series of artworks by Daniel Barrow (1971–), old toys, has-been celebrities, and outmoded styles and genres are resurrected from the pop culture of the artist's youth, becoming narrative trajectories that can accommodate adult desires. In the work of Rodney Graham (1949–), the artist's unreliable historical re-creations—often based on tableaux from movies, TV shows, or advertisements—are similar to the distorted figurations of childhood memories. Across these three art practices, childhood and adulthood are understood as interlocked forms of consciousness, while an immersion in pop-culture forms and media allows movement back and forth between child and adult selves, and between past and present.

Jack Chambers: The Sleep of Realism

The realistic facture of *Diego Asleep* is striking, and indeed Chambers was not the only painter of his time intent on reviving realism: the 1960s and 1970s saw the rise of photo- and hyper-realisms in the United States, for instance, while the new category of "capitalist realism" was proposed by Gerhard Richter and other German artists. In Canada, Jack Chambers, Alex Colville, Mary Pratt, Christopher Pratt, and Ken Danby are some of the artists who set out to paint realistic scenes of everyday life during this period. Terms such as "high realism" and "magic realism" have at various times been used to describe this Canadian phenomenon, but there is no commonly accepted rubric that adequately covers these diverse art practices.[1] Chambers shared with these Canadian and international contemporaries a commitment to older forms of painterly realism, even while acknowledging that photography was the sovereign form of realistic image-making of the late twentieth century. Indeed, for this generation of realists, the artwork would often be the venue for deliberate, confrontational encounters between painting and photography. This in itself signalled a challenge to the tenets of mid-century modernism, because instead of remaining "true" to one particular medium, these artists explored the intersecting techniques, conventions, and ideological suppositions of both painterly and photographic realisms.

Chambers does more than merely mimic the effects of photographic emulsion with anachronistic blobs of oily pigment. If *Diego Asleep* is "like a photograph," this is because the painting is reminiscent of the lurid colour photography found in mass-circulation publications such as *Life* magazine, while also pointing to the social environment of suburban life as captured in family snapshots. The proliferation of affordable photographic technologies in the postwar era was accompanied by the (ostensibly democratic) imperative that everyone should unceasingly document their own families, homes, possessions, pets, and especially children. It is arguably this socio-photographic development that in turn inspired a great deal of this era's realist painting.[2] In Canada, the aesthetic tension in paintings by artists as different as Mary Pratt and Alex Colville is linked to how their artworks both conform to and subtly deviate from the normative poses and scenes of family photo albums. If Chambers was imitating photography, he was also paying homage to the hallowed tradition of painting, the extraordinary realisms of artists like Vermeer and Velázquez, achieved by painstakingly reconstructing the world on a blank canvas. Chambers's paintings of the mundane environments and encounters of family life are rendered uncanny through the overlapping realisms of photography and painting.

Diego Asleep is kin to the family snapshot genre not least because the paterfamilias (Jack) took/made this picture of the family home, with his son as the central focus of

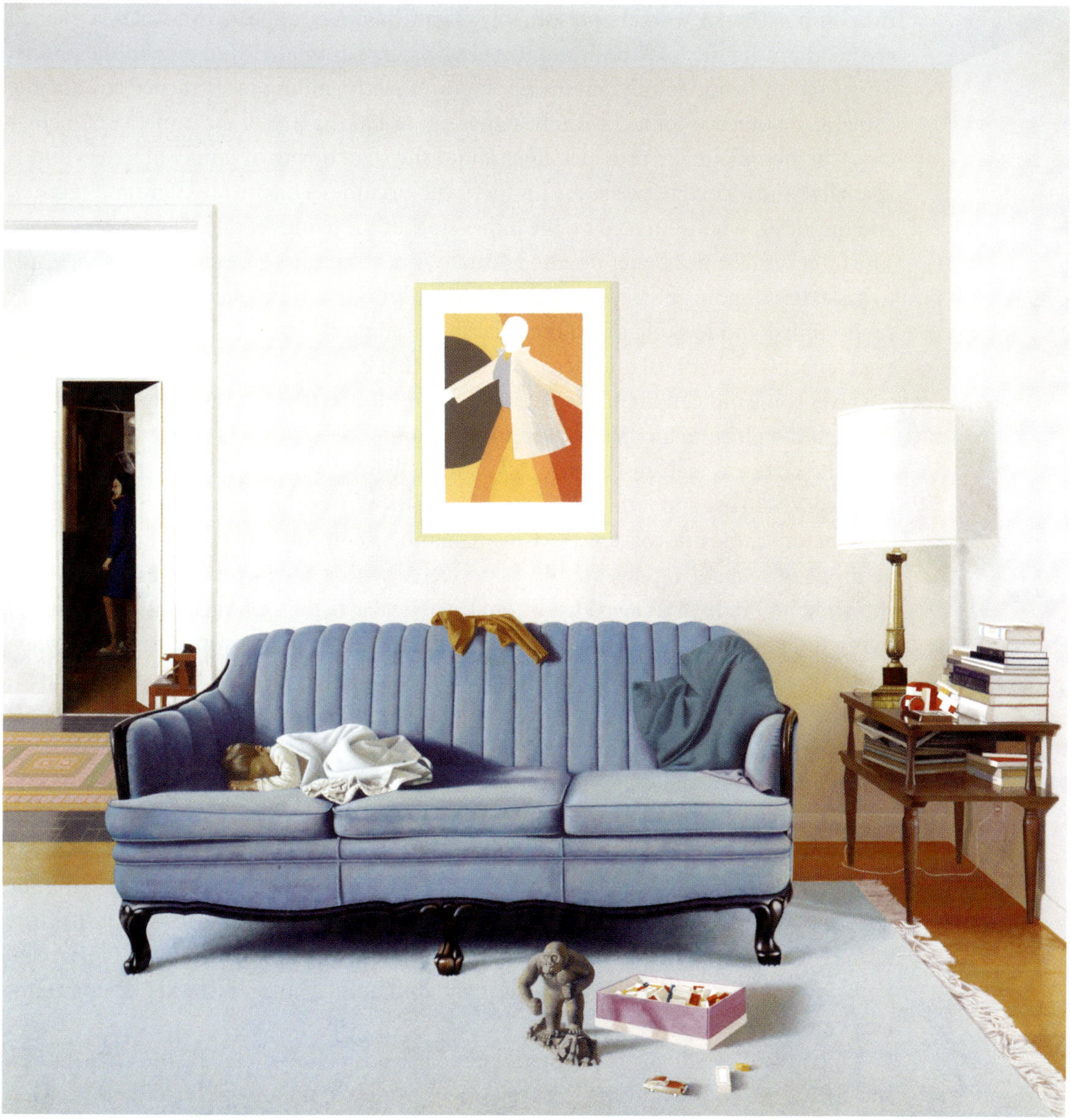

FIGURE 17.1 Jack Chambers, *Diego Asleep #2*, 1972, oil on wood, 121.9 × 121.9 cm. Toronto Dominion Bank Collection.

the composition. A woman, presumably Olga Chambers, appears in a small, darkened room adjoining the back wall, and it looks like she's animatedly talking on the phone. This isn't an iconic family-album photograph, with smiling faces turned toward the camera, making eye contact with the father's gaze and the lens of the camera.[3] Nonetheless, Chambers's image provides clues about the structuring of family life: the child is spatially sandwiched between the mother, who occupies a distinct background register, and the father, who is situated on the "other side" of the living room, in the viewer's space. The father might not be represented visually, but the entire *mise en scène* corresponds to his external point of view. It should be noted too that if the mother is momentarily preoccupied and looking off to the side, she would only have to lift her head to make eye contact with her husband, across the space that belongs to their son; thus, the painting gives some indication of how families are constituted through intersecting gazes, and through the illusionistic spaces of representation.

The virtuoso realism of *Diego Asleep* initially suggests that Jack Chambers (in his dual roles of artist and father) has complete control over the means of representation. This picture came into existence because Chambers faithfully obeyed the rules and conventions of realistic representation as perfected within the European tradition—and the artist had indeed received traditional, classical artistic training during his years of living in Spain. The flawlessly receding angles of walls and furniture bespeak a mastery of perspective, there is expert modelling and shading of objects to suggest three-dimensionality, and a deployment of complex chiaroscuro effects is meant to imitate the ephemeral play of natural illumination. Many hours of labour and centuries' worth of accumulated knowledge have therefore gone into erecting an image that can approximate a snapshot or an individual's fleeting glance. *Diego Asleep*'s maker thus comes across as a masterful manipulator of signs, a socially integrated subject, and a vigilant father figure. This cluster of qualities is reminiscent of the Lacanian symbolic order, which links the realms of representation and signification to the "law of the father." The sleeping child is necessarily positioned within this realm of patriarchal authority, and so his psyche will take shape as it comes up against a set of dominant semiotic and social codes.

A conventionally realistic visual regime has been constructed by the artist/father, but this is not to say that the sleeping boy is pinioned or fully defined by this external, paternalistic gaze. Embedded within this expert performance of realism are intimations that other forms of consciousness operate even within this system of visual representation. The sleeping child is the centrepiece of this disturbance. Unlike the father/artist, the boy doesn't stand tall, projecting his vision and consciousness out into the world. He is prone, unmoving, unseeing, and yet it could be said that Diego has agency even while he is asleep because his unconscious is in full throttle, entering into imaginary and empathetic relations with the world around him. Chambers suggests his son's paradoxically active unconsciousness by creating a picture of stillness that is nonetheless a repository of implied movement, through the bold zigzag of varnished flooring, for instance. A sense of dynamism that is both pictorial and psychic is primarily accomplished, though, by that King Kong toy whose stride traces a line between boy and viewer, and also by the framed artwork hanging on the wall above the sleeping boy, a self-portrait of Greg Curnoe as a multicoloured cartoon-like silhouette, seen in profile and also striding in an exaggerated way, although in this case the implied movement is parallel to the picture plane. I want to suggest that these two comically advancing figures interrupt the claims to realism of the painting as a whole, while they can also be regarded as surrogate bodies or avatars for the sleeping child. These lively presences serve, as well, to complicate the picture of parental authority and familial stability described above.

So the boy is unmoving and unconscious, but hardly lifeless, and an imaginative energy seems to emanate from him, permeating the room and its contents. Diego sleeps, but the object world seems on the verge of awakening. The formless lumps of abandoned clothing take on the mutability of Plasticine. The sofa cradling Diego is on the verge of anthropomorphized movement, as its shiny, black "clawed feet" mimic the crooked legs of the advancing King Kong toy. And then, the toys themselves are full of potentiality for action, storytelling, assembly, and destruction—they are ready to be played with, in other words. The box filled with plastic blocks in the foreground will be patiently conjoined to form a building or bridge or space station, at which point King Kong will surely come along to knock everything down, to gleefully inflict damage on this "built environment" in miniature.

By the time a plastic King Kong toy showed up on a London, Ontario, living room floor and in the foreground of a Jack Chambers painting in the early 1970s, this ape's original appearance in a 1933 Hollywood film had been supplemented by multiple other incarnations—in Japanese films, in an animated TV show, in comic books, and as three-dimensional toys and to-be-assembled model kits. King Kong is a veritable pop-culture icon whose every new appearance or iteration has him storming the bastions of civilization, and if he inevitably fails to decimate New York and destroy its police force, the effort is applauded every time, and he remains a celebrity monster despite his ultimate failure. In the painting, nothing really moves, of course, but Kong does appear to stride with determination toward the picture plane, toward the viewer, and toward the creator of this picture—in order to smash and destroy what lies before him? The human-built world against which King Kong launches himself can be said, in this instance, to include the architectural space that encloses him, as well as the architectonic labour performed by Jack Chambers in constructing this picture. And if the toy monster is regarded as Diego's came dressed in rags and whose traumatized face was supplemented by one detachable plastic tear. If the pop-cultural past is being revived here, it's as a constellation of half-forgotten, half-hidden cultural markers.

Barrow's work, with its focus on childhood, the past, and nostalgia, and in its preoccupation with outmoded styles and genres in pop culture, is an important contribution to what might be called the "Winnipeg school." Indeed, many members of the contemporary Winnipeg art scene make work that explores childhood in some way. Within this local scene, it is the production of the Royal Art Lodge that most overtly resembles the art of children. The Royal Art Lodge is the name of an ongoing collaborative endeavour, begun by a group of young Winnipeggers in 1996; over the years, Lodge members have met with greater or lesser regularity for sessions of drawing, painting, and other activities.[11] Much of the imagery coming out of this project is deliberately crude in its execution, and this is so despite the art school credentials of the members. Stick figures traverse lumpy landscapes; indeterminate beasts confront painterly voids. As more than ten years have passed since the Lodge's emergence, it is now obvious that these artists are dedicated professionals, that they are neither untrained children nor uninformed "outsider" artists. Instead, the Royal Art Lodge stands for a concerted, collective refutation of the artistic skills and techniques honed within the Western tradition. Drawing is at the heart of this project, and within the circumscribed world of the Royal Art Lodge, "bad" drawing is valorized, and even fetishized.[12] It must be recognized that the Royal Art Lodge sends mixed messages: its artists are supposedly not bound by artistic rules and conventions, but they are continually making aesthetic judgments.

The interest in a childish imagination is actually quite widespread, as many contemporary artists across North America, Europe, and Japan are obsessively revisiting childhood and adolescence: David Shrigley, Chris Johanson, Jockum Nordstrom, Kojo Griffin, Sue Williams, and Yoshitomo Nara are some of the most notable. Beyond this recent development, however, the history of twentieth-century modern art includes repeated moments of primitivism, which have often encompassed a desire for childish spontaneity and freedom of expression. In 1947 the French artist Jean Dubuffet would say, "Drawing with one's finger on a fogged up windowpane or ... with the toe of one's shoe in the dust, that revives him (the artist), that gives him a way to invent new forms and modes of expression."[13] This commitment to simple gestures often accompanies a disdain for conventionalized modes of making art, and a determination to break through the calcified surfaces of beauty, good taste, polished presentations, and precious objects. Dubuffet would define a category of *art brut* made by eccentric loners and psychologically unbalanced individuals, and his own artwork would follow in their footsteps. Whether under the rubric of cubism, expressionism, surrealism, or other movements, modern artists repeatedly turned for inspiration to non-European statuary and ritual objects for their erotic charge or edge of violence, and to the art of the insane for similar reasons, as well as for its revelation of unconscious desire. The art of the child has often been categorized alongside these, ostensibly because there is still something wild and uncivilized in a young person's psyche and imagination.

It has been pointed out that Paul Klee would make "an effect of childlike directness one of the distinguishing marks of authentic personal vision."[14] Thus we have another example of a childlike "effect" created by a trained artist, through a kind of strategic amnesia; within this conceptual framework, an artwork's authenticity is measured against all evidence of artistic training. Given this history, we might well ask: Is a deliberate stance of immaturity and outsiderness productive at the present time? If, once again, the calcified traditions and empty signifiers of "high" art are to be reinvigorated through a transfusion of childlike otherness, what are the cultural stakes of this latest foray into primitivism? Wayne Baerwaldt's description of the Royal Art Lodge's "lo-tech, no-tech, do-it-yourself provisional aesthetic"[15] does imply that we should read this body of work in relation to the present-day dominance of high-tech, highly mediatized representations. At a time when virtually all forms of communication and image-making are accomplished through the use of complex technologies, when handwriting is disappearing as a feature of everyday life, the most basic kind of mark- making on paper can seem enormously appealing.

One of the most well-known child-focused artists in Winnipeg is Marcel Dzama, who has also been a member of the Royal Art Lodge from its inception. Diverging from the Lodge's visual rhetoric, Dzama's fanciful watercolour drawings have a kind of Victorian formality, while there are stylistic references to early twentieth-century newspaper comics, greeting card designs, movies, and TV shows. His drawings feature many children, alongside invented plant-like creatures and more familiar pop-culture figures. Other artworks are based on toys: when Dzama was featured as a cultural arbiter in *Artforum*'s prestigious "Top Ten" column in 2001 (contributors are asked to provide some compelling cultural reference points in their life at that moment), the artist accorded the Tomland brand of toys the number two spot, immediately following an appreciation of the Swedish artist Jockum Nordstrom.[16] Dzama proudly proclaimed that the 70s-era toys that had informed his childhood sensibility were still highly influential in his creative life. Dzama has remarked, "I tell myself stories as I draw,"[17] and it is as if the artist is still playing with toys, even as the violence that inevitably erupts among these characters has acquired connotations of (adult) institutions and rituals.

Daniel Barrow's artwork bears comparison with Dzama's in that both artists have created elaborate pictorial and narrative structures within which childhood is evoked. Barrow's artwork suggests a more complicated nostalgia, however, by emphasizing the social and psychic consequences of attempting to resurrect the past. At the foundation of Barrow's artworks is a practice of deceptively simple coloured-in line drawings. These are reminiscent of confessional graphic novel cartooning, and of the private journals of a high school loner. In fact, Barrow's stories draw from a vast pop-cultural archive both for their iconographic material and stylistic flourishes. Barrow has expressed his admiration for the unsung talents of Ken McDermid, a dollar-store colouring-book artist, for instance.[18] As in print advertisements or televised game shows, Barrow's drawings often feature elegant and disembodied hands holding beauty products or paintbrushes, or wielding surgical instruments. And Barrow's characteristically twirling and curving lines achieve a kind of decorative grandeur, when delineating the fluttering scarves, ribbons, and flowers that adorn his characters.

Barrow created a series of interrelated works between 2002 and 2004, which feature a recurring cast of characters: *The Face of Everything* (2002), a forty-five-minute live-animation performance, *Catalogue of the Original* (2004), a nine-minute video ("ten underestimated personalities from the recent past," is how Barrow describes his characters in this context), and *Trading Cards* (2004), a set of three-by-four-inch cards with pictures on one side and text on the flip side. *The Face of Everything* focuses primarily on the life story of Scott Thorson, the adolescent boyfriend of Liberace in the 1970s. In other parts of this project, various odd characters are given the chance to step forward into the limelight. Thus the *Trading Cards* recount Margaret Keane's battles with her ex-husband over the authorship of the "big-eye" paintings of mournful children; we are told the story of ventriloquist Wayland Flowers and his signature puppet Madame, including the entertainer's death from an AIDS-related illness in 1988; and we hear about the career and highly publicized nervous breakdowns of 70s-era child actress Kristy McNichol.

Conventionally, the characters appearing on trading cards correspond to a group of superheroes or athletes, the cast of a television program, or a lineup of military leaders. Trading cards come in series, and it usually takes a while for the child collector to amass the entire set of cards. Barrow's reinvention of the trading card is idiosyncratic, which is not to say that he has fabricated his own characters, but rather, that he has brought together a group of minor entertainers and failed toys as if they were all part of a coherent scheme, all part of the same story. The *Trading Cards* can be shuffled and read in different sequences, but the implication is that the biographies of these people and nonhuman creatures are related and mutually constitutive. The characters are unified thanks to the pre-existence of a visual form (the trading card), but the more important factor here is one person's desire to retroactively give meaning to the pop-cultural universe of his childhood.

Barrow's homage to the trading card is joined to his aesthetic recuperation of things like gossip magazines, game shows, and colouring books. These kinds of cultural products don't usually get much respect, and while the pop art movement had laid the groundwork for the appropriation of such low-brow stuff, Barrow's artwork does not aim for the spectacular transfiguration of mass-produced artifacts to be found in the art practices of Warhol or Lichtenstein. Writing in 1971, Umberto Eco suggests that pop art can "redeem" such low-down kitsch, elevating it to a higher cultural level by giving it a kind of second life as part of an artwork.[19] But Barrow seems to have a real appreciation for the supposed dregs of pop culture that is more in keeping with Dick Hebdige's comment that the most radical insight of pop art was that "popular culture and mass-produced imagery are worthy of consideration in their own right."[20] Alongside his drawing-based art practice, in 2006 Barrow curated *Winnipeg Babysitter*, which consisted of a selection of public access television programming originally shown in the Winnipeg area in the 1980s; he also provided a personalized text to accompany the viewing of these amateur and low-budget productions. This project is yet another example of Barrow's attunement to disregarded fragments of the pop-cultural past.

It seems entirely appropriate to accuse Daniel Barrow of nostalgia, because again and again the production of imagery in his art practice seems to depend on the resurgence of childhood memories in the form of vintage toys or TV shows, infused by a kind of affective excess. I want to suggest that Barrow's approach to childhood and to the past more generally can be compared to the aesthetic attitude of the filmmaker Guy Maddin; indeed, Maddin contends that Winnipeggers are particularly susceptible to nostalgia. *Frieze* magazine's special section on Winnipeg in 2006 included a so-called city report submitted by Maddin, where he informed the international art world that his native city has "stories and memories piled one on top of another," that "the people and buildings that were once here are now gone but are allowed to coexist with those that are still here," and that the "streets are full of drowsy and forgetful wanderers" who are somehow capable of moving backwards and forwards in time.[21] The text goes on to describe fantastical, alternative structures within the city, which provide a spatial equivalent to the multiple temporal and mnemonic registers the author has outlined. Maddin's recent film *My Winnipeg*, 2007, similarly sets out to bring versions of Winnipeg's past back to consciousness, or it would be accurate to say, back to semi-consciousness, since the characters in this film are explicitly identified as spectres and sleepwalkers. Here and in other Maddin films, the past is inevitably distorted and (dis)coloured by the visual style and narrative imperatives of outmoded art forms. It has been proposed that "Maddin patiently unearths and reinhabits the lost languages of minor, transitional moments in film history,"[22] and this understanding of the filmmaker's artistic process could be applied to Barrow, in the sense that he too manages to access the past through the distinctive pictorial vocabularies of long-gone pop-culture media and genres. If the past thereby appears sugar-coated or dripping with cheap sentiment, that is no reason to yearn for a supposedly objective or more well-balanced perspective onto history. It is precisely when the past comes laden with an emotional burden that it has the power to destabilize the present moment. "I just want to make people cry," Barrow has said about his artistic intentions.[23]

One of Barrow's most fraught appropriated images is that of the forlorn child with a tear in his or her eye, appearing in two guises in the *Trading Cards*: as part of the story of Margaret Keane, maker of the big-eye paintings, and as embodied in the Little Miss No-Name doll. The Keane story is told over the course of three cards, the first of which shows a framed painting of a young boy with enormous, wide-open eyes (fig. 17.2), with a very feminine hand holding a paint brush in the lower register. The second card repeats this format with a different painting, this time of a young girl. The text on the reverse side of the cards meanwhile tells of the break-up of the Keane marriage, the couple's fourteen-year legal dispute over the authorship of big-eye imagery, and the eventual victory of Margaret. It is only in the last card that the triumphantly smiling middle-aged Keane appears in front of a third painting of the same genre, now recognized and celebrated as the legitimate author of these artworks. The children in the first two cards look somewhat frightened, but they are dry-eyed, whereas the gender-indeterminate child of the third painting has acquired a large tear in one of its oversized eyes. The artist's addition of a tear is thus revealed to be the crowning authorial touch, the "money shot," in that this liquid materialization of the child's distress has guaranteed the popularity and market success of the big-eye genre since its 1960s heyday.[24]

Barrow introduces an even more perverse version of the figure Anne Higonnet has termed the "innocent child," with his images of the bedraggled Little Miss No-Name doll. In Higonnet's study of artistic and commercial visual cultures from the eighteenth to the twentieth century, she points out various instances when the purported innocence of children unravels, mainly because we come to question the motives of the adult viewer who takes a not-so-innocent pleasure in the vulnerability of those children. Lewis Carroll's 1859 photograph of Alice Liddell as a "beggar maid" is one such troubling picture she addresses,[25] and it is noteworthy that Little Miss No-Name shares many features of the Carroll portrait, including the rags, the semi-nakedness, and the outstretched hand asking for charity. Barrow's text informs us that the television commercial for this doll showed her "shivering in a burlap sack, barefoot in a blizzard," and the first card provides a rather psychedelic snowstorm as a background. Barrow then recounts, however, how this particular doll has become highly collectible, and indeed this contemporary apotheosis of the toy on eBay is an important part of the story the artist tells. All these years later, the most valuable dolls are those whose original state of destitution has remained perfectly intact, and of course it is essential that the left eye still sport that big plastic tear. Does the surge of nostalgia for Little Miss No-Name suggest that her plastic tears merged with real tears in the intervening years?

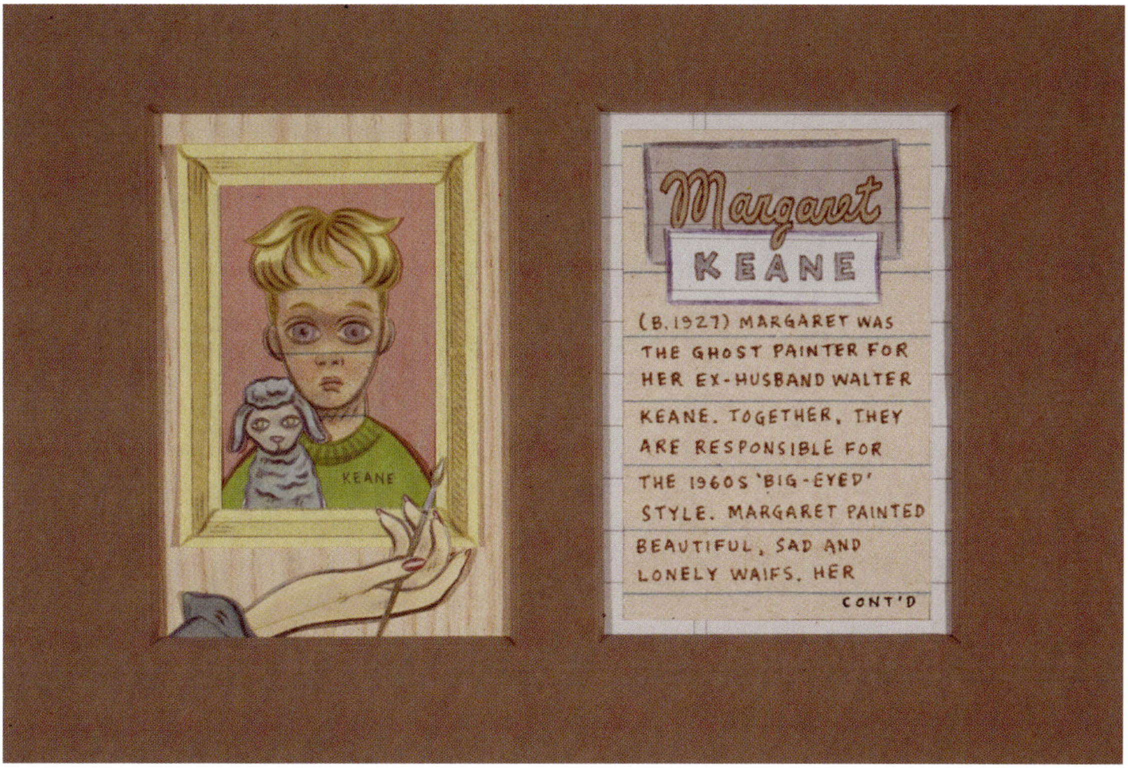

FIGURE 17.2 Daniel Barrow, *Margaret Keane Trading Card*, 2004, multiple edition, 7.6 × 10.2 cm. Collection of the artist.

The King Kong toy belonging to Diego Chambers was quite likely an Aurora Plastics Corp. model first issued in 1964, and this contemporary of Little Miss No-Name (Hasbro first introduced her to the public in 1965) also continues to circulate as a collectible object of desire, for adults who rather desperately want to repossess the toys they had as kids, or perhaps own what they were deprived of. How seriously should we take King Kong or Little Miss No-Name (or one of Dzama's Tomland robots), and what cultural significance might be ascribed to these diminutive figures? Is the attachment to such artifacts a sign of pathological nostalgia, or an unwillingness to assume adult roles and responsibilities? At one level, an artist's use of toys can pay homage to a notion of child's play, whereby the playthings are made to interact in unprogrammed ways, such that a sweet little doll might well set up house with a monstrous creature, who also happens to belong to a rival toy company. But the playlike rearrangement of things also has the potential to become a form of revisionist history.[26]

In Barrow's work the social trajectories and interior lives of both people and objects are given new life, especially through the artist's remarkable live-animation performances. Barrow's drawings are transformed through the layering of images, transparency, and simple lenticular effects, using only an old-fashioned overhead projector. Somehow, through the use of this technological relic and some decidedly low-tech techniques, a quasi-cinematic sense of movement ensues. In *The Face of Everything*, some of the most striking sequences are those showing Scott Thorson, Liberace's young protegé and lover, as he undergoes plastic surgery, supposedly so that he might resemble the older man. Medical instruments appear to float over Thorson's face, while the facial features themselves gradually shift and morph. The subtle transitions from still to flickering, almost-moving image are accompanied by the artist's spoken words, telling the story of a new identity being forged, and an old one coming apart at the seams. Through these performances, Barrow uncovers the reserves of pathos that lie hidden in such everyday tabloid exploits. And if the stories are not overtly autobiographical, there is nevertheless a sense that this constellation of people, objects, styles, and stories have been dredged up out of the past for a reason, that these fragments of pop culture detritus had become lodged in someone's psyche. In Barrow's work it is perhaps the figure of the adolescent Thorson, awkwardly and self-consciously poised between the worlds of childhood and adulthood, who provides an equivalent to Jack Chambers's doubled child/adult perspective. Barrow's characters are not exactly positive role models, but by focusing on queasy makeovers, uneven career paths, and unlikely success stories, the artworks do show how faces and identities are in a continual process of reinvention, and that the desire to attain an adult self is unceasingly fuelled by images from the past.

Rodney Graham: Half-Awake and Partly Adult

I want to propose that yet another kind of composite adult/child consciousness is evident in Rodney Graham's art practice. To begin with, Chambers's *Diego Asleep* and Graham's *Halcion Sleep*, 1994, are comparable because both artworks feature a centrally positioned sleeping child—in a manner of speaking. In the case of Graham's artwork, a videotape loop shows the (adult) artist curled up on the back seat of a moving van, but the artist himself has claimed that *Halcion Sleep* was meant to "enact a regression"[27] based on an early childhood memory, that of drifting in and out of sleep in the back of a family car, on the way home. The artwork shows the artist supposedly drugged and unconscious, after having ingested a double dose of sleeping pills with the brand name Halcion, "chosen for the pleasant thoughts of the past evoked by its name." And so for twenty-six minutes the viewer is presented with the sight of a man's prone, unresponsive, pyjama-clad body, while the flickering nighttime illumination of Vancouver is visible through the vehicle's windows. As was the case when Andy Warhol turned the camera on his lover John Giorno sleeping for his first film, *Sleep*, 1963, there is something startlingly intimate about being given permission to watch a stranger sleep. In this instance, the relationship of viewer to sleeper is complicated by the artist's stated goal, to regress to childhood over the course of this car ride. Of course, Graham arranged to have someone drive the vehicle and another person operate the camera, so it is still Graham's authority as a fully conscious and adult artist which largely determines the structure and meaning of *Halcion Sleep*. Is it possible that the viewer of this video loop might nonetheless begin to perceive the artist's childhood self emerge out of the sleeping man?

Graham's photographic, film, and video work of recent years has featured the artist enacting various roles, often in a state of dramatically altered consciousness or full-on unconsciousness. *Vexation Island*, 1997, shows the artist in the guise of an eighteenth-century shipwrecked gentleman lying prone on the beach of a secluded island, only briefly awakening and rising to his feet, to be immediately knocked unconscious again (and again and again, because this is an endlessly looping film) by a falling coconut. In *Phonokinetoscope*, 2001, Graham pays homage to a legendary bicycle ride undertaken by Dr. Albert Hofmann, the Swiss doctor who discovered and sampled LSD in 1943: the artist is to be seen riding a bicycle around a park after having apparently consumed this very same mind-altering drug. *Awakening*, 2006 (fig. 17.3), re-creates a 1970 photograph of the heavy-metal band Black Sabbath walking through a park, where Graham has assumed the place of an anonymous man asleep on a bench, a man who is pointed to and jeered at by the Ozzy Osbourne look-alike. These artworks can all be regarded as historical re-enactments, and as aesthetic strategies to bring the past to life.

Just as Chambers assembled his realistic painting with consummate and conventionalized artistic technique, so too does Rodney Graham's photographic and film work display authorial control and impeccable production values, even when the artist apparently lies knocked cold on the ground. If *Halcion Sleep* was a rather no-frills production, in subsequent projects Graham has adhered to the standards of high-budget filmmaking, with complex *mise en scènes*, smooth editing, and high-resolution images, and so on. As was the case with Chambers's painting *Diego Asleep*, it is from deep inside a conventionally constructed pictorial space that the artist registers a social and/or psychic disturbance; on the surface, everything looks perfectly okay. The expressive limitations Graham imposes on the visual technologies at his disposal are perhaps most apparent in *Phonokinetoscope*, where in spite of the subject matter under consideration—the consumption of psychotropic drugs—there is never one wayward camera movement that might correspond to a destabilized psychological or perceptual condition.[28] Rather, the camera follows Graham around the park with the utmost sobriety and decorum. It could be said that the camera is made to play straight man to Graham's clown.

In a 2002 interview, Graham announced that his films are "based on both personal childhood models and Hollywood stereotypes—'screen memories,' to adapt Freud's term."[29] The artist has indeed proposed this idiosyncratic understanding of "screen memories" on multiple occasions. In biographical terms, childhood memories and Hollywood screens intersected for Graham because his father, as manager of a British Columbia logging camp, showed movies to the workers. And so as a child (in the 1950s), Graham was physically immersed in a remote landscape, while at the same time encountering a phantasmatic world of pirates, cowboys, costume dramas, and so on. Therefore, these could be considered personalized and historically specific "screen memories." But Graham, attentive to the insights of psychoanalysis, has also referred to screen memories as "clever fictions constructed later by the unconscious to veil other, real memories." A psychoanalytic definition of "screen memories" has nothing to do with movies, whether emanating from Hollywood or elsewhere, and is instead related to the flawed quality of childhood memories. Discussing the way that memory is inevitably a complex psychic operation, Freud says, "mnemonic images are certainly falsified, incomplete, or displaced in time and place."[30] Do Graham's film loops and photographs capture elusive childhood memories in encoded form? The artist seems intent on informing his public that we shouldn't believe what we see, that the manifest content of his artworks, however entertaining it might be, however conventional in its fabrication, veils other, more disturbing content. Graham purports to lay bare the psychological and mnemonic foundations of his artworks, without ever offering any specific information, however, about the supposedly intolerable memories that have thus been camouflaged by the artist's visual fictions. Does some repressed trauma really lie beneath the surface appearance of a singing cowboy in *How I Became a Ramblin' Man* (1999)? Considering the levels of fiction and subterfuge in Graham's practice as a whole, we are under no obligation to accept his assertion of the artworks' traumatic depths. Nonetheless, it is worth noting Freud's remark that personal and collective memory might be structured along similar lines: "The 'childhood memories' of individuals come in general to acquire the significance of 'screen memories' and in doing so offer a remarkable analogy with the childhood memories that a nation preserves in its store of legends and myths."[31] This shift in emphasis raises the possibility that the convoluted memory work evident in Graham's artwork might concern something other than the troubled psyche of one individual. If the past inevitably makes its appearance in a warped form, is there a collective and social dimension to these distorted memories?

In *Awakening*, a photographic document of musicians from only a few decades ago serves as the basis for a new, unreliable memory image. As can be said of his art production in general, here Graham creates a picture of the (pop-cultural) past that is as distorted as would be a recollection of one's own childhood. And once again Graham

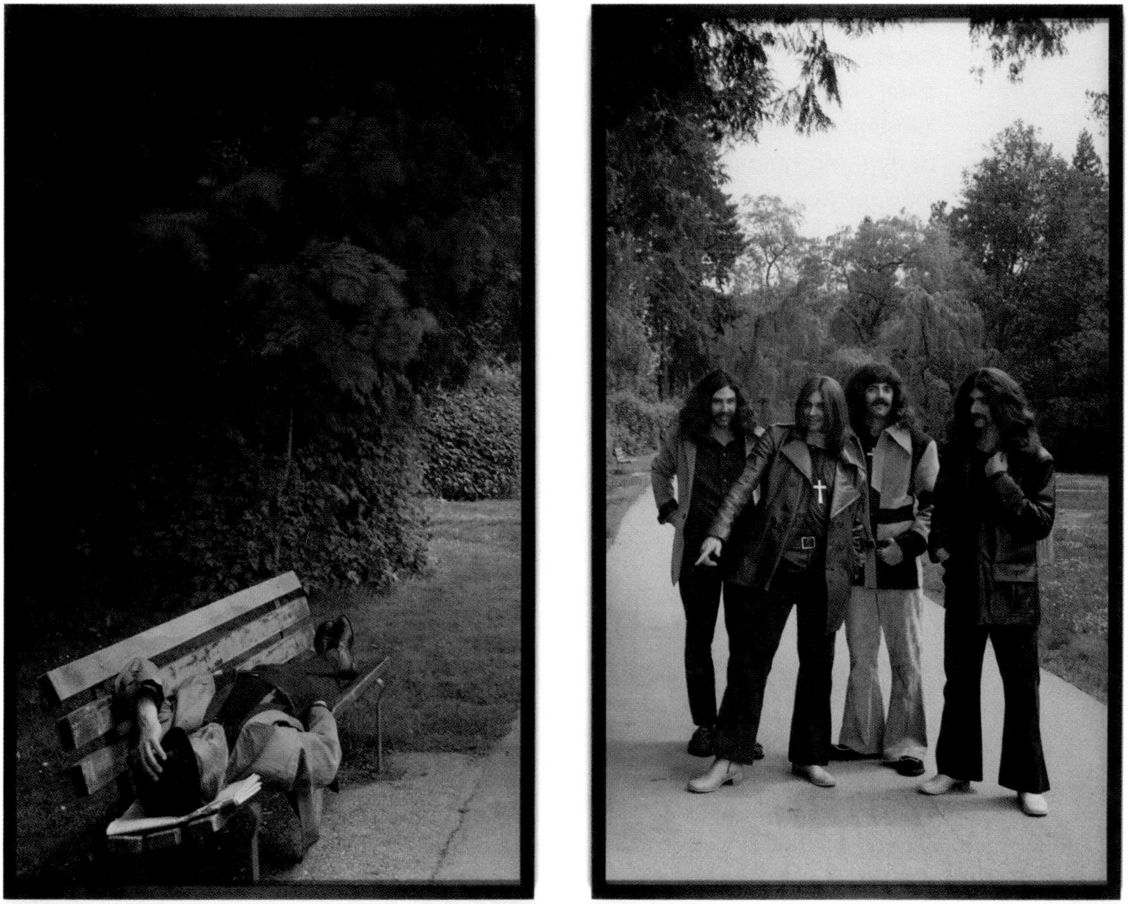

FIGURE 17.3 Rodney Graham, *Awakening*, 2006, two monochrome colour photographs, framed (edition of four), 240 × 146.1 cm. Donald Young Gallery, Chicago.

does not suggest a disturbance of the visual field through a fissure in the technical processes of reproduction: the large black-and-white image is masterfully printed and delivers a high degree of precise visual detail. *Awakening* is "wrong" in other ways: as the figures in the artwork are almost life size, it is quite easy to tell that the contemporary stand-ins for the Black Sabbath musicians wear exaggeratedly fake wigs, too-perfect "period" costumes, and caked-on makeup. This is comical, but the almost-real quality is also uncanny. In fact, Graham's *Awakening* is itself a doubled image, consisting of both a conventionally developed photograph and a "negative" version of the work, where the people have become shimmering, white, ghostlike presences.

Graham's artwork can be compared to Daniel Barrow's in the sense that both artists invite all kinds of kitschy, outmoded kinds of popular entertainment back to contemporary consciousness, back to haunt the present, and the world of art. With *Awakening*'s allusion to the glory days of transgressive youth culture, Graham also shows his willingness to confront nostalgia. And once again we are obliged to consider whether nostalgia constitutes a serious or effective engagement with history. Frank Ankersmit has written, "Characteristically, the strongest form of memory—nostalgia—is always accompanied by an intense and painful awareness of an unbridgeable distance to the object of nostalgic yearning."[32] In Graham's work, it is difficult to judge whether the past is flaring up for some personally or culturally legitimate reason, whether the particular ghosts who have been reanimated by the artist are delivering some meaningful message to us, or whether we are merely being distracted by a parade of clownish historical figures. Is there some other repressed or unbearable memory from circa 1970 that the Black Sabbath episode is screening, and that might be brought to consciousness? If the viewer is left in a state of uncertainty, doubt, or even psychic turmoil, this is surely because the flawed access to childhood memories has provided the template for the artist's engagement with the past.

As was the case with *Halcion Sleep*, where the artist first introduced his own (childhood) unconsciousness into the space of representation, in *Awakening* too Graham represents himself as something other than a fully functioning and rational adult man. This insertion could also correspond to the doubts one has when looking at old (family) snapshots: "Was I really there? Do I really remember being there, or is it only because this photograph of me as a child exists that I think I remember this particular scenario?" *Awakening* more explicitly transfers this unstable sense of self into a collectively remembered past, however. Graham inserts himself into a historical document in the guise of an anonymous man-on-the-street, but he is not a reliable witness to history, not least because he has himself become the object of ridicule. Thus, the contemporary re-enactment of a Black Sabbath stroll through the park can bring on the kind of psychic disturbance Freud suggested was characteristic of the uncanny experience, because the familiar and even kitsch darkness of this musical group has acquired a new pallor. In Graham's artwork, these figures from the "infancy" of heavy metal no longer mock some innocent and unknown man back in 1970, but rather this animus from the past is aimed directly at the artist, and by implication at the viewer, at this very moment.

In artworks by Jack Chambers, Daniel Barrow, and Rodney Graham, childhood is remembered and represented alongside the point of view of an adult subject. It can be said that all three artists are quite conscious of this complication: they recognize the "otherness" of childhood, but they don't attempt to retrieve some authentic essence that would be entirely exempt from adult knowledge, perception, and desires. Chambers painted his sleeping son Diego in such a way that the child's unconscious and unpredictable energy seems forever poised to interrupt the meticulously wrought and realistic picture created by the father. Barrow's world of adolescent yearnings and childish heroes is given narrative shape and ironic flourishes by a worldly sensibility. And Graham's carefully choreographed lapses of consciousness speak to a productive tension between childish regression and a more sophisticated kind of historical and aesthetic knowledge. At the same time, these artists pay close attention to those pop-culture images that infiltrate our psyches, memories, and bodies, as it is through these that imaginative encounters between childhood and adulthood can be staged.

Notes

I would like to thank Kristina Huneault and Zoe Chan for their valuable comments on earlier stages of this essay.

1 See Paul Duval, *High Realism in Canada* (Toronto: Clarke, Irwin, 1974); and Nancy-Lou Patterson, *Magic Realism in Canada* (Guelph, ON: University of Guelph, 1969).

2 Jean-Claude Lebensztejn, the curator of a major exhibition, *Hyperréalismes USA, 1965–75*, held in 2003, notes that "above all, the photography at the source of Hyperrealism could never be artistic photography." "Locus Focus: Jean-Pierre Criqui talks with Jean-Claude Lebensztejn," *Artforum* (Summer 2003): 152. In 1966 Gerhardt Richter would say, "I consider many amateur photographs better than the best Cézannes." Quoted in *Pop*, ed. Mark Francis (London: Phaidon Press, 2005), 32.

3 A painting by the American artist Robert Bechtle, *Agua Caliente Nova* (1975), for instance, more explicitly re-creates this configuration, with mother and children grouped around a parked car at a sunny tourist destination, the kids squinting at the viewer.

4 The original painting includes lines of text radiating from the figure's head; these are references to poetry, a hockey team, and the Mary Worth comic strip. This is apparently a serigraph version of the work that was in Chambers's possession, however. See *Greg Curnoe: Retrospective* (Ottawa: National Gallery of Canada, 1982), 77.

5 Like Chambers, Curnoe featured himself, his lover/wife, and eventually his children as protagonists of domestic scenarios, in artworks such as the *Family Painting* series from 1966.

6 Curnoe's mural was quickly taken down by the federal government agency that had commissioned it, ostensibly because of its anti-American and anti-war sentiments. See Charles Hill, "Greg Curnoe's Homage to the F-34," *National Gallery of Canada Review* 4, 2003.

7 Curnoe included Tintin's smiling face in a collage, *Bowering Westmount #5*, 1967, alongside fellow comic-book heroes Superman, Batman, and Robin.

8 The same year that *Diego Asleep* was painted, Chambers wrote about the temporal dimension he was attempting to capture in his paintings, suggesting that "the viewer on the outside looking in is able to experience the flow of time in which he is traveling and of which he is seldom, if ever, conscious." Jack Chambers, "Perceptualism, Painting and Cinema," *Art & Artists* 7, no. 9 (December 1972): 31.

9 For an account of how children have been increasingly interpellated as consumers since the post-war era, see Stephen Kline, *Out of the Garden: Toys, TV, and Children's Culture in the Age of Marketing* (London: Verso, 1993).

10 Barrow doesn't seem to have a single name for his own productions, as he refers to them as "graphic performance, live illustration, or manual animation." See http://danielbarrow.com.

11 The Royal Art Lodge has had a shifting membership. Michael Dumontier, Hollie Dzama, Marcel Dzama, Neil Farber, Drue Langlois, Myles Langlois, Jonathan Pylypchuk, and Adrian Williams were the eight artists included in the exhibition *The Royal Art Lodge: Ask the Dust* in 2003, while in 2007 the RAL website lists only Dzama, Dumontier, and Farber as members. See http://www.mts.net/~mondmann/.

12 Wayne Baerwaldt and Joseph Wolin, "An Interview with the Royal Art Lodge," *Royal Art Lodge: Ask the Dust Dictionary of Received Ideas* (New York: The Drawing Center, 2003), 14.

13 Jean Dubuffet, quoted in Lucienne Peiry, *Art Brut: The Origins of Outsider Art* (Paris: Flammarion, 2001), 98–99.

14 Marcel Franciscono, "Paul Klee and Children's Art," in *Discovering Child Art: Essays on Childhood, Primitivism and Modernism*, ed. Jonathan David Fineberg (Princeton University Press, 1998), 96.

15 Wayne Baerwaldt, quoted in Sascha Hastings, "Doodle Dandies: The Art World's Newfound Appreciation for Drawing," on the CBC website, http://www.cbc.ca/arts (June 22, 2005).

16 Marcel Dzama, "Top Ten," *Artforum* 40, no. 2 (October 2001): 59.

17 Marcel Dzama, "Dzamatizations: The Drawings of Marcel Dzama," *Border Crossings* 17, no. 3 (July 1998): 36.

18 See the artist's website, http://www.danielbarrow.com, under the "collections" rubric. Accessed February 2007.

19 Umberto Eco, "Lowbrow Highbrow, Highbrow Lowbrow," in *Pop Art: The Critical Dialogue*, ed. Carol Anne Mahsun (1971; repr., Ann Arbor, MI: UMI Research Press, 1989).

20 Dick Hebdige, "In Poor Taste: Notes on Pop," in *Modern Dreams: The Rise and Fall of Pop* (New York: ICA; London: MIT Press, 1988), 78.

21 Guy Maddin, "City Report: Winnipeg," *Frieze* (March 2006): 146.

22 Will Straw, "Careful," in *Canada's Best Features: Critical Essays on 15 Canadian Films*, ed. Eugene P. Walz (New York: Rodopi, 2002), 309.

23 Daniel Barrow, in an artist's talk at Concordia University, Faculty of Fine Arts, March 21, 2007.

24 While the term derives from porn, "money shot" has been used to describe the emotional payoff on talk shows, that anticipated moment of bodily response, of "tears that stream or drip down the face; the suffused blood visible in an angry face; the spittle sprayed from a mouth contorted by rage, spewing bleeped invectives; even the fistfights, bared breasts, and spit-swaps on stage." Kelly Dennis, "Money Shots," *Art Journal* 64, no. 3 (Fall 2005): 119. (This is a review article of Laura Grindstaff, *The Money Shot: Trash, Class, and the Making of TV Talk Shows* [Chicago: University of Chicago Press, 2002].)

25 Anne Higonnet, *Pictures of Innocence: The History and Crisis of Ideal Childhood* (London: Thames & Hudson, 1998), 123.

26 It is worth noting that the Toronto-based curator/collector Ydessa Hendeles put a vintage Minnie Mouse toy on the cover of her *Partners* exhibition catalogue. This exhibition, held at the Haus der Kunst in Munich in 2003, ambitiously addressed the Holocaust through an arrangement of contemporary artworks, documentary photographs, and a few toys. Hendeles asked the art world to take seriously the plight of this absurd mouse toy, forever on the move with her suitcases in hand. See Anja Bock, *Exhibiting Trauma: Ydessa Hendeles at the Haus der Kunst in Munich* (MA thesis, Concordia University, 2004).

27 Rodney Graham, "Halcion Sleep," *Rodney Graham* (London: Whitechapel Art Gallery, 2002), 112.

28 Graham might well have chosen to mimic the visual tricks of 1960s mainstream films such as *The Trip* (1967) or *Darling* (1965), which make liberal use of coloured scrims and strobing lights to visually approximate a drugged person's perceptual experience.

29 Rodney Graham, "Inteview with Anthony Spira," Whitechapel Art Gallery website, http://www.whitechapel.org/content461.html (2002).

30 Sigmund Freud, *The Psychopathology of Everyday Life* (London: Hogarth Press, 1960), 46.

31 Ibid., 47–48.

32 F.R. Ankersmit, *Historical Representation* (Stanford, CA: Stanford University Press, 2001), 178.

comic strip, *Aeroplane Ace* (1938), which do the same. But this snapshot carries considerably more freight. Snow, the adult artist, is using this snapshot of Snow, the child, to make a point about the creative act. His re-presentation of this image as—I must repeat—the penultimate image in his bookwork, functions as a kind of signature to the work. Captioned in the first person (the only first-person artist's statement in the book), the image can be taken as a key to this bookwork that is the summary of Snow's oeuvre to date, proposing a construction of its producer, the artist, as subject. "Infantile freshness. What a strong wind!" exclaims Snow in a text about the creative process written just one year later.[2] He lists the benefits of having a poor memory, a rather doubtful claim, but effective in making the point that his artistic activity occurs in the time and space between familiarity (memory) and anticipation (imagination), both modes of consciousness nourishing his intense present-based perceptions. This position is encapsulated in the photograph, drawing a picture of an adventurous child muse, harboured in the mind/body of an adult artist. Other children will figure in Snow's work: his son Aleck as an infant in *Quintet* (1984), an adolescent Aleck in the film **Corpus Callosum* (2002), and a rebellious schoolroom of children in a crucial segment from the same film.[3]

Taking a page from Snow the modernist and his bookwork, *A Survey*, it seems important to stress one rather obvious point. We (reader and writer) are looking at the photograph of a child identified as Michael Snow. Some philosophers, Kendall L. Walton at the head of the class, would phrase that differently: we are looking *through* the photograph at Michael Snow, *through* this window-like viewing device that is a photograph.[4] Snow, even at an early age, seems to have been skeptical of such claims, and still today, he would encourage us to see and understand the photograph as an image-object that is material, literal, and symbolic—part of a large family of image-object-metaphors for the relationship between sight and mind. So we should take this depiction of a child coolly. And yet, however rigorously we explain the image to ourselves as a paper-based sign representing two distinct episodes of photographic activity (prospective/retrospective), there is no escaping the fact that we are being led through these intellectual hoops by a child. This is not an innocent child, but a knowing child—I am using terms of differentiation proposed by Anne Higonnet, but here in a particular way: this image-child, and other image-children to be examined here, are figured as guides through sensorial experience to uncharted territories of knowledge. In the works I have in mind, the figure of the child functions within the work of art as Snow once defined the *very function* of a work of art: "a directing of the spectator's attention by the artist, or a guidance to concentration."[5] Higonnet's "knowing child" displays knowledge of the visual codes of innocence, participating in photographic works that explore forbidden sexualities and the terrors of violence between children—the very darkest children's

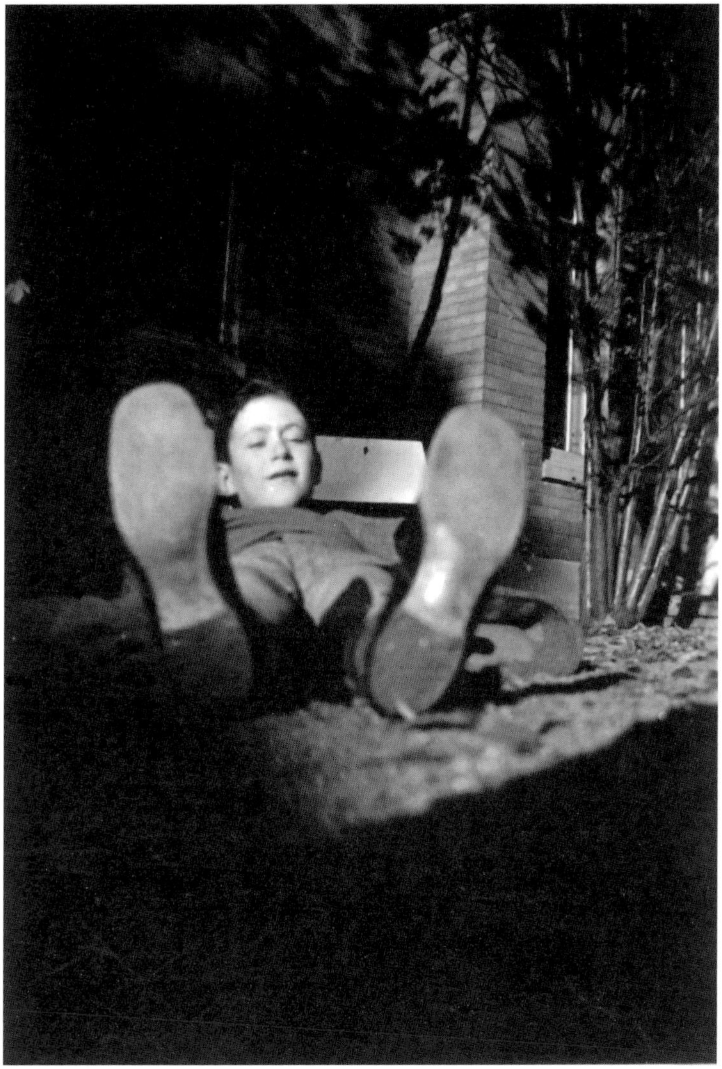

FIGURE 18.1
Denyse Snow Rynard and Michael Snow, untitled snapshot (1936), detail of artist's book, *Michael Snow/A Survey*, published by the Art Gallery of Ontario in collaboration with the Isaacs Gallery (1970).

hours. Questions of reality and fiction matter in Higonnet's framework because real children are pictured in these works, real people respond to them, and increasingly, emerging artists, some barely out of their teens, are generating them, with real-world implications.[6] Without diminishing the importance of Higonnet's work, for it is both urgent and important, I want to suggest that there are other realms of knowledge tapped by the figure of the child. Snow and other artists considered here use photography and film to amplify other ways of knowing: present-based or future-oriented states of consciousness. Children, figures drawn from their own children, point the way.

The differences between these complementary ways of "knowing" can be explored through the portraiture of Robert Minden. In the 1970s and 1980s, Robert Minden photographed the surviving members of two Canadian exile communities, including their descendants: Japanese Canadians and Doukhobor Canadians. He also photographed families, his own and others—intertwining projects that continue to this day under the headings of *Family Arrangements* and *Portrait of My Daughters*.

Minden's approach to photographic portraiture was inflected by his training as a sociologist. Sensitized by the teachings of Erving Goffman to the richness and subtleties of face-to-face communication, Minden was intrigued by the potential of staging human encounters before the camera. As a budding sociologist, he had studied the family. As a budding photographer, he was drawn to "the skin called 'family' … the layeredness of it.… I wanted the photograph to leak, to melt, to reveal those layers."[7] Leaking, melting, and revealing are slow processes, needful of patient observation and a compatibly slow machine. Minden adopted the view camera as an instrument and a prop that heightened and extended the photographic meeting: "We're lousy actors—you can't hold the official version very long."[8] He also learned the craft of fine printing, to enhance the beauty and permanence of the image and to bring out in the print every nuance of what Goffman had called "small behaviours."[9]

Family Arrangements depicts all kinds of families, but pays particular attention to single parents and their children. The series title was carefully chosen, ironically paraphrasing "flower arrangements," with their false, denaturing effect.[10] Minden rejected the role of arranger, instead creating space and time for the families to arrange themselves. The subjects' involvement in this photographic act coaxed out their *small behaviours*—their subtle expressions of *family*. Minden was fascinated with the ways that members of these families positioned themselves before the camera—tiny, lucid details, such as the touch of mother's hand, or the tension in a child's clenched fist. The public nature of these private encounters is frequently underscored by their setting—out-of-doors to satisfy the view camera's hunger for light and sometimes framed in a doorway, on the sill of the family home. The settings are therefore rather formal, while the poses, clothing, and facial expressions are not.

Minden was photographing families around the time that Susan Sontag wrote:

> Photography becomes a rite of family life just when, in the industrializing countries of Europe and America, the very institution of the family starts undergoing radical surgery. As that claustrophobic unit, the nuclear family, was being carved out of a much larger family aggregate, photography came along to memorialize, to restate symbolically, the imperiled continuity and vanished extendedness of family life.[11]

Family Arrangements does something very different. It refutes the judgments on family and photography implicit in Sontag's ascerbic text. Some thirty years later, Minden reflected on the various ways that his photographic theatre had drawn out the vulnerability and heroism of his subjects. His were inarguably "dark pictures of people who were very much holding on and arranging themselves as they could, as they saw fit, and revealing themselves in ways that they had not necessarily chosen to." But while the family portraits can be unsettling, they also speak of love. Minden's critique was never aimed at the parents and children, but at the impossible conditions of their existence as a social unit: "What had failed the test was society's understanding of the family and this was an image of that failure." Different arrangements were bound to come out of these nonconformist *family arrangements*, but how would the children's attempts at redefinition be received? "Can this be the place in which the flowers of diversity bloom or do we beat them down?"[12]

Lark and Her Children, Vancouver (1974) depicts a family standing in the doorway of their home (fig. 18.2). It is the front door; architectural hints are reinforced by a printed sign that says: "Children and Friends please use back door. Others ring or nok." Lark and her children are meeting the photographer at the entrance designated for "Others." There are four children, whose family resemblance to their young mother is striking. They have arranged themselves in a triangle, the mother's face at the apex, the two younger children at arm's reach, the two older girls seated at their mother's feet, young lions guarding a temple. The arrangement forms a photographic archetype, a reminder of Dorothea Lange's iconic *Migrant Mother* (1936).[13] Minden was always attentive to such correspondences; he would later characterize his series as "the underlife of the *Family of Man*."[14] Edward Steichen's famous exhibition also contained dark pictures, but the dominant message was of hope: signs of piety, compassion, literacy, science, technology, and decisive moments organized to affirm its faith in the nuclear family. In the published version of *Family of Man*, "We two form a multitude" is the message repeated under seven photographs of (apparently) heterosexual couples: Adam and Eve (Mom and Pop). Their progeny are the hope of the nuclear age. Lark is of that generation. *Family Arrangements* can be read as the reality that haunts Steichen's dream.

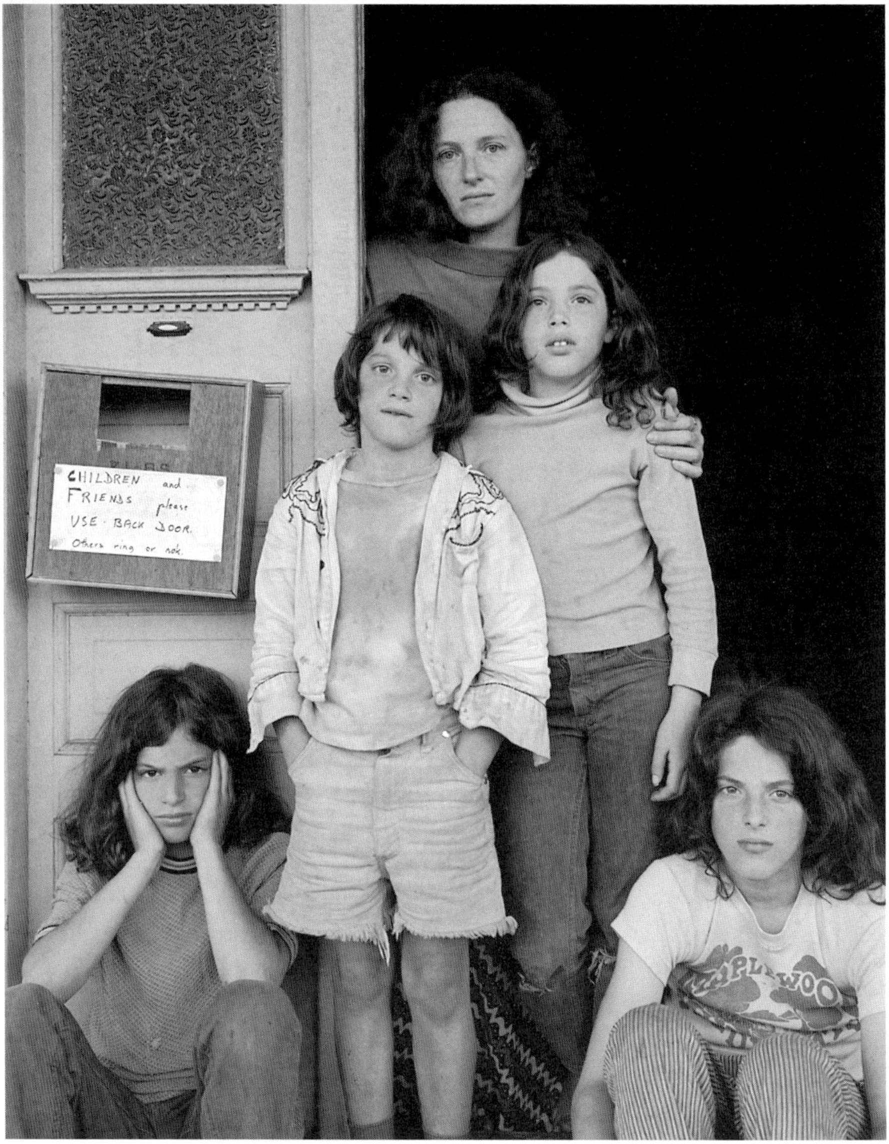

FIGURE 18.2
Robert Minden, *Lark and Her Children, Vancouver* (1974), from the series *Family Arrangements*, gelatin silver print, 35.4 × 27.7 cm.

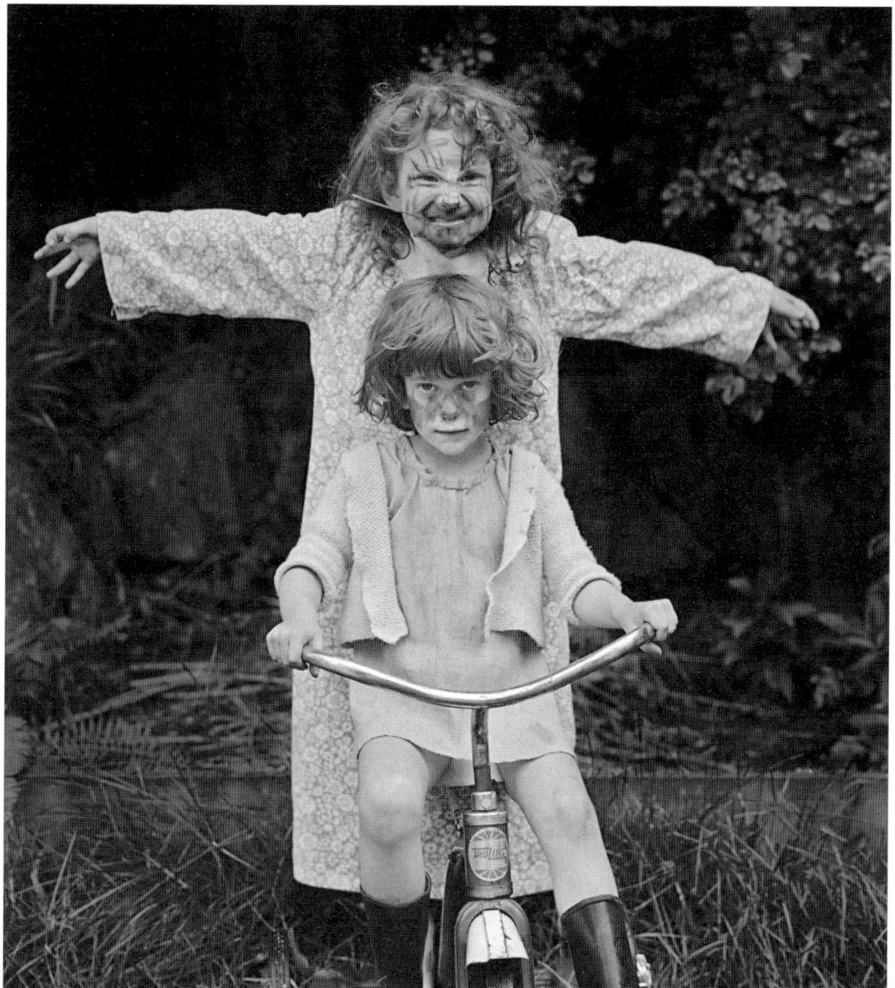

FIGURE 18.3
Robert Minden, *Andrea and Dewi, 1973* (1973), from the series *Portrait of My Daughters*, gelatin silver print, 24 × 18 cm.

Lark stands alone with her children; they are beautiful, not beatific; their childhoods stale-dated, they wear the look of having seen too much. The youngest boy, positioned in the middle of the group, thrusts his hands in his pockets. Nested in the family, he is protected and caught in a net of relations. The poses of his mother and older siblings form circuitries of touch: one is steadied by her mother's grip; one cups his face in his hands; one hugs his knees. They look out; they hold themselves in. They are possessors of a particular way of knowing, children who relate to a camera, communicating *through* it their knowledge of who they are, where they stand, and how they might be perceived, both individually and as members of this group. Registering that image through Minden's camera, they are contributing to the history of the Western family—five and one histories of family photographic experience.[15]

A complementary system of knowledge, also turning on the photographic act, is evoked by Minden's *Portrait of My Daughters*, a series developed in parallel with his better-known projects at Steveston and Grand Forks—projects that kept him away for days, or even weeks. Coming home from these trips, Minden was the photographer-father who sometimes re-encountered his daughters through the camera. The role-playing that factored in his portraits elsewhere was, if anything, heightened in his own backyard. "A lot of [the photographs] were prompted by my daughters, enjoying me as a photographer and enjoying going through the drama." The dynamic of the moment was everything, "sometimes being enthralled by it, sometimes being the catalyst for it," as he later recalled, the "it" being "a kind of improvisational theatre." Any attempt to control the situation was futile; the dynamic was powerful, but evanescent: "Children rarely hold still and you can't make them. Sometimes they would just quickly become enamoured with an idea, 'Oh oh, let's make a picture of this' and go into a grotesque, gargoyle pose between themselves. And it would quickly evaporate."[16]

In a photograph from 1973, imagination takes flight (fig. 18.3). Andrea and Dewi have painted their faces using theatrical makeup or watercolours—whatever bright colours came to hand. They want to be photographed. Minden positions the camera to pose them in front of a dark, leafy screen. Dewi sits on her tricycle, as though pedalling toward the camera. Self-possessed, almost shy, she looks intently into the lens. Andrea, positioned behind Dewi, is in every way her sister's foil. In a flowered nightgown, she is both tall and wide. Arms extended, face contorted into a lion-like snarl, she clenches improvised whiskers between her teeth. Her monstrification reaches its climax and the shutter must be released: *now*.

The energy bursting from this photograph shines light on Minden's entire photographic oeuvre. The crucial point is that appeals to posterity, whether for the Doukhobors or his family, were very much beside the point; a present-based theatre of encounters between strangers, or family members, "reaching through the medium of the camera" was the driving force. "My daughters were so alive to the moment; they were infusing life with their wild games and their tremendous imagination and their incredible storytelling between themselves." Photography admitted their father to a "tribe of childhood. It had different language, a different body language; it had different myths and stories and languages and furies and passions and things that were forbidden."[17] It was here, close to home, and not in the field, that Minden's background as a sociologist and his creative instincts fully coalesced, leading slowly but surely to the improvisational music and storytelling for young audiences that have occupied him, mind and body, for some twenty years. *Portrait of My Daughters* holds the key to those places of exploration.

Many artists work with memories of their own childhood, some tormented by traumatic memories that they have put to work in their art, some nostalgic for the freedoms and phantasms that adults put aside as childish things. The child evoked in André Breton's first "Manifesto of Surrealism" acts on the present as an agent from the past:

> From childhood memories, and from a few others, there emanates a sentiment of being unintegrated, and then later of *having gone astray*, which I hold to be the most fertile that exists. It is perhaps childhood that comes closest to one's "real life": childhood beyond which man has at his disposal, aside from his laisser-passer, only a few complimentary tickets; childhood where everything nevertheless conspires to bring about the effective, risk-free possession of oneself. Thanks to Surrealism, it seems that opportunity knocks a second time. It is as though we were still running toward our salvation, or our perdition. In the shadow we again see a precious terror.[18]

Childhood memory is one thing—a second chance at the unconscious—but there are other conceivable conduits, some more immediate. Years later, in a letter to his eight-month-old daughter, a letter he imagines her reading at age sixteen, by which time he will have died or disappeared, Breton is able to articulate what Mary Ann Caws expresses as his "intense and unshakeable sense of the doubleness of everything—these contrasts that can be bridged only by a sort of miracle, or the daily marvelous."[19] The miracle here is temporal: Breton puts his message of love in a bottle, imagining a future that recollects the co-presence of father and daughter in September 1936, when "the unconscious and the conscious, in you and me, existed in complete duality near each other, keeping each other in total ignorance and yet communicating at will by a single all-powerful thread which was the exchanged glance between us … that thread which is happiness, such as it pierces the web of unhappiness itself."[20] And what is this infant communicating? Or, in this temporal doubleness, what knowledge does Breton imagine her "one day" imparting? Answers to "insidious questions" grownups (himself?) ask children: "'What do we think with, suffer with? How did we get the sun's name? Where does the night come from?' As if they could answer the questions themselves!"[21] He cannot imagine the answers; his own childhood memories will not supply them. And so Breton concludes his letter, and his reader closes the book, with the faint hope that his daughter, "the human creature in its perfect authenticity," might have (before now, for now, sixteen years later, he is gone) taught him about them.[22] Memories from the future dangle before Breton a vast treasury of knowledge. His astonishment and ours at his attachment to "authenticity" echo (astonishingly) in the temporal conundra of Roland Barthes. The photograph, Barthes writes, "is a prophecy in reverse: like Cassandra, but eyes fixed on the past.... From a phenomenological viewpoint, in the photograph, the power of authentication exceeds the power of representation."[23] A photograph is tamed by generalized consumption; it remains mad (and therefore "authentic") if it bursts the restraints of depiction by activating the spectator's imagination, if this violence bestirs a kind of mad questing love. The figure of the child may perform this function, in presence or in absence.

A series of images by photographer and writer Michael Mitchell is accompanied by this text:

> There has been another war. Arriving home after midnight, I discover the troops' blanket tents and dozens of small casualties on the kitchen floor. Despite the late night silence, all the lights blaze. My sons sleep where they dropped. One is curled in a chair while the other, covered by a mother too tired to carry him to bed, lies stretched out on the floor.
>
> I survey the damage room by room. When I find my hardhat keeping strange company in the sink, I begin to set up my view camera. A search for the focus cloth ends under the meat grinder. Viewed on the ground glass, this incredible chaos becomes rich in mystery. I begin to realize that my search for new pictures is really a search for my sons.[24]

Staying Home (1981–1983/1990) documents Mitchell's search as a series of photographic still lifes created by the sons and recognized by the father (fig. 18.4). Mitchell's allusive text only occasionally comments directly on the content of the images. Polyphonic, it is a compilation of true stories woven together from the writer's life: childhood memories; life before fatherhood and after; oscillations between *being there*, listening to his little boy's dreams, and *being away*, "the man who is always in airports"; the imagined thoughts of his boys missing him.[25] The colour photographs are primarily of objects, supplemented with part-objects—a chubby hand or sun-kissed ear poking out from under a duvet. Autobiographical and made up of everyday things, the images are both coded and decipherable by interested strangers. They are "amenable objects," critic Jeanne Randolph's term for artworks met in public and publicly investigated for "the artist's version of experience, intentionality that need be neither explicit nor disguised."[26] Exploring the use of psychoanalytical theory in art criticism, Randolph draws the spectator into a space of mental play explicated by psychoanalyst D.W. Winnicott as a space

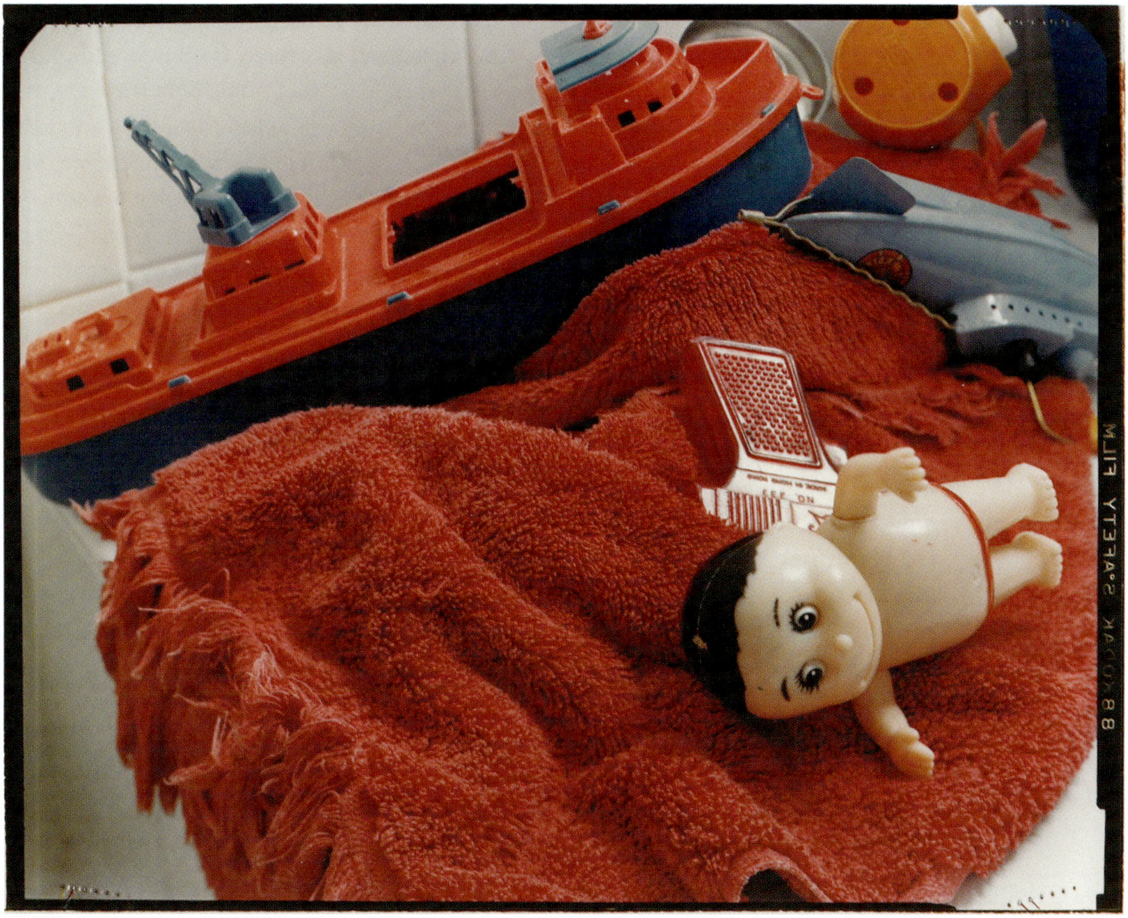

FIGURE 18.4 Michael Mitchell, untitled, from the series *Staying Home* (1981–1983/1990), chromogenic print, 40.5 × 50.6 cm.

between subjectivity and objectivity, "between me-extension [the transitional object] and the not-me." As Randolph explains, "Winnicott did not see how there could be something objectively experienced without some aspect of it having already been anticipated by creative subjectivity."[27] Mitchell's selective documentation of his children's toys is a photographic doubling of objects, textually redoubled: *Staying Home* is an elegant, by which I mean deceptively simple, reification of creation as "an adaptive relationship with the mysterious world." Creation is serious play; as Randolph develops Winnicott's theory, "It is not that the adult artist reverts to a baby-like state when he or she is artistically inventive; it is as though to play were one of the first adult modes that a child acquires."[28] In his boys' spaces of play, Mitchell father-and-son processes his memories, works things through. A boyhood memory of lying in the grass, watching a plane stuttering and gliding between clouds has been recovered from a serendipitous combination of toy planes and puffy white batting; another airfield, at the edge of a brown paper mountain range, reminds Mitchell of a sputtering plane over the Caribbean. The father's wrenching account of his family's boating accident is accompanied by a documentary photograph of an accidental still life: a boy doll floating among foundering ships in a roiled red-towel sea. Such strange coincidences make up Breton's "daily marvelous," Barthes' "prophecy in reverse." The suspended games of the sons spark the memories of the father, who writes: "We photograph something in the present in order to recover the past."[29]

Sandra Semchuk's earliest photographic projects are also explorations of the past, as an expression of identity between personal experience and collective memory. Born in Meadow Lake, Saskatchewan, and raised with a consciousness of her Ukrainian ancestry, Semchuk, become a photographer, worked patiently to portray the people and settings of her childhood, before turning to an even more personal project, a collective portrait involving her most intimate relationships: "grandmother, father, mother, sister, nephews, nieces, husband, daughter."[30] This project evolved into a way of working that Semchuk called "co-operative" self-portraiture, exemplified by her *Co-operative Self-portrait: Rowenna and I. R.R. 6, Saskatoon, Saskatchewan, June 1979* (1979) (fig. 18.5). In this black-and-white panoramic image, Semchuk and her daughter are found dancing in their sun-drenched kitchen. Toe pointed, arm extended, Semchuk controls the remote shutter release but looks to Rowenna for her cue to take the picture. Consciously, or unconsciously, responsibility for the content of the photograph has been split. Space belongs to the mother, time to the daughter. The stage having been set by Semchuk, she cedes direction to the daughter who gestures forcefully toward the camera, looking down her arm directly into the lens. The formula is simple, especially in the description, but the effect is curiously complex. The combination of Rowenna's concentration in the moment and her mother's attunement to it exerts a strange magnetism, indeed, changes the basic dynamic of spectatorship. Semchuk can be felt both inside (looking on) and outside (looking into) the picture. This effect is heightened by her position in the frame: her hand brushes the upper edge, her toes scrape at the bottom; she is in the picture with her daughter, the subject, and also outside it with us, the spectators. Spontaneity, in this case, means responding to another as co-creator—effectively ceding authority to a being who brings another mode of consciousness into the creative act. As Semchuk admits her daughter to the process, so she admits us—she makes herself a bridge. The dialogical nature of the co-operative self-portraits stands in sharp contrast to another, concurrent series of self-portraits (1976–1981) in which Semchuk used the camera as a mechanical diary, relentlessly recording her face as a palimpsest of life experience.

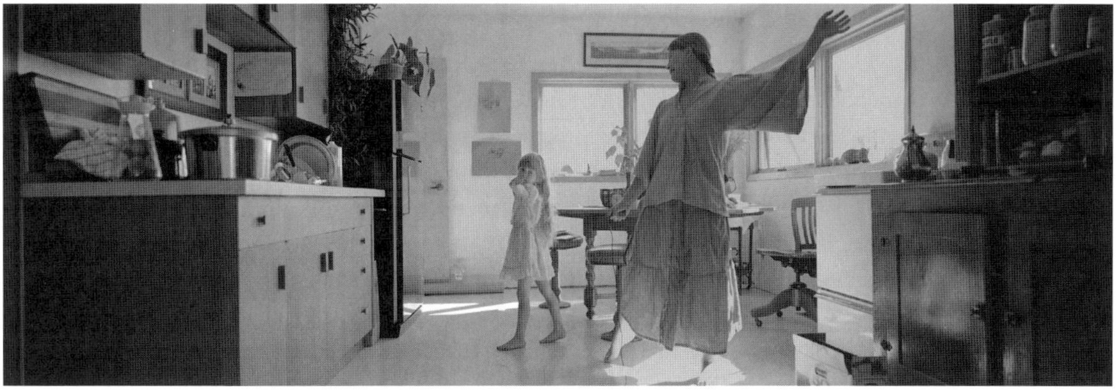

FIGURE 18.5 Sandra Semchuk, with Rowenna Holden, *Co-operative Self-portrait: Rowenna and I. R.R. 6, Saskatoon, Saskatchewan, June 1979*, gelatin silver print, 14.7 × 43.2 cm.

In 1981 Semchuk and her daughter moved to London, Ontario, joining a community of performance artists, including Rae Davis, Robert McKaskell, and Coco Gordon, also Rowenna's godmother. The impact on Semchuk's work was decisive. Its spontaneity returned in ways of working that *Co-operative Self-portrait: Rowenna and I* was rehearsing, but whose predictions were not yet clear. Reflecting on that time, Semchuk writes:

> I was very excited about the idea of visual gestures done with the body that were an articulation of complex and often unconscious sensual perceptions. I was also studying free form Chinese calligraphy as it was passed down from Chin Shek Lam, where the physical act of making the stroke in the moment is an articulation of disposition in motion.[31]

This two-year period of investigation immediately preceded Semchuk's move to New Mexico, where ideas already set in motion flowed into her photographic imagery.[32] Rowenna, then seven, carried the memory of the London performances in her body: "She was the most free of the two of us and, in the small rituals that she did in nature, she articulated complex modalities of awareness and perception."[33] She was also blossoming under the tutelage of an inspired teacher, a Mrs. Sloan: "She was Navaho and brought some of New Mexico's finest First Nations' artists into that grade two classroom to talk about their work."[34] Semchuk remembers precisely the moment that these complementary forces, operating on herself and her child, came out in her own practice:

> Rowenna was playing with the long golden "ropes" of the giant willow trees when I began to use the camera gesturally, in relationship to her movements: "a moving parallel," I called it. It seemed to me that her actions were a way of speaking, a visual poetry. I think my use of the camera was a kind of visual listening to her, trying to move closer,

> recognize or witness her complexity and the spontaneous brilliance of a seven-year-old, without appropriating her.[35]

Semchuk took Rowenna as both teacher and subject, expressing this synergy by embracing movement in her still photographic work. Her technique was to slow the shutter speed, play with the focus, and take the camera "through a kind of stroke"[36]—processes hard to predict, results invisible to the naked eye, thus drawing the artist into a fully embodied mode of automatic writing. As she recalls (a very telling recollection for a still photographer): "When I saw the uncut roll of film, the immediacy of the experience was there."[37] A single summarizing image would never do, nor should the action be frozen. Rather, Semchuk began to develop sequences of rich, calligraphic images. Blurring, or fuzziness, is a double sign, expressing both the daughter's uncontainable energy and the close proximity of her artist-mother. In the middle frame of *Series #10* (1982/1983), made in New Mexico, Semchuk's presence is recorded in a shadow falling across Rowenna's bare chest; elsewhere we see the artist's feet, and guess that the camera is being held out at arm's length. Working at the edge of a dark pool in which Rowenna plays, or floats, simplifies the colour and texture of a work that will ultimately be printed to heighten the elemental contrasts—the sun-warmed skin and the fathomless black water. *Series #10* is a succinct five-part sequence. Semchuk would later develop more complex, irregular-shaped grids, such as *Pinery Net Fishing, Pinery, Ontario* (1984/2005), photographed in collaboration with Rowenna after their return to London (fig. 18.6). Both mother and child appear in this work whose creation is co-credited. For McKaskell, the work eliminates the boundaries between the artist and nature: "By using her camera to record movement rather than things, [Semchuk] transforms an act of play into a ritualistic encounter with nature. The four elements—earth, air, fire and water—are not so much depicted as evoked."[38] The conditions of the work's creation choreograph the spectator's movement, across the landscape, in and out of the frame. Rowenna's embodied knowledge persists in this co-operative self-portrait.

We understand the photograph as synchronized seeing, even though the seeing is *not* direct but mediated by an instrument and materials, a fact underscored by Semchuk's blurs. Lark and her children, who gaze frankly into the lens, are felt to communicate something of their circumstances; we presume on this kind of portrait—often a very static image—for measured doses of intimacy with the other. Social documentary photographers have produced countless images in this vein. What makes such an image memorable is its call on the viewer's connotative powers, through recognition (Barthes' *studium*), and the interruption of that call—a phenomenon that Barthes called "the *punctum*" of the photograph: "a 'detail,' *i.e.*, a partial object."[39] The *punctum* disrupts conventional readings of the photograph, imbuing the image with heightened subjectivity, one might almost say possessing it, so powerful is the viewer's fixation on a detail that no one else seems to have noticed. All of Barthes' examples draw on memory, a private

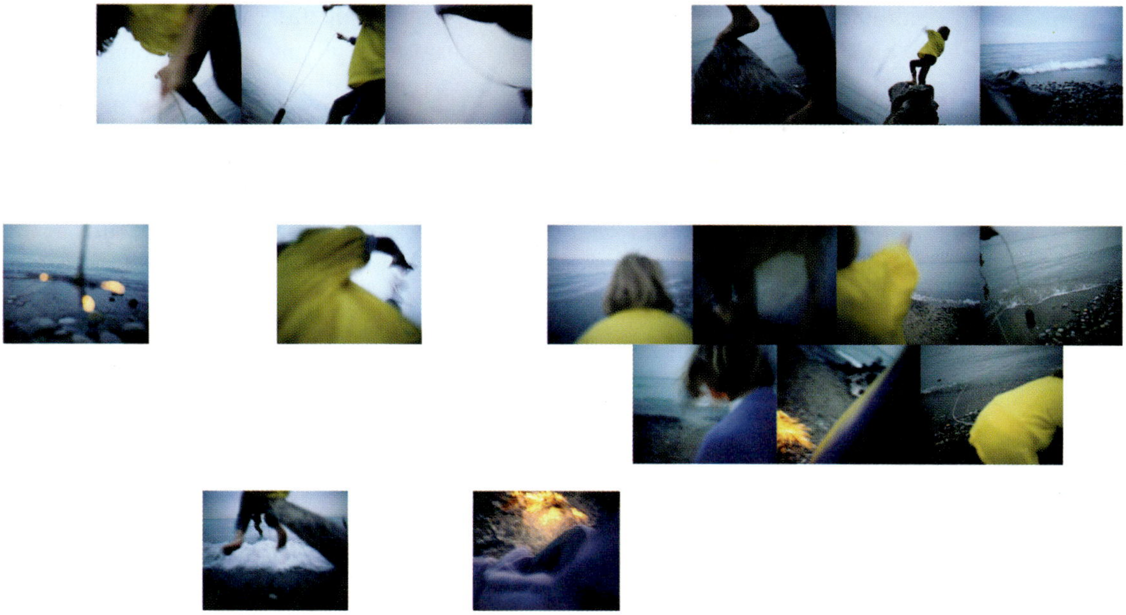

FIGURE 18.6 Sandra Semchuk, with Rowenna Holden, *Pinery Net Fishing, Pinery, Ontario* (1984/2005), 17 chromogenic prints, 612 × 1008 cm installed.

reserve from which he cites liberally, sometimes "mistakenly," as Margaret Olin has intriguingly shown.[40] The *punctum* is a mobilizer of twin forces, memory and imagination whose visual expression—pastness quickened and coloured in the present—may remind us of a child's re-creative imagination.

Michel Campeau began his career in the 1970s as a social documentary photographer, though he felt restless within this frame right from the start and was especially keen to distance himself from any claims of objectivity or truth to be found in external appearances.[41] For Campeau, a frontal portrait of a subject (young or old) gazing into the camera offered as much, or as little, knowledge as the photographic negatives and snapshot albums preserved by his mother—mysterious artifacts of his own childhood that he wanted to understand better and through which he sought connections to an absent father. The only process that made sense was purely subjective, a creative interpretation of the evidence, a fictionalization of the gaps. At age forty, he entered his photographic past through his imagination, accompanied by his first child, a son, Léandre.

The bookwork that emerged was *Les tremblements du coeur* (1988).[42] Léandre is present throughout: a blurry figure, wafting up between his father and an unmade double bed; a newborn, curling up and clenching his fists in one frame, displaying his body to the camera in another (which one shows his character?); playing naked at Grand Lac Noir and fingering the end of his penis (oh dear—has he scratched it on that rock?); squinting, and later wailing, unprofessionally close to the camera at Port-au-Persil. In between, Campeau has inserted fragments of his own family history, leavening that daily bread with images appropriated from the photographic canon, such as Duane Michals's *Self-portrait Shaking Hands with My Father* (c. 1973) and avant-garde cinema, such as the soon-to-be-fallen angel in Wim Wenders's *Wings of Desire* (1987). These borrowings are expressed as memories, imperfectly clear and sucked into the vortex of the present by a phrase or a visual prompt. There are echoes and parallels throughout this book: a snapshot of a boy and his mother in a graveyard, taken *sometime* in the 1950s, part of a cycle of mourning and regeneration; cherubs praying over wildflowers in an overgrown cemetery; a solitary guardian angel whose view over the water has been spoiled by a filling station. A key image of the bookwork, used twice in fact, is Campeau's solitary self-portrait, *Autoportrait à la table lumineuse, Atelier* (1984). He stages himself as an exhausted bourgeois worker, rubbing his tired eyes with his white-gloved hand, sitting at a light table where he has been shuffling images. Behind him, pinned to the studio wall, is yet another narrative sequence (which one is right?).

Photographic theorist, artist, and friend Richard Baillargeon takes the *Atelier* self-portrait as his entrance to *Les tremblements du coeur*, reading the image as a synthesis of photographic production and spectatorship, or more precisely, as an oscillation between the two. The photograph resists neutral contemplation—Baillargeon does not know quite where to stand. His position as spectator has been anticipated by a camera-eye that common sense ascribes to Campeau, and yet, Baillargeon does not feel usurped. Rather, he identifies with this doubled subject.[43] From there, the narrative of presence and absence flows, with Campeau always doubly cast: the absent father's and present son's life stories intertwine.

Where is Léandre in all this? In 1984 he is absent, not yet born, but in 1988 he is making his mark on the *Atelier* self-portrait (fig. 18.7). His chubby arms, wielding a crayon, declare his appropriation of the photograph, which he has reworked vigorously with swirling strokes and proto-letters. Is this picture-upon-picture another *mise en scène*? In other words, was Léandre caught or staged in the desecration of this iconic self-portrait of his worker-father? Possibly both, in a two-stage process of re-creation, recognition, and reintegration into the father's œuvre. For the crayoned photograph was not part of *Les tremblements du coeur.* Retitled *Gribouillage sur la photographie—Autoportrait à la table lumineuse* (1988), it appears in a later bookwork, *Éclipses et Labyrinthes* (1991) whose double title suggests planetary alignments, a plunge into darkness, walking blind, fingering a magic thread.[44] The portrait of the artist, as altered by his son, figures these myths. For while Léandre's crayon has whipped up an expressive storm

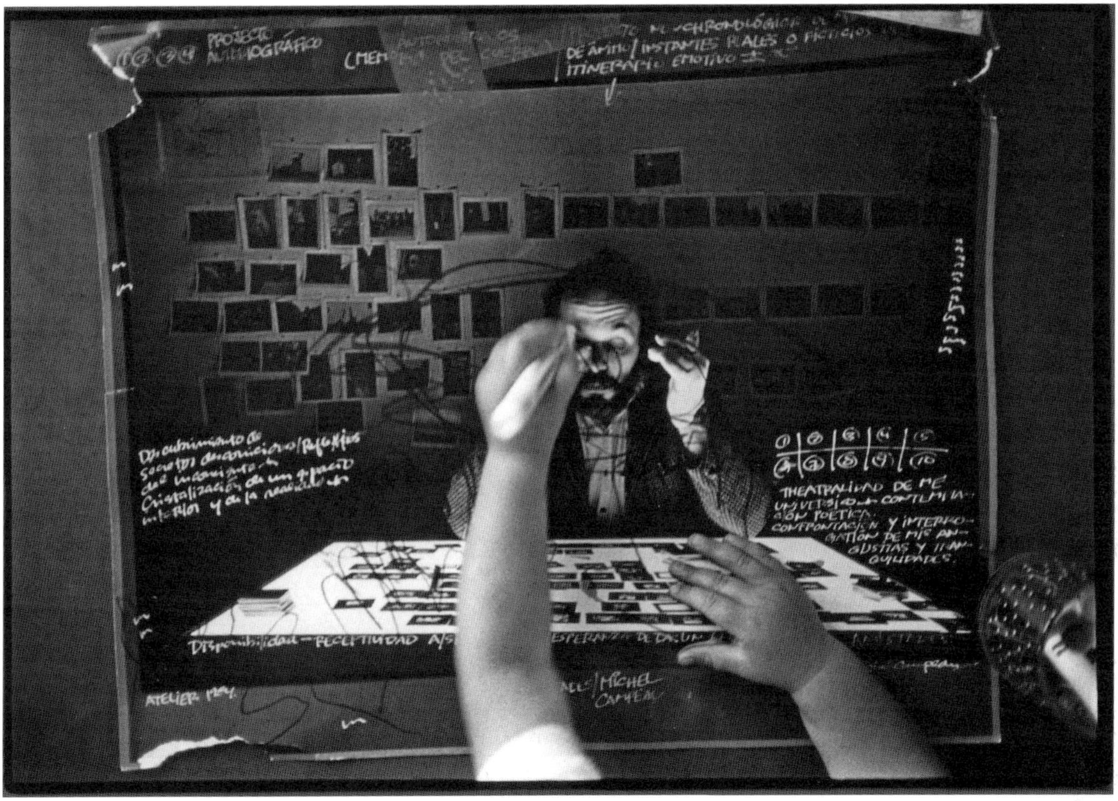

FIGURE 18.7 Michel Campeau, *Gribouillage sur la photographie—Autoportrait à la table lumineuse* (1988), from the artist's book, *Éclipses et Labyrinthes* (Chicoutimi, QC: Séquence, 1991).

around his art-worker–father's head—the very image of a labyrinth—it also stabs him in the eye. The father is blinded; his vision turns inward. Is the moment Oedipal? Perhaps. The myth of childhood is the brilliance of the future; the present will be eclipsed. And yet, the inner child twists through the corridors of the past.

But leaving these dreams and fantasms, Campeau's use of Léandre's grafitti shows us something rather more hopeful on a social level. The portrait of the artist-father here includes the mark of his child, a person who is not remote, but near enough to wreak havoc with the oeuvre that is solitude's castle.

Minden, Mitchell, Semchuk, and Campeau depict the child—in each case, their own child or children—as a very active agent in their work, showing them things, reminding them of things, and awakening them to their imaginations. The child opens up the world of dreams, a realm sometimes entered with difficulty by an adult artist, lumbered

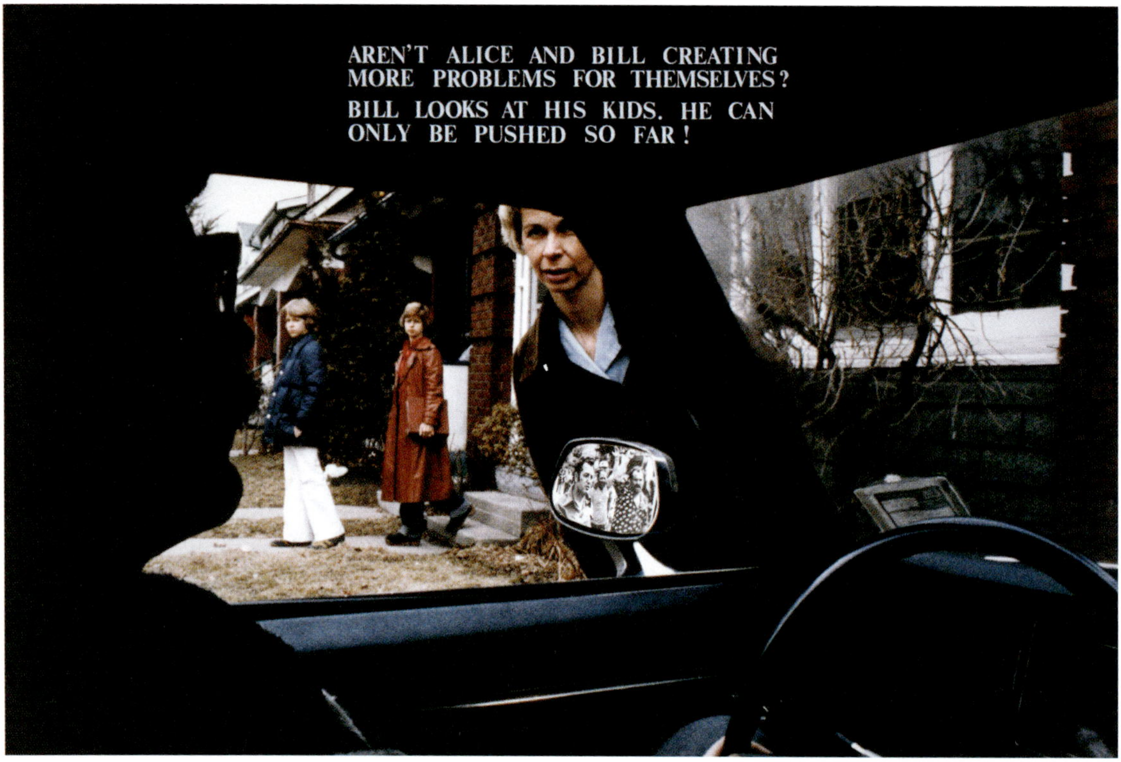

FIGURE 18.8 Carol Condé and Karl Beveridge, detail from *Maybe Wendy's Right* (1979), chromogenic print, 40.2 × 61 cm.

with an instrument of the real. But as Breton (the self-consciously imperfect father) reminds us, the very act of conceiving a child is a leap into the void—an act of faith and hope and dreaming pinned on another life.[45] A parent's imagination is never purely poetic, but frequently quite practical and therefore social and political. Parents may imagine the very real possibilities of social and political justice for their children. These motives are the underpinning of an early work by the activist artists Carole Condé and Karl Beveridge, *Maybe Wendy's Right* (1979).

The work takes the form of a photo-novella. The genre is staged photography, the principal roles played by Condé (wife/mother); Beveridge (husband/father); Simara Beveridge, the artists' daughter who was sixteen at the time (daughter/sister); and Simara's friend Peter Dobson (son/brother).[46] I have attended elsewhere to the work's intermingling of memory and imagination, its dialectical narrative of a working-class Canadian family awakening to the importance of collective action.[47] Here I want to focus on the role of the daughter, Wendy, who leads her father through the shoals of caution and coercion to his ultimate decision to support the strike. The briefest synopsis will lay out the issues at stake.

The crisis at the plant has invaded the home, setting up conflicts between husband and wife, parents and children, and especially, father and daughter. Wendy's eyes are on her father as he talks on the phone about the looming strike—wife and mother Alice watches two brewing storms, the plant's and her family's. Wendy holds up signs of rising food prices. Wendy looks over the TV listings, where she finds nothing to watch, no revolutionary sisters on *Charlie's Angels, Mary Tyler Moore, Wonder Woman.* Wendy reads while her father and brother gaze at the TV, whose screen has been covered with a black-and-white portrait of themselves as a smiling family unit: "Seeing themselves as the boss sees them." As the labour crisis builds, Wendy's gaze fixes on her father; they argue, her pose assertive, his aggressive, a closed fist responding to the double threat to his manhood. Later, tempers cooled, he visits Wendy in her room, where she is studying Marxism. "They talk." And after a restless night, the father's decision has been taken: "Bill looks at his kids. He can only be pushed so far!"

The war is being conducted over economic justice for the worker; the battleground is the family, where in the 1970s, as now, other battles are also taking place. In *Femininity as Alienation: Women and the Family in Marxism and Psychoanalysis* (1977), British political theorist Ann Foreman summarizes the conflicts embodied in the characters of *Maybe Wendy's Right*:

> Capitalism split society into two worlds—the world of business, industry and social interchange, and the world of the family. But the two were not symmetrical. Men strove to rule in the first, but failing that were the victors in the second. Women were their foils in both. Family life provided the relief where, after the threats and assaults that social life made on a man's confidence, the woman confirmed his humanity and subjectivity. Away from the constant fight for survival in the competitive arena of social production his position at the centre of the family's world was guaranteed. Femininity, in capitalist society, takes its meaning from this relationship.[48]

Maybe Wendy's Right turns on a man's decision, but the stickiness of the piece is its investment of hope in the *next* generation. The inequities at the plant, echoed in the dynamic between husband and wife, may never be resolved to the satisfaction of their daughter, but the political imaginations of the artists, poured into the character of Wendy, are at work, breaking open the ideological constructions that have been naturalized to the point that, as Foreman suggests, "real experience ... is only partially understood." Wendy's mother is going through a period of questioning, but she belongs to a generation for whom "the full experience of femininity prevents women from developing a consciousness of their oppression," making them "unknowing accomplices in their own oppression."[49] Alienation does not begin at home, but enters it daily, mirrored in domestic arrangements whose gender-based inequities then rebound from the private back into the public whenever women are able, or obligated, to join the workforce. In the 1970s, Marxist theorists were grappling with this situation, goaded by the radicalization of the women's movement; different strategies and concepts of social justice had these groups at loggerheads. Condé and Beveridge represent the stresses by using the pictorial device of *mise en abyme*, a picture within a picture. This device gives us our last glimpse of Wendy who, framed by the car window, is seen looking back at her father—seen through her father's eyes. She is walking out of the family home, carrying her briefcase (fig. 18.8).

One might take this image to mean that only by leaving the domestic sphere can a woman achieve both economic and sexual freedom, but the picture can be read another way. Perhaps the revolution fomented at home can be spread, and then returned to the domestic sphere. As Foreman was suggesting in 1978, the women's movement had the potential to "help transform the traditionally limited location ... content ... and form of political struggle." Potential areas of intervention included everything from student unions and public housing to sexuality. The women's movement, then dominated by the educated middle class, might also correct itself, by opening up to working-class women. And as Foreman continues to speculate, "Perhaps gradually small workshop discussions, a feature of the women's movement which allows the individual to contribute and recognises the validity of his or her personal experience, could replace more formal types of debate."[50] *Small workshop discussions*, often conducted around the kitchen table, have been nourishing the work of Condé and Beveridge for some thirty years, leading to projects on union histories, industrial safety, socialized medicine, and women's labour. Listening to "Wendy" was the beginning of their photographic activist oeuvre.

For Marian Penner Bancroft, the impetus is showing her daughter Susanna, or rather, looking with her at places, objects, and images that have constructed their family identity and thus constitute their situation in a particular place and time. Broadly speaking, the place is Canada, itself a construction of national myths and local legends, while the time is a confluence of cultural, familial, and individual times. In the early 1980s, Bancroft began to incorporate references to space—both crossings and occupations—using a combination of inherited family photographs, ambiguous landscapes, and natural materials to express the affective and ethical complexities of her own implacements. A first series, entitled *Transfigured Wood*, introduced Bancroft's desire to change the spectator's relationship to the photographic object. As large images, pushing into the spectator's space, works from this series involved the spectator in physical and metaphysical repositioning. If a certain level of discomfort arose, if the message could not be digested easily, Bancroft was satisfied. She increased the level of difficulty with *Mnemonicon (the screen)* (1988) (fig. 18.9).

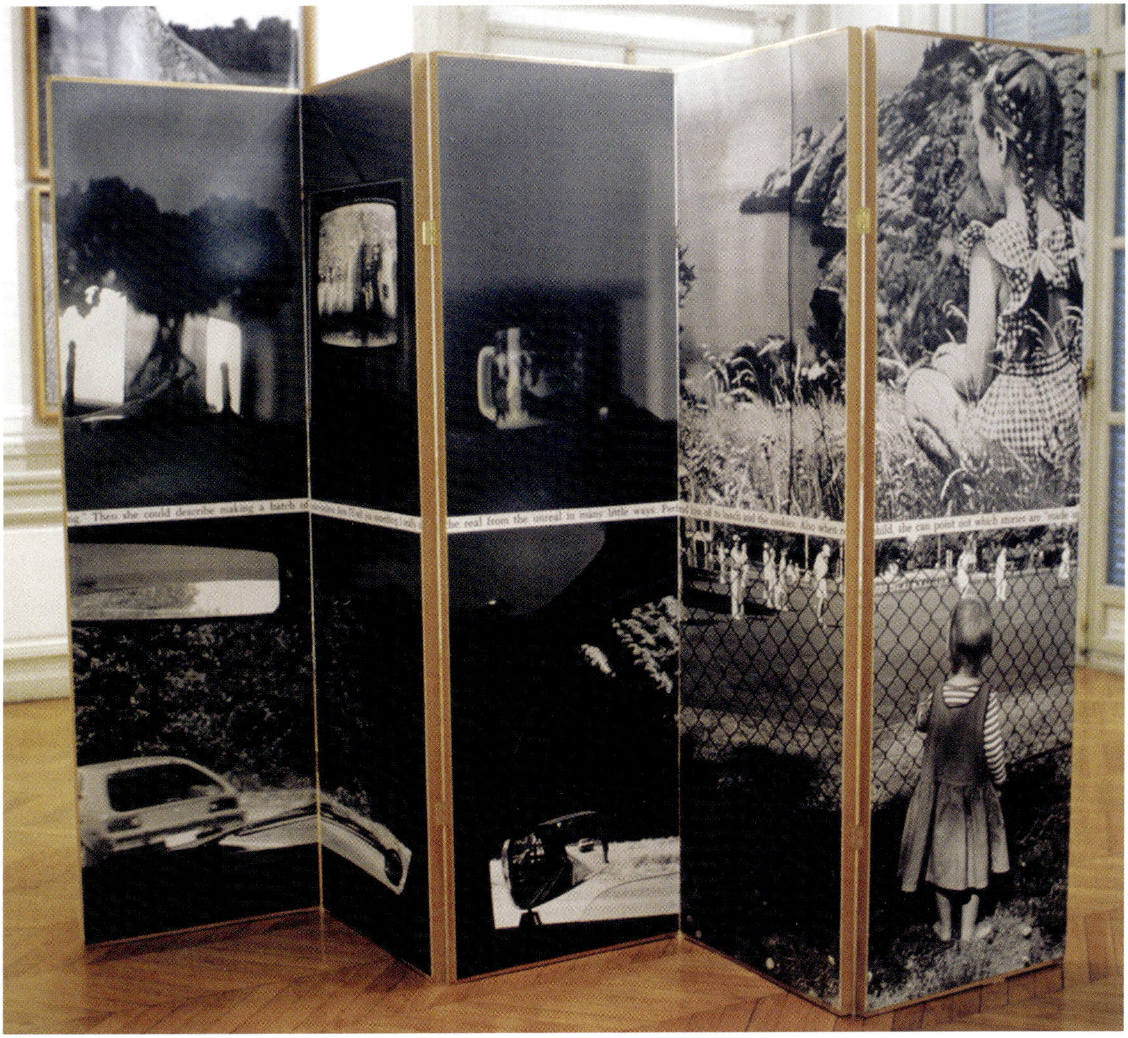

FIGURE 18.9 Marian Penner Bancroft, detail from *Mnemonicon (the screen)* (1988), black-and-white photographs, fir, metal hinges, 203 × 317 × 7.62 cm. Collection of the artist.

A large, free-standing art object, *Mnemonicon (the screen)* must be circled to be seen in its entirety and must be committed to memory to make all the correlations Bancroft had in mind:

> I've placed side by side images from a number of sources for the construction of my white Canadian female identity. These representations come from different places in history, from the utopian landscape found in children's books; the television screen; the presence of the monarchy through the images of the Queen and Prince Philip; the landscape read through a car window while being driven, being in it and not in it all at once; from a mother's care manual of the fifties sitting beside a contemporary image of a child in a chair, these being references to two separate times, that of the child and that of the mother. There is a reference also to Canada as a colonial culture, with the image of the Queen and the image of my daughter watching a lawn bowling tournament through a fence, the elderly players all dressed in white.[51]

Susanna, this very little girl, elsewhere pictured in diapers, stands at the edge of the playing field, her fingers exploring the chainlink fence that separates her from the mysterious game and also frames it. She functions in this image as a *Rückenfigur*, a walker stopped in her tracks by a view. The *Rückenfigur*'s gaze channels the spectator's contemplation. This is a deictic figure—a stand-in for photography's deictic function, which is to point us *at* a subject, thus making us conscious of where we stand in relation *to* that subject. Like Semchuk in the 1979 co-operative self-portrait, that is, literally in the picture and figuratively outside it, the presence of Susanna is powerful—she is the motive force of the piece, a reliable guide to the territory mapped by her mother. And she represents an important tenet of Bancroft's beliefs: that however hard we look, our knowledge of place remains imperfect; a *Rückenfigur* is a partial eclipse of the view.

Figuration is a very copious term, functioning across the semiotic field, iconically, indexically, symbolically, each of these modes leaching into the other; as Richard Shiff explains, "Figuration spreads." Figuration is referential, whether to an object, an act, or a system of knowledge, and these things link together as a *mode* of figuration. To figure an object or an idea is to represent, or characterize, it in a form that can be apprehended. No figuration, then, without cogitation, as Shiff explains: "Figuration occurs to the extent that a simple act of visual attention—looking at something, becoming aware that it has significance—is interpretive."[52]

This principle is elaborated by Michael Snow's *Quintet* (1984) (fig. 18.10). The work consists of a framed oil painting of a nude female figure on which surface (I mean, the painting) is a photograph of a man (modelled by Al Mattis) holding up a child (modelled by Aleck Snow), as though to contemplate the work. The photographic element is both within and without. The frame of the painting is cut away below the photograph, setting up a productive zone of confusion between representational and

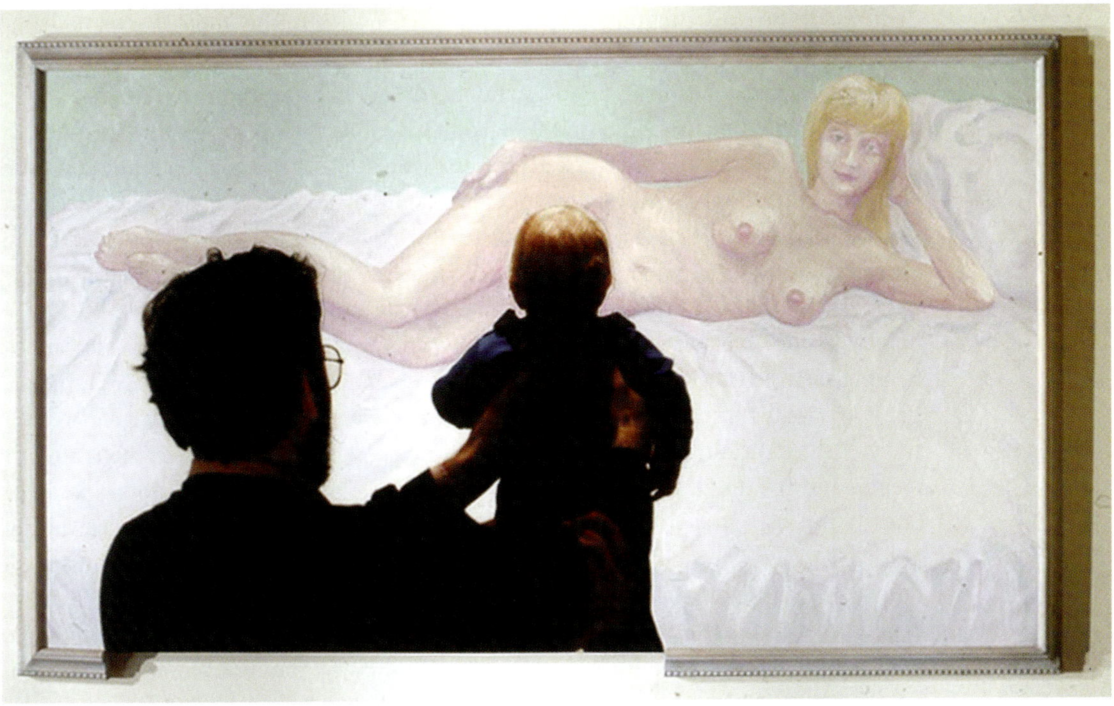

FIGURE 18.10 Michael Snow, *Quintet* (1984), oil on canvas, photograph, 88 × 150 cm. (Collection: Burle & Louise Yolles. Courtesy of the artist)

spectatorial territories. The man and baby are supposed to be with us, but they are also with her. And who is she, but a pale, almost vaporous figure, whose pleasant expression and blonde hair suggest neither maternity nor nights-of-love-with-man-made-laws-forgot: she is a figure of contemplation. Her breasts are displayed, but her pubic region (if ever it was painted) is fully covered by the baby's head. Again, the child as *Rückenfigur* shows us where to look and prevents our seeing. And yet we are engaged, indeed, summoned to the work by its title, *Quintet*, the five parts of the group being the painted woman, the photographed man, the photographed child, the artist, and the spectator.

Louise Dompierre places *Quintet* in a family of works, produced by Snow in the early 1980s, which "propose an understanding of the world as one that is driven and conditioned by the image."[53] Indeed, the basic proposal in this work deals with the nature of image-objects, and especially, the confusion set up by the combination of different media. The photograph, in its transparentness, as a thing we look through, here blocks our gaze; the painting, as a surface and a thing we look at, here impassively returns our gaze. This culturally bounded experience is almost naturalized, perhaps because the dualities of the construction are so ordinary, so founded in the "daily marvelous." But within the terms of this work of art, who is instructing whom? Dompierre reads the work as figuring "apprehension and understanding" of "art and its reception ... reproduction and representation ... sexuality and sexual difference." A father instructs his son "through representation or at a once-removed level from the Real."[54] But the gender of this babe is by no means established by the work, and taking him or her as my surrogate, I am struck by the denial of knowledge in this partial eclipse of the painted figure's body. There are secrets being kept in the mind of this child, the newest born of Snow's figurative quintet.

Many modern artists have acknowledged children's art as a source of inspiration, helping them to break through the social and psychological boundaries of adulthood. In Snow's work, the model is somewhat different. Children, when they appear, direct the spectator's attention, intensifying and extending perception, allowing constellations of feeling and meaning to *form* around the forms in play. In the living room scene of Snow's film **Corpus Callosum* (2002), the adolescent boy, played by Aleck, seen staring at the television is watching clouds drift across the sky—that is, he is watching a digital moving image of clouds through the technological window of television.[55] The living room, a decorated box, will soon come alive with arrivals and departures of people and objects, but a core illusion has been established by the directed attention of an adolescent in an ordinary domestic scene.

Beginning and ending with Snow's photographic illusions, I have looked at a number of ways in which the depiction of a child figures the creative process in an artist's work. This is not to be taken as a picture of innocence; on the contrary, as I have stressed, the children pictured here are active, knowing agents of visual concentration and spectatorial fascination. With no attempt to survey this phenomenon, recourse to the very different work of Robert Minden, Michael Mitchell, Sandra Semchuk, Michel Campeau, Carol Condé and Karl Beveridge, Marian Penner Bancroft, and Michael Snow still suggests certain commonalities. The sources of these images are specific, one might say "local." They are little bits of observation and intuition, some accidental discoveries, that have been allowed to grow into figurative photographic forms. The figure of the child underscores the temporal aspects of the photograph; time is the child's otherness. This awareness of time heightens its expression in the work: the blur, the ruptured edge, the picture-within-a-picture, the juxtaposition of old and new. In a photo-novella, as in a real family, the arrival of a child starts the clock; decisions become more urgent. For the photo diarist, dailiness is not quite large enough, especially when his or her own memories of childhood rush in. A photographic figure that tests time leads the photographic artist away from the real, into the imaginary, there to meet the child in me.

Notes

1 Michael Snow and the Art Gallery of Ontario, *Michael Snow/A Survey* (Toronto: Art Gallery of Ontario and Isaacs Gallery, 1970), unpaginated.

2 Michael Snow, "Passage (Dairy) 1971," in *Collected Writings* (Waterloo, ON: Wilfrid Laurier University Press, 1994), 66.

3 In "The Child in the Machine: On the Use of CGI in Michael Snow's **Corpus Callosum*," Malcolm Turvey describes the performance of Aleck Snow, as well as the classroom scene, as he explores what he sees as the expression of Snow's "childlike consciousness" (40–41) in computer-generated imagery (CGI). A fine description of the classroom scene is given by Erik Bullot in his "Keaton and Snow" (26–27). Both articles appear in *October* 114 (Fall 2005). My article, I hope, supplements these authors' observations and interpretations with an account of Snow's longstanding interest in form.

4 Kendall L. Walton, "Transparent Pictures: On the Nature of Photographic Realism," *Critical Inquiry* 11 (December 1984): 246–278.

5 Michael Snow, interviewed by Pierre Théberge, "Laocoön of the People (1987)" in Snow's *Collected Writings*, 254.

6 Anne Higonnet, *Pictures of Innocence: The History and Crisis of Ideal Childhood* (London: Thames & Hudson, 1998); Higonnet, "The Image of Childhood Today" (keynote address at the symposium "Picturing Her: Images of Girlhood," McCord Museum, December, 1, 2005).

7 Robert Minden, in an interview conducted by the author in Vancouver, December 14–15, 2000.

8 Ibid., 2000.

9 Erving Goffman, *Interaction Ritual* (New York: Pantheon Books, 1982), 1.

10 Minden interview, 2000.

11 Susan Sontag, *On Photography* (New York: Farrar, Straus & Giroux, 1973, 1978), 8–9.

12 Minden interview, 2000.

13 American photographer Dorothea Lange took her most famous photograph, *Migrant Mother*, while working for the Farm Security Administration. Taken to illustrate the plight of tenant farmers during the drought and depression of the 1930s, Lange's photograph focuses on the worried expression of a woman stranded with her three children in the middle of a frozen pea field.

14 Minden interview, 2000; *The Family of Man* (1955), a photographic exhibition organized by Edward Steichen for the Museum of Modern Art in New York, included 508 photographs taken in 68 countries and sequenced to form an extended photo essay with all aspects of human life. A great popular success, both in exhibition and book form, *The Family of Man*'s universalist message was sometimes met with sharp criticism and continues to be cited as a photographic monument of the Cold War.

15 Children need not know the history of photographic portraiture to rehearse its tropes; the conditions simply repeat themselves to be materialized photographically in similar ways. But any child who has been exposed to the complementary technologies of family photography and the bathroom mirror knows something of self-presentation and applies it when asked to pose for a camera. Under normal circumstances (neither flood, nor famine), modern children who do not stick out their tongues or say "Cheese" in front of a camera have been discouraged from doing so, whether by osmosis (mimicking the seriousness of the photographer), photographic experience (snapshots in which they looked silly), or in so many words ("Now let's try one where you don't smile—just look into the camera"). To say that children know that their performance in front of a camera is controllable is not to assert that they always know what to do. I write from the perspective of a "knowing" child who unintentionally sabotaged her First Communion photographs by squeezing her eyes shut to affect an air of piety.

16 Minden interview, 2000.
17 Ibid.
18 André Breton, "Manifesto of Surrealism (1924)" in *Manifestos of Surrealism*, trans. Richard Seaver and Helen R. Lane (Ann Arbor: University of Michigan Press, 1969), 40.
19 Mary Ann Caws, "Reading André Breton," *Context: A Forum for Literary Arts and Culture* 11 (2002). Online edition, http://www.centerforbookculture.org/context/no11/Caws.html (accessed December 28, 2006).
20 André Breton, *Mad Love* (*L'Amour fou*, 1937), trans. Mary Ann Caws (Lincoln: University of Nebraska Press, 1987), 117.
21 Breton, *Mad Love*, 119.
22 Ibid.
23 Roland Barthes, *Camera Lucida: Reflections on Photography* (*La Chambre claire*, 1980), trans. Richard Howard (New York: Hill & Wang, 1981), 87, 89.
24 Michael Mitchell, *Staying Home* (artist's book produced by the Inter City Papers Group, Toronto, 1990), 14.
25 Mitchell, *Staying Home*, 6.
26 Jeanne Randolph, "The Amenable Object," in *Psychoanalysis and Synchronized Swimming* (Toronto: YYZ Books, 1991), 31.
27 Randolph draws freely on Winnicott's *Playing and Reality* (London: Tavistock, 1971), 95–109 in her "Amenable Object," 26–31; citations, 30.
28 Randolph, "Amenable Object," 30.
29 Mitchell, *Staying Home*, 1.
30 Pierre Dessureault, "Between Identity and Recognition," in Canadian Museum of Contemporary Photography, *Sandra Semchuk: How Far Back Is Home?* Exhibition catalogue by Pierre Dessureault (Ottawa: Canadian Museum of Contemporary Photography, 1995), 24.
31 Sandra Semchuk, letter to the author, December 28, 2006.
32 In 1986 Semchuk's work was included in an important exhibition organized by Van Deren Coke and Diana C. du Pont for the San Francisco Museum of Modern Art, *Photography: A Facet of Modernism*. The change in Semchuk's work is well described in terms of modalities. Du Pont attributes Semchuk's flowering to her graduate studies at the University of New Mexico (1982–1983) and the structure of Semchuk's master's thesis, bracketing two periods of production (Saskatchewan, 1972–1982; New Mexico, 1982–1983), contributes to this account. Semchuk herself nevertheless sees the transition through London as crucial to this story, and the significance of her activity there has recently been recognized in a group exhibition, organized by Robert McKaskell for Museum London: *Beyond Bounds: Art in London 1970–1987* (October 2005–August 2006).
33 Semchuk, December 28, 2006.
34 Semchuk, letter to the author, December 31, 2006.
35 Semchuk, December 28, 2006.
36 Semchuk, telephone conversation with Diana du Pont, March 18, 1985, cited in the "Expressionism" section of the exhibition catalogue by Van Deren Coke, with Diana C. du Pont, *Photography: A Facet of Modernism. Photographs from the San Francisco Museum of Modern Art* (New York: Hudson Hills Press, in association with the Museum, 1986), 145.
37 Semchuk, December 28, 2006.
38 McKaskill, didactic material, *Beyond Bounds*.
39 Barthes, *Camera Lucida*, 27–60; citation, 43.
40 Margaret Olin, "Touching Photographs: Roland Barthes's 'Mistaken' Identification," *Representations* 80 (Fall 2002): 99–119.

41 For Campeau's early social documentary portraits of children, see Claire Beaugrand-Champagne, Michel Campeau, Roger Charbonneau and Cedric Pearson, *Disraëli: Une expérience humaine en photographie* (Montreal: Les Publications de l'imagerie populaire, 1974).
42 Michel Campeau, *Les tremblements du coeur* (Quebec and Montreal: VU Centre d'animation et de diffusion de la photographie and Editions Saint-Martin, 1988).
43 Richard Baillargeon, "Le Fait du Temps," in Campeau, *Les tremblements du coeur*, 13–18.
44 Michel Campeau, *Éclipses et Labyrinthes* (Chicoutimi, QC: Séquence, 1991). The altered *Atelier, Gribouillage sur la photographie—Autoportrait à la table lumineuse* (1988), appears on p. 15.
45 In his letter to his daughter (*Mad Love*, 112), Breton confesses: "For a long time, I thought it was the gravest insanity to give life. In any case I held it against those who had given it to me. It may be that you would hold it against me on some days."
46 Carole Condé and Karl Beveridge, letters to the author, November 20 and 28, 2006.
47 See "Agit-prompters," in my *Scissors, Paper, Stone: Expressions of Memory in Contemporary Photographic Art* (Montreal: McGill-Queen's University Press, 2007), 200–216.
48 Ann Foreman, *Femininity as Alienation: Women and the Family in Marxism and Psychoanalysis* (London: Pluto Press, 1977), 93
49 Foreman, *Femininity as Alienation*, 104–105.
50 Ibid., 156–157.
51 Marian Penner Bancroft, Lorna Brown, Kati Campbell, and Sandra Semchuk, "Installation and Photography," *Blackflash* 8, no. 2 (Summer 1990): 6.
52 Richard Shiff, "Figuration," in *Critical Terms for Art History*, ed. Robert S. Nelson and Richard Shiff (Chicago: University of Chicago Press, 1996), 323–324.
53 Louise Dompierre, "Embodied Vision: The Painting, Sculpture, Photo-Work, Sound Installation, Music, Holographic Work, Films and Books of Michael Snow from 1970 to 1993," in Art Gallery of Ontario and the Power Plant, *The Michael Snow Project: Visual Art 1951–1993*, exhibition catalogue by Dennis Reid, Philip Monk, and Louise Dompierre (Toronto: Art Gallery of Ontario and The Power Plant, 1994), 445.
54 Dompierre, "Embodied Vision," 451.
55 Cloud formations are frequently studied by looking up at the sky, often by children lying on their backs. The cloud formations in **Corpus Callosum* were in fact recorded by a video camera aimed directly upward. The concentration given by the boy to the passing clouds on the televisions screen—a lateral relationship—is one of many directional twists in the film.

MONIQUE WESTRA

PATERSON EWEN'S *PORTRAIT OF VINCENT*

Loving Song
OH, come OH, come
To see the beautiful
Flower of heaven
—Vincent Ewen (age eight)[1]

Wearing kneepads, a face mask, and earplugs, Paterson Ewen crawls on his hands and knees on top of a huge, rough-hewn sheet of plywood that straddles two sawhorses. He gouges deep grooves into the wood, vigorously attacking the surface with an electric router. The year is 1974, and Ewen is embarked on a monumental portrait of his son Vincent.[2] The direct and aggressive nature of his technique belies the sensitivity of the subject and the emotional engagement of the artist with this image of his first-born son.

In 1968 Paterson Ewen's life underwent a dramatic change following the breakup of his family, the abrupt cessation of his daytime managerial job, and a severe and prolonged depression, which eventually landed him in a hospital in London, Ontario, far from his native Montreal. Ewen's sixteen-year marriage with dancer and sculptor Françoise Sullivan collapsed under the weight of mutual infidelity and distrust. The couple had four sons, the eldest of whom was Vincent—named after Vincent van Gogh. Vincent was eighteen when his father left and twenty-four when his portrait was done.

In the huge, over eight-foot-high portrait, Vincent stands alone and faces the spectator. In a strange parody of the relaxed standing pose of a classical statue, Vincent rests his weight on one leg—his awkward and self-conscious stance the antithesis of the balanced *contrapposto* of antiquity (fig. 19.1). He is dressed formally in a dark-green, double-breasted jacket with gold buttons, grey trousers, and a white shirt and a tie. He seems to draw his brows together, lending him a somewhat quizzical air. There is a

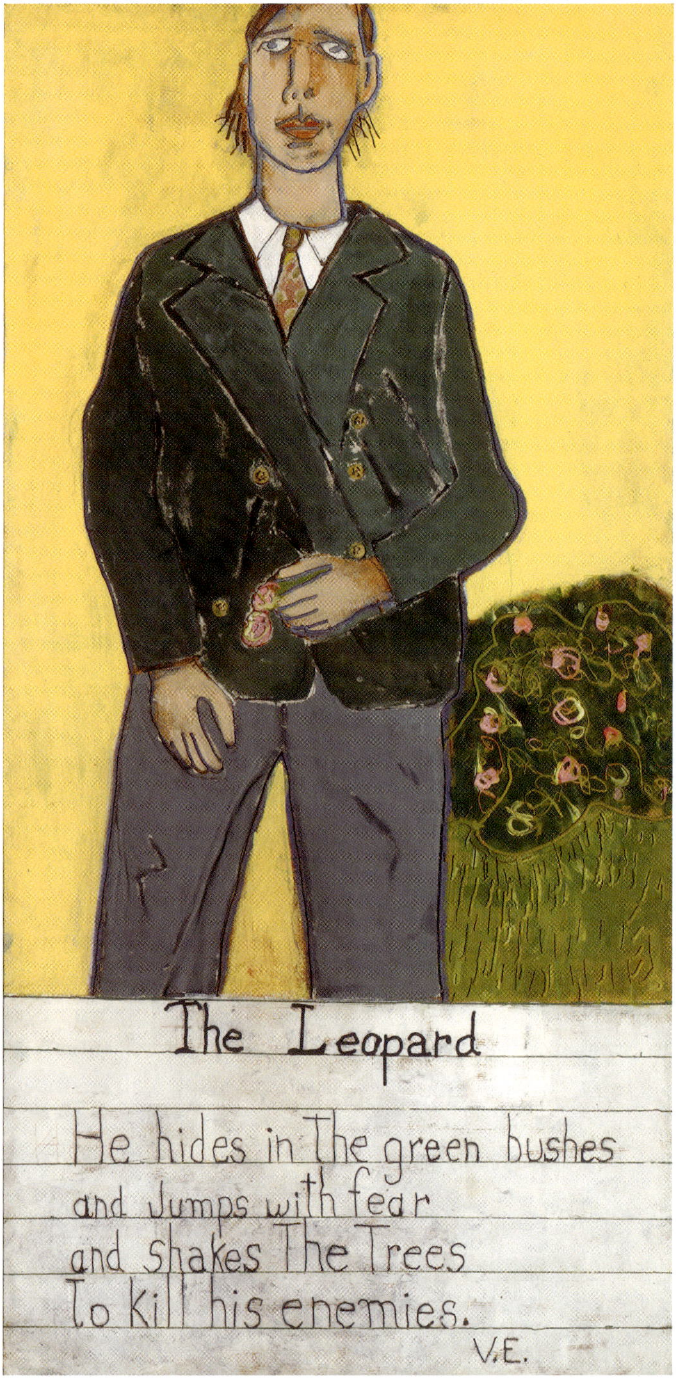

FIGURE 19.1
Paterson Ewen, *Portrait of Vincent*, 1974, canvas, acrylic, metal on plywood, 243.5 × 122 cm. Vancouver Art Gallery, Gallery Shop Funds, VAG 75.14. (Photo: Teresa Healy; copyright: Mary Alison Handford)

muted solemnity to his expression, his large, down-turned eyes set in an unfocused outward gaze. He stands against a colour field of saturated yellow that recalls his namesake. On his left is a squat bush with pink flowers. Two blossoms dangle from his left hand. As in other contemporary works by Paterson Ewen, collaged elements were affixed to the surface: "I used real cloth for the jacket and trousers, and part of the creases in the trousers are actually the cloth folded over, others are painted on very roughly. The buttons are pieces of galvanized iron sprayed with gold spray paint and a few squiggles of black to suggest the indentations."[3] The jacket worn by Vincent in the portrait was one of Ewen's own.

The image is based on a slide, a picture that Ewen had taken of his son at his grandmother's funeral. Ewen explains that "I took a number of photos and this one happened to be the last frame on the roll and consequently it cut him off at about the knees and it cut off a bit of the top of his head."[4] This literal slice across the forehead struck Ewen as a sign for his son's lifelong emotional problems: "I thought this was a true portrait of him and I had to tread a line somewhere between being cruel or sentimental."[5] It is significant that, with the crop above the knees, the stability of a firm foothold is denied, reinforcing the sense of disequilibrium. In the original source photograph, Vincent was holding an umbrella. Ewen put pink flowers in its place to symbolize his son's sensitivity.

In an interview with Doris Shadbolt in 1977, Paterson Ewen described Vincent as "an emotionally disturbed young man" who did not talk until he was five years old.[6] But the child was also a prodigy, writing a series of thirty poems between the ages of six and nine. The poems express with admirable economy and clarity the wonders of nature and the joy of life:

> Winter at Saturday morning
> I hear the chickadee sing
> And the sun was shining
> My heart is beating

In "Groing [*sic*] Bigger," the young poet imagines a fanciful, delicious place:

> Once there was a
> little
> Old hollow family
> And they
> built
> Their house in the
> Forest until
> Some people discovered it

and
Built their house near by
and
suddenly
it turned
into
A cottage cheese village
A
Few months later it turned
Into a maple
Town
A few months later it turned
Into
A
Chocolate
City[7]

Vincent's poetry was admired by McGill University professors and poets Frank Scott and Louis Dudek, who published fifteen of his poems in *Delta*, a respected poetry review, prompting an article in *Time* magazine entitled "Precocious Muse": "His images have a vivid directness often found in children's painting but rarely in children's poetry. He imagines a Halloween witch who 'hated white / she could even bite,' and Greenland as a place where 'Flowers grow like smoky mushrooms.'"[8] One of the published poems is inscribed at the bottom of *Portrait of Vincent*, carefully printed in a child's shaky script on the lined pages of a schoolboy's scribbler. Vincent was eight years old when he wrote "The Leopard." In graphic terms, the poem evokes both the strength and weakness of the predator in the natural world:

He hides in the green bushes
and Jumps with fear
and shakes the trees
to kill his enemies.

This dichotomy is not unlike the disorienting impact of the gigantic portrait, its insistent materiality and towering physical presence paradoxically and simultaneously expressive of an almost palpable sense of vulnerability and insecurity.

Six years after Ewen left Montreal in despair, he was being hailed by the art world and in the public press for his extraordinary new work. In 1974, when he did his remarkable portrait of Vincent, he was living in London, Ontario, then a hotbed of artistic activity centred on Greg Curnoe. Ewen was teaching painting at University of Western Ontario and producing some of the most powerful and original landscape art of the century. Until 1971, he had been an artist of modest-sized easel paintings in oil of landscape-derived abstractions. His sudden transformation in 1971 was an epiphany that is the stuff of legend. Living in Toronto at the time, and increasingly disillusioned with minimalism, canvas, oil, and all the paraphernalia of art, Ewen set out to create a giant woodcut engraving using a four-by-eight-foot sheet of plywood as his block. But as he carved into the raw, unyielding surface, it suddenly occurred to him that the plywood itself was the end, not the means, to artistic expression—a brute and a massive surface from which to elicit images of unparalleled force.

Inspired by simplified diagrams in science books, Ewen began to create gargantuan line drawings of celestial phenomena and cataclysmic meteorological events using workmen's hand tools and an electric router to carve into the wood. In addition to excavating the surface of the plywood with deep grooves, Ewen augmented his imagery through collage. He affixed ordinary hardware items, including chains and bolts, to re-create intangible elements such as lightning, air currents, and energy.

Through his "phenomascapes,"[9] Ewen's imagination soared beyond his immediate environment, beyond his day-to-day life, to engage with the universal, the timeless, and the sublime. From a high vantage point—the vast and distant remove of space—he produced celestial panoramas, which both overwhelm and humble the spectator. In reproduction, these mammoth images read almost like children's line drawings, a style that enhances the feeling of awe. This naivety metamorphoses into cosmic power through scale, colour, and texture.

It was during this exciting phase of his career, when his spectacular paintings were being widely heralded, that he created two disturbing and very personal images—figural compositions that are rare in his oeuvre. Although executed with the same methodology, and in the medium and massive scale of the epic images, the figural works represent striking contrasts: from the universal to the specific, from public to private, from power to weakness, and from infinite to finite.

Portrait of Vincent is linked to *The Bandaged Man*,[10] the first of these portraits, executed one year earlier (fig. 19.2). Consistent with the genesis of most of his grand, epic landscapes, a simplified line drawing provided the source for the image. In an old medical encyclopaedia describing the use of different kinds of bandages, Ewen came across a tiny etching depicting a standing man, covered from head to foot in bandages. He decided to transpose its outline onto a huge sheet of plywood. To replicate the bandages, he applied torn strips of canvas. What is striking here is not his method or style (familiar from his great landscapes), but the fact that he responded to an objective illustration with acute subjectivity. Ewen recognized an allegory of self in the man covered in bandages—a visual metaphor for his years of accumulated pain. In spite of his worldly success as an artist (the fulfillment of a lifelong dream) and a very respectable job as a university professor, Ewen still perceived himself as vulnerable, damaged, and held together by tenuous, outer means. "I was a bit of a wreck at the time after my year in Toronto. And as I went along with *The Bandaged Man* I began to realize it looked more and more like me. It had my body and it became very scary. When I went to bed at night I used to turn it to the wall. There's no question it is a kind of a self-portrait."[11]

As a symbolic self-portrait, *The Bandaged Man* lacks specificity. The features of the artist are subsumed in the neutrality and generic facial representation of the schematic sketch. But in the portrait of his son that followed one year later, the generic yields to the specific, in the representation and in the title. Significantly, the two portraits are similar in pose. Common to both figures are the upright stance, the splayed legs, the contrast between the straight arm on the right with the bent left arm, the frontality and immobility. Stylistically, both portraits are vertically formatted, heavily outlined, and with applied fabric collaged on the surface.

Both giant figures are deceptively simple and childlike in form and presentation. The formal echoes between the two works express a poignant vulnerability that underscores the particular bond between father and son, both of whom (like the artist after whom Vincent was named) endured private pain. Throughout his adult life, Paterson Ewen continued to suffer from alcoholism and debilitating depression and was repeatedly hospitalized for extended periods. *The Bandaged Man*, his surrogate image, was to be superseded sixteen years later by a more explicit *Self-portrait*, a brutal, full-length figure posed in a wide, aggressive stance.[12] These three paintings of family (self/father and son) are anomalies in Ewen's oeuvre, in which a vast and uncontrollable cosmos is like a parallel universe, where humanity in general and his own life in particular play no part. Although related to the rest of his work in terms of technique, medium, and scale, the personal nature of the family pictures seems to demand a separate genre, distinct and unmistakable, in which emotion is heightened and personal stakes are high.

Ewen struggled to create *Portrait of Vincent.*[13] He wanted it to be a true representation of his son but was determined to avoid the sentimentality so characteristic of family portraits. Acutely aware of his son's continuing emotional problems, he did not want to elicit pity in the spectator. Yet, he wanted to express his love, pride, and admiration for this unique individual, of whom he said, "He must have dropped from another planet, a superior one probably."[14] He was able to achieve this by subverting his usual methodology.

In most of his grand paintings, Ewen simulates a childlike drawing style to heighten a sense of primordial wonder in the face of extraordinary natural forces.[15] But in these monumental evocations of a vast cosmos, there is a jarring dissonance between the style of execution and the content. The simplicity implicit in the child's drawing is at variance with the infinitely mysterious and complex phenomenon it describes. However, in

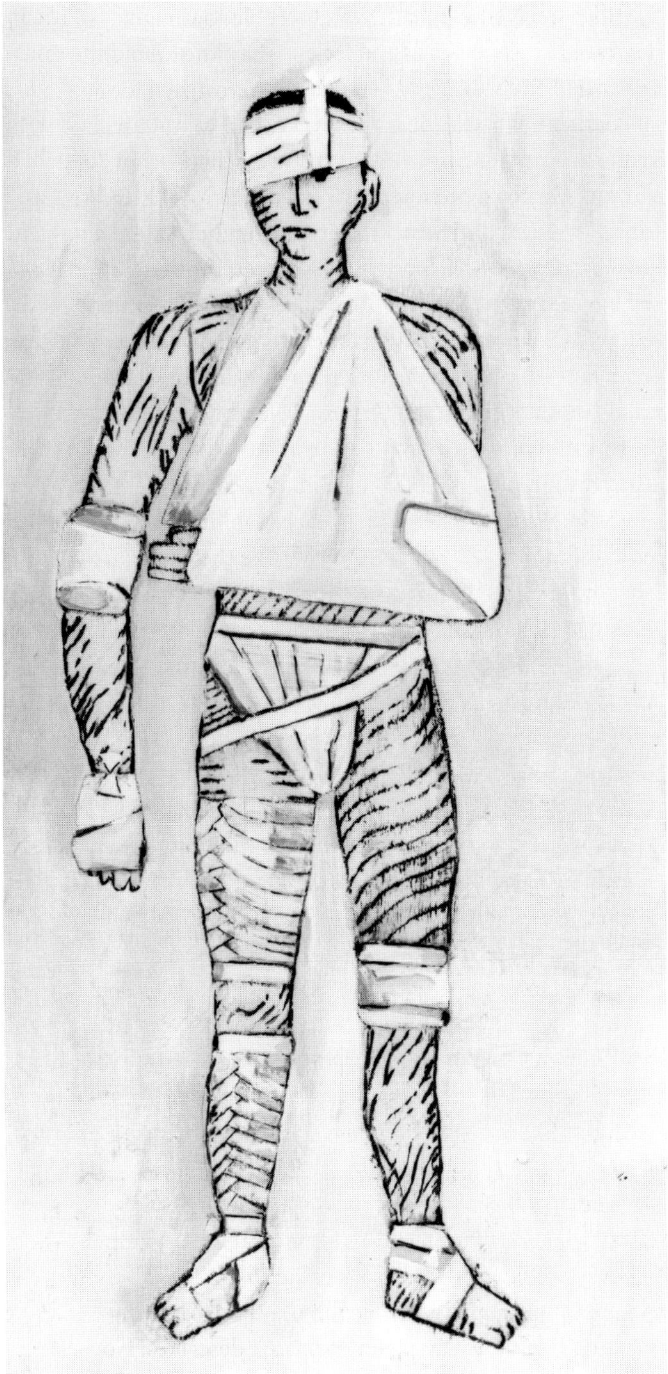

FIGURE 19.2
Paterson Ewen, *The Bandaged Man*, 1973, acrylic and canvas on plywood, 244 × 122 cm. National Gallery of Canada, purchased 1973, no. 17253. (Copyright: Mary Alison Handford)

Ewen's portrait of his son, the opposite is true. In this case, there is a consonance between style and content. Indeed, the childish style is integral to its presentation and interpretation, affecting both the father and the son.

By appropriating the hand of a child, Ewen vicariously sees and speaks as a child with simplicity, honesty, and trust. Thus the intense feelings of the father for his disturbed adult son are sublimated and give way to a pure and unsullied expression. At the same time, a brilliant visual synopsis is effected in which the twenty-four-year-old Vincent Ewen is presented as a child, bringing to the fore his true and quintessential self, an impression that is reinforced by the transcription of the poem beneath his image.[16]

In portraying his beloved son as a colossus man/child and by departing from the general tenor of his overall oeuvre, Paterson Ewen succeeded in creating a compelling portrait with profound emotional resonance. *Portrait of Vincent* is unique in Ewen's body of work and is one of the most original representations by a father of his child within the genre of family portraiture in Canada.

Notes

1 Louis Dudek, ed., "Poems by Vincent Ewen," *Delta* 11 (Spring 1960): 12–13.

2 Paterson Ewen, *Portrait of Vincent*, 1974, canvas, acrylic, metal mixed on plywood, 243.5 × 122 cm, was purchased by the Vancouver Art Gallery in 1975.

3 Doris Shadbolt, *Paterson Ewen: Recent Works* (Vancouver, BC: Vancouver Art Gallery, 1977), non-paginated.

4 Ibid.

5 Ibid.

6 Ibid.

7 Dudek, "Poems by Vincent Ewen," 13.

8 "Precocious Muse," *Time* (September 5, 1960): 11–12.

9 "I call my work 'Phenomascapes' because they are images of what is happening around us as individuals, rain, lightning, hail, wind. They are also images of what is happening in and around our Universe, Galaxies, Solar Eruptions. They are sometimes inner phenomena. I observe, contemplate and then attack." Paterson Ewen, as cited in Phillip Monk, *Paterson Ewen: Phenomena 1971–1987* (Toronto: Art Gallery of Ontario, 1987).

10 Paterson Ewen, *The Bandaged Man*, 1973, acrylic and cloth on plywood, 244 × 122 cm, was purchased by the National Gallery of Canada in 1973.

11 Lisa Rochon, "The Bandaged Man—the Art of Paterson Ewen," *Brick: A Journal of Reviews* (Winter 1988): 22.

12 Paterson Ewen, *Self-portrait*, 1986, acrylic on gouged plywood, 243.9 × 121.8 × 3.8 cm, was purchased by the National Gallery of Canada in 1986.

13 Shadbolt, *Paterson Ewen Recent Works.*

14 Gillian MacKay, "Profile: Paterson Ewen—Capturing the Universe in Process," *Maclean's* (June 28, 1982): 11.

15 In consciously simulating the look of children's art in his paintings, Paterson Ewen takes his place among numerous twentieth-century artists who were inspired by the art of children, including

Kandinsky, Klee, Miro, Matisse, and Picasso. Many artists actually collected examples of children's art, which they used as direct or indirect sources for their own work. (Jonathan Fineberg, *The Innocent Eye: Children's Art and the Modern Artist* (Princeton, NJ: Princeton University Press, 1997.)

16 Ewen's naive style does not reproduce any specific artwork done by a child. In *Portrait of Vincent*, the only direct reference to a child's artistic creation is to a poem, rather than to a picture.

on photography include *Suspended Conversations: The Afterlife of Memory in Photographic Albums* (2001); an edited collection, *Image and Imagination* (2005); and *Scissors, Paper, Stone: Expressions of Memory in Contemporary Photographic Art* (2007), all from McGill-Queen's University Press. An active independent curator, she was artistic director of the international photographic biennale *Le Mois de la Photo à Montréal 2005*.

Loren Lerner is professor and chair of art history at Concordia University. In 2005, Lerner curated *Picturing Her: Images of Girlhood / Salut les filles! La jeune fille en images* at the McCord Museum. Writings on the images of children include "From Victorian Girl Reader to Modern Woman Artist: Reading and Seeing in the Paintings of the Canadian Girl by William Brymner, Emily Coonan, and Prudence Heward," in *Canadian Children's Literature/Littérature canadienne pour la jeunesse* (2007); "Canada Receiving the Homage of Her Children: George Reid's *Ave Canada* and Gustav Hahn's *Hail Dominion*: A Proposal of Murals for the Entrance Hall of Canada's Parliament Buildings," in *Journal of Canadian Art History* (2008); and "When the Children Are Sick, So Is Society: Dr. Norman Bethune and the Montreal Circle of Artists," in *Healing the World's Children* (2008). She received a grant from Fonds québécois de la recherche sur la société et la culture for her research on the representations of children in Canadian art.

Patricia McKeever is a senior scientist and holder of the Bloorview Kids Foundation Chair in Childhood Disability Studies at the Bloorview Research Institute, Bloorview Kid's Rehab in Toronto, and a professor in the Faculty of Nursing, University of Toronto. She is a health sociologist whose scholarship focuses on children with chronic illnesses or disabilities and their built environments. From 2002 to 2008, she co-directed an interdisciplinary-research training program at the University of Toronto entitled Health Care, Technology and Place, funded by the Canadian Institutes of Health Research.

Margaret McNay is an associate professor and associate dean (Undergraduate and Preservice Programs) in the Faculty of Education at the University of Western Ontario with teaching and research interests focusing primarily on teacher education. She was an elementary school teacher in British Columbia before deciding to pursue another, earlier interest in science and to undertake doctoral studies in cell biology. Eventually she returned to the field of education to teach at the university level, first in New Brunswick, later in Alberta, and, since 1987, in Ontario. Upon discovering after his death that her father had been a home child and had been emigrated to Canada by Quarrier's Orphan Homes of Scotland, she began to explore and write about her newly discovered inheritance.

Claudia Mitchell is a James McGill Professor in the Faculty of Education, McGill University, and an honorary professor in the Faculty of Education, University of KwaZulu-Natal. She is the co-author/co-editor of several books on girlhood, childhood culture, and media: the two-volume *Girl Culture: An Encyclopedia*, *Researching Children's Popular Culture*, and *Seven Going on Seventeen: Tween Studies in the Culture of Girlhood* (with Jacqueline Reid-Walsh); *Girlhood: Redefining the Limits* (with Yasmin Jiwani and Candis Steenbergen); and *Combating Gender Violence in and around Schools* (with Fiona Leach). With Reid-Walsh she is co-editor of the new journal *Girlhood Studies: An Interdisciplinary Journal*.

Sharon Murray is a doctoral student in art history at Concordia University specializing in photographic history and theory. Her SSHRC-funded research centres on photographic representations of India created by Canadian overseas missionaries.

Sandra Paikowsky is a professor in the Art History Department of Concordia University. She is also the First Distinguished Scholar at the Gail and Stephen A. Jarislowsky Institute for Studies in Canadian Art at Concordia. A founder of *The Journal of Canadian Art History / Annales d'histoire de l'art canadien*, she is also its publisher and managing editor. From 1981 to 1992 she was director/curator of the Concordia Art Gallery. Her recent research and publications focus on James Wilson Morrice's images of Venice, the history of the Maritime Art Association, and the art writings of Walter Abell.

Carol Payne, photo historian, is on faculty at Carleton University in the art history unit of the School for Studies in Art and Culture. She is currently writing a book on the National Film Board of Canada's Still Photography Division (1941–1984) and co-editing a volume on photo studies in Canada. Both projects have been supported by the Social Sciences and Humanities Research Council of Canada.

Jacqueline Reid-Walsh, a specialist in historical children's literature, popular culture, and new media, teaches at Pennsylvania State University. She has published on topics ranging from girls' reading in the eighteenth century to moveable books to children's websites. With Claudia Mitchell, she co-authored *Researching Children's Popular Culture: The Cultural Spaces of Childhood* (2002) and co-edited *Seven Going on Seventeen: Tween Studies in the Culture of Girlhood* (2005) and *Girl Culture*, a two-volume encyclopaedia (2007). She is also co-editing with Mitchell the new journal, *Girlhood Studies: An Interdisciplinary Journal*.

Johanne Sloan is an associate professor in the Department of Art History, Concordia University. She is the co-editor, with Rhona Richman Kenneally, of the book *Expo 67: Not Just a Souvenir* (University of Toronto Press, 2009). She is currently completing a book project that revisits Joyce Wieland's 1976 film *The Far Shore*.

David Theodore is a doctoral student at Harvard University. He was formerly research associate and college lecturer at the School of Architecture, McGill University, where he taught courses in architectural design and studied the history of health care. An active design journalist and critic, he serves as a regional correspondent for *The Canadian Architect*, a contributing editor at *Azure*, and a contributor to the *Phaidon Atlas of 21st-Century World Architecture* (2008).

Elspeth Tulloch is the director of graduate studies in English at Université Laval, Quebec City, where she teaches Canadian literature. She is continuing her work on the National Film Board adaptations with a grant from the Fonds québécois de la recherche sur la société et la culture.

Abigail A. Van Slyck holds the Dayton Chair in Art History at Connecticut College, where she also directs the Architectural Studies program. She is the author of two books: *A Manufactured Wilderness: Summer Camps and the Shaping of American Youth, 1890–1960* (2006; winner of the Abbott Lowell Cummings Award) and *Free to All: Carnegie Libraries and American Culture, 1890–1920* (1995; Japanese translation, 2005).

Andrea N. Walsh is an associate professor in the Department of Anthropology at the University of Victoria. She is a visual anthropologist, curator, and multimedia artist of Irish, Scottish, Canadian, and Nlakapamux ancestry who specializes in twentieth-century and contemporary First Nations visual and material culture.

Monique Westra has been active as a teacher, writer, and curator for thirty years. She has been an art curator at the Glenbow Museum in Calgary since 2002. She is particularly interested in the theme of the family in contemporary Canadian art.

Kai Wood Mah is assistant professor of design and architectural history at the School of the Art Institute of Chicago. His essay is based on his research on educational architecture and the experience of urban life.

INDEX

Please note: Page numbers in italics refer to illustrations.

A

Aboriginal peoples. *See* First Nations *entries*

Algonquin Provincial Park, 27, *28–29*, 30, 32, 33. *See also* Camp Ahmek (Ontario)

Ange gardien, 13

art education, for First Nations students, 78, 289–91, 302n40

atrium, as architectural space, 261, 271; in hospitals, 260–61, 270–72. *See also* SickKids (Toronto) atrium, photographs by patients at

B

Baillargeon, Richard, 402

Ballantyne, R.M., 147; *Dusty Diamonds Cut and Polished*, 133, 147–49, *148*

Bancroft, Marian Penner, 406–8; *Mnemonicon (the screen)*, 406, *407*, 408; *Transfigured Wood*, 406

Barbie (doll), 109, 111, 114; and Barbie-play, 115–16, 123–24

Barnardo, Thomas John, 134, 147–48, 166; and "Barnardo children," 162, 164, *165*, 168–69; farms of, *144*, 144–45, 158, 162, *163*, 164; homes of, 133, 158

Barnardo, Thomas John, and photography of children: "artistic fiction" of, 135–37, 144–45; and "before and after" photographs, 142–43, *143*; for documentation purposes, 134–35, 162, 164, 166; on farms, *144*, 144–45, *146*, 162, *163*, 164; photographers of, 135, 169; and "Raw Material" photograph, 136, *137*; at school, 164, *165*, 166–67

Barnes, Thomas, 135; photographs attributed to, *137*, *143*

Barrow, Daniel, and pop culture aesthetic, 365, 371–78, 382, 383; *Catalogue of the Original*, 374; *The Face of Everything*, 374, 378; and Little Miss No-Name, 371–72, 376–77; *Trading Cards*, 374, 376, *377*

Barthes, Roland, 396, 398, 400–1

Battleford Industrial School (Saskatchewan), 68, 74, 78

"before and after" photographs: of home children, 142–43, *143*, 144, 145, 147; of residential school students, 52–56, *53*, *55*, *59*; as sign of progress, 56, 251–52; as transformative/"civilizing," 52–56, *53*, 141–43, *143*

Berczy, William: *The Woolsey Family*, 20

Beveridge, Karl. *See* Condé, Carol, and Karl Beveridge

Black children, in Quebec art, 20, *21*, 22

Blashfield, Edwin, 339

Blewett, Jean: "Back on the Farm," 330

Blum, Jack, and Sharon Corder, 174

boyhood: and child labour, 64–65, *66*, 68–69, *70*, 140–41, 142–45, 162–64; in residential schools, 52–54, 59–61, *62*, 64–65, *66*, 68–69, *70*, 74–77; Rousseau's concept of, 330; in rural Canada, as evoked by Reid's *The Story*, 328–32, *329*; and summer camp experience, 27–46

"Boy Ploughing" (photograph), *144*, *163*; as staged, 144, 162; symbolism of, 144–45, 162, 164; visual geometry of, 162

Bramley, Frank: *A Hopeless Dawn*, 333–34

Bressami, Father Joseph, 9, 23n4

Breton, André, 404; first "Manifesto of Surrealism," 395–96, 398

Brown, John George, 330

Brownell, Franklin, 327

Bryce, Peter H., and report on residential schools, *72–73*, 74

Brymner, William, 327, 350

C

Call Them Canadians (NFB picture book), 89, 99, *100*, 101–2

Camp Ahmek (Ontario), 27–46; awards system at, 39, 40; and Behaviour Frequency Scale, 40–41; and camping movement, 31–32; and Camp Wapomeo, *28*, 30, 32; and conflicting theories of childhood, 45–46; council ring of, 33, *34*, 35–38, *37*; Dimock and Hendry's work at, 39–43; First Nations motifs/rituals of, 32–38, 44–46; landscape planning/naming of, 43–45; leaders/counsellors at, 31–32, 42–43; and

Camp Ahmek (Ontario) (*continued*)
manliness vs. masculinity, 32, 45; map of, 27, *28–29*, 44–45; medical staff at, 43, *43*; original anti-modernist approach of, 31–38, 45; Seton cabin at, 27, 33; Seton's involvement in, 33–37; and switch to child psychology approach, 38–45; as tightly controlled environment, 31, 43–45, 46; totem pole of, *34*, 35; and view of women, 31, 41–42. *See also* Statten, Taylor
Camp Couchiching (Ontario), 30, 33, 46–47n9
Campeau, Léandre, 401–3, *403*
Campeau, Michel, 401–3; *Autoportrait à la table lumineuse, Atelier*, 402; *Gribouillage sur la photographie—Autoportrait à la table lumineuse*, 402–3, *403*; *Les tremblements du coeur*, 401–2
Camping and Character: A Camp Experiment in Character Education (Dimock and Hendry), 39, 41–42
camps, summer, 27, 31–32. *See also* Camp Ahmek (Ontario)
Camp Wapomeo (Algonquin Park), 30, 32; map of, *28*
Canada: A Year of the Land (NFB picture book), 89
"Canada Will Start Trials of Polio Vaccine April 18" (NFB photo story), 92–96, *93*, *95*
"Canada's Future Belongs to Them" (NFB photo story), 85, *86*, 87, 88, 89, 91, 98, 102, 103
Canadian Association of Broadcasters, 177
Canadian Centre for Architecture, 110, 125
Canadian children's literature, 111
Canadian dolls. *See* dolls, Canadian
Canadian Junior Red Cross, 279; creation of, 281–82; and First Nations children, 285–86; and good citizenship, 282, 284–86, 287–88, 289; at Inkameep Day School, 288–91; magazine of, 279, 282; in schools, 287–88; and "Twelve Rules of Health," 279, 281–84, *283*, 292, *293*. See also *Canadian Red Cross Junior* (magazine); Okanagan children, "health rules" drawings by; "Twelve Rules of Health"
Canadian Museum of Civilization, 110, 112
Canadian Radio-television and Telecommunications Commission (CRTC), sex-role stereotyping task force of, 176–81
Canadian Red Cross, 279; and creation of Junior Red Cross, 281–82; and progressive education movement, 287–88; public health mandate of, 280–82, 284–85, 287, 296–97; and public health standards for children, 279–80, 281–82, 296–97
Canadian Red Cross Junior (magazine), 279, 282; on good citizenship, 282, 284–86; and representation of First Nations peoples, 286–87; in schools, 287–88; and "Twelve Rules of Health," 282–84. *See also* Okanagan children, "health rules" drawings by; "Twelve Rules of Health"
Canadian Short Story Video Series (Atlantis Films/NFB), 174, 177–81, 195, 196n19. *See also* "Jack of Hearts" *entries*
Caniff, William, 305, 315
Canoe Lake (Algonquin Park), 27, *28*, 30, 35
Carlisle Indian Industrial School (Pennsylvania), 49–50, 52
Carroll, Lewis, 376
Cartier, George-Étienne, monuments to, 219, 222
cartoons/comic strips, as political, 202–4. See also *Weltschmerz* (comic strip)
Cassatt, Marie: *Modern Woman*, 339
Central Ontario School of Art and Design, 335, 339
Ces visages qui sont un pays (NFB picture book), 89, 99
Challener, Frederick Sproston, 327
Chambers, Jack, 366–71; *Hybrid*, 370; and pop culture, 365, 369–71; and realism, 365, 366, 368, 370–71; *Sunday Morning*, 370. See also *Diego Asleep*
Champlain, Samuel de, 3, 5, 9–10
childhood: ambivalence toward, xviii–xix, 205–7, 213–14; and child-like art, 372–73; concept of, xvi, xviii, xxiii, 330; conflicting theories of, 45–46; memories of, as seen from adult perspective, xxii–xxiv, 365–83, 395–96; and nationhood, 85–103, 325, 331–32, 338–43; visual representation of, xv–xxiv
childhood, and nationhood, 85–86; in NFB photo stories, 85–103; in work of Reid, 325, 331–32, 338–43
child labour: by home children, 140–41, 142–45, *143–44*, 162, *163*, 164; by residential school students, 64–65, *66*, 68–69, *70*
Children's Memorial Hospital (Montreal), 259–60; leisure images at, 266–70, *267–69*, 275; pneumothorax treatment at, 261, 263, *263*
Church of England Waifs and Strays Society, 133, 142, 154
citizenship: and home children movement, 141–42, 145; and rural life, 145, 331–32; and work of Canadian Junior Red Cross, 282, 284–86, 287–88, 289; in work of Reid, *331*, 331–33, 343
Codex canadiensis, 5, *7*
Condé, Carol, and Karl Beveridge: *Maybe Wendy's Right*, *404*, 404–6
Confederation Park/Boulevard (Ottawa), 219, 220, 222, 226
construction toys, 110, 125. *See also* doll-play; dolls; dolls, Canadian; toys and amusements
conversion, religious: in art of New France, 9–10, *11*, 12, 15; of Hindu girls, 237, 244–45, 246, 249, 251–54; of home children, 138–40, 142; at residential schools, 69, *71*, 72; YMCA emphasis on, 30
Corder, Sharon. *See* Blum, Jack, and Sharon Corder
Côte-de-Beaupré region (Quebec), 347, 350–51, 352, 358, 361–62

Courtenay, Vincent R., 219, 222
cradleboards, for First Nations infants, 5, *6–7*, 9
Crow Island School (Winnetka, Ill.), 307
Cullen, Maurice, 350
Curnoe, Greg, 370, 418; *Homage to the R-34*, 370; *Myself Walking North in the Tweed Coat*, 370–71
Curtis, Edward S., 49, 80n3
Cyprien Tanguay, *17*
Cyrice Têtu et sa fille Caroline, *18*

D

Danby, Ken, 366
Dance, Girl, Dance (film), 189–90
Davin, Nicholas Flood, 50, 51
Diego Asleep (Chambers), 365, 366, *367*, 368–71, 378, 379, 382–83; and artist/father's control over, 368; and child's "active unconsciousness," 368–69, 382–83; and family snapshot genre, 366, 368; high culture and pop culture in, 370–71; King Kong toy in, 365, 369–70, 377; realism of, 365, 366, 368, 370–71
Dimock, Hedley S., 39–43, 48n44; camping book of (with Hendry), 39, 41–42
diphtheria, 315
doll-play, 109–10, 114–24; with Barbie, 115–16, 123–24; cowgirl, 115; curatorial, 115, 119–20, *121–22*; with Eaton's catalogue, 110, 116–19; memories of, 114–16; phases of, 124
dolls, 109–25; Barbie, 109, 111, 114, 115–16, 123–24; as Black, 112, 114; bride doll, 19, 120, *122*; as Canadian, 110, 111–14; collections of, 110, 125; and doll-play, 109–10, 114–24; as gendered objects, 110, 124–25; Little Miss No-Name, 371–72, 376–77; paper, 110, 113, 114, 118–19; as personal artifacts, 109–10, 111–12; physical genres/compositions of, 115, 119–20, *121–22*, 128n55
dolls, Canadian, 110, 111–14; defining, 111; Eaton's Beauty doll, 110, 113, 116–19, *117*, 120; and Eaton's catalogue, 110, 113, 115–19; famous examples of, 110, 113; First Nations/Inuit, 112; religious, 114; wartime, 113, 114, 116
Douglas, William, 161, *161*, 167, *168*
drama program, for First Nations students, 292, 296, *296*, *297*
Dubuffet, Jean, 372
Duck Lake Boarding School (Saskatchewan): photograph of two children at, 74–75, *75*; student labour at, 65, *66*
Du Creux, François: *Historiae canadensis seu Novae Franciae Libri Decem*, 5, *6*, *8*, 9
Dudek, Louis, 418
Dzama, Marcel, 373, *377*

E

Eakins, Thomas, 327
Eaton Centre (Toronto), 271, 273
Eaton's Beauty doll, 110, 113, 116–19, *117*, 120
Eaton's catalogue, 113, 115–16; doll-play with, 110, 116–19; as "text of desire," 117
education. *See* public education; residential schools *and entry following*
E.E.J.M. Home for Working & Destitute Lads, 142–43, *143*
Emigration Home for Destitute Little Girls, 134, 147. *See also* Rye, Maria Susan
Evelina Children's Hospital (London), 271–72
Ewen, Paterson, 415, 418–19; *The Bandaged Man*, 419–20, *421*; "phenomascapes" of, 419, 420; *Portrait of Vincent*, 415, *416*, 417, 418–20, 422; *Self-portrait*, 420
Ewen, Vincent: poetry of, *416*, 417–18; portrait of, 415, *416*, 417, 418–20, 422
ex votos, 12, 13, *14*, 14–15

F

Fairknowe (Quarrier children's home in Ontario), 158, *159*, 159–62, *161*, 167, *168*
The Family of Man (Steichen), 106n53, 391
family portrait: as "conversation piece," 20; as "co-operative self-portraiture," 398–401, *399*, *401*; as *ex voto*, 13, *14*, 14–15; and family snapshot genre, 366, 368; as genre painting, 327, *333*, 333–38, *337*; of nineteenth century, 16, *17–19*, 20; as photographic creation, 390–91, *392–93*, *394–95*
Fegan, James, and children's homes of, 133, 134, 154
Fildes, Samuel Luke: *The Doctor*, 333
film adaptation, of literary texts, 174–76. *See also* "Jack of Hearts" *entries*
First Nations children, in art of New France, 3–10; as carried/breastfed by mothers, 3, *4*, 5, *8*; as compared to white children, 10–15; as converted, 9–10, *11*, 12, 15; on cradleboards, 5, *6–7*, 9. *See also* New France, art of; white children, in art of New France
First Nations children, "health rules" drawings by, 279–80, 291–300; illustrated, *294–95*; and Red Cross curriculum/practices, 288–91; and significance of animal imagery, 291–92, 296, 298; as subversion of "Canadianization" attempts, 296–300; and teacher's respect for First Nations culture, 290–91, 292, 299
First Nations children, residential school experience of. *See* residential schools *and entry following*
First Nations culture, 285–86; and government assimilation/oppression policy, 50–51, 63; and public health/education systems, 296–300; as represented in *Canadian Red Cross Junior*, 286–87; and significance of animal imagery, 291–92, 296, 298; teacher's respect for, 290–91, 292, 299. *See also* residential schools *and entry following*
First Nations culture, as targeted by residential schools: clothing, 52–56, *53*, *55*, 60–61, *62*; hair, 52–53, *53*, 59–60, *60*, *77*; names, 59, 60–61; and

First Nations culture, as targeted by residential schools (*continued*)
religious training, 69, *71*, 72. *See also* residential schools *and entry following*
First Nations motifs/rituals, in summer camps. *See* Camp Ahmek (Ontario)
Fort Marion (Florida), 49–50
Foucault, Michel, 63
François, Claude, *11*, *13*
Frère Luc. *See* François, Claude
Freud, Sigmund, 20, 380, 382
Froebel, Friedrich, 320

G

Gaultier, Angélique, 13, *14*, 14–15
genre painting: family portrait as, 327, *333*, 333–38, *337*; in work of Reid, 327–28, 333–34, 338
Georgetown School (Ontario), *306*, 306–7
Gifford, Dorothy, *93*, 93, 94, *95*, 96, *97*, 98, 101
girlhood: in colonial India, 233–54; and dolls/doll-play, 109–25; at residential schools, 58, *58*, 65, *66–67*, 68–69, *73*, 73–75, *75*
girlhood, narratives of, as adapted for film, 173–74, 177–81, 195; and CRTC sex-role stereotyping task force, 176–81; and feminist criticism/scholarship, 180–81. *See also* "Jack of Hearts" *entries*
Goffman, Erving, 390
Graham, Rodney, 365, 378–82, 383; *Awakening*, 379, 380–82, *381*; *Halcion Sleep*, 378–79; *How I Became a Ramblin' Man*, 380; *Photokinetoscope*, 379; "screen"/childhood memories of, 380, 382; *Vexation Island*, 379
Great Britain, immigrant children from. *See* home children *entries*; *see also* orphaned and destitute children, of Great Britain
Grierson, John, 88, 89–90, 96. *See also* NFB *entries*
Growing Up in Montréal (exhibition), xvii, 125
guardian angel, as image in art, 12, *13*

H

Hahn, Gustav: *Hail Dominion*, 339–40
Hall, G. Stanley, 33, 45
Hamel, Théophile, and work of, 16, *18–19*
Hannum, Mary and Robert, photograph of, 243, 248, 249, *250*, 251; as compared to photograph of Muktie and Savitni, 248–49, 251–53
Hannum, William and Annabel, 234, 247–48; children of, 243, 248, 249, *250*, 251
Harper, Stephen, 86
Harris, Mike, as depicted in *Weltschmerz*, 202, *205*, *207*, 209–11, *211*, *212*, 214–15; as cannibal, 210–11, *211*; as squeegee-wielding bully, *205*, 206, 210; and war on squeegee kids, 201–2, 204–5, 207, 209
Harris, Robert, 327; *A Meeting of the School Trustees*, 332–33
Haydon, Brownlee, 38, 45
Hébert, Louis-Philippe, 219, 222
Hendry, Charles E., 39–43, 48n44; camping book of (with Dimock), 39, 41–42
Heward, Prudence, and work of, 20, 22
Higonnet, Anne, 91, 101, 376, 388, 390. *See also* "knowing child"; "Romantic child"
Hine, Lewis W., 142
Historiae canadensis seu Novae Franciae Libri Decem (Du Creux), 5, *6*, *8*, 9
Hodgins, J. George, 305, 309, 310, 313, 320
Holy Family, as image in art, 10, *11*, 12
home children. *See also* orphaned and destitute children, of Great Britain
home children, experience of, 153–70; for author's father, 153–54, 155, 167, *168*, 170; and Canadian guidelines/legislation, 159–60, 160–61; at children's homes in Canada, 158, *159*, 159–62, *161*; as farm labourers, 138, 140–41, *144*, 144–45, *146*, 149, 155–56, 158, 160–61, 162, *163*, 164; as immigrants, 156–62, *157–59*, *161*; on journey, 156–59, *157–58*, *165*, 166; and loss of identity, 162, 168–69; as "others," 164, *165*, 166–67, 169; studies of, 154; and treatment by adoptive families/classmates, 156, 164, 166. *See also* orphaned and destitute children, of Great Britain
home children, photography of, 133–49, 154–55; as "artistic fiction," 133, 135–37, *137*, 142, *143*, *144*, 144–47, *146*, 148–49; "before and after," 142–43, *143*, 144, 145, 147; at children's homes in Canada, 158, *159*, 159–62, *161*; for documentation purposes, 134–35, 162, 164, 166; and facial expressions of subjects, 158, *158–59*, 160–62, *161*, 164, *165*, 167, *168*, 168–69; and "family" groupings, 157, *157*, *159*, 160; on farms, *144*, 144–45, *146*, 162, *163*, 164; as immigrants, 156–62, *157–59*, *161*; in outdoor settings, 145, 147; as promotional material, 134–37, 142–43, *143*; at school, 164, *165*, 166–67; and scrubbed/polished appearance of subjects, 143, *143*, 160, *161*, 167, *168*, 169; on ship, 156–57, *157*; and "staging" techniques, 135, 144, 162; at train station, *158*, 158–59
home children movement, 133–34, 153, 155–56; as depicted in fiction, 133, 147–49, *148*; evangelical zeal of, 134, 135–36, 138–40, 142; and good citizenship, 141–42, 145; imperialist agenda of, 134, 137–38, 141–42, 149; organizations/leaders of, 133–34, 154–55. *See also specific organizations and leaders*
Homer, Winslow, 330
Hôpital Ste-Justine (Montreal), *262*, 265–66
Hospital for Sick Children (Toronto), 260. *See also* SickKids (Toronto) atrium, photographs by patients at; Victoria Hospital for Sick Children (Toronto)
hospitalized children, early leisure images of, 259, *260*, 266–70; interior, 268–69, *269*; exterior, 266–68, *267–68*; and parties/amusements, 259, *260*, 269–70; and tuberculosis

patients, *265*, 266. *See also specific hospitals*
hospitalized children, early therapeutic images of, 259, 261–66; as about to undergo procedures, 263–65, *264*; and hospital exteriors, 261, *262*, 266; and hospital interiors, 261, *262*, *264–65*, 264–66; and medical staff, 261, *263–65*, 263–66; and state-of-the-art treatment, 261, 263, *263*. *See also specific hospitals*
hospitalized children, modern photographs by. *See* SickKids (Toronto) atrium, photographs by patients at
Houle, Robert, 80; *Sandy Bay*, 79
Huggan, Isabel: *The Elizabeth Stories*, 174, 181; "Jack of Hearts," and film adaptation of, 173–95. *See also* "Jack of Hearts" *entries*
Hugonnard, Fr. Joseph, 64, 72, 79–80. *See also* Qu'Appelle Industrial School (Saskatchewan)

I

Images of Women (report of CRTC task force), 176–81
Indian Act, 51, 57, 286
Indian Affairs, Department of, 51, 54, 57, 63–64, 65, 72
Indians. *See* First Nations *entries*
Inkameep Day School (B.C.), 279, 280, 286; art program at, 289–91, 302n40; drama program at, 292, 296, *296*, *297*; establishment of, 290; Junior Red Cross at, 288–91; school medical inspections at, 296; and teacher's respect for First Nations culture, 290–91, 292, 299. *See also* Canadian Junior Red Cross; *Canadian Red Cross Junior* (magazine); Okanagan children, "health rules" drawings by; "Twelve Rules of Health"

J

"Jack of Hearts" (Huggan short story), 173–95; and CRTC sex-role stereotyping task force, 176–81; and narratives of girlhood, 173–74
"Jack of Hearts" (Huggan short story), film changes to: attitudes to costuming/clothing, 186–88, 190–92; and casting of lead, 197n32; optimistic ending of, 192–95; and recital fiasco, 188–90; removal of ring, 193; role of family friend, 182–84, 192–94; timing of family friend's arrival, 183–84, 198n37
"Jack of Hearts" (Huggan short story), protagonist of: ballet costume of, 190, 191, *192*; ballet dreams of, 186–88, *187*; chief tormentor of, 188, *189*, *192*; male ballet role assigned to, *178*, 181–82, *183*, *192*; "masculinity" of, 181–82, 197n32; and relationship with father, 182, 184, 192–93; and relationship with mother, 182, 190–91, 193; and recital show of defiance, 182, 184, 188–90; as ridiculed by peers, *182*, 187–88, *189*; as ridiculed by recital audience, 188–89, *189*; and role of family friend, 182–84, *185*, 192–94; as taught poker by family friend, 182, 184, 193, 194, 199n69; and women's clothing/jewellery, 182, 186, 190–94
Jackson, A.Y., 22
Jarvis Collegiate (Toronto), Reid murals at, 341–42, *342*
Jefferson, Amanda, 233, *239*; and adoption of Muktie and Savitni, 234–35, 237, 245, 246, 248–49, 251–53, 254; culture/value system of, 238, 242–44; and mission in Kolhapur, 233–34, 237–38, *239–42*, 242–43; and mission in Ratnagiri, 233, 234, 235, 243, 247, *247*; and powers/prestige of missionary work, 251–52; and relationship with Minor, 233, 234, 245–46. *See also* Minor, Emily; missionary work; Muktie and Savitni (girls in India)
Jefferson, Amanda, photograph album of, 233–34; buildings/surrounding area in, 238, 244; captions in, 237–38, 242–43; and family aspect of, 243–44; "famine people" in, 243, *247*; fellow missionaries in, 237, 238, *239*, 243, 244; images from, *236*, *239–42*, *247*; and Jefferson's culture/value system, 238, 242–44; missionaries' children in, 243, 248, 249, *250*, 251; "Native Christians" in, 237, 238, *240*, 243, 244; organization of, 237–44; servants/workers and tradespeople in, 237, 238, *241–42*, 242–43, 244, *247*. *See also* Muktie and Savitni (girls in India)
Jesuit Relations, 5, 9
Johnson, Eastman, 330, 332

K

Kamloops Indian Residential School (B.C.), 57–58
Kane, Paul, 9
Keane, Margaret, 374, 376, *377*
Kennedy, Dan (residential School student), 57, 59
kindergarten, 318, 320; at Toronto Normal School, 307, *308*; at Wellesley Street School, 318, *319*, 320; as women's sphere, 320
King Kong (movie/action figure), 365, 369–70, 377
Klee, Paul, 373
Kolhapur (India), Presbyterian mission in, 233–34, 237–38, *239–42*, 242–43
"knowing child": in NFB photographs, 99–102, *101*; in Snow childhood photograph, 387–90, *389*
Korean War, memorial to (Ottawa), 219, 220, *221*, 222–23, 226, 228

L

Lambeth, Michel, and NFB photograph by, 98, 99, *100*, 101, 102
Lange, Dorothea: *Migrant Mother*, 391, 411n13
Lastman, Mel, 202, 208; as depicted in *Weltschmerz*, 202, *212*, 212–13
Laurence, Margaret: "To Set Our House in Order," 177, 179, 180
Laurier, Sir Wilfrid, 339
Laval, François de, 10, 12
Lind, Gareth, and *Weltschmerz* comic strip, 201–15; depictions of politicians by, 202, *205*, *207*, 209–11, *211*,

Lind, Gareth (*continued*) *212*, 212–15; and Ontario's war on squeegee kids, 201–2, 204–5, 207, 209; and visual rhetoric, 201–3, 209–13. *See also* squeegee kids; *Weltschmerz* (comic strip)
Little Miss No-Name (doll), 371–72, *376–77*
London (Ontario), artistic community in, 370, 399, 418–19
Luc, Frère, and work of, 10, *11*, 12, *13*, 15
Lund, Chris, and NFB photograph by, 92–94, *93*, *95*, 96, 98

M

Macfie, Jack: photograph of residential school students, 61, *62*
MacMonnies, Frederick: *Columbian Fountain*, 339
Macpherson, Annie, 133, 134, 138, 154, 166; as depicted in fiction, 147, 148; on emigration, 140; Ontario children's homes of, 155, 158, *158*
Madame Têtu et son fils Amable, *19*
Maddin, Guy, 375
Map, Camps Ahmek and Wapomeo, *28–29*
March, Vernon: National War Memorial (Ottawa), 223, *224*, 226, 228
Margaret Keane Trading Card, *377*
masculinity, 32, 45, 318
Matisse, Henri, 347, 350, 356
Maurice, Fr. William, 52
Mavor, James, 340–41
Maynard, Fredelle, 117–18
McCord Museum of Canadian History, xvii, 110, 114, 125
McGuinty, Dalton, 210, *211*
McLeod, A.J., 63–64, 65
McNaught, William K., 332
McNay, James, 167, *168*
Michals, Duane: *Self-portrait Shaking Hands with My Father*, 402
Middlemore, John Throgmorton, 134, 158
Miller, Muriel, 325–26, 341
Minden, Robert, 390–95, 403; *Andrea and Dewi* (photograph), *393*, 394–95; *Family Arrangements* (project), 390–91, *392*, 394; *Lark and Her Children, Vancouver* (photograph), 391, *392*, 394, 400; *Portrait of My Daughters* (project), 390, *393*, 394–95
Minor, Emily, 233–34, *239*; and adoption of Muktie and Savitni, 234–35, 237, 245, 246, 248–49, 251–53, 254; and relationship with Jefferson, 233, 234, 245–46. *See also* Jefferson, Amanda, *and entry following*; missionary work; Muktie and Savitni (girls in India)
missionary work, 233–34; and adoption of native children, 247–48; and contrast of cultures/religions, 237–38, 242–45; and conversion, 233–34, 237, 248; photography of, 235, 237; women's role in, 234, 245–49
Mitchell, Michael, 396–98, 403; *Staying Home*, 396–98, *397*
Monk, Lorraine, 98, *99*, 101, 103
Montagnais, 3, *4*, 12
Montreal Children's Hospital, 260. *See also* Children's Memorial Hospital (Montreal)
monuments, commemorative, children as depicted in: and Korean War memorial (Ottawa), 219, 220, *221*, 222–23, 226, 228; and Niederwald Monument (Germany), 223, 225; as "others," 219–20, 225–26, 228; in Roman Empire, 223; and Vietnamese memorial (Ottawa), 226, *227*. *See also* Ottawa, commemorative monuments of
Moore, Thomas (residential school student), 52–54, *53*, 59
Morrice, James Wilson, 347, 349; and Côte-de-Beaupré region, 347, 350–51, 358, 361–62; girls or young women, in paintings of, 356, *357*, 358, *360*; painting technique of, 361; and rural Quebec landscape, 350–51, 355–56, 358, 360–62; walking figures, in paintings of, 358. See also *Return from School*
Morrice, James Wilson, works by: *La Communiante*, 358, *360*; *The Barber Shop*, 358; *The Ferry*, 354; *Girl Knitting (near St-Malo, Brittany)*, 356; *Girl Wearing Clogs*, 356, *357*; *On the Road*, 350, 361; portrait of sister, 356; *Sugar Bush*, 356, 358, *359*; *Towards Evening Beaupré*, 356; *Wharf on the St. Lawrence*, 354. See also *Return from School*
Morris, Edmund, 49, 80n4
Muhlstock, Louis: *Evelyn Pleasant, Clark Street, Montreal*, 20, *21*, 22
Muktie and Savitni (girls in India): adoption of, 234–35, 237, 245, 246, 248–49, 251–53, 254; as both Christian and "Hindoo," 237, 244–45, 246, 249, 251–54; as compared to missionaries' children, 248–49, *250*, 251–53; and conversion image of, 237, 252–54; facial expressions of, 251, 254; new identities of, 251–54; as part of Jefferson-Minor family, 248–49, 252–53; photograph of, 234–35, *236*, 237, 252–54; Western-style clothing of, 234–35, 249, 252; and white middle-class culture, 251–54. *See also* Jefferson, Amanda, *and entry following*; Minor, Emily
Munro, Alice: "Boys and Girls," 173
murals and mural painting, 338–43, 370

N

National Capital Commission, 220
National Children's Home and Orphanage of London, 133
National Film Board of Canada. *See* NFB
National War Memorial (Ottawa), 223, *224*, 226, 228
nationhood, and childhood, 85–86; and government policies, 86; in NFB photo stories, 85–103; in work of Reid, 325, 331–32, 338–43
New France, art of, 3–15; and *ex votos*, 12, *13*–15; First Nations children/families in, 3–12, 15; guardian angel in, 12, *13*; Holy Family in, 10, *11*, 12; religious conversion in, 9–10, *11*, 12, 15; religious imagery/themes in,

9–15, 16; white children/families in, 10–15. *See also* First Nations children, in art of New France; Quebec, art of; white children, in art of New France

NFB: and concern with childhood, 90; and emphasis on Canadian unity, 88, 90; establishment of, 88; short story adaptations by, 174, 177–81, 195, 196n19. *See also* "Jack of Hearts" *entries*

NFB Still Photography Division, 87, 88; adult audience of, 90–91; and cinéma-vérité, 87, 102; and direct appeal of documentary photograph, 89–90; and documentary film division, 87, 88–91, 96–97; and emphasis on Canadian unity, 88–89; in mid- to late 1960s, 87, 98–103; Monk's tenure at, 98, 99, 101, 103; in paternalistic postwar era, 87, 96–98; and portrayal of Aboriginal children, 97; and relationship with government, 87, 88, 97–98; stock library of, 91, 98

NFB Still Photography Division, children depicted by, 85–103; and expository mode of representation, 87, 96–98, 102; as free spirits/individuals, 87, 102–3; and gaze towards camera, 92, *93*, 96, 99, *100*, 101–2; as "knowing," 99–102; and observational mode of representation, 87, 98–103; as "Romantic," 91–92, 101; and spontaneity of images, 87, 98, 101–3; and staged/didactic images, 87, 92–98; as symbolic of citizenry/nationhood, 85–87, 92, 99, 101–3; as symbolic of national achievements/aspirations, 92, 93; as typologies, 94, 99, 101

NFB Still Photography Division, photo stories by, 89, 98; "Canada Will Start Trials of Polio Vaccine April 18," 92–96, *93*, *95*; "Canada's Future Belongs to Them," 85, *86*, 87, 88, 89, 91, 98, 102, 103; and expository mode of representation, 87, 96–98, 102; and observational mode of representation, 87, 98–103; and recontextualization of photographs, 91, 92–96, 97, 104–5n23; and spontaneity of images, 87, 98, 101–3; and staged/didactic images, 87, 92–98; "Sudbury's Polio Clinic: A Whole Community of Volunteers Pitches in to Operate," 94–95; variety of topics covered by, 90–91, 95–96

NFB Still Photography Division, picture books by, 89, 98; *Call Them Canadians*, 89, 99, *100*, 101–2; *Canada: A Year of the Land*, 89; *Ces visages qui sont un pays*, 89, 99; life cycle model of, 99, 106n53; and observational mode of representation, 87, 98–103; and recontextualization of photographs, 101; and spontaneity of images, 87, 98, 101–3

Nicolas, Louis: *Codex Canadiensis*, *7*

Niederwald Monument (Germany), 223, 225

Notman, William, and work of, 259, *260*, 270

Novae Franciae Accurata Delineatio (map), 9

O

Okanagan children, "health rules" drawings by, 279–80, 291–300; illustrated, *294–95*; and Red Cross curriculum/practices, 288–91; and significance of animal imagery, 291–92, 296, 298; as subversion of "Canadianization" attempts, 296–300; and teacher's respect for First Nations culture, 290–91, 292, 299

Ontario: children's homes in, 155, *158–59*, 158–62, *161*, 167, *168*; Reid's bequest of paintings to, 342–43; residential school in, 51–52, 58, *58*, 61, 69, *70*, *76*, 77, 78; and war on squeegee kids, 201–2, 204–5, 207, 209

Ontario Society of Artists, 326, 327, 339

orphaned and destitute children, of Great Britain, 133–34; and Canada as ideal home for, 137–42, *139*; as depicted in child welfare literature, 135–37, 141; as depicted in fiction, 133, 147–49, *148*; public fascination with, 134; as "raw material," 136, *137*, 140; as "savages" to be civilized, 141–43; as "street-Arabs," 133, 136, 141, 147–49, *148*; training of, 140–41. *See also* home children *and entries following*

Orphan Homes of Scotland, 133, 140, 154, 156, 159. *See also* home children *and entries following*; Quarrier, William

Osoyoos reserve (B.C.), 279, 280, 291, 299; day school of, 290. *See also* Inkameep Day School; Okanagan children, "health rules" drawings by

"others"/outsiders: children on commemorative monuments as, 219–20, 225–26, 228; home children as, 164, *165*, 166–67; squeegee kids as, 211–12

Ottawa, commemorative monuments of, 219–28; early examples, 219; Korean War memorial, 219, 220, *221*, 222–23, 226, 228; National War Memorial, *224*, 226, 228; Vietnamese memorial, 226, *227*; women in, 226, 228. *See also* monuments, commemorative, children as depicted in

P

Papineau, Louis-Joseph, family portraits of, 16

Pellan, Alfred: *La Fillette en rouge*, 20

Pham Thế Trung: *Refuge—Mother and Child*, 226, *227*

photograph albums, 243–44. *See also* Jefferson, Amanda, photograph album of

photography of children: of home children, 133–49, 154–55; by hospitalized children, 260–61, 270–76; of hospitalized children, 259–60, 261–70; and lives/work of contemporary artists, 387–410; by NFB Still Photography Division, 85–103; and poses in, 52–54, *53*, 69,

photography of children (*continued*) *70*, 234–35, *236*, 248–49, *250*, 251; at residential schools, 49–80; as staged, 92–93, *93*, 136, *137*, 142–145, *144*, *146*, 162, *163*, 164
photography of children, and children's gaze towards camera: and child in stroller, 99, *100*, 101–2; in family portraits, 390–91, *392–93*, 394–95; and home children, 158, *158–59*, 160–62, *161*, 164, *165*, 167, *168*, 168–69; and residential school students, 52–54, *53*, 69, *70*, 74–75, *75*; and sister's childhood photograph of Snow, 387–90, *389*; and young polio patient, 92, *93*, 96
photography of children, by contemporary artists, 387–410; and child as active agent in, 403–4; and child as *Rückenfigur*, 408–10; as "co-operative self-portraiture," 398–401, *399*, *401*; as family portraits, 390–91, *392–93*, 394–95; and "knowing child," 387–90, *389*; as self-portraits, 398–403; in socio-political context, *404*, 404–6; as still lifes, 396–98, *397*; temporal aspects of, 410
Photo League (New York), 98
Picturing Her: Images of Girlhood (exhibition), xvii
Plamondon, Antoine, and work of, 16, *17*, 20
Poitras, Edward: *1885*, 79–80
polio vaccine, NFB photo story on, 93–96, *93*, *95*
political cartoons/comic strips, 201–4, 214–15. See also *Weltschmerz* (comic strip)
pop culture: and work of Barrow, 365, 371–78, 382, 383; in work of Chambers, 365, 369–71
Portman, John, and Hyatt hotel architecture, 271
Portrait of Vincent (Ewen), 415, *416*, 417, 418–20, 422
Pratt, Richard, 49–50, 52
public education: and "Canadianization" of students, 297–300; and progressive education movement, 287–88, 290; and public health movement, 287–88, 296–97; and Quebec's fee-based system, 352–53; and school interiors, 305–20
public health movement: and "Canadianization" of student bodies, 297–98; First Nations' experience with, 296–300; and mandate of Red Cross, 280–82, 284–85, 287, 296–97; and public education, 287–88, 296–97; and standards for children, 279–80, 281–82, 296–97; and Toronto schools, 315
Puvis de Chavannes, Pierre, 338

Q

Qu'Appelle Industrial School (Saskatchewan): "before and after" photographs taken at, *55*, 55–56; girls' domestic activities at, 65, *66*, 68; illegal confinement at, 64; school photograph taken at, 79–80; sewing room of, 65, *66*, 68; student health at, 72
Quarrier, William, 134, 140, 154, 157, *157*, 166, 170; Ontario children's home of, 158, *159*, 159–62, *161*, 167, *168*; and Orphan Homes of Scotland, 133, 140, 154, 156, 159; and photographs of children, 142, 155, 156–62, *157*, *159*, *161*, 167, *168*
Quebec, art of, 3–22; Black children in, 20, *21*, 22; and *ex voto*, 12, 13, *14*, 14–15; and family portrait, 13–15, 16, *17–19*, 20; First Nations children/families in, 3–10; and modern depictions of children, 20–22; religious imagery in, 9–15, 16, 22; rural children in, 20, 22; white children/families in, 10–20. *See also* First Nations children, in art of New France; Morrice, James Wilson, *and entry following*; New France, art of; white children, in art of New France
Quebec, rural: difficulty of life in, 351; education/schools in, 352–53, *353*; Roman Catholic influence in, 351–52; as subject of art, 350–51; women in, 353–54

R

Raddall, Thomas H.: "The Trumpeter," 178–79, 180
Ratnagiri (India), Presbyterian mission in, 233, 234, 235, 243, 247, *247*
realism, 90, 338, 366; in work of Chambers, 365, 366, 368, 370–71
Regina Industrial School, 63, 65, 69; and transformation of students, 52–54, *53*, 59
Regnard-Duplessis, Marie-Andrée, 12
Reid, George, 325–43; art education of, 327; and bequest of paintings to Ontario, 342–43; at Chicago Exposition, 336–39; criticism of, 338, 340; on educational purpose of art, 341–43; as educator, 335, 339; father of, 326–27, 332; and genre painting, 327–28, 333–34, 338; later landscapes by, 343; Miller biography of, 325–26, 341; on moral purpose of art, 336; and mural painting, 338–43; and Royal Academy, 335, 338, 339
Reid, George, murals by, 338–43; as allegorical, 338–43; children in, 339, 340, 341–42; criticism of, 340; at Jarvis Collegiate, 341–42, *342*; as proposed for Parliament Buildings (*Canada Receiving the Homage of Her Children*), 339–40
Reid, George, paintings by: *Ave Canada* (mural), 339–41, 343; *Family Prayer*, 336; *Forbidden Fruit*, 336, 343; *The Foreclosure of the Mortgage*, 336–38, *337*, 343; *Lullaby*, 336, 343; *Mortgaging the Homestead*, 327, *333*, 333–36, 343; *The Other Side of the Question*, 327, *331*, 331–33; *Patriotism* (mural), 341–42, *342*, 343; *Sacrifice* (mural), 341, 343; *The Story*, 327, 328–32, *329*, 336, 343; *The Visit of the Clockmaker*, 336, 343
Reid, George, themes of: Canadian nationhood, 325, 338–43; child-

hood, 325, 328–32, *329*, 336, 343; children as nation's future, 325, 331–32, 339, 343; family life, 327, *333*, 333–38, *337*, 340, 343; good citizenship, *331*, 331–33, 343; rural life, 327–38, *329*, *333*, *337*, 341, 343
Rejlander, Oscar Gustav, 142
reserves, First Nation, 286. *See also* Osoyoos reserve (B.C.)
residential schools: American roots of, 49–50, 64; assimilation rituals of, 59–61, *62*; autobiographical accounts of, 52; and "Canadianization" of students, 298–300; and confinement of students, 63–64; and control of children, 50–51; deaths at, 72, 74; girls' activities at, 65, *66*, 68–69, *73*, 73–74; and girls' future as domestic servants, *67*, 68; as grafted onto missionary system, 50; panopticon of, 63, 64, 77, 78; as part of assimilation/oppression policy, 50–51, 63; as prisons, 63–64; promotion of, 52–56, 65, 68; and relationship with parents, *55*, 55–56, 57, 63, 72, 77; religious training at, 69, *71*, 72; and seizure/transportation of students, 57–58; sexual abuse at, 74–77; and students' advocates/protectors, 77–78; and students' escapes/escape attempts, 57, 74; students' health at, *73*, 73–74, *76*, 77; students' labour at, 64–65, *66*, 68–69, *70*; and students' names, 59, 60–61; students' recreation at, *73*, 73–74, 76, 78; and students' resistance/resilience, 78, *79*
residential schools, photography of, 49–80; "before and after" (students), 52–54, *53*, 59; "before and after" (students and parents), *55*, 55–56; contemporary art based on, 79–80; and facial expressions of students, *53*, 53–54, *55*, 58, *58*, *70*, 74–75, *75*, 78; and girls' activities, 65, *66*, 68–69; as haunting images, 74–77, *75*, *76*; as published in government reports, 52–56; and religious training, 69, *71*, 72; research projects on, 78–79; and seizure/transportation of students, 57–58, *58*; at Spanish Indian Residential School, 51–52, 58, *58*, 69, *70*, 78; as staged, 52–56, 73–74, 79–80; and students' bunching together, 61, *62*; and students' haircuts, 52–53, *53*, 59–60, *60*, 77; and students' health, *73*, 73–74, *76*, 77; and students' labour, 64–65, *66*, 68–69, *70*; and students' uniforms, 52–53, *53*, 60–61, *62*; and traditional clothing, 52–56, *53*, *55*. *See also* Duck Lake Boarding School; Qu'Appelle Industrial School; Spanish Indian Residential School; St. Joseph's Industrial School
The Response (National War Memorial, Ottawa), 223, *224*, 226, 228
Return from School (Morrice), 347, *348*; compositional analysis of, 354–56, 358, 360–62; history of, 349–50; oil study for, 347, *349*, 352; societal context of, 350–54; unusual subject matter of, 350; walking figures in, 358, 360–61
Reynolds, George, 135
Ridpath, Jack, *34*, 35
Riel, Louis, 79–80
Riggins, Stephen, 109–10, 114–15, 116, 119
Riverin, Angélique (Gaultier), 13, *14*, 14–15
Roberts, Sir Charles G.D., 328
Robertson, James W., 280, 281, 282, 298
Robinau de Bécancour, Marie-Anne, 15
Robinson, Albert H., 22
Robinson, Henry Peach, 142
Roman Empire, commemorative monuments of, 223
"Romantic child," 91–92, 101
Rousseau, Jean-Jacques, xvi, xviii, 330
Roy, Gabrielle: *The Tin Flute*, 270
Royal Art Lodge (Winnipeg artists' collective), 372–73, 384n11
Royal Canadian Academy of Arts, 335, 338, 339
Royal Edward Institute (Montreal), *265*, 266
Royal Victoria Hospital (Montreal): children's ward tea party in, 259, *260*, 270
Rückenfigur, child as, 408–10
rural life: and good citizenship, 145, 331–32; for home children, 138, 140–41, *144*, 144–45, *146*, 149, 158, 160–61, 162, *163*, 164; and migration to city, 330, 341; and mortgaged farms, 334–35; in Quebec, 350–54; transformation of, 341. *See also* Morrice, James Wilson; *see also* Reid, George, *and entries following*
Rye, Maria Susan, and home run by, 133, 134, 135, 138, 144, 147

S

Safe Streets Act (Ontario), 204, 207
Sainte Famille à la huronne, *11*
school interiors, 305–9. *See also* Wellesley Street School (Toronto)
Scott, Cynthia, 174
Scott, Duncan Campbell, 51
Scott, Frank, 418
Semchuk, Sandra, 398–401, 403; *Co-operative Self-portrait: Rowenna and I. R.R.6, Saskatoon, Saskatchewan, June 1979*, 398–99, *399*, 408; *Pinery Net Fishing, Pinery, Ontario*, 400, *401*; *Series #10*, 400
Seton, Ernest Thompson, 33–37; Camp Ahmek cabin of, 27, 33; Camp Ahmek council ring of, 33, *34*, 35–38; on campfire, 35–37; Connecticut council ring of, 35, *36*; stories by, 328–29; and Woodcraft Indians, 33, *36*; and Woodcraft League, 33, 35
Shaw, Harold V., map of Camp Ahmek by, 27, *28–29*, 44–45
Sherwood, William A.: "A National Spirit in Art," 327–28, 341
SickKids (Toronto) atrium, photographs by patients at, 260–61, 270–76; and atrium architecture, 260–61, 270–72; of exterior cityscapes, 272–73, *273*; of hospital as place of confinement, *274–75*, 274–76. *See also* Victoria Hospital for Sick Children (Toronto)

Simmie, Lois: "Red Shoes," 177, 179
Smith, Jori, 22
Snow Rynard, Denyse, 387, *389*
Snow, Michael: **Corpus Callosum*, 388, 410; *Quintet*, 388, 408–10, *409*; sister's childhood photograph of, 387–90, *389*; *Walking Woman* figures, 370, 387
Sontag, Susan, 391
Spanish Indian Residential School (Ontario), 51–52, 61, 78; boys doing construction work at, 69, *70*; empty dormitory beds at, *76*, 77; girls arriving at, *58*, 58
squeegee kids, 201–15; and ambivalence toward children, 205–7, 213–14; appearances of, 206, *207*, 207–8; as depicted by *Weltschmerz*, 206, 207–9, 211–12, 214–15; as "kids" but not "children," 205–6, 214; Ontario's war on, 201–2, 204–5, 207, 209; as "others," 211–12; as threats to order/undisciplined, 204–5, 206–7, 208, 213; and toplessness, *205*, 209; as visible nuisance, 204–5. See also *Weltschmerz* (comic strip)
St. Joseph's Industrial School (Alberta), 59–60, *60*, 77
St. Lawrence Ward School (Toronto), 310, 311, *313*
Statten, Ethel, 30, 31, 32, 46–47n9
Statten, Taylor, 30–46; as Camp Ahmek "Chief," 35–36, *37*, 38; and Camp Couchiching, 30, 33; and Camp Tuxis, 30, 39; and founding/management of Camp Ahmek, 30–31; as "Great Beaver," 32, 34; Seton's influence on, 33–37; and switch to child psychology approach, 38–46. *See also* Camp Ahmek (Ontario)
Steichen, Edward: *The Family of Man*, 106n53, 391
Stephenson, Thomas Bowman, 134, 154
Storm, William G., 309, *311*, *312*, *313*, 316
Stratford (Ontario), Macpherson children's home in, 158, *158*
Sudbury General Hospital (Ontario), polio clinic of: and NFB photo of child patient, 92–96, *93*, *95*; NFB photo story on, 94–95
summer camps. *See* camps, summer
Sunnylea Public School (Etobicoke, Ont.), 307
Svendsen, Linda: "Esso," 178, 179–80

T

Tanguay, Cyprien, 16, *17*
Têtu, Cyrice, family portraits of, 16, *18–19*
Thorson, Scott, 374, 378
Toronto Normal School, model kindergarten in, 307, *308*
toys and amusements: construction toys, 110, 125; King Kong figure, 365, 369–70, 377; as still life components, 396–98, *397*; Tomland, 373, 377; trading cards, 374, 376, *377*. *See also* doll-play; dolls; dolls, Canadian
Toy Story 2 (animated film), 115
"Twelve Rules of Health" (Red Cross), 279, 281–84; dangers of disobeying, 282–83; and good citizenship, 282, 284–86, 289; as illustrated by Red Cross, 282, *283*, 292, *293*; as illustrated by Okanagan children, 279–80, 291–300, *294–95*; and morality, 282, 284; and social acceptance/exclusion, 283–84; wartime implications of, 285

V

Victoria Hospital for Sick Children (Toronto), 260, *264*, 264–65
Vietnamese commemorative monument (Ottawa), 226, *227*

W

Waddington, Miriam, 101
Walker, Horatio, 351, 356
Walsh, Anthony, 290–91, 292, 299, 302n40
Warhol, Andy, 375, 379
Wellesley Street School (Toronto), 305–20; alterations and additions to, 316, 318, *319*; basement of, 316, *317*; and evolution of school interiors, 305–9; exterior of, *310*, 310–11; gender separation at, *311–12*, 312–14, *314*, 318; ground floor plan of, *314*, *319*; and health/safety concerns, 312–16, 318; kindergarten room at, 318, *319*, 320; location of, 311; as "modern," 309; outdoor privies at, 312, *312*, 315–16; site plan of, 312, *312*
Weltschmerz (comic strip), 201–15; enthymematic form of, 208–9; Mike Harris as depicted in, 202, *205*, *207*, 209–11, *211*, *212*, 213, 214–15; Mel Lastman as depicted in, 202, *212*, 212–13; and Ontario's war on squeegee kids, 201–2, 204–5, 207, 209; as political, 201–2, 204, 208–15; squeegee kids as depicted in, 206, 207–9, 211–12, 214–15; visual rhetoric of, 201–3, 209–13. *See also* squeegee kids
Wenders, Wim: *Wings of Desire*, 402
West Edmonton Mall, 271
white children, in art of New France, 10–15; and *ex votos*, 12, 13, *14*, 14–15; and guardian angel, 12, *13*; and Holy Family, 10, *11*, 12. *See also* First Nations children, in art of New France; New France, art of
Winters, Claude, 161, *161*, 167, *168*
Wood, Frank, 32
World's Columbian Exposition (Chicago), 336, *337*, 338–39

Y

Yoo Young Mun: *Monument to Canadian Fallen*, 219, 220, *221*, 222–23, 226, 228

Z

Zeidler Partnership Architects, 260, 271

Books in the Studies in Childhood and Family in Canada Series Published by Wilfrid Laurier University Press

Making Do: Women, Family, and Home in Montreal during the Great Depression by Denyse Baillargeon, translated by Yvonne Klein • 1999 / xii + 232 pp. / ISBN: 0-88920-326-1 / ISBN-13: 978-0-88920-326-6

Children in English-Canadian Society: Framing the Twentieth-Century Consensus by Neil Sutherland with a new foreword by Cynthia Comacchio • 2000 / xxiv + 336 pp. / illus. / ISBN: 0-88920-351-2 / ISBN-13: 978-0-88920-351-8

Love Strong as Death: Lucy Peel's Canadian Journal, 1833–1836 edited by J.I. Little • 2001 / x + 229 pp. / illus. / ISBN: 0-88920-389-x / ISBN-13: 978-0-88920-389-230-x

The Challenge of Children's Rights for Canada by Katherine Covell and R. Brian Howe • 2001 / viii + 244 pp. / ISBN: 0-88920-380-6 / ISBN-13: 978-0-88920-380-8

NFB Kids: Portrayals of Children by the National Film Board of Canada, 1939–1989 by Brian J. Low • 2002 / vi + 288 pp. / illus. / ISBN: 0-88920-386-5 / ISBN-13: 978-0-88920-386-0

Something to Cry About: An Argument against Corporal Punishment of Children in Canada by Susan M. Turner • 2002 / xx + 317 pp. / ISBN: 0-88920-382-2 / ISBN-13: 978-0-88920-382-2

Freedom to Play: We Made Our Own Fun edited by Norah L. Lewis • 2002 / xiv + 210 pp. / ISBN: 0-88920-406-3 / ISBN-13: 978-0-88920-406-5

The Dominion of Youth: Adolescence and the Making of Modern Canada, 1920–1950 by Cynthia Comacchio • 2006 / x + 302 pp. / illus. / ISBN: 0-88920-488-8 / ISBN-13: 978-0-88920-488-1

Evangelical Balance Sheet: Character, Family, and Business in Mid-Victorian Nova Scotia by B. Anne Wood • 2006 / xxx + 198 pp. / illus. / ISBN: 0-88920-500-0 / ISBN-13: 978-0-88920-500-0

A Question of Commitment: Children's Rights in Canada edited by R. Brian Howe and Katherine Covell • 2007 / xiv + 442 pp. / ISBN: 978-1-55458-003-3

Taking Responsibility for Children edited by Samantha Brennan and Robert Noggle • 2007 / xxii + 188 pp. / ISBN: 978-1-55458-015-6

Home Words: Discourses of Children's Literature in Canada edited by Mavis Reimer • 2008 / xx + 280 pp. / ISBN: 978-1-55458-016-3

Depicting Canada's Children edited by Loren Lerner • 2009 / xxvi + 442 pp. / illus. / ISBN: 978-1-55458-050-7